ALA-APA Non-MLS Salary Survey

A Survey of Library Positions Not Requiring an ALA-Accredited Master's Degree

2006

Jenifer Grady and Denise Davis

Project Directors

ALA-APA Survey Report

AMERICAN LIBRARY ASSOCIATION-ALLIED PROFESSIONAL ASSOCIATION
AMERICAN LIBRARY ASSOCIATION, OFFICE FOR RESEARCH AND STATISTICS

ISBN   0-8389-8397-9

Printed in the United States of America.

Acknowledgments

Thanks are due to the many respondents who completed our questionnaire. Without their cooperation, this report would not be possible. We are especially appreciative because this is the first *Non-MLS (Master's Degree in Library and Information Studies) Salary Survey* that we have conducted. We included a large sample of public and academic libraries, including smaller public libraries, in our quest to gather state level data.

We pay homage to the Editor of *Library Mosaics: The Magazine for Support Staff* Raymond Roney and his staff: Ruth Roney, Circulation Manager; Ed Martinez, Consulting Editor; and Charlie Fox, Editorial Director. They started the national effort for collection and publication of library support staff salary statistics. For sixteen years, *Library Mosaics* was one of two national sources, the other being from the United States Census Bureau, which reported salary data for library-specific positions in all regions of the country. *Library Mosaics* asked public and academic libraries to supply data for their Clerks, Assistants, Technicians and Other Support Staff. Although the magazine is no longer being published, it is an important resource for support staff salaries from 1989 through 2003.[1] Our survey builds and expands on their success.

We are grateful to members of Association of Research Libraries (ARL) for participating in the *Non-MLS Salary Survey* because data on the majority of the sixty-two (62) positions are not collected by ARL. For the *Survey of Librarian Salaries*, ARL members give us permission to use their data. For this survey, ARL members, just as other libraries, had to complete it for the first time in its entirety. We especially thank Martha Kyrillidou, ARL Senior Program Officer for Statistics and Measurement, for her support and promotion of this project.

We are excited about working with the staff at The Management Association of Illinois for this inaugural *Non-MLS Salary Survey*. We appreciate the creativity, suggestions and survey execution by The Association's former director Denise Vuilleumier, Kristy Williams CCP, Manager of Compensation Services, and Jeanne Hannon, Coordinator of Compensation Services, who managed the mailings, processed the returns and analyzed the results. They are to be commended for manifesting the *Non-MLS Salary Survey* as it was envisioned and helping to shape this complex project. On behalf of the respondents, we thank The Association for providing so many methods for submitting salary data.

Finally, thanks are due to ALA-APA intern Alexander Hawley and ALA Production Services for formatting this edition. □

1. *Library Mosaics* conducted six support staff salary surveys, published in 1989, 1990, 1993, 1996, 2000 and 2003. The magazine was published by Yenor, Inc., PO Box 5171, Culver City, CA 90231; 310-645-4889.

Table of Contents

Discussion

Appendixes

Introduction

THIS IS THE inaugural issue of the *ALA-APA Non-MLS Salary Survey: A Survey of Library Positions Not Requiring an ALA-Accredited Master's Degree*. The American Library Association-Allied Professional Association: the Organization for the Advancement of Library Employees (ALA-APA) and American Library Association (ALA) Office for Research and Statistics launched this survey as a companion to the long-standing *Survey of Librarian Salaries*.

The purpose of the *Non-MLS Salary Survey* was to capture salaries for all staff who were not in one of the six positions of the *Survey of Librarian Salaries* and who were in positions that do not require an MLS.[1] The *Non-MLS Salary Survey* included sixty-two (62) titles and position descriptions based on feedback from the 2003 *Library Mosaics* Support Staff Salary survey, answers to a question about support staff position titles asked in the *2005 Survey of Librarian Salaries*, a review of titles in public and academic libraries and the advice of The Management Association of Illinois. These titles and positions descriptions are in Appendix A of this report. Salary data were reported by appropriate library staff for each incumbent in a position.

This survey improves access for Non-MLS library staff, employers, researchers, salary-reporting agencies, salary publishers (print and Web-based) and interested others to accurate data about the salaries paid in these positions and in a particular type of library.

The *Non-MLS Salary Survey* was inspired by several factors:

- The ALA 3rd Congress on Professional Education (COPE 3) focused on support staff. Recommendation 2.4.2 states that "ALA should commit to including support staff salaries in its annual salary survey by 2004."[2] The 2005 survey asked for support staff titles, which were incorporated into this survey.
- Support staff represent 67% of the positions held in libraries.
- *Library Mosaics: The Magazine for Support Staff*, no longer in publication, was a valuable source for national data on salaries for library support staff. *Library Mosaics* last published its biennial salary survey in 2004.
- The U.S. Bureau of Labor Statistics reports information and the U.S Census Bureau collects earnings data only on Librarians; Library Technicians; Library Assistants, Clerical; and Other Education, Training, and Library Workers.[3]
- Based on graduation rates from Schools of Library and Information Studies, the number of "librarians" who report their salaries to the U.S. Census Bureau is greatly inflated, which leads to a presumption is that a large percentage of those who self-identify as "librarians" do not hold an MLS and may be more appropriately categorized as support staff.
- The American Library Association Office for Research and Statistics has collected, published and reported on salary data about librarians with ALA-accredited Master's Degrees in Library and/or Information Science since 1982.
- Thirty-three (33) state libraries collect library-related salary data, but some states only include librarians or select titles or total salary expenditures.[4] There is no uniformity/standard for salary collection.
- Data may be difficult to find or gain access to even in states where salary data are collected.

---

1. Positions reported in the *Survey of Librarian Salaries* are Director/Dean, Deputy/Associate/Assistant Directors, Department Heads/Coordinators/Senior Managers, Managers/Supervisors of Support Staff, Librarians who do not supervise, Beginning Librarians.
2. Steering Committee. 2003. 3rd Congress on Professional Education: Focus on Library Support Staff. http://www.ala.org/ala/hrdrbucket/3rdcongressonpro/COPE3Final_Report.pdf (accessed July 7, 2006).
3. U.S. Census Bureau. 2000. Earnings by Occupation and Education. http://www.census.gov/hhes/income/earnings/call2usboth.html (accessed July 7, 2006).
4. ALA Office for Research and Statistics. 2005. Directory of State Libraries Reporting Salary Data. http://www.ala.org/ala/ors/reports/2006StateSalarySurveySummary.pdf (accessed July 7, 2006). *See* Appendix D.

Three thousand four hundred and eighteen (3,418) public and academic libraries were asked to complete this survey. The survey was laborious, much more so than the *Survey of Librarian Salaries* because there were ten times as many positions, many of which had never been asked about in the past. We established a proportional random sample to collect salary data at a regional level at minimum, a state-level at best.

Respondents could complete the survey in several ways: through a secure Web site, on an MS Excel spreadsheet that could be faxed or emailed to The Management Association of Illinois (The Association), by emailing or faxing a report generated by a Human Resources software or other program to The Association or by calling The Association with the information. The Association for Research Libraries (ARL) and all but the largest public libraries (serving 500,000 or more) completed the survey electronically via the established website.

Details of the 2006 ALA-APA *Non-MLS Salary Survey:*

- It was based on salaries paid to incumbents in positions as of February 1st, 2006.
- It shows salaries paid to staff in positions that do not require **a master's degree from a program in library and information studies accredited by ALA,** although some incumbents may hold an MLS. (See Discussion and Appendix B.)
- It was **completed by** Directors, Human Resources or administrative **staff of libraries,** not individual library employees.
- It was based on a survey of **full-time and part-time** positions.
- It was based on a survey of **public and academic** libraries only.
- It was based on a survey of libraries with at least **two staff members.**
- The nation was stratified into the **geographic areas:** North Atlantic, Great Lakes & Plains, Southeast, West & Southwest (see Appendix B for list of states).

- It shows the **first quartile, median, and third quartile** for salaries paid in each type/size of library in addition to the **mean** and **range** (minimum and maximum) for each position reported.
- In addition to regional- and state-level breakouts, there is also **data based on education level required for the position**—high school diploma, associate's degree, bachelor's degree, master's degree, and doctoral degree.
- **The Management Association of Illinois** in Downers Grove, Illinois, prepared the Web- and paper-based surveys and response sheet, **answered respondent questions, and performed the mailing, processing, and computer analysis of the survey responses.**
- It included **sixty-two (62) positions** that might be present in both public and academic libraries, which are listed in the Results section (full descriptions are in Appendix A).

This annual salary survey, like the *Survey of Librarian Salaries,* will periodically include "Supplementary Questions" to gather information on an issue related to library personnel. For 2006, the questions were:

- Are employees (support staff, professionals) represented by a bargaining unit?
- If yes, which union/local?
- How many of your staff report being a member of the following U.S. Census Bureau categories of race/ethnicity (assumption)?

The results of the supplemental questions will be reported separately in upcoming issues of the ALA-APA monthly electronic newsletter, *Library Worklife: HR E-News for Today's Leaders,* http://www.ala-apa.org/newsletter/current.html, as well as on the ALA Office for Research and Statistics' Reports Web site, http://www.ala.org/ala/ors/reports/reports.htm.

Results

The survey questionnaire was mailed to a stratified sample of 3,418 public and academic libraries, including a sample of the membership of the Association of Research Libraries (ARL). The samples were drawn from the National Center for Education Statistics (NCES) data files *Academic Libraries: 2004* and *Public Libraries in the United States: Fiscal Year 2003*.[1] Surveys were sent to a sample of 1,435 public and 1,983 academic libraries, using a proportional sampling procedure that took into account the size of the population in each group by state and geographic region and the expected response rate to the survey. Libraries received a letter in February 2006 directing them to the complete the survey by using the Web site.

By April 30, 2006, usable responses had been received from 836 libraries (567 public, 269 academic), 24.5 percent of those sampled. The response rate for 2005 is lower than the preferred minimum of 50 percent and even lower than our 25 percent benchmark, for several reasons:

- This is the first year of this survey;
- Notice of the survey was insufficient for some respondents;
- The survey had a relatively quick deadline of less than six weeks;
- Initial mailing to directors was complicated by address formatting, or insufficient information (i.e., "Attention Library Director" was omitted from address).

Further, the survey requested salary data for sixty-two (62) positions, a labor-intensive process, particularly for libraries with a large staff and several incumbents in the same position with different salaries, necessitating entry of each one. The Web version of the survey required that each employee's salary be entered individually. This was a manual task for staff at many libraries.

Response was particularly low for academic libraries: Two-Year Colleges (11.7 percent), ARL members (16.2 percent), and Four-Year Colleges (21.4 percent).

Regional- and state-level salaries are reported in this first survey for each position and by type of library, acknowledging that in most cases, especially for state-level data, there was *not a statistically significant response rate*. Salary data based on the level of education required for each position (High School Diploma, Associates Degree, Bachelor's Degree, Master's Degree and Doctoral Degree) are reported— not the degree held by each incumbent. These data are not representative, so use caution in reviewing them or re-using them in any way. We look forward to increased participation in future editions (See Caveats below and Discussion).

The results of this survey are presented on the following pages in sixty-two sets of tables for public libraries and sixty-two sets of tables for academic libraries. Each set reflects salaries for each position title (see Discussion section).

The tables present the number of positions for which salaries are reported (N), the minimum salary and the maximum salary (range), the mean (arithmetic average), the first quartile, median and third quartile for each of the four U.S. Census regions, for states and degrees required. This pattern is repeated for each type and size of library.

Caveats

Caveats should be observed in reading the tables. The intent of the survey is to collect and present a statistically valid report of region- and state-level data for each position and library type. This was not possible with an overall response rate of 24.5 percent. Although we received at least one response from either a public or academic library in forty-nine states (49), separating those responses by library class and region reduced the significance of individual library responses.

Very Large public libraries (serving 500,000+) had the highest response rate at 48.7 percent, followed by Large public libraries at 32.9 percent. Universities

---

1. The academic libraries sample was drawn from the 2004 post-survey file provided by the U.S. Census Bureau for the purposes of this study.

libraries were the largest respondent group among academic libraries at 25.1 percent.

The Range of Average Minimum and Maximum Salaries is a mean from those libraries that reported a minimum (beginning) and maximum (cap) range for each position. All libraries did not include these data in their responses.

The Degree Required tables include data from libraries that reported the minimum degree required to hold a position. All libraries did not include these data in their responses.

The higher the number of cases (N), the more reliable the results of the sample in giving a true picture of the total population. For three regions, the response rate for Very Large public libraries was sufficient: Great Lakes & Plains at 73 percent, N=8; Southeast at 50 percent, N=9; and West & Southwest at 49 percent, N=17. The response rate was above 40 percent for only one other region, Large public libraries (serving 250,000–499,999) in the North Atlantic at 40.4 percent, N=19. Response rates are defined as the percentage of responses divided by the surveys sent by category. For example, eleven surveys were sent to Very Large public libraries in the Great Lakes & Plains region and eight responded (8/11 = 73 percent).

Another caveat is that when the mean and the median are not close together, the mean is being influenced by some unusual values. When the mean is much higher than the median, there are several very high salaries. When the mean is much lower than the median, there are several very low salaries.

The following example illustrates how to interpret the tables:

On the first page of the public library tables, there were forty-one (41) Associate Director—Adult Services salaries reported by Very Small public libraries from the North Atlantic region. The minimum salary for the range reported for this position was $12,480 and the maximum was $68,252. When all of the salaries were added together and the result was divided by the total number (41), the average or mean salary was $30,338. When all of the salaries were arrayed from low to high, 25 percent of Associate Director—Adult Services salaries fell below $23,150 (Q1), 50 percent fell below or at $28,600 (median), and 75 percent fell below $35,360 (Q3). The mean and median were close with a difference of $1,738.

On the first page of the academic library tables, there were four (4) Associate Director—Adult Services salaries reported by Two-Year Colleges from the North Atlantic region. The minimum salary for the range reported for this position was $29,120 and the maximum was $52,000. When all of the salaries were added together and the result was divided by the total number (4), the average or mean salary was $35,060. When all of the salaries were arrayed from low to high, 25 percent of Associate Director—Adult Services salaries fell below $29,120 (Q1), 50 percent fell below or at $29,560 (median), and 75 percent fell below $41,000 (Q3). The mean and median were $5,500 apart, which is not definitive with this small a response rate. □

ASSOCIATE LIBRARIAN OF ADULT SERVICES (NON-MLS DEGREED)

Provides assistance to patrons including topical research and material location. Assists patrons with the use of library resources and equipment. Screens the collection for outdated or unused materials following established guidelines. May perform managerial and administrative duties. Provides access to materials, services and programs intended to meet the needs of the adult users of a public library.

Very Small Public Library
(Serving a population of less than 10,000)
Regional Data

	Min	Q1	Mean	Median	Q3	Max	N	Range Avg Min	Range Avg Max
North Atlantic	12,480	23,150	30,338	28,600	35,360	68,252	41	27,067	34,950
Great Lakes & Plains	10,909	14,560	22,711	20,000	29,120	48,360	81	16,827	24,185
Southeast	10,712	13,680	22,919	20,800	32,121	36,218	14	10,712	15,600
West & Southwest	10,712	14,560	20,813	18,772	25,345	41,600	32	16,355	19,203
ALL REGIONS	10,712	15,878	24,228	22,661	30,899	68,252	168	19,388	25,604

State Data

	Min	Q1	Mean	Median	Q3	Max	N	Range Avg Min	Range Avg Max
AL	12,501	18,838	25,677	26,218	33,293	36,218	8	.	.
CO	15,766	18,242	24,140	25,358	30,038	30,077	4	26,707	36,088
CT	17,139	23,570	29,678	30,756	35,786	40,061	4	29,120	31,512
IA	12,480	19,200	28,420	25,504	40,541	48,360	9	14,352	14,352
ID	18,514	18,514	22,257	22,257	26,000	26,000	2	.	.
IL	13,520	13,520	20,014	17,264	24,800	44,455	21	15,662	20,800
IN	10,909	11,261	17,627	13,782	21,754	36,516	8	11,613	19,067
KS	11,440	14,602	17,254	16,640	19,760	25,132	13	13,461	20,099
KY	10,712	10,712	17,904	20,200	22,800	22,800	3	10,712	15,600
MA	23,504	30,389	37,866	37,419	41,746	68,252	10	32,469	37,745
ME	23,150	23,150	26,204	24,773	29,257	32,119	4	18,935	34,528
MI	18,200	19,760	24,559	23,920	28,135	33,422	6	.	.
MN	18,720	24,721	31,856	33,384	36,504	46,910	8	31,564	44,127
MO	30,670	30,670	30,670	30,670	30,670	30,670	1	.	.
MS	13,296	13,296	13,488	13,488	13,680	13,680	2	.	.
MT	16,744	16,744	20,005	18,772	23,265	25,730	4	14,914	19,760
ND	12,168	13,458	14,968	15,246	15,246	18,720	5	.	.
NE	24,000	24,000	24,000	24,000	24,000	24,000	1	.	.
NH	22,360	22,620	27,254	25,740	31,889	35,177	4	21,639	28,711
NJ	19,275	22,137	25,899	25,000	29,660	34,320	4	33,280	41,600
NM	20,160	20,160	28,907	24,960	41,600	41,600	3	24,960	41,600
NY	26,582	26,582	29,269	27,241	33,983	33,983	3	.	.
OH	23,920	23,920	30,326	30,326	36,731	36,731	2	14,872	23,920
PA	12,480	15,600	25,392	27,200	28,746	45,714	7	.	.
SD	15,360	15,360	24,310	24,310	33,259	33,259	2	.	.
TX	10,712	12,480	18,051	16,120	21,320	33,488	18	13,150	13,150
VT	19,240	21,320	32,699	35,360	43,200	44,375	5	.	.
WA	33,280	33,280	33,280	33,280	33,280	33,280	1	29,120	33,280
WI	24,024	29,202	31,445	31,200	31,200	41,600	5	20,800	27,040
WV	34,759	34,759	34,759	34,759	34,759	34,759	1	.	.

Degree Required Data

	Min	Q1	Mean	Median	Q3	Max	N	Range Avg Min	Range Avg Max
High School	10,712	13,520	19,978	18,720	23,920	42,350	95	15,815	20,793
Associate's	12,501	20,160	27,863	25,600	36,878	44,455	19	26,304	34,720
Bachelor's	15,360	26,395	31,768	31,200	35,568	48,360	38	28,109	37,534
Master's	28,000	28,000	47,721	46,910	68,252	68,252	3	.	.
Doctoral	.	.	.	.	.	.	.	.	.

ASSOCIATE LIBRARIAN OF ADULT SERVICES (NON-MLS DEGREED) - CONTINUED
Small Public Library
(Serving a population of 10,000 to 25,000)
Regional Data

	Min	Q1	Mean	Median	Q3	Max	N	Range Avg Min	Range Avg Max
North Atlantic	16,328	28,080	34,243	33,280	41,600	48,527	17	29,274	38,004
Great Lakes & Plains	16,640	26,589	29,297	29,120	32,926	39,674	38	23,528	32,559
Southeast	12,480	19,860	22,485	21,840	23,899	31,907	17	20,800	22,880
West & Southwest	23,287	29,857	33,559	30,903	34,897	56,160	16	33,471	49,795
ALL REGIONS	12,480	23,670	29,711	29,562	33,280	56,160	88	27,951	37,832

State Data

	Min	Q1	Mean	Median	Q3	Max	N	Range Avg Min	Range Avg Max
AL	19,860	19,860	19,860	19,860	19,860	19,860	1	.	.
AR	21,175	21,175	21,175	21,175	21,175	21,175	1	.	.
AZ	30,410	30,410	34,466	34,757	38,230	38,230	3	26,666	40,005
CO	30,000	30,000	30,000	30,000	30,000	30,000	1	.	.
GA	12,480	12,480	16,740	16,740	21,000	21,000	2	.	.
IA	26,229	26,229	26,229	26,229	26,229	26,229	1	.	.
IL	23,920	29,120	31,382	31,000	33,280	39,520	13	22,880	31,200
IN	30,597	30,597	31,762	31,762	32,926	32,926	2	.	.
KS	24,960	24,960	28,526	25,750	34,869	34,869	3	18,720	31,200
KY	22,318	22,318	27,113	27,113	31,907	31,907	2	.	.
LA	19,739	19,739	24,575	24,575	29,411	29,411	2	20,800	22,880
MA	48,527	48,527	48,527	48,527	48,527	48,527	1	.	.
ME	32,135	32,135	32,135	32,135	32,135	32,135	1	.	.
MI	26,589	28,895	33,544	33,956	38,193	39,674	4	.	.
MT	33,280	33,280	33,280	33,280	33,280	33,280	1	.	.
NC	15,831	15,831	15,831	15,831	15,831	15,831	1	.	.
ND	16,640	16,640	16,640	16,640	16,640	16,640	1	.	.
NJ	33,280	34,081	37,205	36,543	40,329	42,453	4	32,185	39,395
NM	30,139	30,139	46,793	54,080	56,160	56,160	3	43,680	64,480
NY	39,520	40,560	43,160	42,640	45,760	47,840	4	35,880	44,720
OH	18,304	22,048	25,310	26,895	27,934	32,635	11	26,666	39,998
OK	24,040	24,040	28,379	28,379	32,718	32,718	2	.	.
OR	35,037	35,037	35,037	35,037	35,037	35,037	1	.	.
PA	16,328	22,880	25,022	26,624	28,080	31,200	5	12,480	22,880
RI	23,442	23,442	27,446	27,446	31,450	31,450	2	20,093	30,046
TN	21,424	21,840	24,045	23,192	23,899	29,869	5	.	.
TX	23,287	23,287	27,619	29,713	30,861	30,945	5	.	.
VA	28,267	28,267	28,267	28,267	28,267	28,267	1	.	.
WI	27,955	27,955	33,583	33,285	39,510	39,510	3	27,144	30,555
WV	17,160	17,160	20,020	20,020	22,880	22,880	2	.	.

Degree Required Data

	Min	Q1	Mean	Median	Q3	Max	N	Range Avg Min	Range Avg Max
High School	12,480	21,840	25,466	23,442	29,869	38,230	37	21,807	30,989
Associate's	17,160	25,355	29,197	30,854	32,240	39,520	8	18,720	31,200
Bachelor's	19,860	29,120	35,131	33,280	39,510	56,160	33	31,433	41,467
Master's	23,920	23,920	31,797	31,797	39,674	39,674	2	.	.
Doctoral	.	.	.	.	.	.		.	.

ASSOCIATE LIBRARIAN OF ADULT SERVICES (NON-MLS DEGREED) - CONTINUED
Medium Public Library
(Serving a population of 25,000 to 99,999)
Regional Data

	Min	Q1	Mean	Median	Q3	Max	N	Range Avg Min	Range Avg Max
North Atlantic	13,000	25,709	33,801	34,767	43,181	54,579	40	34,286	44,846
Great Lakes & Plains	18,720	22,880	30,116	27,102	35,360	74,322	75	28,569	39,864
Southeast	12,480	19,344	22,991	24,159	26,988	39,111	58	20,010	29,557
West & Southwest	11,520	18,138	27,307	24,190	34,029	73,840	103	23,327	30,740
ALL REGIONS	11,520	20,800	28,105	25,820	34,070	74,322	276	26,626	36,045

State Data

	Min	Q1	Mean	Median	Q3	Max	N	Range Avg Min	Range Avg Max
AL	12,813	14,934	21,130	22,319	27,585	28,000	5		
AR	21,320	21,320	24,221	22,558	27,122	30,448	4		
CA	11,520	15,360	32,419	35,573	42,804	56,035	14	29,675	29,120
CO	28,000	28,000	37,677	37,677	47,353	47,353	2		
CT	42,682	44,679	47,918	47,206	51,158	54,579	4	44,096	54,579
GA	14,560	16,640	19,224	18,013	19,344	30,600	9		
IA	29,120	35,360	40,917	35,360	41,538	74,322	7	30,368	34,528
ID	13,520	16,640	24,699	21,944	27,040	73,840	71	18,038	24,910
IL	24,960	31,200	36,136	34,767	38,418	49,379	14	30,883	46,628
IN	23,462	23,462	28,445	24,731	37,142	37,142	3	23,275	32,469
KS	26,000	26,000	26,000	26,000	26,000	26,000	1	18,741	25,813
LA	14,076	22,447	23,515	23,920	25,397	29,370	15	20,010	29,557
MA	36,587	37,555	41,282	43,680	43,680	44,908	5	38,466	41,420
ME	31,928	32,406	37,232	34,902	43,555	44,200	8	30,992	44,200
MI	26,686	26,686	26,686	26,686	26,686	26,686	1		
MN	48,330	48,330	48,330	48,330	48,330	48,330	1		
MO	34,965	34,965	38,924	40,830	40,976	40,976	3		
MS	29,333	29,333	29,333	29,333	29,333	29,333	1		
NC	24,960	24,960	26,138	24,960	27,888	29,442	14		
ND	22,714	22,714	22,714	22,714	22,714	22,714	1	20,467	30,722
NJ	41,933	41,933	41,933	41,933	41,933	41,933	1	29,120	49,920
NY	22,818	25,709	36,413	36,026	47,118	50,784	4	43,451	45,490
OH	18,720	20,800	25,894	24,960	29,120	47,632	43	22,880	29,120
OR	49,712	49,712	49,712	49,712	49,712	49,712	1		
PA	13,000	19,448	26,029	25,594	31,200	41,000	18		
SC	39,111	39,111	39,111	39,111	39,111	39,111	1		
TN	12,480	12,480	16,293	14,560	22,224	23,189	7		
TX	24,000	24,500	27,278	25,500	30,056	34,112	4		
UT	28,413	28,600	30,599	28,807	32,961	34,216	5	27,310	40,955
VA	27,770	27,770	28,378	28,378	28,986	28,986	2		
WI	27,102	27,102	27,102	27,102	27,102	27,102	1	26,021	34,091
WY	34,029	34,029	36,334	36,650	37,190	39,458	6	34,029	43,930

Degree Required Data

	Min	Q1	Mean	Median	Q3	Max	N	Range Avg Min	Range Avg Max
High School	11,520	18,720	23,528	22,880	26,000	56,035	147	21,089	28,511
Associate's	15,300	20,613	28,896	27,829	32,250	54,579	32	28,056	38,138
Bachelor's	21,320	30,600	35,815	34,778	40,976	74,322	81	30,616	41,501
Master's	36,587	37,142	47,088	43,451	49,608	73,840	7	40,914	52,146
Doctoral									

ASSOCIATE LIBRARIAN OF ADULT SERVICES (NON-MLS DEGREED) - CONTINUED
Large Public Library
(Serving a population of 100,000 to 499,999)
Regional Data

	Min	Q1	Mean	Median	Q3	Max	N	Range Avg Min	Range Avg Max
North Atlantic	10,837	15,419	27,411	26,208	35,006	65,146	65	20,800	35,360
Great Lakes & Plains	16,640	25,501	29,860	30,305	34,029	55,376	216	27,181	39,389
Southeast	18,720	30,012	35,970	35,180	41,945	61,817	56	20,337	28,246
West & Southwest	17,077	25,095	33,972	31,296	41,764	72,101	64	23,512	31,788
ALL REGIONS	10,837	24,690	30,973	30,804	35,551	72,101	401	26,271	37,679

State Data

	Min	Q1	Mean	Median	Q3	Max	N	Range Avg Min	Range Avg Max
AL	25,630	25,630	25,630	25,630	25,630	25,630	1		
AZ	53,019	53,019	53,019	53,019	53,019	53,019	1		
CA	31,762	47,258	49,485	50,953	52,707	72,101	13	34,663	42,883
CO	22,880	26,874	31,884	29,432	36,444	44,693	14	21,359	32,263
FL	29,946	30,032	36,214	34,375	38,123	50,013	14		
GA	29,120	32,032	33,365	32,698	37,086	37,139	7		
IL	28,662	28,662	31,365	30,290	33,196	41,923	18		
IN	27,698	27,698	30,461	30,461	33,224	33,224	2		
KS	28,995	31,366	34,389	34,590	37,398	42,432	48	28,995	48,318
MD	24,690	25,823	35,334	30,170	38,033	65,146	20		
MI	26,395	28,850	31,761	32,157	33,769	38,191	56	27,054	33,634
MN	28,496	31,866	41,188	40,244	50,905	55,376	6		
MO	22,339	23,005	24,810	23,920	25,626	32,469	22	22,339	31,580
MS	20,364	20,364	24,088	20,700	31,200	31,200	3		
NC	25,481	30,910	33,656	32,016	39,346	40,528	5		
NE	30,264	32,320	35,299	36,113	38,422	38,422	8	29,376	37,513
NJ	10,837	12,792	22,984	19,517	35,006	42,354	39		
NM	35,857	35,857	35,857	35,857	35,857	35,857	1	35,838	49,109
NY	41,613	41,613	41,613	41,613	41,613	41,613	1		
OH	16,640	18,096	23,564	21,341	28,215	46,842	56	28,200	44,418
OK	17,077	21,694	23,113	23,026	24,981	29,474	15	19,791	25,807
OR	26,208	26,208	26,208	26,208	26,208	26,208	1		
PA	20,800	24,960	27,405	27,040	30,509	33,717	5	20,800	35,360
TN	18,720	21,045	27,626	22,880	34,790	42,651	9	20,337	28,246
TX	24,545	30,538	32,777	31,296	35,560	45,228	19	19,490	33,342
VA	23,732	40,448	44,646	42,089	48,459	61,817	17		

Degree Required Data

	Min	Q1	Mean	Median	Q3	Max	N	Range Avg Min	Range Avg Max
High School	16,640	20,072	25,448	23,088	29,120	61,817	86	21,144	29,073
Associate's	20,800	26,520	33,751	29,869	46,321	47,258	15	24,879	35,159
Bachelor's	18,720	28,922	33,814	32,417	36,941	72,101	252	27,116	39,027
Master's	29,946	29,946	33,142	32,342	37,139	37,139	3	.	.
Doctoral	.	.	.	.	.	.			

ASSOCIATE LIBRARIAN OF ADULT SERVICES (NON-MLS DEGREED) - CONTINUED
Very Large Public Library
(Serving a population of 500,000 or more)
Regional Data

	Min	Q1	Mean	Median	Q3	Max	N	Range Avg Min	Range Avg Max
North Atlantic	31,990	36,621	39,507	37,565	42,353	60,707	83	.	.
Great Lakes & Plains	26,077	33,694	37,538	36,050	42,557	45,302	86	31,272	46,947
Southeast	23,958	25,215	29,401	28,352	33,444	41,179	60	.	.
West & Southwest	30,326	35,402	45,121	39,272	57,782	70,928	26	43,102	53,297
ALL REGIONS	23,958	32,635	37,038	36,465	41,392	70,928	255	36,996	50,019

State Data

	Min	Q1	Mean	Median	Q3	Max	N	Range Avg Min	Range Avg Max
CA	34,606	48,926	55,901	57,782	64,522	70,928	12	47,777	57,841
FL	35,307	35,307	35,307	35,307	35,307	35,307	3	.	.
GA	35,566	35,566	35,566	35,566	35,566	35,566	1	.	.
MD	34,697	37,565	41,165	37,565	44,506	60,707	47	.	.
MO	26,077	27,581	30,256	30,314	30,846	36,406	6	24,856	37,294
NC	23,958	25,005	28,974	28,209	31,359	41,179	56	.	.
NJ	31,990	35,427	37,343	36,621	38,791	46,857	36	.	.
OH	31,699	33,694	38,084	36,584	42,838	45,302	80	31,699	47,590
OR	41,392	41,392	41,392	41,392	41,392	41,392	2	33,654	41,392
TX	30,326	31,491	34,963	36,119	37,690	39,374	12	26,832	40,206

Degree Required Data

	Min	Q1	Mean	Median	Q3	Max	N	Range Avg Min	Range Avg Max
High School	39,170	39,170	39,170	39,170	39,170	39,170	1	.	.
Associate's	31,387	33,394	37,393	38,397	41,392	41,392	4	30,243	40,799
Bachelor's	23,958	31,792	36,970	35,761	41,459	70,928	204	37,957	51,530
Master's	35,566	35,566	41,593	41,593	47,619	47,619	2	39,007	47,619
Doctoral	.	.	.	.	.	.			

ASSOCIATE LIBRARIAN OF ADULT SERVICES (NON-MLS DEGREED) - CONTINUED
ALL PUBLIC LIBRARIES
Regional Data

	Min	Q1	Mean	Median	Q3	Max	N	Range Avg Min	Range Avg Max
North Atlantic	10,837	26,582	33,491	35,427	39,414	68,252	246	29,832	39,198
Great Lakes & Plains	10,909	23,920	30,019	30,784	35,103	74,322	496	26,427	38,183
Southeast	10,712	23,189	28,366	27,585	32,792	61,817	205	19,583	27,387
West & Southwest	10,712	21,278	30,552	28,807	36,837	73,840	241	25,990	33,924
ALL REGIONS	10,712	23,281	30,561	30,563	36,705	74,322	1,188	26,403	36,681

State Data

	Min	Q1	Mean	Median	Q3	Max	N	Range Avg Min	Range Avg Max
AL	12,501	18,741	23,771	22,319	31,036	36,218	15		
AR	21,175	21,320	23,612	21,320	23,795	30,448	5		
AZ	30,410	32,583	39,104	36,494	45,625	53,019	4	26,666	40,005
CA	11,520	34,606	45,333	47,619	57,013	72,101	39	41,128	49,046
CO	15,766	26,874	30,871	29,869	33,644	47,353	21	21,894	32,646
CT	17,139	30,756	38,798	41,371	47,206	54,579	8	36,608	43,046
FL	29,946	31,846	36,054	35,307	37,985	50,013	17		
GA	12,480	16,973	25,033	23,339	32,698	37,139	19		
IA	12,480	25,504	33,437	35,360	40,541	74,322	17	25,792	28,763
ID	13,520	16,765	24,632	21,944	26,790	73,840	73	18,038	24,910
IL	13,520	24,800	28,769	29,996	33,812	49,379	66	28,431	42,121
IN	10,909	13,004	23,387	24,731	32,926	37,142	15	14,529	22,417
KS	11,440	28,995	30,563	32,427	36,733	42,432	65	26,727	44,158
KY	10,712	20,200	21,587	22,318	22,800	31,907	5	10,712	15,600
LA	14,076	22,447	23,640	23,920	25,397	29,411	17	20,168	28,221
MA	23,504	33,894	39,600	38,694	43,680	68,252	16	34,468	38,970
MD	24,690	34,697	39,424	37,565	44,094	65,146	67		
ME	23,150	31,928	33,447	32,135	35,942	44,200	13	27,704	41,562
MI	18,200	27,997	31,147	32,157	33,758	39,674	67	27,054	33,634
MN	18,720	29,120	36,687	35,568	47,502	55,376	15	31,564	44,127
MO	22,339	23,452	27,337	25,563	30,440	40,976	32	22,449	31,829
MS	13,296	13,680	21,429	20,532	29,333	31,200	6		
MT	16,744	16,744	22,660	20,800	25,730	33,280	5	14,914	19,760
NC	15,831	24,960	28,587	27,954	30,729	41,179	76		
ND	12,168	13,458	16,313	15,246	18,720	22,714	7	20,467	30,722
NE	24,000	31,098	34,044	35,622	38,422	38,422	9	29,376	37,513
NH	22,360	22,620	27,254	25,740	31,889	35,177	4	21,639	28,711
NJ	10,837	19,517	30,179	34,944	37,675	46,857	84	31,791	41,941
NM	20,160	24,960	37,565	35,857	54,080	56,160	7	37,040	54,917
NY	22,818	27,921	37,309	40,560	43,566	50,784	12	37,394	44,874
OH	16,640	22,048	30,306	31,158	36,050	47,632	192	29,442	44,702
OK	17,077	21,902	23,732	23,234	24,981	32,718	17	19,791	25,807
OR	26,208	35,037	38,748	41,392	41,392	49,712	5	33,654	41,392
PA	12,480	19,448	25,954	27,040	31,200	45,714	35	18,027	31,200
RI	23,442	23,442	27,446	27,446	31,450	31,450	2	20,093	30,046
SC	39,111	39,111	39,111	39,111	39,111	39,111	1		
SD	15,360	15,360	24,310	24,310	33,259	33,259	2		
TN	12,480	18,720	22,996	22,224	23,899	42,651	21	20,337	28,246
TX	10,712	22,691	27,835	30,784	33,488	45,228	58	15,959	19,342
UT	28,413	28,600	30,599	28,807	32,961	34,216	5	27,310	40,955
VA	23,732	37,531	42,200	41,945	46,685	61,817	20		
VT	19,240	21,320	32,699	35,360	43,200	44,375	5		
WA	33,280	33,280	33,280	33,280	33,280	33,280	1	29,120	33,280
WI	24,024	27,955	31,675	31,200	33,285	41,600	9	24,655	30,562
WV	17,160	17,160	24,933	22,880	34,759	34,759	3		
WY	34,029	34,029	36,334	36,650	37,190	39,458	6	34,029	43,930

Degree Required Data

	Min	Q1	Mean	Median	Q3	Max	N	Range Avg Min	Range Avg Max
High School	10,712	17,701	23,296	22,271	27,040	61,817	366	18,991	25,683
Associate's	12,501	23,150	30,044	28,166	36,878	54,579	78	26,408	36,282
Bachelor's	15,360	29,207	35,083	33,837	38,430	74,322	608	29,328	41,037
Master's	23,920	35,566	42,293	39,674	47,619	73,840	17	40,278	50,637
Doctoral	.	.	.	.	.	.		.	.

ASSOCIATE LIBRARIAN OF ARCHIVES AND SPECIAL COLLECTIONS (NON-MLS DEGREED)

Provides assistance to patrons including topical research and material location. Assists patrons with the use of library resources and equipment. Screens the collection for outdated or unused materials following established guidelines. May perform managerial and administrative duties. Manages and maintains collection; identifies and appraises records, authenticates, describes and documents, facilitates access and use, preserves and conserves, and exhibits collection.

Very Small Public Library
(Serving a population of less than 10,000)
Regional Data

	Min	Q1	Mean	Median	Q3	Max	N	Range Avg Min	Range Avg Max
Great Lakes & Plains	16,848	19,364	24,197	20,800	22,880	48,360	9	.	.
Southeast	21,403	21,403	21,403	21,403	21,403	21,403	1	.	.
West & Southwest	12,480	13,520	18,216	16,640	22,911	27,102	4	17,425	19,510
ALL REGIONS	12,480	18,720	22,288	20,400	22,880	48,360	14	17,425	19,510

State Data

	Min	Q1	Mean	Median	Q3	Max	N	Range Avg Min	Range Avg Max
AL	21,403	21,403	21,403	21,403	21,403	21,403	1	.	.
CO	27,102	27,102	27,102	27,102	27,102	27,102	1	23,941	32,282
IA	20,800	20,800	34,580	34,580	48,360	48,360	2	.	.
IL	18,720	19,760	23,100	21,840	26,440	30,000	4	.	.
ND	16,848	16,848	18,106	18,106	19,364	19,364	2	.	.
NE	20,000	20,000	20,000	20,000	20,000	20,000	1	.	.
TX	12,480	12,480	15,253	14,560	18,720	18,720	3	15,253	15,253

Degree Required Data

	Min	Q1	Mean	Median	Q3	Max	N	Range Avg Min	Range Avg Max
High School	12,480	16,848	18,516	19,364	20,800	21,403	7	15,600	15,600
Associate's	14,560	16,640	19,240	19,760	21,840	22,880	4	14,560	14,560
Bachelor's	27,102	27,102	37,731	37,731	48,360	48,360	2	23,941	32,282
Master's	.	.	.	.	.	.		.	.
Doctoral	.	.	.	.	.	.		.	.

ASSOCIATE LIBRARIAN OF ARCHIVES AND SPECIAL COLLECTIONS (NON-MLS DEGREED) - CONTINUED
Small Public Library
(Serving a population of 10,000 to 25,000)
Regional Data

	Min	Q1	Mean	Median	Q3	Max	N	Range Avg Min	Range Avg Max
North Atlantic	28,080	28,080	28,080	28,080	28,080	28,080	1	28,080	35,360
Great Lakes & Plains	20,636	22,798	29,349	28,621	35,901	39,520	4	35,360	41,600
Southeast	15,126	15,126	21,544	21,544	27,963	27,963	2	15,600	27,976
West & Southwest	37,500	37,500	37,500	37,500	37,500	37,500	1	.	.
ALL REGIONS	15,126	22,798	28,258	28,021	34,891	39,520	8	26,347	34,979

State Data

	Min	Q1	Mean	Median	Q3	Max	N	Range Avg Min	Range Avg Max
AL	15,126	15,126	15,126	15,126	15,126	15,126	1	.	.
CO	37,500	37,500	37,500	37,500	37,500	37,500	1	.	.
IL	20,636	20,636	26,459	26,459	32,282	32,282	2	.	.
IN	39,520	39,520	39,520	39,520	39,520	39,520	1	35,360	41,600
KY	27,963	27,963	27,963	27,963	27,963	27,963	1	15,600	27,976
ME	28,080	28,080	28,080	28,080	28,080	28,080	1	28,080	35,360
MI	24,960	24,960	24,960	24,960	24,960	24,960	1	.	.

Degree Required Data

	Min	Q1	Mean	Median	Q3	Max	N	Range Avg Min	Range Avg Max
High School	15,126	17,881	22,171	22,798	26,461	27,963	4	15,600	27,976
Associate's									
Bachelor's	28,080	30,181	34,345	34,891	38,510	39,520	4	31,720	38,480
Master's									
Doctoral									

ASSOCIATE LIBRARIAN OF ARCHIVES AND SPECIAL COLLECTIONS (NON-MLS DEGREED) - CONTINUED
Medium Public Library
(Serving a population of 25,000 to 99,999)
Regional Data

	Min	Q1	Mean	Median	Q3	Max	N	Range Avg Min	Range Avg Max
North Atlantic	13,000	27,000	35,155	35,942	48,677	52,871	7	25,974	36,660
Great Lakes & Plains	22,484	25,334	38,137	34,726	48,016	66,456	8	51,792	80,704
Southeast	21,578	21,578	24,835	24,126	28,800	28,800	3	.	.
ALL REGIONS	13,000	25,334	34,760	30,364	47,986	66,456	18	34,580	51,341

State Data

	Min	Q1	Mean	Median	Q3	Max	N	Range Avg Min	Range Avg Max
AR	21,578	21,578	21,578	21,578	21,578	21,578	1	.	.
IL	41,475	41,475	51,972	47,986	66,456	66,456	3	51,792	80,704
IN	25,334	25,334	31,673	26,655	38,012	48,047	4	.	.
MA	36,665	36,665	46,071	48,677	52,871	52,871	3	28,912	37,440
ME	31,928	31,928	33,935	33,935	35,942	35,942	2	30,992	44,200
MI	22,484	22,484	22,484	22,484	22,484	22,484	1	.	.
MS	28,800	28,800	28,800	28,800	28,800	28,800	1	.	.
PA	13,000	13,000	20,000	20,000	27,000	27,000	2	13,000	20,800
SC	24,126	24,126	24,126	24,126	24,126	24,126	1	.	.

Degree Required Data

	Min	Q1	Mean	Median	Q3	Max	N	Range Avg Min	Range Avg Max
High School	13,000	13,000	23,748	21,578	36,665	36,665	3	20,956	29,120
Associate's	48,047	48,047	48,047	48,047	48,047	48,047	1	.	.
Bachelor's	22,484	25,334	32,167	27,488	35,942	52,871	10	30,992	44,200
Master's	28,800	35,138	46,179	44,730	57,221	66,456	4	51,792	80,704
Doctoral	.	.	.	.	.	.		.	.

ASSOCIATE LIBRARIAN OF ARCHIVES AND SPECIAL COLLECTIONS (NON-MLS DEGREED) - CONTINUED
Large Public Library
(Serving a population of 100,000 to 499,999)
Regional Data

	Min	Q1	Mean	Median	Q3	Max	N	Range Avg Min	Range Avg Max
North Atlantic	12,792	12,955	24,990	20,930	35,137	49,088	8	.	.
Great Lakes & Plains	24,939	28,018	30,864	28,018	35,006	40,817	14	23,408	29,613
Southeast	33,000	33,000	42,832	42,832	52,664	52,664	2	.	.
West & Southwest	29,702	31,179	40,107	37,819	45,540	56,293	5	24,419	41,808
ALL REGIONS	12,792	25,958	31,663	30,274	37,232	56,293	29	23,577	31,645

State Data

	Min	Q1	Mean	Median	Q3	Max	N	Range Avg Min	Range Avg Max
CO	56,293	56,293	56,293	56,293	56,293	56,293	1	.	.
FL	33,000	33,000	33,000	33,000	33,000	33,000	1	.	.
GA	52,664	52,664	52,664	52,664	52,664	52,664	1	.	.
MD	30,274	30,274	39,681	39,681	49,088	49,088	2	.	.
MI	24,939	26,988	30,009	28,018	32,949	40,817	12	23,067	28,018
MO	34,757	34,757	35,994	35,994	37,232	37,232	2	24,773	35,994
NJ	12,792	12,792	16,112	13,117	20,506	21,353	5	.	.
NY	40,000	40,000	40,000	40,000	40,000	40,000	1	.	.
TX	29,702	30,441	36,060	34,499	41,679	45,540	4	24,419	41,808

Degree Required Data

	Min	Q1	Mean	Median	Q3	Max	N	Range Avg Min	Range Avg Max
High School	31,179	31,179	33,814	33,814	36,448	36,448	2	24,419	41,808
Associate's	29,702	29,702	29,702	29,702	29,702	29,702	1	24,419	41,808
Bachelor's	24,939	28,018	32,845	30,274	37,232	49,088	17	23,408	29,613
Master's	33,000	36,500	45,489	46,332	54,479	56,293	4	.	.
Doctoral								.	.

ASSOCIATE LIBRARIAN OF ARCHIVES AND SPECIAL COLLECTIONS (NON-MLS DEGREED) - CONTINUED
Very Large Public Library
(Serving a population of 500,000 or more)
Regional Data

	Min	Q1	Mean	Median	Q3	Max	N	Range Avg Min	Range Avg Max
Great Lakes & Plains	33,010	41,246	48,636	43,733	44,034	81,159	5	31,699	47,590
Southeast	18,720	20,800	28,834	27,040	31,200	72,769	53	28,758	44,936
West & Southwest	28,745	28,745	28,745	28,745	28,745	28,745	1	.	.
ALL REGIONS	18,720	22,880	30,511	28,416	33,010	81,159	59	29,003	45,157

State Data

	Min	Q1	Mean	Median	Q3	Max	N	Range Avg Min	Range Avg Max
FL	28,416	28,416	31,166	28,416	28,416	44,915	6	.	.
GA	18,720	20,800	25,721	24,960	29,120	39,520	41	27,040	41,600
MO	41,246	41,246	41,246	41,246	41,246	41,246	1	.	.
NC	32,995	32,995	35,466	34,095	39,308	39,308	3	.	.
OH	33,010	38,371	50,484	43,883	62,596	81,159	4	31,699	47,590
TX	28,745	28,745	28,745	28,745	28,745	28,745	1	.	.
VA	51,757	51,757	60,085	55,729	72,769	72,769	3	39,638	66,063

Degree Required Data

	Min	Q1	Mean	Median	Q3	Max	N	Range Avg Min	Range Avg Max
High School	28,745	28,745	40,251	40,251	51,757	51,757	2	33,331	55,551
Associate's	55,729	55,729	64,249	64,249	72,769	72,769	2	42,791	71,319
Bachelor's	18,720	20,800	28,664	28,416	31,200	81,159	53	27,506	42,199
Master's								.	.
Doctoral								.	.

ASSOCIATE LIBRARIAN OF ARCHIVES AND SPECIAL COLLECTIONS (NON-MLS DEGREED) - CONTINUED
ALL PUBLIC LIBRARIES
Regional Data

	Min	Q1	Mean	Median	Q3	Max	N	Range Avg Min	Range Avg Max
North Atlantic	12,792	16,812	29,630	29,177	38,333	52,871	16	26,395	36,400
Great Lakes & Plains	16,848	24,950	32,888	28,018	40,168	81,159	40	29,095	39,621
Southeast	15,126	21,403	28,736	27,040	31,200	72,769	61	28,186	44,198
West & Southwest	12,480	18,720	30,876	29,702	37,819	56,293	11	19,757	26,943
ALL REGIONS	12,480	21,491	30,329	28,049	35,183	81,159	128	27,249	39,889

State Data

	Min	Q1	Mean	Median	Q3	Max	N	Range Avg Min	Range Avg Max
AL	15,126	15,126	18,265	18,265	21,403	21,403	2		
AR	21,578	21,578	21,578	21,578	21,578	21,578	1		
CO	27,102	27,102	40,298	37,500	56,293	56,293	3	23,941	32,282
FL	28,416	28,416	31,428	28,416	33,000	44,915	7		
GA	18,720	20,800	26,362	26,000	29,120	52,664	42	27,040	41,600
IA	20,800	20,800	34,580	34,580	48,360	48,360	2		
IL	18,720	20,800	33,470	30,000	41,475	66,456	9	51,792	80,704
IN	25,334	25,334	33,242	27,976	39,520	48,047	5	35,360	41,600
KY	27,963	27,963	27,963	27,963	27,963	27,963	1	15,600	27,976
MA	36,665	36,665	46,071	48,677	52,871	52,871	3	28,912	37,440
MD	30,274	30,274	39,681	39,681	49,088	49,088	2		
ME	28,080	28,080	31,983	31,928	35,942	35,942	3	30,021	41,253
MI	22,484	25,958	29,111	28,018	30,892	40,817	14	23,067	28,018
MO	34,757	34,757	37,745	37,232	41,246	41,246	3	24,773	35,994
MS	28,800	28,800	28,800	28,800	28,800	28,800	1		
NC	32,995	32,995	35,466	34,095	39,308	39,308	3		
ND	16,848	16,848	18,106	18,106	19,364	19,364	2		
NE	20,000	20,000	20,000	20,000	20,000	20,000	1		
NJ	12,792	12,792	16,112	13,117	20,506	21,353	5		
NY	40,000	40,000	40,000	40,000	40,000	40,000	1		
OH	33,010	38,371	50,484	43,883	62,596	81,159	4	31,699	47,590
PA	13,000	13,000	20,000	20,000	27,000	27,000	2	13,000	20,800
SC	24,126	24,126	24,126	24,126	24,126	24,126	1		
TX	12,480	16,640	27,343	29,224	34,499	45,540	8	18,920	25,875
VA	51,757	51,757	60,085	55,729	72,769	72,769	3	39,638	66,063

Degree Required Data

	Min	Q1	Mean	Median	Q3	Max	N	Range Avg Min	Range Avg Max
High School	12,480	18,720	24,315	21,102	28,745	51,757	18	20,923	30,682
Associate's	14,560	19,760	35,401	26,291	51,888	72,769	8	31,140	49,751
Bachelor's	18,720	24,126	30,373	28,416	34,095	81,159	86	26,673	38,221
Master's	28,800	36,500	45,834	44,730	54,479	66,456	8	51,792	80,704
Doctoral									

ASSOCIATE LIBRARIAN OF CHILDREN'S SERVICES/YOUNG ADULT SERVICES (NON-MLS DEGREED)

Provides assistance to patrons including topical research and material location. Assists patrons with the use of library resources and equipment. Screens the collection for outdated or unused materials following established guidelines. May perform managerial and administrative duties. Provides services intended for children and youth through twelfth grade; develops collection, provides homework and reader's advisory services, and develops age appropriate programs.

Very Small Public Library
(Serving a population of less than 10,000)
Regional Data

	Min	Q1	Mean	Median	Q3	Max	N	Range Avg Min	Range Avg Max
North Atlantic	12,480	30,007	33,205	34,226	39,021	47,165	24	28,803	38,305
Great Lakes & Plains	11,202	18,720	24,614	23,462	28,150	57,720	49	18,952	26,163
Southeast	20,135	25,148	29,191	30,206	33,235	36,218	4	.	.
West & Southwest	13,920	16,536	25,497	19,460	26,707	56,901	6	21,622	26,312
ALL REGIONS	11,202	19,556	27,382	25,759	33,654	57,720	83	23,364	31,378

State Data

	Min	Q1	Mean	Median	Q3	Max	N	Range Avg Min	Range Avg Max
AL	20,135	20,135	28,838	30,160	36,218	36,218	3	.	.
AZ	56,901	56,901	56,901	56,901	56,901	56,901	1	.	.
CO	16,536	16,536	21,622	21,622	26,707	26,707	2	21,622	26,312
CT	30,000	34,382	38,166	38,584	42,151	45,714	5	31,782	34,382
IA	18,720	21,819	25,324	25,533	28,986	31,200	8	22,027	26,166
IL	20,550	24,939	28,152	24,960	29,120	39,133	9	.	.
IN	11,202	17,221	21,424	18,720	24,128	39,459	9	15,762	23,916
KS	11,440	17,054	21,331	21,314	25,667	31,200	6	15,600	24,405
MA	30,014	33,654	36,301	34,382	39,458	47,165	7	30,306	40,281
ME	25,210	27,636	30,407	30,507	33,178	35,406	4	22,703	35,589
MI	18,720	18,720	19,245	19,459	19,556	19,556	3	.	.
MO	57,720	57,720	57,720	57,720	57,720	57,720	1	47,507	57,720
ND	14,310	14,310	14,310	14,310	14,310	14,310	1	.	.
NE	15,590	15,590	20,677	17,680	28,762	28,762	3	.	.
NH	28,600	28,600	28,600	28,600	28,600	28,600	1	27,477	36,213
NJ	38,542	38,542	39,291	39,291	40,040	40,040	2	33,280	45,760
NY	40,019	40,019	40,019	40,019	40,019	40,019	1	37,440	52,000
OH	22,859	22,859	31,504	23,920	47,734	47,734	3	14,872	23,920
PA	12,480	12,480	21,478	19,818	32,136	32,136	3	.	.
SD	22,630	22,630	25,875	25,875	29,120	29,120	2	.	.
TX	13,920	13,920	17,613	17,680	21,239	21,239	3	.	.
VT	18,720	18,720	18,720	18,720	18,720	18,720	1	18,720	18,720
WI	16,640	18,065	22,810	23,265	27,555	28,069	4	16,640	19,760
WV	30,251	30,251	30,251	30,251	30,251	30,251	1	.	.

Degree Required Data

	Min	Q1	Mean	Median	Q3	Max	N	Range Avg Min	Range Avg Max
High School	11,202	16,847	19,516	18,720	22,745	30,160	28	16,712	22,069
Associate's	11,440	20,592	28,127	28,392	34,070	57,720	19	26,070	33,147
Bachelor's	19,556	27,322	31,799	30,507	37,380	47,165	28	29,292	41,803
Master's	37,333	37,333	46,650	45,714	56,901	56,901	3	.	.
Doctoral									

ASSOCIATE LIBRARIAN OF CHILDREN'S SERVICES/YOUNG ADULT SERVICES (NON-MLS DEGREED) - CONTINUED
Small Public Library
(Serving a population of 10,000 to 25,000)
Regional Data

	Min	Q1	Mean	Median	Q3	Max	N	Range Avg Min	Range Avg Max
North Atlantic	18,720	24,981	34,141	34,307	43,191	53,477	12	26,597	41,835
Great Lakes & Plains	17,160	25,688	30,629	31,200	35,360	50,960	45	24,434	32,365
Southeast	14,098	18,043	20,728	18,720	22,318	31,953	9	15,600	31,928
West & Southwest	13,455	22,626	30,321	26,229	38,094	56,160	12	29,111	41,087
ALL REGIONS	13,455	23,254	29,980	28,664	35,360	56,160	78	25,359	36,547

State Data

	Min	Q1	Mean	Median	Q3	Max	N	Range Avg Min	Range Avg Max
AL	18,210	18,210	18,210	18,210	18,210	18,210	1		
AR	18,043	18,043	18,043	18,043	18,043	18,043	1		
CO	37,500	37,500	40,500	40,500	43,500	43,500	2		
IA	23,254	23,254	23,254	23,254	23,254	23,254	1		
IL	17,160	26,344	31,707	33,124	37,440	41,600	20	20,107	27,733
IN	24,960	24,960	28,047	27,539	31,641	31,641	3	20,800	27,040
KS	24,960	26,480	30,670	31,430	34,860	34,861	4	18,720	31,200
KY	22,318	22,318	27,136	27,136	31,953	31,953	2	15,600	31,928
MA	44,783	44,783	44,783	44,783	44,783	44,783	1		
MI	23,777	29,328	30,724	30,264	34,000	36,712	6	29,328	29,328
MN	50,960	50,960	50,960	50,960	50,960	50,960	1	38,230	50,960
MO	18,720	18,720	18,720	18,720	18,720	18,720	1	18,720	24,960
MT	26,770	26,770	26,770	26,770	26,770	26,770	1		
NC	14,098	14,098	14,733	14,733	15,369	15,369	2		
ND	17,680	17,680	17,680	17,680	17,680	17,680	1		
NE	39,250	39,250	39,250	39,250	39,250	39,250	1		
NH	34,091	34,091	43,784	43,784	53,477	53,477	2	37,950	56,358
NJ	34,522	34,522	40,674	41,600	45,900	45,900	3	35,360	62,400
NM	13,455	18,476	29,700	24,593	40,924	56,160	4	29,111	41,087
OH	22,339	25,950	28,310	26,666	33,003	35,235	6	26,666	39,998
OK	21,860	21,860	21,860	21,860	21,860	21,860	1		
OR	38,688	38,688	38,688	38,688	38,688	38,688	1		
PA	18,720	19,760	24,856	22,880	29,952	34,944	4	16,640	26,347
RI	25,002	25,002	27,945	27,945	30,888	30,888	2	25,002	38,688
TX	22,252	22,252	25,577	23,000	31,478	31,478	3		
WI	33,285	33,285	33,285	33,285	33,285	33,285	1		
WV	18,720	18,720	22,187	20,800	27,040	27,040	3		

Degree Required Data

	Min	Q1	Mean	Median	Q3	Max	N	Range Avg Min	Range Avg Max
High School	13,455	17,862	22,218	22,285	26,495	33,003	16	18,138	25,875
Associate's	17,160	23,376	30,838	32,084	37,440	50,960	16	22,161	31,158
Bachelor's	18,210	26,666	31,601	30,888	35,235	56,160	37	26,062	37,719
Master's	37,000	37,000	38,146	38,189	39,250	39,250	3	.	.
Doctoral	.	.	.	.	.	.	.	.	.

ASSOCIATE LIBRARIAN OF CHILDREN'S SERVICES/YOUNG ADULT SERVICES (NON-MLS DEGREED) - CONTINUED
Medium Public Library
(Serving a population of 25,000 to 99,999)
Regional Data

	Min	Q1	Mean	Median	Q3	Max	N	Range Avg Min	Range Avg Max
North Atlantic	11,752	25,917	34,643	36,309	43,680	55,337	33	38,082	45,266
Great Lakes & Plains	16,224	25,127	35,150	34,889	42,411	53,103	62	26,172	38,054
Southeast	17,056	24,303	27,158	25,680	31,432	36,592	16	31,200	23,920
West & Southwest	18,179	25,000	33,045	34,796	40,395	50,232	18	27,132	34,871
ALL REGIONS	11,752	25,000	33,735	33,947	41,844	55,337	129	28,510	38,004

State Data

	Min	Q1	Mean	Median	Q3	Max	N	Range Avg Min	Range Avg Max
AR	18,658	18,658	23,834	24,202	28,642	28,642	3	.	.
CA	23,026	25,355	35,489	34,258	44,574	50,232	5	25,917	33,171
CO	25,480	25,480	36,932	35,334	49,983	49,983	3	18,720	31,200
CT	42,515	42,515	47,063	44,096	54,579	54,579	3	44,096	54,579
DE	55,337	55,337	55,337	55,337	55,337	55,337	1	.	.
IA	35,360	35,360	39,722	35,360	48,445	48,445	3	31,200	35,360
ID	18,179	18,970	21,965	21,840	24,960	26,000	4	18,179	25,210
IL	23,920	30,784	38,513	39,562	46,734	51,774	27	28,657	44,098
IN	21,133	21,133	29,804	33,280	35,000	35,000	3	24,825	33,446
KS	16,224	16,224	18,720	18,720	21,216	21,216	2	16,442	19,458
LA	24,403	24,403	24,403	24,403	24,403	24,403	1	.	.
MA	37,441	43,680	44,481	43,680	46,728	51,676	6	39,250	41,985
ME	44,200	44,200	44,200	44,200	44,200	44,200	1	30,992	44,200
MI	22,484	22,484	23,705	24,315	24,315	24,315	3	20,446	24,315
MN	48,330	48,330	48,330	48,330	48,330	48,330	3	.	.
MS	31,164	31,164	31,164	31,164	31,164	31,164	1		6,240
NC	21,799	25,548	28,539	27,798	31,699	36,592	6	31,200	41,600
ND	24,461	24,461	31,221	31,221	37,981	37,981	2	24,211	36,327
NE	41,600	41,600	41,600	41,600	41,600	41,600	1	29,120	41,600
NJ	35,314	35,314	38,728	38,728	42,141	42,141	2	29,120	49,920
NY	16,640	18,907	26,976	19,573	36,309	43,451	5	43,451	45,490
OH	19,067	24,960	31,076	30,888	34,778	53,103	17	25,110	39,387
PA	11,752	24,000	28,286	27,415	32,960	41,243	14	.	.
RI	27,248	27,248	27,248	27,248	27,248	27,248	1	.	.
SC	25,435	25,435	29,691	29,691	33,947	33,947	2	.	.
TN	17,056	17,056	25,626	25,626	34,196	34,196	2	.	.
TX	25,000	25,000	33,846	36,142	40,395	40,395	3	.	.
VA	25,596	25,596	25,596	25,596	25,596	25,596	1	.	.
WI	44,966	44,966	44,966	44,966	44,966	44,966	1	.	.
WY	37,523	37,523	39,055	38,646	40,997	40,997	3	37,523	44,803

Degree Required Data

	Min	Q1	Mean	Median	Q3	Max	N	Range Avg Min	Range Avg Max
High School	17,056	24,331	30,013	26,520	34,029	50,232	24	21,379	32,849
Associate's	18,887	25,548	32,537	25,918	39,531	54,579	13	30,985	38,126
Bachelor's	16,640	25,596	35,664	36,142	43,680	55,337	75	29,932	40,586
Master's	28,642	31,316	35,701	35,796	40,167	42,411	8	31,200	41,600
Doctoral	.	.	.	.	.	.		.	.

ASSOCIATE LIBRARIAN OF CHILDREN'S SERVICES/YOUNG ADULT SERVICES (NON-MLS DEGREED) - CONTINUED
Large Public Library
(Serving a population of 100,000 to 499,999)
Regional Data

	Min	Q1	Mean	Median	Q3	Max	N	Range Avg Min	Range Avg Max
North Atlantic	10,837	14,399	29,478	30,867	37,558	71,958	69	33,616	41,676
Great Lakes & Plains	18,574	27,310	32,568	32,731	37,544	48,852	107	26,697	39,914
Southeast	18,720	26,125	31,355	30,185	36,733	49,067	32	28,028	38,381
West & Southwest	19,261	29,151	35,819	34,158	44,693	52,998	37	26,125	36,848
ALL REGIONS	10,837	25,481	32,030	32,261	37,856	71,958	245	27,321	39,640

State Data

	Min	Q1	Mean	Median	Q3	Max	N	Range Avg Min	Range Avg Max
AZ	52,998	52,998	52,998	52,998	52,998	52,998	1	.	.
CA	29,856	34,248	41,571	46,321	46,321	47,632	11	30,243	39,811
CO	28,995	34,226	38,940	39,004	44,693	44,693	9	24,700	38,095
FL	26,999	27,539	31,374	30,723	34,069	39,333	8		
GA	24,960	24,960	32,968	32,968	40,976	40,976	2		
IL	26,110	31,740	37,431	35,484	42,410	48,499	19		
IN	32,288	32,288	32,288	32,288	32,288	32,288	1		
KS	28,995	30,347	33,972	33,446	35,776	44,325	25	29,133	48,549
LA	26,770	26,770	26,770	26,770	26,770	26,770	1	23,629	33,405
MA	32,635	32,635	38,612	41,600	41,600	41,600	3		
MD	24,690	30,867	37,490	34,757	45,344	65,520	31		
MI	27,791	35,141	38,053	40,817	40,817	48,852	9	30,784	38,792
MN	36,570	37,304	39,949	39,983	42,594	43,259	4		
MO	19,469	22,339	24,970	23,005	27,310	36,712	19	21,606	30,913
MS	30,481	30,481	30,481	30,481	30,481	30,481	1		
NC	25,481	28,109	28,702	29,120	29,890	30,910	5	27,321	43,139
NE	28,664	28,664	32,222	31,098	36,604	36,604	9	28,664	36,604
NJ	10,837	12,480	15,227	13,117	14,399	40,137	25		
NM	48,805	48,805	48,805	48,805	48,805	48,805	1	35,838	49,109
NY	37,558	37,558	50,032	40,581	71,958	71,958	3	35,811	43,940
OH	18,574	19,240	24,618	22,610	27,685	42,890	14	22,069	33,093
OK	19,261	19,261	20,103	20,103	20,946	20,946	2	17,368	22,547
OR	26,208	26,208	26,208	26,208	26,208	26,208	1		
PA	21,320	30,509	32,174	33,717	35,173	36,650	7	31,970	39,978
TN	18,720	18,720	20,157	18,720	22,266	22,361	5		
TX	23,395	26,737	29,111	29,468	31,740	34,158	12	24,419	41,808
VA	23,732	35,425	38,487	38,115	43,730	49,067	10	33,842	33,842
WI	37,544	37,544	40,093	41,991	41,991	41,991	7	32,926	37,544

Degree Required Data

	Min	Q1	Mean	Median	Q3	Max	N	Range Avg Min	Range Avg Max
High School	18,574	21,299	31,022	27,791	41,991	71,958	37	27,778	32,493
Associate's	19,469	22,339	32,867	30,185	46,321	46,321	18	20,708	30,472
Bachelor's	22,069	29,120	34,702	33,738	38,037	65,520	154	28,231	41,468
Master's	31,678	32,673	36,420	37,440	39,333	40,976	5	32,448	54,080
Doctoral	.	.	.	.	.	.	.	.	.

ASSOCIATE LIBRARIAN OF CHILDREN'S SERVICES/YOUNG ADULT SERVICES (NON-MLS DEGREED) - CONTINUED
Very Large Public Library
(Serving a population of 500,000 or more)
Regional Data

	Min	Q1	Mean	Median	Q3	Max	N	Range Avg Min	Range Avg Max
North Atlantic	31,990	34,697	44,907	44,094	53,483	60,707	29	.	.
Great Lakes & Plains	24,971	34,713	40,092	39,060	45,302	55,821	109	31,699	47,590
Southeast	23,958	28,299	32,041	31,961	35,019	47,771	44	.	.
West & Southwest	23,130	34,714	38,043	37,848	41,392	50,170	38	33,600	41,072
ALL REGIONS	23,130	32,907	38,763	37,063	44,038	60,707	220	33,168	42,553

State Data

	Min	Q1	Mean	Median	Q3	Max	N	Range Avg Min	Range Avg Max
CA	29,797	29,797	35,067	36,376	36,376	41,679	6	29,797	36,376
CO	30,700	35,138	36,801	37,316	39,498	40,830	15	.	.
FL	26,263	28,416	35,262	35,307	37,355	47,771	11	.	.
MD	34,696	40,142	46,746	45,050	53,483	60,707	25	.	.
MO	24,971	24,971	24,971	24,971	24,971	24,971	3	.	.
NC	23,958	27,276	30,967	31,657	33,699	40,359	33	.	.
NJ	31,990	31,995	33,416	32,000	34,838	37,675	4	.	.
OH	31,699	34,713	40,520	39,060	45,302	55,821	106	31,699	47,590
OR	41,392	41,392	45,681	48,797	48,797	50,170	11	36,281	43,786
TX	23,130	27,560	30,123	31,470	31,970	35,140	6	23,130	34,694

Degree Required Data

	Min	Q1	Mean	Median	Q3	Max	N	Range Avg Min	Range Avg Max
High School	.	.	.	.	.	.	.	.	.
Associate's	31,464	35,140	41,039	41,392	48,797	48,797	11	33,654	41,392
Bachelor's	23,958	33,191	38,848	36,479	44,094	60,707	198	32,890	43,217
Master's	37,355	37,355	41,150	37,355	45,917	47,771	5	.	.
Doctoral	.	.	.	.	.	.	.	.	.

ASSOCIATE LIBRARIAN OF CHILDREN'S SERVICES/YOUNG ADULT SERVICES (NON-MLS DEGREED) - CONTINUED
ALL PUBLIC LIBRARIES
Regional Data

	Min	Q1	Mean	Median	Q3	Max	N	Range Avg Min	Range Avg Max
North Atlantic	10,837	25,002	34,049	34,522	42,515	71,958	167	31,523	41,364
Great Lakes & Plains	11,202	26,833	33,921	34,174	40,229	57,720	372	25,637	37,421
Southeast	14,098	25,596	30,009	29,832	34,095	49,067	105	26,485	33,328
West & Southwest	13,455	27,560	34,978	35,334	41,392	56,901	111	29,469	37,913
ALL REGIONS	10,837	26,208	33,561	33,694	40,229	71,958	755	27,476	38,055

State Data

	Min	Q1	Mean	Median	Q3	Max	N	Range Avg Min	Range Avg Max
AL	18,210	19,173	26,181	25,148	33,189	36,218	4	.	.
AR	18,043	18,350	22,386	21,430	26,422	28,642	4	.	.
AZ	52,998	52,998	54,950	54,950	56,901	56,901	2	.	.
CA	23,026	33,509	38,415	36,376	46,321	50,232	22	28,615	36,166
CO	16,536	34,226	36,694	37,500	40,274	49,983	31	22,273	32,003
CT	30,000	36,483	41,503	42,333	44,905	54,579	8	37,939	44,481
DE	55,337	55,337	55,337	55,337	55,337	55,337	1	.	.
FL	26,263	28,416	33,625	32,673	37,355	47,771	19	.	.
GA	24,960	24,960	32,968	32,968	40,976	40,976	2	.	.
IA	18,720	23,150	28,751	27,877	33,280	48,445	12	26,614	30,763
ID	18,179	18,970	21,965	21,840	24,960	26,000	4	18,179	25,210
IL	17,160	27,040	35,181	35,360	41,736	51,774	75	26,947	40,825
IN	11,202	18,720	24,916	24,544	31,965	39,459	16	18,658	26,689
KS	11,440	28,995	30,741	32,011	34,859	44,325	37	26,669	43,776
KY	22,318	22,318	27,136	27,136	31,953	31,953	2	15,600	31,928
LA	24,403	24,403	25,586	25,586	26,770	26,770	2	23,629	33,405
MA	30,014	34,382	40,095	41,600	43,680	51,676	17	34,281	41,038
MD	24,690	33,738	41,622	40,142	49,943	65,520	56	.	.
ME	25,210	30,063	33,166	30,950	35,406	44,200	5	25,466	38,459
MI	18,720	24,315	31,222	31,200	36,712	48,852	21	26,067	29,216
MN	36,570	39,983	44,468	45,795	48,330	50,960	8	38,230	50,960
MO	18,720	22,339	26,074	23,400	26,853	57,720	24	22,702	31,906
MS	30,481	30,481	30,823	30,823	31,164	31,164	2	.	6,240
MT	26,770	26,770	26,770	26,770	26,770	26,770	1	.	.
NC	14,098	27,276	29,698	29,861	33,102	40,359	46	28,614	42,626
ND	14,310	15,995	23,608	21,070	31,221	37,981	4	24,211	36,327
NE	15,590	28,664	30,920	30,681	36,604	41,600	14	28,710	37,103
NH	28,600	28,600	38,723	34,091	53,477	53,477	3	34,459	49,643
NJ	10,837	13,117	22,011	14,399	33,261	45,900	36	32,587	52,693
NM	13,455	23,498	33,521	25,688	48,805	56,160	5	30,793	43,092
NY	16,640	19,573	36,111	37,558	40,581	71,958	9	37,665	45,862
OH	18,574	32,712	37,209	35,761	43,982	55,821	146	26,737	40,850
OK	19,261	19,261	20,689	20,946	21,860	21,860	3	17,368	22,547
OR	26,208	41,392	43,645	41,392	48,797	50,170	13	36,281	43,786
PA	11,752	21,160	28,039	29,710	33,998	41,243	28	25,400	34,136
RI	25,002	25,002	27,713	27,248	30,888	30,888	3	25,002	38,688
SC	25,435	25,435	29,691	29,691	33,947	33,947	2	.	.
SD	22,630	22,630	25,875	25,875	29,120	29,120	2	.	.
TN	17,056	18,720	21,720	18,720	22,361	34,196	7	.	.
TX	13,920	23,395	28,192	29,151	31,970	40,395	27	23,774	38,251
VA	23,732	33,842	37,315	37,356	43,730	49,067	11	33,842	33,842
VT	18,720	18,720	18,720	18,720	18,720	18,720	1	18,720	18,720
WI	16,640	28,069	34,626	37,544	41,991	44,966	13	26,412	30,430
WV	18,720	19,760	24,203	23,920	28,646	30,251	4	.	.
WY	37,523	37,523	39,055	38,646	40,997	40,997	3	37,523	44,803

Degree Required Data

	Min	Q1	Mean	Median	Q3	Max	N	Range Avg Min	Range Avg Max
High School	11,202	18,720	26,382	23,920	30,509	71,958	105	20,346	27,477
Associate's	11,440	23,254	32,388	31,200	41,392	57,720	77	26,179	34,467
Bachelor's	16,640	30,274	36,119	34,818	41,382	65,520	492	29,042	41,101
Master's	28,642	35,796	38,660	37,397	41,652	56,901	24	31,824	47,840
Doctoral									

ASSOCIATE LIBRARIAN OF GOVERNMENT DOCUMENTS (NON-MLS DEGREED)

Provides assistance to patrons including topical research and material location. Assists patrons with the use of library resources and equipment. Screens the collection for outdated or unused materials following established guidelines. May perform managerial and administrative duties. Provides access to publications of the U.S. federal government such as transcripts of hearings and text of bills, resolutions, statutes, reports, charters, treaties, periodicals and statistics.

Very Small Public Library
(Serving a population of less than 10,000)
Regional Data

	Min	Q1	Mean	Median	Q3	Max	N	Range Avg Min	Range Avg Max
Great Lakes & Plains	12,480	12,480	12,480	12,480	12,480	12,480	1	12,480	12,480
ALL REGIONS	12,480	12,480	12,480	12,480	12,480	12,480	1	12,480	12,480

State Data

	Min	Q1	Mean	Median	Q3	Max	N	Range Avg Min	Range Avg Max
IA	12,480	12,480	12,480	12,480	12,480	12,480	1	12,480	12,480

Degree Required Data

	Min	Q1	Mean	Median	Q3	Max	N	Range Avg Min	Range Avg Max
High School	12,480	12,480	12,480	12,480	12,480	12,480	1	12,480	12,480
Associate's									
Bachelor's									
Master's									
Doctoral									

ASSOCIATE LIBRARIAN OF GOVERNMENT DOCUMENTS (NON-MLS DEGREED) - CONTINUED
Small Public Library
(Serving a population of 10,000 to 25,000)
Regional Data

	Min	Q1	Mean	Median	Q3	Max	N	Range Avg Min	Range Avg Max
Southeast	21,840	21,840	21,840	21,840	21,840	21,840	1	15,600	21,840
West & Southwest	23,366	23,366	23,366	23,366	23,366	23,366	1		
ALL REGIONS	21,840	21,840	22,603	22,603	23,366	23,366	2	15,600	21,840

State Data

	Min	Q1	Mean	Median	Q3	Max	N	Range Avg Min	Range Avg Max
KY	21,840	21,840	21,840	21,840	21,840	21,840	1	15,600	21,840
TX	23,366	23,366	23,366	23,366	23,366	23,366	1	.	.

Degree Required Data

	Min	Q1	Mean	Median	Q3	Max	N	Range Avg Min	Range Avg Max
High School	21,840	21,840	21,840	21,840	21,840	21,840	1	15,600	21,840
Associate's	.	.	.	.	.	.		.	.
Bachelor's	23,366	23,366	23,366	23,366	23,366	23,366	1	.	.
Master's	.	.	.	.	.	.		.	.
Doctoral	.	.	.	.	.	.		.	.

ASSOCIATE LIBRARIAN OF GOVERNMENT DOCUMENTS (NON-MLS DEGREED) - CONTINUED
Large Public Library
(Serving a population of 100,000 to 499,999)
Regional Data

	Min	Q1	Mean	Median	Q3	Max	N	Range Avg Min	Range Avg Max
North Atlantic	10,837	11,658	12,069	12,480	12,480	12,480	4	.	.
Great Lakes & Plains	18,158	18,699	22,994	19,365	31,418	33,218	7	19,684	27,532
Southeast	25,481	25,481	43,552	48,108	57,068	57,068	3	.	.
West & Southwest	28,995	28,995	28,995	28,995	28,995	28,995	1	28,995	45,594
ALL REGIONS	10,837	12,480	24,593	19,365	31,418	57,068	15	21,014	30,112

State Data

	Min	Q1	Mean	Median	Q3	Max	N	Range Avg Min	Range Avg Max
CO	28,995	28,995	28,995	28,995	28,995	28,995	1	28,995	45,594
MI	31,418	31,418	31,418	31,418	31,418	31,418	1	.	.
MO	18,158	18,699	21,590	19,365	20,738	33,218	6	19,684	27,532
NC	25,481	25,481	25,481	25,481	25,481	25,481	1	.	.
NJ	10,837	11,658	12,069	12,480	12,480	12,480	4	.	.
VA	48,108	48,108	52,588	52,588	57,068	57,068	2	.	.

Degree Required Data

	Min	Q1	Mean	Median	Q3	Max	N	Range Avg Min	Range Avg Max
High School	18,158	18,699	25,121	19,365	31,418	48,108	7	18,158	26,395
Associate's	.	.	.	.	.	.		.	.
Bachelor's	25,481	27,238	36,190	31,106	45,143	57,068	4	28,153	39,406
Master's	.	.	.	.	.	.		.	.
Doctoral	.	.	.	.	.	.		.	.

ASSOCIATE LIBRARIAN OF GOVERNMENT DOCUMENTS (NON-MLS DEGREED) - CONTINUED
Very Large Public Library
(Serving a population of 500,000 or more)
Regional Data

	Min	Q1	Mean	Median	Q3	Max	N	Range Avg Min	Range Avg Max
Great Lakes & Plains	51,152	51,152	51,152	51,152	51,152	51,152	1	.	.
Southeast	23,869	23,869	26,143	26,143	28,416	28,416	2	.	.
West & Southwest	29,320	29,320	41,294	41,294	53,268	53,268	2	.	.
ALL REGIONS	23,869	28,416	37,205	29,320	51,152	53,268	5	.	.

State Data

	Min	Q1	Mean	Median	Q3	Max	N	Range Avg Min	Range Avg Max
CA	53,268	53,268	53,268	53,268	53,268	53,268	1	.	.
FL	23,869	23,869	26,143	26,143	28,416	28,416	2	.	.
OH	51,152	51,152	51,152	51,152	51,152	51,152	1	.	.
TX	29,320	29,320	29,320	29,320	29,320	29,320	1	.	.

Degree Required Data

	Min	Q1	Mean	Median	Q3	Max	N	Range Avg Min	Range Avg Max
High School	29,320	29,320	29,320	29,320	29,320	29,320	1	.	.
Associate's	.	.	.	.	.	.		.	.
Bachelor's	28,416	28,416	44,279	51,152	53,268	53,268	3	.	.
Master's	.	.	.	.	.	.		.	.
Doctoral	.	.	.	.	.	.		.	.

ASSOCIATE LIBRARIAN OF GOVERNMENT DOCUMENTS (NON-MLS DEGREED) - CONTINUED
ALL PUBLIC LIBRARIES
Regional Data

	Min	Q1	Mean	Median	Q3	Max	N	Range Avg Min	Range Avg Max
North Atlantic	10,837	11,658	12,069	12,480	12,480	12,480	4	.	.
Great Lakes & Plains	12,480	18,699	24,955	19,365	31,418	51,152	9	18,655	25,382
Southeast	21,840	23,869	34,130	26,948	48,108	57,068	6	15,600	21,840
West & Southwest	23,366	26,181	33,737	29,157	41,294	53,268	4	28,995	45,594
ALL REGIONS	10,837	18,158	26,635	23,366	31,418	57,068	23	19,464	27,234

State Data

	Min	Q1	Mean	Median	Q3	Max	N	Range Avg Min	Range Avg Max
CA	53,268	53,268	53,268	53,268	53,268	53,268	1		
CO	28,995	28,995	28,995	28,995	28,995	28,995	1	28,995	45,594
FL	23,869	23,869	26,143	26,143	28,416	28,416	2		
IA	12,480	12,480	12,480	12,480	12,480	12,480	1	12,480	12,480
KY	21,840	21,840	21,840	21,840	21,840	21,840	1	15,600	21,840
MI	31,418	31,418	31,418	31,418	31,418	31,418	1		
MO	18,158	18,699	21,590	19,365	20,738	33,218	6	19,684	27,532
NC	25,481	25,481	25,481	25,481	25,481	25,481	1		
NJ	10,837	11,658	12,069	12,480	12,480	12,480	4		
OH	51,152	51,152	51,152	51,152	51,152	51,152	1		
TX	23,366	23,366	26,343	26,343	29,320	29,320	2		
VA	48,108	48,108	52,588	52,588	57,068	57,068	2		

Degree Required Data

	Min	Q1	Mean	Median	Q3	Max	N	Range Avg Min	Range Avg Max
High School	12,480	18,699	23,949	20,051	29,320	48,108	10	16,982	23,757
Associate's									
Bachelor's	23,366	26,948	37,620	31,106	52,210	57,068	8	28,153	39,406
Master's									
Doctoral									

ASSOCIATE LIBRARIAN OF INSTRUCTIONAL SERVICE/LITERACY (NON-MLS DEGREED)

Provides assistance to patrons including topical research and material location. Assists patrons with the use of library resources and equipment. Screens the collection for outdated or unused materials following established guidelines. May perform managerial and administrative duties. Advances learning, teaching and research with respect to information literacy in higher education; assists patrons to develop the ability to read and write.

Medium Public Library
(Serving a population of 25,000 to 99,999)
Regional Data

	Min	Q1	Mean	Median	Q3	Max	N	Range Avg Min	Range Avg Max
North Atlantic	49,400	49,400	49,400	49,400	49,400	49,400	1		
West & Southwest	30,000	48,194	59,491	54,024	82,618	82,618	5	55,716	71,143
ALL REGIONS	30,000	48,194	57,809	51,712	82,618	82,618	6	55,716	71,143

State Data

	Min	Q1	Mean	Median	Q3	Max	N	Range Avg Min	Range Avg Max
CA	30,000	48,194	59,491	54,024	82,618	82,618	5	55,716	71,143
MA	49,400	49,400	49,400	49,400	49,400	49,400	1		

Degree Required Data

	Min	Q1	Mean	Median	Q3	Max	N	Range Avg Min	Range Avg Max
High School	.	.	.	.	.	.		.	
Associate's	30,000	30,000	30,000	30,000	30,000	30,000	1	.	
Bachelor's	48,194	48,194	48,194	48,194	48,194	48,194	1	31,200	48,194
Master's	49,400	51,712	67,165	68,321	82,618	82,618	4	67,974	82,618
Doctoral	.	.	.	.	.	.		.	

ASSOCIATE LIBRARIAN OF INSTRUCTIONAL SERVICE/LITERACY (NON-MLS DEGREED) - CONTINUED
Large Public Library
(Serving a population of 100,000 to 499,999)
Regional Data

	Min	Q1	Mean	Median	Q3	Max	N	Range Avg Min	Range Avg Max
North Atlantic	18,720	27,040	32,286	30,669	38,279	52,000	12	37,558	37,558
Great Lakes & Plains	33,614	33,614	33,614	33,614	33,614	33,614	1	.	.
Southeast	10,920	34,603	37,060	36,556	47,425	48,391	8	33,842	33,842
West & Southwest	35,105	43,222	54,399	51,740	69,326	71,580	20	46,027	60,214
ALL REGIONS	10,920	34,653	44,037	40,831	52,000	71,580	41	44,650	56,946

State Data

	Min	Q1	Mean	Median	Q3	Max	N	Range Avg Min	Range Avg Max
AZ	39,270	39,270	45,843	45,843	52,416	52,416	2	.	.
CA	38,106	48,859	58,692	59,779	69,680	71,580	14	46,976	61,388
CO	40,789	40,789	40,789	40,789	40,789	40,789	1	32,635	48,963
FL	35,464	35,464	35,464	35,464	35,464	35,464	1	.	.
IL	33,614	33,614	33,614	33,614	33,614	33,614	1	.	.
MD	32,218	33,435	36,676	36,827	39,916	40,831	4	.	.
MS	10,920	10,920	10,920	10,920	10,920	10,920	1	.	.
NJ	18,720	20,129	29,024	29,120	29,120	52,000	7	.	.
NY	37,558	37,558	37,558	37,558	37,558	37,558	1	37,558	37,558
TX	35,105	35,105	44,606	48,984	49,728	49,728	3	48,984	58,552
VA	33,842	35,364	41,682	42,194	48,110	48,391	6	33,842	33,842

Degree Required Data

	Min	Q1	Mean	Median	Q3	Max	N	Range Avg Min	Range Avg Max
High School	33,842	35,364	40,341	37,648	46,739	48,110	5	33,842	33,842
Associate's	38,106	38,106	40,050	40,050	41,995	41,995	2	38,106	46,301
Bachelor's	32,218	38,279	47,599	46,420	54,621	70,889	20	46,295	56,864
Master's	35,464	35,464	53,522	53,522	71,580	71,580	2	.	.
Doctoral	.	.	.	.	.	.		.	

ASSOCIATE LIBRARIAN OF INSTRUCTIONAL SERVICE/LITERACY (NON-MLS DEGREED) - CONTINUED
Very Large Public Library
(Serving a population of 500,000 or more)
Regional Data

	Min	Q1	Mean	Median	Q3	Max	N	Range Avg Min	Range Avg Max
Southeast	19,995	31,960	33,373	31,960	37,323	47,043	6	.	
West & Southwest	34,440	45,504	44,450	45,504	48,168	48,636	5	.	
ALL REGIONS	19,995	31,960	38,408	37,323	47,043	48,636	11	.	

State Data

	Min	Q1	Mean	Median	Q3	Max	N	Range Avg Min	Range Avg Max
CA	45,504	45,504	46,548	45,504	48,636	48,636	3	.	
FL	19,995	31,960	33,373	31,960	37,323	47,043	6	.	
TX	34,440	34,440	41,304	41,304	48,168	48,168	2	.	

Degree Required Data

	Min	Q1	Mean	Median	Q3	Max	N	Range Avg Min	Range Avg Max
High School	.	.	.	.	.			.	
Associate's	48,636	48,636	48,636	48,636	48,636	48,636	1	.	
Bachelor's	34,440	45,504	44,132	45,504	47,043	48,168	5	.	
Master's	.	.	.	.	.			.	
Doctoral	.	.	.	.	.			.	

ASSOCIATE LIBRARIAN OF INSTRUCTIONAL SERVICE/LITERACY (NON-MLS DEGREED) - CONTINUED
ALL PUBLIC LIBRARIES
Regional Data

	Min	Q1	Mean	Median	Q3	Max	N	Range Avg Min	Range Avg Max
North Atlantic	18,720	29,120	33,602	32,218	39,001	52,000	13	37,558	37,558
Great Lakes & Plains	33,614	33,614	33,614	33,614	33,614	33,614	1		
Southeast	10,920	31,960	35,480	35,414	46,739	48,391	14	33,842	33,842
West & Southwest	30,000	44,450	53,590	49,356	68,973	82,618	30	47,844	62,264
ALL REGIONS	10,920	33,842	44,394	43,222	51,064	82,618	58	46,495	59,312

State Data

	Min	Q1	Mean	Median	Q3	Max	N	Range Avg Min	Range Avg Max
AZ	39,270	39,270	45,843	45,843	52,416	52,416	2		
CA	30,000	45,504	57,218	55,425	69,680	82,618	22	48,849	63,479
CO	40,789	40,789	40,789	40,789	40,789	40,789	1	32,635	48,963
FL	19,995	31,960	33,672	31,960	37,323	47,043	7		
IL	33,614	33,614	33,614	33,614	33,614	33,614	1		
MA	49,400	49,400	49,400	49,400	49,400	49,400	1		
MD	32,218	33,435	36,676	36,827	39,916	40,831	4		
MS	10,920	10,920	10,920	10,920	10,920	10,920	1		
NJ	18,720	20,129	29,024	29,120	29,120	52,000	7		
NY	37,558	37,558	37,558	37,558	37,558	37,558	1	37,558	37,558
TX	34,440	35,105	43,285	48,168	48,984	49,728	5	48,984	58,552
VA	33,842	35,364	41,682	42,194	48,110	48,391	6	33,842	33,842

Degree Required Data

	Min	Q1	Mean	Median	Q3	Max	N	Range Avg Min	Range Avg Max
High School	33,842	35,364	40,341	37,648	46,739	48,110	5	33,842	33,842
Associate's	30,000	34,053	39,684	40,050	45,316	48,636	4	38,106	46,301
Bachelor's	32,218	39,001	46,955	46,274	51,064	70,889	26	44,618	55,900
Master's	35,464	49,400	62,617	62,802	82,618	82,618	6	67,974	82,618
Doctoral	.	.	.	.	.	.			

ASSOCIATE LIBRARIAN OF REFERENCE/INFORMATION SERVICES (NON-MLS DEGREED)

Provides assistance to patrons including topical research and material location. Assists patrons with the use of library resources and equipment. Screens the collection for outdated or unused materials following established guidelines. May perform managerial and administrative duties. Assists patrons with questions; instructs in the selection and use of appropriate tools and techniques for finding information; conducts searches for materials; contributes to reference collection development.

Very Small Public Library
(Serving a population of less than 10,000)
Regional Data

	Min	Q1	Mean	Median	Q3	Max	N	Range Avg Min	Range Avg Max
North Atlantic	28,233	28,233	32,528	33,946	35,406	35,406	3	27,789	41,662
Great Lakes & Plains	15,205	17,618	27,438	20,241	35,432	57,720	8	47,507	57,720
Southeast	10,712	10,712	16,210	17,784	20,135	20,135	3	10,712	6,396
West & Southwest	22,872	22,872	22,872	22,872	22,872	22,872	1		
ALL REGIONS	10,712	17,784	25,906	20,550	33,946	57,720	15	28,669	28,044

State Data

	Min	Q1	Mean	Median	Q3	Max	N	Range Avg Min	Range Avg Max
AL	17,784	17,784	18,960	18,960	20,135	20,135	2	.	2,080
IA	19,931	19,931	19,931	19,931	19,931	19,931	1	.	.
IN	32,864	32,864	32,864	32,864	32,864	32,864	1	.	.
KY	10,712	10,712	10,712	10,712	10,712	10,712	1	10,712	10,712
ME	28,233	28,233	32,528	33,946	35,406	35,406	3	27,789	41,662
MI	38,000	38,000	38,000	38,000	38,000	38,000	1	.	.
MO	57,720	57,720	57,720	57,720	57,720	57,720	1	47,507	57,720
NE	15,205	15,205	15,205	15,205	15,205	15,205	1	.	.
OH	16,786	16,786	18,595	18,450	20,550	20,550	3	.	.
TX	22,872	22,872	22,872	22,872	22,872	22,872	1	.	.

Degree Required Data

	Min	Q1	Mean	Median	Q3	Max	N	Range Avg Min	Range Avg Max
High School	10,712	15,205	16,340	16,786	18,450	20,550	5	10,712	10,712
Associate's	17,784	17,784	32,792	22,872	57,720	57,720	3	47,507	57,720
Bachelor's	19,931	28,233	31,396	33,405	35,406	38,000	6	27,789	41,662
Master's	.	.	.	.	.	.	.	.	.
Doctoral	.	.	.	.	.	.	.	.	.

ASSOCIATE LIBRARIAN OF REFERENCE/INFORMATION SERVICES (NON-MLS DEGREED) - CONTINUED
Small Public Library
(Serving a population of 10,000 to 25,000)
Regional Data

	Min	Q1	Mean	Median	Q3	Max	N	Range Avg Min	Range Avg Max
North Atlantic	16,640	18,720	30,798	30,316	42,600	46,197	6	27,217	41,253
Great Lakes & Plains	14,560	26,000	31,386	32,781	36,400	46,384	16	34,112	46,825
Southeast	14,873	14,873	20,923	18,013	29,884	29,884	3	15,600	29,848
West & Southwest	21,000	25,106	35,863	34,706	43,500	56,160	6	31,689	46,155
ALL REGIONS	14,560	18,720	31,126	30,861	38,667	56,160	31	29,488	43,129

State Data

	Min	Q1	Mean	Median	Q3	Max	N	Range Avg Min	Range Avg Max
AZ	38,550	38,550	38,550	38,550	38,550	38,550	1	.	.
CO	43,500	43,500	43,500	43,500	43,500	43,500	1	.	.
IA	18,221	18,221	18,221	18,221	18,221	18,221	1	.	.
IL	14,560	18,000	29,954	32,781	35,520	46,080	6	.	.
IN	27,040	27,040	28,226	28,226	29,411	29,411	2	24,960	39,520
KS	34,859	34,859	34,859	34,859	34,859	34,859	1	.	.
KY	29,884	29,884	29,884	29,884	29,884	29,884	1	15,600	29,848
MI	24,960	24,960	24,960	24,960	24,960	24,960	1	.	.
MN	36,400	36,400	39,463	37,534	42,526	46,384	4	36,400	48,651
MS	14,873	14,873	16,443	16,443	18,013	18,013	2	.	.
MT	25,106	25,106	25,106	25,106	25,106	25,106	1	.	.
NH	41,912	41,912	44,054	44,054	46,197	46,197	2	39,114	59,280
NJ	42,600	42,600	42,600	42,600	42,600	42,600	1	39,312	58,240
NM	21,000	21,000	38,580	38,580	56,160	56,160	2	31,689	46,155
OH	30,118	30,118	30,118	30,118	30,118	30,118	1	.	.
PA	16,640	16,640	18,027	18,720	18,720	18,720	3	15,253	23,573
TX	30,861	30,861	30,861	30,861	30,861	30,861	1	.	.

Degree Required Data

	Min	Q1	Mean	Median	Q3	Max	N	Range Avg Min	Range Avg Max
High School	14,560	15,756	22,307	21,487	29,647	30,118	8	14,040	25,324
Associate's	18,221	18,221	19,610	19,610	21,000	21,000	2	19,698	27,830
Bachelor's	18,000	30,861	35,583	36,400	42,600	56,160	21	33,187	47,757
Master's	.	.	.	.	.	.		.	.
Doctoral	.	.	.	.	.	.		.	.

ASSOCIATE LIBRARIAN OF REFERENCE/INFORMATION SERVICES (NON-MLS DEGREED) - CONTINUED
Medium Public Library
(Serving a population of 25,000 to 99,999)
Regional Data

	Min	Q1	Mean	Median	Q3	Max	N	Range Avg Min	Range Avg Max
North Atlantic	24,960	29,000	35,839	33,280	43,680	52,871	13	30,326	42,952
Great Lakes & Plains	20,530	24,981	30,375	27,248	32,282	70,489	31	23,118	34,385
Southeast	19,943	23,247	27,122	25,980	28,404	39,111	13	15,600	24,960
West & Southwest	20,925	20,925	28,045	23,993	31,200	52,562	10	22,984	28,374
ALL REGIONS	19,943	24,403	30,456	27,269	33,280	70,489	67	23,902	33,966

State Data

	Min	Q1	Mean	Median	Q3	Max	N	Range Avg Min	Range Avg Max
AR	22,339	22,339	22,339	22,339	22,339	22,339	1	15,600	24,960
CA	20,925	20,925	26,548	20,925	23,026	52,562	6	21,979	26,738
CO	30,000	30,000	30,000	30,000	30,000	30,000	1	.	.
GA	21,880	21,880	22,564	22,564	23,247	23,247	2	.	.
ID	31,200	31,200	33,103	33,103	35,006	35,006	2	31,200	37,440
IL	25,312	25,312	25,312	25,312	25,312	25,312	1	.	.
IN	20,530	21,871	24,284	23,670	26,697	29,266	4	20,530	21,133
KS	27,248	27,248	27,248	27,248	27,248	27,248	1	21,070	29,058
LA	24,403	24,403	24,403	24,403	24,403	24,403	1	.	.
MA	43,680	43,680	46,744	43,680	52,871	52,871	3	41,600	43,680
ME	44,200	44,200	44,200	44,200	44,200	44,200	1	30,992	44,200
MI	34,112	34,112	34,112	34,112	34,112	34,112	1	29,432	34,112
MO	27,872	27,872	27,872	27,872	27,872	27,872	1	25,251	36,795
MS	27,733	27,733	31,159	31,159	34,584	34,584	2	.	.
NC	19,943	25,980	25,257	25,980	25,980	28,404	5	.	.
ND	32,282	32,282	32,282	32,282	32,282	32,282	1	24,107	36,150
NE	29,120	29,120	29,120	29,120	29,120	29,120	1	29,120	41,600
NY	40,603	40,603	40,603	40,603	40,603	40,603	1	.	.
OH	22,090	24,981	32,980	29,203	35,360	70,489	17	21,080	35,171
PA	24,960	26,208	29,655	29,000	30,933	39,520	7	18,720	41,600
RI	33,280	33,280	33,280	33,280	33,280	33,280	1	.	.
SC	39,111	39,111	39,111	39,111	39,111	39,111	1	.	.
TN	33,000	33,000	33,000	33,000	33,000	33,000	1	.	.
TX	24,960	24,960	24,960	24,960	24,960	24,960	1	20,800	29,120
WI	26,936	26,936	26,972	26,946	27,009	27,061	4	26,021	34,091

Degree Required Data

	Min	Q1	Mean	Median	Q3	Max	N	Range Avg Min	Range Avg Max
High School	20,925	20,925	28,927	25,980	35,006	47,840	15	20,102	24,918
Associate's	19,943	22,090	25,058	23,546	28,483	32,282	8	21,029	37,432
Bachelor's	20,530	25,709	32,697	28,404	39,111	70,489	37	26,184	36,451
Master's	23,247	27,872	28,810	29,000	30,933	33,000	5	25,251	36,795
Doctoral	.	.	.	.	.	.	.	.	.

ASSOCIATE LIBRARIAN OF REFERENCE/INFORMATION SERVICES (NON-MLS DEGREED) - CONTINUED
Large Public Library
(Serving a population of 100,000 to 499,999)
Regional Data

	Min	Q1	Mean	Median	Q3	Max	N	Range Avg Min	Range Avg Max
North Atlantic	12,480	30,285	35,157	34,752	41,496	54,143	92	28,895	43,180
Great Lakes & Plains	17,160	22,693	30,145	29,702	36,604	50,197	66	25,557	34,621
Southeast	13,776	24,024	29,839	28,704	31,385	58,385	57	22,740	40,654
West & Southwest	20,000	31,054	37,099	38,106	41,600	56,048	74	32,291	41,409
ALL REGIONS	12,480	28,609	33,461	31,867	38,792	58,385	289	28,192	39,981

State Data

	Min	Q1	Mean	Median	Q3	Max	N	Range Avg Min	Range Avg Max
AL	21,632	21,632	23,809	21,632	28,163	28,163	3	18,429	27,643
CA	25,605	31,054	37,666	38,106	41,995	56,048	50	32,708	41,565
CO	25,709	25,709	27,352	27,352	28,995	28,995	2	24,700	38,095
FL	28,933	29,910	31,862	30,426	32,607	37,433	5	.	.
GA	32,136	32,136	42,400	42,400	52,664	52,664	2	.	.
IL	28,949	29,962	35,854	33,220	40,835	50,197	13	.	.
KS	49,774	49,774	49,774	49,774	49,774	49,774	1	32,448	54,080
LA	22,194	23,546	26,338	25,397	30,098	31,990	26	22,832	41,558
MD	26,166	30,335	35,599	34,752	41,496	54,143	82	28,895	43,180
MI	24,939	32,282	34,471	33,862	38,792	40,817	13	30,012	37,715
MO	19,469	20,051	21,547	21,102	21,466	28,288	10	19,606	28,488
MS	13,776	13,776	20,055	20,055	26,333	26,333	2	.	.
NC	25,481	26,109	28,922	27,423	31,734	35,360	4	33,280	56,160
NE	28,664	28,664	33,103	34,582	36,604	36,604	10	28,807	36,786
NJ	12,480	13,117	29,859	31,867	39,424	45,730	7	.	.
NM	20,000	20,000	35,907	35,907	51,813	51,813	2	41,205	56,451
NY	40,739	40,739	41,176	41,176	41,613	41,613	2	.	.
OH	17,160	20,925	25,214	23,400	28,038	41,475	19	22,069	33,093
OK	22,298	22,298	22,298	22,298	22,298	22,298	1	19,115	24,794
OR	26,208	26,208	26,208	26,208	26,208	26,208	1	.	.
PA	23,920	23,920	23,920	23,920	23,920	23,920	1	.	.
TX	30,923	30,923	36,625	34,757	44,196	44,196	3	30,909	53,414
VA	28,469	28,609	36,314	31,385	41,067	58,385	15	.	.
WA	32,593	37,440	38,475	38,130	41,600	41,952	15	32,500	40,040

Degree Required Data

	Min	Q1	Mean	Median	Q3	Max	N	Range Avg Min	Range Avg Max
High School	17,160	26,208	34,367	31,366	43,680	58,385	39	36,016	45,277
Associate's	19,469	23,005	30,743	30,098	38,106	46,301	63	26,663	39,599
Bachelor's	20,000	29,453	34,532	33,220	38,792	56,048	153	28,190	40,362
Master's	28,933	29,910	34,244	30,675	32,607	52,664	6	.	.
Doctoral	.	.	.	.	.	.	.	.	.

ASSOCIATE LIBRARIAN OF REFERENCE/INFORMATION SERVICES (NON-MLS DEGREED) - CONTINUED
Very Large Public Library
(Serving a population of 500,000 or more)
Regional Data

	Min	Q1	Mean	Median	Q3	Max	N	Range Avg Min	Range Avg Max
North Atlantic	32,000	32,000	33,143	33,143	34,286	34,286	2	.	.
Great Lakes & Plains	26,813	32,323	38,275	36,360	43,181	52,687	108	32,042	46,842
Southeast	22,733	30,078	32,995	31,000	35,561	56,436	177	.	.
West & Southwest	20,080	35,714	38,881	39,562	41,392	53,256	147	33,179	45,364
ALL REGIONS	20,080	31,699	36,303	35,714	41,392	56,436	434	32,771	45,895

State Data

	Min	Q1	Mean	Median	Q3	Max	N	Range Avg Min	Range Avg Max
AZ	32,552	32,552	37,404	36,774	41,538	43,638	50	32,552	50,606
CA	32,736	41,679	47,137	50,946	53,256	53,256	6	.	.
CO	30,693	35,582	39,528	39,676	42,034	51,965	22	.	.
FL	22,733	26,275	32,780	28,416	37,355	56,436	71	.	.
GA	30,078	30,078	33,277	32,033	35,561	42,700	102	.	.
IN	26,813	27,349	30,998	30,884	33,123	38,292	14	.	.
MO	39,374	39,374	39,633	39,633	39,891	39,891	2	30,888	47,882
NC	27,276	28,459	29,619	29,756	30,779	31,687	4	.	.
NJ	32,000	32,000	33,143	33,143	34,286	34,286	2	.	.
OH	31,699	32,594	39,561	37,679	45,920	52,687	86	31,699	47,590
OR	33,654	37,877	39,523	41,392	41,392	41,392	66	33,654	41,392
TX	20,080	20,080	28,117	32,136	32,136	32,136	3	.	.
WI	35,544	36,362	36,369	36,362	36,362	37,221	6	35,547	39,437

Degree Required Data

	Min	Q1	Mean	Median	Q3	Max	N	Range Avg Min	Range Avg Max
High School	20,080	20,080	20,080	20,080	20,080	20,080	1	.	.
Associate's	32,736	37,346	39,557	41,392	41,392	48,636	68	33,654	41,392
Bachelor's	26,275	31,928	37,195	35,880	41,763	56,436	239	32,264	48,479
Master's	35,919	37,355	39,764	39,400	41,582	47,771	11	.	.
Doctoral								.	.

ASSOCIATE LIBRARIAN OF REFERENCE/INFORMATION SERVICES (NON-MLS DEGREED) - CONTINUED
ALL PUBLIC LIBRARIES
Regional Data

	Min	Q1	Mean	Median	Q3	Max	N	Range Avg Min	Range Avg Max
North Atlantic	12,480	30,207	34,905	34,116	41,554	54,143	116	28,801	42,849
Great Lakes & Plains	14,560	27,872	34,003	33,010	38,792	70,489	229	28,903	41,341
Southeast	10,712	28,416	31,640	30,493	33,447	58,385	253	21,943	37,859
West & Southwest	20,000	33,654	37,728	38,106	41,392	56,160	238	32,439	43,376
ALL REGIONS	10,712	29,848	34,474	33,447	40,206	70,489	836	29,978	42,165

State Data

	Min	Q1	Mean	Median	Q3	Max	N	Range Avg Min	Range Avg Max
AL	17,784	20,135	21,869	21,632	21,632	28,163	5	18,429	21,252
AR	22,339	22,339	22,339	22,339	22,339	22,339	1	15,600	24,960
AZ	32,552	32,552	37,426	37,669	41,538	43,638	51	32,552	50,606
CA	20,925	30,659	37,507	38,106	44,096	56,048	62	31,470	39,854
CO	25,709	30,700	38,378	39,052	42,034	51,965	26	24,700	38,095
FL	22,733	26,444	32,720	28,416	36,637	56,436	76	.	.
GA	21,880	30,078	33,247	32,033	35,561	52,664	106	.	.
IA	18,221	18,221	19,076	19,076	19,931	19,931	2	.	.
ID	31,200	31,200	33,103	33,103	35,006	35,006	2	31,200	37,440
IL	14,560	29,957	33,557	32,626	40,835	50,197	20	.	.
IN	20,530	27,040	29,544	29,266	32,864	38,292	21	22,745	30,326
KS	27,248	27,248	37,294	34,859	49,774	49,774	3	26,759	41,569
KY	10,712	10,712	20,298	20,298	29,884	29,884	2	13,156	20,280
LA	22,194	23,546	26,266	24,403	30,098	31,990	27	22,832	41,558
MA	43,680	43,680	46,744	43,680	52,871	52,871	3	41,600	43,680
MD	26,166	30,335	35,599	34,752	41,496	54,143	82	28,895	43,180
ME	28,233	31,089	35,446	34,676	39,803	44,200	4	29,390	42,931
MI	24,939	30,150	34,075	33,987	38,792	40,817	16	29,960	37,387
MN	36,400	36,400	39,463	37,534	42,526	46,384	4	36,400	48,651
MO	19,469	20,051	27,166	21,466	28,288	57,720	14	23,054	32,867
MS	13,776	14,873	22,552	22,173	27,733	34,584	6	.	.
MT	25,106	25,106	25,106	25,106	25,106	25,106	1	.	.
NC	19,943	25,980	27,727	27,276	29,642	35,360	13	33,280	56,160
ND	32,282	32,282	32,282	32,282	32,282	32,282	1	24,107	36,150
NE	15,205	28,664	31,279	31,497	36,604	36,604	12	28,835	37,223
NH	41,912	41,912	44,054	44,054	46,197	46,197	2	39,114	59,280
NJ	12,480	29,944	31,790	33,143	39,424	45,730	10	39,312	58,240
NM	20,000	20,500	37,243	36,407	53,987	56,160	4	34,861	49,587
NY	40,603	40,603	40,985	40,739	41,613	41,613	3	.	.
OH	16,786	31,699	35,936	33,956	43,181	70,489	126	29,275	44,458
OK	22,298	22,298	22,298	22,298	22,298	22,298	1	19,115	24,794
OR	26,208	36,816	39,324	41,392	41,392	41,392	67	33,654	41,392
PA	16,640	18,720	25,963	26,208	29,939	39,520	11	16,640	30,784
RI	33,280	33,280	33,280	33,280	33,280	33,280	1	.	.
SC	39,111	39,111	39,111	39,111	39,111	39,111	1	.	.
TN	33,000	33,000	33,000	33,000	33,000	33,000	1	.	.
TX	20,080	24,960	30,325	30,923	32,136	44,196	9	25,854	41,267
VA	28,469	28,609	36,314	31,385	41,067	58,385	15	.	.
WA	32,593	37,440	38,475	38,130	41,600	41,952	15	32,500	40,040
WI	26,936	26,957	32,610	35,953	36,362	37,221	10	31,737	37,299

Degree Required Data

	Min	Q1	Mean	Median	Q3	Max	N	Range Avg Min	Range Avg Max
High School	10,712	20,925	30,213	29,848	36,745	58,385	68	28,161	35,843
Associate's	17,784	27,044	34,478	37,658	41,392	57,720	144	30,076	40,468
Bachelor's	18,000	30,196	35,786	34,143	40,835	70,489	456	30,437	44,726
Master's	23,247	30,426	35,769	36,637	40,754	52,664	22	25,251	36,795
Doctoral	.	.	.	.	.	.	.	.	.

ASSOCIATE LIBRARIAN OF OUTREACH/BOOKMOBILE (NON-MLS DEGREED)

Provides assistance to patrons including topical research and material location. Assists patrons with the use of library resources and equipment. Screens the collection for outdated or unused materials following established guidelines. May perform managerial and administrative duties. Provides services and programs to homebound, disabled, institutionalized or other underserved patrons.

Very Small Public Library
(Serving a population of less than 10,000)
Regional Data

	Min	Q1	Mean	Median	Q3	Max	N	Range Avg Min	Range Avg Max
North Atlantic	12,480	12,480	20,800	20,800	29,120	29,120	2	.	.
Great Lakes & Plains	11,154	20,832	33,467	22,163	55,464	57,720	5	29,994	38,220
ALL REGIONS	11,154	12,480	29,848	22,163	55,464	57,720	7	29,994	38,220

State Data

	Min	Q1	Mean	Median	Q3	Max	N	Range Avg Min	Range Avg Max
IN	11,154	11,154	11,154	11,154	11,154	11,154	1	12,480	18,720
MO	57,720	57,720	57,720	57,720	57,720	57,720	1	47,507	57,720
ND	55,464	55,464	55,464	55,464	55,464	55,464	1		
NE	20,832	20,832	20,832	20,832	20,832	20,832	1		
PA	12,480	12,480	12,480	12,480	12,480	12,480	1		
VT	29,120	29,120	29,120	29,120	29,120	29,120	1		
WI	22,163	22,163	22,163	22,163	22,163	22,163	1		

Degree Required Data

	Min	Q1	Mean	Median	Q3	Max	N	Range Avg Min	Range Avg Max
High School	11,154	12,480	24,419	20,832	22,163	55,464	5	12,480	18,720
Associate's	57,720	57,720	57,720	57,720	57,720	57,720	1	47,507	57,720
Bachelor's	29,120	29,120	29,120	29,120	29,120	29,120	1		
Master's	.	.	.	.	.	.			
Doctoral	.	.	.	.	.	.			

ASSOCIATE LIBRARIAN OF OUTREACH/BOOKMOBILE (NON-MLS DEGREED) - CONTINUED
Small Public Library
(Serving a population of 10,000 to 25,000)
Regional Data

	Min	Q1	Mean	Median	Q3	Max	N	Range Avg Min	Range Avg Max
North Atlantic	18,720	18,720	18,720	18,720	18,720	18,720	1	16,640	24,960
Great Lakes & Plains	20,000	20,000	24,354	24,960	28,101	28,101	3	20,436	29,130
Southeast	12,480	15,673	18,530	19,157	21,388	23,328	4	15,808	21,476
West & Southwest	25,106	25,106	27,553	27,553	30,000	30,000	2	.	.
ALL REGIONS	12,480	18,866	22,101	21,664	25,106	30,000	10	17,826	25,235

State Data

	Min	Q1	Mean	Median	Q3	Max	N	Range Avg Min	Range Avg Max
CO	30,000	30,000	30,000	30,000	30,000	30,000	1	.	.
GA	12,480	12,480	12,480	12,480	12,480	12,480	1	.	.
IN	28,101	28,101	28,101	28,101	28,101	28,101	1	20,072	33,301
KY	19,448	19,448	21,388	21,388	23,328	23,328	2	15,600	24,856
LA	18,866	18,866	18,866	18,866	18,866	18,866	1	16,016	18,096
MI	24,960	24,960	24,960	24,960	24,960	24,960	1	20,800	24,960
MT	25,106	25,106	25,106	25,106	25,106	25,106	1	.	.
ND	20,000	20,000	20,000	20,000	20,000	20,000	1	.	.
PA	18,720	18,720	18,720	18,720	18,720	18,720	1	16,640	24,960

Degree Required Data

	Min	Q1	Mean	Median	Q3	Max	N	Range Avg Min	Range Avg Max
High School	12,480	18,866	21,026	20,000	24,960	28,101	7	18,122	25,303
Associate's	.	.	.	.	.	.		.	.
Bachelor's	18,720	18,720	24,609	25,106	30,000	30,000	3	16,640	24,960
Master's	.	.	.	.	.	.		.	.
Doctoral	.	.	.	.	.	.		.	.

ASSOCIATE LIBRARIAN OF OUTREACH/BOOKMOBILE (NON-MLS DEGREED) - CONTINUED
Medium Public Library
(Serving a population of 25,000 to 99,999)
Regional Data

	Min	Q1	Mean	Median	Q3	Max	N	Range Avg Min	Range Avg Max
North Atlantic	15,538	15,538	26,755	26,600	38,126	38,126	3	30,992	44,200
Great Lakes & Plains	18,200	30,790	38,561	38,875	48,589	57,434	19	28,579	43,430
Southeast	20,363	21,612	23,556	22,400	27,200	28,235	7	13,520	24,960
West & Southwest	27,040	27,040	31,415	33,093	34,112	34,112	3	29,806	35,110
ALL REGIONS	15,538	24,982	33,502	31,990	41,022	57,434	32	27,437	40,828

State Data

	Min	Q1	Mean	Median	Q3	Max	N	Range Avg Min	Range Avg Max
AR	20,363	20,363	20,363	20,363	20,363	20,363	1	13,520	24,960
ID	27,040	27,040	27,040	27,040	27,040	27,040	1		
IL	26,498	37,003	42,257	43,126	49,213	54,330	9	33,105	50,070
IN	26,790	28,839	40,826	39,541	52,814	57,434	4		
KS	18,200	18,200	18,200	18,200	18,200	18,200	1	15,392	21,216
ME	38,126	38,126	38,126	38,126	38,126	38,126	1	30,992	44,200
MI	18,278	18,278	18,278	18,278	18,278	18,278	1		
MN	48,330	48,330	48,330	48,330	48,330	48,330	1		
MO	30,790	30,790	34,854	34,854	38,917	38,917	2		
MS	27,200	27,200	27,200	27,200	27,200	27,200	1		
NC	21,612	21,612	23,820	21,612	28,235	28,235	3		
OH	34,528	34,528	34,528	34,528	34,528	34,528	1	19,136	32,448
PA	15,538	15,538	21,069	21,069	26,600	26,600	2		
SC	23,467	23,467	23,467	23,467	23,467	23,467	1		
TX	34,112	34,112	34,112	34,112	34,112	34,112	1		
WV	22,400	22,400	22,400	22,400	22,400	22,400	1		
WY	33,093	33,093	33,093	33,093	33,093	33,093	1	29,806	35,110

Degree Required Data

	Min	Q1	Mean	Median	Q3	Max	N	Range Avg Min	Range Avg Max
High School	15,538	21,612	33,287	29,513	48,262	57,434	12	27,865	36,906
Associate's	18,278	22,400	30,239	33,280	34,112	43,126	5	24,960	41,600
Bachelor's	23,467	26,790	35,696	34,528	38,917	54,330	13	30,460	46,201
Master's	37,003	37,003	37,003	37,003	37,003	37,003	1		
Doctoral									

ASSOCIATE LIBRARIAN OF OUTREACH/BOOKMOBILE (NON-MLS DEGREED) - CONTINUED
Large Public Library
(Serving a population of 100,000 to 499,999)
Regional Data

	Min	Q1	Mean	Median	Q3	Max	N	Range Avg Min	Range Avg Max
North Atlantic	13,117	26,915	33,585	32,658	41,224	54,728	14	28,110	34,350
Great Lakes & Plains	16,952	23,338	29,896	27,987	33,614	51,000	26	21,932	33,824
Southeast	23,338	26,790	37,720	36,510	43,892	52,988	10	20,606	32,295
West & Southwest	20,800	27,602	34,847	32,690	37,647	57,305	12	34,805	45,212
ALL REGIONS	13,117	25,667	32,949	32,146	39,424	57,305	62	24,306	35,091

State Data

	Min	Q1	Mean	Median	Q3	Max	N	Range Avg Min	Range Avg Max
AL	23,338	23,338	24,502	24,502	25,667	25,667	2	18,429	27,643
AZ	53,019	53,019	53,019	53,019	53,019	53,019	1	.	.
CA	57,305	57,305	57,305	57,305	57,305	57,305	1	46,654	57,304
CO	28,995	28,995	34,568	34,568	40,141	40,141	2	24,482	36,733
GA	52,664	52,664	52,664	52,664	52,664	52,664	1	.	.
IL	27,024	27,024	36,339	33,614	48,380	48,380	3	.	.
IN	32,300	32,300	32,300	32,300	32,300	32,300	1	.	.
MD	28,800	41,224	45,034	50,209	50,209	54,728	5	.	.
MN	51,000	51,000	51,000	51,000	51,000	51,000	2	.	.
MO	16,952	24,752	27,678	25,501	31,054	47,362	9	22,115	31,392
NC	37,440	37,440	37,440	37,440	37,440	37,440	1	24,960	41,600
NE	28,664	28,664	29,139	28,664	30,087	30,087	3	18,210	39,681
NJ	13,117	13,117	21,008	15,746	28,899	39,424	4	.	.
NM	20,800	20,800	20,800	20,800	20,800	20,800	1	.	.
NY	37,558	37,558	37,558	37,558	37,558	37,558	1	37,558	37,558
OH	16,994	18,574	23,147	22,672	26,250	34,216	7	22,246	35,183
OR	26,208	26,208	26,208	26,208	26,208	26,208	1	.	.
PA	26,915	29,058	30,858	31,720	32,658	33,076	4	24,960	33,280
TX	32,052	32,052	33,602	33,602	35,152	35,152	2	.	.
VA	26,790	35,364	39,682	39,529	43,892	52,988	6	.	.
WA	25,835	29,263	31,124	32,690	32,985	33,280	4	33,280	41,600
WI	35,422	35,422	35,422	35,422	35,422	35,422	1	30,826	35,422

Degree Required Data

	Min	Q1	Mean	Median	Q3	Max	N	Range Avg Min	Range Avg Max
High School	16,952	19,989	26,710	26,229	32,690	37,440	18	18,684	33,637
Associate's	24,752	25,501	28,258	27,310	31,054	33,280	7	22,942	32,109
Bachelor's	20,800	30,644	37,551	33,915	46,136	57,305	28	27,754	36,079
Master's	47,362	47,362	50,342	51,000	52,664	52,664	3	38,730	56,264
Doctoral	.	.	.	.	.	.		.	.

ASSOCIATE LIBRARIAN OF OUTREACH/BOOKMOBILE (NON-MLS DEGREED) - CONTINUED
Very Large Public Library
(Serving a population of 500,000 or more)
Regional Data

	Min	Q1	Mean	Median	Q3	Max	N	Range Avg Min	Range Avg Max
Great Lakes & Plains	25,376	27,320	34,373	29,248	34,424	57,495	10	31,699	47,590
Southeast	35,273	35,273	43,062	40,016	53,896	53,896	3	33,331	55,551
West & Southwest	32,736	36,376	40,914	41,538	45,947	48,152	9	36,758	48,386
ALL REGIONS	25,376	29,528	38,233	35,825	45,947	57,495	22	35,404	48,944

State Data

	Min	Q1	Mean	Median	Q3	Max	N	Range Avg Min	Range Avg Max
AZ	37,669	37,669	42,453	41,538	48,152	48,152	3	32,552	50,606
CA	32,736	32,736	34,556	34,556	36,376	36,376	2	29,797	36,376
MO	25,376	25,745	27,449	27,539	28,969	29,528	6	.	.
NC	35,273	35,273	37,645	37,645	40,016	40,016	2	.	.
OH	34,424	34,424	44,757	43,555	55,091	57,495	4	31,699	47,590
OR	44,595	44,595	45,497	45,947	45,947	45,947	3	43,285	50,170
TX	35,265	35,265	35,265	35,265	35,265	35,265	1	.	.
VA	53,896	53,896	53,896	53,896	53,896	53,896	1	33,331	55,551

Degree Required Data

	Min	Q1	Mean	Median	Q3	Max	N	Range Avg Min	Range Avg Max
High School	53,896	53,896	53,896	53,896	53,896	53,896	1	33,331	55,551
Associate's	32,736	32,736	34,000	34,000	35,265	35,265	2	.	.
Bachelor's	25,376	28,969	37,855	36,376	45,947	57,495	19	35,634	48,209
Master's	.	.	.	.	.	.	.	.	.
Doctoral	.	.	.	.	.	.	.	.	.

ASSOCIATE LIBRARIAN OF OUTREACH/BOOKMOBILE (NON-MLS DEGREED) - CONTINUED
ALL PUBLIC LIBRARIES
Regional Data

	Min	Q1	Mean	Median	Q3	Max	N	Range Avg Min	Range Avg Max
North Atlantic	12,480	18,547	30,539	30,160	38,775	54,728	20	26,678	34,426
Great Lakes & Plains	11,154	25,376	33,239	30,087	43,126	57,720	63	24,761	37,188
Southeast	12,480	22,006	31,058	26,995	38,728	53,896	24	20,041	31,478
West & Southwest	20,800	30,000	35,990	33,696	41,538	57,305	26	35,594	46,314
ALL REGIONS	11,154	25,376	32,977	31,200	40,016	57,720	133	26,638	38,031

State Data

	Min	Q1	Mean	Median	Q3	Max	N	Range Avg Min	Range Avg Max
AL	23,338	23,338	24,502	24,502	25,667	25,667	2	18,429	27,643
AR	20,363	20,363	20,363	20,363	20,363	20,363	1	13,520	24,960
AZ	37,669	39,603	45,094	44,845	50,586	53,019	4	32,552	50,606
CA	32,736	32,736	42,139	36,376	57,305	57,305	3	38,226	46,840
CO	28,995	28,995	33,046	30,000	40,141	40,141	3	24,482	36,733
GA	12,480	12,480	32,572	32,572	52,664	52,664	2	.	.
ID	27,040	27,040	27,040	27,040	27,040	27,040	1	.	.
IL	26,498	33,447	40,778	41,001	48,901	54,330	12	33,105	50,070
IN	11,154	26,790	33,551	30,888	48,193	57,434	7	16,276	26,010
KS	18,200	18,200	18,200	18,200	18,200	18,200	1	15,392	21,216
KY	19,448	19,448	21,388	21,388	23,328	23,328	2	15,600	24,856
LA	18,866	18,866	18,866	18,866	18,866	18,866	1	16,016	18,096
MD	28,800	41,224	45,034	50,209	50,209	54,728	5	.	.
ME	38,126	38,126	38,126	38,126	38,126	38,126	1	30,992	44,200
MI	18,278	18,278	21,619	21,619	24,960	24,960	2	20,800	24,960
MN	48,330	48,330	50,110	51,000	51,000	51,000	3	.	.
MO	16,952	25,501	30,068	27,539	31,054	57,720	18	24,654	34,025
MS	27,200	27,200	27,200	27,200	27,200	27,200	1	.	.
MT	25,106	25,106	25,106	25,106	25,106	25,106	1	.	.
NC	21,612	21,612	30,698	31,754	37,440	40,016	6	24,960	41,600
ND	20,000	20,000	37,732	37,732	55,464	55,464	2	.	.
NE	20,832	24,748	27,062	28,664	29,376	30,087	4	18,210	39,681
NJ	13,117	13,117	21,008	15,746	28,899	39,424	4	.	.
NM	20,800	20,800	20,800	20,800	20,800	20,800	1	.	.
NY	37,558	37,558	37,558	37,558	37,558	37,558	1	37,558	37,558
OH	16,994	21,330	31,299	30,233	34,476	57,495	12	25,405	39,599
OR	26,208	35,402	40,674	45,271	45,947	45,947	4	43,285	50,170
PA	12,480	17,129	24,596	26,758	31,720	33,076	8	22,880	31,200
SC	23,467	23,467	23,467	23,467	23,467	23,467	1	.	.
TX	32,052	33,082	34,145	34,632	35,208	35,265	4	.	.
VA	26,790	35,364	41,712	43,478	52,988	53,896	7	33,331	55,551
VT	29,120	29,120	29,120	29,120	29,120	29,120	1	.	.
WA	25,835	29,263	31,124	32,690	32,985	33,280	4	33,280	41,600
WI	22,163	22,163	28,793	28,793	35,422	35,422	2	30,826	35,422
WV	22,400	22,400	22,400	22,400	22,400	22,400	1	.	.
WY	33,093	33,093	33,093	33,093	33,093	33,093	1	29,806	35,110

Degree Required Data

	Min	Q1	Mean	Median	Q3	Max	N	Range Avg Min	Range Avg Max
High School	11,154	19,448	27,986	25,835	33,093	57,434	43	20,793	32,604
Associate's	18,278	25,501	31,648	31,054	34,112	57,720	15	25,896	36,009
Bachelor's	18,720	28,279	36,526	34,424	44,244	57,495	64	30,687	42,026
Master's	37,003	42,182	47,007	49,181	51,832	52,664	4	38,730	56,264
Doctoral	.	.	.	.	.	.		.	.

ASSOCIATE LIBRARIAN OF MEDIA SERVICES (NON-MLS DEGREED)

Provides assistance to patrons including topical research and material location. Assists patrons with the use of library resources and equipment. Screens the collection for outdated or unused materials following established guidelines. May perform managerial and administrative duties. Develops and manages non-print library materials such as files, video recordings, audio recordings, CD-ROMs, computer software, etc.

Very Small Public Library
(Serving a population of less than 10,000)
Regional Data

	Min	Q1	Mean	Median	Q3	Max	N	Range Avg Min	Range Avg Max
Great Lakes & Plains	29,890	29,890	29,890	29,890	29,890	29,890	1	29,016	35,069
West & Southwest	23,962	23,962	23,962	23,962	23,962	23,962	1	.	.
ALL REGIONS	23,962	23,962	26,926	26,926	29,890	29,890	2	29,016	35,069

State Data

	Min	Q1	Mean	Median	Q3	Max	N	Range Avg Min	Range Avg Max
IL	29,890	29,890	29,890	29,890	29,890	29,890	1	29,016	35,069
TX	23,962	23,962	23,962	23,962	23,962	23,962	1	.	.

Degree Required Data

	Min	Q1	Mean	Median	Q3	Max	N	Range Avg Min	Range Avg Max
High School	.	.	.	.	.	.	.	.	.
Associate's	.	.	.	.	.	.	.	.	.
Bachelor's	29,890	29,890	29,890	29,890	29,890	29,890	1	29,016	35,069
Master's	.	.	.	.	.	.	.	.	.
Doctoral	.	.	.	.	.	.	.	.	.

ASSOCIATE LIBRARIAN OF MEDIA SERVICES (NON-MLS DEGREED) - CONTINUED
Small Public Library
(Serving a population of 10,000 to 25,000)
Regional Data

	Min	Q1	Mean	Median	Q3	Max	N	Range Avg Min	Range Avg Max
North Atlantic	53,103	53,103	53,103	53,103	53,103	53,103	1	.	.
Great Lakes & Plains	26,728	26,728	26,884	26,884	27,040	27,040	2	.	.
ALL REGIONS	26,728	26,728	35,624	27,040	53,103	53,103	3	.	.

State Data

	Min	Q1	Mean	Median	Q3	Max	N	Range Avg Min	Range Avg Max
IL	26,728	26,728	26,728	26,728	26,728	26,728	1	.	.
MA	53,103	53,103	53,103	53,103	53,103	53,103	1	.	.
MI	27,040	27,040	27,040	27,040	27,040	27,040	1	.	.

Degree Required Data

	Min	Q1	Mean	Median	Q3	Max	N	Range Avg Min	Range Avg Max
High School	27,040	27,040	27,040	27,040	27,040	27,040	1	.	.
Associate's	.	.	.	.	.	.		.	.
Bachelor's	53,103	53,103	53,103	53,103	53,103	53,103	1	.	.
Master's	26,728	26,728	26,728	26,728	26,728	26,728	1	.	.
Doctoral	.	.	.	.	.	.		.	.

ASSOCIATE LIBRARIAN OF MEDIA SERVICES (NON-MLS DEGREED) - CONTINUED
Medium Public Library
(Serving a population of 25,000 to 99,999)
Regional Data

	Min	Q1	Mean	Median	Q3	Max	N	Range Avg Min	Range Avg Max
North Atlantic	51,670	51,670	51,670	51,670	51,670	51,670	1	.	.
Great Lakes & Plains	46,176	46,176	46,176	46,176	46,176	46,176	1	20,259	37,752
West & Southwest	100,224	100,224	100,224	100,224	100,224	100,224	1	.	.
ALL REGIONS	46,176	46,176	66,023	51,670	100,224	100,224	3	20,259	37,752

State Data

	Min	Q1	Mean	Median	Q3	Max	N	Range Avg Min	Range Avg Max
CT	51,670	51,670	51,670	51,670	51,670	51,670	1	.	.
OH	46,176	46,176	46,176	46,176	46,176	46,176	1	20,259	37,752
OR	100,224	100,224	100,224	100,224	100,224	100,224	1	.	.

Degree Required Data

	Min	Q1	Mean	Median	Q3	Max	N	Range Avg Min	Range Avg Max
High School	46,176	46,176	46,176	46,176	46,176	46,176	1	20,259	37,752
Associate's	.	.	.	.	.	.		.	.
Bachelor's	51,670	51,670	51,670	51,670	51,670	51,670	1	.	.
Master's	100,224	100,224	100,224	100,224	100,224	100,224	1	.	.
Doctoral	.	.	.	.	.	.		.	.

ASSOCIATE LIBRARIAN OF MEDIA SERVICES (NON-MLS DEGREED) - CONTINUED
Large Public Library
(Serving a population of 100,000 to 499,999)
Regional Data

	Min	Q1	Mean	Median	Q3	Max	N	Range Avg Min	Range Avg Max
North Atlantic	16,507	16,507	37,430	39,139	56,646	56,646	3	.	.
Great Lakes & Plains	22,256	25,293	29,071	27,290	34,590	37,710	6	26,000	42,640
Southeast	24,620	24,620	37,171	40,448	46,444	46,444	3	.	.
West & Southwest	25,917	25,917	39,272	44,640	47,258	47,258	3	38,168	47,258
ALL REGIONS	16,507	25,293	34,403	34,590	44,640	56,646	15	29,042	43,794

State Data

	Min	Q1	Mean	Median	Q3	Max	N	Range Avg Min	Range Avg Max
CA	44,640	44,640	45,949	45,949	47,258	47,258	2	38,168	47,258
FL	46,444	46,444	46,444	46,444	46,444	46,444	1		
MD	56,646	56,646	56,646	56,646	56,646	56,646	1		
MS	24,620	24,620	24,620	24,620	24,620	24,620	1		
NJ	16,507	16,507	27,823	27,823	39,139	39,139	2		
NM	25,917	25,917	25,917	25,917	25,917	25,917	1		
OH	22,256	25,293	29,071	27,290	34,590	37,710	6	26,000	42,640
VA	40,448	40,448	40,448	40,448	40,448	40,448	1		

Degree Required Data

	Min	Q1	Mean	Median	Q3	Max	N	Range Avg Min	Range Avg Max
High School	22,256	24,956	29,704	26,375	32,729	47,258	8	30,056	44,179
Associate's	44,640	44,640	44,640	44,640	44,640	44,640	1		
Bachelor's	40,448	40,448	47,846	46,444	56,646	56,646	3		
Master's									
Doctoral									

ASSOCIATE LIBRARIAN OF MEDIA SERVICES (NON-MLS DEGREED) - CONTINUED
Very Large Public Library
(Serving a population of 500,000 or more)
Regional Data

	Min	Q1	Mean	Median	Q3	Max	N	Range Avg Min	Range Avg Max
North Atlantic	60,707	60,707	60,707	60,707	60,707	60,707	1		
Great Lakes & Plains	32,323	33,842	43,290	36,525	37,170	101,615	21	31,699	47,590
Southeast	23,869	26,328	26,960	27,221	28,416	28,966	5		
West & Southwest	41,205	41,205	44,096	44,096	46,987	46,987	2	31,065	47,476
ALL REGIONS	23,869	33,114	41,131	36,046	41,205	101,615	29	31,629	47,578

State Data

	Min	Q1	Mean	Median	Q3	Max	N	Range Avg Min	Range Avg Max
AZ	46,987	46,987	46,987	46,987	46,987	46,987	1	32,552	50,606
FL	23,869	26,328	26,960	27,221	28,416	28,966	5		
MD	60,707	60,707	60,707	60,707	60,707	60,707	1		
MO	43,870	43,870	43,870	43,870	43,870	43,870	1		
OH	32,323	33,842	43,261	36,286	37,170	101,615	20	31,699	47,590
TX	41,205	41,205	41,205	41,205	41,205	41,205	1	29,578	44,346

Degree Required Data

	Min	Q1	Mean	Median	Q3	Max	N	Range Avg Min	Range Avg Max
High School									
Associate's									
Bachelor's	28,416	33,842	43,439	36,525	44,096	101,615	24	31,629	47,578
Master's	43,870	43,870	43,870	43,870	43,870	43,870	1		
Doctoral									

ASSOCIATE LIBRARIAN OF MEDIA SERVICES (NON-MLS DEGREED) - CONTINUED
ALL PUBLIC LIBRARIES
Regional Data

	Min	Q1	Mean	Median	Q3	Max	N	Range Avg Min	Range Avg Max
North Atlantic	16,507	39,139	46,295	52,386	56,646	60,707	6	.	.
Great Lakes & Plains	22,256	32,323	39,141	35,963	37,170	101,615	31	30,212	45,818
Southeast	23,869	25,474	30,789	27,818	34,707	46,444	8	.	.
West & Southwest	23,962	25,917	47,170	44,640	47,258	100,224	7	33,433	47,403
ALL REGIONS	16,507	28,082	39,762	36,046	45,408	101,615	52	30,615	46,017

State Data

	Min	Q1	Mean	Median	Q3	Max	N	Range Avg Min	Range Avg Max
AZ	46,987	46,987	46,987	46,987	46,987	46,987	1	32,552	50,606
CA	44,640	44,640	45,949	45,949	47,258	47,258	2	38,168	47,258
CT	51,670	51,670	51,670	51,670	51,670	51,670	1	.	.
FL	23,869	26,328	30,207	27,818	28,966	46,444	6	.	.
IL	26,728	26,728	28,309	28,309	29,890	29,890	2	29,016	35,069
MA	53,103	53,103	53,103	53,103	53,103	53,103	1	.	.
MD	56,646	56,646	58,676	58,676	60,707	60,707	2	.	.
MI	27,040	27,040	27,040	27,040	27,040	27,040	1	.	.
MO	43,870	43,870	43,870	43,870	43,870	43,870	1	.	.
MS	24,620	24,620	24,620	24,620	24,620	24,620	1	.	.
NJ	16,507	16,507	27,823	27,823	39,139	39,139	2	.	.
NM	25,917	25,917	25,917	25,917	25,917	25,917	1	.	.
OH	22,256	33,114	40,216	36,046	37,170	101,615	27	30,272	46,356
OR	100,224	100,224	100,224	100,224	100,224	100,224	1	.	.
TX	23,962	23,962	32,583	32,583	41,205	41,205	2	29,578	44,346
VA	40,448	40,448	40,448	40,448	40,448	40,448	1	.	.

Degree Required Data

	Min	Q1	Mean	Median	Q3	Max	N	Range Avg Min	Range Avg Max
High School	22,256	25,293	31,085	26,936	37,710	47,258	10	27,607	42,572
Associate's	44,640	44,640	44,640	44,640	44,640	44,640	1	.	.
Bachelor's	28,416	33,842	44,025	37,128	51,670	101,615	30	31,491	46,919
Master's	26,728	26,728	56,941	43,870	100,224	100,224	3	.	.
Doctoral	.	.	.	.	.	.			

ASSOCIATE LIBRARIAN OF TECHNICAL ASSISTANCE (NON-MLS DEGREED)

Provides assistance to patrons including topical research and material location. Assists patrons with the use of library resources and equipment. Screens the collection for outdated or unused materials following established guidelines. May perform managerial and administrative duties. Acquires, organizes (bibliographic control), physically processes and maintains library collections.

Very Small Public Library
(Serving a population of less than 10,000)
Regional Data

	Min	Q1	Mean	Median	Q3	Max	N	Range Avg Min	Range Avg Max
North Atlantic	26,894	33,987	40,880	35,360	39,520	68,640	5	36,572	49,098
Great Lakes & Plains	14,560	18,500	25,683	25,660	30,326	39,104	16	23,639	33,023
Southeast	21,403	21,403	25,083	25,083	28,762	28,762	2		
West & Southwest	33,738	33,738	34,869	34,869	36,000	36,000	2	23,941	33,738
ALL REGIONS	14,560	22,880	29,409	28,642	34,677	68,640	25	28,369	38,934

State Data

	Min	Q1	Mean	Median	Q3	Max	N	Range Avg Min	Range Avg Max
AL	21,403	21,403	21,403	21,403	21,403	21,403	1		
CO	33,738	33,738	33,738	33,738	33,738	33,738	1	23,941	33,738
CT	33,987	33,987	36,754	36,754	39,520	39,520	2	27,040	39,520
IA	34,677	34,677	34,677	34,677	34,677	34,677	1		
IL	18,096	22,880	27,052	25,660	31,117	38,896	6	22,828	34,174
IN	27,040	27,040	27,841	27,841	28,642	28,642	2	19,739	29,744
KS	14,560	15,600	19,344	16,640	23,088	29,536	4	22,880	31,200
ME	26,894	26,894	31,127	31,127	35,360	35,360	2	25,303	32,677
MI	18,903	18,903	18,903	18,903	18,903	18,903	1		
MN	39,104	39,104	39,104	39,104	39,104	39,104	1	33,821	39,104
MO	22,880	22,880	22,880	22,880	22,880	22,880	1		
NJ	68,640	68,640	68,640	68,640	68,640	68,640	1	68,640	91,520
TX	36,000	36,000	36,000	36,000	36,000	36,000	1		
WV	28,762	28,762	28,762	28,762	28,762	28,762	1		

Degree Required Data

	Min	Q1	Mean	Median	Q3	Max	N	Range Avg Min	Range Avg Max
High School	14,560	18,903	28,870	22,880	33,987	68,640	13	36,280	47,850
Associate's	24,960	26,361	30,029	29,089	34,677	36,000	6	20,093	32,309
Bachelor's	26,894	28,762	32,331	31,117	35,360	39,520	5	26,666	34,986
Master's									
Doctoral									

ASSOCIATE LIBRARIAN OF TECHNICAL ASSISTANCE (NON-MLS DEGREED) - CONTINUED
Small Public Library
(Serving a population of 10,000 to 25,000)
Regional Data

	Min	Q1	Mean	Median	Q3	Max	N	Range Avg Min	Range Avg Max
North Atlantic	20,667	23,000	33,566	35,714	35,942	52,509	5	28,465	42,422
Great Lakes & Plains	19,000	21,253	27,025	27,040	31,200	41,600	15	23,449	36,213
Southeast	15,788	16,952	21,035	19,302	24,170	28,965	5	17,784	19,864
West & Southwest	22,880	25,106	31,022	29,640	36,483	41,000	5	25,778	39,783
ALL REGIONS	15,788	21,253	27,783	26,853	31,387	52,509	30	24,018	35,256

State Data

	Min	Q1	Mean	Median	Q3	Max	N	Range Avg Min	Range Avg Max
AL	28,965	28,965	28,965	28,965	28,965	28,965	1	.	.
AR	15,788	15,788	15,788	15,788	15,788	15,788	1	.	.
AZ	36,483	36,483	36,483	36,483	36,483	36,483	1	35,776	53,664
CO	41,000	41,000	41,000	41,000	41,000	41,000	1	.	.
CT	35,942	35,942	35,942	35,942	35,942	35,942	1	35,942	49,130
IA	23,254	23,254	23,254	23,254	23,254	23,254	1	.	.
IL	19,000	20,280	27,254	27,144	31,294	41,600	8	.	.
IN	29,120	29,120	31,023	31,023	32,927	32,927	2	24,960	37,440
KS	21,253	21,253	21,253	21,253	21,253	21,253	1	18,720	31,200
LA	16,952	16,952	20,561	20,561	24,170	24,170	2	17,784	19,864
MI	29,120	29,120	29,120	29,120	29,120	29,120	1	.	.
MS	19,302	19,302	19,302	19,302	19,302	19,302	1	.	.
MT	25,106	25,106	25,106	25,106	25,106	25,106	1	.	.
ND	25,000	25,000	25,000	25,000	25,000	25,000	1	.	.
NJ	52,509	52,509	52,509	52,509	52,509	52,509	1	.	.
NM	29,640	29,640	29,640	29,640	29,640	29,640	1	22,090	35,339
OH	26,666	26,666	26,666	26,666	26,666	26,666	1	26,666	39,998
PA	20,667	20,667	21,833	21,833	23,000	23,000	2	.	.
RI	35,714	35,714	35,714	35,714	35,714	35,714	1	20,987	35,714
TX	22,880	22,880	22,880	22,880	22,880	22,880	1	19,469	30,347

Degree Required Data

	Min	Q1	Mean	Median	Q3	Max	N	Range Avg Min	Range Avg Max
High School	15,788	19,302	25,900	26,020	31,200	35,942	14	22,917	31,982
Associate's	19,760	19,760	27,538	21,253	41,600	41,600	3	18,720	31,200
Bachelor's	20,667	23,254	30,354	27,248	36,483	52,509	11	26,718	40,362
Master's	.	.	.	.	.	.		.	.
Doctoral	.	.	.	.	.	.		.	.

ASSOCIATE LIBRARIAN OF TECHNICAL ASSISTANCE (NON-MLS DEGREED) - CONTINUED
Medium Public Library
(Serving a population of 25,000 to 99,999)
Regional Data

	Min	Q1	Mean	Median	Q3	Max	N	Range Avg Min	Range Avg Max
North Atlantic	25,772	34,882	36,653	36,665	37,440	51,126	13	36,275	41,728
Great Lakes & Plains	16,640	28,558	33,582	31,200	35,942	59,363	21	25,769	35,180
Southeast	15,657	18,089	26,769	29,333	33,000	37,440	7		
West & Southwest	20,800	24,960	29,679	27,258	33,107	45,984	8	22,880	35,013
ALL REGIONS	15,657	27,000	32,786	31,200	36,924	59,363	49	27,756	36,845

State Data

	Min	Q1	Mean	Median	Q3	Max	N	Range Avg Min	Range Avg Max
CA	29,557	29,557	29,557	29,557	29,557	29,557	1	18,720	31,200
CT	42,702	42,702	45,899	43,867	51,126	51,126	3	41,330	46,925
DE	35,669	35,669	35,669	35,669	35,669	35,669	1		
IA	31,200	31,200	32,587	31,200	35,360	35,360	3	28,427	32,587
ID	20,800	22,880	26,000	24,960	29,120	33,280	4	24,440	37,440
IL	16,640	29,120	35,391	31,200	39,733	59,363	9	24,595	36,448
IN	28,891	28,891	28,891	28,891	28,891	28,891	1		
MA	36,067	36,665	36,907	36,924	37,440	37,440	5	34,667	37,440
ME	34,882	34,882	34,882	34,882	34,882	34,882	1	30,992	44,200
MI	23,816	23,816	23,816	23,816	23,816	23,816	1		
MN	48,330	48,330	49,355	49,355	50,380	50,380	2		
MO	18,374	18,374	26,106	28,558	31,387	31,387	3		
MS	29,333	29,333	33,387	33,387	37,440	37,440	2		
NC	24,209	24,209	26,931	26,931	29,652	29,652	2		
OH	32,085	32,085	32,085	32,085	32,085	32,085	1		
OR	45,984	45,984	45,984	45,984	45,984	45,984	1		
PA	25,772	25,772	27,902	27,000	30,933	30,933	3		
SC	18,089	18,089	18,089	18,089	18,089	18,089	1		
TN	33,000	33,000	33,000	33,000	33,000	33,000	1		
TX	24,960	24,960	28,947	28,947	32,933	32,933	2	20,800	29,120
VA	15,657	15,657	15,657	15,657	15,657	15,657	1		
WI	27,123	27,123	27,123	27,123	27,123	27,123	1	26,021	34,091

Degree Required Data

	Min	Q1	Mean	Median	Q3	Max	N	Range Avg Min	Range Avg Max
High School	18,089	24,960	30,964	30,267	36,924	48,330	14	26,000	34,944
Associate's	15,657	21,292	31,874	30,426	41,218	59,363	16	26,954	34,403
Bachelor's	23,816	29,848	35,834	35,121	36,754	59,072	16	33,951	47,091
Master's	33,000	33,000	33,000	33,000	33,000	33,000	1		
Doctoral									

ASSOCIATE LIBRARIAN OF TECHNICAL ASSISTANCE (NON-MLS DEGREED) - CONTINUED
Large Public Library
(Serving a population of 100,000 to 499,999)
Regional Data

	Min	Q1	Mean	Median	Q3	Max	N	Range Avg Min	Range Avg Max
North Atlantic	39,424	39,424	42,899	42,051	46,374	48,069	4	.	.
Great Lakes & Plains	25,958	28,018	31,537	28,018	28,018	47,674	5	30,326	45,334
Southeast	14,532	25,168	30,760	27,864	38,334	48,656	15	22,922	25,993
West & Southwest	22,422	28,482	33,482	29,856	43,618	44,693	9	25,709	39,863
ALL REGIONS	14,532	26,790	33,091	29,692	39,424	48,656	33	25,834	35,482

State Data

	Min	Q1	Mean	Median	Q3	Max	N	Range Avg Min	Range Avg Max
AL	20,301	20,301	20,301	20,301	20,301	20,301	1	18,429	27,643
AZ	43,618	43,618	43,618	43,618	43,618	43,618	1		
CA	29,856	29,856	29,856	29,856	29,856	29,856	1	.	.
CO	22,422	28,995	34,426	31,325	44,693	44,693	5	25,709	39,863
FL	48,656	48,656	48,656	48,656	48,656	48,656	1		
GA	37,440	37,440	39,208	39,208	40,976	40,976	2	.	.
KS	47,674	47,674	47,674	47,674	47,674	47,674	1	37,586	62,650
MI	25,958	26,988	27,503	28,018	28,018	28,018	4	23,067	28,018
MS	14,532	14,532	14,532	14,532	14,532	14,532	1	.	.
NC	25,481	25,481	32,413	32,413	39,346	39,346	2		
NJ	39,424	39,424	42,306	39,424	48,069	48,069	3	.	.
OR	27,252	27,252	27,252	27,252	27,252	27,252	1		
PA	44,678	44,678	44,678	44,678	44,678	44,678	1	.	.
TX	28,482	28,482	28,482	28,482	28,482	28,482	1		
VA	25,168	25,168	29,334	27,327	33,090	38,334	8	25,168	25,168

Degree Required Data

	Min	Q1	Mean	Median	Q3	Max	N	Range Avg Min	Range Avg Max
High School	22,422	25,168	31,134	29,774	36,964	44,678	12	24,253	28,156
Associate's	39,346	39,346	39,346	39,346	39,346	39,346	1	.	.
Bachelor's	20,301	26,790	35,218	28,995	44,693	48,656	11	27,019	40,976
Master's	40,976	40,976	40,976	40,976	40,976	40,976	1	.	.
Doctoral									

ASSOCIATE LIBRARIAN OF TECHNICAL ASSISTANCE (NON-MLS DEGREED) - CONTINUED
Very Large Public Library
(Serving a population of 500,000 or more)
Regional Data

	Min	Q1	Mean	Median	Q3	Max	N	Range Avg Min	Range Avg Max
North Atlantic	49,149	49,149	50,873	50,873	52,598	52,598	2	.	.
Great Lakes & Plains	32,331	32,331	40,606	35,741	50,111	57,495	7	.	.
Southeast	23,869	24,916	27,845	26,489	29,864	52,390	91		
West & Southwest	28,365	32,576	34,374	34,518	36,636	39,633	6	29,797	36,376
ALL REGIONS	23,869	25,156	29,492	27,234	31,440	57,495	106	29,797	36,376

State Data

	Min	Q1	Mean	Median	Q3	Max	N	Range Avg Min	Range Avg Max
CA	36,376	36,376	36,376	36,376	36,376	36,376	1	29,797	36,376
CO	28,365	32,576	33,974	32,660	36,636	39,633	5	.	.
FL	23,869	23,869	26,623	25,518	28,416	31,440	5	.	.
MI	32,331	32,331	35,328	32,331	35,741	43,905	5	.	.
NC	23,958	24,916	27,916	26,498	29,864	52,390	86	.	.
NJ	49,149	49,149	50,873	50,873	52,598	52,598	2	.	.
OH	50,111	50,111	53,803	53,803	57,495	57,495	2	.	.

Degree Required Data

	Min	Q1	Mean	Median	Q3	Max	N	Range Avg Min	Range Avg Max
High School	28,365	32,331	34,651	32,618	36,636	43,905	10	.	.
Associate's	.	.	.	.	.	.	.	.	.
Bachelor's	23,958	25,021	28,591	26,633	29,939	57,495	90	29,797	36,376
Master's	.	.	.	.	.	.	.	.	.
Doctoral	.	.	.	.	.	.	.	.	.

ASSOCIATE LIBRARIAN OF TECHNICAL ASSISTANCE (NON-MLS DEGREED) - CONTINUED
ALL PUBLIC LIBRARIES
Regional Data

	Min	Q1	Mean	Median	Q3	Max	N	Range Avg Min	Range Avg Max
North Atlantic	20,667	34,882	38,692	36,924	43,867	68,640	29	35,072	44,301
Great Lakes & Plains	14,560	24,388	30,679	29,120	33,802	59,363	64	25,286	35,656
Southeast	14,532	24,796	27,817	26,498	29,866	52,390	120	20,867	23,541
West & Southwest	20,800	27,252	32,329	31,950	36,483	45,984	30	24,598	36,867
ALL REGIONS	14,532	25,021	30,425	28,416	34,141	68,640	243	26,947	36,789

State Data

	Min	Q1	Mean	Median	Q3	Max	N	Range Avg Min	Range Avg Max
AL	20,301	20,301	23,556	21,403	28,965	28,965	3	18,429	27,643
AR	15,788	15,788	15,788	15,788	15,788	15,788	1	.	.
AZ	36,483	36,483	40,050	40,050	43,618	43,618	2	35,776	53,664
CA	29,557	29,557	31,930	29,856	36,376	36,376	3	24,259	33,788
CO	22,422	30,160	34,728	33,199	40,317	44,693	12	25,119	37,821
CT	33,987	35,942	41,191	41,111	43,867	51,126	6	36,410	45,625
DE	35,669	35,669	35,669	35,669	35,669	35,669	1	.	.
FL	23,869	23,869	30,295	26,967	31,440	48,656	6	.	.
GA	37,440	37,440	39,208	39,208	40,976	40,976	2	.	.
IA	23,254	31,200	31,138	31,200	34,677	35,360	5	28,427	32,587
ID	20,800	22,880	26,000	24,960	29,120	33,280	4	24,440	37,440
IL	16,640	20,800	30,385	29,120	35,942	59,363	23	24,202	35,942
IN	27,040	28,642	29,324	28,891	29,120	32,927	5	21,479	32,309
KS	14,560	16,640	24,384	18,947	29,536	47,674	6	26,395	41,683
LA	16,952	16,952	20,561	20,561	24,170	24,170	2	17,784	19,864
MA	36,067	36,665	36,907	36,924	37,440	37,440	5	34,667	37,440
ME	26,894	26,894	32,379	34,882	35,360	35,360	3	27,199	36,518
MI	18,903	26,988	29,874	28,569	32,331	43,905	12	23,067	28,018
MN	39,104	39,104	45,938	48,330	50,380	50,380	3	33,821	39,104
MO	18,374	20,627	25,300	25,719	29,973	31,387	4	.	.
MS	14,532	16,917	25,152	24,318	33,387	37,440	4	.	.
MT	25,106	25,106	25,106	25,106	25,106	25,106	1	.	.
NC	23,958	24,916	27,994	26,498	29,864	52,390	90	.	.
ND	25,000	25,000	25,000	25,000	25,000	25,000	1	.	.
NJ	39,424	39,424	49,973	49,149	52,598	68,640	7	68,640	91,520
NM	29,640	29,640	29,640	29,640	29,640	29,640	1	22,090	35,339
OH	26,666	29,375	41,589	41,098	53,803	57,495	4	26,666	39,998
OR	27,252	27,252	36,618	36,618	45,984	45,984	2	.	.
PA	20,667	23,000	28,675	26,386	30,933	44,678	6	.	.
RI	35,714	35,714	35,714	35,714	35,714	35,714	1	20,987	35,714
SC	18,089	18,089	18,089	18,089	18,089	18,089	1	.	.
TN	33,000	33,000	33,000	33,000	33,000	33,000	1	.	.
TX	22,880	24,960	29,051	28,482	32,933	36,000	5	20,134	29,734
VA	15,657	25,168	27,814	26,790	29,692	38,334	9	25,168	25,168
WI	27,123	27,123	27,123	27,123	27,123	27,123	1	26,021	34,091
WV	28,762	28,762	28,762	28,762	28,762	28,762	1	.	.

Degree Required Data

	Min	Q1	Mean	Median	Q3	Max	N	Range Avg Min	Range Avg Max
High School	14,560	24,170	30,024	29,692	35,942	68,640	63	26,930	35,692
Associate's	15,657	24,209	31,235	29,604	39,346	59,363	26	24,738	33,674
Bachelor's	20,301	25,533	30,297	27,854	32,085	59,072	133	28,659	40,590
Master's	33,000	33,000	36,988	36,988	40,976	40,976	2	.	.
Doctoral	.	.	.	.	.	.		.	.

LIBRARY TECHNICAL ASSISTANT OF ADULT SERVICES

Provides basic assistance to patrons referring patrons to Librarian for professional assistance. Locates materials and information for patrons. May complete routine copy cataloging. Assists with special programming. Provides access to materials, services and programs intended to meet the needs of the adult users of a public library.

Very Small Public Library
(Serving a population of less than 10,000)
Regional Data

	Min	Q1	Mean	Median	Q3	Max	N	Range Avg Min	Range Avg Max
North Atlantic	19,656	22,173	26,028	24,762	29,120	34,320	14	22,880	28,898
Great Lakes & Plains	14,933	18,034	22,539	21,112	23,046	57,720	18	20,996	28,208
Southeast	13,374	13,374	19,521	19,521	25,668	25,668	2		
West & Southwest	19,240	26,936	28,371	31,200	31,200	33,280	5	26,000	29,770
ALL REGIONS	13,374	19,656	24,385	22,984	29,120	57,720	39	22,849	28,840

State Data

	Min	Q1	Mean	Median	Q3	Max	N	Range Avg Min	Range Avg Max
AL	13,374	13,374	13,374	13,374	13,374	13,374	1		
CT	21,632	24,502	25,372	24,648	24,877	31,200	5	21,762	29,562
IA	18,720	20,800	21,341	21,424	22,714	23,046	5	15,506	21,934
ID	19,240	19,240	19,240	19,240	19,240	19,240	1	16,640	19,240
IL	14,933	14,933	16,827	16,827	18,720	18,720	2		
IN	22,048	22,048	22,048	22,048	22,048	22,048	1		
KS	24,024	24,024	24,024	24,024	24,024	24,024	1	18,720	27,040
MA	19,656	19,656	23,758	22,173	22,984	34,320	5	20,030	25,738
ME	29,120	29,120	29,120	29,120	29,120	29,120	3	29,120	33,280
MI	15,080	15,340	18,850	16,640	22,360	27,040	4		
MN	18,034	18,034	20,433	20,800	22,464	22,464	3		
MO	57,720	57,720	57,720	57,720	57,720	57,720	1	47,507	57,720
TX	26,936	26,936	26,936	26,936	26,936	26,936	1		
VT	31,387	31,387	31,387	31,387	31,387	31,387	1		
WA	31,200	31,200	31,893	31,200	33,280	33,280	3	29,120	33,280
WI	24,856	24,856	24,856	24,856	24,856	24,856	1	18,720	24,960
WV	25,668	25,668	25,668	25,668	25,668	25,668	1		

Degree Required Data

	Min	Q1	Mean	Median	Q3	Max	N	Range Avg Min	Range Avg Max
High School	13,374	18,377	20,595	21,112	22,880	25,668	20	17,258	22,797
Associate's	18,720	22,984	30,100	29,120	33,280	57,720	10	29,028	34,558
Bachelor's	21,632	24,502	28,012	29,120	31,200	31,387	7	24,960	32,240
Master's									
Doctoral									

LIBRARY TECHNICAL ASSISTANT OF ADULT SERVICES - CONTINUED
Small Public Library
(Serving a population of 10,000 to 25,000)
Regional Data

	Min	Q1	Mean	Median	Q3	Max	N	Range Avg Min	Range Avg Max
North Atlantic	16,702	22,506	28,919	27,040	35,423	44,803	14	21,388	31,184
Great Lakes & Plains	14,955	16,313	22,772	22,000	28,184	50,000	27	20,623	34,151
Southeast	16,217	18,613	21,755	21,268	24,898	28,267	4	.	.
West & Southwest	13,440	17,618	26,064	21,320	33,218	43,680	9	25,990	38,990
ALL REGIONS	13,440	17,000	24,839	22,693	29,120	50,000	54	22,156	34,619

State Data

	Min	Q1	Mean	Median	Q3	Max	N	Range Avg Min	Range Avg Max
AL	16,217	16,217	16,217	16,217	16,217	16,217	1	.	.
AZ	20,779	20,779	26,638	25,917	33,218	33,218	3	20,779	31,179
CT	44,803	44,803	44,803	44,803	44,803	44,803	1	35,443	44,803
IL	14,955	15,080	21,385	19,200	22,880	50,000	17	22,880	40,560
IN	23,171	23,525	26,125	26,031	28,725	29,266	4	17,853	27,040
MA	27,040	27,040	33,748	31,232	42,973	42,973	6	.	.
ME	22,506	22,506	22,506	22,506	22,506	22,506	2	.	.
MI	16,640	16,640	19,760	19,760	22,880	22,880	2	.	.
MT	21,320	21,320	21,320	21,320	21,320	21,320	1	.	.
NM	41,600	41,600	42,640	42,640	43,680	43,680	2	31,200	46,800
NY	26,166	26,166	29,682	29,682	33,197	33,197	2	.	.
OH	19,906	19,906	19,906	19,906	19,906	19,906	1	19,906	29,848
RI	16,702	16,702	17,735	16,702	19,802	19,802	3	16,702	26,645
TX	13,440	13,440	16,019	17,000	17,618	17,618	3	.	.
VA	21,008	21,008	23,601	21,528	28,267	28,267	3	.	.
WI	29,120	29,120	29,123	29,120	29,128	29,128	3	.	.

Degree Required Data

	Min	Q1	Mean	Median	Q3	Max	N	Range Avg Min	Range Avg Max
High School	13,440	16,313	22,131	20,779	23,878	50,000	33	20,763	31,701
Associate's	22,880	27,040	30,700	29,120	35,423	42,973	11	22,880	29,120
Bachelor's	19,906	24,960	29,328	33,197	33,218	35,360	5	21,889	44,616
Master's	22,506	22,506	22,506	22,506	22,506	22,506	2	.	.
Doctoral	.	.	.	.	.	.		.	.

LIBRARY TECHNICAL ASSISTANT OF ADULT SERVICES - CONTINUED
Medium Public Library
(Serving a population of 25,000 to 99,999)
Regional Data

	Min	Q1	Mean	Median	Q3	Max	N	Range Avg Min	Range Avg Max
North Atlantic	17,680	29,952	34,454	34,561	37,440	68,200	45	31,508	40,722
Great Lakes & Plains	15,994	19,115	27,308	26,042	32,365	58,818	59	23,141	34,700
Southeast	12,480	15,870	18,864	16,650	22,687	29,867	32	14,227	20,010
West & Southwest	12,480	24,960	34,222	32,760	43,809	53,768	36	27,733	37,876
ALL REGIONS	12,480	19,666	29,054	27,040	36,421	68,200	172	25,061	35,034

State Data

	Min	Q1	Mean	Median	Q3	Max	N	Range Avg Min	Range Avg Max
CA	38,064	38,064	45,882	47,229	49,982	53,768	14	40,713	49,677
CT	26,874	26,874	36,928	31,845	42,370	59,085	9	36,400	45,282
DE	51,688	51,688	51,688	51,688	51,688	51,688	1	.	.
IA	17,410	21,528	34,095	35,000	39,769	51,074	7	.	.
ID	16,640	17,680	21,320	21,840	24,960	24,960	4	20,280	29,120
IL	16,640	24,648	26,820	26,312	29,806	44,907	14	23,066	34,379
IN	32,813	32,813	32,813	32,813	32,813	32,813	1	.	.
KS	17,285	17,285	18,200	18,200	19,115	19,115	2	16,338	22,547
LA	15,000	15,725	17,960	16,397	19,469	26,682	19	14,227	20,010
MA	20,446	34,561	34,289	34,561	37,440	43,789	13	37,465	38,596
ME	30,514	30,971	33,599	34,341	36,421	36,421	9	28,857	41,138
MI	15,994	15,994	19,146	19,146	22,298	22,298	2	19,510	22,298
MN	36,619	36,619	40,563	40,563	44,507	44,507	2	.	.
MO	20,883	20,946	23,251	21,736	25,958	26,042	7	20,883	30,430
MS	12,480	14,560	17,177	16,640	18,200	26,133	8	.	.
NC	28,768	28,768	28,768	28,768	28,768	28,768	1	.	.
ND	16,640	16,640	17,801	18,065	18,637	18,762	6	16,640	24,960
NY	22,381	25,203	35,292	36,733	37,715	68,200	10	26,359	39,026
OH	17,493	28,995	29,936	30,222	32,365	58,818	18	26,859	41,175
OR	38,208	38,208	38,208	38,208	38,208	38,208	1	.	.
PA	17,680	17,680	21,771	17,680	29,952	29,952	3	.	.
SC	23,978	23,978	26,578	25,891	29,867	29,867	3	.	.
TX	12,480	21,840	27,421	26,208	32,760	42,336	17	21,040	32,400
WV	16,480	16,480	16,480	16,480	16,480	16,480	1	.	.

Degree Required Data

	Min	Q1	Mean	Median	Q3	Max	N	Range Avg Min	Range Avg Max
High School	12,480	17,451	28,878	25,203	38,064	68,200	100	23,764	31,488
Associate's	15,994	20,946	25,161	25,584	28,670	38,514	21	23,884	36,557
Bachelor's	17,680	28,768	31,118	30,742	34,341	51,688	38	28,593	41,410
Master's	.	.	.	.	.	.	.	.	.
Doctoral	.	.	.	.	.	.	.	.	.

LIBRARY TECHNICAL ASSISTANT OF ADULT SERVICES - CONTINUED
Large Public Library
(Serving a population of 100,000 to 499,999)
Regional Data

	Min	Q1	Mean	Median	Q3	Max	N	Range Avg Min	Range Avg Max
North Atlantic	16,640	27,146	33,214	30,248	40,473	50,182	36	27,019	46,987
Great Lakes & Plains	17,680	22,235	28,196	25,788	33,280	47,040	70	21,767	30,998
Southeast	16,600	23,081	26,603	25,954	29,181	42,312	87	22,806	30,241
West & Southwest	15,517	17,680	26,044	25,638	32,656	57,305	89	21,119	28,425
ALL REGIONS	15,517	22,235	27,666	26,458	32,656	57,305	282	21,647	30,015

State Data

	Min	Q1	Mean	Median	Q3	Max	N	Range Avg Min	Range Avg Max
AL	23,026	23,026	23,026	23,026	23,026	23,026	1	23,254	28,163
AZ	29,307	31,106	34,351	34,268	37,596	39,562	4	.	.
CA	26,458	26,458	33,058	32,999	35,485	57,305	26	28,870	35,184
CO	21,112	22,422	24,554	22,870	27,893	30,264	14	21,163	31,921
FL	20,629	26,796	29,183	28,580	33,230	38,539	20	23,650	34,320
GA	16,910	21,320	22,718	21,944	23,920	28,704	10	16,910	16,910
IL	20,925	27,093	33,170	31,949	38,133	47,040	12	29,196	35,182
IN	28,725	28,725	28,725	28,725	28,725	28,725	1	.	.
MD	31,803	36,112	40,791	41,841	44,217	50,182	8	23,712	35,568
MI	24,045	24,045	24,045	24,045	24,045	24,045	1	20,717	31,762
MN	19,032	20,946	22,460	22,235	23,608	25,875	11	.	.
MS	16,600	16,900	19,113	17,915	21,326	24,021	4	.	.
NC	20,910	23,598	23,921	23,608	24,315	26,819	13	23,150	36,733
NE	21,640	21,640	23,697	23,180	24,831	28,496	13	20,908	28,496
NJ	27,033	27,146	30,300	29,055	30,261	41,149	19	.	.
NM	15,600	18,007	19,501	20,607	20,995	21,190	4	18,637	25,501
NY	41,613	41,613	43,102	43,847	43,847	43,847	3	.	.
OH	17,680	21,788	24,440	24,367	26,822	33,280	20	17,680	30,160
OK	15,517	15,746	16,791	17,046	17,597	19,261	26	14,407	20,331
OR	26,208	26,208	36,996	42,390	42,390	42,390	3	21,195	27,934
PA	16,640	20,800	27,393	29,294	30,509	37,822	6	28,122	50,794
SC	20,820	23,534	27,283	26,346	29,363	36,333	30	.	.
TN	22,544	22,544	24,389	23,333	27,290	27,290	3	18,158	23,899
TX	19,323	24,190	29,305	31,822	34,151	36,946	12	17,472	31,491
VA	29,181	29,181	33,582	30,028	40,762	42,312	6	29,182	29,182
WI	35,172	38,564	39,913	40,983	40,983	43,774	12	.	.

Degree Required Data

	Min	Q1	Mean	Median	Q3	Max	N	Range Avg Min	Range Avg Max
High School	15,517	18,741	25,322	23,629	29,037	43,774	110	16,766	25,498
Associate's	16,600	22,235	27,152	24,021	30,933	57,305	71	23,672	31,628
Bachelor's	19,032	25,262	31,713	29,363	36,946	50,182	51	28,340	49,494
Master's	.	.	.	.	.	.			
Doctoral	.	.	.	.	.	.			

LIBRARY TECHNICAL ASSISTANT OF ADULT SERVICES - CONTINUED
Very Large Public Library
(Serving a population of 500,000 or more)
Regional Data

	Min	Q1	Mean	Median	Q3	Max	N	Range Avg Min	Range Avg Max
North Atlantic	32,240	32,240	32,240	32,240	32,240	32,240	1	.	.
Great Lakes & Plains	24,898	25,875	30,958	30,451	35,714	39,978	102	25,803	35,005
Southeast	22,454	23,128	29,634	24,515	36,194	56,136	183	33,331	55,551
West & Southwest	21,964	25,442	43,242	57,044	57,044	61,958	65	48,657	59,150
ALL REGIONS	21,964	23,943	32,546	27,706	36,400	61,958	351	31,986	44,099

State Data

	Min	Q1	Mean	Median	Q3	Max	N	Range Avg Min	Range Avg Max
CA	56,186	57,044	58,985	57,044	61,958	61,958	35	48,657	59,150
FL	22,733	24,183	28,885	25,226	34,910	42,328	84	.	.
GA	28,920	28,920	28,920	28,920	28,920	28,920	1	.	.
NC	22,454	22,454	23,419	22,454	23,128	56,136	63	.	.
NJ	32,240	32,240	32,240	32,240	32,240	32,240	1	.	.
OH	24,898	25,875	30,958	30,451	35,714	39,978	102	25,803	35,005
TX	21,964	22,962	24,875	25,438	26,090	29,188	30	.	.
VA	33,331	35,693	42,638	41,209	48,228	55,551	35	33,331	55,551

Degree Required Data

	Min	Q1	Mean	Median	Q3	Max	N	Range Avg Min	Range Avg Max
High School	22,454	23,128	30,562	27,706	36,379	56,136	195	27,698	41,060
Associate's	.	.	.	.	.	.	.	.	.
Bachelor's	21,964	23,065	25,436	25,442	26,602	38,438	33	30,597	44,054
Master's	.	.	.	.	.	.	.	.	.
Doctoral	.	.	.	.	.	.	.	.	.

LIBRARY TECHNICAL ASSISTANT OF ADULT SERVICES - CONTINUED
ALL PUBLIC LIBRARIES
Regional Data

	Min	Q1	Mean	Median	Q3	Max	N	Range Avg Min	Range Avg Max
North Atlantic	16,640	27,033	32,251	31,086	37,440	68,200	110	27,557	36,942
Great Lakes & Plains	14,933	22,776	28,127	26,667	33,238	58,818	276	24,044	33,820
Southeast	12,480	22,454	27,491	24,263	32,453	56,136	308	27,546	43,867
West & Southwest	12,480	22,100	33,025	27,373	42,336	61,958	204	29,571	38,272
ALL REGIONS	12,480	22,672	29,527	26,468	35,000	68,200	898	26,598	36,837

State Data

	Min	Q1	Mean	Median	Q3	Max	N	Range Avg Min	Range Avg Max
AL	13,374	13,374	17,539	16,217	23,026	23,026	3	23,254	28,163
AZ	20,779	25,917	31,046	32,906	35,630	39,562	7	20,779	31,179
CA	26,458	35,485	47,551	53,768	57,044	61,958	75	40,622	49,438
CO	21,112	22,422	24,554	22,870	27,893	30,264	14	21,163	31,921
CT	21,632	24,877	33,601	31,200	42,370	59,085	15	28,961	37,362
DE	51,688	51,688	51,688	51,688	51,688	51,688	1	.	.
FL	20,629	24,183	28,943	26,329	34,646	42,328	104	23,650	34,320
GA	16,910	21,320	23,282	22,048	27,040	28,920	11	16,910	16,910
IA	17,410	21,112	28,781	22,880	37,115	51,074	12	15,506	21,934
ID	16,640	18,720	20,904	19,240	24,960	24,960	5	19,552	27,144
IL	14,933	18,720	26,016	24,960	29,848	50,000	45	25,447	35,578
IN	22,048	23,171	26,869	28,184	29,266	32,813	7	17,853	27,040
KS	17,285	17,285	20,141	19,115	24,024	24,024	3	17,132	24,045
LA	15,000	15,725	17,960	16,397	19,469	26,682	19	14,227	20,010
MA	19,656	25,012	31,960	34,561	37,440	43,789	24	28,748	32,167
MD	31,803	36,112	40,791	41,841	44,217	50,182	8	23,712	35,568
ME	22,506	29,120	31,054	30,742	35,360	36,421	14	28,922	39,173
MI	15,080	15,994	19,695	17,680	22,880	27,040	9	20,114	27,030
MN	18,034	20,873	24,343	22,350	24,305	44,507	16	.	.
MO	20,883	21,341	27,560	23,598	26,000	57,720	8	34,195	44,075
MS	12,480	15,580	17,822	16,920	18,675	26,133	12	.	.
MT	21,320	21,320	21,320	21,320	21,320	21,320	1	.	.
NC	20,910	22,454	23,574	22,454	23,128	56,136	77	23,150	36,733
ND	16,640	16,640	17,801	18,065	18,637	18,762	6	16,640	24,960
NE	21,640	21,640	23,697	23,180	24,831	28,496	13	20,908	28,496
NJ	27,033	27,146	30,397	29,055	31,251	41,149	20	.	.
NM	15,600	20,413	27,214	20,995	41,600	43,680	6	24,918	36,150
NY	22,381	25,203	36,106	36,733	41,613	68,200	15	26,359	39,026
OH	17,493	25,293	29,824	28,995	34,798	58,818	141	24,869	35,087
OK	15,517	15,746	16,791	17,046	17,597	19,261	26	14,407	20,331
OR	26,208	32,208	37,299	40,299	42,390	42,390	4	21,195	27,934
PA	16,640	17,680	25,519	28,804	29,952	37,822	9	28,122	50,794
RI	16,702	16,702	17,735	16,702	19,802	19,802	3	16,702	26,645
SC	20,820	23,978	27,219	26,336	29,363	36,333	33	.	.
TN	22,544	22,544	24,389	23,333	27,290	27,290	3	18,158	23,899
TX	12,480	22,960	26,017	25,576	27,789	42,336	63	20,564	32,279
VA	21,008	34,766	40,105	38,126	46,839	55,551	44	33,215	54,818
VT	31,387	31,387	31,387	31,387	31,387	31,387	1	.	.
WA	31,200	31,200	31,893	31,200	33,280	33,280	3	29,120	33,280
WI	24,856	32,150	36,949	39,249	40,983	43,774	16	18,720	24,960
WV	16,480	16,480	21,074	21,074	25,668	25,668	2	.	.

Degree Required Data

	Min	Q1	Mean	Median	Q3	Max	N	Range Avg Min	Range Avg Max
High School	12,480	21,798	27,893	25,293	34,798	68,200	458	23,897	34,703
Associate's	15,994	22,528	27,388	24,877	30,264	57,720	113	24,252	32,684
Bachelor's	17,680	24,960	29,716	28,786	33,383	51,688	134	27,570	41,150
Master's	22,506	22,506	22,506	22,506	22,506	22,506	2	.	.
Doctoral									

LIBRARY TECHNICAL ASSISTANT OF ARCHIVES AND SPECIAL COLLECTIONS

Provides basic assistance to patrons referring patrons to Librarian for professional assistance. Locates materials and information for patrons. May complete routine copy cataloging. Assists with special programming. Manages and maintains collection; identifies and appraises records, authenticates, describes and documents, facilitates access and use, preserves and conserves, and exhibits collection.

Very Small Public Library
(Serving a population of less than 10,000)
Regional Data

	Min	Q1	Mean	Median	Q3	Max	N	Range Avg Min	Range Avg Max
Great Lakes & Plains	21,893	21,893	21,893	21,893	21,893	21,893	1	.	.
ALL REGIONS	21,893	21,893	21,893	21,893	21,893	21,893	1	.	.

State Data

	Min	Q1	Mean	Median	Q3	Max	N	Range Avg Min	Range Avg Max
OH	21,893	21,893	21,893	21,893	21,893	21,893	1	.	.

Degree Required Data

	Min	Q1	Mean	Median	Q3	Max	N	Range Avg Min	Range Avg Max
High School	.	.	.	.	.	.		.	.
Associate's	21,893	21,893	21,893	21,893	21,893	21,893	1	.	.
Bachelor's	.	.	.	.	.	.		.	.
Master's	.	.	.	.	.	.			
Doctoral	.	.	.	.	.	.			

LIBRARY TECHNICAL ASSISTANT OF ARCHIVES AND SPECIAL COLLECTIONS - CONTINUED
Small Public Library
(Serving a population of 10,000 to 25,000)
Regional Data

	Min	Q1	Mean	Median	Q3	Max	N	Range Avg Min	Range Avg Max
North Atlantic	23,920	23,920	23,920	23,920	23,920	23,920	1	19,760	26,520
Great Lakes & Plains	24,960	24,960	24,960	24,960	24,960	24,960	1	.	.
ALL REGIONS	23,920	23,920	24,440	24,440	24,960	24,960	2	19,760	26,520

State Data

	Min	Q1	Mean	Median	Q3	Max	N	Range Avg Min	Range Avg Max
ME	23,920	23,920	23,920	23,920	23,920	23,920	1	19,760	26,520
MI	24,960	24,960	24,960	24,960	24,960	24,960	1	.	.

Degree Required Data

	Min	Q1	Mean	Median	Q3	Max	N	Range Avg Min	Range Avg Max
High School	24,960	24,960	24,960	24,960	24,960	24,960	1	.	.
Associate's	.	.	.	.	.	.		.	.
Bachelor's	23,920	23,920	23,920	23,920	23,920	23,920	1	19,760	26,520
Master's	.	.	.	.	.	.		.	.
Doctoral	.	.	.	.	.	.		.	.

LIBRARY TECHNICAL ASSISTANT OF ARCHIVES AND SPECIAL COLLECTIONS - CONTINUED
Medium Public Library
(Serving a population of 25,000 to 99,999)
Regional Data

	Min	Q1	Mean	Median	Q3	Max	N	Range Avg Min	Range Avg Max
North Atlantic	36,924	42,747	50,771	53,394	59,085	59,085	6	.	.
Great Lakes & Plains	18,720	20,800	25,643	23,400	31,537	33,760	5	20,162	25,757
Southeast	23,754	23,754	23,754	23,754	23,754	23,754	1	.	.
ALL REGIONS	18,720	23,577	38,050	35,342	53,394	59,085	12	20,162	25,757

State Data

	Min	Q1	Mean	Median	Q3	Max	N	Range Avg Min	Range Avg Max
CT	51,496	53,394	56,239	57,188	59,085	59,085	4	.	.
IN	18,720	18,720	23,686	20,800	31,537	31,537	3	18,720	19,760
MA	36,924	36,924	39,835	39,835	42,747	42,747	2	.	.
OH	23,400	23,400	28,580	28,580	33,760	33,760	2	23,046	37,752
WV	23,754	23,754	23,754	23,754	23,754	23,754	1	.	.

Degree Required Data

	Min	Q1	Mean	Median	Q3	Max	N	Range Avg Min	Range Avg Max
High School	18,720	31,537	40,744	36,924	55,291	59,085	9	18,720	19,760
Associate's	23,400	23,400	33,073	33,073	42,747	42,747	2	23,046	37,752
Bachelor's	.	.	.	.	.	.		.	.
Master's	23,754	23,754	23,754	23,754	23,754	23,754	1	.	.
Doctoral	.	.	.	.	.	.		.	.

LIBRARY TECHNICAL ASSISTANT OF ARCHIVES AND SPECIAL COLLECTIONS - CONTINUED
Large Public Library
(Serving a population of 100,000 to 499,999)
Regional Data

	Min	Q1	Mean	Median	Q3	Max	N	Range Avg Min	Range Avg Max
North Atlantic	17,160	17,160	27,359	27,359	37,558	37,558	2	37,558	37,558
Southeast	15,912	25,792	30,090	29,182	37,202	42,307	15	23,920	27,647
West & Southwest	21,611	21,999	26,548	25,834	28,995	34,299	5	28,995	45,594
ALL REGIONS	15,912	25,792	29,037	29,182	34,299	42,307	22	26,259	31,129

State Data

	Min	Q1	Mean	Median	Q3	Max	N	Range Avg Min	Range Avg Max
CO	28,995	28,995	28,995	28,995	28,995	28,995	1	28,995	45,594
GA	16,910	16,910	16,910	16,910	16,910	16,910	1	16,910	16,910
NC	15,912	25,792	24,997	25,792	25,792	31,695	5	19,531	30,711
NY	17,160	17,160	27,359	27,359	37,558	37,558	2	37,558	37,558
TX	21,611	21,805	25,936	23,917	30,067	34,299	4		
VA	29,181	29,182	34,385	30,795	40,123	42,307	9	29,182	29,182

Degree Required Data

	Min	Q1	Mean	Median	Q3	Max	N	Range Avg Min	Range Avg Max
High School	16,910	25,834	30,447	29,182	37,202	42,307	13	26,114	26,114
Associate's	15,912	20,852	26,925	28,744	32,997	34,299	4	19,531	30,711
Bachelor's	28,995	28,995	33,277	33,277	37,558	37,558	2	33,277	41,576
Master's	17,160	17,160	17,160	17,160	17,160	17,160	1		
Doctoral									

LIBRARY TECHNICAL ASSISTANT OF ARCHIVES AND SPECIAL COLLECTIONS - CONTINUED
Very Large Public Library
(Serving a population of 500,000 or more)
Regional Data

	Min	Q1	Mean	Median	Q3	Max	N	Range Avg Min	Range Avg Max
Great Lakes & Plains	24,898	24,898	31,450	29,474	39,978	39,978	3	25,868	34,417
Southeast	28,379	35,494	42,047	40,564	42,328	63,746	11	38,247	63,746
West & Southwest	31,847	34,331	45,688	46,930	57,044	57,044	4	42,505	51,827
ALL REGIONS	24,898	31,847	41,090	40,271	42,328	63,746	18	35,202	48,278

State Data

	Min	Q1	Mean	Median	Q3	Max	N	Range Avg Min	Range Avg Max
CA	57,044	57,044	57,044	57,044	57,044	57,044	2	46,930	57,044
FL	28,379	35,494	37,225	40,564	40,564	42,328	9		
OH	24,898	24,898	31,450	29,474	39,978	39,978	3	25,868	34,417
OR	36,816	36,816	36,816	36,816	36,816	36,816	1	33,654	41,392
TX	31,847	31,847	31,847	31,847	31,847	31,847	1		
VA	63,746	63,746	63,746	63,746	63,746	63,746	2	38,247	63,746

Degree Required Data

	Min	Q1	Mean	Median	Q3	Max	N	Range Avg Min	Range Avg Max
High School	24,898	29,474	42,281	35,912	63,746	63,746	6	30,820	46,148
Associate's	36,816	36,816	36,816	36,816	36,816	36,816	1	33,654	41,392
Bachelor's	28,379	35,494	37,225	40,564	40,564	42,328	9	.	.
Master's	.	.	.	.	.	.	.	.	.
Doctoral	.	.	.	.	.	.	.	.	.

LIBRARY TECHNICAL ASSISTANT OF ARCHIVES AND SPECIAL COLLECTIONS - CONTINUED
ALL PUBLIC LIBRARIES
Regional Data

	Min	Q1	Mean	Median	Q3	Max	N	Range Avg Min	Range Avg Max
North Atlantic	17,160	36,924	42,585	42,747	55,291	59,085	9	28,659	32,039
Great Lakes & Plains	18,720	21,893	26,942	24,929	31,537	39,978	10	23,015	30,087
Southeast	15,912	28,379	34,727	31,695	40,564	63,746	27	27,502	36,671
West & Southwest	21,611	25,834	35,054	31,847	36,816	57,044	9	39,127	50,268
ALL REGIONS	15,912	25,792	34,651	31,695	40,564	63,746	55	28,597	36,952

State Data

	Min	Q1	Mean	Median	Q3	Max	N	Range Avg Min	Range Avg Max
CA	57,044	57,044	57,044	57,044	57,044	57,044	2	46,930	57,044
CO	28,995	28,995	28,995	28,995	28,995	28,995	1	28,995	45,594
CT	51,496	53,394	56,239	57,188	59,085	59,085	4	.	.
FL	28,379	35,494	37,225	40,564	40,564	42,328	9	.	.
GA	16,910	16,910	16,910	16,910	16,910	16,910	1	16,910	16,910
IN	18,720	18,720	23,686	20,800	31,537	31,537	3	18,720	19,760
MA	36,924	36,924	39,835	39,835	42,747	42,747	2	.	.
ME	23,920	23,920	23,920	23,920	23,920	23,920	1	19,760	26,520
MI	24,960	24,960	24,960	24,960	24,960	24,960	1	.	.
NC	15,912	25,792	24,997	25,792	25,792	31,695	5	19,531	30,711
NY	17,160	17,160	27,359	27,359	37,558	37,558	2	37,558	37,558
OH	21,893	23,400	28,900	27,186	33,760	39,978	6	25,163	35,251
OR	36,816	36,816	36,816	36,816	36,816	36,816	1	33,654	41,392
TX	21,611	21,999	27,118	25,834	31,847	34,299	5	.	.
VA	29,181	29,182	39,723	37,202	42,307	63,746	11	32,808	43,008
WV	23,754	23,754	23,754	23,754	23,754	23,754	1	.	.

Degree Required Data

	Min	Q1	Mean	Median	Q3	Max	N	Range Avg Min	Range Avg Max
High School	16,910	25,834	35,902	31,537	42,307	63,746	29	26,909	34,065
Associate's	15,912	22,647	29,069	28,744	35,558	42,747	8	23,941	35,142
Bachelor's	23,920	29,619	35,458	36,941	40,564	42,328	12	28,771	36,557
Master's	17,160	17,160	20,457	20,457	23,754	23,754	2	.	.
Doctoral	.	.	.	.	.	.	.	.	.

LIBRARY TECHNICAL ASSISTANT OF CHILDREN'S SERVICES/YOUNG ADULT SERVICES

Provides basic assistance to patrons referring patrons to Librarian for professional assistance. Locates materials and information for patrons. May complete routine copy cataloging. Assists with special programming. Provides services intended for children and youths through twelfth grade; develops collection, provides homework and reader's advisory services, and develops age appropriate programs.

Very Small Public Library
(Serving a population of less than 10,000)
Regional Data

	Min	Q1	Mean	Median	Q3	Max	N	Range Avg Min	Range Avg Max
North Atlantic	16,640	19,760	21,993	21,840	24,648	31,078	9	19,665	24,149
Great Lakes & Plains	15,600	16,640	23,709	18,720	21,923	57,720	7	31,034	37,180
West & Southwest	16,536	17,368	21,575	20,436	25,782	28,891	4	18,852	22,339
ALL REGIONS	15,600	16,640	22,510	20,020	23,660	57,720	20	21,356	25,868

State Data

	Min	Q1	Mean	Median	Q3	Max	N	Range Avg Min	Range Avg Max
CO	16,536	16,536	22,714	22,714	28,891	28,891	2	19,958	24,409
CT	24,648	24,648	24,648	24,648	24,648	24,648	1	24,648	24,648
ID	18,200	18,200	18,200	18,200	18,200	18,200	1	16,640	18,200
IL	18,720	18,720	18,720	18,720	18,720	18,720	1		
MA	16,640	19,760	20,072	20,280	21,840	21,840	5	18,720	22,880
ME	25,210	25,210	25,210	25,210	25,210	25,210	1	19,406	29,994
MI	15,600	15,600	15,600	15,600	15,600	15,600	1		
MN	16,640	16,640	19,282	19,282	21,923	21,923	2		
MO	57,720	57,720	57,720	57,720	57,720	57,720	1	47,507	57,720
NY	16,640	16,640	16,640	16,640	16,640	16,640	1		
SD	18,720	18,720	18,720	18,720	18,720	18,720	1		
TX	22,672	22,672	22,672	22,672	22,672	22,672	1		
VT	31,078	31,078	31,078	31,078	31,078	31,078	1		
WI	16,640	16,640	16,640	16,640	16,640	16,640	1	14,560	16,640

Degree Required Data

	Min	Q1	Mean	Median	Q3	Max	N	Range Avg Min	Range Avg Max
High School	15,600	16,640	19,378	18,200	21,923	28,891	11	18,387	22,558
Associate's	16,640	19,760	26,347	21,060	21,840	57,720	6	25,309	29,016
Bachelor's	25,210	25,210	28,144	28,144	31,078	31,078	2	19,406	29,994
Master's									
Doctoral									

LIBRARY TECHNICAL ASSISTANT OF CHILDREN'S SERVICES/YOUNG ADULT SERVICES - CONTINUED
Small Public Library
(Serving a population of 10,000 to 25,000)
Regional Data

	Min	Q1	Mean	Median	Q3	Max	N	Range Avg Min	Range Avg Max
North Atlantic	17,680	23,795	30,746	28,330	37,960	46,343	21	28,917	39,049
Great Lakes & Plains	14,892	20,800	25,167	24,960	29,128	39,520	25	21,650	41,545
West & Southwest	11,327	12,391	20,553	17,762	28,714	35,360	4	24,950	37,430
ALL REGIONS	11,327	22,000	27,141	26,530	31,200	46,343	50	24,239	40,417

State Data

	Min	Q1	Mean	Median	Q3	Max	N	Range Avg Min	Range Avg Max
AZ	22,069	22,069	22,069	22,069	22,069	22,069	1	20,779	31,179
CT	44,803	44,803	44,803	44,803	44,803	44,803	1	35,443	35,443
IA	16,120	16,120	16,120	16,120	16,120	16,120	1	.	.
IL	14,892	23,067	26,379	24,960	27,664	39,520	14	22,880	49,920
IN	16,640	16,640	20,041	20,041	23,442	23,442	2	17,160	23,920
MA	27,040	27,040	31,023	27,040	35,007	42,973	4	.	.
ME	21,320	21,320	21,715	21,320	22,506	22,506	3	16,640	22,048
MI	31,200	31,200	31,200	31,200	31,200	31,200	1	.	.
NH	37,960	37,960	37,960	37,960	37,960	37,960	2	37,211	56,389
NJ	22,000	26,021	33,531	32,829	41,167	46,343	6	29,397	40,026
NM	13,455	13,455	24,408	24,408	35,360	35,360	2	29,120	43,680
NY	23,795	26,062	29,206	29,016	32,350	34,999	4	.	.
OH	18,906	18,906	19,836	19,906	20,696	20,696	3	20,301	25,272
PA	17,680	17,680	17,680	17,680	17,680	17,680	1	.	.
TX	11,327	11,327	11,327	11,327	11,327	11,327	1	.	.
WI	25,584	27,356	28,242	29,128	29,128	29,129	4	21,029	25,584

Degree Required Data

	Min	Q1	Mean	Median	Q3	Max	N	Range Avg Min	Range Avg Max
High School	11,327	22,069	26,612	26,062	31,200	46,343	10	23,135	33,795
Associate's	16,120	26,312	28,757	27,352	29,128	42,973	12	21,029	25,584
Bachelor's	16,640	21,320	26,915	24,960	33,029	39,520	24	24,051	42,853
Master's	22,506	22,506	22,506	22,506	22,506	22,506	1	.	.
Doctoral	.	.	.	.	.	.		.	.

LIBRARY TECHNICAL ASSISTANT OF CHILDREN'S SERVICES/YOUNG ADULT SERVICES - CONTINUED
Medium Public Library
(Serving a population of 25,000 to 99,999)
Regional Data

	Min	Q1	Mean	Median	Q3	Max	N	Range Avg Min	Range Avg Max
North Atlantic	21,070	34,561	39,075	38,201	43,400	59,085	22	35,513	42,173
Great Lakes & Plains	14,560	21,278	27,850	25,969	32,261	58,818	62	23,358	36,012
Southeast	12,480	15,657	18,976	19,916	21,900	23,985	10	10,712	19,032
West & Southwest	17,395	23,046	29,064	25,231	31,596	51,376	30	26,967	37,599
ALL REGIONS	12,480	21,736	29,420	26,527	34,906	59,085	124	25,567	36,774

State Data

	Min	Q1	Mean	Median	Q3	Max	N	Range Avg Min	Range Avg Max
CA	29,786	37,224	44,417	49,067	49,982	51,376	6	40,452	49,500
CO	18,429	20,010	21,445	21,975	22,880	23,400	4	18,720	31,200
CT	36,358	40,820	49,952	52,183	59,085	59,085	4	36,400	45,282
GA	20,800	20,800	20,800	20,800	20,800	20,800	1		
IA	19,781	26,811	33,455	31,006	40,961	51,167	6	24,960	27,040
ID	24,960	24,960	29,120	31,200	31,200	31,200	3	24,960	35,360
IL	14,560	21,466	26,083	25,220	28,621	43,597	30	23,256	36,259
IN	18,582	18,582	20,691	18,741	19,719	27,830	5	18,013	21,611
LA	12,480	12,480	17,804	19,032	21,900	21,900	3	10,712	19,032
MA	21,070	34,561	37,691	39,097	42,525	43,903	10	37,515	40,909
ME	33,342	33,342	37,783	37,783	42,224	42,224	2	29,619	42,224
MN	44,507	44,507	44,507	44,507	44,507	44,507	1		
MO	21,736	23,889	27,425	27,581	30,961	32,802	4		
MS	14,560	14,560	18,148	18,148	21,736	21,736	2		
ND	16,640	16,640	18,252	18,252	19,864	19,864	2	16,640	24,960
NY	37,430	37,430	42,269	38,962	50,413	50,413	3		
OH	21,278	28,933	33,235	30,742	35,194	58,818	12	26,083	41,593
PA	23,072	23,072	26,852	26,284	31,200	31,200	3		
SC	23,467	23,467	23,467	23,467	23,467	23,467	1		
TN	23,985	23,985	23,985	23,985	23,985	23,985	1		
TX	18,720	24,814	26,844	25,501	31,596	33,180	11	23,944	37,488
UT	17,395	17,395	22,404	23,046	26,770	26,770	3	22,630	33,925
VA	15,657	15,657	15,902	15,902	16,148	16,148	2		
WI	20,821	20,821	25,261	25,261	29,702	29,702	2	18,762	24,586
WY	23,026	23,026	23,261	23,026	23,733	23,733	3	21,944	26,978

Degree Required Data

	Min	Q1	Mean	Median	Q3	Max	N	Range Avg Min	Range Avg Max
High School	14,560	19,864	31,721	27,830	40,961	59,085	49	27,321	35,621
Associate's	19,282	21,653	25,122	24,960	25,896	41,257	31	22,906	35,967
Bachelor's	12,480	23,046	30,213	30,347	33,342	43,903	38	27,427	39,585
Master's									
Doctoral									

LIBRARY TECHNICAL ASSISTANT OF CHILDREN'S SERVICES/YOUNG ADULT SERVICES - CONTINUED
Large Public Library
(Serving a population of 100,000 to 499,999)
Regional Data

	Min	Q1	Mean	Median	Q3	Max	N	Range Avg Min	Range Avg Max
North Atlantic	22,880	35,402	36,376	37,558	39,118	49,013	33	28,327	36,231
Great Lakes & Plains	16,640	20,946	26,075	23,754	31,616	44,579	59	22,705	31,010
Southeast	17,100	23,150	28,258	26,578	31,200	71,336	66	24,332	35,883
West & Southwest	15,517	21,899	29,241	29,099	35,485	56,160	54	23,083	31,644
ALL REGIONS	15,517	22,458	29,165	27,782	35,443	71,336	212	23,352	32,373

State Data

	Min	Q1	Mean	Median	Q3	Max	N	Range Avg Min	Range Avg Max
AL	19,469	19,469	23,754	25,896	25,896	25,896	3	18,429	27,643
AZ	29,307	33,946	36,178	38,251	39,562	39,562	9	.	.
CA	23,816	27,789	35,093	32,625	42,817	56,160	14	30,092	37,869
CO	22,235	22,235	27,366	28,995	30,867	30,867	3	23,268	35,596
FL	22,452	24,523	28,015	27,315	30,859	36,275	8	23,650	34,320
GA	20,924	21,840	22,696	22,568	23,920	24,356	6	.	.
IL	25,230	27,685	31,529	31,833	34,880	36,875	19	26,401	31,817
LA	30,493	30,493	32,646	32,646	34,798	34,798	2	30,493	41,558
MD	23,712	38,050	38,767	38,457	41,310	49,013	21	23,712	35,568
MI	30,493	30,493	30,493	30,493	30,493	30,493	2	24,357	30,493
MN	20,946	20,946	22,266	22,266	23,587	23,587	2	.	.
MS	17,100	17,450	17,935	17,960	18,419	18,719	4	.	.
NC	17,914	23,150	30,145	26,132	34,951	71,336	18	24,701	39,419
NJ	22,880	24,825	28,669	27,272	32,513	37,251	4	.	.
NM	16,640	16,640	16,640	16,640	16,640	16,640	1	.	.
NY	37,558	37,558	37,558	37,558	37,558	37,558	1	37,558	37,558
OH	16,640	17,576	20,932	21,393	22,932	30,493	32	19,397	30,376
OK	15,517	15,517	16,141	15,662	15,912	18,096	5	14,352	20,488
OR	30,279	30,279	35,074	36,408	38,536	38,536	3	21,195	27,934
PA	26,551	30,509	33,438	35,402	35,402	35,402	7	.	.
SC	24,828	25,372	27,008	26,336	28,811	30,935	7	.	.
TN	19,258	27,040	29,366	31,378	31,378	38,783	9	.	.
TX	17,472	21,507	25,129	24,753	27,435	33,966	19	18,481	32,417
VA	29,182	29,182	33,389	30,494	38,046	42,312	9	29,182	29,182
WI	38,648	39,238	41,010	40,406	42,781	44,579	4	.	.

Degree Required Data

	Min	Q1	Mean	Median	Q3	Max	N	Range Avg Min	Range Avg Max
High School	15,517	20,874	26,181	24,856	30,494	56,160	90	22,774	32,919
Associate's	17,800	22,651	28,346	27,133	32,656	45,614	50	23,128	31,397
Bachelor's	19,469	28,811	34,776	35,402	38,783	71,336	59	24,368	33,216
Master's	.	.	.	.	.	.	.	.	.
Doctoral	.	.	.	.	.	.	.	.	.

LIBRARY TECHNICAL ASSISTANT OF CHILDREN'S SERVICES/YOUNG ADULT SERVICES - CONTINUED
Very Large Public Library
(Serving a population of 500,000 or more)
Regional Data

	Min	Q1	Mean	Median	Q3	Max	N	Range Avg Min	Range Avg Max
Great Lakes & Plains	24,898	25,397	28,793	25,875	34,112	36,400	7	25,539	35,550
Southeast	22,454	22,454	30,856	26,620	37,988	53,173	81	33,331	55,551
West & Southwest	29,664	29,676	40,556	34,955	57,044	57,044	6	41,576	52,950
ALL REGIONS	22,454	22,545	31,322	27,649	37,662	57,044	94	32,653	52,192

State Data

	Min	Q1	Mean	Median	Q3	Max	N	Range Avg Min	Range Avg Max
CA	57,044	57,044	57,044	57,044	57,044	57,044	2	46,930	57,044
FL	23,869	25,245	26,830	27,518	28,416	28,416	4		
NC	22,454	22,454	23,400	22,454	23,128	29,796	43		
OH	24,898	25,397	28,793	25,875	34,112	36,400	7	25,539	35,550
TX	29,664	29,670	32,312	32,196	34,955	35,194	4	30,867	44,762
VA	33,331	34,405	40,760	39,449	45,257	53,173	34	33,331	55,551

Degree Required Data

	Min	Q1	Mean	Median	Q3	Max	N	Range Avg Min	Range Avg Max
High School	22,454	22,454	30,898	26,802	37,662	53,173	87	32,000	52,136
Associate's									
Bachelor's	26,620	27,518	29,542	28,416	31,566	34,715	4	30,867	44,762
Master's									
Doctoral									

LIBRARY TECHNICAL ASSISTANT OF CHILDREN'S SERVICES/YOUNG ADULT SERVICES - CONTINUED
ALL PUBLIC LIBRARIES
Regional Data

	Min	Q1	Mean	Median	Q3	Max	N	Range Avg Min	Range Avg Max
North Atlantic	16,640	26,551	34,161	35,402	40,488	59,085	85	28,651	35,914
Great Lakes & Plains	14,560	20,946	26,637	25,230	30,933	58,818	160	23,161	34,926
Southeast	12,480	22,454	29,007	25,896	34,197	71,336	157	29,692	48,094
West & Southwest	11,327	22,260	29,212	27,612	34,715	57,044	98	25,722	35,216
ALL REGIONS	11,327	22,454	29,165	27,019	35,360	71,336	500	25,804	38,041

State Data

	Min	Q1	Mean	Median	Q3	Max	N	Range Avg Min	Range Avg Max
AL	19,469	19,469	23,754	25,896	25,896	25,896	3	18,429	27,643
AZ	22,069	30,763	34,767	36,941	39,562	39,562	10	20,779	31,179
CA	23,816	29,765	39,632	39,048	49,067	57,044	22	35,791	44,303
CO	16,536	21,590	23,701	22,360	28,891	30,867	9	21,023	31,144
CT	24,648	36,358	44,877	45,042	59,085	59,085	6	33,223	37,664
FL	22,452	24,706	27,620	27,518	29,580	36,275	12	23,650	34,320
GA	20,800	20,924	22,425	22,464	23,920	24,356	7	.	.
IA	16,120	19,781	30,979	27,040	40,961	51,167	7	24,960	27,040
ID	18,200	21,580	26,390	28,080	31,200	31,200	4	22,880	31,070
IL	14,560	23,951	27,649	26,853	32,191	43,597	64	24,177	37,390
IN	16,640	18,582	20,505	18,741	23,442	27,830	7	17,444	23,150
LA	12,480	19,032	23,741	21,900	30,493	34,798	5	20,602	30,295
MA	16,640	21,840	31,651	34,561	41,257	43,903	19	28,117	31,895
MD	23,712	38,050	38,767	38,457	41,310	49,013	21	23,712	35,568
ME	21,320	21,320	27,654	23,858	33,342	42,224	6	22,385	31,708
MI	15,600	23,046	26,946	30,493	30,846	31,200	4	24,357	30,493
MN	16,640	20,946	25,521	21,923	23,587	44,507	5	.	.
MO	21,736	26,042	33,484	29,120	32,802	57,720	5	47,507	57,720
MS	14,560	17,100	18,006	17,960	18,719	21,736	6	.	.
NC	17,914	22,454	25,390	23,128	25,275	71,336	61	24,701	39,419
ND	16,640	16,640	18,252	18,252	19,864	19,864	2	16,640	24,960
NH	37,960	37,960	37,960	37,960	37,960	37,960	2	37,211	56,389
NJ	22,000	26,021	31,586	29,287	37,251	46,343	10	29,397	40,026
NM	13,455	13,455	21,818	16,640	35,360	35,360	3	29,120	43,680
NY	16,640	28,330	33,092	34,999	37,558	50,413	9	37,558	37,558
OH	16,640	20,696	24,624	22,350	27,643	58,818	54	22,160	33,717
OK	15,517	15,517	16,141	15,662	15,912	18,096	5	14,352	20,488
OR	30,279	30,279	35,074	36,408	38,536	38,536	3	21,195	27,934
PA	17,680	26,284	30,209	31,200	35,402	35,402	11	.	.
SC	23,467	25,100	26,566	25,861	28,101	30,935	8	.	.
SD	18,720	18,720	18,720	18,720	18,720	18,720	1	.	.
TN	19,258	23,985	28,828	29,209	31,378	38,783	10	.	.
TX	11,327	21,813	26,000	25,543	30,562	35,194	36	23,544	37,201
UT	17,395	17,395	22,404	23,046	26,770	26,770	3	22,630	33,925
VA	15,657	33,331	38,181	38,046	43,688	53,173	45	33,212	54,797
VT	31,078	31,078	31,078	31,078	31,078	31,078	1	.	.
WI	16,640	25,584	31,288	29,129	39,829	44,579	11	18,117	22,270
WY	23,026	23,026	23,261	23,026	23,733	23,733	3	21,944	26,978

Degree Required Data

	Min	Q1	Mean	Median	Q3	Max	N	Range Avg Min	Range Avg Max
High School	11,327	22,256	28,656	25,230	34,972	59,085	247	27,054	40,315
Associate's	16,120	22,194	27,265	25,584	30,933	57,720	99	23,191	32,733
Bachelor's	12,480	25,896	31,656	31,200	38,050	71,336	127	25,747	40,102
Master's	22,506	22,506	22,506	22,506	22,506	22,506	1	.	.
Doctoral	.	.	.	.	.	.		.	.

LIBRARY TECHNICAL ASSISTANT OF GOVERNMENT DOCUMENTS

Provides basic assistance to patrons referring patrons to Librarian for professional assistance. Locates materials and information for patrons. May complete routine copy cataloging. Assists with special programming. Provides access to publications of the U.S. federal government such as transcripts of hearings and text of bills, resolutions, statutes, reports, charters, treaties, periodicals and statistics.

Small Public Library
(Serving a population of 10,000 to 25,000)
Regional Data

	Min	Q1	Mean	Median	Q3	Max	N	Range Avg Min	Range Avg Max
North Atlantic	37,706	37,706	37,706	37,706	37,706	37,706	1	.	.
ALL REGIONS	37,706	37,706	37,706	37,706	37,706	37,706	1	.	.

State Data

	Min	Q1	Mean	Median	Q3	Max	N	Range Avg Min	Range Avg Max
NJ	37,706	37,706	37,706	37,706	37,706	37,706	1	.	.

Degree Required Data

	Min	Q1	Mean	Median	Q3	Max	N	Range Avg Min	Range Avg Max
High School	.	.	.	.	.	.		.	.
Associate's	.	.	.	.	.	.		.	.
Bachelor's	37,706	37,706	37,706	37,706	37,706	37,706	1	.	.
Master's	.	.	.	.	.	.		.	.
Doctoral	.	.	.	.	.	.		.	.

LIBRARY TECHNICAL ASSISTANT OF GOVERNMENT DOCUMENTS - CONTINUED
Medium Public Library
(Serving a population of 25,000 to 99,999)
Regional Data

	Min	Q1	Mean	Median	Q3	Max	N	Range Avg Min	Range Avg Max
Great Lakes & Plains	28,101	28,101	28,101	28,101	28,101	28,101	1	.	.
ALL REGIONS	28,101	28,101	28,101	28,101	28,101	28,101	1	.	.

State Data

	Min	Q1	Mean	Median	Q3	Max	N	Range Avg Min	Range Avg Max
MO	28,101	28,101	28,101	28,101	28,101	28,101	1	.	.

Degree Required Data

	Min	Q1	Mean	Median	Q3	Max	N	Range Avg Min	Range Avg Max
High School	.	.	.	.	.	.		.	.
Associate's	.	.	.	.	.	.		.	.
Bachelor's	28,101	28,101	28,101	28,101	28,101	28,101	1	.	.
Master's	.	.	.	.	.	.		.	.
Doctoral	.	.	.	.	.	.		.	.

LIBRARY TECHNICAL ASSISTANT OF GOVERNMENT DOCUMENTS - CONTINUED
Large Public Library
(Serving a population of 100,000 to 499,999)
Regional Data

	Min	Q1	Mean	Median	Q3	Max	N	Range Avg Min	Range Avg Max
North Atlantic	35,402	35,402	35,402	35,402	35,402	35,402	2	.	.
Southeast	22,880	27,040	30,010	29,182	29,182	41,766	5	26,031	33,311
West & Southwest	26,125	26,125	26,125	26,125	26,125	26,125	1	19,490	33,342
ALL REGIONS	22,880	26,582	30,872	29,182	35,402	41,766	8	24,723	33,317

State Data

	Min	Q1	Mean	Median	Q3	Max	N	Range Avg Min	Range Avg Max
NC	22,880	22,880	24,960	24,960	27,040	27,040	2	22,880	37,440
PA	35,402	35,402	35,402	35,402	35,402	35,402	2	.	.
TX	26,125	26,125	26,125	26,125	26,125	26,125	1	19,490	33,342
VA	29,182	29,182	33,377	29,182	41,766	41,766	3	29,182	29,182

Degree Required Data

	Min	Q1	Mean	Median	Q3	Max	N	Range Avg Min	Range Avg Max
High School	22,880	26,125	29,363	28,111	29,182	41,766	6	24,723	33,317
Associate's	.	.	.	.	.	.			
Bachelor's	35,402	35,402	35,402	35,402	35,402	35,402	2	.	.
Master's	.	.	.	.	.	.			
Doctoral	.	.	.	.	.	.			

LIBRARY TECHNICAL ASSISTANT OF GOVERNMENT DOCUMENTS - CONTINUED
Very Large Public Library
(Serving a population of 500,000 or more)
Regional Data

	Min	Q1	Mean	Median	Q3	Max	N	Range Avg Min	Range Avg Max
Great Lakes & Plains	25,293	27,706	32,660	28,350	36,400	48,582	7	25,293	36,400
West & Southwest	28,746	42,895	49,969	57,044	57,044	57,044	4	46,930	57,044
ALL REGIONS	25,293	28,279	38,954	34,008	57,044	57,044	11	33,407	44,142

State Data

	Min	Q1	Mean	Median	Q3	Max	N	Range Avg Min	Range Avg Max
CA	57,044	57,044	57,044	57,044	57,044	57,044	3	46,930	57,044
MI	28,279	28,279	28,279	28,279	28,279	28,279	1	.	.
OH	25,293	27,706	33,390	31,179	36,400	48,582	6	25,293	36,400
TX	28,746	28,746	28,746	28,746	28,746	28,746	1	.	.

Degree Required Data

	Min	Q1	Mean	Median	Q3	Max	N	Range Avg Min	Range Avg Max
High School	25,293	27,992	32,170	28,548	35,204	48,582	8	25,293	36,400
Associate's				.					
Bachelor's				.					
Master's				.					
Doctoral				.					

LIBRARY TECHNICAL ASSISTANT OF GOVERNMENT DOCUMENTS - CONTINUED
ALL PUBLIC LIBRARIES
Regional Data

	Min	Q1	Mean	Median	Q3	Max	N	Range Avg Min	Range Avg Max
North Atlantic	35,402	35,402	36,170	35,402	37,706	37,706	3		.
Great Lakes & Plains	25,293	27,903	32,090	28,315	35,204	48,582	8	25,293	36,400
Southeast	22,880	27,040	30,010	29,182	29,182	41,766	5	26,031	33,311
West & Southwest	26,125	28,746	45,200	57,044	57,044	57,044	5	40,070	51,119
ALL REGIONS	22,880	28,101	35,299	29,182	37,706	57,044	21	30,067	39,978

State Data

	Min	Q1	Mean	Median	Q3	Max	N	Range Avg Min	Range Avg Max
CA	57,044	57,044	57,044	57,044	57,044	57,044	3	46,930	57,044
MI	28,279	28,279	28,279	28,279	28,279	28,279	1		.
MO	28,101	28,101	28,101	28,101	28,101	28,101	1		.
NC	22,880	22,880	24,960	24,960	27,040	27,040	2	22,880	37,440
NJ	37,706	37,706	37,706	37,706	37,706	37,706	1		.
OH	25,293	27,706	33,390	31,179	36,400	48,582	6	25,293	36,400
PA	35,402	35,402	35,402	35,402	35,402	35,402	2		.
TX	26,125	26,125	27,435	27,435	28,746	28,746	2	19,490	33,342
VA	29,182	29,182	33,377	29,182	41,766	41,766	3	29,182	29,182

Degree Required Data

	Min	Q1	Mean	Median	Q3	Max	N	Range Avg Min	Range Avg Max
High School	22,880	27,040	30,967	28,548	34,008	48,582	14	25,008	34,859
Associate's				.					
Bachelor's	28,101	31,751	34,153	35,402	36,554	37,706	4		
Master's				.					
Doctoral				.					

LIBRARY TECHNICAL ASSISTANT OF INSTRUCTIONAL SERVICES/LITERACY

Provides basic assistance to patrons referring patrons to Librarian for professional assistance. Locates materials and information for patrons. May complete routine copy cataloging. Assists with special programming. Advances learning, teaching and research with respect to information literacy in higher education; assists patrons to develop the ability to read and write.

Medium Public Library
(Serving a population of 25,000 to 99,999)
Regional Data

	Min	Q1	Mean	Median	Q3	Max	N	Range Avg Min	Range Avg Max
Southeast	17,680	17,680	17,902	17,680	18,346	18,346	3	14,934	21,715
West & Southwest	36,213	44,200	49,559	51,251	57,221	57,221	6	39,211	49,819
ALL REGIONS	17,680	18,346	39,007	44,200	57,221	57,221	9	31,119	40,451

State Data

	Min	Q1	Mean	Median	Q3	Max	N	Range Avg Min	Range Avg Max
CA	36,213	44,200	49,559	51,251	57,221	57,221	6	39,211	49,819
LA	17,680	17,680	17,902	17,680	18,346	18,346	3	14,934	21,715

Degree Required Data

	Min	Q1	Mean	Median	Q3	Max	N	Range Avg Min	Range Avg Max
High School	17,680	17,680	24,747	18,013	31,814	45,282	4	20,509	27,607
Associate's	44,200	44,200	44,200	44,200	44,200	44,200	1	27,040	45,760
Bachelor's	36,213	46,717	51,969	57,221	57,221	57,221	4	42,749	51,969
Master's	.	.	.	.	.	.	.	.	.
Doctoral	.	.	.	.	.	.	.	.	.

LIBRARY TECHNICAL ASSISTANT OF INSTRUCTIONAL SERVICES/LITERACY - CONTINUED
Large Public Library
(Serving a population of 100,000 to 499,999)
Regional Data

	Min	Q1	Mean	Median	Q3	Max	N	Range Avg Min	Range Avg Max
North Atlantic	37,558	37,558	37,558	37,558	37,558	37,558	1	37,558	37,558
Southeast	29,182	29,182	32,779	30,793	38,046	39,348	9	29,182	29,182
West & Southwest	32,531	32,531	34,892	32,531	38,168	38,700	10	29,245	36,213
ALL REGIONS	29,182	30,793	34,075	32,531	38,168	39,348	20	29,865	34,153

State Data

	Min	Q1	Mean	Median	Q3	Max	N	Range Avg Min	Range Avg Max
CA	32,531	32,531	34,892	32,531	38,168	38,700	10	29,245	36,213
NY	37,558	37,558	37,558	37,558	37,558	37,558	1	37,558	37,558
VA	29,182	29,182	32,779	30,793	38,046	39,348	9	29,182	29,182

Degree Required Data

	Min	Q1	Mean	Median	Q3	Max	N	Range Avg Min	Range Avg Max
High School	29,182	30,793	33,388	32,531	38,046	39,348	17	27,435	31,192
Associate's	38,168	38,168	38,168	38,168	38,168	38,168	2	38,168	47,258
Bachelor's	37,558	37,558	37,558	37,558	37,558	37,558	1	37,558	37,558
Master's			.						.
Doctoral			.						.

LIBRARY TECHNICAL ASSISTANT OF INSTRUCTIONAL SERVICES/LITERACY - CONTINUED
Very Large Public Library
(Serving a population of 500,000 or more)
Regional Data

	Min	Q1	Mean	Median	Q3	Max	N	Range Avg Min	Range Avg Max
Southeast	28,120	28,120	28,120	28,120	28,120	28,120	1	.	.
West & Southwest	39,170	39,170	44,425	39,170	54,936	54,936	3	.	.
ALL REGIONS	28,120	33,645	40,349	39,170	47,053	54,936	4	.	.

State Data

	Min	Q1	Mean	Median	Q3	Max	N	Range Avg Min	Range Avg Max
CA	39,170	39,170	44,425	39,170	54,936	54,936	3	.	.
FL	28,120	28,120	28,120	28,120	28,120	28,120	1	.	.

Degree Required Data

	Min	Q1	Mean	Median	Q3	Max	N	Range Avg Min	Range Avg Max
High School	39,170	39,170	39,170	39,170	39,170	39,170	2	.	.
Associate's	54,936	54,936	54,936	54,936	54,936	54,936	1	.	.
Bachelor's	.	.	.	.	.	.		.	.
Master's			.						.
Doctoral			.						.

LIBRARY TECHNICAL ASSISTANT OF INSTRUCTIONAL SERVICES/LITERACY - CONTINUED
ALL PUBLIC LIBRARIES
Regional Data

	Min	Q1	Mean	Median	Q3	Max	N	Range Avg Min	Range Avg Max
North Atlantic	37,558	37,558	37,558	37,558	37,558	37,558	1	37,558	37,558
Southeast	17,680	28,120	28,987	29,182	30,793	39,348	13	23,076	25,982
West & Southwest	32,531	32,531	41,029	38,700	45,282	57,221	19	33,516	42,044
ALL REGIONS	17,680	30,793	36,180	36,213	39,170	57,221	33	30,378	36,730

State Data

	Min	Q1	Mean	Median	Q3	Max	N	Range Avg Min	Range Avg Max
CA	32,531	32,531	41,029	38,700	45,282	57,221	19	33,516	42,044
FL	28,120	28,120	28,120	28,120	28,120	28,120	1	.	.
LA	17,680	17,680	17,902	17,680	18,346	18,346	3	14,934	21,715
NY	37,558	37,558	37,558	37,558	37,558	37,558	1	37,558	37,558
VA	29,182	29,182	32,779	30,793	38,046	39,348	9	29,182	29,182

Degree Required Data

	Min	Q1	Mean	Median	Q3	Max	N	Range Avg Min	Range Avg Max
High School	17,680	29,182	32,388	32,531	38,700	45,282	23	25,456	30,167
Associate's	38,168	38,168	43,868	41,184	49,568	54,936	4	34,459	46,758
Bachelor's	36,213	37,558	49,087	57,221	57,221	57,221	5	41,711	49,087
Master's	.	.	.	.	.	.	.	.	.
Doctoral	.	.	.	.	.	.	.	.	.

LIBRARY TECHNICAL ASSISTANT OF REFERENCE/INFORMATION SERVICES

Provides basic assistance to patrons referring patrons to Librarian for professional assistance. Locates materials and information for patrons. May complete routine copy cataloging. Assists with special programming.Assists patrons with questions; instructs in the selection and use of appropriate tools and techniques for finding information; conducts searches for materials; contributes to reference collection development.

Very Small Public Library
(Serving a population of less than 10,000)
Regional Data

	Min	Q1	Mean	Median	Q3	Max	N	Range Avg Min	Range Avg Max
North Atlantic	46,370	46,370	46,370	46,370	46,370	46,370	1	.	.
Great Lakes & Plains	16,640	16,640	17,160	17,160	17,680	17,680	2	.	.
ALL REGIONS	16,640	16,640	26,897	17,680	46,370	46,370	3	.	.

State Data

	Min	Q1	Mean	Median	Q3	Max	N	Range Avg Min	Range Avg Max
IL	16,640	16,640	16,640	16,640	16,640	16,640	1		
MI	17,680	17,680	17,680	17,680	17,680	17,680	1		
NJ	46,370	46,370	46,370	46,370	46,370	46,370	1		

Degree Required Data

	Min	Q1	Mean	Median	Q3	Max	N	Range Avg Min	Range Avg Max
High School	16,640	16,640	16,640	16,640	16,640	16,640	1	.	.
Associate's	.	.	.	.	.	.	.	.	.
Bachelor's	46,370	46,370	46,370	46,370	46,370	46,370	1	.	.
Master's	.	.	.	.	.	.	.	.	.
Doctoral	.	.	.	.	.	.	.	.	.

LIBRARY TECHNICAL ASSISTANT OF REFERENCE/INFORMATION SERVICES - CONTINUED
Small Public Library
(Serving a population of 10,000 to 25,000)
Regional Data

	Min	Q1	Mean	Median	Q3	Max	N	Range Avg Min	Range Avg Max
North Atlantic	16,120	18,720	26,947	29,717	36,147	36,366	7	16,640	27,040
Great Lakes & Plains	16,598	25,840	26,804	29,245	30,181	33,218	13	22,946	28,363
West & Southwest	33,217	33,217	39,499	41,600	43,680	43,680	3	31,200	46,800
ALL REGIONS	16,120	19,344	28,503	29,245	33,217	43,680	23	23,583	30,585

State Data

	Min	Q1	Mean	Median	Q3	Max	N	Range Avg Min	Range Avg Max
AZ	33,217	33,217	33,217	33,217	33,217	33,217	1	.	.
IL	25,840	25,840	25,840	25,840	25,840	25,840	1	20,800	29,120
IN	16,640	16,640	16,640	16,640	16,640	16,640	1	16,640	22,880
MA	32,212	32,212	34,180	34,180	36,147	36,147	2	.	.
MI	29,245	29,245	30,308	29,245	31,574	33,218	9	25,462	30,463
MN	16,598	16,598	16,598	16,598	16,598	16,598	2	15,850	21,278
NJ	29,717	29,717	33,041	33,041	36,366	36,366	2	.	.
NM	41,600	41,600	42,640	42,640	43,680	43,680	2	31,200	46,800
PA	16,120	16,120	18,061	18,720	19,344	19,344	3	16,640	27,040

Degree Required Data

	Min	Q1	Mean	Median	Q3	Max	N	Range Avg Min	Range Avg Max
High School	16,598	29,245	30,096	29,245	31,574	43,680	13	24,866	31,563
Associate's	25,840	25,840	31,103	31,103	36,366	36,366	2	20,800	29,120
Bachelor's	16,640	18,720	27,776	30,964	33,217	36,147	6	16,640	24,960
Master's	.	.	.	.	.	.	.	.	.
Doctoral	.	.	.	.	.	.	.	.	.

LIBRARY TECHNICAL ASSISTANT OF REFERENCE/INFORMATION SERVICES - CONTINUED
Medium Public Library
(Serving a population of 25,000 to 99,999)
Regional Data

	Min	Q1	Mean	Median	Q3	Max	N	Range Avg Min	Range Avg Max
North Atlantic	20,259	24,794	30,983	34,486	37,440	37,934	5	25,993	30,978
Great Lakes & Plains	16,640	22,880	30,768	29,794	38,848	47,840	22	20,531	34,406
Southeast	16,640	22,984	23,413	22,984	24,540	30,645	17	21,133	35,568
West & Southwest	21,316	23,307	30,175	26,572	32,760	49,982	16	26,176	36,752
ALL REGIONS	16,640	22,984	28,544	25,220	32,760	49,982	60	23,544	35,119

State Data

	Min	Q1	Mean	Median	Q3	Max	N	Range Avg Min	Range Avg Max
CA	43,784	43,784	47,251	47,986	49,982	49,982	3	42,897	52,506
CO	23,920	23,920	26,052	26,052	28,184	28,184	2	18,720	31,200
DE	24,794	24,794	24,794	24,794	24,794	24,794	1	.	.
IA	31,200	31,200	38,804	40,832	43,644	45,114	6	27,040	31,200
ID	24,960	24,960	24,960	24,960	24,960	24,960	2	24,960	35,360
IL	16,640	20,800	25,304	26,406	29,754	33,375	12	19,348	34,989
IN	18,360	18,360	24,040	24,040	29,720	29,720	2	.	.
MA	37,440	37,440	37,687	37,687	37,934	37,934	2	37,440	37,440
MN	44,507	44,507	44,507	44,507	44,507	44,507	1	.	.
MS	18,720	18,720	18,720	18,720	18,720	18,720	1	.	.
NC	22,984	22,984	24,140	22,984	24,540	30,645	13	.	.
OH	47,840	47,840	47,840	47,840	47,840	47,840	1	.	.
PA	20,259	20,259	27,373	27,373	34,486	34,486	2	20,270	27,747
SC	16,640	16,640	16,640	16,640	16,640	16,640	1	.	.
TN	21,299	21,299	21,299	21,299	21,299	21,299	1	21,133	35,568
TX	21,316	23,088	26,559	23,525	32,760	32,760	9	20,423	31,191
VA	27,546	27,546	27,546	27,546	27,546	27,546	1	.	.

Degree Required Data

	Min	Q1	Mean	Median	Q3	Max	N	Range Avg Min	Range Avg Max
High School	18,360	24,960	35,630	38,391	44,146	49,982	16	33,883	43,035
Associate's	16,640	22,984	24,635	23,088	27,342	34,486	32	19,315	32,994
Bachelor's	16,640	24,794	27,983	31,200	32,760	32,760	9	22,954	32,314
Master's	47,840	47,840	47,840	47,840	47,840	47,840	1	.	.
Doctoral	.	.	.	.	.	.		.	.

LIBRARY TECHNICAL ASSISTANT OF REFERENCE/INFORMATION SERVICES - CONTINUED
Large Public Library
(Serving a population of 100,000 to 499,999)
Regional Data

	Min	Q1	Mean	Median	Q3	Max	N	Range Avg Min	Range Avg Max
North Atlantic	16,432	32,686	32,770	34,409	35,402	45,555	49	.	.
Great Lakes & Plains	18,616	23,712	26,545	25,282	29,276	36,338	28	23,096	31,880
Southeast	16,910	25,208	29,735	29,621	33,633	38,783	90	23,167	35,832
West & Southwest	20,322	27,324	30,313	28,954	33,280	72,101	55	25,583	34,250
ALL REGIONS	16,432	25,334	30,146	29,193	34,409	72,101	222	24,327	33,978

State Data

	Min	Q1	Mean	Median	Q3	Max	N	Range Avg Min	Range Avg Max
CA	24,336	27,324	29,535	28,018	29,307	72,101	36	24,592	33,618
CO	28,995	28,995	28,995	28,995	28,995	28,995	1	28,995	45,594
FL	21,798	24,284	27,872	26,205	32,720	33,787	20		
GA	16,910	24,960	26,096	24,960	28,683	34,652	8	16,910	17,950
IL	25,230	25,230	29,222	28,371	31,928	36,338	13	25,230	32,947
MD	16,432	33,646	33,602	34,409	38,802	45,555	28		
MN	18,616	19,032	23,400	19,032	30,160	30,160	5		
NC	22,880	22,880	29,234	29,120	35,360	37,440	15	22,880	37,440
NJ	22,880	22,880	28,487	28,487	34,095	34,095	2		
NY	40,739	40,739	41,176	41,176	41,613	41,613	2		
OH	21,362	23,213	24,636	23,733	25,334	30,493	10	20,322	30,493
OR	39,240	40,200	41,385	41,160	42,570	43,980	4		
PA	16,640	26,551	30,915	35,402	35,402	35,402	17		
SC	24,222	25,200	27,547	26,475	27,062	36,333	10	24,232	36,338
TN	25,208	28,911	32,623	32,859	38,783	38,783	31		
TX	20,322	20,874	21,261	21,552	21,552	22,006	5		
VA	29,182	30,059	30,776	30,494	30,793	33,633	6	29,182	29,182
WA	29,120	32,690	33,677	35,360	35,360	35,360	9	29,120	35,360

Degree Required Data

	Min	Q1	Mean	Median	Q3	Max	N	Range Avg Min	Range Avg Max
High School	16,432	24,960	28,126	27,331	33,280	37,440	90	25,495	35,102
Associate's	16,640	21,362	22,971	23,691	25,106	30,493	13	20,011	29,353
Bachelor's	17,701	28,911	33,654	34,409	38,783	72,101	91	25,185	38,189
Master's									
Doctoral									

LIBRARY TECHNICAL ASSISTANT OF REFERENCE/INFORMATION SERVICES - CONTINUED
Very Large Public Library
(Serving a population of 500,000 or more)
Regional Data

	Min	Q1	Mean	Median	Q3	Max	N	Range Avg Min	Range Avg Max
Great Lakes & Plains	24,898	24,898	27,785	25,397	29,474	47,167	169	25,710	37,503
Southeast	22,412	24,360	29,230	26,954	34,358	44,702	174		
West & Southwest	25,917	40,932	44,221	43,524	54,314	61,958	85	41,841	52,058
ALL REGIONS	22,412	24,898	31,637	27,859	36,324	61,958	428	28,248	39,793

State Data

	Min	Q1	Mean	Median	Q3	Max	N	Range Avg Min	Range Avg Max
CA	30,367	42,198	46,856	43,530	57,044	61,958	72	47,806	58,112
FL	22,412	24,263	29,988	27,372	36,324	42,328	120	.	.
GA	22,508	24,670	27,546	26,662	29,556	44,702	54	.	.
OH	24,898	24,898	26,929	24,898	27,498	47,167	153	24,898	37,398
TX	28,634	28,634	28,634	28,634	28,634	28,634	1	.	.
UT	25,917	25,918	29,710	28,738	33,332	36,360	12	24,690	34,653
WI	33,316	34,289	35,976	35,806	37,928	38,474	16	33,322	38,480

Degree Required Data

	Min	Q1	Mean	Median	Q3	Max	N	Range Avg Min	Range Avg Max
High School	22,508	24,898	30,505	25,709	36,084	47,167	205	24,898	37,398
Associate's	58,994	61,958	61,365	61,958	61,958	61,958	5	50,960	61,958
Bachelor's	33,316	34,289	35,976	35,806	37,928	38,474	16	33,322	38,480
Master's	.	.	.	.	.	.		.	.
Doctoral	.	.	.	.	.	.		.	.

LIBRARY TECHNICAL ASSISTANT OF REFERENCE/INFORMATION SERVICES - CONTINUED
ALL PUBLIC LIBRARIES
Regional Data

	Min	Q1	Mean	Median	Q3	Max	N	Range Avg Min	Range Avg Max
North Atlantic	16,120	26,551	32,188	34,409	35,402	46,370	62	23,655	29,994
Great Lakes & Plains	16,598	24,898	27,772	25,397	29,952	47,840	234	24,950	36,161
Southeast	16,640	24,476	29,040	27,060	33,280	44,702	281	23,070	35,820
West & Southwest	20,322	28,018	37,908	36,984	43,536	72,101	159	31,594	41,258
ALL REGIONS	16,120	24,898	30,818	28,423	35,360	72,101	736	26,581	37,420

State Data

	Min	Q1	Mean	Median	Q3	Max	N	Range Avg Min	Range Avg Max
AZ	33,217	33,217	33,217	33,217	33,217	33,217	1		
CA	24,336	29,411	41,249	42,456	43,536	72,101	111	34,744	44,308
CO	23,920	23,920	27,033	28,184	28,995	28,995	3	23,858	38,397
DE	24,794	24,794	24,794	24,794	24,794	24,794	1		
FL	21,798	24,283	29,686	26,638	35,391	42,328	140		
GA	16,910	24,670	27,359	26,264	29,556	44,702	62	16,910	17,950
IA	31,200	31,200	38,804	40,832	43,644	45,114	6	27,040	31,200
ID	24,960	24,960	24,960	24,960	24,960	24,960	2	24,960	35,360
IL	16,640	25,230	26,890	27,331	29,869	36,338	27	22,465	33,693
IN	16,640	16,640	21,573	18,360	29,720	29,720	3	16,640	22,880
MA	32,212	34,180	35,933	36,794	37,687	37,934	4	37,440	37,440
MD	16,432	33,646	33,602	34,409	38,802	45,555	28		
MI	17,680	29,245	29,045	29,245	31,574	33,218	10	25,462	30,463
MN	16,598	17,607	24,338	19,032	30,160	44,507	8	15,850	21,278
MS	18,720	18,720	18,720	18,720	18,720	18,720	1		
NC	22,880	22,984	26,869	24,540	29,883	37,440	28	22,880	37,440
NJ	22,880	29,717	33,885	34,095	36,366	46,370	5		
NM	41,600	41,600	42,640	42,640	43,680	43,680	2	31,200	46,800
NY	40,739	40,739	41,176	41,176	41,613	41,613	2		
OH	21,362	24,898	26,916	24,898	27,352	47,840	164	24,612	36,967
OR	39,240	40,200	41,385	41,160	42,570	43,980	4		
PA	16,120	19,344	28,840	33,586	35,402	35,402	22	19,060	27,511
SC	16,640	24,648	26,555	26,229	27,062	36,333	11	24,232	36,338
TN	21,299	28,294	32,269	32,119	38,783	38,783	32	21,133	35,568
TX	20,322	21,320	24,931	23,088	28,634	32,760	15	20,423	31,191
UT	25,917	25,918	29,710	28,738	33,332	36,360	12	24,690	34,653
VA	27,546	29,182	30,314	30,494	30,793	33,633	7	29,182	29,182
WA	29,120	32,690	33,677	35,360	35,360	35,360	9	29,120	35,360
WI	33,316	34,289	35,976	35,806	37,928	38,474	16	33,322	38,480

Degree Required Data

	Min	Q1	Mean	Median	Q3	Max	N	Range Avg Min	Range Avg Max
High School	16,432	24,898	30,039	27,269	34,652	49,982	325	25,309	36,788
Associate's	16,640	22,984	27,999	23,733	27,865	61,958	52	24,545	36,147
Bachelor's	16,640	29,717	33,358	34,340	36,333	72,101	123	28,434	36,091
Master's	47,840	47,840	47,840	47,840	47,840	47,840	1		
Doctoral									

LIBRARY TECHNICAL ASSISTANT OF OUTREACH/BOOKMOBILE

Provides basic assistance to patrons referring patrons to Librarian for professional assistance. Locates materials and information for patrons. May complete routine copy cataloging. Assists with special programming. Provides services and programs to homebound, disabled, institutionalized or other underserved patrons.

Very Small Public Library
(Serving a population of less than 10,000)
Regional Data

	Min	Q1	Mean	Median	Q3	Max	N	Range Avg Min	Range Avg Max
North Atlantic	29,120	29,120	29,120	29,120	29,120	29,120	1	.	.
Great Lakes & Plains	24,720	24,720	24,720	24,720	24,720	24,720	1	.	.
ALL REGIONS	24,720	24,720	26,920	26,920	29,120	29,120	2	.	.

State Data

	Min	Q1	Mean	Median	Q3	Max	N	Range Avg Min	Range Avg Max
KS	24,720	24,720	24,720	24,720	24,720	24,720	1	.	.
VT	29,120	29,120	29,120	29,120	29,120	29,120	1	.	.

Degree Required Data

	Min	Q1	Mean	Median	Q3	Max	N	Range Avg Min	Range Avg Max
High School	24,720	24,720	24,720	24,720	24,720	24,720	1	.	.
Associate's	.	.	.	.	.	.			
Bachelor's	29,120	29,120	29,120	29,120	29,120	29,120	1	.	.
Master's	.	.	.	.	.	.			
Doctoral	.	.	.	.	.	.			

LIBRARY TECHNICAL ASSISTANT OF OUTREACH/BOOKMOBILE - CONTINUED
Small Public Library
(Serving a population of 10,000 to 25,000)
Regional Data

	Min	Q1	Mean	Median	Q3	Max	N	Range Avg Min	Range Avg Max
Great Lakes & Plains	21,840	21,840	25,875	25,875	29,910	29,910	2	28,038	37,378
Southeast	12,480	12,480	12,480	12,480	12,480	12,480	1	.	.
ALL REGIONS	12,480	12,480	21,410	21,840	29,910	29,910	3	28,038	37,378

State Data

	Min	Q1	Mean	Median	Q3	Max	N	Range Avg Min	Range Avg Max
GA	12,480	12,480	12,480	12,480	12,480	12,480	1	.	.
IL	21,840	21,840	21,840	21,840	21,840	21,840	1	.	.
MN	29,910	29,910	29,910	29,910	29,910	29,910	1	28,038	37,378

Degree Required Data

	Min	Q1	Mean	Median	Q3	Max	N	Range Avg Min	Range Avg Max
High School	12,480	12,480	21,195	21,195	29,910	29,910	2	28,038	37,378
Associate's									
Bachelor's	21,840	21,840	21,840	21,840	21,840	21,840	1		
Master's									
Doctoral									

LIBRARY TECHNICAL ASSISTANT OF OUTREACH/BOOKMOBILE - CONTINUED
Medium Public Library
(Serving a population of 25,000 to 99,999)
Regional Data

	Min	Q1	Mean	Median	Q3	Max	N	Range Avg Min	Range Avg Max
North Atlantic	22,946	22,946	22,946	22,946	22,946	22,946	1		
Great Lakes & Plains	15,746	22,974	28,090	27,040	30,846	42,095	21	24,431	34,991
Southeast	15,600	19,820	24,654	26,111	29,489	30,796	4		
West & Southwest	24,440	26,926	33,296	32,812	39,666	43,118	4	29,182	35,563
ALL REGIONS	15,600	22,974	28,154	27,040	30,846	43,118	30	25,619	35,134

State Data

	Min	Q1	Mean	Median	Q3	Max	N	Range Avg Min	Range Avg Max
CA	29,411	29,411	36,247	36,213	43,118	43,118	3	31,235	37,974
IA	38,004	38,004	40,517	41,452	42,095	42,095	3		
IL	20,800	20,800	27,118	27,040	30,846	35,180	11	24,190	35,227
IN	20,000	21,487	24,960	24,682	28,432	30,475	4		
MS	15,600	15,600	15,600	15,600	15,600	15,600	1		
NC	28,182	28,182	29,489	29,489	30,796	30,796	2		
OH	15,746	15,746	23,400	24,107	30,347	30,347	3	25,636	33,810
PA	22,946	22,946	22,946	22,946	22,946	22,946	1		
SC	24,039	24,039	24,039	24,039	24,039	24,039	1		
WY	24,440	24,440	24,440	24,440	24,440	24,440	1	23,026	28,330

Degree Required Data

	Min	Q1	Mean	Median	Q3	Max	N	Range Avg Min	Range Avg Max
High School	15,600	24,107	29,722	28,797	36,213	43,118	18	27,906	37,102
Associate's	15,746	20,800	23,867	20,800	30,796	35,180	7	18,720	29,120
Bachelor's	24,960	26,000	27,347	27,040	28,694	30,347	4	25,969	34,278
Master's									
Doctoral									

LIBRARY TECHNICAL ASSISTANT OF OUTREACH/BOOKMOBILE - CONTINUED
Large Public Library
(Serving a population of 100,000 to 499,999)
Regional Data

	Min	Q1	Mean	Median	Q3	Max	N	Range Avg Min	Range Avg Max
North Atlantic	19,736	20,763	27,532	26,522	33,465	39,020	8	28,683	50,960
Great Lakes & Plains	20,717	23,213	27,952	28,860	31,978	36,604	16	23,137	32,210
Southeast	14,830	23,440	27,505	26,397	33,787	37,915	19	23,156	29,723
West & Southwest	22,422	23,981	35,461	34,000	45,614	54,080	8	28,408	38,574
ALL REGIONS	14,830	23,150	28,897	27,721	33,833	54,080	51	24,542	34,013

State Data

	Min	Q1	Mean	Median	Q3	Max	N	Range Avg Min	Range Avg Max
CA	29,203	37,409	43,628	45,614	49,847	54,080	4	35,402	44,782
CO	22,422	22,422	22,547	22,547	22,672	22,672	2	21,414	32,365
FL	21,798	23,650	27,374	26,397	31,699	34,592	9	23,650	34,320
GA	14,830	14,830	14,830	14,830	14,830	14,830	1	14,830	15,870
IL	32,000	32,000	32,000	32,000	32,000	32,000	1	31,200	37,440
MD	19,736	20,725	28,499	26,528	38,457	39,020	6	.	.
MN	34,600	34,600	35,300	35,300	36,000	36,000	2	.	.
NC	23,081	23,260	26,890	23,519	30,519	37,440	4	24,960	39,520
NE	21,640	21,640	30,066	31,955	36,604	36,604	3	26,079	33,901
OH	20,717	23,150	24,856	23,317	27,706	30,493	9	20,322	30,493
OR	38,796	38,796	38,796	38,796	38,796	38,796	1	.	.
PA	20,800	20,800	24,631	24,631	28,462	28,462	2	28,683	50,960
TX	25,289	25,289	25,289	25,289	25,289	25,289	1	.	.
VA	23,732	29,182	30,769	29,182	33,833	37,915	5	29,182	29,182
WI	30,722	30,722	30,722	30,722	30,722	30,722	1	.	.

Degree Required Data

	Min	Q1	Mean	Median	Q3	Max	N	Range Avg Min	Range Avg Max
High School	14,830	23,150	28,424	26,397	33,833	54,080	27	26,599	34,557
Associate's	20,717	21,640	27,442	23,598	30,493	45,614	15	21,809	31,381
Bachelor's	23,732	28,467	33,187	34,279	38,627	39,020	8	28,671	41,389
Master's	.	.	.	.	.	.		.	.
Doctoral	.	.	.	.	.	.		.	.

LIBRARY TECHNICAL ASSISTANT OF OUTREACH/BOOKMOBILE - CONTINUED
Very Large Public Library
(Serving a population of 500,000 or more)
Regional Data

	Min	Q1	Mean	Median	Q3	Max	N	Range Avg Min	Range Avg Max
Great Lakes & Plains	25,293	25,418	32,639	32,542	36,400	48,582	18	25,769	34,824
Southeast	23,869	33,571	37,342	37,836	42,180	49,970	19	28,793	47,989
West & Southwest	26,304	26,304	36,735	34,714	49,187	49,187	3	25,024	30,549
ALL REGIONS	23,869	31,282	35,180	34,907	40,271	49,970	40	26,394	37,500

State Data

	Min	Q1	Mean	Median	Q3	Max	N	Range Avg Min	Range Avg Max
CA	26,304	26,304	37,746	37,746	49,187	49,187	2	25,024	30,549
CO	34,714	34,714	34,714	34,714	34,714	34,714	1		
FL	23,869	31,908	36,324	35,162	40,564	49,970	14		
OH	25,293	25,418	32,639	32,542	36,400	48,582	18	25,769	34,824
VA	35,100	37,836	40,192	42,262	42,340	43,420	5	28,793	47,989

Degree Required Data

	Min	Q1	Mean	Median	Q3	Max	N	Range Avg Min	Range Avg Max
High School	25,293	27,914	34,456	34,117	39,978	49,187	26	26,394	37,500
Associate's									
Bachelor's	34,000	34,357	40,216	38,447	46,075	49,970	4		
Master's									
Doctoral									

LIBRARY TECHNICAL ASSISTANT OF OUTREACH/BOOKMOBILE - CONTINUED
ALL PUBLIC LIBRARIES
Regional Data

	Min	Q1	Mean	Median	Q3	Max	N	Range Avg Min	Range Avg Max
North Atlantic	19,736	20,800	27,232	26,522	29,120	39,020	10	28,683	50,960
Great Lakes & Plains	15,746	24,315	29,329	29,130	33,176	48,582	58	24,766	34,284
Southeast	12,480	23,819	31,237	31,717	37,836	49,970	43	26,288	39,871
West & Southwest	22,422	25,289	35,139	34,714	45,614	54,080	15	28,376	36,344
ALL REGIONS	12,480	24,039	30,505	29,962	36,000	54,080	126	25,615	35,733

State Data

	Min	Q1	Mean	Median	Q3	Max	N	Range Avg Min	Range Avg Max
CA	26,304	29,411	39,861	43,118	45,614	54,080	9	31,589	39,006
CO	22,422	22,422	26,603	22,672	34,714	34,714	3	21,414	32,365
FL	21,798	26,397	32,822	33,571	38,725	49,970	23	23,650	34,320
GA	12,480	12,480	13,655	13,655	14,830	14,830	2	14,830	15,870
IA	38,004	38,004	40,517	41,452	42,095	42,095	3	.	.
IL	20,800	21,840	27,088	27,040	30,846	35,180	13	24,828	35,428
IN	20,000	21,487	24,960	24,682	28,432	30,475	4	.	.
KS	24,720	24,720	24,720	24,720	24,720	24,720	1	.	.
MD	19,736	20,725	28,499	26,528	38,457	39,020	6	.	.
MN	29,910	29,910	33,503	34,600	36,000	36,000	3	28,038	37,378
MS	15,600	15,600	15,600	15,600	15,600	15,600	1	.	.
NC	23,081	23,440	27,756	25,890	30,796	37,440	6	24,960	39,520
NE	21,640	21,640	30,066	31,955	36,604	36,604	3	26,079	33,901
OH	15,746	24,315	29,380	28,132	33,134	48,582	30	24,451	33,703
OR	38,796	38,796	38,796	38,796	38,796	38,796	1	.	.
PA	20,800	20,800	24,069	22,946	28,462	28,462	3	28,683	50,960
SC	24,039	24,039	24,039	24,039	24,039	24,039	1	.	.
TX	25,289	25,289	25,289	25,289	25,289	25,289	1	.	.
VA	23,732	29,182	35,480	36,468	42,262	43,420	10	28,858	44,855
VT	29,120	29,120	29,120	29,120	29,120	29,120	1	.	.
WI	30,722	30,722	30,722	30,722	30,722	30,722	1	.	.
WY	24,440	24,440	24,440	24,440	24,440	24,440	1	23,026	28,330

Degree Required Data

	Min	Q1	Mean	Median	Q3	Max	N	Range Avg Min	Range Avg Max
High School	12,480	24,582	30,614	29,661	36,000	54,080	74	26,793	37,013
Associate's	15,746	20,800	26,304	23,199	30,493	45,614	22	21,096	30,859
Bachelor's	21,840	27,040	32,595	31,151	38,457	49,970	18	27,127	37,326
Master's	.	.	.	.	.	.			
Doctoral	.	.	.	.	.	.			

LIBRARY TECHNICAL ASSISTANT OF MEDIA SERVICES

Provides basic assistance to patrons referring patrons to Librarian for professional assistance. Locates materials and information for patrons. May complete routine copy cataloging. Assists with special programming. Develops and manages non-print library materials such as files, video recordings, audio recordings, CD-ROMs, computer software, etc.

Small Public Library
(Serving a population of 10,000 to 25,000)
Regional Data

	Min	Q1	Mean	Median	Q3	Max	N	Range Avg Min	Range Avg Max
North Atlantic	42,973	42,973	42,973	42,973	42,973	42,973	1	.	.
Great Lakes & Plains	22,734	22,734	22,734	22,734	22,734	22,734	1	18,720	30,160
ALL REGIONS	22,734	22,734	32,854	32,854	42,973	42,973	2	18,720	30,160

State Data

	Min	Q1	Mean	Median	Q3	Max	N	Range Avg Min	Range Avg Max
IN	22,734	22,734	22,734	22,734	22,734	22,734	1	18,720	30,160
MA	42,973	42,973	42,973	42,973	42,973	42,973	1	.	.

Degree Required Data

	Min	Q1	Mean	Median	Q3	Max	N	Range Avg Min	Range Avg Max
High School	22,734	22,734	22,734	22,734	22,734	22,734	1	18,720	30,160
Associate's	42,973	42,973	42,973	42,973	42,973	42,973	1	.	.
Bachelor's	.	.	.	.	.	.	.	.	.
Master's	.	.	.	.	.	.	.	.	.
Doctoral	.	.	.	.	.	.	.	.	.

LIBRARY TECHNICAL ASSISTANT OF MEDIA SERVICES - CONTINUED
Medium Public Library
(Serving a population of 25,000 to 99,999)
Regional Data

	Min	Q1	Mean	Median	Q3	Max	N	Range Avg Min	Range Avg Max
North Atlantic	31,762	31,762	34,865	35,443	37,390	37,390	3	34,154	40,789
Great Lakes & Plains	18,720	21,707	30,917	30,503	41,746	45,094	14	22,804	33,102
Southeast	17,368	17,368	17,368	17,368	17,368	17,368	1	.	.
West & Southwest	56,436	56,436	56,436	56,436	56,436	56,436	1	.	.
ALL REGIONS	17,368	21,707	32,170	33,987	41,746	56,436	19	23,750	33,743

State Data

	Min	Q1	Mean	Median	Q3	Max	N	Range Avg Min	Range Avg Max
CA	56,436	56,436	56,436	56,436	56,436	56,436	1	.	.
CT	31,762	31,762	33,602	33,602	35,443	35,443	2	34,154	40,789
IL	18,720	20,213	30,281	30,503	38,282	45,094	12	23,005	33,500
IN	24,960	24,960	24,960	24,960	24,960	24,960	1	20,800	29,120
MA	37,390	37,390	37,390	37,390	37,390	37,390	1	.	.
MN	44,507	44,507	44,507	44,507	44,507	44,507	1	.	.
SC	17,368	17,368	17,368	17,368	17,368	17,368	1	.	.

Degree Required Data

	Min	Q1	Mean	Median	Q3	Max	N	Range Avg Min	Range Avg Max
High School	17,368	18,720	29,359	21,840	39,975	56,436	8	19,727	25,214
Associate's	21,707	21,707	21,707	21,707	21,707	21,707	1	.	.
Bachelor's	27,019	33,987	36,762	34,819	41,746	45,094	9	26,624	39,835
Master's	.	.	.	.	.	.	.	.	.
Doctoral	.	.	.	.	.	.	.	.	.

LIBRARY TECHNICAL ASSISTANT OF MEDIA SERVICES - CONTINUED
Large Public Library
(Serving a population of 100,000 to 499,999)
Regional Data

	Min	Q1	Mean	Median	Q3	Max	N	Range Avg Min	Range Avg Max
North Atlantic	32,968	32,968	34,935	34,935	36,901	36,901	2	29,456	34,329
West & Southwest	20,467	20,467	25,563	27,226	28,995	28,995	3	24,242	39,468
ALL REGIONS	20,467	27,226	29,312	28,995	32,968	36,901	5	26,849	36,898

State Data

	Min	Q1	Mean	Median	Q3	Max	N	Range Avg Min	Range Avg Max
CO	28,995	28,995	28,995	28,995	28,995	28,995	1	28,995	45,594
NY	32,968	32,968	34,935	34,935	36,901	36,901	2	29,456	34,329
TX	20,467	20,467	23,847	23,847	27,226	27,226	2	19,490	33,342

Degree Required Data

	Min	Q1	Mean	Median	Q3	Max	N	Range Avg Min	Range Avg Max
High School	20,467	23,847	29,391	30,097	34,935	36,901	4	26,134	34,000
Associate's	.	.	.	.	.	.		.	.
Bachelor's	28,995	28,995	28,995	28,995	28,995	28,995	1	28,995	45,594
Master's	.	.	.	.	.	.		.	.
Doctoral	.	.	.	.	.	.		.	.

LIBRARY TECHNICAL ASSISTANT OF MEDIA SERVICES - CONTINUED
Very Large Public Library
(Serving a population of 500,000 or more)
Regional Data

	Min	Q1	Mean	Median	Q3	Max	N	Range Avg Min	Range Avg Max
Great Lakes & Plains	24,898	24,898	29,226	24,898	28,642	54,872	18	25,080	37,661
Southeast	42,522	42,522	42,522	42,522	42,522	42,522	1	29,027	48,378
West & Southwest	48,542	57,044	58,175	57,044	57,304	74,412	10	48,290	58,690
ALL REGIONS	24,898	24,898	39,667	29,474	57,044	74,412	29	33,822	45,846

State Data

	Min	Q1	Mean	Median	Q3	Max	N	Range Avg Min	Range Avg Max
CA	48,542	57,044	58,175	57,044	57,304	74,412	10	48,290	58,690
IN	54,872	54,872	54,872	54,872	54,872	54,872	1		
OH	24,898	24,898	27,717	24,898	25,480	48,582	17	25,080	37,661
VA	42,522	42,522	42,522	42,522	42,522	42,522	1	29,027	48,378

Degree Required Data

	Min	Q1	Mean	Median	Q3	Max	N	Range Avg Min	Range Avg Max
High School	24,898	24,898	28,540	24,898	28,642	48,582	18	25,312	38,291
Associate's	61,958	61,958	61,958	61,958	61,958	61,958	1	50,960	61,958
Bachelor's	48,542	51,707	58,783	56,088	65,858	74,412	4	50,119	60,892
Master's									
Doctoral									

LIBRARY TECHNICAL ASSISTANT OF MEDIA SERVICES - CONTINUED
ALL PUBLIC LIBRARIES
Regional Data

	Min	Q1	Mean	Median	Q3	Max	N	Range Avg Min	Range Avg Max
North Atlantic	31,762	32,968	36,239	36,172	37,390	42,973	6	31,022	36,482
Great Lakes & Plains	18,720	24,898	29,747	24,960	34,653	54,872	33	23,959	35,602
Southeast	17,368	17,368	29,945	29,945	42,522	42,522	2	29,027	48,378
West & Southwest	20,467	48,542	51,062	57,044	57,044	74,412	14	44,282	55,486
ALL REGIONS	17,368	24,898	35,888	31,762	45,094	74,412	55	30,098	41,375

State Data

	Min	Q1	Mean	Median	Q3	Max	N	Range Avg Min	Range Avg Max
CA	48,542	56,436	58,017	57,044	57,304	74,412	11	48,290	58,690
CO	28,995	28,995	28,995	28,995	28,995	28,995	1	28,995	45,594
CT	31,762	31,762	33,602	33,602	35,443	35,443	2	34,154	40,789
IL	18,720	20,213	30,281	30,503	38,282	45,094	12	23,005	33,500
IN	22,734	22,734	34,189	24,960	54,872	54,872	3	19,760	29,640
MA	37,390	37,390	40,181	40,181	42,973	42,973	2		
MN	44,507	44,507	44,507	44,507	44,507	44,507	1		
NY	32,968	32,968	34,935	34,935	36,901	36,901	2	29,456	34,329
OH	24,898	24,898	27,717	24,898	25,480	48,582	17	25,080	37,661
SC	17,368	17,368	17,368	17,368	17,368	17,368	1		
TX	20,467	20,467	23,847	23,847	27,226	27,226	2	19,490	33,342
VA	42,522	42,522	42,522	42,522	42,522	42,522	1	29,027	48,378

Degree Required Data

	Min	Q1	Mean	Median	Q3	Max	N	Range Avg Min	Range Avg Max
High School	17,368	24,898	28,674	24,898	32,968	56,436	31	24,079	34,969
Associate's	21,707	21,707	42,213	42,973	61,958	61,958	3	50,960	61,958
Bachelor's	27,019	33,987	42,499	39,568	48,542	74,412	14	33,247	46,101
Master's									
Doctoral									

LIBRARY TECHNICAL ASSISTANT OF ACQUISITIONS

Provides basic assistance to patrons referring patrons to Librarian for professional assistance. Locates materials and information for patrons. May complete routine copy cataloging. Assists with special programming.Selects, orders, and receives new materials and maintains accurate records of such transactions.

Very Small Public Library
(Serving a population of less than 10,000)
Regional Data

	Min	Q1	Mean	Median	Q3	Max	N	Range Avg Min	Range Avg Max
North Atlantic	28,704	28,704	29,151	29,151	29,598	29,598	2	.	.
Great Lakes & Plains	18,720	19,906	28,312	22,214	23,000	57,720	5	26,929	34,840
West & Southwest	22,714	22,714	22,714	22,714	22,714	22,714	1	22,714	22,714
ALL REGIONS	18,720	21,060	27,822	22,857	29,151	57,720	8	25,875	31,808

State Data

	Min	Q1	Mean	Median	Q3	Max	N	Range Avg Min	Range Avg Max
CO	22,714	22,714	22,714	22,714	22,714	22,714	1	22,714	22,714
CT	28,704	28,704	28,704	28,704	28,704	28,704	1	.	.
IL	19,906	19,906	19,906	19,906	19,906	19,906	1	14,560	21,840
MI	23,000	23,000	23,000	23,000	23,000	23,000	1	.	.
MO	18,720	18,720	38,220	38,220	57,720	57,720	2	47,507	57,720
NY	29,598	29,598	29,598	29,598	29,598	29,598	1	.	.
WI	22,214	22,214	22,214	22,214	22,214	22,214	1	18,720	24,960

Degree Required Data

	Min	Q1	Mean	Median	Q3	Max	N	Range Avg Min	Range Avg Max
High School	19,906	21,060	23,608	22,464	26,156	29,598	4	18,665	23,171
Associate's	23,000	23,000	36,475	28,704	57,720	57,720	3	47,507	57,720
Bachelor's	.	.	.	.	.	.			
Master's	.	.	.	.	.	.			
Doctoral	.	.	.	.	.	.			

LIBRARY TECHNICAL ASSISTANT OF ACQUISITIONS - CONTINUED
Small Public Library
(Serving a population of 10,000 to 25,000)
Regional Data

	Min	Q1	Mean	Median	Q3	Max	N	Range Avg Min	Range Avg Max
North Atlantic	18,720	36,691	38,878	42,806	45,900	46,343	6	26,042	35,922
Great Lakes & Plains	18,720	19,906	26,629	24,336	35,200	37,274	6	21,382	28,896
West & Southwest	25,230	25,376	32,983	31,511	40,590	43,680	4	24,946	37,426
ALL REGIONS	18,720	24,159	32,811	35,946	42,806	46,343	16	23,606	33,301

State Data

	Min	Q1	Mean	Median	Q3	Max	N	Range Avg Min	Range Avg Max
AZ	25,230	25,230	25,376	25,376	25,522	25,522	2	20,779	31,179
CO	37,500	37,500	37,500	37,500	37,500	37,500	1	.	.
CT	42,640	42,640	42,640	42,640	42,640	42,640	1	35,443	44,803
IL	35,200	35,200	35,200	35,200	35,200	35,200	1	.	.
IN	18,720	18,720	18,720	18,720	18,720	18,720	1	16,640	22,880
MA	42,973	42,973	42,973	42,973	42,973	42,973	1	.	.
MN	37,274	37,274	37,274	37,274	37,274	37,274	1	27,955	37,274
NJ	36,691	36,691	42,978	45,900	46,343	46,343	3	.	.
NM	43,680	43,680	43,680	43,680	43,680	43,680	1	33,280	49,920
OH	19,906	19,906	21,497	21,497	23,088	23,088	2	19,906	29,848
PA	18,720	18,720	18,720	18,720	18,720	18,720	1	16,640	27,040
WI	25,584	25,584	25,584	25,584	25,584	25,584	1	21,029	25,584

Degree Required Data

	Min	Q1	Mean	Median	Q3	Max	N	Range Avg Min	Range Avg Max
High School	23,088	25,230	33,975	36,691	43,680	46,343	7	25,698	37,388
Associate's	18,720	19,313	26,796	22,745	34,278	42,973	4	19,191	26,104
Bachelor's	18,720	26,960	34,330	36,350	41,700	45,900	4	16,640	27,040
Master's	.	.	.	.	.	.		.	.
Doctoral	.	.	.	.	.	.		.	.

LIBRARY TECHNICAL ASSISTANT OF ACQUISITIONS - CONTINUED
Medium Public Library
(Serving a population of 25,000 to 99,999)
Regional Data

	Min	Q1	Mean	Median	Q3	Max	N	Range Avg Min	Range Avg Max
North Atlantic	19,967	30,593	36,826	35,994	38,399	59,085	10	30,964	40,151
Great Lakes & Plains	23,275	29,120	34,865	35,764	42,773	45,447	19	26,154	37,758
Southeast	22,090	22,090	23,927	23,927	25,764	25,764	2	.	.
West & Southwest	23,150	23,150	31,513	27,355	38,854	50,232	8	23,341	28,385
ALL REGIONS	19,967	25,764	34,119	32,427	41,746	59,085	39	26,025	35,176

State Data

	Min	Q1	Mean	Median	Q3	Max	N	Range Avg Min	Range Avg Max
CA	23,150	23,150	31,506	23,150	45,282	50,232	7	23,341	28,385
CT	30,593	35,651	43,391	36,337	55,291	59,085	5	34,154	40,789
IA	42,773	42,773	42,773	42,773	42,773	42,773	1	.	.
IL	24,128	29,120	32,958	33,638	35,764	41,746	10	26,401	37,939
KS	23,275	23,275	23,275	23,275	23,275	23,275	1	18,741	24,981
MA	35,091	35,091	36,745	36,745	38,399	38,399	2	29,120	37,440
ME	36,421	36,421	36,421	36,421	36,421	36,421	1	29,619	42,224
MI	26,020	26,020	26,020	26,020	26,020	26,020	1		
MN	44,507	44,507	44,507	44,507	44,507	44,507	2		
NC	25,764	25,764	25,764	25,764	25,764	25,764	1	.	.
OH	30,222	30,222	30,982	30,982	31,741	31,741	2	28,995	43,514
PA	19,967	19,967	20,696	20,696	21,424	21,424	2	.	.
SC	22,090	22,090	22,090	22,090	22,090	22,090	1	.	.
TX	31,560	31,560	31,560	31,560	31,560	31,560	1	.	.
WI	44,361	44,361	44,904	44,904	45,447	45,447	2	.	.

Degree Required Data

	Min	Q1	Mean	Median	Q3	Max	N	Range Avg Min	Range Avg Max
High School	21,424	23,150	36,117	35,651	44,507	59,085	17	24,118	29,510
Associate's	24,128	25,764	27,339	26,020	29,224	31,560	5	24,128	34,840
Bachelor's	19,967	29,120	33,406	31,741	37,440	45,447	13	28,020	40,643
Master's	.	.	.	.	.	.		.	.
Doctoral	.	.	.	.	.	.		.	.

LIBRARY TECHNICAL ASSISTANT OF ACQUISITIONS - CONTINUED
Large Public Library
(Serving a population of 100,000 to 499,999)
Regional Data

	Min	Q1	Mean	Median	Q3	Max	N	Range Avg Min	Range Avg Max
North Atlantic	30,576	34,980	38,463	40,605	40,967	43,046	6	26,822	32,204
Great Lakes & Plains	22,714	28,309	33,191	31,637	36,670	52,105	19	24,648	31,618
Southeast	14,830	22,040	25,034	25,751	29,175	32,739	16	19,282	27,023
West & Southwest	17,077	27,788	35,614	35,485	41,880	52,000	23	28,477	37,060
ALL REGIONS	14,830	27,045	32,517	32,106	38,173	52,105	64	25,430	33,068

State Data

	Min	Q1	Mean	Median	Q3	Max	N	Range Avg Min	Range Avg Max
AL	16,973	16,973	16,973	16,973	16,973	16,973	1	18,429	27,643
AZ	39,562	39,562	39,562	39,562	39,562	39,562	2		
CA	34,248	35,485	41,345	41,880	42,147	52,000	9	34,561	42,482
FL	30,742	30,742	31,831	32,011	32,739	32,739	3	21,050	30,534
GA	14,830	14,830	14,830	14,830	14,830	14,830	1	14,830	15,870
IL	23,250	26,987	30,159	28,587	36,800	37,000	7	24,404	29,072
IN	29,617	29,617	29,617	29,617	29,617	29,617	1		
KS	32,843	32,843	32,843	32,843	32,843	32,843	1	21,632	36,067
MA	43,046	43,046	43,046	43,046	43,046	43,046	1		
MI	31,418	31,418	41,285	41,285	51,152	51,152	2		
MN	32,200	32,200	42,153	42,153	52,105	52,105	2		
MS	17,025	17,025	21,671	21,671	26,316	26,316	2		
NC	25,186	26,393	27,784	28,181	29,175	29,588	4		
NJ	40,605	40,605	40,605	40,605	40,605	40,605	2		
NM	21,190	21,190	31,637	31,637	42,084	42,084	2	24,679	33,790
NY	34,980	34,980	34,980	34,980	34,980	34,980	1	29,183	33,831
OH	22,714	25,511	29,832	29,973	34,154	36,670	4	23,920	36,400
OK	17,077	17,077	17,077	17,077	17,077	17,077	1	15,787	22,547
OR	23,795	23,795	25,524	25,524	27,252	27,252	2	23,795	31,366
PA	30,576	30,576	35,772	35,772	40,967	40,967	2	24,461	30,576
SC	20,820	23,260	23,753	23,413	24,827	26,445	5		
TX	27,102	27,102	30,486	27,788	36,566	36,566	3	21,736	40,102
WA	34,978	35,169	36,261	35,360	37,353	39,346	4	29,120	35,360
WI	35,422	35,422	35,422	35,422	35,422	35,422	2	30,826	35,422

Degree Required Data

	Min	Q1	Mean	Median	Q3	Max	N	Range Avg Min	Range Avg Max
High School	14,830	27,102	31,924	31,418	35,422	52,105	33	24,925	32,923
Associate's	20,820	25,186	32,334	30,909	37,000	51,152	21	27,543	33,825
Bachelor's	16,973	27,788	34,592	39,562	40,967	43,046	7	18,429	27,643
Master's									
Doctoral									

LIBRARY TECHNICAL ASSISTANT OF ACQUISITIONS - CONTINUED
Very Large Public Library
(Serving a population of 500,000 or more)
Regional Data

	Min	Q1	Mean	Median	Q3	Max	N	Range Avg Min	Range Avg Max
North Atlantic	37,952	37,952	37,952	37,952	37,952	37,952	1		
Great Lakes & Plains	26,478	34,008	38,635	39,250	47,167	48,582	15	26,161	35,833
Southeast	28,381	28,381	33,046	31,657	39,099	39,099	3		
West & Southwest	28,704	37,565	47,199	46,613	57,044	61,958	23	41,758	54,165
ALL REGIONS	26,478	34,798	42,909	40,747	49,270	61,958	42	35,403	46,696

State Data

	Min	Q1	Mean	Median	Q3	Max	N	Range Avg Min	Range Avg Max
AZ	28,704	33,134	36,327	37,565	39,520	41,475	4	27,331	42,494
CA	28,905	49,270	53,230	57,044	61,958	61,958	13	47,316	57,490
CO	30,701	30,701	37,296	39,182	42,004	42,004	3	.	.
FL	28,381	28,381	33,046	31,657	39,099	39,099	3	.	.
MD	37,952	37,952	37,952	37,952	37,952	37,952	1	.	.
OH	26,478	34,008	38,635	39,250	47,167	48,582	15	26,161	35,833
OR	46,613	46,613	46,613	46,613	46,613	46,613	1	43,950	54,038
TX	35,104	35,104	44,894	44,894	54,683	54,683	2	41,683	67,725

Degree Required Data

	Min	Q1	Mean	Median	Q3	Max	N	Range Avg Min	Range Avg Max
High School	26,478	34,798	39,097	37,952	46,144	54,683	25	27,424	39,491
Associate's	.	.	.	.	.	.		.	.
Bachelor's	30,701	34,942	39,625	40,593	44,308	46,613	4	43,950	54,038
Master's	39,099	39,099	39,099	39,099	39,099	39,099	1	.	.
Doctoral	.	.	.	.	.	.		.	.

LIBRARY TECHNICAL ASSISTANT OF ACQUISITIONS - CONTINUED
ALL PUBLIC LIBRARIES
Regional Data

	Min	Q1	Mean	Median	Q3	Max	N	Range Avg Min	Range Avg Max
North Atlantic	18,720	30,593	37,142	36,691	42,640	59,085	25	28,374	36,672
Great Lakes & Plains	18,720	27,643	33,967	33,426	39,614	57,720	64	25,301	34,350
Southeast	14,830	23,260	26,073	26,316	29,588	39,099	21	19,282	27,023
West & Southwest	17,077	28,905	39,177	39,182	46,613	61,958	59	32,827	42,544
ALL REGIONS	14,830	27,581	35,275	35,104	41,880	61,958	169	28,418	37,619

State Data

	Min	Q1	Mean	Median	Q3	Max	N	Range Avg Min	Range Avg Max
AL	16,973	16,973	16,973	16,973	16,973	16,973	1	18,429	27,643
AZ	25,230	27,113	34,398	37,565	39,562	41,475	8	25,147	38,723
CA	23,150	35,485	44,298	45,282	57,044	61,958	29	37,429	45,601
CO	22,714	30,701	34,420	37,500	39,182	42,004	5	22,714	22,714
CT	28,704	30,593	41,186	36,337	55,291	59,085	7	34,798	42,796
FL	28,381	30,742	32,438	31,834	32,739	39,099	6	21,050	30,534
GA	14,830	14,830	14,830	14,830	14,830	14,830	1	14,830	15,870
IA	42,773	42,773	42,773	42,773	42,773	42,773	1	.	.
IL	19,906	27,581	31,358	30,909	35,764	41,746	19	24,680	32,728
IN	18,720	18,720	24,169	24,169	29,617	29,617	2	16,640	22,880
KS	23,275	23,275	28,059	28,059	32,843	32,843	2	20,186	30,524
MA	35,091	36,745	39,877	40,686	43,009	43,046	4	29,120	37,440
MD	37,952	37,952	37,952	37,952	37,952	37,952	1	.	.
ME	36,421	36,421	36,421	36,421	36,421	36,421	1	29,619	42,224
MI	23,000	24,510	32,897	28,719	41,285	51,152	4	.	.
MN	32,200	37,274	42,119	44,507	44,507	52,105	5	27,955	37,274
MO	18,720	18,720	38,220	38,220	57,720	57,720	2	47,507	57,720
MS	17,025	17,025	21,671	21,671	26,316	26,316	2	.	.
NC	25,186	25,764	27,380	27,600	28,761	29,588	5	.	.
NJ	36,691	40,605	42,029	40,605	45,900	46,343	5	.	.
NM	21,190	21,190	35,651	42,084	43,680	43,680	3	27,546	39,166
NY	29,598	29,598	32,289	32,289	34,980	34,980	2	29,183	33,831
OH	19,906	28,309	34,948	34,798	40,019	48,582	23	25,844	36,490
OK	17,077	17,077	17,077	17,077	17,077	17,077	1	15,787	22,547
OR	23,795	23,795	32,553	27,252	46,613	46,613	3	33,873	42,702
PA	18,720	19,967	26,331	21,424	30,576	40,967	5	20,550	28,808
SC	20,820	22,090	23,476	23,337	24,827	26,445	6	.	.
TX	27,102	27,788	35,467	33,332	36,566	54,683	6	31,710	53,914
WA	34,978	35,169	36,261	35,360	37,353	39,346	4	29,120	35,360
WI	22,214	25,584	34,742	35,422	44,361	45,447	6	23,525	28,655

Degree Required Data

	Min	Q1	Mean	Median	Q3	Max	N	Range Avg Min	Range Avg Max
High School	14,830	27,102	34,618	34,798	41,475	59,085	86	25,261	34,176
Associate's	18,720	24,827	31,283	28,761	36,800	57,720	33	26,459	34,076
Bachelor's	16,973	29,671	34,723	35,810	41,357	46,613	28	27,562	39,442
Master's	39,099	39,099	39,099	39,099	39,099	39,099	1	.	.
Doctoral	.	.	.	.	.	.	.	.	.

LIBRARY TECHNICAL ASSISTANT OF CATALOGING

Provides basic assistance to patrons referring patrons to Librarian for professional assistance. Locates materials and information for patrons. May complete routine copy cataloging. Assists with special programming. Prepares bibliographic records to represent the items acquired by the library, including bibliographic description, subject analysis, and classification.

Very Small Public Library
(Serving a population of less than 10,000)
Regional Data

	Min	Q1	Mean	Median	Q3	Max	N	Range Avg Min	Range Avg Max
North Atlantic	27,435	28,080	29,842	29,578	31,387	32,728	5	25,282	35,370
Great Lakes & Plains	14,560	15,282	20,741	18,720	24,496	31,200	12	19,916	29,640
West & Southwest	14,016	14,016	23,489	22,714	33,738	33,738	3	23,327	28,226
ALL REGIONS	14,016	17,056	23,428	23,972	29,151	33,738	20	22,842	31,079

State Data

	Min	Q1	Mean	Median	Q3	Max	N	Range Avg Min	Range Avg Max
AZ	14,016	14,016	14,016	14,016	14,016	14,016	1	.	.
CO	22,714	22,714	28,226	28,226	33,738	33,738	2	23,327	28,226
CT	27,435	27,435	27,435	27,435	27,435	27,435	1	.	.
IA	24,968	24,968	24,968	24,968	24,968	24,968	1	.	.
IL	18,720	18,720	24,960	24,960	31,200	31,200	2	24,960	35,360
IN	28,724	28,724	28,724	28,724	28,724	28,724	1	.	.
KS	15,172	15,172	16,946	16,946	18,720	18,720	2	.	.
MA	29,578	29,578	29,578	29,578	29,578	29,578	1	28,725	37,461
MI	15,392	15,392	15,392	15,392	15,392	15,392	1	.	.
MO	18,720	18,720	21,372	21,372	24,024	24,024	2	.	.
ND	14,560	14,560	14,560	14,560	14,560	14,560	1	.	.
NE	14,768	14,768	14,768	14,768	14,768	14,768	1	.	.
NJ	32,728	32,728	32,728	32,728	32,728	32,728	1	.	.
NY	28,080	28,080	28,080	28,080	28,080	28,080	1	21,840	33,280
OH	23,920	23,920	23,920	23,920	23,920	23,920	1	14,872	23,920
VT	31,387	31,387	31,387	31,387	31,387	31,387	1	.	.

Degree Required Data

	Min	Q1	Mean	Median	Q3	Max	N	Range Avg Min	Range Avg Max
High School	14,016	15,172	22,444	22,714	28,080	33,738	13	21,665	29,802
Associate's	18,720	18,720	22,571	24,024	24,968	24,968	3	.	.
Bachelor's	29,578	29,578	31,231	31,387	32,728	32,728	3	28,725	37,461
Master's	.	.	.	.	.	.		.	.
Doctoral	.	.	.	.	.	.		.	.

LIBRARY TECHNICAL ASSISTANT OF CATALOGING - CONTINUED
Small Public Library
(Serving a population of 10,000 to 25,000)
Regional Data

	Min	Q1	Mean	Median	Q3	Max	N	Range Avg Min	Range Avg Max
North Atlantic	14,560	26,458	30,656	29,799	34,632	46,343	14	23,034	32,760
Great Lakes & Plains	19,198	20,904	26,731	25,584	30,160	43,326	13	23,468	32,614
Southeast	14,560	17,680	22,787	21,892	27,893	32,802	4	.	.
West & Southwest	11,852	21,195	27,595	25,376	35,360	41,000	7	25,646	38,126
ALL REGIONS	11,852	21,195	27,921	26,718	33,280	46,343	38	23,759	33,765

State Data

	Min	Q1	Mean	Median	Q3	Max	N	Range Avg Min	Range Avg Max
AZ	21,195	21,195	21,195	21,195	21,195	21,195	1	20,779	31,179
CO	41,000	41,000	41,000	41,000	41,000	41,000	1	.	.
IA	20,592	20,592	20,592	20,592	20,592	20,592	1	.	.
IL	20,904	22,932	26,286	27,040	29,640	30,160	4	22,187	35,360
IN	20,800	20,800	20,800	20,800	20,800	20,800	1	18,720	22,880
MA	30,603	32,516	35,659	34,531	38,802	42,973	4	27,914	34,632
MI	19,198	19,198	26,250	29,120	30,430	30,430	3	25,480	30,430
MN	43,326	43,326	43,326	43,326	43,326	43,326	1	32,490	43,326
NC	14,560	14,560	19,448	20,800	22,984	22,984	3	.	.
NH	26,458	26,458	27,726	27,726	28,995	28,995	2	24,502	35,152
NJ	34,222	34,222	39,980	39,374	46,343	46,343	3	.	.
NM	11,852	18,614	26,467	29,328	34,320	35,360	4	28,080	41,600
OH	22,818	22,818	26,657	26,657	30,496	30,496	2	.	.
PA	14,560	17,680	21,044	21,580	24,409	26,458	4	16,640	27,040
RI	26,978	26,978	26,978	26,978	26,978	26,978	1	21,611	31,824
TX	25,100	25,100	25,100	25,100	25,100	25,100	1	.	.
VA	32,802	32,802	32,802	32,802	32,802	32,802	1	.	.
WI	25,584	25,584	25,584	25,584	25,584	25,584	1	21,029	25,584

Degree Required Data

	Min	Q1	Mean	Median	Q3	Max	N	Range Avg Min	Range Avg Max
High School	11,852	20,904	27,180	26,458	33,280	46,343	22	26,478	36,634
Associate's	20,800	20,800	29,786	25,584	42,973	42,973	3	19,874	24,232
Bachelor's	20,592	22,818	28,360	29,120	30,603	41,000	11	20,962	32,989
Master's	.	.	.	.	.	.	.	.	.
Doctoral	.	.	.	.	.	.	.	.	.

LIBRARY TECHNICAL ASSISTANT OF CATALOGING - CONTINUED
Medium Public Library
(Serving a population of 25,000 to 99,999)
Regional Data

	Min	Q1	Mean	Median	Q3	Max	N	Range Avg Min	Range Avg Max
North Atlantic	15,500	22,839	31,869	27,290	34,561	59,085	25	27,633	35,422
Great Lakes & Plains	24,274	27,019	32,503	28,392	41,844	46,738	11	25,691	36,220
Southeast	14,560	15,600	18,200	17,680	20,800	22,880	4	.	.
West & Southwest	14,560	23,920	29,211	28,600	37,086	39,912	9	18,522	27,841
ALL REGIONS	14,560	22,880	30,407	27,310	34,561	59,085	49	24,198	33,598

State Data

	Min	Q1	Mean	Median	Q3	Max	N	Range Avg Min	Range Avg Max
CA	19,635	19,635	32,829	38,940	39,912	39,912	3	14,560	20,800
CO	28,600	28,600	28,600	28,600	28,600	28,600	1	18,720	31,200
CT	53,281	56,183	57,634	59,085	59,085	59,085	4	.	.
GA	22,880	22,880	22,880	22,880	22,880	22,880	1	.	.
ID	23,920	23,920	30,503	30,503	37,086	37,086	2	18,179	25,438
IL	25,686	27,019	35,810	34,494	46,426	46,738	6	29,169	43,340
MA	29,994	32,277	35,996	37,138	39,714	39,714	4	28,080	36,157
MI	31,995	31,995	31,995	31,995	31,995	31,995	1	.	.
MO	29,702	29,702	29,702	29,702	29,702	29,702	1	.	.
MS	16,640	16,640	17,680	17,680	18,720	18,720	2	.	.
PA	15,500	19,313	24,312	25,438	27,165	33,585	16	.	.
RI	33,218	33,218	33,218	33,218	33,218	33,218	1	26,291	33,218
TX	14,560	14,560	23,747	23,747	32,933	32,933	2	.	.
UT	27,310	27,310	27,310	27,310	27,310	27,310	1	22,630	33,925
VA	14,560	14,560	14,560	14,560	14,560	14,560	1	.	.
WI	24,274	24,274	26,991	28,309	28,392	28,392	3	22,214	29,099

Degree Required Data

	Min	Q1	Mean	Median	Q3	Max	N	Range Avg Min	Range Avg Max
High School	14,560	19,635	32,723	33,218	39,714	59,085	17	23,454	31,699
Associate's	15,500	22,839	29,193	27,092	32,933	53,281	18	25,505	35,293
Bachelor's	22,880	27,010	28,388	28,506	30,597	31,995	8	25,085	34,736
Master's	30,933	30,933	30,933	30,933	30,933	30,933	1	.	.
Doctoral	.	.	.	.	.	.		.	.

LIBRARY TECHNICAL ASSISTANT OF CATALOGING - CONTINUED
Large Public Library
(Serving a population of 100,000 to 499,999)
Regional Data

	Min	Q1	Mean	Median	Q3	Max	N	Range Avg Min	Range Avg Max
North Atlantic	21,570	28,144	34,470	38,260	38,617	46,883	7	.	.
Great Lakes & Plains	18,200	29,536	30,777	29,536	30,933	39,467	17	24,200	29,690
Southeast	16,910	21,169	26,778	26,408	31,769	38,334	12	19,944	27,771
West & Southwest	16,640	24,648	31,897	31,907	39,562	47,258	31	23,916	32,367
ALL REGIONS	16,640	24,673	30,965	30,302	38,229	47,258	67	23,341	30,585

State Data

	Min	Q1	Mean	Median	Q3	Max	N	Range Avg Min	Range Avg Max
AL	20,301	20,301	20,301	20,301	20,301	20,301	1	18,429	27,643
AZ	39,562	39,562	39,562	39,562	39,562	39,562	2		
CA	31,907	39,176	40,928	41,561	43,394	47,258	8	32,219	40,893
CO	23,130	23,130	24,287	24,648	25,085	25,085	3	21,819	32,913
FL	23,982	23,982	28,267	28,267	32,552	32,552	2	21,050	30,534
GA	16,910	16,910	16,910	16,910	16,910	16,910	1	16,910	17,888
IL	29,440	30,909	33,380	30,933	36,150	39,467	5	26,678	31,549
MD	21,570	24,857	33,714	33,202	42,572	46,883	4		
MI	30,888	30,888	33,392	30,888	38,400	38,400	3		
MO	29,536	29,536	29,536	29,536	29,536	29,536	6	24,294	29,536
NC	34,392	34,392	34,392	34,392	34,392	34,392	1		
NJ	38,387	38,387	38,502	38,502	38,617	38,617	2		
NM	16,640	20,413	22,957	21,190	23,991	32,553	5	20,072	27,473
OH	18,200	18,200	20,935	20,935	23,670	23,670	2	17,722	25,501
OK	20,654	20,654	20,654	20,654	20,654	20,654	1	19,115	24,794
OR	21,195	21,195	30,801	27,252	43,956	43,956	3	21,195	27,934
PA	29,429	29,429	29,429	29,429	29,429	29,429	1		
SC	22,036	24,673	27,228	28,142	30,302	30,987	5	24,232	36,338
TN	18,720	18,720	18,720	18,720	18,720	18,720	1	17,992	23,691
TX	27,456	28,059	29,692	29,338	31,387	32,573	6	17,472	31,491
VA	38,334	38,334	38,334	38,334	38,334	38,334	1		
WA	32,690	32,690	34,470	33,280	37,440	37,440	3	31,200	37,440
WI	37,045	37,045	37,045	37,045	37,045	37,045	1		

Degree Required Data

	Min	Q1	Mean	Median	Q3	Max	N	Range Avg Min	Range Avg Max
High School	18,720	27,758	30,870	29,536	34,715	46,883	28	23,648	30,909
Associate's	16,640	22,583	30,641	30,605	39,795	47,258	24	24,018	30,572
Bachelor's	20,301	30,888	33,377	34,392	38,400	39,562	9	21,330	31,990
Master's	29,429	29,429	29,429	29,429	29,429	29,429	1		
Doctoral									

LIBRARY TECHNICAL ASSISTANT OF CATALOGING - CONTINUED
Very Large Public Library
(Serving a population of 500,000 or more)
Regional Data

	Min	Q1	Mean	Median	Q3	Max	N	Range Avg Min	Range Avg Max
North Atlantic	41,600	41,600	41,600	41,600	41,600	41,600	2	31,200	41,600
Great Lakes & Plains	31,974	33,217	35,676	34,537	39,250	40,543	6	24,898	37,398
Southeast	16,640	18,720	23,223	19,995	28,557	32,205	5		
West & Southwest	25,872	38,272	44,590	38,272	57,044	61,958	39	40,960	52,016
ALL REGIONS	16,640	35,345	41,392	38,272	57,044	61,958	52	39,592	50,653

State Data

	Min	Q1	Mean	Median	Q3	Max	N	Range Avg Min	Range Avg Max
AZ	34,882	36,650	36,662	36,650	37,565	37,565	5	27,331	42,494
CA	38,272	38,272	48,128	44,013	57,044	61,958	30	46,016	55,901
FL	19,995	19,995	26,919	28,557	32,205	32,205	3	.	.
GA	16,640	16,640	17,680	17,680	18,720	18,720	2	.	.
IN	31,974	33,217	34,962	33,265	35,809	40,543	5	.	.
MD	41,600	41,600	41,600	41,600	41,600	41,600	2	31,200	41,600
OH	39,250	39,250	39,250	39,250	39,250	39,250	1	24,898	37,398
TX	25,872	26,602	27,966	28,059	29,331	29,875	4	23,150	33,592

Degree Required Data

	Min	Q1	Mean	Median	Q3	Max	N	Range Avg Min	Range Avg Max
High School	16,640	25,872	31,132	34,882	37,565	39,250	11	26,386	40,495
Associate's	.	.	.	.	.	.		.	.
Bachelor's	31,974	33,217	36,858	35,809	41,600	41,600	7	31,200	41,600
Master's	.	.	.	.	.	.		.	.
Doctoral	.	.	.	.	.	.		.	.

LIBRARY TECHNICAL ASSISTANT OF CATALOGING - CONTINUED
ALL PUBLIC LIBRARIES
Regional Data

	Min	Q1	Mean	Median	Q3	Max	N	Range Avg Min	Range Avg Max
North Atlantic	14,560	26,458	32,068	29,994	38,387	59,085	53	26,051	35,341
Great Lakes & Plains	14,560	23,920	28,664	29,536	31,974	46,738	59	24,061	32,009
Southeast	14,560	18,720	24,056	22,880	30,302	38,334	25	19,944	27,771
West & Southwest	11,852	27,456	36,566	37,565	41,000	61,958	89	31,717	41,593
ALL REGIONS	11,852	24,274	32,064	30,463	38,272	61,958	226	27,901	36,987

State Data

	Min	Q1	Mean	Median	Q3	Max	N	Range Avg Min	Range Avg Max
AL	20,301	20,301	20,301	20,301	20,301	20,301	1	18,429	27,643
AZ	14,016	34,882	33,072	36,650	37,565	39,562	9	26,239	40,609
CA	19,635	38,272	45,604	42,147	57,044	61,958	41	42,547	52,085
CO	22,714	23,130	28,416	25,085	33,738	41,000	7	21,805	31,065
CT	27,435	53,281	51,594	59,085	59,085	59,085	5		
FL	19,995	23,982	27,458	28,557	32,205	32,552	5	21,050	30,534
GA	16,640	16,775	18,788	17,815	20,800	22,880	4	16,910	17,888
IA	20,592	20,592	22,780	22,780	24,968	24,968	2		
ID	23,920	23,920	30,503	30,503	37,086	37,086	2	18,179	25,438
IL	18,720	27,019	31,578	30,160	36,150	46,738	17	26,035	35,767
IN	20,800	28,724	32,048	33,217	35,809	40,543	7	18,720	22,880
KS	15,172	15,172	16,946	16,946	18,720	18,720	2		
MA	29,578	30,603	35,133	34,561	39,714	42,973	9	28,176	36,113
MD	21,570	28,144	36,343	39,930	41,600	46,883	6	31,200	41,600
MI	15,392	24,159	28,289	30,659	31,442	38,400	8	25,480	30,430
MN	43,326	43,326	43,326	43,326	43,326	43,326	1	32,490	43,326
MO	18,720	29,536	27,740	29,536	29,536	29,702	9	24,294	29,536
MS	16,640	16,640	17,680	17,680	18,720	18,720	2		
NC	14,560	17,680	23,184	21,892	28,688	34,392	4		
ND	14,560	14,560	14,560	14,560	14,560	14,560	1		
NE	14,768	14,768	14,768	14,768	14,768	14,768	1		
NH	26,458	26,458	27,726	27,726	28,995	28,995	2	24,502	35,152
NJ	32,728	34,222	38,279	38,502	39,374	46,343	6		
NM	11,852	20,413	24,517	23,991	32,553	35,360	9	22,360	31,509
NY	28,080	28,080	28,080	28,080	28,080	28,080	1	21,840	33,280
OH	18,200	22,818	26,392	23,795	30,496	39,250	6	18,803	28,080
OK	20,654	20,654	20,654	20,654	20,654	20,654	1	19,115	24,794
OR	21,195	21,195	30,801	27,252	43,956	43,956	3	21,195	27,934
PA	14,560	19,739	23,933	24,960	27,040	33,585	21	16,640	27,040
RI	26,978	26,978	30,098	30,098	33,218	33,218	2	23,951	32,521
SC	22,036	24,673	27,228	28,142	30,302	30,987	5	24,232	36,338
TN	18,720	18,720	18,720	18,720	18,720	18,720	1	17,992	23,691
TX	14,560	27,331	27,893	28,787	29,875	32,933	13	20,311	32,542
UT	27,310	27,310	27,310	27,310	27,310	27,310	1	22,630	33,925
VA	14,560	14,560	28,565	32,802	38,334	38,334	3		
VT	31,387	31,387	31,387	31,387	31,387	31,387	1		
WA	32,690	32,690	34,470	33,280	37,440	37,440	3	31,200	37,440
WI	24,274	25,584	28,721	28,309	28,392	37,045	5	21,918	28,220

Degree Required Data

	Min	Q1	Mean	Median	Q3	Max	N	Range Avg Min	Range Avg Max
High School	11,852	21,570	29,152	29,120	34,632	59,085	91	24,421	33,692
Associate's	15,500	22,749	29,540	27,092	38,584	53,281	48	23,980	31,069
Bachelor's	20,301	27,310	31,346	30,888	34,430	41,600	38	24,142	34,907
Master's	29,429	29,429	30,181	30,181	30,933	30,933	2		
Doctoral									

ADULT SERVICES CLERK

Performs routine duties requiring the use of a variety of forms, reports or procedures. Provides basic patron assistance: sets up computer stations, locates materials, provides information. Maintains departmental or area records. Performs miscellaneous clerical duties such as filing, typing, sorting or photocopying. Provides access to materials, services and programs intended to meet the needs of the adult users of a public library.

Very Small Public Library
(Serving a population of less than 10,000)
Regional Data

	Min	Q1	Mean	Median	Q3	Max	N	Range Avg Min	Range Avg Max
North Atlantic	11,440	20,800	22,933	24,908	27,310	27,435	14	23,058	26,885
Great Lakes & Plains	13,374	14,872	18,930	17,160	20,800	36,480	28	14,269	22,381
Southeast	19,663	19,663	19,663	19,663	19,663	19,663	1	.	.
West & Southwest	16,070	16,070	19,951	16,224	27,560	27,560	3	20,082	24,253
ALL REGIONS	11,440	16,224	20,231	19,191	24,648	36,480	46	20,286	25,341

State Data

	Min	Q1	Mean	Median	Q3	Max	N	Range Avg Min	Range Avg Max
CO	16,224	16,224	21,892	21,892	27,560	27,560	2	20,082	24,253
CT	16,640	16,640	20,644	20,644	24,648	24,648	2	24,648	24,648
IA	13,374	13,374	18,013	18,720	21,946	21,946	3	.	.
IL	13,520	13,832	16,494	16,640	17,680	20,800	5	20,384	24,544
IN	14,560	15,184	18,708	19,842	22,048	22,921	7	13,520	18,720
KS	14,560	14,560	23,744	16,640	36,480	36,480	5	12,480	22,880
MA	16,640	20,800	24,338	25,459	27,310	27,435	10	22,899	27,109
MI	15,600	15,600	16,120	16,120	16,640	16,640	2	.	.
NE	14,560	14,560	14,560	14,560	14,560	14,560	1	.	.
PA	11,440	11,440	11,440	11,440	11,440	11,440	1	.	.
SD	16,640	16,640	17,680	17,680	18,720	18,720	2	.	.
TX	16,070	16,070	16,070	16,070	16,070	16,070	1	.	.
VT	24,960	24,960	24,960	24,960	24,960	24,960	1	.	.
WI	18,720	18,720	20,561	20,800	22,163	22,163	3	.	.
WV	19,663	19,663	19,663	19,663	19,663	19,663	1	.	.

Degree Required Data

	Min	Q1	Mean	Median	Q3	Max	N	Range Avg Min	Range Avg Max
High School	11,440	15,600	19,299	18,200	21,946	36,480	38	18,256	24,070
Associate's	27,435	27,435	27,435	27,435	27,435	27,435	1	21,944	29,016
Bachelor's	24,960	27,310	26,890	27,310	27,310	27,560	5	26,468	28,553
Master's	.	.	.	.	.	.		.	.
Doctoral	.	.	.	.	.	.		.	.

ADULT SERVICES CLERK - CONTINUED
Small Public Library
(Serving a population of 10,000 to 25,000)
Regional Data

	Min	Q1	Mean	Median	Q3	Max	N	Range Avg Min	Range Avg Max
North Atlantic	12,480	28,558	32,917	32,594	36,203	63,231	22	27,489	35,200
Great Lakes & Plains	14,040	15,600	19,175	16,640	20,800	42,224	45	18,317	26,108
Southeast	15,080	15,600	17,436	17,223	19,744	19,744	6	14,213	18,304
West & Southwest	18,824	19,011	23,508	22,675	24,828	33,280	20	21,366	31,289
ALL REGIONS	12,480	16,640	23,245	19,744	28,558	63,231	93	21,493	29,636

State Data

	Min	Q1	Mean	Median	Q3	Max	N	Range Avg Min	Range Avg Max
AZ	18,824	18,824	18,976	18,824	19,198	19,510	7	18,824	28,246
CO	20,800	20,800	20,800	20,800	20,800	20,800	1	20,800	20,800
CT	32,594	32,594	32,594	32,594	32,594	32,594	6	32,594	43,680
IA	16,120	16,120	16,120	16,120	16,120	16,120	1	.	.
IL	14,040	15,600	17,347	16,120	17,680	29,120	25	16,510	26,520
KS	14,560	14,560	15,600	15,600	16,640	16,640	2	12,480	18,720
KY	15,600	15,600	18,363	19,744	19,744	19,744	3	14,213	18,304
MI	23,774	23,774	25,330	25,938	25,938	27,227	5	22,818	27,227
MN	40,123	40,123	40,123	40,123	40,123	40,123	1	30,098	40,123
MS	16,620	16,620	17,223	17,223	17,826	17,826	2	.	.
NJ	27,165	28,558	32,394	28,558	36,203	40,103	9	23,920	28,558
NM	22,797	25,043	29,467	31,200	33,280	33,280	6	24,426	36,587
NY	27,040	29,120	38,884	33,280	41,749	63,231	5	27,040	33,280
OH	15,600	15,600	19,555	17,118	18,820	42,224	11	15,600	23,400
OK	19,572	19,572	19,572	19,572	19,572	19,572	1	.	.
PA	12,480	12,480	21,320	21,320	30,160	30,160	2	12,480	16,640
TX	22,553	24,328	24,030	24,328	24,328	24,612	5	.	.
WV	15,080	15,080	15,080	15,080	15,080	15,080	1	.	.

Degree Required Data

	Min	Q1	Mean	Median	Q3	Max	N	Range Avg Min	Range Avg Max
High School	12,480	16,640	22,583	18,824	27,040	63,231	67	20,351	28,117
Associate's	15,080	17,326	22,734	23,368	28,142	29,120	4	23,400	40,279
Bachelor's	20,800	28,558	31,837	32,594	36,203	40,103	10	27,737	34,826
Master's	.	.	.	.	.	.		.	.
Doctoral	.	.	.	.	.	.		.	.

ADULT SERVICES CLERK - CONTINUED
Medium Public Library
(Serving a population of 25,000 to 99,999)
Regional Data

	Min	Q1	Mean	Median	Q3	Max	N	Range Avg Min	Range Avg Max
North Atlantic	13,600	17,200	22,346	21,070	26,335	50,934	34	24,242	36,369
Great Lakes & Plains	12,813	17,140	21,449	20,155	20,654	49,689	44	18,084	24,060
Southeast	11,429	12,240	15,922	17,209	18,271	21,011	20	12,480	18,720
West & Southwest	11,440	18,755	21,643	22,220	24,960	33,104	34	19,479	24,389
ALL REGIONS	11,429	16,755	20,893	20,155	24,190	50,934	132	18,845	24,752

State Data

	Min	Q1	Mean	Median	Q3	Max	N	Range Avg Min	Range Avg Max
AR	12,480	14,342	16,240	17,025	18,138	18,429	4	12,480	18,720
CA	16,141	20,925	20,478	20,925	20,925	23,026	6	17,212	21,098
CO	33,104	33,104	33,104	33,104	33,104	33,104	1	.	.
CT	21,965	22,880	24,780	22,880	27,269	31,762	9	23,310	33,932
IA	13,499	13,832	19,916	19,562	26,000	27,040	4	24,960	27,040
ID	24,960	24,960	24,960	24,960	24,960	24,960	1	24,960	37,440
IL	17,160	18,720	21,889	18,720	23,517	36,858	9	20,007	27,423
IN	24,877	24,877	24,877	24,877	24,877	24,877	1	.	.
KS	12,813	12,813	12,813	12,813	12,813	12,813	1	11,586	16,120
LA	11,429	11,429	13,324	11,429	17,778	17,778	7	.	.
MA	19,906	20,488	20,790	21,070	21,091	21,112	4	.	.
MI	20,259	20,259	20,259	20,259	20,259	20,259	2	17,430	20,259
MN	33,702	33,702	37,335	37,335	40,968	40,968	2	.	.
MO	14,248	14,539	16,272	14,830	18,970	20,134	10	15,696	22,504
NJ	26,335	26,335	35,650	29,681	50,934	50,934	3	.	.
NY	20,075	20,130	25,596	27,664	28,288	31,824	5	27,040	43,680
OH	16,952	19,344	23,433	20,571	20,654	49,689	15	18,429	24,182
PA	13,600	15,538	16,821	16,869	18,444	19,760	13	.	.
SC	13,374	16,640	17,800	18,113	18,981	21,011	9	.	.
TX	11,440	11,440	12,257	12,480	12,480	13,000	7	11,440	14,040
UT	18,755	21,144	21,965	21,210	21,414	28,059	6	22,630	33,925
WY	24,190	24,918	25,950	24,918	26,437	29,744	13	24,190	29,744

Degree Required Data

	Min	Q1	Mean	Median	Q3	Max	N	Range Avg Min	Range Avg Max
High School	11,429	16,141	20,731	20,176	23,026	50,934	102	18,397	24,052
Associate's	14,200	19,594	21,913	21,070	24,232	36,858	17	24,111	32,748
Bachelor's	15,538	18,720	20,015	18,720	18,970	31,762	8	18,803	24,454
Master's	.	.	.	.	.	.	.	.	.
Doctoral	.	.	.	.	.	.	.	.	.

ADULT SERVICES CLERK - CONTINUED
Large Public Library
(Serving a population of 100,000 to 499,999)
Regional Data

	Min	Q1	Mean	Median	Q3	Max	N	Range Avg Min	Range Avg Max
North Atlantic	14,560	23,046	24,552	24,253	27,144	32,968	8	24,933	30,041
Great Lakes & Plains	19,248	21,445	25,479	24,981	24,981	43,318	69	20,018	26,102
Southeast	14,830	18,595	26,371	25,168	31,007	40,174	15	21,722	22,069
West & Southwest	17,514	22,422	27,604	28,164	31,140	41,424	18	22,916	30,155
ALL REGIONS	14,560	21,756	25,881	24,981	29,099	43,318	110	20,833	26,386

State Data

	Min	Q1	Mean	Median	Q3	Max	N	Range Avg Min	Range Avg Max
CA	22,176	28,164	29,372	28,164	31,140	38,700	10	26,978	33,561
CO	17,514	18,117	19,412	18,855	20,706	22,422	4	18,855	26,749
GA	14,830	14,830	14,830	14,830	14,830	14,830	2	14,830	15,870
IL	21,674	23,667	28,044	27,099	30,608	37,572	12	20,939	27,407
IN	19,248	19,248	19,248	19,248	19,248	19,248	1		
MI	19,323	19,802	23,331	24,981	24,981	29,682	46	19,717	25,817
MS	15,336	15,336	15,336	15,336	15,336	15,336	1		
NC	18,595	18,595	18,595	18,595	18,595	18,595	1		
NY	22,048	22,048	28,038	29,099	32,968	32,968	3	25,841	29,328
OR	41,424	41,424	41,424	41,424	41,424	41,424	1		
PA	14,560	24,045	22,460	24,045	24,461	25,189	5	24,253	30,576
TX	24,323	24,323	28,030	26,692	33,076	33,076	3		
VA	25,168	25,168	30,179	27,747	35,771	40,174	11	25,168	25,168
WI	21,756	23,109	32,907	36,756	37,977	43,318	10	28,038	31,096

Degree Required Data

	Min	Q1	Mean	Median	Q3	Max	N	Range Avg Min	Range Avg Max
High School	14,560	23,109	27,488	26,512	31,634	43,318	58	22,785	27,169
Associate's	19,323	20,592	24,261	24,981	24,981	40,174	51	19,918	26,019
Bachelor's									
Master's									
Doctoral									

ADULT SERVICES CLERK - CONTINUED
Very Large Public Library
(Serving a population of 500,000 or more)
Regional Data

	Min	Q1	Mean	Median	Q3	Max	N	Range Avg Min	Range Avg Max
Great Lakes & Plains	20,904	20,904	22,503	21,882	22,901	30,056	142	20,956	30,178
West & Southwest	30,867	37,336	41,006	37,336	47,362	47,362	164	34,248	41,375
ALL REGIONS	20,904	21,882	32,419	35,682	37,336	47,362	306	28,039	36,145

State Data

	Min	Q1	Mean	Median	Q3	Max	N	Range Avg Min	Range Avg Max
CA	30,867	37,336	41,103	37,336	47,362	47,362	162	34,334	41,472
OH	20,904	20,904	22,503	21,882	22,901	30,056	142	20,956	30,178
OR	32,656	32,656	33,155	33,155	33,654	33,654	2	27,373	33,654

Degree Required Data

	Min	Q1	Mean	Median	Q3	Max	N	Range Avg Min	Range Avg Max
High School	20,904	20,904	22,835	21,882	22,901	39,984	141	20,997	30,108
Associate's	.	.	.	.	.	.			
Bachelor's	.	.	.	.	.	.			
Master's	.	.	.	.	.	.			
Doctoral	.	.	.	.	.	.			

ADULT SERVICES CLERK - CONTINUED
ALL PUBLIC LIBRARIES
Regional Data

	Min	Q1	Mean	Median	Q3	Max	N	Range Avg Min	Range Avg Max
North Atlantic	11,440	20,075	25,659	25,074	29,120	63,231	78	25,277	31,786
Great Lakes & Plains	12,813	19,802	22,226	21,382	23,774	49,689	328	20,035	28,034
Southeast	11,429	15,336	19,959	18,070	25,168	40,174	42	17,994	20,433
West & Southwest	11,440	28,164	35,514	37,336	47,362	47,362	239	31,069	38,061
ALL REGIONS	11,429	20,592	27,100	23,421	37,336	63,231	687	24,905	32,264

State Data

	Min	Q1	Mean	Median	Q3	Max	N	Range Avg Min	Range Avg Max
AR	12,480	14,342	16,240	17,025	18,138	18,429	4	12,480	18,720
AZ	18,824	18,824	18,976	18,824	19,198	19,510	7	18,824	28,246
CA	16,141	37,336	39,749	37,336	47,362	47,362	178	33,634	40,650
CO	16,224	18,117	21,917	19,895	24,991	33,104	8	19,735	24,561
CT	16,640	22,880	27,051	27,269	32,594	32,594	17	29,014	38,852
GA	14,830	14,830	14,830	14,830	14,830	14,830	2	14,830	15,870
IA	13,374	13,832	18,728	17,420	23,453	27,040	8	24,960	27,040
ID	24,960	24,960	24,960	24,960	24,960	24,960	1	24,960	37,440
IL	13,520	15,912	20,582	18,720	23,517	37,572	51	19,006	26,960
IN	14,560	16,556	19,453	19,842	22,048	24,877	9	13,520	18,720
KS	12,813	14,560	20,342	15,600	26,560	36,480	8	12,331	20,367
KY	15,600	15,600	18,363	19,744	19,744	19,744	3	14,213	18,304
LA	11,429	11,429	13,324	11,429	17,778	17,778	7	.	.
MA	16,640	20,800	23,324	22,984	27,310	27,435	14	22,899	27,109
MI	15,600	19,802	23,139	24,981	24,981	29,682	55	19,927	25,738
MN	33,702	33,702	38,264	40,123	40,968	40,968	3	30,098	40,123
MO	14,248	14,539	16,272	14,830	18,970	20,134	10	15,696	22,504
MS	15,336	15,336	16,594	16,620	17,826	17,826	3	.	.
NC	18,595	18,595	18,595	18,595	18,595	18,595	1	.	.
NE	14,560	14,560	14,560	14,560	14,560	14,560	1	.	.
NJ	26,335	28,108	33,208	29,120	37,371	50,934	12	23,920	28,558
NM	22,797	25,043	29,467	31,200	33,280	33,280	6	24,426	36,587
NY	20,075	27,040	31,270	29,099	32,968	63,231	13	26,526	33,072
OH	15,600	20,904	22,393	21,382	22,901	49,689	168	20,646	29,556
OK	19,572	19,572	19,572	19,572	19,572	19,572	1	.	.
OR	32,656	32,656	35,911	33,654	41,424	41,424	3	27,373	33,654
PA	11,440	14,588	18,336	17,000	19,760	30,160	21	21,898	27,789
SC	13,374	16,640	17,800	18,113	18,981	21,011	9	.	.
SD	16,640	16,640	17,680	17,680	18,720	18,720	2	.	.
TX	11,440	12,480	19,132	19,312	24,328	33,076	16	11,440	14,040
UT	18,755	21,144	21,965	21,210	21,414	28,059	6	22,630	33,925
VA	25,168	25,168	30,179	27,747	35,771	40,174	11	25,168	25,168
VT	24,960	24,960	24,960	24,960	24,960	24,960	1	.	.
WI	18,720	22,163	30,058	31,096	37,279	43,318	13	28,038	31,096
WV	15,080	15,080	17,371	17,371	19,663	19,663	2	.	.
WY	24,190	24,918	25,950	24,918	26,437	29,744	13	24,190	29,744

Degree Required Data

	Min	Q1	Mean	Median	Q3	Max	N	Range Avg Min	Range Avg Max
High School	11,429	18,824	22,599	21,382	24,918	63,231	406	20,376	28,027
Associate's	14,200	19,802	23,674	24,960	24,981	40,174	73	20,463	27,204
Bachelor's	15,538	18,970	26,649	27,310	32,594	40,103	23	24,070	29,368
Master's	.	.	.	.	.	.	.	.	.
Doctoral	.	.	.	.	.	.	.	.	.

ARCHIVES AND SPECIAL COLLECTIONS CLERK

Performs routine duties requiring the use of a variety of forms, reports or procedures. Provides basic patron assistance: sets up computer stations, locates materials, provides information. Maintains departmental or area records. Performs miscellaneous clerical duties such as filing, typing, sorting or photocopying. Manages and maintains collection; identifies and appraises records, authenticates, describes and documents, facilitates access and use, preserves and conserves, and exhibits collection.

Very Small Public Library
(Serving a population of less than 10,000)
Regional Data

	Min	Q1	Mean	Median	Q3	Max	N	Range Avg Min	Range Avg Max
Great Lakes & Plains	16,120	16,120	18,390	18,390	20,660	20,660	2	.	
ALL REGIONS	16,120	16,120	18,390	18,390	20,660	20,660	2	.	

State Data

	Min	Q1	Mean	Median	Q3	Max	N	Range Avg Min	Range Avg Max
IA	16,120	16,120	18,390	18,390	20,660	20,660	2	.	

Degree Required Data

	Min	Q1	Mean	Median	Q3	Max	N	Range Avg Min	Range Avg Max
High School	16,120	16,120	18,390	18,390	20,660	20,660	2	.	
Associate's	.	.	.	.	.	.	.	.	
Bachelor's	.	.	.	.	.	.	.	.	
Master's	.	.	.	.	.	.	.	.	
Doctoral	.	.	.	.	.	.	.	.	

ARCHIVES AND SPECIAL COLLECTIONS CLERK - CONTINUED
Small Public Library
(Serving a population of 10,000 to 25,000)
Regional Data

	Min	Q1	Mean	Median	Q3	Max	N	Range Avg Min	Range Avg Max
North Atlantic	26,849	26,849	26,849	26,849	26,849	26,849	1	.	.
Great Lakes & Plains	17,576	17,576	25,428	25,428	33,280	33,280	2	33,280	33,280
ALL REGIONS	17,576	17,576	25,902	26,849	33,280	33,280	3	33,280	33,280

State Data

	Min	Q1	Mean	Median	Q3	Max	N	Range Avg Min	Range Avg Max
KS	17,576	17,576	17,576	17,576	17,576	17,576	1	.	.
NJ	26,849	26,849	26,849	26,849	26,849	26,849	1	.	.
OH	33,280	33,280	33,280	33,280	33,280	33,280	1	33,280	33,280

Degree Required Data

	Min	Q1	Mean	Median	Q3	Max	N	Range Avg Min	Range Avg Max
High School	17,576	17,576	25,902	26,849	33,280	33,280	3	33,280	33,280
Associate's									
Bachelor's									
Master's									
Doctoral									

ARCHIVES AND SPECIAL COLLECTIONS CLERK - CONTINUED
Medium Public Library
(Serving a population of 25,000 to 99,999)
Regional Data

	Min	Q1	Mean	Median	Q3	Max	N	Range Avg Min	Range Avg Max
North Atlantic	20,510	20,510	20,510	20,510	20,510	20,510	1	24,960	31,200
Great Lakes & Plains	15,246	15,246	16,650	17,328	17,376	17,376	3		
Southeast	12,480	12,480	13,572	13,572	14,664	14,664	2	10,712	12,480
ALL REGIONS	12,480	14,664	16,267	16,287	17,376	20,510	6	17,836	21,840

State Data

	Min	Q1	Mean	Median	Q3	Max	N	Range Avg Min	Range Avg Max
IA	15,246	15,246	15,246	15,246	15,246	15,246	1		
LA	12,480	12,480	12,480	12,480	12,480	12,480	1	10,712	12,480
MA	20,510	20,510	20,510	20,510	20,510	20,510	1	24,960	31,200
MS	14,664	14,664	14,664	14,664	14,664	14,664	1		
OH	17,328	17,328	17,352	17,352	17,376	17,376	2		

Degree Required Data

	Min	Q1	Mean	Median	Q3	Max	N	Range Avg Min	Range Avg Max
High School	12,480	14,664	16,267	16,287	17,376	20,510	6	17,836	21,840
Associate's									
Bachelor's									
Master's									
Doctoral									

ARCHIVES AND SPECIAL COLLECTIONS CLERK - CONTINUED
Large Public Library
(Serving a population of 100,000 to 499,999)
Regional Data

	Min	Q1	Mean	Median	Q3	Max	N	Range Avg Min	Range Avg Max
North Atlantic	21,370	21,370	21,370	21,370	21,370	21,370	1	21,165	24,537
Great Lakes & Plains	30,493	30,493	30,493	30,493	30,493	30,493	1	20,322	30,493
Southeast	20,654	20,654	24,960	20,654	33,570	33,570	3	20,654	20,654
West & Southwest	21,549	21,549	21,549	21,549	21,549	21,549	1	17,742	30,306
ALL REGIONS	20,654	20,654	24,715	21,459	30,493	33,570	6	20,107	25,329

State Data

	Min	Q1	Mean	Median	Q3	Max	N	Range Avg Min	Range Avg Max
NY	21,370	21,370	21,370	21,370	21,370	21,370	1	21,165	24,537
OH	30,493	30,493	30,493	30,493	30,493	30,493	1	20,322	30,493
TX	21,549	21,549	21,549	21,549	21,549	21,549	1	17,742	30,306
VA	20,654	20,654	24,960	20,654	33,570	33,570	3	20,654	20,654

Degree Required Data

	Min	Q1	Mean	Median	Q3	Max	N	Range Avg Min	Range Avg Max
High School	20,654	20,654	21,057	21,012	21,459	21,549	4	20,054	24,038
Associate's	30,493	30,493	32,031	32,031	33,570	33,570	2	20,322	30,493
Bachelor's	.	.	.	.	.	.		.	.
Master's	.	.	.	.	.	.		.	.
Doctoral	.	.	.	.	.	.		.	.

ARCHIVES AND SPECIAL COLLECTIONS CLERK - CONTINUED
Very Large Public Library
(Serving a population of 500,000 or more)
Regional Data

	Min	Q1	Mean	Median	Q3	Max	N	Range Avg Min	Range Avg Max
Great Lakes & Plains	18,996	22,381	27,201	22,381	29,474	45,079	10	23,743	33,699
Southeast	25,949	29,330	35,772	33,305	39,745	52,999	6	29,070	48,450
West & Southwest	37,336	37,336	37,336	37,336	37,336	37,336	3	30,867	37,336
ALL REGIONS	18,996	22,381	31,508	29,474	37,336	52,999	19	26,743	38,990

State Data

	Min	Q1	Mean	Median	Q3	Max	N	Range Avg Min	Range Avg Max
CA	37,336	37,336	37,336	37,336	37,336	37,336	3	30,867	37,336
FL	25,949	25,949	25,949	25,949	25,949	25,949	1	.	.
MO	18,996	18,996	18,996	18,996	18,996	18,996	1	.	.
OH	22,381	22,381	26,817	22,381	28,777	45,079	8	22,170	33,016
VA	29,330	29,884	37,737	36,726	39,745	52,999	5	29,070	48,450
WI	38,474	38,474	38,474	38,474	38,474	38,474	1	34,757	38,480

Degree Required Data

	Min	Q1	Mean	Median	Q3	Max	N	Range Avg Min	Range Avg Max
High School	18,996	29,330	35,479	36,726	39,745	52,999	9	28,716	44,398
Associate's	.	.	.	.	.	.		.	.
Bachelor's	.	.	.	.	.	.		.	.
Master's	.	.	.	.	.	.		.	.
Doctoral	.	.	.	.	.	.		.	.

ARCHIVES AND SPECIAL COLLECTIONS CLERK - CONTINUED
ALL PUBLIC LIBRARIES
Regional Data

	Min	Q1	Mean	Median	Q3	Max	N	Range Avg Min	Range Avg Max
North Atlantic	20,510	20,510	22,910	21,370	26,849	26,849	3	23,062	27,868
Great Lakes & Plains	15,246	17,576	24,449	22,381	29,474	45,079	18	24,355	33,336
Southeast	12,480	20,654	28,787	29,330	36,726	52,999	11	24,671	37,005
West & Southwest	21,549	29,442	33,389	37,336	37,336	37,336	4	27,586	35,578
ALL REGIONS	12,480	20,582	26,640	22,381	33,425	52,999	36	24,891	34,477

State Data

	Min	Q1	Mean	Median	Q3	Max	N	Range Avg Min	Range Avg Max
CA	37,336	37,336	37,336	37,336	37,336	37,336	3	30,867	37,336
FL	25,949	25,949	25,949	25,949	25,949	25,949	1		
IA	15,246	15,246	17,342	16,120	20,660	20,660	3		
KS	17,576	17,576	17,576	17,576	17,576	17,576	1		
LA	12,480	12,480	12,480	12,480	12,480	12,480	1	10,712	12,480
MA	20,510	20,510	20,510	20,510	20,510	20,510	1	24,960	31,200
MO	18,996	18,996	18,996	18,996	18,996	18,996	1		
MS	14,664	14,664	14,664	14,664	14,664	14,664	1		
NJ	26,849	26,849	26,849	26,849	26,849	26,849	1		
NY	21,370	21,370	21,370	21,370	21,370	21,370	1	21,165	24,537
OH	17,328	22,381	26,084	22,381	29,983	45,079	12	23,199	32,765
TX	21,549	21,549	21,549	21,549	21,549	21,549	1	17,742	30,306
VA	20,654	24,992	32,945	31,727	38,235	52,999	8	26,665	40,508
WI	38,474	38,474	38,474	38,474	38,474	38,474	1	34,757	38,480

Degree Required Data

	Min	Q1	Mean	Median	Q3	Max	N	Range Avg Min	Range Avg Max
High School	12,480	17,476	25,651	21,015	31,582	52,999	24	25,013	34,564
Associate's	30,493	30,493	32,031	32,031	33,570	33,570	2	20,322	30,493
Bachelor's									
Master's									
Doctoral									

CHILDREN'S SERVICES/YOUNG ADULT SERVICES CLERK

Performs routine duties requiring the use of a variety of forms, reports or procedures. Provides basic patron assistance: sets up computer stations, locates materials, provides information. Maintains departmental or area records. Performs miscellaneous clerical duties such as filing, typing, sorting or photocopying. Provides services intended for children and youths through twelfth grade; develops collection, provides homework and reader's advisory services, and develops age appropriate programs.

Very Small Public Library
(Serving a population of less than 10,000)
Regional Data

	Min	Q1	Mean	Median	Q3	Max	N	Range Avg Min	Range Avg Max
North Atlantic	16,640	20,800	24,086	25,979	27,435	27,685	6	24,634	26,991
Great Lakes & Plains	11,794	13,000	16,614	16,640	20,146	21,549	8	15,260	22,783
West & Southwest	16,224	16,224	20,623	20,623	25,022	25,022	2	20,082	24,253
ALL REGIONS	11,794	16,432	19,917	20,146	24,835	27,685	16	19,981	24,729

State Data

	Min	Q1	Mean	Median	Q3	Max	N	Range Avg Min	Range Avg Max
CO	16,224	16,224	20,623	20,623	25,022	25,022	2	20,082	24,253
CT	16,640	16,640	20,644	20,644	24,648	24,648	2	24,648	24,648
IA	12,480	14,560	17,353	18,222	20,146	20,489	4	.	.
IN	13,520	13,520	13,520	13,520	13,520	13,520	1	13,520	18,720
KS	11,794	11,794	11,794	11,794	11,794	11,794	1	10,712	11,794
MA	27,310	27,310	27,373	27,373	27,435	27,435	2	24,627	28,163
MN	21,549	21,549	21,549	21,549	21,549	21,549	1	21,549	37,835
NJ	20,800	20,800	24,242	24,242	27,685	27,685	2	.	.
WI	16,640	16,640	16,640	16,640	16,640	16,640	1	.	.

Degree Required Data

	Min	Q1	Mean	Median	Q3	Max	N	Range Avg Min	Range Avg Max
High School	11,794	16,640	20,173	20,489	24,648	27,685	13	18,934	24,360
Associate's	.	.	.	.	.	.	.	.	.
Bachelor's	27,310	27,310	27,310	27,310	27,310	27,310	1	27,310	27,310
Master's	.	.	.	.	.	.	.	.	.
Doctoral	.	.	.	.	.	.	.	.	.

CHILDREN'S SERVICES/YOUNG ADULT SERVICES CLERK - CONTINUED
Small Public Library
(Serving a population of 10,000 to 25,000)
Regional Data

	Min	Q1	Mean	Median	Q3	Max	N	Range Avg Min	Range Avg Max
North Atlantic	13,432	22,443	26,426	27,040	30,417	41,749	16	23,005	29,099
Great Lakes & Plains	14,580	16,120	18,778	17,680	21,029	24,960	22	15,615	21,662
Southeast	14,311	14,311	14,311	14,311	14,311	14,311	1	.	.
West & Southwest	18,354	24,294	30,075	26,070	31,200	59,120	8	22,609	33,615
ALL REGIONS	13,432	17,160	23,210	21,112	27,040	59,120	47	20,178	27,547

State Data

	Min	Q1	Mean	Median	Q3	Max	N	Range Avg Min	Range Avg Max
AL	14,311	14,311	14,311	14,311	14,311	14,311	1		
IA	16,120	16,120	16,120	16,120	16,120	16,120	1		
IL	14,580	16,640	18,353	17,680	20,800	24,960	11	15,947	22,187
IN	19,094	20,062	21,580	21,715	23,098	23,795	4	17,160	23,920
KS	16,074	16,074	16,074	16,074	16,074	16,074	1	12,480	18,720
MA	29,995	29,995	33,565	33,030	37,670	37,670	3		
MN	15,912	15,912	15,912	15,912	15,912	15,912	2	15,912	21,216
NJ	13,432	21,091	23,926	26,582	27,685	30,839	5	21,091	27,685
NM	18,354	24,939	26,547	27,040	29,120	33,280	5	22,609	33,615
NY	23,795	24,627	28,549	27,040	27,040	41,749	6	27,040	33,280
OH	18,180	18,180	20,301	18,512	24,211	24,211	3		
PA	14,560	14,560	15,600	15,600	16,640	16,640	2	16,640	20,800
TX	23,648	23,648	35,956	25,100	59,120	59,120	3		

Degree Required Data

	Min	Q1	Mean	Median	Q3	Max	N	Range Avg Min	Range Avg Max
High School	13,432	16,640	21,952	21,029	25,100	41,749	41	20,227	27,240
Associate's	17,160	17,160	17,160	17,160	17,160	17,160	1	16,640	24,960
Bachelor's	30,839	30,839	31,935	31,935	33,030	33,030	2		
Master's									
Doctoral									

CHILDREN'S SERVICES/YOUNG ADULT SERVICES CLERK - CONTINUED
Medium Public Library
(Serving a population of 25,000 to 99,999)
Regional Data

	Min	Q1	Mean	Median	Q3	Max	N	Range Avg Min	Range Avg Max
North Atlantic	15,538	17,369	23,559	20,129	29,390	35,173	21	22,845	29,848
Great Lakes & Plains	11,586	16,952	20,517	19,698	21,902	47,528	50	18,605	27,320
Southeast	16,894	18,311	19,992	20,701	21,674	21,674	4		
West & Southwest	12,480	19,812	27,751	32,338	34,870	35,487	8	19,765	24,118
ALL REGIONS	11,586	17,243	21,958	20,010	26,291	47,528	83	19,781	27,632

State Data

	Min	Q1	Mean	Median	Q3	Max	N	Range Avg Min	Range Avg Max
AR	21,674	21,674	21,674	21,674	21,674	21,674	2	.	.
CA	26,624	26,624	31,122	32,484	34,258	34,258	3	28,090	34,195
CO	32,192	32,192	34,387	35,482	35,487	35,487	3	.	.
CT	28,954	28,954	30,794	29,526	32,635	35,173	4	29,047	33,103
IA	12,792	12,792	15,791	13,166	13,166	27,040	5	24,960	27,040
IL	13,936	16,640	21,441	19,812	23,920	47,528	22	20,206	30,370
IN	19,094	19,094	21,452	22,630	22,630	22,630	3	.	.
KS	11,586	11,586	11,586	11,586	11,586	11,586	1	11,586	16,120
MA	34,802	34,802	34,802	34,802	34,802	34,802	1	.	.
MN	40,968	40,968	40,968	40,968	40,968	40,968	1	.	.
NC	19,728	19,728	19,728	19,728	19,728	19,728	1	.	.
NJ	29,682	29,682	31,332	31,332	32,982	32,982	2	.	.
NY	16,307	16,307	20,808	18,686	25,469	29,390	6	17,332	27,877
OH	16,248	17,918	19,578	19,542	20,613	24,736	16	17,301	25,622
PA	15,538	16,640	17,565	17,680	18,889	19,157	7	16,640	21,341
RI	26,291	26,291	26,291	26,291	26,291	26,291	1	26,291	33,218
TX	12,480	12,480	12,740	12,740	13,000	13,000	2	11,440	14,040
VA	16,894	16,894	16,894	16,894	16,894	16,894	1	.	.
WI	20,010	20,010	22,506	22,506	25,002	25,002	2	.	.

Degree Required Data

	Min	Q1	Mean	Median	Q3	Max	N	Range Avg Min	Range Avg Max
High School	11,586	17,555	21,872	20,176	25,002	40,968	63	19,330	26,445
Associate's	16,640	17,680	23,415	19,424	24,471	47,528	8	20,854	32,623
Bachelor's	16,894	16,894	21,967	21,967	27,040	27,040	2	22,880	27,040
Master's	.	.	.	.	.	.		.	.
Doctoral	.	.	.	.	.	.		.	.

CHILDREN'S SERVICES/YOUNG ADULT SERVICES CLERK - CONTINUED
Large Public Library
(Serving a population of 100,000 to 499,999)
Regional Data

	Min	Q1	Mean	Median	Q3	Max	N	Range Avg Min	Range Avg Max
North Atlantic	14,560	18,720	24,328	23,326	27,501	47,086	12	17,761	27,113
Great Lakes & Plains	15,600	23,129	25,796	24,981	28,517	37,572	13	19,523	29,740
Southeast	16,889	20,363	25,265	24,816	28,184	46,510	22	21,597	28,323
West & Southwest	13,520	18,075	25,032	24,894	30,580	38,700	23	26,743	35,895
ALL REGIONS	13,520	19,656	25,127	24,937	28,517	47,086	70	21,268	30,145

State Data

	Min	Q1	Mean	Median	Q3	Max	N	Range Avg Min	Range Avg Max
CA	28,995	30,597	33,457	33,800	35,194	38,700	5	29,552	36,676
FL	16,889	16,889	19,333	18,658	21,694	23,213	6	21,050	30,534
IL	21,668	24,024	28,191	28,517	29,625	37,572	7	21,847	27,803
MI	24,981	24,981	24,981	24,981	24,981	24,981	2	19,802	24,981
MN	15,600	15,600	15,600	15,600	15,600	15,600	1		
NC	20,363	20,467	21,751	21,087	23,036	24,468	4	19,968	31,699
NE	21,640	21,640	21,640	21,640	21,640	21,640	1	12,272	40,310
NJ	26,770	26,770	26,770	26,770	26,770	26,770	1		
NM	13,520	13,520	20,810	20,810	28,100	28,100	2		
NY	21,895	24,625	30,263	28,233	29,474	47,086	5	21,763	25,229
OH	27,685	27,685	27,685	27,685	27,685	27,685	1		
PA	14,560	14,560	18,977	18,720	22,027	25,272	6	14,560	28,621
SC	19,490	19,490	23,837	23,837	28,184	28,184	2	19,115	28,683
TX	16,266	16,765	20,518	18,772	23,639	30,580	12	17,742	30,306
VA	25,163	25,168	30,515	27,704	35,771	46,510	10	25,168	25,168
WA	26,270	26,609	30,154	28,608	33,698	37,128	4	25,626	37,128
WI	23,129	23,129	23,129	23,129	23,129	23,129	1		

Degree Required Data

	Min	Q1	Mean	Median	Q3	Max	N	Range Avg Min	Range Avg Max
High School	13,520	20,363	25,044	25,166	28,995	38,700	58	21,325	30,344
Associate's	21,351	21,351	30,776	24,468	46,510	46,510	3		
Bachelor's	24,981	24,981	25,126	25,126	25,272	25,272	2	19,802	24,981
Master's	.	.	.	.	.	.			
Doctoral	.	.	.	.	.	.			

CHILDREN'S SERVICES/YOUNG ADULT SERVICES CLERK - CONTINUED
Very Large Public Library
(Serving a population of 500,000 or more)
Regional Data

	Min	Q1	Mean	Median	Q3	Max	N	Range Avg Min	Range Avg Max
North Atlantic	25,967	27,314	28,908	28,626	30,469	34,143	11		
Great Lakes & Plains	14,607	22,838	25,443	24,309	26,166	45,079	30	22,381	33,509
Southeast	22,880	22,880	25,454	24,960	27,040	30,618	13	22,880	31,200
West & Southwest	30,784	30,867	35,235	33,654	33,654	47,216	5	30,451	37,132
ALL REGIONS	14,607	23,010	26,922	26,140	29,801	47,216	59	24,767	33,247

State Data

	Min	Q1	Mean	Median	Q3	Max	N	Range Avg Min	Range Avg Max
CA	30,867	30,867	39,042	39,042	47,216	47,216	2	35,069	42,349
FL	26,770	26,770	29,182	30,160	30,618	30,618	3		
GA	22,880	22,880	24,336	22,880	27,040	27,040	10	22,880	31,200
IN	14,607	23,431	24,333	24,309	25,174	35,367	22		
NJ	25,967	27,314	28,908	28,626	30,469	34,143	11		
OH	22,381	22,381	28,496	24,758	33,114	45,079	8	22,381	33,509
OR	30,784	30,784	32,698	33,654	33,654	33,654	3	27,373	33,654

Degree Required Data

	Min	Q1	Mean	Median	Q3	Max	N	Range Avg Min	Range Avg Max
High School	14,607	23,010	26,246	24,545	27,040	45,079	42	23,917	31,766
Associate's	.	.	.	.	.	.		.	.
Bachelor's	.	.	.	.	.	.		.	.
Master's	.	.	.	.	.	.		.	.
Doctoral	.	.	.	.	.	.		.	.

CHILDREN'S SERVICES/YOUNG ADULT SERVICES CLERK - CONTINUED
ALL PUBLIC LIBRARIES
Regional Data

	Min	Q1	Mean	Median	Q3	Max	N	Range Avg Min	Range Avg Max
North Atlantic	13,432	18,889	25,333	26,676	29,446	47,086	66	21,491	28,523
Great Lakes & Plains	11,586	17,555	21,712	21,382	24,447	47,528	123	18,354	26,956
Southeast	14,311	21,087	24,525	23,046	27,040	46,510	40	22,399	30,121
West & Southwest	12,480	18,990	27,299	26,994	33,280	59,120	46	24,858	32,608
ALL REGIONS	11,586	18,512	23,925	23,431	27,685	59,120	275	21,056	28,957

State Data

	Min	Q1	Mean	Median	Q3	Max	N	Range Avg Min	Range Avg Max
AL	14,311	14,311	14,311	14,311	14,311	14,311	1	.	.
AR	21,674	21,674	21,674	21,674	21,674	21,674	2	.	.
CA	26,624	30,597	33,873	33,142	35,194	47,216	10	30,566	37,474
CO	16,224	25,022	28,881	32,192	35,482	35,487	5	20,082	24,253
CT	16,640	24,648	27,411	28,954	30,098	35,173	6	28,167	31,412
FL	16,889	17,659	22,616	21,694	26,770	30,618	9	21,050	30,534
GA	22,880	22,880	24,336	22,880	27,040	27,040	10	22,880	31,200
IA	12,480	12,792	16,449	14,643	19,803	27,040	10	24,960	27,040
IL	13,936	17,243	21,773	20,259	24,502	47,528	40	19,744	28,473
IN	13,520	22,630	23,318	23,816	24,451	35,367	30	15,340	21,320
KS	11,586	11,586	13,151	11,794	16,074	16,074	3	11,593	15,545
MA	27,310	27,435	31,707	31,513	34,802	37,670	6	24,627	28,163
MI	24,981	24,981	24,981	24,981	24,981	24,981	2	19,802	24,981
MN	15,600	15,912	21,988	15,912	21,549	40,968	5	17,791	26,756
NC	19,728	20,363	21,347	20,571	21,603	24,468	5	19,968	31,699
NE	21,640	21,640	21,640	21,640	21,640	21,640	1	12,272	40,310
NJ	13,432	26,582	27,407	27,685	29,682	34,143	21	21,091	27,685
NM	13,520	18,354	24,908	27,040	29,120	33,280	7	22,609	33,615
NY	16,307	21,895	26,321	25,469	28,233	47,086	17	21,591	28,388
OH	16,248	18,439	22,493	20,613	23,525	45,079	28	18,496	27,478
OR	30,784	30,784	32,698	33,654	33,654	33,654	3	27,373	33,654
PA	14,560	15,538	17,867	17,680	18,889	25,272	15	15,154	26,464
RI	26,291	26,291	26,291	26,291	26,291	26,291	1	26,291	33,218
SC	19,490	19,490	23,837	23,837	28,184	28,184	2	19,115	28,683
TX	12,480	16,702	22,328	18,990	23,754	59,120	17	13,541	19,462
VA	16,894	25,168	29,277	26,993	35,771	46,510	11	25,168	25,168
WA	26,270	26,609	30,154	28,608	33,698	37,128	4	25,626	37,128
WI	16,640	18,325	21,195	21,570	24,066	25,002	4	.	.

Degree Required Data

	Min	Q1	Mean	Median	Q3	Max	N	Range Avg Min	Range Avg Max
High School	11,586	18,720	23,480	23,010	27,040	45,079	217	20,635	28,229
Associate's	16,640	17,680	24,734	20,740	25,754	47,528	12	20,152	31,346
Bachelor's	16,894	24,981	26,481	27,040	30,839	33,030	7	23,331	26,444
Master's	.	.	.	.	.	.		.	.
Doctoral	.	.	.	.	.	.		.	.

GOVERNMENT DOCUMENTS CLERK

Performs routine duties requiring the use of a variety of forms, reports or procedures. Provides basic patron assistance: sets up computer stations, locates materials, provides information. Maintains departmental or area records. Performs miscellaneous clerical duties such as filing, typing, sorting or photocopying. Provides access to publications of the U.S. federal government such as transcripts of hearings and text of bills, resolutions, statutes, reports, charters, treaties, periodicals and statistics.

Medium Public Library
(Serving a population of 25,000 to 99,999)
Regional Data

	Min	Q1	Mean	Median	Q3	Max	N	Range Avg Min	Range Avg Max
North Atlantic	17,056	17,056	23,370	23,370	29,683	29,683	2	14,560	20,800
ALL REGIONS	17,056	17,056	23,370	23,370	29,683	29,683	2	14,560	20,800

State Data

	Min	Q1	Mean	Median	Q3	Max	N	Range Avg Min	Range Avg Max
NJ	17,056	17,056	23,370	23,370	29,683	29,683	2	14,560	20,800

Degree Required Data

	Min	Q1	Mean	Median	Q3	Max	N	Range Avg Min	Range Avg Max
High School	17,056	17,056	23,370	23,370	29,683	29,683	2	14,560	20,800
Associate's	.	.	.	.	.	.	.	.	.
Bachelor's	.	.	.	.	.	.	.	.	.
Master's	.	.	.	.	.	.	.	.	.
Doctoral	.	.	.	.	.	.	.	.	.

GOVERNMENT DOCUMENTS CLERK - CONTINUED
Large Public Library
(Serving a population of 100,000 to 499,999)
Regional Data

	Min	Q1	Mean	Median	Q3	Max	N	Range Avg Min	Range Avg Max
North Atlantic	26,513	26,513	29,541	30,576	31,533	31,533	3	24,461	30,576
Great Lakes & Plains	39,399	39,399	39,399	39,399	39,399	39,399	1	.	.
ALL REGIONS	26,513	28,545	32,005	31,054	35,466	39,399	4	24,461	30,576

State Data

	Min	Q1	Mean	Median	Q3	Max	N	Range Avg Min	Range Avg Max
MA	31,533	31,533	31,533	31,533	31,533	31,533	1	.	.
MD	26,513	26,513	26,513	26,513	26,513	26,513	1	.	.
PA	30,576	30,576	30,576	30,576	30,576	30,576	1	24,461	30,576
WI	39,399	39,399	39,399	39,399	39,399	39,399	1	.	.

Degree Required Data

	Min	Q1	Mean	Median	Q3	Max	N	Range Avg Min	Range Avg Max
High School	26,513	28,545	32,005	31,054	35,466	39,399	4	24,461	30,576
Associate's	.	.	.	.	.	.	.	.	.
Bachelor's	.	.	.	.	.	.	.	.	.
Master's	.	.	.	.	.	.	.	.	.
Doctoral	.	.	.	.	.	.	.	.	.

GOVERNMENT DOCUMENTS CLERK - CONTINUED
Very Large Public Library
(Serving a population of 500,000 or more)
Regional Data

	Min	Q1	Mean	Median	Q3	Max	N	Range Avg Min	Range Avg Max
Great Lakes & Plains	31,637	31,637	31,980	31,980	32,323	32,323	2	22,402	33,613
Southeast	19,995	19,995	19,995	19,995	19,995	19,995	1		
West & Southwest	20,080	20,080	29,582	33,654	35,012	35,012	3	27,373	33,654
ALL REGIONS	19,995	20,080	28,784	31,980	33,654	35,012	6	24,887	33,634

State Data

	Min	Q1	Mean	Median	Q3	Max	N	Range Avg Min	Range Avg Max
CO	35,012	35,012	35,012	35,012	35,012	35,012	1	.	.
FL	19,995	19,995	19,995	19,995	19,995	19,995	1	.	.
MO	31,637	31,637	31,637	31,637	31,637	31,637	1	22,402	33,613
OH	32,323	32,323	32,323	32,323	32,323	32,323	1	.	.
OR	33,654	33,654	33,654	33,654	33,654	33,654	1	27,373	33,654
TX	20,080	20,080	20,080	20,080	20,080	20,080	1	.	.

Degree Required Data

	Min	Q1	Mean	Median	Q3	Max	N	Range Avg Min	Range Avg Max
High School	20,080	26,201	30,267	32,989	34,333	35,012	4	27,373	33,654
Associate's	31,637	31,637	31,637	31,637	31,637	31,637	1	22,402	33,613
Bachelor's	.	.	.	.	.	.	.	.	.
Master's	.	.	.	.	.	.	.	.	.
Doctoral	.	.	.	.	.	.	.	.	.

GOVERNMENT DOCUMENTS CLERK - CONTINUED
ALL PUBLIC LIBRARIES
Regional Data

	Min	Q1	Mean	Median	Q3	Max	N	Range Avg Min	Range Avg Max
North Atlantic	17,056	26,513	27,072	29,683	30,576	31,533	5	19,510	25,688
Great Lakes & Plains	31,637	31,637	34,453	32,323	39,399	39,399	3	22,402	33,613
Southeast	19,995	19,995	19,995	19,995	19,995	19,995	1		
West & Southwest	20,080	20,080	29,582	33,654	35,012	35,012	3	27,373	33,654
ALL REGIONS	17,056	23,297	28,955	31,054	32,989	39,399	12	22,199	29,661

State Data

	Min	Q1	Mean	Median	Q3	Max	N	Range Avg Min	Range Avg Max
CO	35,012	35,012	35,012	35,012	35,012	35,012	1		
FL	19,995	19,995	19,995	19,995	19,995	19,995	1		
MA	31,533	31,533	31,533	31,533	31,533	31,533	1		
MD	26,513	26,513	26,513	26,513	26,513	26,513	1		
MO	31,637	31,637	31,637	31,637	31,637	31,637	1	22,402	33,613
NJ	17,056	17,056	23,370	23,370	29,683	29,683	2	14,560	20,800
OH	32,323	32,323	32,323	32,323	32,323	32,323	1		
OR	33,654	33,654	33,654	33,654	33,654	33,654	1	27,373	33,654
PA	30,576	30,576	30,576	30,576	30,576	30,576	1	24,461	30,576
TX	20,080	20,080	20,080	20,080	20,080	20,080	1		
WI	39,399	39,399	39,399	39,399	39,399	39,399	1		

Degree Required Data

	Min	Q1	Mean	Median	Q3	Max	N	Range Avg Min	Range Avg Max
High School	17,056	26,513	29,583	31,054	33,654	39,399	10	22,131	28,343
Associate's	31,637	31,637	31,637	31,637	31,637	31,637	1	22,402	33,613
Bachelor's									
Master's									
Doctoral									

INSTRUCTIONAL SERVICES/LITERACY CLERK

Performs routine duties requiring the use of a variety of forms, reports or procedures. Provides basic patron assistance: sets up computer stations, locates materials, provides information. Maintains departmental or area records. Performs miscellaneous clerical duties such as filing, typing, sorting or photocopying. Advances learning, teaching and research with respect to information literacy in higher education; assists patrons to develop the ability to read and write.

Medium Public Library
(Serving a population of 25,000 to 99,999)
Regional Data

	Min	Q1	Mean	Median	Q3	Max	N	Range Avg Min	Range Avg Max
North Atlantic	26,125	26,125	26,125	26,125	26,125	26,125	1	16,973	30,742
West & Southwest	15,891	26,291	33,864	36,566	42,328	42,328	15	30,751	37,602
ALL REGIONS	15,891	26,291	33,381	35,693	42,328	42,328	16	29,833	37,145

State Data

	Min	Q1	Mean	Median	Q3	Max	N	Range Avg Min	Range Avg Max
CA	15,891	26,291	33,864	36,566	42,328	42,328	15	30,751	37,602
NY	26,125	26,125	26,125	26,125	26,125	26,125	1	16,973	30,742

Degree Required Data

	Min	Q1	Mean	Median	Q3	Max	N	Range Avg Min	Range Avg Max
High School	15,891	26,291	34,393	36,566	42,328	42,328	14	30,570	38,178
Associate's	.	.	.	.	.	.	.	.	.
Bachelor's	.	.	.	.	.	.	.	.	.
Master's	.	.	.	.	.	.	.	.	.
Doctoral	.	.	.	.	.	.	.	.	.

INSTRUCTIONAL SERVICES/LITERACY CLERK - CONTINUED
Large Public Library
(Serving a population of 100,000 to 499,999)
Regional Data

	Min	Q1	Mean	Median	Q3	Max	N	Range Avg Min	Range Avg Max
Southeast	25,163	25,438	26,506	26,619	27,573	27,621	4	.	.
West & Southwest	24,877	24,877	31,468	34,104	35,922	37,560	5	23,310	28,558
ALL REGIONS	24,877	25,163	29,262	27,525	34,104	37,560	9	23,310	28,558

State Data

	Min	Q1	Mean	Median	Q3	Max	N	Range Avg Min	Range Avg Max
CA	24,877	24,877	31,468	34,104	35,922	37,560	5	23,310	28,558
VA	25,163	25,438	26,506	26,619	27,573	27,621	4	.	.

Degree Required Data

	Min	Q1	Mean	Median	Q3	Max	N	Range Avg Min	Range Avg Max
High School	24,877	25,163	29,262	27,525	34,104	37,560	9	23,310	28,558
Associate's	.	.	.	.	.	.	.	.	.
Bachelor's	.	.	.	.	.	.	.	.	.
Master's	.	.	.	.	.	.	.	.	.
Doctoral	.	.	.	.	.	.	.	.	.

INSTRUCTIONAL SERVICES/LITERACY CLERK - CONTINUED
Very Large Public Library
(Serving a population of 500,000 or more)
Regional Data

	Min	Q1	Mean	Median	Q3	Max	N	Range Avg Min	Range Avg Max
West & Southwest	31,737	36,945	43,989	39,984	55,640	55,640	5	45,786	55,640
ALL REGIONS	31,737	36,945	43,989	39,984	55,640	55,640	5	45,786	55,640

State Data

	Min	Q1	Mean	Median	Q3	Max	N	Range Avg Min	Range Avg Max
CA	31,737	36,945	43,989	39,984	55,640	55,640	5	45,786	55,640

Degree Required Data

	Min	Q1	Mean	Median	Q3	Max	N	Range Avg Min	Range Avg Max
High School	31,737	31,737	36,222	36,945	39,984	39,984	3	.	.
Associate's	.	.	.	.	.	.		.	.
Bachelor's	55,640	55,640	55,640	55,640	55,640	55,640	2	45,786	55,640
Master's	.	.	.	.	.	.		.	.
Doctoral	.	.	.	.	.	.		.	.

INSTRUCTIONAL SERVICES/LITERACY CLERK - CONTINUED
ALL PUBLIC LIBRARIES
Regional Data

	Min	Q1	Mean	Median	Q3	Max	N	Range Avg Min	Range Avg Max
North Atlantic	26,125	26,125	26,125	26,125	26,125	26,125	1	16,973	30,742
Southeast	25,163	25,438	26,506	26,619	27,573	27,621	4	.	.
West & Southwest	15,891	26,291	35,410	36,566	42,328	55,640	25	31,159	38,073
ALL REGIONS	15,891	26,291	33,913	34,462	39,984	55,640	30	30,450	37,706

State Data

	Min	Q1	Mean	Median	Q3	Max	N	Range Avg Min	Range Avg Max
CA	15,891	26,291	35,410	36,566	42,328	55,640	25	31,159	38,073
NY	26,125	26,125	26,125	26,125	26,125	26,125	1	16,973	30,742
VA	25,163	25,438	26,506	26,619	27,573	27,621	4	.	.

Degree Required Data

	Min	Q1	Mean	Median	Q3	Max	N	Range Avg Min	Range Avg Max
High School	15,891	26,125	32,828	34,462	38,397	42,328	26	29,208	36,374
Associate's	.	.	.	.	.	.		.	.
Bachelor's	55,640	55,640	55,640	55,640	55,640	55,640	2	45,786	55,640
Master's	.	.	.	.	.	.		.	.
Doctoral	.	.	.	.	.	.		.	.

REFERENCE/INFORMATION SERVICES CLERK

Performs routine duties requiring the use of a variety of forms, reports or procedures. Provides basic patron assistance: sets up computer stations, locates materials, provides information. Maintains departmental or area records. Performs miscellaneous clerical duties such as filing, typing, sorting or photocopying.Assists patrons with questions; instructs in the selection and use of appropriate tools and techniques for finding information; conducts searches for materials; contributes to reference collection development.

Very Small Public Library
(Serving a population of less than 10,000)
Regional Data

	Min	Q1	Mean	Median	Q3	Max	N	Range Avg Min	Range Avg Max
North Atlantic	29,578	29,578	32,905	32,905	36,233	36,233	2	28,725	37,461
Great Lakes & Plains	14,560	14,560	20,103	17,680	28,069	28,069	3		
West & Southwest	25,022	25,022	25,917	25,376	27,352	27,352	3	23,941	32,282
ALL REGIONS	14,560	21,351	25,484	26,364	28,824	36,233	8	25,137	33,576

State Data

	Min	Q1	Mean	Median	Q3	Max	N	Range Avg Min	Range Avg Max
CO	25,022	25,022	25,917	25,376	27,352	27,352	3	23,941	32,282
IN	14,560	14,560	14,560	14,560	14,560	14,560	1		
MA	29,578	29,578	29,578	29,578	29,578	29,578	1	28,725	37,461
MI	17,680	17,680	17,680	17,680	17,680	17,680	1		
PA	36,233	36,233	36,233	36,233	36,233	36,233	1		
WI	28,069	28,069	28,069	28,069	28,069	28,069	1		

Degree Required Data

	Min	Q1	Mean	Median	Q3	Max	N	Range Avg Min	Range Avg Max
High School	14,560	25,022	24,076	25,376	27,352	28,069	5	23,941	32,282
Associate's									
Bachelor's	29,578	29,578	32,905	32,905	36,233	36,233	2	28,725	37,461
Master's									
Doctoral									

REFERENCE/INFORMATION SERVICES CLERK - CONTINUED
Small Public Library
(Serving a population of 10,000 to 25,000)
Regional Data

	Min	Q1	Mean	Median	Q3	Max	N	Range Avg Min	Range Avg Max
North Atlantic	18,720	18,720	18,720	18,720	18,720	18,720	1	16,640	24,960
Great Lakes & Plains	14,560	16,120	17,476	16,952	18,200	22,576	7	14,820	21,320
West & Southwest	18,870	20,800	31,572	35,360	39,520	39,520	6	24,308	33,748
ALL REGIONS	14,560	16,952	23,606	18,795	33,280	39,520	14	21,348	30,010

State Data

	Min	Q1	Mean	Median	Q3	Max	N	Range Avg Min	Range Avg Max
CO	20,800	20,800	20,800	20,800	20,800	20,800	1	20,800	20,800
IA	16,120	16,120	16,120	16,120	16,120	16,120	1	.	.
IL	14,560	14,560	14,560	14,560	14,560	14,560	1	.	.
IN	17,285	17,285	17,742	17,742	18,200	18,200	2	17,160	23,920
KS	16,640	16,640	18,723	16,952	22,576	22,576	3	12,480	18,720
NM	18,870	33,280	33,726	37,440	39,520	39,520	5	25,010	36,338
PA	18,720	18,720	18,720	18,720	18,720	18,720	1	16,640	24,960

Degree Required Data

	Min	Q1	Mean	Median	Q3	Max	N	Range Avg Min	Range Avg Max
High School	14,560	16,796	23,926	18,460	35,360	39,520	12	21,416	31,161
Associate's	22,576	22,576	22,576	22,576	22,576	22,576	1	.	.
Bachelor's	20,800	20,800	20,800	20,800	20,800	20,800	1	20,800	20,800
Master's	.	.	.	.	.	.	.	.	.
Doctoral	.	.	.	.	.	.	.	.	.

REFERENCE/INFORMATION SERVICES CLERK - CONTINUED
Medium Public Library
(Serving a population of 25,000 to 99,999)
Regional Data

	Min	Q1	Mean	Median	Q3	Max	N	Range Avg Min	Range Avg Max
North Atlantic	15,579	17,139	23,833	18,200	27,934	41,504	9	20,368	29,684
Great Lakes & Plains	26,853	30,572	31,491	31,200	33,067	35,764	5	27,040	31,200
Southeast	19,110	19,110	19,110	19,110	19,110	19,110	1	.	.
West & Southwest	11,440	11,960	14,547	14,560	17,108	17,680	8	13,173	17,680
ALL REGIONS	11,440	16,474	22,063	17,680	30,572	41,504	23	17,935	24,984

State Data

	Min	Q1	Mean	Median	Q3	Max	N	Range Avg Min	Range Avg Max
CT	16,474	16,474	16,994	16,994	17,514	17,514	2	15,392	17,472
IA	31,200	31,200	31,200	31,200	31,200	31,200	1	27,040	31,200
ID	16,640	16,640	16,640	16,640	16,640	16,640	2	16,640	24,960
IL	26,853	28,712	31,564	31,819	34,415	35,764	4	.	.
MA	41,504	41,504	41,504	41,504	41,504	41,504	1	37,565	43,222
ME	33,862	33,862	33,862	33,862	33,862	33,862	1	23,754	33,862
NY	15,579	15,579	20,218	17,139	27,934	27,934	3	14,851	30,742
PA	18,200	18,200	18,200	18,200	18,200	18,200	1	.	.
RI	26,291	26,291	26,291	26,291	26,291	26,291	1	26,291	33,218
TN	19,110	19,110	19,110	19,110	19,110	19,110	1	.	.
TX	11,440	11,440	11,960	11,960	12,480	12,480	4	11,440	14,040
WY	17,576	17,576	17,628	17,628	17,680	17,680	2	.	.

Degree Required Data

	Min	Q1	Mean	Median	Q3	Max	N	Range Avg Min	Range Avg Max
High School	11,440	15,579	18,655	17,139	19,110	33,862	17	15,725	23,102
Associate's	18,200	18,200	18,200	18,200	18,200	18,200	1		
Bachelor's	31,200	31,200	36,352	36,352	41,504	41,504	2	32,302	37,211
Master's									
Doctoral									

REFERENCE/INFORMATION SERVICES CLERK - CONTINUED
Large Public Library
(Serving a population of 100,000 to 499,999)
Regional Data

	Min	Q1	Mean	Median	Q3	Max	N	Range Avg Min	Range Avg Max
North Atlantic	23,015	25,293	30,473	27,227	32,198	48,230	7	29,030	35,804
Great Lakes & Plains	18,200	22,069	24,615	23,546	27,955	34,778	10	20,459	32,897
Southeast	10,712	18,470	22,642	22,170	26,295	36,487	23	21,416	26,015
West & Southwest	12,480	18,616	25,278	24,378	30,597	41,424	13	21,671	30,345
ALL REGIONS	10,712	20,488	24,695	24,378	27,955	48,230	53	21,895	30,166

State Data

	Min	Q1	Mean	Median	Q3	Max	N	Range Avg Min	Range Avg Max
CA	30,597	30,597	32,344	32,344	34,092	34,092	2	28,995	35,922
KS	21,632	22,069	25,189	23,421	28,330	34,778	7	21,632	36,067
MS	10,712	10,712	11,995	10,712	14,560	14,560	3		
NC	24,480	24,480	24,480	24,480	24,480	24,480	1		
NJ	23,015	23,015	24,893	24,893	26,770	26,770	2		
NM	16,640	16,900	20,582	18,824	24,263	28,038	4	16,640	22,776
NY	27,227	27,227	37,728	37,728	48,230	48,230	2	25,938	43,014
OH	18,200	18,200	23,275	23,670	27,955	27,955	3	17,722	25,501
OR	41,424	41,424	41,424	41,424	41,424	41,424	1		
PA	25,293	25,293	29,356	30,576	32,198	32,198	3	30,576	32,198
SC	19,594	19,594	20,738	21,237	21,382	21,382	3	19,115	28,683
TN	17,347	17,846	19,940	18,470	22,170	24,580	7	17,243	22,714
TX	12,480	12,480	15,548	15,548	18,616	18,616	2	15,111	21,393
VA	25,168	25,168	28,724	26,553	33,356	36,487	9	27,316	27,316
WA	24,378	24,378	27,269	24,690	30,160	35,318	4	24,378	35,318

Degree Required Data

	Min	Q1	Mean	Median	Q3	Max	N	Range Avg Min	Range Avg Max
High School	10,712	19,594	24,239	24,378	28,038	41,424	45	22,197	30,207
Associate's	24,480	24,480	24,480	24,480	24,480	24,480	1		
Bachelor's	25,293	25,293	25,293	25,293	25,293	25,293	1		
Master's									
Doctoral									

REFERENCE/INFORMATION SERVICES CLERK - CONTINUED
Very Large Public Library
(Serving a population of 500,000 or more)
Regional Data

	Min	Q1	Mean	Median	Q3	Max	N	Range Avg Min	Range Avg Max
North Atlantic	32,274	32,274	33,284	33,789	33,789	33,789	3	.	.
Great Lakes & Plains	19,677	22,381	26,676	22,381	26,624	48,881	145	22,381	33,509
Southeast	22,970	26,333	27,787	27,914	28,985	32,594	28	19,032	34,195
West & Southwest	30,784	30,784	32,365	32,656	33,654	33,654	3	27,373	33,654
ALL REGIONS	19,677	22,381	27,056	22,838	29,016	48,881	179	22,367	33,540

State Data

	Min	Q1	Mean	Median	Q3	Max	N	Range Avg Min	Range Avg Max
FL	22,970	26,333	27,787	27,914	28,985	32,594	28	19,032	34,195
NJ	32,274	32,274	33,284	33,789	33,789	33,789	3	.	.
OH	19,677	22,381	26,676	22,381	26,624	48,881	145	22,381	33,509
OR	30,784	30,784	32,365	32,656	33,654	33,654	3	27,373	33,654

Degree Required Data

	Min	Q1	Mean	Median	Q3	Max	N	Range Avg Min	Range Avg Max
High School	25,438	28,184	35,762	32,656	45,079	48,881	53	27,373	33,654
Associate's	.	.	.	.	.	.	.	.	.
Bachelor's	.	.	.	.	.	.	.	.	.
Master's	.	.	.	.	.	.	.	.	.
Doctoral	.	.	.	.	.	.	.	.	.

REFERENCE/INFORMATION SERVICES CLERK - CONTINUED
ALL PUBLIC LIBRARIES
Regional Data

	Min	Q1	Mean	Median	Q3	Max	N	Range Avg Min	Range Avg Max
North Atlantic	15,579	18,720	27,827	27,581	33,789	48,230	22	22,723	31,331
Great Lakes & Plains	14,560	22,381	26,202	22,381	27,602	48,881	170	22,154	33,258
Southeast	10,712	22,570	25,345	26,333	28,163	36,487	52	20,671	28,571
West & Southwest	11,440	17,160	24,523	24,378	32,656	41,424	33	21,238	28,813
ALL REGIONS	10,712	22,381	25,970	22,838	28,766	48,881	277	21,938	32,099

State Data

	Min	Q1	Mean	Median	Q3	Max	N	Range Avg Min	Range Avg Max
CA	30,597	30,597	32,344	32,344	34,092	34,092	2	28,995	35,922
CO	20,800	22,911	24,638	25,199	26,364	27,352	4	23,156	29,411
CT	16,474	16,474	16,994	16,994	17,514	17,514	2	15,392	17,472
FL	22,970	26,333	27,787	27,914	28,985	32,594	28	19,032	34,195
IA	16,120	16,120	23,660	23,660	31,200	31,200	2	27,040	31,200
ID	16,640	16,640	16,640	16,640	16,640	16,640	2	16,640	24,960
IL	14,560	26,853	28,163	30,572	33,067	35,764	5		
IN	14,560	14,560	16,682	17,285	18,200	18,200	3	17,160	23,920
KS	16,640	21,632	23,249	22,374	23,920	34,778	10	20,488	33,899
MA	29,578	29,578	35,541	35,541	41,504	41,504	2	33,145	40,342
ME	33,862	33,862	33,862	33,862	33,862	33,862	1	23,754	33,862
MI	17,680	17,680	17,680	17,680	17,680	17,680	1		
MS	10,712	10,712	11,995	10,712	14,560	14,560	3		
NC	24,480	24,480	24,480	24,480	24,480	24,480	1		
NJ	23,015	26,770	29,927	32,274	33,789	33,789	5		
NM	16,640	18,870	27,884	28,038	37,440	39,520	9	23,615	34,078
NY	15,579	17,139	27,222	27,227	27,934	48,230	5	17,623	33,810
OH	18,200	22,381	26,607	22,381	27,082	48,881	148	22,265	33,310
OR	30,784	31,720	34,630	33,155	37,539	41,424	4	27,373	33,654
PA	18,200	18,720	26,870	27,934	32,198	36,233	6	25,931	29,786
RI	26,291	26,291	26,291	26,291	26,291	26,291	1	26,291	33,218
SC	19,594	19,594	20,738	21,237	21,382	21,382	3	19,115	28,683
TN	17,347	18,158	19,836	18,790	21,433	24,580	8	17,243	22,714
TX	11,440	11,440	13,156	12,480	12,480	18,616	6	12,664	16,491
VA	25,168	25,168	28,724	26,553	33,356	36,487	9	27,316	27,316
WA	24,378	24,378	27,269	24,690	30,160	35,318	4	24,378	35,318
WI	28,069	28,069	28,069	28,069	28,069	28,069	1		
WY	17,576	17,576	17,628	17,628	17,680	17,680	2		

Degree Required Data

	Min	Q1	Mean	Median	Q3	Max	N	Range Avg Min	Range Avg Max
High School	10,712	19,352	28,112	26,811	33,810	48,881	132	20,931	28,968
Associate's	18,200	18,200	21,752	22,576	24,480	24,480	3		
Bachelor's	20,800	25,293	30,768	30,389	36,233	41,504	6	28,532	33,171
Master's									
Doctoral									

OUTREACH/BOOKMOBILE CLERK

Performs routine duties requiring the use of a variety of forms, reports or procedures. Provides basic patron assistance: sets up computer stations, locates materials, provides information. Maintains departmental or area records. Performs miscellaneous clerical duties such as filing, typing, sorting or photocopying. Provides services and programs to homebound, disabled, institutionalized or other underserved patrons.

Very Small Public Library
(Serving a population of less than 10,000)
Regional Data

	Min	Q1	Mean	Median	Q3	Max	N	Range Avg Min	Range Avg Max
North Atlantic	24,274	24,274	24,274	24,274	24,274	24,274	1	.	.
ALL REGIONS	24,274	24,274	24,274	24,274	24,274	24,274	1	.	.

State Data

	Min	Q1	Mean	Median	Q3	Max	N	Range Avg Min	Range Avg Max
NY	24,274	24,274	24,274	24,274	24,274	24,274	1	.	.

Degree Required Data

	Min	Q1	Mean	Median	Q3	Max	N	Range Avg Min	Range Avg Max
High School	.	.	.	.	.	.		.	.
Associate's	.	.	.	.	.	.		.	.
Bachelor's	24,274	24,274	24,274	24,274	24,274	24,274	1		
Master's	.	.	.	.	.	.		.	.
Doctoral	.	.	.	.	.	.		.	.

OUTREACH/BOOKMOBILE CLERK - CONTINUED
Small Public Library
(Serving a population of 10,000 to 25,000)
Regional Data

	Min	Q1	Mean	Median	Q3	Max	N	Range Avg Min	Range Avg Max
North Atlantic	13,520	13,520	13,520	13,520	13,520	13,520	1	.	.
ALL REGIONS	13,520	13,520	13,520	13,520	13,520	13,520	1	.	.

State Data

	Min	Q1	Mean	Median	Q3	Max	N	Range Avg Min	Range Avg Max
PA	13,520	13,520	13,520	13,520	13,520	13,520	1	.	.

Degree Required Data

	Min	Q1	Mean	Median	Q3	Max	N	Range Avg Min	Range Avg Max
High School	13,520	13,520	13,520	13,520	13,520	13,520	1		
Associate's	.	.	.	.	.	.		.	.
Bachelor's	.	.	.	.	.	.		.	.
Master's	.	.	.	.	.	.		.	.
Doctoral	.	.	.	.	.	.		.	.

OUTREACH/BOOKMOBILE CLERK - CONTINUED
Medium Public Library
(Serving a population of 25,000 to 99,999)
Regional Data

	Min	Q1	Mean	Median	Q3	Max	N	Range Avg Min	Range Avg Max
North Atlantic	17,482	17,482	22,365	22,365	27,248	27,248	2		
Great Lakes & Plains	18,387	19,604	27,293	25,636	33,071	48,100	32	22,018	34,512
West & Southwest	18,179	18,179	21,570	21,570	24,960	24,960	2	18,179	27,269
ALL REGIONS	17,482	19,271	26,701	25,490	32,187	48,100	36	21,835	34,167

State Data

	Min	Q1	Mean	Median	Q3	Max	N	Range Avg Min	Range Avg Max
IL	19,157	20,790	27,929	26,634	33,071	42,266	20	23,533	38,113
IN	18,720	18,720	22,325	22,672	25,438	25,730	6	18,720	29,120
MN	40,968	40,968	40,968	40,968	40,968	40,968	1		
NE	18,720	18,720	18,720	18,720	18,720	18,720	2	16,640	18,720
OH	18,387	18,387	34,140	35,932	48,100	48,100	3	16,640	22,880
PA	17,482	17,482	17,482	17,482	17,482	17,482	1		
RI	27,248	27,248	27,248	27,248	27,248	27,248	1		
TX	18,179	18,179	18,179	18,179	18,179	18,179	1	18,179	27,269
WY	24,960	24,960	24,960	24,960	24,960	24,960	1		

Degree Required Data

	Min	Q1	Mean	Median	Q3	Max	N	Range Avg Min	Range Avg Max
High School	17,482	18,720	26,207	25,438	31,304	48,100	23	21,547	32,383
Associate's	21,466	21,466	23,504	23,504	25,542	25,542	2	23,015	47,237
Bachelor's	26,624	26,624	33,873	33,873	41,122	41,122	2	26,624	40,851
Master's									
Doctoral									

OUTREACH/BOOKMOBILE CLERK - CONTINUED
Large Public Library
(Serving a population of 100,000 to 499,999)
Regional Data

	Min	Q1	Mean	Median	Q3	Max	N	Range Avg Min	Range Avg Max
North Atlantic	22,880	22,880	24,409	24,409	25,938	25,938	2	20,800	24,960
Great Lakes & Plains	19,260	22,609	24,885	23,900	26,439	33,134	16	21,085	32,187
Southeast	20,654	24,441	24,574	24,669	25,168	27,936	5	18,762	27,186
West & Southwest	16,640	19,063	23,574	22,943	26,874	34,195	8	22,402	26,326
ALL REGIONS	16,640	21,029	24,466	24,441	26,853	34,195	31	21,010	29,509

State Data

	Min	Q1	Mean	Median	Q3	Max	N	Range Avg Min	Range Avg Max
CA	16,640	16,640	22,831	24,960	26,894	26,894	3	22,402	26,326
FL	20,654	20,654	22,662	22,662	24,669	24,669	2	18,762	27,186
IL	19,552	19,552	23,103	24,024	25,735	25,735	3	19,552	37,565
IN	19,260	19,260	19,260	19,260	19,260	19,260	1		
KS	24,960	24,960	26,052	26,052	27,144	27,144	2	21,632	36,067
MI	23,733	23,733	23,733	23,733	23,733	23,733	2	23,046	28,808
MN	30,188	30,188	31,194	31,194	32,200	32,200	2		
NC	27,936	27,936	27,936	27,936	27,936	27,936	1		
NM	19,926	20,426	25,475	23,889	30,524	34,195	4		
OH	21,029	21,029	21,559	21,559	22,090	22,090	2	19,344	28,995
PA	22,880	22,880	24,409	24,409	25,938	25,938	2	20,800	24,960
TX	18,200	18,200	18,200	18,200	18,200	18,200	1		
VA	24,441	24,441	24,805	24,805	25,168	25,168	2		
WI	23,128	23,452	26,130	24,128	28,807	33,134	4		

Degree Required Data

	Min	Q1	Mean	Median	Q3	Max	N	Range Avg Min	Range Avg Max
High School	16,640	20,925	24,292	23,776	25,938	34,195	25	20,176	29,632
Associate's	22,880	22,880	23,661	23,661	24,441	24,441	2	20,800	24,960
Bachelor's	27,936	27,936	27,936	27,936	27,936	27,936	1		
Master's	.	.	.	.	.	.		.	.
Doctoral	.	.	.	.	.	.		.	.

OUTREACH/BOOKMOBILE CLERK - CONTINUED
Very Large Public Library
(Serving a population of 500,000 or more)
Regional Data

	Min	Q1	Mean	Median	Q3	Max	N	Range Avg Min	Range Avg Max
North Atlantic	25,958	25,958	25,958	25,958	25,958	25,958	1	.	.
Great Lakes & Plains	22,381	34,130	36,395	36,400	45,079	45,079	7	26,383	35,381
Southeast	24,752	25,688	28,663	27,326	29,453	42,646	11	25,563	42,605
West & Southwest	36,650	36,650	46,847	46,847	57,044	57,044	2	37,131	49,769
ALL REGIONS	22,381	26,395	32,843	29,453	36,400	57,044	21	28,039	40,624

State Data

	Min	Q1	Mean	Median	Q3	Max	N	Range Avg Min	Range Avg Max
AZ	36,650	36,650	36,650	36,650	36,650	36,650	1	27,331	42,494
CA	57,044	57,044	57,044	57,044	57,044	57,044	1	46,930	57,044
FL	24,752	25,397	26,939	27,206	28,330	29,453	7		
NJ	25,958	25,958	25,958	25,958	25,958	25,958	1		
OH	22,381	36,400	37,068	36,400	45,079	45,079	5	24,322	35,436
VA	26,395	26,861	31,679	28,838	36,497	42,646	4	25,563	42,605
WI	34,130	34,130	34,713	34,713	35,296	35,296	2	29,474	35,298

Degree Required Data

	Min	Q1	Mean	Median	Q3	Max	N	Range Avg Min	Range Avg Max
High School	24,752	27,206	32,462	29,901	36,400	45,079	18	26,568	39,590
Associate's									
Bachelor's									
Master's									
Doctoral									

OUTREACH/BOOKMOBILE CLERK - CONTINUED
ALL PUBLIC LIBRARIES
Regional Data

	Min	Q1	Mean	Median	Q3	Max	N	Range Avg Min	Range Avg Max
North Atlantic	13,520	17,482	22,471	24,274	25,958	27,248	7	20,800	24,960
Great Lakes & Plains	18,387	21,466	27,751	25,542	33,134	48,100	55	22,496	34,139
Southeast	20,654	24,960	27,385	26,801	28,133	42,646	16	23,296	37,465
West & Southwest	16,640	19,063	27,119	24,960	30,545	57,044	12	26,608	34,297
ALL REGIONS	13,520	22,090	27,191	25,615	30,349	57,044	90	23,113	34,400

State Data

	Min	Q1	Mean	Median	Q3	Max	N	Range Avg Min	Range Avg Max
AZ	36,650	36,650	36,650	36,650	36,650	36,650	1	27,331	42,494
CA	16,640	20,800	31,385	25,927	41,969	57,044	4	28,534	34,005
FL	20,654	24,752	25,988	25,688	27,747	29,453	9	18,762	27,186
IL	19,157	20,114	27,300	26,000	33,071	42,266	23	23,284	38,078
IN	18,720	18,720	21,887	22,256	25,438	25,730	7	18,720	29,120
KS	24,960	24,960	26,052	26,052	27,144	27,144	2	21,632	36,067
MI	23,733	23,733	23,733	23,733	23,733	23,733	2	23,046	28,808
MN	30,188	30,188	34,452	32,200	40,968	40,968	3		
NC	27,936	27,936	27,936	27,936	27,936	27,936	1		
NE	18,720	18,720	18,720	18,720	18,720	18,720	2	16,640	18,720
NJ	25,958	25,958	25,958	25,958	25,958	25,958	1		
NM	19,926	20,426	25,475	23,889	30,524	34,195	4		
NY	24,274	24,274	24,274	24,274	24,274	24,274	1		
OH	18,387	22,090	33,088	36,166	45,079	48,100	10	21,382	31,197
PA	13,520	15,501	19,955	20,181	24,409	25,938	4	20,800	24,960
RI	27,248	27,248	27,248	27,248	27,248	27,248	1		
TX	18,179	18,179	18,190	18,190	18,200	18,200	2	18,179	27,269
VA	24,441	25,168	29,388	26,861	30,349	42,646	6	25,563	42,605
WI	23,128	23,776	28,991	28,807	34,130	35,296	6	29,474	35,298
WY	24,960	24,960	24,960	24,960	24,960	24,960	1		

Degree Required Data

	Min	Q1	Mean	Median	Q3	Max	N	Range Avg Min	Range Avg Max
High School	13,520	20,925	26,984	25,730	31,304	48,100	67	22,501	33,515
Associate's	21,466	22,173	23,582	23,661	24,992	25,542	4	22,277	39,811
Bachelor's	24,274	25,449	29,989	27,280	34,529	41,122	4	26,624	40,851
Master's	.	.	.	.	.	.		.	
Doctoral	.	.	.	.	.	.		.	

MEDIA SERVICES CLERK

Performs routine duties requiring the use of a variety of forms, reports or procedures. Provides basic patron assistance: sets up computer stations, locates materials, provides information. Maintains departmental or area records. Performs miscellaneous clerical duties such as filing, typing, sorting or photocopying. Develops and manages non-print library materials such as files, video recordings, audio recordings, CD-ROMs, computer software, etc.

Very Small Public Library
(Serving a population of less than 10,000)
Regional Data

	Min	Q1	Mean	Median	Q3	Max	N	Range Avg Min	Range Avg Max
Great Lakes & Plains	37,835	37,835	37,835	37,835	37,835	37,835	1	21,549	37,835
ALL REGIONS	37,835	37,835	37,835	37,835	37,835	37,835	1	21,549	37,835

State Data

	Min	Q1	Mean	Median	Q3	Max	N	Range Avg Min	Range Avg Max
MN	37,835	37,835	37,835	37,835	37,835	37,835	1	21,549	37,835

Degree Required Data

	Min	Q1	Mean	Median	Q3	Max	N	Range Avg Min	Range Avg Max
High School	37,835	37,835	37,835	37,835	37,835	37,835	1	21,549	37,835
Associate's	.	.	.	.	.	.		.	
Bachelor's	.	.	.	.	.	.		.	
Master's	.	.	.	.	.	.		.	
Doctoral	.	.	.	.	.	.		.	

MEDIA SERVICES CLERK - CONTINUED
Small Public Library
(Serving a population of 10,000 to 25,000)
Regional Data

	Min	Q1	Mean	Median	Q3	Max	N	Range Avg Min	Range Avg Max
North Atlantic	26,978	26,978	26,978	26,978	26,978	26,978	1	25,022	49,920
ALL REGIONS	26,978	26,978	26,978	26,978	26,978	26,978	1	25,022	49,920

State Data

	Min	Q1	Mean	Median	Q3	Max	N	Range Avg Min	Range Avg Max
NJ	26,978	26,978	26,978	26,978	26,978	26,978	1	25,022	49,920

Degree Required Data

	Min	Q1	Mean	Median	Q3	Max	N	Range Avg Min	Range Avg Max
High School	26,978	26,978	26,978	26,978	26,978	26,978	1	25,022	49,920
Associate's									
Bachelor's									
Master's									
Doctoral									

MEDIA SERVICES CLERK - CONTINUED
Medium Public Library
(Serving a population of 25,000 to 99,999)
Regional Data

	Min	Q1	Mean	Median	Q3	Max	N	Range Avg Min	Range Avg Max
North Atlantic	19,843	20,966	24,273	23,670	28,576	28,912	6	16,823	32,356
Great Lakes & Plains	18,970	19,157	21,141	19,313	22,381	28,844	12	19,614	35,707
ALL REGIONS	18,970	19,157	22,185	19,791	25,334	28,912	18	18,617	34,510

State Data

	Min	Q1	Mean	Median	Q3	Max	N	Range Avg Min	Range Avg Max
IL	18,970	19,157	21,141	19,313	22,381	28,844	12	19,614	35,707
MA	28,576	28,576	28,576	28,576	28,576	28,576	1		
NY	19,843	20,966	23,412	22,006	25,334	28,912	5	16,823	32,356

Degree Required Data

	Min	Q1	Mean	Median	Q3	Max	N	Range Avg Min	Range Avg Max
High School	18,970	19,157	20,834	19,344	20,966	28,912	13	18,075	33,186
Associate's	19,739	22,381	24,978	25,665	27,575	28,844	4	21,871	42,453
Bachelor's	28,576	28,576	28,576	28,576	28,576	28,576	1		
Master's									
Doctoral									

MEDIA SERVICES CLERK - CONTINUED
Large Public Library
(Serving a population of 100,000 to 499,999)
Regional Data

	Min	Q1	Mean	Median	Q3	Max	N	Range Avg Min	Range Avg Max
North Atlantic	16,640	16,640	23,684	24,960	29,453	29,453	3	16,640	27,955
Southeast	14,200	15,047	27,035	29,796	34,107	42,024	5		
West & Southwest	14,685	24,894	30,468	35,194	35,922	39,666	13	27,485	34,949
ALL REGIONS	14,200	24,648	28,681	29,453	35,922	42,024	21	24,527	33,042

State Data

	Min	Q1	Mean	Median	Q3	Max	N	Range Avg Min	Range Avg Max
CA	28,995	35,195	35,342	35,922	35,922	39,666	8	29,313	36,352
MS	14,200	14,200	14,624	14,624	15,047	15,047	2	.	.
NM	19,926	19,926	22,287	22,287	24,648	24,648	2	.	.
PA	16,640	16,640	23,684	24,960	29,453	29,453	3	16,640	27,955
TX	14,685	14,685	22,924	24,894	29,192	29,192	3	14,685	25,126
VA	29,796	29,796	35,309	34,107	42,024	42,024	3	.	.

Degree Required Data

	Min	Q1	Mean	Median	Q3	Max	N	Range Avg Min	Range Avg Max
High School	14,200	18,283	27,623	29,094	35,922	39,666	16	26,280	34,338
Associate's	24,960	29,453	32,068	29,796	34,107	42,024	5	16,640	27,206
Bachelor's	.	.	.	.	.	.	.	.	.
Master's	.	.	.	.	.	.	.	.	.
Doctoral	.	.	.	.	.	.	.	.	.

MEDIA SERVICES CLERK - CONTINUED
Very Large Public Library
(Serving a population of 500,000 or more)
Regional Data

	Min	Q1	Mean	Median	Q3	Max	N	Range Avg Min	Range Avg Max
Great Lakes & Plains	22,381	22,381	27,008	22,381	31,272	39,558	10	22,381	33,509
West & Southwest	46,098	46,098	47,255	47,255	48,412	48,412	2	39,910	48,412
ALL REGIONS	22,381	22,381	30,383	25,574	37,880	48,412	12	26,276	36,821

State Data

	Min	Q1	Mean	Median	Q3	Max	N	Range Avg Min	Range Avg Max
CA	46,098	46,098	47,255	47,255	48,412	48,412	2	39,910	48,412
OH	22,381	22,381	27,008	22,381	31,272	39,558	10	22,381	33,509

Degree Required Data

	Min	Q1	Mean	Median	Q3	Max	N	Range Avg Min	Range Avg Max
High School	31,272	31,272	35,677	36,201	39,558	39,558	3	.	.
Associate's	.	.	.	.	.	.	.	.	.
Bachelor's	.	.	.	.	.	.	.	.	.
Master's	.	.	.	.	.	.	.	.	.
Doctoral	.	.	.	.	.	.	.	.	.

MEDIA SERVICES CLERK - CONTINUED
ALL PUBLIC LIBRARIES
Regional Data

	Min	Q1	Mean	Median	Q3	Max	N	Range Avg Min	Range Avg Max
North Atlantic	16,640	20,966	24,367	25,147	28,576	29,453	10	17,673	32,841
Great Lakes & Plains	18,970	19,282	24,418	22,381	28,766	39,558	23	20,867	34,927
Southeast	14,200	15,047	27,035	29,796	34,107	42,024	5	.	.
West & Southwest	14,685	24,894	32,706	35,196	35,922	48,412	15	29,970	37,642
ALL REGIONS	14,200	19,843	27,001	25,022	34,107	48,412	53	22,597	35,160

State Data

	Min	Q1	Mean	Median	Q3	Max	N	Range Avg Min	Range Avg Max
CA	28,995	35,196	37,725	35,922	39,666	48,412	10	31,668	39,032
IL	18,970	19,157	21,141	19,313	22,381	28,844	12	19,614	35,707
MA	28,576	28,576	28,576	28,576	28,576	28,576	1	.	.
MN	37,835	37,835	37,835	37,835	37,835	37,835	1	21,549	37,835
MS	14,200	14,200	14,624	14,624	15,047	15,047	2	.	.
NJ	26,978	26,978	26,978	26,978	26,978	26,978	1	25,022	49,920
NM	19,926	19,926	22,287	22,287	24,648	24,648	2	.	.
NY	19,843	20,966	23,412	22,006	25,334	28,912	5	16,823	32,356
OH	22,381	22,381	27,008	22,381	31,272	39,558	10	22,381	33,509
PA	16,640	16,640	23,684	24,960	29,453	29,453	3	16,640	27,955
TX	14,685	14,685	22,924	24,894	29,192	29,192	3	14,685	25,126
VA	29,796	29,796	35,309	34,107	42,024	42,024	3	.	.

Degree Required Data

	Min	Q1	Mean	Median	Q3	Max	N	Range Avg Min	Range Avg Max
High School	14,200	19,157	26,019	24,771	35,196	39,666	34	21,739	34,567
Associate's	19,739	25,022	28,917	28,844	29,796	42,024	9	19,256	34,830
Bachelor's	28,576	28,576	28,576	28,576	28,576	28,576	1	.	.
Master's	.	.	.	.	.	.		.	.
Doctoral	.	.	.	.	.	.		.	.

ACQUISITIONS CLERK

Performs routine duties requiring the use of a variety of forms, reports or procedures. Provides basic patron assistance: sets up computer stations, locates materials, provides information. Maintains departmental or area records. Performs miscellaneous clerical duties such as filing, typing, sorting or photocopying. Orders and receives new materials; works with collections staff to determine most appropriate sources; checks shipments to ensure correct quantity, material and quality.

Very Small Public Library
(Serving a population of less than 10,000)
Regional Data

	Min	Q1	Mean	Median	Q3	Max	N	Range Avg Min	Range Avg Max
North Atlantic	27,310	27,310	27,310	27,310	27,310	27,310	2	27,310	27,310
Great Lakes & Plains	20,800	20,800	20,800	20,800	20,800	20,800	1	20,384	24,544
West & Southwest	23,424	23,424	28,581	28,581	33,738	33,738	2	23,941	33,738
ALL REGIONS	20,800	23,424	26,516	27,310	27,310	33,738	5	24,736	28,226

State Data

	Min	Q1	Mean	Median	Q3	Max	N	Range Avg Min	Range Avg Max
CO	33,738	33,738	33,738	33,738	33,738	33,738	1	23,941	33,738
IL	20,800	20,800	20,800	20,800	20,800	20,800	1	20,384	24,544
MA	27,310	27,310	27,310	27,310	27,310	27,310	2	27,310	27,310
TX	23,424	23,424	23,424	23,424	23,424	23,424	1	.	.

Degree Required Data

	Min	Q1	Mean	Median	Q3	Max	N	Range Avg Min	Range Avg Max
High School	20,800	20,800	25,987	23,424	33,738	33,738	3	22,162	29,141
Associate's									
Bachelor's	27,310	27,310	27,310	27,310	27,310	27,310	2	27,310	27,310
Master's									
Doctoral									

ACQUISITIONS CLERK - CONTINUED
Small Public Library
(Serving a population of 10,000 to 25,000)
Regional Data

	Min	Q1	Mean	Median	Q3	Max	N	Range Avg Min	Range Avg Max
North Atlantic	23,296	25,480	30,790	31,429	37,616	37,960	7	25,719	35,916
Great Lakes & Plains	16,120	18,720	23,033	20,800	22,576	42,848	13	18,561	24,932
Southeast	12,480	12,480	12,480	12,480	12,480	12,480	1	.	.
ALL REGIONS	12,480	18,720	25,116	22,576	31,429	42,848	21	20,470	27,861

State Data

	Min	Q1	Mean	Median	Q3	Max	N	Range Avg Min	Range Avg Max
GA	12,480	12,480	12,480	12,480	12,480	12,480	1		
KS	22,576	22,576	22,576	22,576	22,576	22,576	1		
MI	16,120	18,200	21,273	20,800	21,320	33,280	11	17,212	23,140
MN	42,848	42,848	42,848	42,848	42,848	42,848	1	32,053	42,848
NH	37,960	37,960	37,960	37,960	37,960	37,960	1	32,136	48,714
NJ	23,296	24,388	29,455	28,454	34,523	37,616	4	23,580	31,651
NY	27,038	27,038	29,874	29,874	32,711	32,711	2		

Degree Required Data

	Min	Q1	Mean	Median	Q3	Max	N	Range Avg Min	Range Avg Max
High School	12,480	18,720	24,491	21,948	29,234	42,848	20	20,470	27,861
Associate's									
Bachelor's	37,616	37,616	37,616	37,616	37,616	37,616	1		
Master's									
Doctoral									

ACQUISITIONS CLERK - CONTINUED
Medium Public Library
(Serving a population of 25,000 to 99,999)
Regional Data

	Min	Q1	Mean	Median	Q3	Max	N	Range Avg Min	Range Avg Max
North Atlantic	25,103	30,472	38,252	37,440	45,853	54,912	27	26,998	32,781
Great Lakes & Plains	13,520	19,240	23,062	23,338	24,856	41,059	17	21,082	31,115
Southeast	19,074	20,689	22,807	22,967	25,210	25,938	6	17,285	25,147
West & Southwest	20,692	40,934	41,983	43,784	45,822	50,253	25	40,302	49,460
ALL REGIONS	13,520	25,103	34,817	35,195	43,784	54,912	75	31,129	40,104

State Data

	Min	Q1	Mean	Median	Q3	Max	N	Range Avg Min	Range Avg Max
AR	22,214	22,214	23,712	23,712	25,210	25,210	2		
CA	34,128	41,829	44,127	43,784	46,842	50,253	21	40,302	49,460
CT	26,874	26,874	36,365	31,855	49,639	51,096	6	29,432	30,472
IL	15,600	17,680	23,130	19,968	23,338	41,059	9	21,200	32,609
IN	20,800	20,800	22,828	22,828	24,856	24,856	2	20,800	29,120
LA	19,074	19,074	21,397	21,397	23,720	23,720	2	17,285	25,147
MA	26,208	26,208	31,824	31,824	37,440	37,440	2	30,420	31,824
MO	26,562	26,562	26,562	26,562	26,562	26,562	1		
NC	25,938	25,938	25,938	25,938	25,938	25,938	1		
NJ	36,576	38,629	40,337	38,629	38,629	50,934	6		
NY	25,103	31,922	40,282	38,290	49,642	54,912	12	22,360	34,892
OH	13,520	23,962	22,335	24,107	24,274	25,813	5	20,914	28,626
RI	25,563	25,563	25,563	25,563	25,563	25,563	1		
TN	20,689	20,689	20,689	20,689	20,689	20,689	1		
TX	20,692	25,105	30,723	31,942	36,342	38,316	4		

Degree Required Data

	Min	Q1	Mean	Median	Q3	Max	N	Range Avg Min	Range Avg Max
High School	13,520	26,010	36,361	38,629	45,597	54,912	64	32,794	41,282
Associate's	19,968	19,968	22,062	22,880	23,338	23,338	3	19,982	33,966
Bachelor's	19,074	19,074	25,805	25,103	33,238	33,238	3	17,285	25,147
Master's	.	.	.	.	.	.	.	.	.
Doctoral	.	.	.	.	.	.	.	.	.

ACQUISITIONS CLERK - CONTINUED
Large Public Library
(Serving a population of 100,000 to 499,999)
Regional Data

	Min	Q1	Mean	Median	Q3	Max	N	Range Avg Min	Range Avg Max
North Atlantic	15,538	28,233	34,556	32,968	42,786	51,462	29	24,794	34,199
Great Lakes & Plains	20,072	24,357	28,320	27,539	30,094	43,318	25	20,420	31,128
Southeast	18,952	22,523	27,630	26,643	31,822	38,334	16	.	.
West & Southwest	16,640	22,901	27,048	26,208	31,138	37,128	35	22,796	29,589
ALL REGIONS	15,538	23,920	29,513	28,233	33,509	51,462	105	22,521	31,043

State Data

	Min	Q1	Mean	Median	Q3	Max	N	Range Avg Min	Range Avg Max
AZ	35,880	35,880	35,880	35,880	35,880	35,880	2	.	.
CA	20,467	20,467	26,284	23,691	31,138	35,693	11	22,734	28,216
FL	19,771	19,771	22,744	22,253	26,207	26,207	3	.	.
GA	26,000	26,000	26,000	26,000	26,000	26,000	1	.	.
IL	20,935	23,150	25,169	25,509	27,123	28,787	6	19,781	29,328
KS	27,706	27,976	30,742	29,921	33,509	35,422	4	21,632	36,067
MD	28,996	30,763	32,063	31,929	33,200	35,564	6	.	.
MI	26,978	26,978	27,860	27,539	27,710	30,094	5	.	.
MN	31,704	31,704	31,704	31,704	31,704	31,704	1	.	.
MO	29,536	29,536	29,536	29,536	29,536	29,536	1	24,294	29,536
NC	18,952	18,952	20,279	20,279	21,606	21,606	2	.	.
NJ	15,538	15,538	21,666	23,706	25,756	25,756	3	.	.
NM	16,640	16,640	23,275	22,901	30,284	30,284	3	.	.
NY	25,958	32,594	37,368	37,297	43,198	51,462	13	25,875	34,429
OH	20,072	20,384	22,160	22,069	23,920	24,357	5	18,151	26,874
OR	26,208	26,208	26,208	26,208	26,208	26,208	1	.	.
PA	26,411	28,122	36,993	34,031	51,360	51,360	7	21,549	33,509
TN	22,794	22,794	22,794	22,794	22,794	22,794	1	.	.
TX	19,739	21,570	24,925	23,847	28,618	32,651	10	17,472	31,491
VA	23,732	27,711	31,611	29,596	37,916	38,334	9	.	.
WA	23,922	27,497	30,066	29,120	33,124	37,128	8	23,795	31,789
WI	37,232	37,232	40,895	42,137	43,318	43,318	3	.	.

Degree Required Data

	Min	Q1	Mean	Median	Q3	Max	N	Range Avg Min	Range Avg Max
High School	15,538	23,922	28,619	28,145	32,325	51,360	78	22,131	30,372
Associate's	20,322	23,150	29,590	30,137	35,880	37,916	6	.	.
Bachelor's	23,732	23,732	30,824	30,824	37,916	37,916	2	.	.
Master's	22,992	22,992	22,992	22,992	22,992	22,992	1	.	.
Doctoral	.	.	.	.	.	.	.	.	.

ACQUISITIONS CLERK - CONTINUED
Very Large Public Library
(Serving a population of 500,000 or more)
Regional Data

	Min	Q1	Mean	Median	Q3	Max	N	Range Avg Min	Range Avg Max
North Atlantic	25,459	27,149	30,826	28,485	33,374	44,197	19	.	.
Great Lakes & Plains	18,554	24,627	28,380	27,976	31,864	39,978	24	22,128	30,335
Southeast	25,915	26,768	33,673	35,525	39,077	40,733	8	25,286	42,143
West & Southwest	25,228	30,276	34,272	33,339	37,336	49,812	20	29,049	35,372
ALL REGIONS	18,554	26,559	31,291	31,272	35,026	49,812	71	26,334	34,692

State Data

	Min	Q1	Mean	Median	Q3	Max	N	Range Avg Min	Range Avg Max
CA	27,375	37,336	37,152	37,336	38,388	49,812	10	29,887	36,230
FL	26,978	31,651	36,036	38,217	40,421	40,733	4	.	.
GA	38,044	38,044	38,044	38,044	38,044	38,044	1	.	.
IN	29,348	29,348	29,348	29,348	29,348	29,348	1	.	.
MD	27,149	27,149	27,728	27,728	28,306	28,306	2	.	.
MO	18,554	19,843	23,689	23,747	26,713	30,355	8	18,179	27,269
NJ	25,459	27,643	31,191	29,057	33,374	44,197	17	.	.
OH	22,381	25,151	30,817	31,864	33,939	39,978	15	22,786	30,846
OR	32,656	32,656	33,155	33,155	33,654	33,654	4	27,373	33,654
TX	25,228	25,228	27,354	27,354	29,479	29,479	2	.	.
UT	29,928	30,276	31,650	31,824	33,024	33,024	4	.	.
VA	25,915	25,915	29,067	26,559	34,726	34,726	3	25,286	42,143

Degree Required Data

	Min	Q1	Mean	Median	Q3	Max	N	Range Avg Min	Range Avg Max
High School	18,554	26,197	30,154	29,928	33,024	49,812	45	24,068	33,009
Associate's	29,479	29,479	29,479	29,479	29,479	29,479	1	.	.
Bachelor's	.	.	.	.	.	.	.	.	.
Master's	.	.	.	.	.	.	.	.	.
Doctoral	.	.	.	.	.	.	.	.	.

ACQUISITIONS CLERK - CONTINUED
ALL PUBLIC LIBRARIES
Regional Data

	Min	Q1	Mean	Median	Q3	Max	N	Range Avg Min	Range Avg Max
North Atlantic	15,538	27,668	34,414	32,757	38,629	54,912	84	25,834	33,462
Great Lakes & Plains	13,520	20,858	26,268	25,151	30,224	43,318	80	20,422	29,257
Southeast	12,480	22,253	27,768	26,207	34,726	40,733	31	23,285	37,894
West & Southwest	16,640	26,208	33,401	33,024	40,934	50,253	82	30,781	38,389
ALL REGIONS	12,480	25,064	31,018	29,348	37,128	54,912	277	25,830	34,143

State Data

	Min	Q1	Mean	Median	Q3	Max	N	Range Avg Min	Range Avg Max
AR	22,214	22,214	23,712	23,712	25,210	25,210	2	.	.
AZ	35,880	35,880	35,880	35,880	35,880	35,880	2	.	.
CA	20,467	31,138	37,793	39,661	44,782	50,253	42	32,827	40,284
CO	33,738	33,738	33,738	33,738	33,738	33,738	1	23,941	33,738
CT	26,874	26,874	36,365	31,855	49,639	51,096	6	29,432	30,472
FL	19,771	22,253	30,339	26,978	40,109	40,733	7	.	.
GA	12,480	12,480	25,508	26,000	38,044	38,044	3	.	.
IL	15,600	19,604	23,749	23,015	26,874	41,059	16	20,777	31,117
IN	20,800	20,800	25,001	24,856	29,348	29,348	3	20,800	29,120
KS	22,576	27,706	29,109	28,246	31,595	35,422	5	21,632	36,067
LA	19,074	19,074	21,397	21,397	23,720	23,720	2	17,285	25,147
MA	26,208	26,759	29,567	27,310	32,375	37,440	4	28,865	29,567
MD	27,149	28,651	30,979	31,148	32,763	35,564	8	.	.
MI	16,120	18,720	23,331	21,060	27,290	33,280	16	17,212	23,140
MN	31,704	31,704	37,276	37,276	42,848	42,848	2	32,053	42,848
MO	18,554	20,916	24,561	25,193	27,228	30,355	10	21,237	28,402
NC	18,952	18,952	22,165	21,606	25,938	25,938	3	.	.
NH	37,960	37,960	37,960	37,960	37,960	37,960	1	32,136	48,714
NJ	15,538	25,896	31,836	31,846	37,616	50,934	30	23,580	31,651
NM	16,640	16,640	23,275	22,901	30,284	30,284	3	.	.
NY	25,103	31,042	38,108	35,360	43,954	54,912	27	24,996	34,545
OH	13,520	23,962	27,389	25,151	31,864	39,978	25	21,141	29,246
OR	26,208	32,656	31,766	32,656	33,654	33,654	5	27,373	33,654
PA	26,411	28,122	36,993	34,031	51,360	51,360	7	21,549	33,509
RI	25,563	25,563	25,563	25,563	25,563	25,563	1	.	.
TN	20,689	20,689	21,741	21,741	22,794	22,794	2	.	.
TX	19,739	22,992	26,487	25,228	29,517	38,316	17	17,472	31,491
UT	29,928	30,276	31,650	31,824	33,024	33,024	4	.	.
VA	23,732	26,818	30,975	28,883	36,321	38,334	12	25,286	42,143
WA	23,922	27,497	30,066	29,120	33,124	37,128	8	23,795	31,789
WI	37,232	37,232	40,895	42,137	43,318	43,318	3	.	.

Degree Required Data

	Min	Q1	Mean	Median	Q3	Max	N	Range Avg Min	Range Avg Max
High School	12,480	24,323	30,877	29,120	36,400	54,912	210	25,788	34,069
Associate's	19,968	22,880	27,321	23,866	35,880	37,916	10	19,982	33,966
Bachelor's	19,074	24,417	28,912	27,310	35,427	37,916	8	23,969	26,589
Master's	22,992	22,992	22,992	22,992	22,992	22,992	1	.	.
Doctoral	.	.	.	.	.	.	.	.	.

CIRCULATION CLERK

Performs routine duties requiring the use of a variety of forms, reports or procedures. Provides basic patron assistance: sets up computer stations, locates materials, provides information. Maintains departmental or area records. Performs miscellaneous clerical duties such as filing, typing, sorting or photocopying. Checks in and out materials; inspects materials for damage, verifies due date and calculates fine; assists patrons with basic informational questions; sorts materials and prepares for reshelving; issues and updates identification cards according to established procedures.

Very Small Public Library
(Serving a population of less than 10,000)
Regional Data

	Min	Q1	Mean	Median	Q3	Max	N	Range Avg Min	Range Avg Max
North Atlantic	10,712	20,475	23,348	24,773	27,373	38,617	40	22,669	28,540
Great Lakes & Plains	10,712	14,560	18,856	16,640	18,720	52,312	78	18,422	23,950
Southeast	17,410	17,410	23,338	21,840	30,763	30,763	3	21,840	31,200
West & Southwest	13,957	14,560	18,573	18,048	21,756	26,686	11	15,787	19,456
ALL REGIONS	10,712	15,038	20,295	17,441	22,849	52,312	132	19,870	25,499

State Data

	Min	Q1	Mean	Median	Q3	Max	N	Range Avg Min	Range Avg Max
AL	21,840	21,840	26,302	26,302	30,763	30,763	2	21,840	31,200
AZ	18,048	18,048	18,048	18,048	18,048	18,048	1	.	.
CO	13,957	14,092	18,694	17,066	23,296	26,686	4	16,094	20,160
CT	15,080	15,080	19,864	19,864	24,648	24,648	2	24,648	24,648
IA	16,598	16,598	18,075	17,451	19,552	20,800	4	15,600	18,720
ID	14,560	14,560	15,080	15,080	15,600	15,600	2	.	.
IL	13,520	14,560	17,514	16,640	20,800	23,254	27	16,035	24,355
IN	14,560	14,560	15,600	14,560	15,600	20,800	8	13,867	18,027
KS	11,794	11,794	15,024	14,560	18,096	18,720	7	12,605	15,533
MA	27,310	27,310	31,121	27,435	38,617	38,617	3	24,627	28,163
ME	20,800	20,800	24,372	23,005	27,945	30,680	4	21,902	27,872
MI	16,640	16,640	16,640	16,640	16,640	16,640	5	.	.
MN	17,264	17,264	21,731	17,264	26,198	35,131	4	18,335	22,407
MO	14,310	17,368	37,241	52,312	52,312	52,312	7	43,014	49,988
MT	16,120	16,120	16,120	16,120	16,120	16,120	1	14,560	16,640
NE	14,560	15,080	15,505	15,080	15,080	18,269	9	.	.
NH	23,462	23,462	23,462	23,462	23,462	23,462	1	17,909	23,462
NJ	20,800	26,000	27,712	27,248	31,200	36,254	14	26,000	31,200
NY	14,997	20,995	22,448	23,026	25,147	26,250	8	21,840	33,280
OH	16,952	17,087	18,484	17,640	19,880	21,703	4	14,976	19,396
PA	10,712	11,128	13,074	14,560	14,560	14,560	7	10,712	10,920
SD	10,712	10,712	10,712	10,712	10,712	10,712	1	.	.
TX	20,712	20,712	21,732	21,756	22,728	22,728	3	.	.
VT	20,800	20,800	20,800	20,800	20,800	20,800	1	.	.
WI	19,834	19,834	20,317	20,317	20,800	20,800	2	.	.
WV	17,410	17,410	17,410	17,410	17,410	17,410	1	.	.

Degree Required Data

	Min	Q1	Mean	Median	Q3	Max	N	Range Avg Min	Range Avg Max
High School	10,712	15,080	20,299	17,472	22,728	52,312	113	19,968	25,510
Associate's	18,057	18,057	20,187	20,800	21,703	21,703	3	.	.
Bachelor's	14,997	25,210	27,333	27,310	30,680	38,617	7	24,440	32,399
Master's	.	.	.	.	.	.	.	.	.
Doctoral	.	.	.	.	.	.	.	.	.

CIRCULATION CLERK - CONTINUED
Small Public Library
(Serving a population of 10,000 to 25,000)
Regional Data

	Min	Q1	Mean	Median	Q3	Max	N	Range Avg Min	Range Avg Max
North Atlantic	11,336	18,949	25,722	24,960	30,800	49,920	146	21,740	28,824
Great Lakes & Plains	12,480	16,557	21,414	20,010	24,014	60,348	152	17,399	25,806
Southeast	13,656	14,560	20,055	15,933	18,980	46,436	17	13,052	15,132
West & Southwest	11,325	18,750	25,015	21,217	31,200	38,913	35	24,269	34,070
ALL REGIONS	11,325	17,139	23,505	21,424	27,955	60,348	350	19,656	27,458

State Data

	Min	Q1	Mean	Median	Q3	Max	N	Range Avg Min	Range Avg Max
AZ	23,193	23,193	24,856	24,856	26,520	26,520	2		
CO	20,800	20,800	20,800	20,800	20,800	20,800	1	20,800	20,800
CT	31,574	31,574	35,266	35,266	38,958	38,958	4	31,574	38,958
IA	16,120	16,120	16,120	16,120	16,120	16,120	1		
IL	13,520	15,392	23,687	21,112	29,120	60,348	57	18,915	32,793
IN	14,560	16,640	17,713	17,368	18,720	22,672	28	15,037	20,193
KS	13,853	16,384	17,958	18,096	20,800	20,800	7	15,600	21,840
KY	15,933	15,933	15,933	15,933	15,933	15,933	2		
LA	13,998	14,071	16,630	14,612	19,188	23,296	4	13,052	15,132
MA	14,976	25,043	30,131	27,165	37,668	49,920	31	23,237	27,640
ME	14,622	14,622	18,253	18,720	21,424	22,506	7	16,640	22,048
MI	12,480	16,474	20,019	20,155	22,880	29,120	15	19,646	23,806
MN	15,912	23,816	29,615	29,827	34,154	40,123	9	26,742	35,721
MO	12,480	12,480	14,203	13,487	15,610	17,992	8	12,480	20,800
NC	13,656	14,560	22,051	16,224	22,932	46,436	11		
ND	13,520	13,520	13,520	13,520	13,520	13,520	1		
NE	13,520	13,520	21,060	21,060	28,600	28,600	2	12,688	18,450
NH	24,502	27,664	30,014	28,954	32,178	37,960	13	26,981	39,670
NJ	17,197	23,296	29,123	26,978	35,327	49,143	42	21,793	30,926
NM	13,650	20,800	27,426	29,120	33,280	37,440	15	25,792	37,024
NY	17,514	21,424	24,359	23,400	28,933	33,449	11	21,424	23,270
OH	16,120	21,154	22,172	22,007	24,211	29,557	19	13,598	29,692
OK	13,975	13,975	20,473	17,492	29,952	29,952	3		
OR	31,623	34,563	36,502	37,736	38,441	38,913	4		
PA	11,336	14,560	16,892	16,640	20,176	24,960	26	15,398	19,546
RI	17,160	18,221	19,335	18,741	20,124	23,920	12		
TX	11,325	18,720	18,619	18,750	20,800	21,217	10	18,387	25,938
WI	19,864	20,842	21,932	22,984	22,984	22,984	5	18,907	22,984

Degree Required Data

	Min	Q1	Mean	Median	Q3	Max	N	Range Avg Min	Range Avg Max
High School	11,325	17,680	23,657	21,840	27,778	60,348	304	19,540	27,489
Associate's	13,520	14,581	19,118	16,640	18,720	36,283	21	15,451	21,097
Bachelor's	20,800	24,700	35,315	38,886	44,711	45,130	8	20,800	20,800
Master's	22,506	22,506	22,506	22,506	22,506	22,506	1		
Doctoral									

CIRCULATION CLERK - CONTINUED
Medium Public Library
(Serving a population of 25,000 to 99,999)
Regional Data

	Min	Q1	Mean	Median	Q3	Max	N	Range Avg Min	Range Avg Max
North Atlantic	10,712	19,656	26,586	25,345	30,472	56,800	330	22,098	29,245
Great Lakes & Plains	13,936	18,907	22,960	21,840	25,044	56,299	301	20,418	30,060
Southeast	10,712	12,584	16,079	15,600	19,492	27,192	83	13,589	16,902
West & Southwest	11,440	18,179	23,459	21,871	26,957	45,136	94	20,179	28,035
ALL REGIONS	10,712	18,429	23,792	22,672	27,664	56,800	808	20,560	28,698

State Data

	Min	Q1	Mean	Median	Q3	Max	N	Range Avg Min	Range Avg Max
AR	16,203	17,846	19,997	19,531	22,214	23,691	13	12,480	20,800
CA	16,536	25,043	28,450	27,248	32,406	38,160	26	24,461	30,038
CO	16,640	18,720	21,560	20,800	23,400	31,696	18	18,720	31,200
CT	22,880	27,269	33,860	30,098	39,375	50,369	35	28,536	33,941
DE	18,200	19,240	20,280	20,800	21,320	21,320	4	.	.
GA	14,560	14,560	14,803	14,612	14,872	15,600	6	.	.
ID	16,640	20,800	21,389	20,800	21,840	31,200	10	18,431	26,195
IL	14,144	19,791	25,356	24,752	29,224	56,299	136	22,170	35,750
IN	16,640	18,013	20,505	19,313	22,880	27,040	38	16,998	27,161
LA	10,712	10,712	10,754	10,712	10,712	11,336	15	10,712	12,480
MA	19,656	22,880	26,029	23,483	24,960	39,572	53	22,601	26,240
ME	25,210	27,539	29,212	27,539	32,885	32,885	5	23,754	33,862
MI	18,408	19,334	19,796	20,259	20,259	20,259	4	17,430	20,259
MN	18,242	20,634	22,118	22,963	23,878	23,878	17	.	.
MS	12,584	13,052	14,987	14,269	14,560	27,192	12	.	.
NC	14,552	17,742	19,555	19,718	19,728	25,428	18	17,614	22,577
NE	18,720	18,720	18,928	18,720	18,720	20,800	10	18,720	19,344
NJ	13,362	19,282	28,864	29,683	35,928	51,038	35	21,429	35,714
NY	14,040	20,405	27,416	27,664	29,783	56,800	118	18,971	29,921
OH	13,936	18,744	21,221	21,299	22,818	39,229	79	19,662	25,727
OR	35,328	35,328	37,264	37,264	39,200	39,200	2	.	.
PA	10,712	16,391	17,941	17,139	18,720	34,040	55	16,640	21,341
RI	26,291	27,248	29,987	28,662	33,218	36,571	25	26,291	33,218
TN	18,389	18,389	18,941	18,941	19,492	19,492	2	.	.
TX	11,440	17,326	20,102	20,010	23,899	29,550	37	17,711	25,325
UT	45,136	45,136	45,136	45,136	45,136	45,136	1	30,077	45,136
VA	14,560	14,560	15,682	15,656	15,657	20,627	14	.	.
WI	18,429	19,427	21,312	20,260	23,171	25,148	17	19,452	25,488
WV	10,712	10,712	11,752	12,272	12,272	12,272	3	.	.

Degree Required Data

	Min	Q1	Mean	Median	Q3	Max	N	Range Avg Min	Range Avg Max
High School	10,712	18,013	23,222	21,610	26,957	56,800	622	20,562	28,435
Associate's	14,560	15,656	21,240	20,436	25,428	45,136	42	20,904	31,059
Bachelor's	14,664	18,013	24,893	22,880	30,784	39,572	18	21,910	28,261
Master's	29,224	29,224	29,224	29,224	29,224	29,224	2	29,224	48,776
Doctoral	.	.	.	.	.	.		.	.

CIRCULATION CLERK - CONTINUED
Large Public Library
(Serving a population of 100,000 to 499,999)
Regional Data

	Min	Q1	Mean	Median	Q3	Max	N	Range Avg Min	Range Avg Max
North Atlantic	11,316	23,150	28,005	27,227	30,761	57,559	439	23,180	33,134
Great Lakes & Plains	15,205	21,133	24,582	24,294	26,708	45,338	534	20,595	29,290
Southeast	12,400	17,492	22,037	20,579	24,278	47,075	416	18,000	28,432
West & Southwest	12,480	22,269	28,059	26,677	31,138	57,970	448	24,618	32,505
ALL REGIONS	11,316	20,874	25,672	24,294	28,995	57,970	1,837	21,605	30,605

State Data

	Min	Q1	Mean	Median	Q3	Max	N	Range Avg Min	Range Avg Max
AL	15,142	15,142	19,086	15,891	24,398	24,856	5	16,640	24,760
AZ	25,293	27,893	31,873	33,696	35,381	35,880	15		
CA	19,032	28,246	33,961	31,138	39,520	57,970	140	29,480	35,906
CO	16,453	17,618	27,932	26,742	33,964	49,211	18	16,081	23,742
FL	16,888	18,886	21,908	20,259	23,525	35,339	105	18,779	27,225
GA	12,480	14,560	16,817	16,640	16,640	24,960	40	14,830	15,870
IL	19,552	21,528	26,111	25,854	29,314	41,391	98	21,445	29,192
IN	17,524	17,524	18,310	18,310	19,095	19,095	2		
KS	21,632	21,632	24,268	23,161	25,917	32,885	66	21,704	36,187
LA	15,954	16,224	18,235	16,962	19,074	26,520	56	16,224	31,366
MA	23,504	24,170	26,060	26,790	27,622	27,622	15		
MD	17,682	21,570	25,818	24,555	28,309	52,666	180	21,154	31,699
MI	20,717	23,733	25,814	24,814	28,330	33,218	52	22,453	29,987
MN	15,205	16,245	22,578	17,264	26,014	45,338	61		
MO	16,952	20,051	22,549	24,294	24,294	25,501	103	19,969	25,703
MS	12,400	13,000	15,132	14,639	16,625	21,687	14		
NC	16,328	20,150	21,733	20,800	23,834	30,949	55	20,342	32,377
NE	21,640	22,397	25,832	24,831	28,496	36,604	21	21,647	29,268
NJ	11,316	22,880	25,716	24,280	27,358	41,372	53		
NM	18,076	19,926	21,222	21,466	22,277	25,085	11		
NY	23,214	30,031	34,838	32,968	40,469	57,559	92	27,280	35,216
OH	17,722	19,718	21,727	21,133	23,608	30,098	86	18,256	27,807
OR	18,865	36,396	36,847	36,408	40,789	55,896	23	18,866	24,868
PA	17,680	24,454	27,150	28,122	28,200	33,004	99	20,451	32,155
SC	19,119	19,490	20,568	20,012	21,605	23,415	26	19,115	28,683
TN	14,560	16,744	20,020	17,950	21,978	31,377	32	16,744	22,069
TX	12,480	19,677	22,665	21,708	25,334	38,376	115	17,223	30,428
VA	19,176	23,950	30,061	27,537	34,934	47,075	83	23,941	23,941
WA	20,010	22,651	24,982	24,378	27,040	32,011	126	21,369	30,259
WI	19,905	29,611	32,811	35,266	37,279	39,587	45	28,967	32,538

Degree Required Data

	Min	Q1	Mean	Median	Q3	Max	N	Range Avg Min	Range Avg Max
High School	12,400	20,717	24,878	24,294	28,122	55,896	1,533	21,221	30,419
Associate's	17,061	26,581	32,419	32,538	37,144	51,688	100	23,953	30,971
Bachelor's	24,398	36,110	39,064	38,663	44,693	50,953	14	23,547	32,124
Master's	43,783	43,784	45,515	46,613	46,619	46,619	9	39,541	46,613
Doctoral									

CIRCULATION CLERK - CONTINUED
Very Large Public Library
(Serving a population of 500,000 or more)
Regional Data

	Min	Q1	Mean	Median	Q3	Max	N	Range Avg Min	Range Avg Max
North Atlantic	22,807	25,522	27,909	26,647	29,536	44,621	303		
Great Lakes & Plains	16,453	26,135	30,311	29,037	33,093	61,581	535	24,424	32,034
Southeast	17,696	21,778	26,292	26,395	27,742	44,429	407	25,236	42,431
West & Southwest	19,510	26,043	31,280	30,784	34,537	49,270	444	27,248	34,389
ALL REGIONS	16,453	25,459	29,166	27,865	33,014	61,581	1,689	25,934	36,986

State Data

	Min	Q1	Mean	Median	Q3	Max	N	Range Avg Min	Range Avg Max
AZ	25,646	25,646	25,646	25,646	25,646	25,646	1	22,152	32,365
CA	22,424	36,680	38,917	38,376	45,019	49,270	120	35,746	43,383
CO	25,099	29,056	32,269	33,106	35,076	38,888	49		
FL	17,696	19,995	22,113	20,623	24,405	44,429	195	18,766	33,719
IN	18,944	20,805	21,613	21,613	22,557	24,042	70		
MD	22,807	27,149	30,135	28,508	32,714	44,621	113		
MI	20,473	28,279	27,689	28,279	28,279	28,279	31		
MO	16,453	16,598	18,626	18,990	19,441	21,867	22	15,116	22,674
NJ	22,859	25,459	26,585	25,896	27,971	36,873	190		
OH	20,904	27,728	33,109	31,206	36,192	61,581	321	21,977	31,962
OR	27,373	29,869	31,177	30,784	33,654	33,654	129	27,373	33,654
TX	19,962	24,690	26,587	25,896	29,120	31,470	31	23,150	33,592
UT	19,510	21,466	24,257	24,132	26,688	30,000	114	20,943	28,937
VA	26,395	26,395	30,137	27,295	33,850	42,743	212	26,395	43,992
WI	20,558	27,877	30,849	32,647	33,014	37,696	91	26,248	33,186

Degree Required Data

	Min	Q1	Mean	Median	Q3	Max	N	Range Avg Min	Range Avg Max
High School	16,453	26,395	30,278	29,056	33,654	61,581	1,195	26,073	37,664
Associate's	47,292	47,292	48,281	48,281	49,270	49,270	2	46,930	57,044
Bachelor's									
Master's									
Doctoral									

CIRCULATION CLERK - CONTINUED
ALL PUBLIC LIBRARIES
Regional Data

	Min	Q1	Mean	Median	Q3	Max	N	Range Avg Min	Range Avg Max
North Atlantic	10,712	22,859	27,197	26,291	30,459	57,559	1,258	22,475	30,601
Great Lakes & Plains	10,712	20,446	25,612	24,294	29,407	61,581	1,600	20,722	29,321
Southeast	10,712	18,262	23,341	22,422	26,844	47,075	926	21,712	35,380
West & Southwest	11,325	22,852	28,821	27,893	33,654	57,970	1,032	25,214	32,765
ALL REGIONS	10,712	20,800	26,277	25,522	30,287	61,581	4,816	22,424	31,646

State Data

	Min	Q1	Mean	Median	Q3	Max	N	Range Avg Min	Range Avg Max
AL	15,142	15,142	21,148	21,840	24,856	30,763	7	18,126	26,600
AR	16,203	17,846	19,997	19,531	22,214	23,691	13	12,480	20,800
AZ	18,048	26,520	30,079	30,742	35,381	35,880	19	22,152	32,365
CA	16,536	29,661	35,539	35,664	39,910	57,970	286	30,881	37,590
CO	13,957	21,590	28,529	29,437	34,060	49,211	90	17,433	26,333
CT	15,080	27,269	33,315	30,472	38,958	50,369	41	28,896	34,410
DE	18,200	19,240	20,280	20,800	21,320	21,320	4	.	.
FL	16,888	19,386	22,041	20,344	24,388	44,429	300	18,773	30,029
GA	12,480	14,560	16,554	16,120	16,640	24,960	46	14,830	15,870
IA	16,120	16,598	17,684	16,598	18,304	20,800	5	15,600	18,720
ID	14,560	16,983	20,337	20,800	21,320	31,200	12	18,431	26,195
IL	13,520	19,698	24,624	23,377	29,120	60,348	318	21,265	32,700
IN	14,560	18,512	20,202	20,760	22,214	27,040	146	15,755	22,972
KS	11,794	21,632	22,907	22,422	25,490	32,885	80	20,772	34,045
KY	15,933	15,933	15,933	15,933	15,933	15,933	2	.	.
LA	10,712	15,954	16,653	16,598	18,262	26,520	75	14,952	26,723
MA	14,976	23,483	27,430	25,002	31,775	49,920	102	22,794	26,590
MD	17,682	23,566	27,483	27,019	30,539	52,666	293	21,154	31,699
ME	14,622	18,720	23,208	21,965	27,539	32,885	16	20,995	28,384
MI	12,480	22,381	24,891	25,189	28,279	33,218	107	21,700	28,413
MN	15,205	16,640	23,151	23,036	26,014	45,338	91	24,155	31,624
MO	12,480	17,451	22,190	24,294	24,294	52,312	140	19,802	25,898
MS	12,400	13,000	15,065	14,269	15,988	27,192	26	.	.
MT	16,120	16,120	16,120	16,120	16,120	16,120	1	14,560	16,640
NC	13,656	18,805	21,308	20,674	23,063	46,436	84	19,460	29,206
ND	13,520	13,520	13,520	13,520	13,520	13,520	1	.	.
NE	13,520	18,720	21,748	21,640	25,700	36,604	42	20,452	25,829
NH	23,462	27,602	29,546	28,746	32,178	37,960	14	26,333	38,513
NJ	11,316	24,280	27,052	25,954	28,475	51,038	334	22,896	31,581
NM	13,650	19,926	24,801	22,277	29,120	37,440	26	25,792	37,024
NY	14,040	23,566	30,077	29,099	32,968	57,559	229	23,224	32,419
OH	13,936	22,298	28,817	27,728	33,093	61,581	509	19,049	27,610
OK	13,975	13,975	20,473	17,492	29,952	29,952	3	.	.
OR	18,865	29,869	32,214	31,699	33,654	55,896	158	26,761	33,022
PA	10,712	16,640	22,488	21,757	28,122	34,040	187	18,610	27,458
RI	17,160	20,280	26,533	27,248	33,218	36,571	37	26,291	33,218
SC	19,119	19,490	20,568	20,012	21,605	23,415	26	19,115	28,683
SD	10,712	10,712	10,712	10,712	10,712	10,712	1	.	.
TN	14,560	16,744	19,956	18,170	21,535	31,377	34	16,744	22,069
TX	11,325	19,261	22,581	22,076	25,792	38,376	196	17,664	27,372
UT	19,510	21,466	24,439	24,336	26,712	45,136	115	21,048	29,123
VA	14,560	26,395	29,461	27,293	33,726	47,075	309	26,328	43,440
VT	20,800	20,800	20,800	20,800	20,800	20,800	1	.	.
WA	20,010	22,651	24,982	24,378	27,040	32,011	126	21,369	30,259
WI	18,429	25,978	29,977	30,701	33,014	39,587	160	25,647	32,306
WV	10,712	11,492	13,166	12,272	14,841	17,410	4	.	.

Degree Required Data

	Min	Q1	Mean	Median	Q3	Max	N	Range Avg Min	Range Avg Max
High School	10,712	20,800	26,082	25,518	30,306	61,581	3,767	22,112	31,414
Associate's	13,520	19,386	27,932	26,688	35,147	51,688	168	22,366	30,098
Bachelor's	14,664	22,880	31,251	30,680	39,410	50,953	47	22,531	29,233
Master's	22,506	36,504	40,882	44,493	46,616	46,619	12	36,102	47,334
Doctoral									

ACCOUNTING (PAYABLES) CLERK

Performs routine duties requiring the use of a variety of forms, reports or procedures. Provides basic patron assistance: sets up computer stations, locates materials, provides information. Maintains departmental or area records. Performs miscellaneous clerical duties such as filing, typing, sorting or photocopying. Checks in and out materials; inspects materials for damage, verifies due date and calculates fine; assists patrons with basic informational questions; sorts materials and prepares for reshelving; issues and updates identification cards according to established procedures.

Very Small Public Library
(Serving a population of less than 10,000)
Regional Data

	Min	Q1	Mean	Median	Q3	Max	N	Range Avg Min	Range Avg Max
North Atlantic	27,893	27,893	27,893	27,893	27,893	27,893	1		
Great Lakes & Plains	12,480	16,000	23,160	27,040	27,414	32,864	5	24,960	35,360
West & Southwest	27,934	27,934	27,934	27,934	27,934	27,934	1	23,941	32,282
ALL REGIONS	12,480	16,000	24,518	27,414	27,934	32,864	7	24,450	33,821

State Data

	Min	Q1	Mean	Median	Q3	Max	N	Range Avg Min	Range Avg Max
CO	27,934	27,934	27,934	27,934	27,934	27,934	1	23,941	32,282
CT	27,893	27,893	27,893	27,893	27,893	27,893	1		
IL	12,480	12,480	18,507	16,000	27,040	27,040	3	24,960	35,360
IN	27,414	27,414	27,414	27,414	27,414	27,414	1		
KS	32,864	32,864	32,864	32,864	32,864	32,864	1		

Degree Required Data

	Min	Q1	Mean	Median	Q3	Max	N	Range Avg Min	Range Avg Max
High School	12,480	27,040	25,546	27,414	27,934	32,864	5	24,450	33,821
Associate's	16,000	16,000	21,946	21,946	27,893	27,893	2		
Bachelor's									
Master's									
Doctoral									

ACCOUNTING (PAYABLES) CLERK - CONTINUED
Small Public Library
(Serving a population of 10,000 to 25,000)
Regional Data

	Min	Q1	Mean	Median	Q3	Max	N	Range Avg Min	Range Avg Max
North Atlantic	22,048	23,774	31,955	34,882	37,617	42,640	7	36,400	40,498
Great Lakes & Plains	16,640	18,023	36,244	22,433	36,200	120,000	8	21,767	28,756
Southeast	15,580	15,580	15,580	15,580	15,580	15,580	1	.	.
ALL REGIONS	15,580	18,460	33,076	26,714	36,457	120,000	16	29,084	34,627

State Data

	Min	Q1	Mean	Median	Q3	Max	N	Range Avg Min	Range Avg Max
IL	17,992	17,992	17,992	17,992	17,992	17,992	1	.	.
ME	22,048	22,048	22,048	22,048	22,048	22,048	1	.	.
MI	18,866	18,866	24,648	24,648	30,430	30,430	2	25,480	30,430
MS	15,580	15,580	15,580	15,580	15,580	15,580	1	.	.
ND	16,640	16,640	16,640	16,640	16,640	16,640	1	.	.
NJ	27,429	31,155	33,806	35,090	36,457	37,617	4	31,200	38,355
NY	42,640	42,640	42,640	42,640	42,640	42,640	1	41,600	42,640
OH	18,054	22,027	51,506	33,984	80,984	120,000	4	18,054	27,082
PA	23,774	23,774	23,774	23,774	23,774	23,774	1	.	.

Degree Required Data

	Min	Q1	Mean	Median	Q3	Max	N	Range Avg Min	Range Avg Max
High School	15,580	17,992	24,449	23,774	30,430	35,298	11	28,340	34,393
Associate's	.	.	.	.	.	.		.	.
Bachelor's	18,054	37,617	52,056	41,969	42,640	120,000	5	29,827	34,861
Master's	.	.	.	.	.	.		.	.
Doctoral	.	.	.	.	.	.		.	.

ACCOUNTING (PAYABLES) CLERK - CONTINUED
Medium Public Library
(Serving a population of 25,000 to 99,999)
Regional Data

	Min	Q1	Mean	Median	Q3	Max	N	Range Avg Min	Range Avg Max
North Atlantic	23,852	26,670	35,480	36,612	37,977	59,696	12	32,919	37,953
Great Lakes & Plains	19,615	21,258	28,697	26,530	35,803	46,488	10	22,991	33,589
Southeast	25,487	25,487	29,702	30,620	33,000	33,000	3	.	.
West & Southwest	25,000	31,928	36,400	35,048	40,955	49,067	5	32,219	42,276
ALL REGIONS	19,615	25,104	32,795	32,084	37,440	59,696	30	28,122	37,269

State Data

	Min	Q1	Mean	Median	Q3	Max	N	Range Avg Min	Range Avg Max
CA	49,067	49,067	49,067	49,067	49,067	49,067	1	40,934	50,253
CT	36,159	36,159	36,159	36,159	36,159	36,159	1	.	.
IA	35,803	35,803	35,803	35,803	35,803	35,803	1	.	.
ID	31,928	31,928	31,928	31,928	31,928	31,928	1	26,603	37,253
IL	19,615	19,781	29,475	26,884	37,200	46,488	6	24,180	36,405
IN	27,040	27,040	27,040	27,040	27,040	27,040	1	20,800	29,120
MA	23,852	37,066	36,571	37,498	38,399	45,114	6	32,919	37,953
MI	26,020	26,020	26,020	26,020	26,020	26,020	1	.	.
NC	30,620	30,620	30,620	30,620	30,620	30,620	1	.	.
NY	24,898	25,001	34,483	26,670	43,966	59,696	4	.	.
PA	32,240	32,240	32,240	32,240	32,240	32,240	1	.	.
TN	33,000	33,000	33,000	33,000	33,000	33,000	1	.	.
TX	25,000	25,000	25,000	25,000	25,000	25,000	1	.	.
UT	40,955	40,955	40,955	40,955	40,955	40,955	1	27,310	40,955
VA	25,487	25,487	25,487	25,487	25,487	25,487	1	.	.
WI	21,258	21,258	21,258	21,258	21,258	21,258	1	20,426	26,790
WY	35,048	35,048	35,048	35,048	35,048	35,048	1	34,029	40,643

Degree Required Data

	Min	Q1	Mean	Median	Q3	Max	N	Range Avg Min	Range Avg Max
High School	19,781	27,040	35,304	32,240	45,114	59,696	15	28,698	38,159
Associate's	19,615	24,128	29,581	26,020	36,159	40,955	9	27,618	36,026
Bachelor's	23,852	24,426	29,461	28,464	34,497	37,066	4	26,603	37,253
Master's	33,000	33,000	33,000	33,000	33,000	33,000	1	.	.
Doctoral	.	.	.	.	.	.		.	.

ACCOUNTING (PAYABLES) CLERK - CONTINUED
Large Public Library
(Serving a population of 100,000 to 499,999)
Regional Data

	Min	Q1	Mean	Median	Q3	Max	N	Range Avg Min	Range Avg Max
North Atlantic	21,965	28,865	35,848	32,698	40,560	63,001	17	25,813	40,801
Great Lakes & Plains	18,158	22,485	29,439	30,607	33,353	42,890	16	21,746	30,500
Southeast	23,920	27,626	31,099	32,208	33,761	36,513	11	25,178	25,698
West & Southwest	19,885	21,174	27,378	24,835	31,368	45,926	37	22,813	29,322
ALL REGIONS	18,158	23,046	30,068	29,192	33,761	63,001	81	22,967	30,750

State Data

	Min	Q1	Mean	Median	Q3	Max	N	Range Avg Min	Range Avg Max
CA	19,885	19,885	26,457	23,046	29,515	45,926	23	22,999	28,718
CO	21,174	21,174	22,214	22,422	23,046	23,046	3	21,414	32,365
GA	23,920	23,920	23,920	23,920	23,920	23,920	1	23,920	24,960
IL	42,890	42,890	42,890	42,890	42,890	42,890	1	.	.
MA	31,533	31,533	31,533	31,533	31,533	31,533	1	.	.
MD	28,143	28,143	29,212	29,212	30,282	30,282	2	.	.
MI	29,121	29,121	29,859	29,859	30,597	30,597	2	20,717	31,762
MN	33,488	33,488	34,294	34,294	35,100	35,100	2	.	.
MO	18,158	21,466	26,915	27,716	33,218	33,218	6	22,953	30,122
NJ	28,865	28,865	28,865	28,865	28,865	28,865	1	.	.
NY	28,755	32,698	43,687	44,206	49,254	63,001	6	28,621	46,124
OH	21,112	22,755	27,668	29,037	30,618	34,819	5	20,505	30,701
OR	31,368	31,368	31,368	31,368	31,368	31,368	1	.	.
PA	21,965	27,079	32,638	35,007	37,253	40,560	7	23,941	37,253
TX	20,966	24,835	28,721	29,192	32,787	36,260	7	21,445	36,712
VA	26,437	27,626	31,817	32,481	33,761	36,513	10	26,437	26,437
WA	29,120	29,120	35,134	34,978	41,304	41,304	3	22,880	29,120

Degree Required Data

	Min	Q1	Mean	Median	Q3	Max	N	Range Avg Min	Range Avg Max
High School	18,158	27,626	31,315	31,396	35,007	45,926	42	25,664	34,405
Associate's	21,965	23,920	30,744	30,282	34,978	41,304	11	21,549	28,683
Bachelor's	36,260	36,260	41,439	41,439	46,619	46,619	2	.	.
Master's	.	.	.	.	.	.		.	.
Doctoral	.	.	.	.	.	.		.	.

ACCOUNTING (PAYABLES) CLERK - CONTINUED
Very Large Public Library
(Serving a population of 500,000 or more)
Regional Data

	Min	Q1	Mean	Median	Q3	Max	N	Range Avg Min	Range Avg Max
North Atlantic	41,844	41,844	51,061	51,061	60,278	60,278	2	.	.
Great Lakes & Plains	27,706	30,356	31,971	31,714	33,550	36,400	16	23,351	34,473
Southeast	21,660	28,377	33,548	33,696	37,664	50,442	11	27,711	46,185
West & Southwest	23,254	29,286	33,714	35,485	37,003	48,204	15	27,388	37,574
ALL REGIONS	21,660	29,497	33,827	33,488	36,448	60,278	44	25,405	36,980

State Data

	Min	Q1	Mean	Median	Q3	Max	N	Range Avg Min	Range Avg Max
AZ	23,254	23,254	27,276	29,286	29,286	29,286	3	24,260	37,024
CA	28,787	31,894	36,830	36,462	39,170	48,204	6	29,786	35,866
CO	37,642	37,642	37,642	37,642	37,642	37,642	1	.	.
FL	21,660	28,377	33,148	33,467	37,664	50,442	9	.	.
IN	29,514	29,514	29,514	29,514	29,514	29,514	1	.	.
MD	41,844	41,844	41,844	41,844	41,844	41,844	1	.	.
MI	28,279	31,125	31,108	31,125	31,125	33,888	5	.	.
MO	30,261	30,261	30,261	30,261	30,261	30,261	1	.	.
NJ	60,278	60,278	60,278	60,278	60,278	60,278	1	.	.
OH	27,706	32,302	32,913	33,509	33,550	36,400	9	23,351	34,473
TX	26,940	28,210	32,227	32,482	36,244	37,003	4	29,578	44,346
UT	36,360	36,360	36,360	36,360	36,360	36,360	1	.	.
VA	34,264	34,264	35,348	35,348	36,433	36,433	2	27,711	46,185

Degree Required Data

	Min	Q1	Mean	Median	Q3	Max	N	Range Avg Min	Range Avg Max
High School	23,254	29,699	32,997	33,311	36,400	48,204	34	24,933	36,664
Associate's	29,479	29,479	39,961	39,961	50,442	50,442	2	.	.
Bachelor's	35,485	35,485	35,485	35,485	35,485	35,485	1	29,578	44,346
Master's	38,641	38,641	38,641	38,641	38,641	38,641	1	.	.
Doctoral	.	.	.	.	.	.	.	.	.

ACCOUNTING (PAYABLES) CLERK - CONTINUED
ALL PUBLIC LIBRARIES
Regional Data

	Min	Q1	Mean	Median	Q3	Max	N	Range Avg Min	Range Avg Max
North Atlantic	21,965	28,143	35,612	35,007	40,560	63,001	39	30,062	39,886
Great Lakes & Plains	12,480	22,755	30,460	30,430	33,509	120,000	55	22,585	32,355
Southeast	15,580	27,626	31,377	32,481	34,264	50,442	26	26,444	35,942
West & Southwest	19,885	23,046	29,804	29,156	36,260	49,067	58	24,675	32,283
ALL REGIONS	12,480	24,835	31,509	30,524	36,088	120,000	178	24,654	33,415

State Data

	Min	Q1	Mean	Median	Q3	Max	N	Range Avg Min	Range Avg Max
AZ	23,254	23,254	27,276	29,286	29,286	29,286	3	24,260	37,024
CA	19,885	20,883	29,285	24,835	36,462	49,067	30	24,472	30,371
CO	21,174	22,422	26,444	23,046	27,934	37,642	5	22,256	32,337
CT	27,893	27,893	32,026	32,026	36,159	36,159	2	.	.
FL	21,660	28,377	33,148	33,467	37,664	50,442	9	.	.
GA	23,920	23,920	23,920	23,920	23,920	23,920	1	23,920	24,960
IA	35,803	35,803	35,803	35,803	35,803	35,803	1	.	.
ID	31,928	31,928	31,928	31,928	31,928	31,928	1	26,603	37,253
IL	12,480	17,992	26,659	24,128	37,200	46,488	11	24,336	36,196
IN	27,040	27,040	27,989	27,414	29,514	29,514	3	20,800	29,120
KS	32,864	32,864	32,864	32,864	32,864	32,864	1	.	.
MA	23,852	31,533	35,851	37,440	38,399	45,114	7	32,919	37,953
MD	28,143	28,143	33,423	30,282	41,844	41,844	3	.	.
ME	22,048	22,048	22,048	22,048	22,048	22,048	1	.	.
MI	18,866	28,279	29,058	30,514	31,125	33,888	10	23,098	31,096
MN	33,488	33,488	34,294	34,294	35,100	35,100	2	.	.
MO	18,158	21,466	27,393	30,261	33,218	33,218	7	22,953	30,122
MS	15,580	15,580	15,580	15,580	15,580	15,580	1	.	.
NC	30,620	30,620	30,620	30,620	30,620	30,620	1	.	.
ND	16,640	16,640	16,640	16,640	16,640	16,640	1	.	.
NJ	27,429	28,865	37,395	35,090	37,617	60,278	6	31,200	38,355
NY	24,898	28,236	40,245	41,794	49,254	63,001	11	32,947	44,963
OH	18,054	27,706	35,588	32,729	34,819	120,000	18	22,049	32,723
OR	31,368	31,368	31,368	31,368	31,368	31,368	1	.	.
PA	21,965	27,079	31,609	32,240	37,253	40,560	9	23,941	37,253
TN	33,000	33,000	33,000	33,000	33,000	33,000	1	.	.
TX	20,966	25,802	29,579	29,336	34,136	37,003	12	25,511	40,529
UT	36,360	36,360	38,658	38,658	40,955	40,955	2	27,310	40,955
VA	25,487	27,626	31,874	32,753	34,264	36,513	13	27,286	39,602
WA	29,120	29,120	35,134	34,978	41,304	41,304	3	22,880	29,120
WI	21,258	21,258	21,258	21,258	21,258	21,258	1	20,426	26,790
WY	35,048	35,048	35,048	35,048	35,048	35,048	1	34,029	40,643

Degree Required Data

	Min	Q1	Mean	Median	Q3	Max	N	Range Avg Min	Range Avg Max
High School	12,480	27,429	31,433	31,125	35,298	59,696	107	25,935	35,736
Associate's	16,000	24,024	30,343	29,258	35,603	50,442	24	25,342	33,272
Bachelor's	18,054	28,464	41,374	36,663	42,304	120,000	12	28,959	37,830
Master's	33,000	33,000	35,821	35,821	38,641	38,641	2	.	.
Doctoral	.	.	.	.	.	.	.	.	.

SHELVER/PAGE

Moves and unloads carts. Shelves materials in appropriate locations. Shelf-reads assigned areas and straightens collection as needed. Removes out-of-place materials for reshelving.

Very Small Public Library
(Serving a population of less than 10,000)
Regional Data

	Min	Q1	Mean	Median	Q3	Max	N	Range Avg Min	Range Avg Max
North Atlantic	13,520	14,820	16,851	16,620	17,732	24,440	24	16,443	19,789
Great Lakes & Plains	10,712	11,825	13,538	12,688	14,238	26,400	44	13,402	20,253
Southeast	16,224	16,224	16,224	16,224	16,224	16,224	1	.	.
West & Southwest	11,981	11,981	14,696	15,315	16,070	17,514	6	12,688	14,851
ALL REGIONS	10,712	12,480	14,727	14,040	16,600	26,400	75	14,804	19,506

State Data

	Min	Q1	Mean	Median	Q3	Max	N	Range Avg Min	Range Avg Max
CO	11,981	11,981	11,981	11,981	11,981	11,981	2	10,712	12,397
CT	14,560	14,976	15,548	15,496	16,120	16,640	4	15,253	15,253
IA	11,232	11,336	12,418	12,688	12,688	14,560	15	10,712	13,832
IL	11,757	13,520	14,496	13,520	14,560	20,800	11	13,215	21,219
IN	11,752	11,773	12,314	11,794	12,854	13,915	4		
KS	18,013	18,013	22,206	22,206	26,400	26,400	2	12,480	18,720
MA	16,640	16,700	19,643	16,702	23,733	24,440	5	18,694	24,227
ME	20,800	20,800	20,800	20,800	20,800	20,800	1	20,800	20,800
MI	10,712	10,712	11,856	12,376	12,480	12,480	3		
MN	12,480	14,435	15,538	16,390	16,640	16,890	4	16,390	25,147
ND	10,712	10,712	10,712	10,712	10,712	10,712	1		
NH	17,056	17,056	17,420	17,420	17,784	17,784	2	16,411	21,653
NJ	13,520	13,520	16,640	17,680	18,720	18,720	3	14,664	20,107
NY	14,040	14,040	15,043	14,248	14,248	18,637	5	14,248	14,872
OH	10,712	10,712	11,336	11,336	11,960	11,960	2	10,712	14,040
TX	14,560	15,315	16,054	16,070	16,792	17,514	4	16,640	19,760
VT	15,080	15,298	15,813	15,786	16,329	16,600	4		
WI	11,856	11,856	12,595	12,595	13,333	13,333	2	11,856	13,936
WV	16,224	16,224	16,224	16,224	16,224	16,224	1		

Degree Required Data

	Min	Q1	Mean	Median	Q3	Max	N	Range Avg Min	Range Avg Max
High School	10,712	13,333	15,879	15,600	17,680	24,440	23	15,565	19,074
Associate's									
Bachelor's									
Master's									
Doctoral									

SHELVER/PAGE - CONTINUED
Small Public Library
(Serving a population of 10,000 to 25,000)
Regional Data

	Min	Q1	Mean	Median	Q3	Max	N	Range Avg Min	Range Avg Max
North Atlantic	12,480	14,560	16,480	15,912	17,680	35,360	79	20,971	25,592
Great Lakes & Plains	10,712	13,250	15,135	14,030	16,276	42,000	92	13,186	15,725
Southeast	14,791	15,484	16,703	17,242	17,242	17,680	7	.	.
West & Southwest	15,585	15,585	17,349	15,662	20,800	20,800	3	17,349	19,407
ALL REGIONS	10,712	13,520	15,820	15,080	17,420	42,000	181	17,008	21,301

State Data

	Min	Q1	Mean	Median	Q3	Max	N	Range Avg Min	Range Avg Max
CO	20,800	20,800	20,800	20,800	20,800	20,800	1	20,800	20,800
CT	15,392	15,392	16,434	16,494	17,451	18,450	9	15,392	18,450
IA	16,120	16,120	16,120	16,120	16,120	16,120	1	.	.
IL	13,000	13,520	16,652	14,560	18,720	42,000	39	13,618	15,048
IN	11,586	11,898	12,703	12,522	13,541	14,019	11	11,960	15,600
KS	11,488	12,480	13,444	13,312	14,248	16,224	11	10,400	13,173
MA	14,851	17,420	18,768	17,531	17,805	35,360	17	52,765	53,315
ME	13,520	13,520	13,520	13,520	13,520	13,520	1	.	.
MI	10,712	12,480	13,383	13,520	14,560	14,560	7	11,960	15,808
MN	16,952	16,952	16,952	16,952	16,952	16,952	5	16,952	16,952
NC	14,791	14,791	15,138	15,138	15,484	15,484	2	.	.
ND	12,480	12,480	12,480	12,480	12,480	12,480	1	.	.
NE	10,712	10,712	10,712	10,712	10,712	10,712	1	10,712	10,712
NH	15,080	15,496	16,278	16,141	16,370	18,283	10	14,760	27,356
NJ	12,792	13,250	16,519	16,341	18,699	23,213	14	13,546	20,056
NM	15,585	15,585	15,585	15,585	15,585	15,585	1	15,585	21,759
NY	14,040	14,560	15,696	14,560	15,080	27,040	19	15,680	15,680
OH	11,794	12,480	14,604	12,865	17,124	21,800	12	12,505	18,820
OR	15,662	15,662	15,662	15,662	15,662	15,662	1	15,662	15,662
PA	12,480	12,480	13,000	12,480	13,520	14,560	4	11,995	14,560
RI	14,040	14,040	15,434	14,040	17,160	17,888	5	14,040	24,856
VA	17,242	17,242	17,330	17,242	17,242	17,680	5	.	.
WI	14,789	15,122	15,594	15,761	16,067	16,067	4	14,789	16,910

Degree Required Data

	Min	Q1	Mean	Median	Q3	Max	N	Range Avg Min	Range Avg Max
High School	11,794	13,520	16,191	14,791	18,699	42,000	79	13,977	17,727
Associate's	.	.	.	.	.	.	.	.	.
Bachelor's	20,800	20,800	20,800	20,800	20,800	20,800	1	20,800	20,800
Master's	.	.	.	.	.	.	.	.	.
Doctoral	.	.	.	.	.	.	.	.	.

SHELVER/PAGE - CONTINUED
Medium Public Library
(Serving a population of 25,000 to 99,999)
Regional Data

	Min	Q1	Mean	Median	Q3	Max	N	Range Avg Min	Range Avg Max
North Atlantic	10,920	14,353	15,479	15,184	16,536	24,960	237	14,354	18,257
Great Lakes & Plains	10,712	13,520	15,865	14,560	17,472	38,459	309	14,946	21,460
Southeast	10,707	11,596	12,939	12,771	14,518	14,810	16	11,648	16,208
West & Southwest	12,480	15,787	18,267	18,158	20,758	25,418	114	16,995	21,735
ALL REGIONS	10,707	14,040	16,065	15,205	18,096	38,459	676	15,185	20,497

State Data

	Min	Q1	Mean	Median	Q3	Max	N	Range Avg Min	Range Avg Max
AR	11,128	11,804	13,047	13,270	14,290	14,518	4	11,596	15,600
CA	14,040	18,158	19,614	20,030	20,956	25,418	68	18,545	22,704
CT	15,392	15,392	16,002	15,943	16,640	16,640	30	15,392	18,850
DE	13,520	13,520	15,080	15,080	16,640	16,640	2	.	.
IA	12,480	12,480	14,213	14,560	14,560	16,640	6	12,480	16,640
ID	12,480	12,480	13,639	13,520	14,560	16,390	11	13,115	16,111
IL	13,520	14,248	17,077	15,205	19,531	38,459	161	15,817	24,730
IN	12,064	12,480	12,728	12,480	12,834	14,560	22	12,558	16,198
LA	12,064	12,314	13,489	13,541	14,664	14,810	4	11,149	15,683
MA	14,040	17,160	17,778	18,720	18,720	18,720	16	15,898	18,307
ME	14,560	14,560	14,560	14,560	14,560	14,560	21	.	.
MI	10,712	10,712	10,712	10,712	10,712	10,712	6	10,712	10,712
MO	10,712	10,712	10,842	10,712	10,920	11,378	15	10,712	12,563
MS	10,707	10,709	11,153	10,712	11,596	12,480	4	.	.
NC	12,979	12,979	12,979	12,979	12,979	12,979	1	12,480	13,978
ND	17,347	17,347	17,514	17,514	17,680	17,680	2	13,998	17,503
NJ	12,978	15,600	15,232	15,600	15,600	15,772	23	15,600	15,600
NY	14,040	14,248	15,794	15,080	15,704	24,960	105	14,214	20,142
OH	11,149	13,416	15,894	14,976	18,262	26,960	91	15,571	18,983
PA	10,920	10,920	12,299	11,814	13,447	18,720	32	11,024	13,840
RI	19,864	20,426	20,719	20,987	20,987	21,090	8	20,666	20,666
SC	14,603	14,603	14,603	14,603	14,603	14,603	2	.	.
TN	14,082	14,082	14,082	14,082	14,082	14,082	1	12,917	21,757
TX	14,560	15,288	17,506	16,869	18,242	24,981	31	15,606	22,375
UT	12,480	13,104	13,988	13,728	14,872	16,016	4	12,480	16,016
WI	13,146	13,146	13,236	13,218	13,229	13,458	6	13,146	15,912

Degree Required Data

	Min	Q1	Mean	Median	Q3	Max	N	Range Avg Min	Range Avg Max
High School	10,707	14,560	16,847	15,642	19,531	38,459	331	16,042	22,556
Associate's	13,520	13,520	13,929	14,061	14,206	14,206	3	.	.
Bachelor's	.	.	.	.	.	.	.	.	.
Master's	.	.	.	.	.	.	.	.	.
Doctoral	.	.	.	.	.	.	.	.	.

SHELVER/PAGE - CONTINUED
Large Public Library
(Serving a population of 100,000 to 499,999)
Regional Data

	Min	Q1	Mean	Median	Q3	Max	N	Range Avg Min	Range Avg Max
North Atlantic	12,480	14,040	15,449	14,560	14,602	24,048	136	14,958	16,569
Great Lakes & Plains	10,712	12,854	15,946	15,184	18,803	31,893	457	14,562	19,724
Southeast	10,712	12,126	14,985	14,560	17,088	47,456	269	15,404	19,187
West & Southwest	10,711	15,891	18,385	16,818	18,782	41,424	358	16,430	19,112
ALL REGIONS	10,711	13,728	16,394	15,829	18,512	47,456	1,220	15,220	19,029

State Data

	Min	Q1	Mean	Median	Q3	Max	N	Range Avg Min	Range Avg Max
AL	11,357	11,534	12,090	12,095	12,646	12,813	4	11,918	16,682
CA	14,061	16,162	17,926	17,451	18,782	35,922	163	16,780	19,727
CO	14,560	14,560	16,357	15,579	16,515	31,741	55	10,712	16,182
FL	13,312	14,754	15,224	15,198	16,063	17,088	64		
IL	13,520	14,040	18,291	19,032	21,032	31,893	85	14,668	16,658
IN	14,248	14,248	14,248	14,248	14,248	14,248	1	13,811	16,557
KS	18,512	18,512	19,430	18,855	19,708	25,875	80	18,551	30,932
LA	11,211	11,211	11,701	11,211	12,126	12,626	9	11,211	15,600
MA	14,040	14,040	14,040	14,040	14,040	14,040	1	14,040	14,040
MD	13,624	14,040	17,604	17,763	20,132	22,460	5	13,624	17,763
MI	10,712	12,064	12,636	12,854	13,250	15,974	102	12,002	14,359
MO	14,851	16,890	17,401	17,555	18,803	20,051	81	15,868	19,658
MS	10,712	10,712	11,431	10,712	11,128	15,142	65		
NC	12,813	13,083	14,013	14,560	14,560	15,184	44	14,111	21,797
NE	10,712	10,712	11,141	10,712	11,544	12,688	47	10,743	15,733
NJ	12,792	14,602	14,950	14,602	15,361	17,680	8		
NM	12,480	12,480	17,341	18,076	21,466	21,466	3		
NY	12,480	13,520	16,262	14,040	21,278	24,048	62	15,745	18,096
OH	13,000	13,520	14,443	13,998	15,080	18,013	50	13,406	16,953
OK	14,102	14,310	14,465	14,310	14,747	14,872	7	13,042	16,931
OR	17,829	33,030	33,571	33,048	34,667	41,424	20	15,600	18,595
PA	12,480	14,560	14,519	14,560	14,560	20,800	60	14,201	14,919
SC	15,725	15,839	16,793	16,234	16,463	21,549	8	15,725	23,566
TN	11,482	11,482	14,606	14,560	16,640	23,064	13	11,482	15,122
TX	10,711	16,809	16,594	17,272	17,389	22,776	39	13,047	18,801
VA	17,805	17,805	19,661	17,805	17,805	47,456	62	17,805	17,805
WA	16,078	16,640	18,146	16,640	19,018	22,248	71	16,596	17,164
WI	15,331	19,324	19,980	21,258	21,278	21,612	11	18,907	21,500

Degree Required Data

	Min	Q1	Mean	Median	Q3	Max	N	Range Avg Min	Range Avg Max
High School	10,712	14,040	17,174	15,142	19,745	47,456	455	15,372	18,322
Associate's	31,893	31,893	31,893	31,893	31,893	31,893	1	27,040	31,200
Bachelor's									
Master's									
Doctoral									

SHELVER/PAGE - CONTINUED
Very Large Public Library
(Serving a population of 500,000 or more)
Regional Data

	Min	Q1	Mean	Median	Q3	Max	N	Range Avg Min	Range Avg Max
North Atlantic	12,480	14,560	16,409	15,766	18,720	32,763	496	13,048	19,288
Great Lakes & Plains	13,416	15,080	16,324	16,016	17,576	27,331	793	16,447	20,273
Southeast	13,312	18,424	19,665	18,977	21,424	28,772	557	18,468	31,313
West & Southwest	12,854	17,222	24,715	23,650	32,630	41,850	808	25,004	31,261
ALL REGIONS	12,480	15,309	19,596	18,116	21,424	41,850	2,654	19,284	26,206

State Data

	Min	Q1	Mean	Median	Q3	Max	N	Range Avg Min	Range Avg Max
AZ	15,683	16,827	18,146	17,014	19,947	24,253	234	19,976	31,031
CA	14,040	32,630	30,851	32,630	34,216	41,850	356	29,409	35,252
FL	13,312	18,116	20,198	21,424	21,424	25,688	293	18,256	32,806
MD	12,480	14,560	16,712	16,640	18,720	32,763	368	13,048	19,288
MI	15,912	17,160	17,363	17,576	17,576	17,992	131	16,848	17,576
MO	13,874	14,664	16,073	16,328	16,869	21,216	73	14,139	21,214
NJ	14,040	14,560	15,539	14,560	15,600	25,896	128		
OH	13,416	15,080	15,993	15,080	17,222	27,331	531	17,511	22,439
OR	21,653	23,650	24,918	25,813	26,582	26,582	112	21,653	26,582
TX	12,854	23,150	23,634	24,398	25,730	26,770	14	22,672	32,011
UT	15,309	15,517	17,599	17,326	18,283	22,506	92	16,360	21,827
VA	18,424	18,424	19,073	18,424	18,943	28,772	264	18,530	30,883
WI	15,184	16,328	17,324	18,533	18,533	18,533	58	15,184	18,533

Degree Required Data

	Min	Q1	Mean	Median	Q3	Max	N	Range Avg Min	Range Avg Max
High School	13,416	15,080	17,216	16,848	19,427	39,036	782	17,573	23,480
Associate's	.	.	.	.	.	.	.	.	.
Bachelor's	.	.	.	.	.	.	.	.	.
Master's	.	.	.	.	.	.	.	.	.
Doctoral	.	.	.	.	.	.	.	.	.

SHELVER/PAGE - CONTINUED
ALL PUBLIC LIBRARIES
Regional Data

	Min	Q1	Mean	Median	Q3	Max	N	Range Avg Min	Range Avg Max
North Atlantic	10,920	14,560	16,065	15,080	17,807	35,360	972	14,447	19,138
Great Lakes & Plains	10,712	13,645	16,002	15,080	17,576	42,000	1,695	15,318	20,148
Southeast	10,707	16,438	18,029	18,424	20,472	47,456	850	17,613	28,137
West & Southwest	10,711	16,827	22,323	19,864	26,582	41,850	1,289	22,068	27,312
ALL REGIONS	10,707	14,560	18,068	16,909	19,386	47,456	4,806	17,496	23,230

State Data

	Min	Q1	Mean	Median	Q3	Max	N	Range Avg Min	Range Avg Max
AL	11,357	11,534	12,090	12,095	12,646	12,813	4	11,918	16,682
AR	11,128	11,804	13,047	13,270	14,290	14,518	4	11,596	15,600
AZ	15,683	16,827	18,146	17,014	19,947	24,253	234	19,976	31,031
CA	14,040	18,158	25,960	24,149	34,216	41,850	587	24,670	29,520
CO	11,981	14,560	16,283	15,496	16,515	31,741	58	13,234	15,444
CT	14,560	15,392	16,050	15,808	16,640	18,450	43	15,371	18,130
DE	13,520	13,520	15,080	15,080	16,640	16,640	2	.	.
FL	13,312	17,484	19,307	21,154	21,424	25,688	357	18,256	32,806
IA	11,232	12,480	13,076	12,688	14,560	16,640	22	12,227	16,239
ID	12,480	12,480	13,639	13,520	14,560	16,390	11	13,115	16,111
IL	11,757	14,040	17,274	15,205	19,926	42,000	296	15,315	22,087
IN	11,586	12,480	12,717	12,501	13,291	14,560	38	12,419	16,016
KS	11,488	18,512	18,782	18,512	19,656	26,400	93	18,188	30,153
LA	11,211	11,211	12,251	12,126	12,563	14,810	13	11,192	15,626
MA	14,040	17,264	18,353	17,531	18,720	35,360	39	28,498	30,623
MD	12,480	14,560	16,724	16,640	18,720	32,763	373	13,053	19,274
ME	13,520	14,560	14,786	14,560	14,560	20,800	23	20,800	20,800
MI	10,712	12,854	15,088	16,848	17,576	17,992	249	14,826	16,191
MN	12,480	16,390	16,323	16,952	16,952	16,952	9	16,741	20,025
MO	10,712	14,851	16,245	16,474	17,555	21,216	169	14,664	19,700
MS	10,707	10,712	11,415	10,712	11,128	15,142	69	.	.
NC	12,813	13,083	14,039	14,560	14,560	15,484	47	14,067	21,585
ND	10,712	11,596	14,555	14,914	17,514	17,680	4	13,998	17,503
NE	10,712	10,712	11,132	10,712	11,544	12,688	48	10,742	15,628
NH	15,080	15,704	16,468	16,370	17,274	18,283	12	15,035	26,406
NJ	12,792	14,560	15,569	14,872	15,600	25,896	176	14,742	17,694
NM	12,480	14,033	16,902	16,831	19,771	21,466	4	15,585	21,759
NY	12,480	14,040	15,916	14,851	16,640	27,040	191	14,974	18,839
OH	10,712	14,040	15,829	15,080	17,222	27,331	686	16,348	20,803
OK	14,102	14,310	14,465	14,310	14,747	14,872	7	13,042	16,931
OR	15,662	23,650	26,149	26,582	26,582	41,424	133	21,250	26,025
PA	10,920	12,480	13,716	14,560	14,560	20,800	96	13,176	14,584
RI	14,040	17,160	18,686	19,864	20,987	21,090	13	18,678	21,923
SC	14,603	15,725	16,355	16,078	16,390	21,549	10	15,725	23,566
TN	11,482	11,482	14,569	14,560	16,640	23,064	14	11,721	16,227
TX	10,711	16,118	18,011	17,272	18,387	26,770	88	15,304	21,849
UT	12,480	15,309	17,449	17,326	18,283	22,506	96	16,198	21,585
VA	17,242	18,424	19,157	18,424	18,903	47,456	331	18,418	28,871
VT	15,080	15,298	15,813	15,786	16,329	16,600	4	.	.
WA	16,078	16,640	18,146	16,640	19,018	22,248	71	16,596	17,164
WI	11,856	15,184	17,179	17,410	18,533	21,612	81	15,110	18,323
WV	16,224	16,224	16,224	16,224	16,224	16,224	1	.	.

Degree Required Data

	Min	Q1	Mean	Median	Q3	Max	N	Range Avg Min	Range Avg Max
High School	10,707	14,560	17,065	15,933	19,386	47,456	1,670	16,415	21,602
Associate's	13,520	13,790	18,420	14,134	23,050	31,893	4	27,040	31,200
Bachelor's	20,800	20,800	20,800	20,800	20,800	20,800	1	20,800	20,800
Master's	.	.	.	.	.	.	.	.	.
Doctoral	.	.	.	.	.	.	.	.	.

BOOKMOBILE DRIVER

Loads and unloads materials. Drives to and from specified locations. Assists patrons with material selection. Checks in and out materials.

Very Small Public Library
(Serving a population of less than 10,000)
Regional Data

	Min	Q1	Mean	Median	Q3	Max	N	Range Avg Min	Range Avg Max
Great Lakes & Plains	20,832	20,832	20,832	20,832	20,832	20,832	1	.	.
ALL REGIONS	20,832	20,832	20,832	20,832	20,832	20,832	1	.	.

State Data

	Min	Q1	Mean	Median	Q3	Max	N	Range Avg Min	Range Avg Max
NE	20,832	20,832	20,832	20,832	20,832	20,832	1	.	.

Degree Required Data

	Min	Q1	Mean	Median	Q3	Max	N	Range Avg Min	Range Avg Max
High School	20,832	20,832	20,832	20,832	20,832	20,832	1	.	.
Associate's	.	.	.	.	.	.	.	.	.
Bachelor's	.	.	.	.	.	.	.	.	.
Master's	.	.	.	.	.	.	.	.	.
Doctoral	.	.	.	.	.	.	.	.	.

BOOKMOBILE DRIVER - CONTINUED
Small Public Library
(Serving a population of 10,000 to 25,000)
Regional Data

	Min	Q1	Mean	Median	Q3	Max	N	Range Avg Min	Range Avg Max
Great Lakes & Plains	13,520	13,520	13,520	13,520	13,520	13,520	1	.	.
ALL REGIONS	13,520	13,520	13,520	13,520	13,520	13,520	1	.	.

State Data

	Min	Q1	Mean	Median	Q3	Max	N	Range Avg Min	Range Avg Max
IL	13,520	13,520	13,520	13,520	13,520	13,520	1	.	.

Degree Required Data

	Min	Q1	Mean	Median	Q3	Max	N	Range Avg Min	Range Avg Max
High School	.	.	.	.	.	.		.	.
Associate's	.	.	.	.	.	.		.	.
Bachelor's	.	.	.	.	.	.		.	.
Master's	.	.	.	.	.	.		.	.
Doctoral	.	.	.	.	.	.		.	.

BOOKMOBILE DRIVER - CONTINUED
Medium Public Library
(Serving a population of 25,000 to 99,999)
Regional Data

	Min	Q1	Mean	Median	Q3	Max	N	Range Avg Min	Range Avg Max
Great Lakes & Plains	18,158	20,800	27,017	25,251	30,306	50,380	19	23,198	35,277
Southeast	20,363	20,363	20,363	20,363	20,363	20,363	1	14,560	24,960
West & Southwest	11,432	11,432	17,156	17,156	22,880	22,880	2	16,640	24,960
ALL REGIONS	11,432	20,363	25,818	24,066	29,910	50,380	22	22,304	34,063

State Data

	Min	Q1	Mean	Median	Q3	Max	N	Range Avg Min	Range Avg Max
AR	20,363	20,363	20,363	20,363	20,363	20,363	1	14,560	24,960
IL	26,624	26,624	31,334	29,910	34,861	41,122	7	27,637	43,460
IN	18,720	18,720	19,413	18,720	20,800	20,800	3	19,413	29,120
MN	25,251	25,251	32,797	27,778	40,343	50,380	4	.	.
NE	22,880	22,880	22,880	22,880	22,880	22,880	2	20,800	22,880
OH	18,158	18,158	19,601	19,136	21,507	21,507	3	18,221	30,604
TX	22,880	22,880	22,880	22,880	22,880	22,880	1	16,640	24,960
UT	11,432	11,432	11,432	11,432	11,432	11,432	1	.	.

Degree Required Data

	Min	Q1	Mean	Median	Q3	Max	N	Range Avg Min	Range Avg Max
High School	11,432	19,136	24,497	22,880	27,019	41,122	17	22,788	34,632
Associate's	.	.	.	.	.	.		.	.
Bachelor's	50,380	50,380	50,380	50,380	50,380	50,380	1	.	.
Master's	.	.	.	.	.	.		.	.
Doctoral	.	.	.	.	.	.		.	.

BOOKMOBILE DRIVER - CONTINUED
Large Public Library
(Serving a population of 100,000 to 499,999)
Regional Data

	Min	Q1	Mean	Median	Q3	Max	N	Range Avg Min	Range Avg Max
North Atlantic	21,278	23,262	27,744	25,981	30,267	40,766	12	21,187	31,533
Great Lakes & Plains	16,640	19,968	27,028	24,190	30,805	45,302	17	19,386	28,759
Southeast	17,914	21,326	23,982	24,960	26,528	28,887	9	21,393	31,491
West & Southwest	25,626	25,948	30,878	30,202	35,204	38,688	8	27,218	37,811
ALL REGIONS	16,640	22,173	27,288	25,950	30,680	45,302	46	23,377	33,624

State Data

	Min	Q1	Mean	Median	Q3	Max	N	Range Avg Min	Range Avg Max
CA	30,680	30,680	34,216	33,280	38,688	38,688	3	31,200	39,520
IL	24,024	24,024	24,024	24,024	24,024	24,024	1	.	.
MD	40,766	40,766	40,766	40,766	40,766	40,766	1	.	.
MI	35,818	35,818	35,818	35,818	35,818	35,818	1	.	.
MN	35,000	35,000	39,654	39,654	44,308	44,308	2	.	.
MO	27,310	27,310	27,310	27,310	27,310	27,310	1	19,469	28,288
NC	17,914	17,914	21,400	21,326	24,960	24,960	3	24,960	39,520
NJ	22,880	25,630	29,331	29,055	31,479	37,890	6	.	.
OH	16,640	18,262	21,061	19,968	22,173	28,995	9	19,344	28,995
PA	21,278	21,278	23,236	23,645	23,645	26,333	5	21,187	31,533
SC	26,528	26,528	27,781	27,929	28,887	28,887	3	.	.
TN	19,094	19,094	19,094	19,094	19,094	19,094	1	17,826	23,462
VA	23,732	23,732	24,600	24,600	25,467	25,467	2	.	.
WA	25,626	25,626	28,875	26,270	29,723	37,128	5	25,626	37,128
WI	27,352	27,352	34,486	30,805	45,302	45,302	3	.	.

Degree Required Data

	Min	Q1	Mean	Median	Q3	Max	N	Range Avg Min	Range Avg Max
High School	16,640	21,986	27,436	25,626	31,142	45,302	36	23,621	33,957
Associate's	17,914	17,914	22,183	21,326	27,310	27,310	3	19,469	28,288
Bachelor's	23,732	26,528	28,579	27,929	28,887	35,818	5	.	.
Master's	.	.	.	.	.	.	.	.	.
Doctoral	.	.	.	.	.	.	.	.	.

BOOKMOBILE DRIVER - CONTINUED
Very Large Public Library
(Serving a population of 500,000 or more)
Regional Data

	Min	Q1	Mean	Median	Q3	Max	N	Range Avg Min	Range Avg Max
North Atlantic	20,800	20,800	20,800	20,800	20,800	20,800	1	16,640	22,880
Great Lakes & Plains	22,381	23,374	26,896	26,593	29,678	33,072	15	22,386	33,535
Southeast	20,852	27,163	35,666	33,849	45,329	55,461	7	.	.
West & Southwest	26,936	32,435	44,522	44,100	57,044	57,044	9	39,777	49,549
ALL REGIONS	20,800	26,056	33,581	29,950	36,451	57,044	32	31,349	41,301

State Data

	Min	Q1	Mean	Median	Q3	Max	N	Range Avg Min	Range Avg Max
AZ	26,936	26,936	26,936	26,936	26,936	26,936	1	22,152	32,365
CA	36,754	44,100	51,505	57,044	57,044	57,044	6	43,301	52,986
CO	32,299	32,299	32,299	32,299	32,299	32,299	1	.	.
FL	20,852	27,163	35,666	33,849	45,329	55,461	7	.	.
IN	26,111	26,111	26,111	26,111	26,111	26,111	1	.	.
MD	20,800	20,800	20,800	20,800	20,800	20,800	1	16,640	22,880
MI	26,593	28,135	29,164	29,677	30,193	30,708	4	.	.
MO	23,284	23,373	25,603	24,631	27,268	30,222	7	22,402	33,613
OH	22,381	22,381	27,151	26,000	33,072	33,072	3	22,381	33,509
TX	32,435	32,435	32,435	32,435	32,435	32,435	1	.	.

Degree Required Data

	Min	Q1	Mean	Median	Q3	Max	N	Range Avg Min	Range Avg Max
High School	20,800	24,631	30,328	27,268	32,435	55,461	23	22,446	32,305
Associate's	57,044	57,044	57,044	57,044	57,044	57,044	1	46,930	57,044
Bachelor's	.	.	.	.	.	.		.	.
Master's	.	.	.	.	.	.		.	.
Doctoral	.	.	.	.	.	.		.	.

BOOKMOBILE DRIVER - CONTINUED
ALL PUBLIC LIBRARIES
Regional Data

	Min	Q1	Mean	Median	Q3	Max	N	Range Avg Min	Range Avg Max
North Atlantic	20,800	22,880	27,210	25,630	29,055	40,766	13	20,429	30,091
Great Lakes & Plains	13,520	21,798	26,615	26,000	29,910	50,380	53	22,530	34,071
Southeast	17,914	21,326	28,580	26,528	30,860	55,461	17	19,115	29,314
West & Southwest	11,432	26,270	35,896	32,435	44,100	57,044	19	31,845	41,924
ALL REGIONS	11,432	22,880	28,747	26,609	32,299	57,044	102	24,920	35,666

State Data

	Min	Q1	Mean	Median	Q3	Max	N	Range Avg Min	Range Avg Max
AR	20,363	20,363	20,363	20,363	20,363	20,363	1	14,560	24,960
AZ	26,936	26,936	26,936	26,936	26,936	26,936	1	22,152	32,365
CA	30,680	36,754	45,742	44,100	57,044	57,044	9	39,844	49,139
CO	32,299	32,299	32,299	32,299	32,299	32,299	1		
FL	20,852	27,163	35,666	33,849	45,329	55,461	7		
IL	13,520	26,624	28,542	27,019	33,176	41,122	9	27,637	43,460
IN	18,720	18,720	21,088	19,760	23,456	26,111	4	19,413	29,120
MD	20,800	20,800	30,783	30,783	40,766	40,766	2	16,640	22,880
MI	26,593	29,676	30,495	29,678	30,708	35,818	5		
MN	25,251	25,251	35,083	32,653	44,308	50,380	6		
MO	23,284	23,374	25,816	25,848	27,289	30,222	8	20,935	30,950
NC	17,914	17,914	21,400	21,326	24,960	24,960	3	24,960	39,520
NE	20,832	20,832	22,197	22,880	22,880	22,880	3	20,800	22,880
NJ	22,880	25,630	29,331	29,055	31,479	37,890	6		
OH	16,640	18,262	21,987	21,507	24,190	33,072	15	20,062	31,291
PA	21,278	21,278	23,236	23,645	23,645	26,333	5	21,187	31,533
SC	26,528	26,528	27,781	27,929	28,887	28,887	3		
TN	19,094	19,094	19,094	19,094	19,094	19,094	1	17,826	23,462
TX	22,880	22,880	27,658	27,658	32,435	32,435	2	16,640	24,960
UT	11,432	11,432	11,432	11,432	11,432	11,432	1		
VA	23,732	23,732	24,600	24,600	25,467	25,467	2		
WA	25,626	25,626	28,875	26,270	29,723	37,128	5	25,626	37,128
WI	27,352	27,352	34,486	30,805	45,302	45,302	3		

Degree Required Data

	Min	Q1	Mean	Median	Q3	Max	N	Range Avg Min	Range Avg Max
High School	11,432	22,381	27,565	26,111	30,805	55,461	77	23,068	33,938
Associate's	17,914	19,620	30,899	24,318	42,177	57,044	4	33,199	42,666
Bachelor's	23,732	26,528	32,212	28,408	35,818	50,380	6		
Master's									
Doctoral									

COPY CATALOGER

Performs copy cataloging for print and non-print materials using OCLC, AACRII, MARC, DDC and local consortium standards. Edits previously cataloged materials. Serves a resource for other library personnel concerning cataloging rules and practices.

Very Small Public Library
(Serving a population of less than 10,000)
Regional Data

	Min	Q1	Mean	Median	Q3	Max	N	Range Avg Min	Range Avg Max
North Atlantic	30,763	30,763	39,874	39,874	48,984	48,984	2	26,603	39,894
Great Lakes & Plains	20,800	20,800	22,318	22,318	23,837	23,837	2	14,560	22,880
ALL REGIONS	20,800	22,318	31,096	27,300	39,874	48,984	4	20,582	31,387

State Data

	Min	Q1	Mean	Median	Q3	Max	N	Range Avg Min	Range Avg Max
KS	20,800	20,800	22,318	22,318	23,837	23,837	2	14,560	22,880
ME	30,763	30,763	30,763	30,763	30,763	30,763	1	26,603	39,894
NJ	48,984	48,984	48,984	48,984	48,984	48,984	1	.	.

Degree Required Data

	Min	Q1	Mean	Median	Q3	Max	N	Range Avg Min	Range Avg Max
High School	20,800	20,800	31,207	23,837	48,984	48,984	3	14,560	22,880
Associate's	.	.	.	.	.	.		.	.
Bachelor's	30,763	30,763	30,763	30,763	30,763	30,763	1	26,603	39,894
Master's	.	.	.	.	.	.		.	.
Doctoral	.	.	.	.	.	.		.	.

COPY CATALOGER - CONTINUED
Small Public Library
(Serving a population of 10,000 to 25,000)
Regional Data

	Min	Q1	Mean	Median	Q3	Max	N	Range Avg Min	Range Avg Max
North Atlantic	20,384	20,384	20,384	20,384	20,384	20,384	1	16,640	22,048
Great Lakes & Plains	14,352	21,216	31,750	27,040	34,859	62,400	9	23,227	48,533
ALL REGIONS	14,352	20,384	30,613	26,010	34,859	62,400	10	22,286	44,750

State Data

	Min	Q1	Mean	Median	Q3	Max	N	Range Avg Min	Range Avg Max
IL	14,352	21,216	34,355	30,160	47,840	62,400	6	24,960	52,416
KS	34,859	34,859	34,859	34,859	34,859	34,859	1	.	.
ME	20,384	20,384	20,384	20,384	20,384	20,384	1	16,640	22,048
MO	19,781	19,781	19,781	19,781	19,781	19,781	1	14,560	29,120
OH	24,981	24,981	24,981	24,981	24,981	24,981	1	.	.

Degree Required Data

	Min	Q1	Mean	Median	Q3	Max	N	Range Avg Min	Range Avg Max
High School	14,352	17,066	19,874	20,082	22,682	24,981	4	15,600	25,584
Associate's	21,216	27,040	37,773	34,070	47,840	62,400	6	24,960	52,416
Bachelor's	.	.	.	.	.	.		.	.
Master's	.	.	.	.	.	.		.	.
Doctoral	.	.	.	.	.	.		.	.

COPY CATALOGER - CONTINUED
Medium Public Library
(Serving a population of 25,000 to 99,999)
Regional Data

	Min	Q1	Mean	Median	Q3	Max	N	Range Avg Min	Range Avg Max
North Atlantic	15,538	21,424	34,513	36,400	45,261	47,646	11	36,400	45,282
Great Lakes & Plains	20,571	25,480	30,749	30,649	33,280	48,090	14	24,478	32,299
Southeast	20,888	23,462	26,205	23,748	32,386	33,000	6	23,150	33,696
West & Southwest	12,480	22,824	31,107	29,329	37,190	52,021	14	30,160	40,105
ALL REGIONS	12,480	23,700	31,175	30,098	36,400	52,021	45	28,843	37,887

State Data

	Min	Q1	Mean	Median	Q3	Max	N	Range Avg Min	Range Avg Max
AR	23,462	23,462	23,629	23,629	23,795	23,795	2	.	.
CA	29,266	29,266	35,152	29,349	46,842	46,842	3	30,105	37,287
CO	29,310	29,310	29,310	29,310	29,310	29,310	1	.	.
CT	36,400	40,227	42,749	44,658	45,271	45,282	4	36,400	45,282
IL	23,271	24,648	31,480	25,522	41,827	48,090	6	22,880	32,188
IN	32,469	32,469	32,469	32,469	32,469	32,469	1	.	.
LA	32,386	32,386	32,386	32,386	32,386	32,386	1	23,150	33,696
MA	34,802	34,802	34,802	34,802	34,802	34,802	1	.	.
NC	23,700	23,700	23,700	23,700	23,700	23,700	1	.	.
ND	32,739	32,739	32,739	32,739	32,739	32,739	1	27,955	41,933
NJ	27,337	27,337	27,337	27,337	27,337	27,337	1	.	.
NY	41,902	41,902	44,774	44,774	47,646	47,646	2	.	.
OH	20,571	27,976	29,401	30,649	33,280	33,280	6	24,385	29,162
PA	15,538	15,538	18,987	20,000	21,424	21,424	3	.	.
TN	33,000	33,000	33,000	33,000	33,000	33,000	1	.	.
TX	12,480	19,688	25,056	22,824	31,886	42,301	7	11,440	14,040
UT	36,130	36,130	44,075	44,075	52,021	52,021	2	37,669	56,493
VA	20,888	20,888	20,888	20,888	20,888	20,888	1	.	.
WY	37,190	37,190	37,190	37,190	37,190	37,190	1	34,029	41,850

Degree Required Data

	Min	Q1	Mean	Median	Q3	Max	N	Range Avg Min	Range Avg Max
High School	12,480	23,271	29,890	27,337	36,400	47,646	23	28,769	35,762
Associate's	19,688	21,104	29,218	26,312	35,569	48,090	8	22,880	29,120
Bachelor's	20,000	27,414	31,648	32,562	35,466	42,301	8	26,466	37,598
Master's	33,000	33,000	42,510	42,510	52,021	52,021	2	42,182	63,253
Doctoral	.	.	.	.	.	.		.	.

COPY CATALOGER - CONTINUED
Large Public Library
(Serving a population of 100,000 to 499,999)
Regional Data

	Min	Q1	Mean	Median	Q3	Max	N	Range Avg Min	Range Avg Max
North Atlantic	23,716	31,533	31,934	32,968	35,076	37,511	17	24,461	34,015
Great Lakes & Plains	18,700	24,864	31,452	33,218	37,572	44,579	29	24,480	37,516
Southeast	17,992	23,212	31,343	28,413	34,778	72,172	22	24,423	37,457
West & Southwest	16,702	24,510	31,348	29,436	36,402	52,000	32	30,489	39,869
ALL REGIONS	16,702	24,510	31,477	32,053	36,396	72,172	100	26,287	37,582

State Data

	Min	Q1	Mean	Median	Q3	Max	N	Range Avg Min	Range Avg Max
CA	29,856	35,485	40,883	39,437	47,840	52,000	9	35,247	43,704
FL	29,785	29,785	32,282	32,282	34,778	34,778	2	.	.
GA	22,880	22,880	23,046	23,046	23,212	23,212	2	.	.
IL	20,935	24,864	32,758	36,861	37,572	39,454	6	25,230	32,947
IN	18,700	20,421	23,903	24,413	27,386	28,087	4	.	.
KS	36,525	36,525	38,036	38,459	39,125	39,125	3	28,995	48,318
LA	33,197	33,197	33,197	33,197	33,197	33,197	1	37,024	51,293
MA	31,533	31,533	31,533	31,533	31,533	31,533	1	.	.
MD	23,716	23,716	31,413	32,430	35,568	37,511	7	23,712	35,568
MI	33,218	33,218	33,218	33,218	33,218	33,218	2	22,069	33,218
MN	19,989	21,278	25,492	24,271	29,706	33,438	4	.	.
MO	23,109	23,109	28,683	28,683	34,258	34,258	2	22,381	32,521
MS	20,333	20,333	23,057	23,057	25,781	25,781	2	.	.
NC	19,999	23,937	25,696	24,960	27,040	33,280	6	22,880	37,440
NM	24,648	24,648	24,648	24,648	24,648	24,648	1	.	.
NY	29,099	30,847	32,434	32,781	34,022	35,076	4	28,122	32,968
OH	20,613	25,522	29,349	27,019	31,990	41,600	5	22,721	34,431
OR	21,195	31,824	33,357	36,396	36,408	36,408	8	21,195	27,934
PA	23,899	33,509	32,344	33,509	35,402	35,402	5	21,549	33,509
TN	17,992	23,124	28,495	31,200	31,378	38,783	5	17,992	23,691
TX	16,702	22,235	24,548	24,767	26,770	34,346	14	18,481	32,417
VA	41,802	42,888	50,733	44,480	58,579	72,172	4	.	.
WI	44,177	44,177	44,445	44,579	44,579	44,579	3	.	.

Degree Required Data

	Min	Q1	Mean	Median	Q3	Max	N	Range Avg Min	Range Avg Max
High School	16,702	23,899	30,121	29,016	35,402	52,000	75	25,937	36,822
Associate's	19,999	23,109	35,147	30,150	43,973	72,172	10	20,786	29,571
Bachelor's	31,200	33,197	35,831	36,525	38,783	39,454	11	29,586	46,201
Master's	.	.	.	.	.	.		.	.
Doctoral	.	.	.	.	.	.		.	.

COPY CATALOGER - CONTINUED
Very Large Public Library
(Serving a population of 500,000 or more)
Regional Data

	Min	Q1	Mean	Median	Q3	Max	N	Range Avg Min	Range Avg Max
North Atlantic	37,952	37,952	39,898	39,898	41,844	41,844	2		
Great Lakes & Plains	26,678	32,820	38,500	38,474	42,218	48,582	28	31,343	35,485
Southeast	19,995	29,141	40,566	49,225	50,573	53,896	5	33,331	55,551
West & Southwest	21,029	27,343	36,136	37,877	41,392	53,268	19	28,392	36,975
ALL REGIONS	19,995	31,864	37,912	38,474	43,524	53,896	54	30,396	38,220

State Data

	Min	Q1	Mean	Median	Q3	Max	N	Range Avg Min	Range Avg Max
AZ	30,451	30,451	30,451	30,451	30,451	30,451	1	22,152	32,365
CA	43,524	43,524	48,476	48,636	53,268	53,268	3		
CO	46,969	46,969	46,969	46,969	46,969	46,969	1		
FL	19,995	19,995	24,568	24,568	29,141	29,141	2		
MD	37,952	37,952	39,898	39,898	41,844	41,844	2		
OH	26,678	32,594	38,745	39,978	45,793	48,582	22	28,782	33,238
OR	37,877	41,392	40,806	41,392	41,392	41,392	6	33,654	41,392
TX	27,343	27,343	32,090	32,090	36,837	36,837	2	26,832	40,206
UT	21,029	24,586	25,787	26,016	28,536	28,538	6	20,467	28,600
VA	49,225	49,225	51,231	50,573	53,896	53,896	3	33,331	55,551
WI	34,509	37,221	37,604	38,474	38,474	38,474	6	34,757	38,480

Degree Required Data

	Min	Q1	Mean	Median	Q3	Max	N	Range Avg Min	Range Avg Max
High School	26,678	31,864	39,518	38,474	47,167	53,896	26	33,068	42,990
Associate's	36,837	39,634	41,289	41,392	41,392	48,636	8	32,680	41,223
Bachelor's	29,141	37,565	39,594	39,978	39,978	53,268	13	28,782	33,238
Master's									
Doctoral									

COPY CATALOGER - CONTINUED
ALL PUBLIC LIBRARIES
Regional Data

	Min	Q1	Mean	Median	Q3	Max	N	Range Avg Min	Range Avg Max
North Atlantic	15,538	29,099	33,408	33,509	37,511	48,984	33	27,201	36,534
Great Lakes & Plains	14,352	25,974	33,549	33,249	39,454	62,400	82	26,549	37,298
Southeast	17,992	23,462	31,806	29,141	34,778	72,172	33	26,968	42,509
West & Southwest	12,480	25,163	32,696	30,451	39,437	53,268	65	29,583	38,791
ALL REGIONS	12,480	24,981	32,997	32,820	38,783	72,172	213	27,656	38,281

State Data

	Min	Q1	Mean	Median	Q3	Max	N	Range Avg Min	Range Avg Max
AR	23,462	23,462	23,629	23,629	23,795	23,795	2		
AZ	30,451	30,451	30,451	30,451	30,451	30,451	1	22,152	32,365
CA	29,266	34,248	41,256	43,524	47,840	53,268	15	33,704	41,779
CO	29,310	29,310	38,140	38,140	46,969	46,969	2		
CT	36,400	40,227	42,749	44,658	45,271	45,282	4	36,400	45,282
FL	19,995	24,568	28,425	29,463	32,282	34,778	4		
GA	22,880	22,880	23,046	23,046	23,212	23,212	2		
IL	14,352	24,648	32,864	30,160	39,454	62,400	18	24,474	44,925
IN	18,700	22,141	25,616	26,684	28,087	32,469	5		
KS	20,800	23,837	32,267	35,692	38,459	39,125	6	25,386	41,959
LA	32,386	32,386	32,791	32,791	33,197	33,197	2	30,087	42,494
MA	31,533	31,533	33,167	33,167	34,802	34,802	2		
MD	23,716	32,115	33,299	34,836	37,511	41,844	9	23,712	35,568
ME	20,384	20,384	25,574	25,574	30,763	30,763	2	21,622	30,971
MI	33,218	33,218	33,218	33,218	33,218	33,218	2	22,069	33,218
MN	19,989	21,278	25,492	24,271	29,706	33,438	4		
MO	19,781	19,781	25,716	23,109	34,258	34,258	3	19,774	31,387
MS	20,333	20,333	23,057	23,057	25,781	25,781	2		
NC	19,999	23,700	25,411	24,960	27,040	33,280	7	22,880	37,440
ND	32,739	32,739	32,739	32,739	32,739	32,739	1	27,955	41,933
NJ	27,337	27,337	38,161	38,161	48,984	48,984	2		
NM	24,648	24,648	24,648	24,648	24,648	24,648	1		
NY	29,099	32,594	36,548	34,022	41,902	47,646	6	28,122	32,968
OH	20,571	30,936	35,309	33,050	39,978	48,582	34	26,541	32,620
OR	21,195	36,396	36,550	36,408	41,392	41,392	14	31,875	39,469
PA	15,538	20,712	27,335	28,704	34,455	35,402	8	21,549	33,509
TN	17,992	23,124	29,246	31,289	33,000	38,783	6	17,992	23,691
TX	12,480	21,319	25,358	24,892	27,435	42,301	23	18,808	29,770
UT	21,029	24,953	30,359	27,624	32,334	52,021	8	27,348	39,757
VA	20,888	42,888	47,189	47,105	52,235	72,172	8	33,331	55,551
WI	34,509	38,474	39,884	38,474	44,177	44,579	9	34,757	38,480
WY	37,190	37,190	37,190	37,190	37,190	37,190	1	34,029	41,850

Degree Required Data

	Min	Q1	Mean	Median	Q3	Max	N	Range Avg Min	Range Avg Max
High School	12,480	23,899	31,657	30,936	36,408	53,896	131	27,408	37,179
Associate's	19,688	24,293	35,693	35,848	41,815	72,172	32	27,425	41,779
Bachelor's	20,000	32,594	36,146	36,525	39,978	53,268	33	28,269	38,147
Master's	33,000	33,000	42,510	42,510	52,021	52,021	2	42,182	63,253
Doctoral									

BOOK REPAIRER

Checks the condition of the materials and determines the most suitable method of repairing. Recreates packaging, labels and barcodes.

Very Small Public Library
(Serving a population of less than 10,000)
Regional Data

	Min	Q1	Mean	Median	Q3	Max	N	Range Avg Min	Range Avg Max
Great Lakes & Plains	16,640	16,640	19,448	19,448	22,256	22,256	2	14,560	22,880
ALL REGIONS	16,640	16,640	19,448	19,448	22,256	22,256	2	14,560	22,880

State Data

	Min	Q1	Mean	Median	Q3	Max	N	Range Avg Min	Range Avg Max
KS	16,640	16,640	19,448	19,448	22,256	22,256	2	14,560	22,880

Degree Required Data

	Min	Q1	Mean	Median	Q3	Max	N	Range Avg Min	Range Avg Max
High School	16,640	16,640	19,448	19,448	22,256	22,256	2	14,560	22,880
Associate's	.	.	.	.	.	.		.	.
Bachelor's	.	.	.	.	.	.		.	.
Master's	.	.	.	.	.	.		.	.
Doctoral	.	.	.	.	.	.		.	.

BOOK REPAIRER - CONTINUED
Small Public Library
(Serving a population of 10,000 to 25,000)
Regional Data

	Min	Q1	Mean	Median	Q3	Max	N	Range Avg Min	Range Avg Max
North Atlantic	27,867	27,867	27,867	27,867	27,867	27,867	1	.	.
Great Lakes & Plains	14,560	14,560	18,928	17,264	24,960	24,960	3	22,880	52,000
ALL REGIONS	14,560	15,912	21,163	21,112	26,414	27,867	4	22,880	52,000

State Data

	Min	Q1	Mean	Median	Q3	Max	N	Range Avg Min	Range Avg Max
IL	24,960	24,960	24,960	24,960	24,960	24,960	1	22,880	52,000
KS	17,264	17,264	17,264	17,264	17,264	17,264	1	.	.
MI	14,560	14,560	14,560	14,560	14,560	14,560	1	.	.
NY	27,867	27,867	27,867	27,867	27,867	27,867	1	.	.

Degree Required Data

	Min	Q1	Mean	Median	Q3	Max	N	Range Avg Min	Range Avg Max
High School	14,560	14,560	19,897	17,264	27,867	27,867	3	.	.
Associate's	24,960	24,960	24,960	24,960	24,960	24,960	1	22,880	52,000
Bachelor's	.	.	.	.	.	.		.	.
Master's	.	.	.	.	.	.		.	.
Doctoral	.	.	.	.	.	.		.	.

BOOK REPAIRER - CONTINUED
Medium Public Library
(Serving a population of 25,000 to 99,999)
Regional Data

	Min	Q1	Mean	Median	Q3	Max	N	Range Avg Min	Range Avg Max
North Atlantic	15,538	21,424	26,759	23,764	37,253	38,813	6	26,513	38,293
Great Lakes & Plains	16,058	17,472	20,977	22,610	22,942	24,170	6	18,013	24,593
Southeast	20,454	20,454	20,570	20,570	20,686	20,686	2	.	.
ALL REGIONS	15,538	20,454	23,397	22,547	24,170	38,813	14	20,846	29,159

State Data

	Min	Q1	Mean	Median	Q3	Max	N	Range Avg Min	Range Avg Max
CT	22,818	22,818	30,035	30,035	37,253	37,253	2	30,118	37,253
IL	16,058	16,058	19,233	17,472	24,170	24,170	3	17,430	26,465
LA	20,454	20,454	20,454	20,454	20,454	20,454	1	.	.
MN	22,277	22,277	22,721	22,942	22,942	22,942	3	18,595	22,721
MS	20,686	20,686	20,686	20,686	20,686	20,686	1	.	.
NY	24,710	24,710	31,762	31,762	38,813	38,813	2	24,710	38,813
PA	15,538	15,538	18,481	18,481	21,424	21,424	2	.	.

Degree Required Data

	Min	Q1	Mean	Median	Q3	Max	N	Range Avg Min	Range Avg Max
High School	15,538	17,472	23,658	21,055	24,710	38,813	10	21,972	32,379
Associate's	.	.	.	.	.	.		.	.
Bachelor's	22,818	22,818	22,818	22,818	22,818	22,818	1	.	.
Master's	.	.	.	.	.	.		.	.
Doctoral	.	.	.	.	.	.		.	.

BOOK REPAIRER - CONTINUED
Large Public Library
(Serving a population of 100,000 to 499,999)
Regional Data

	Min	Q1	Mean	Median	Q3	Max	N	Range Avg Min	Range Avg Max
Great Lakes & Plains	13,250	13,645	21,047	19,230	24,700	36,604	7	17,119	22,317
Southeast	23,941	23,941	25,317	24,507	25,273	33,180	21	23,941	23,941
West & Southwest	14,705	16,907	25,881	25,002	33,264	41,600	7	19,562	25,074
ALL REGIONS	13,250	23,941	24,576	24,507	25,273	41,600	35	21,305	23,826

State Data

	Min	Q1	Mean	Median	Q3	Max	N	Range Avg Min	Range Avg Max
CA	18,554	18,554	24,846	24,846	31,138	31,138	2	20,280	24,846
IN	19,230	19,230	19,230	19,230	19,230	19,230	1		
MI	13,250	13,250	13,447	13,447	13,645	13,645	2	12,480	15,600
MN	24,616	24,616	24,658	24,658	24,700	24,700	2		
MO	15,288	15,288	15,288	15,288	15,288	15,288	1	14,851	21,466
NE	36,604	36,604	36,604	36,604	36,604	36,604	1	28,664	36,604
OR	41,600	41,600	41,600	41,600	41,600	41,600	1	15,600	18,595
TX	14,705	14,705	14,705	14,705	14,705	14,705	1		
VA	23,941	23,941	25,317	24,507	25,273	33,180	21	23,941	23,941
WA	16,907	16,907	25,057	25,002	33,264	33,264	3	22,090	32,011

Degree Required Data

	Min	Q1	Mean	Median	Q3	Max	N	Range Avg Min	Range Avg Max
High School	13,250	23,941	24,183	24,229	25,273	41,600	32	20,926	22,767
Associate's									
Bachelor's	36,604	36,604	36,604	36,604	36,604	36,604	1	28,664	36,604
Master's									
Doctoral									

BOOK REPAIRER - CONTINUED
Very Large Public Library
(Serving a population of 500,000 or more)
Regional Data

	Min	Q1	Mean	Median	Q3	Max	N	Range Avg Min	Range Avg Max
Great Lakes & Plains	22,381	25,064	29,163	26,832	28,725	47,167	13	20,904	30,056
Southeast	31,565	31,565	31,565	31,565	31,565	31,565	1		
West & Southwest	22,152	23,254	28,192	27,050	30,451	55,926	82	23,513	33,393
ALL REGIONS	22,152	23,254	28,358	27,050	30,451	55,926	96	23,224	33,023

State Data

	Min	Q1	Mean	Median	Q3	Max	N	Range Avg Min	Range Avg Max
AZ	22,152	23,254	26,525	26,936	28,974	34,882	70	22,152	32,365
CA	27,164	37,336	40,235	39,036	46,228	55,926	9	36,146	43,803
FL	31,565	31,565	31,565	31,565	31,565	31,565	1		
OH	22,381	25,064	29,163	26,832	28,725	47,167	13	20,904	30,056
OR	33,654	33,654	33,654	33,654	33,654	33,654	2	27,373	33,654
TX	25,522	25,522	25,522	25,522	25,522	25,522	1	22,672	32,011

Degree Required Data

	Min	Q1	Mean	Median	Q3	Max	N	Range Avg Min	Range Avg Max
High School	22,152	23,254	27,565	26,936	29,702	55,926	87	22,415	32,402
Associate's									
Bachelor's									
Master's									
Doctoral									

BOOK REPAIRER - CONTINUED
ALL PUBLIC LIBRARIES
Regional Data

	Min	Q1	Mean	Median	Q3	Max	N	Range Avg Min	Range Avg Max
North Atlantic	15,538	21,424	26,917	24,710	37,253	38,813	7	26,513	38,293
Great Lakes & Plains	13,250	17,472	24,129	22,942	26,832	47,167	31	19,229	27,830
Southeast	20,454	23,941	25,182	24,229	25,273	33,180	24	23,941	23,941
West & Southwest	14,705	23,254	28,010	26,936	30,451	55,926	89	23,325	32,997
ALL REGIONS	13,250	22,942	26,713	25,273	29,702	55,926	151	22,690	31,478

State Data

	Min	Q1	Mean	Median	Q3	Max	N	Range Avg Min	Range Avg Max
AZ	22,152	23,254	26,525	26,936	28,974	34,882	70	22,152	32,365
CA	18,554	30,867	37,437	37,336	46,228	55,926	11	32,620	39,590
CT	22,818	22,818	30,035	30,035	37,253	37,253	2	30,118	37,253
FL	31,565	31,565	31,565	31,565	31,565	31,565	1	.	.
IL	16,058	16,765	20,665	20,821	24,565	24,960	4	18,793	32,848
IN	19,230	19,230	19,230	19,230	19,230	19,230	1	.	.
KS	16,640	16,640	18,720	17,264	22,256	22,256	3	14,560	22,880
LA	20,454	20,454	20,454	20,454	20,454	20,454	1	.	.
MI	13,250	13,250	13,818	13,645	14,560	14,560	3	12,480	15,600
MN	22,277	22,942	23,496	22,942	24,616	24,700	5	18,595	22,721
MO	15,288	15,288	15,288	15,288	15,288	15,288	1	14,851	21,466
MS	20,686	20,686	20,686	20,686	20,686	20,686	1	.	.
NE	36,604	36,604	36,604	36,604	36,604	36,604	1	28,664	36,604
NY	24,710	24,710	30,463	27,867	38,813	38,813	3	24,710	38,813
OH	22,381	25,064	29,163	26,832	28,725	47,167	13	20,904	30,056
OR	33,654	33,654	36,303	33,654	41,600	41,600	3	23,449	28,635
PA	15,538	15,538	18,481	18,481	21,424	21,424	2	.	.
TX	14,705	14,705	20,113	20,113	25,522	25,522	2	22,672	32,011
VA	23,941	23,941	25,317	24,507	25,273	33,180	21	23,941	23,941
WA	16,907	16,907	25,057	25,002	33,264	33,264	3	22,090	32,011

Degree Required Data

	Min	Q1	Mean	Median	Q3	Max	N	Range Avg Min	Range Avg Max
High School	13,250	23,254	26,173	25,273	28,974	55,926	134	22,113	31,012
Associate's	24,960	24,960	24,960	24,960	24,960	24,960	1	22,880	52,000
Bachelor's	22,818	22,818	29,711	29,711	36,604	36,604	2	28,664	36,604
Master's	.	.	.	.	.	.		.	.
Doctoral	.	.	.	.	.	.		.	.

PROCESSING ASSISTANT

Prepares materials for placement throughout the library. Prepares spines, labels and barcodes. May send materials to outside bindery for processing. May perform simple repairs as needed. Transfers processed materials to appropriate department.

Very Small Public Library
(Serving a population of less than 10,000)
Regional Data

	Min	Q1	Mean	Median	Q3	Max	N	Range Avg Min	Range Avg Max
Great Lakes & Plains	18,720	19,605	20,722	20,645	21,840	22,880	4	18,720	29,120
Southeast	28,350	28,350	28,350	28,350	28,350	28,350	1	21,840	31,200
ALL REGIONS	18,720	20,489	22,248	20,800	22,880	28,350	5	19,760	29,813

State Data

	Min	Q1	Mean	Median	Q3	Max	N	Range Avg Min	Range Avg Max
AL	28,350	28,350	28,350	28,350	28,350	28,350	1	21,840	31,200
IA	18,720	18,720	19,605	19,605	20,489	20,489	2	.	.
IL	20,800	20,800	21,840	21,840	22,880	22,880	2	18,720	29,120

Degree Required Data

	Min	Q1	Mean	Median	Q3	Max	N	Range Avg Min	Range Avg Max
High School	18,720	19,760	22,688	21,840	25,615	28,350	4	19,760	29,813
Associate's	20,489	20,489	20,489	20,489	20,489	20,489	1	.	.
Bachelor's	.	.	.	.	.	.		.	.
Master's	.	.	.	.	.	.		.	.
Doctoral	.	.	.	.	.	.		.	.

PROCESSING ASSISTANT - CONTINUED
Small Public Library
(Serving a population of 10,000 to 25,000)
Regional Data

	Min	Q1	Mean	Median	Q3	Max	N	Range Avg Min	Range Avg Max
North Atlantic	16,120	16,120	17,472	16,120	20,176	20,176	3	10,712	16,640
Great Lakes & Plains	15,912	16,640	20,381	19,937	24,263	24,960	12	20,946	29,023
Southeast	11,495	11,495	11,495	11,495	11,495	11,495	1		
West & Southwest	29,120	29,120	29,120	29,120	29,120	29,120	2	24,960	35,360
ALL REGIONS	11,495	16,640	20,374	19,448	24,357	29,120	18	19,702	27,814

State Data

	Min	Q1	Mean	Median	Q3	Max	N	Range Avg Min	Range Avg Max
IL	16,640	16,640	19,232	18,200	22,827	24,960	7	18,373	31,200
IN	21,154	21,154	21,154	21,154	21,154	21,154	1	.	.
MI	15,912	15,912	20,041	20,041	24,170	24,170	2	24,170	24,170
MN	24,357	24,357	24,357	24,357	24,357	24,357	2	23,192	28,184
MS	11,495	11,495	11,495	11,495	11,495	11,495	1	.	.
NM	29,120	29,120	29,120	29,120	29,120	29,120	2	24,960	35,360
PA	16,120	16,120	17,472	16,120	20,176	20,176	3	10,712	16,640

Degree Required Data

	Min	Q1	Mean	Median	Q3	Max	N	Range Avg Min	Range Avg Max
High School	11,495	16,120	20,064	18,720	24,357	29,120	15	19,195	26,178
Associate's	16,640	16,640	21,923	24,170	24,960	24,960	3	20,883	31,630
Bachelor's	.	.	.	.	.	.	.	.	.
Master's	.	.	.	.	.	.	.	.	.
Doctoral	.	.	.	.	.	.	.	.	.

PROCESSING ASSISTANT - CONTINUED
Medium Public Library
(Serving a population of 25,000 to 99,999)
Regional Data

	Min	Q1	Mean	Median	Q3	Max	N	Range Avg Min	Range Avg Max
North Atlantic	10,920	20,966	25,776	20,966	31,679	47,646	29	24,143	32,282
Great Lakes & Plains	14,248	19,115	23,635	22,859	26,562	38,418	43	18,877	27,984
Southeast	16,120	17,014	20,635	19,718	23,317	28,593	13	14,054	18,484
West & Southwest	12,480	13,000	20,989	21,944	24,440	34,752	11	16,684	21,208
ALL REGIONS	10,920	18,918	23,572	21,138	27,536	47,646	96	18,985	26,814

State Data

	Min	Q1	Mean	Median	Q3	Max	N	Range Avg Min	Range Avg Max
CA	23,026	23,026	23,026	23,026	23,026	23,026	1	19,906	24,170
CO	18,179	18,179	21,310	21,310	24,440	24,440	2	18,720	31,200
CT	16,640	20,966	20,486	20,966	20,966	20,966	9	.	.
IA	33,513	33,513	33,513	33,513	33,513	33,513	1	.	.
IL	14,248	16,806	24,142	23,421	28,829	38,418	15	20,322	32,051
IN	16,640	19,531	22,061	20,800	24,856	28,384	9	17,503	23,083
LA	17,014	17,014	17,014	17,014	17,014	17,014	2	11,690	17,867
MA	20,654	28,660	33,079	37,053	37,498	37,555	4	31,172	36,386
MI	22,298	22,298	22,298	22,298	22,298	22,298	1	19,510	22,298
MO	26,562	26,562	26,562	26,562	26,562	26,562	1	.	.
MS	16,120	16,952	21,134	20,686	23,317	28,593	5	.	.
NC	19,718	19,718	22,190	22,190	24,662	24,662	2	18,782	19,718
ND	24,877	24,877	24,877	24,877	24,877	24,877	1	17,909	26,874
NE	24,960	24,960	24,960	24,960	24,960	24,960	1	18,720	24,960
NJ	16,676	16,676	19,779	19,780	22,880	22,880	3	22,859	39,998
NY	27,040	31,129	34,472	31,768	37,648	47,646	8	27,040	43,680
OH	18,034	19,115	21,094	20,571	20,800	27,560	10	17,555	26,071
PA	10,920	15,392	19,140	20,134	21,424	27,830	5	12,792	16,567
TN	19,115	19,115	20,213	20,213	21,310	21,310	2	.	.
TX	12,480	12,480	20,225	15,860	29,916	34,752	6	12,740	15,730
VA	27,512	27,512	27,512	27,512	27,512	27,512	1	.	.
WI	17,389	21,070	28,122	29,495	35,173	36,108	4	16,786	21,986
WV	16,235	16,235	16,235	16,235	16,235	16,235	1	.	.
WY	21,944	21,944	21,944	21,944	21,944	21,944	2	21,944	25,688

Degree Required Data

	Min	Q1	Mean	Median	Q3	Max	N	Range Avg Min	Range Avg Max
High School	12,480	18,648	22,858	20,966	24,981	47,646	77	18,431	25,987
Associate's	16,235	20,571	26,091	23,761	33,135	37,555	8	24,985	36,421
Bachelor's	22,298	22,298	22,298	22,298	22,298	22,298	1	19,510	22,298
Master's	.	.	.	.	.	.	.	.	.
Doctoral	.	.	.	.	.	.	.	.	.

PROCESSING ASSISTANT - CONTINUED
Large Public Library
(Serving a population of 100,000 to 499,999)
Regional Data

	Min	Q1	Mean	Median	Q3	Max	N	Range Avg Min	Range Avg Max
North Atlantic	12,480	23,995	28,494	28,210	32,968	50,606	50	21,325	30,429
Great Lakes & Plains	11,939	21,601	26,447	24,866	31,096	39,399	56	19,431	27,325
Southeast	14,754	15,538	24,716	25,440	31,200	39,504	17	14,622	19,295
West & Southwest	12,480	21,329	25,544	23,871	30,268	39,520	54	23,063	29,402
ALL REGIONS	11,939	21,590	26,584	26,362	31,200	50,606	177	21,004	28,573

State Data

	Min	Q1	Mean	Median	Q3	Max	N	Range Avg Min	Range Avg Max
AZ	35,880	35,880	35,880	35,880	35,880	35,880	1	.	.
CA	24,960	27,324	30,893	31,138	33,738	39,520	19	26,098	33,082
CO	22,422	22,422	22,422	22,422	22,422	22,422	1	22,422	34,133
FL	14,754	14,828	17,837	14,902	20,846	26,790	4	.	.
GA	14,830	14,830	14,830	14,830	14,830	14,830	1	14,830	15,870
IL	21,756	22,670	29,824	29,088	37,572	38,771	6	.	.
IN	20,340	20,340	20,340	20,340	20,340	20,340	1	.	.
KS	24,128	24,554	27,362	25,740	30,170	33,842	4	21,263	35,448
LA	18,845	18,845	18,845	18,845	18,845	18,845	1	16,224	22,922
MA	27,622	27,622	27,622	27,622	27,622	27,622	2	.	.
MD	21,154	25,493	30,921	29,114	35,773	50,606	26	21,154	31,699
MI	11,939	24,689	24,050	26,978	27,710	28,933	5	16,879	20,374
MN	18,866	18,866	30,233	32,553	39,279	39,279	3	.	.
MO	14,851	21,590	20,141	21,590	21,590	21,590	9	18,151	22,922
NC	15,538	15,538	22,359	25,440	26,099	26,099	3	12,813	19,094
NE	22,397	22,397	26,142	27,533	28,496	28,496	3	20,908	28,496
NM	22,796	22,796	26,360	28,101	28,184	28,184	3	.	.
NY	27,581	31,512	31,931	32,968	32,968	32,968	8	28,122	32,968
OH	19,490	23,317	26,026	24,752	27,643	37,898	13	18,101	29,286
OR	16,806	16,806	19,991	16,806	26,362	26,362	3	16,806	22,214
PA	12,480	14,560	22,148	19,864	29,349	34,092	14	15,527	27,097
TN	28,788	28,788	29,994	29,994	31,200	31,200	2	.	.
TX	12,480	20,043	21,491	22,547	23,264	27,866	13	12,480	12,480
VA	18,012	24,107	31,347	33,477	39,504	39,504	6	.	.
WA	20,509	20,800	22,549	21,329	23,234	30,268	14	21,122	26,723
WI	21,092	22,401	30,277	31,096	35,955	39,399	12	24,599	27,934

Degree Required Data

	Min	Q1	Mean	Median	Q3	Max	N	Range Avg Min	Range Avg Max
High School	12,480	22,532	27,551	26,831	32,553	50,606	131	21,389	29,884
Associate's	16,640	22,397	25,629	26,362	28,995	35,880	13	19,803	28,235
Bachelor's	18,845	18,845	18,845	18,845	18,845	18,845	1	16,224	22,922
Master's	.	.	.	.	.	.		.	.
Doctoral	.	.	.	.	.	.		.	.

PROCESSING ASSISTANT - CONTINUED
Very Large Public Library
(Serving a population of 500,000 or more)
Regional Data

	Min	Q1	Mean	Median	Q3	Max	N	Range Avg Min	Range Avg Max
North Atlantic	14,560	18,720	27,910	27,713	35,609	44,621	30	12,480	18,720
Great Lakes & Plains	17,475	23,297	28,002	27,215	32,820	45,079	71	26,699	35,106
Southeast	19,995	24,102	27,253	25,740	29,675	38,445	20	23,067	38,445
West & Southwest	17,826	38,388	43,067	48,412	48,412	56,186	62	38,790	47,306
ALL REGIONS	14,560	24,253	33,009	31,864	44,257	56,186	183	31,637	40,336

State Data

	Min	Q1	Mean	Median	Q3	Max	N	Range Avg Min	Range Avg Max
CA	26,083	48,412	47,258	48,412	48,412	56,186	48	39,820	48,341
CO	30,508	32,856	34,900	33,246	36,537	41,352	5	.	.
FL	19,995	24,315	24,821	25,210	25,917	26,520	10	.	.
GA	23,448	23,586	26,630	26,552	29,675	29,969	4	.	.
IN	22,306	23,971	25,739	25,140	27,785	29,801	19	.	.
MD	14,560	18,720	27,910	27,713	35,609	44,621	30	12,480	18,720
MO	17,475	19,218	20,925	19,492	23,297	25,193	17	.	.
OH	20,093	29,661	32,215	32,820	36,400	45,079	29	24,137	34,999
OR	33,654	33,654	33,654	33,654	33,654	33,654	1	27,373	33,654
TX	23,268	23,268	28,746	26,133	36,837	36,837	3	26,832	40,206
UT	17,826	22,056	21,469	22,488	22,488	22,488	5	16,869	22,506
VA	23,067	23,951	31,722	33,785	37,300	38,445	6	23,067	38,445
WI	30,568	33,014	34,860	33,014	35,296	44,257	6	30,541	35,266

Degree Required Data

	Min	Q1	Mean	Median	Q3	Max	N	Range Avg Min	Range Avg Max
High School	17,475	24,773	29,710	29,241	35,296	45,079	117	26,237	36,309
Associate's	36,837	36,837	36,837	36,837	36,837	36,837	1	26,832	40,206
Bachelor's	.	.	.	.	.	.		.	.
Master's	.	.	.	.	.	.		.	.
Doctoral	.	.	.	.	.	.		.	.

PROCESSING ASSISTANT - CONTINUED
ALL PUBLIC LIBRARIES
Regional Data

	Min	Q1	Mean	Median	Q3	Max	N	Range Avg Min	Range Avg Max
North Atlantic	10,920	20,810	27,339	27,365	32,968	50,606	112	18,973	27,015
Great Lakes & Plains	11,939	20,800	25,876	24,754	30,846	45,079	186	20,719	29,202
Southeast	11,495	18,980	24,487	24,489	28,472	39,504	52	18,944	28,862
West & Southwest	12,480	22,880	33,633	31,138	48,412	56,186	129	31,204	38,671
ALL REGIONS	10,920	21,092	28,156	26,250	33,014	56,186	479	24,348	32,438

State Data

	Min	Q1	Mean	Median	Q3	Max	N	Range Avg Min	Range Avg Max
AL	28,350	28,350	28,350	28,350	28,350	28,350	1	21,840	31,200
AZ	35,880	35,880	35,880	35,880	35,880	35,880	1	.	.
CA	23,026	34,467	42,330	48,412	48,412	56,186	68	36,058	44,124
CO	18,179	23,431	29,943	31,682	34,892	41,352	8	20,571	32,666
CT	16,640	20,966	20,486	20,966	20,966	20,966	9	.	.
FL	14,754	19,995	22,826	24,742	25,917	26,790	14	.	.
GA	14,830	23,448	24,270	23,723	29,381	29,969	5	14,830	15,870
IA	18,720	18,720	24,241	20,489	33,513	33,513	3	.	.
IL	14,248	18,200	23,979	22,843	27,622	38,771	30	19,789	31,556
IN	16,640	22,306	24,303	24,311	27,053	29,801	30	17,503	23,083
KS	24,128	24,554	27,362	25,740	30,170	33,842	4	21,263	35,448
LA	17,014	17,014	17,625	17,014	18,845	18,845	3	13,201	19,552
MA	20,654	27,622	31,260	32,144	37,441	37,555	6	31,172	36,386
MD	14,560	23,150	29,308	28,287	35,691	50,606	56	15,853	23,767
MI	11,939	19,105	22,828	24,429	27,344	28,933	8	19,360	21,804
MN	18,866	24,357	27,882	24,357	32,553	39,279	5	23,192	28,184
MO	14,851	19,218	20,873	21,590	22,351	26,562	27	18,151	22,922
MS	11,495	16,120	19,527	18,819	23,317	28,593	6	.	.
NC	15,538	19,718	22,291	24,662	25,440	26,099	5	15,798	19,406
ND	24,877	24,877	24,877	24,877	24,877	24,877	1	17,909	26,874
NE	22,397	23,679	25,847	26,246	28,014	28,496	4	20,361	27,612
NJ	16,676	16,676	19,779	19,780	22,880	22,880	3	22,859	39,998
NM	22,796	28,101	27,464	28,184	29,120	29,120	5	24,960	35,360
NY	27,040	31,129	33,201	32,968	32,968	47,646	16	27,986	34,307
OH	18,034	23,015	28,529	27,602	32,820	45,079	52	20,205	30,491
OR	16,806	16,806	23,407	21,584	30,008	33,654	4	19,448	25,074
PA	10,920	15,392	20,827	19,417	28,122	34,092	22	14,269	23,599
TN	19,115	20,213	25,103	25,049	29,994	31,200	4	.	.
TX	12,480	18,611	22,135	22,770	23,820	36,837	22	15,045	19,268
UT	17,826	22,056	21,469	22,488	22,488	22,488	5	16,869	22,506
VA	18,012	24,107	31,225	32,226	37,300	39,504	13	23,067	38,445
WA	20,509	20,800	22,549	21,329	23,234	30,268	14	21,122	26,723
WI	17,389	24,752	31,135	32,544	35,296	44,257	22	27,383	31,739
WV	16,235	16,235	16,235	16,235	16,235	16,235	1	.	.
WY	21,944	21,944	21,944	21,944	21,944	21,944	2	21,944	25,688

Degree Required Data

	Min	Q1	Mean	Median	Q3	Max	N	Range Avg Min	Range Avg Max
High School	11,495	21,154	26,852	26,100	32,581	50,606	344	21,165	29,600
Associate's	16,235	20,489	25,577	24,811	28,995	37,555	26	21,813	31,740
Bachelor's	18,845	18,845	20,571	20,571	22,298	22,298	2	17,867	22,610
Master's	.	.	.	.	.	.	.	.	.
Doctoral	.	.	.	.	.	.	.	.	.

SERIALS PROCESSING ASSISTANT

Orders, receives and prepares library subscriptions. Updates online systems to reflect holdings, locations and identity. Monitors subscription status, processes invoices and renewals, and resolves issues with vendors as needed.

Very Small Public Library
(Serving a population of less than 10,000)
Regional Data

	Min	Q1	Mean	Median	Q3	Max	N	Range Avg Min	Range Avg Max
West & Southwest	16,806	16,806	16,806	16,806	16,806	16,806	1	15,600	16,806
ALL REGIONS	16,806	16,806	16,806	16,806	16,806	16,806	1	15,600	16,806

State Data

	Min	Q1	Mean	Median	Q3	Max	N	Range Avg Min	Range Avg Max
CO	16,806	16,806	16,806	16,806	16,806	16,806	1	15,600	16,806

Degree Required Data

	Min	Q1	Mean	Median	Q3	Max	N	Range Avg Min	Range Avg Max
High School	16,806	16,806	16,806	16,806	16,806	16,806	1	15,600	16,806
Associate's	.	.	.	.	.	.		.	.
Bachelor's	.	.	.	.	.	.		.	.
Master's	.	.	.	.	.	.		.	.
Doctoral	.	.	.	.	.	.		.	.

SERIALS PROCESSING ASSISTANT - CONTINUED
Small Public Library
(Serving a population of 10,000 to 25,000)
Regional Data

	Min	Q1	Mean	Median	Q3	Max	N	Range Avg Min	Range Avg Max
North Atlantic	20,176	20,176	20,176	20,176	20,176	20,176	1	.	.
Great Lakes & Plains	15,912	19,906	25,258	23,920	28,371	39,520	6	23,254	40,186
ALL REGIONS	15,912	19,906	24,532	20,800	28,371	39,520	7	23,254	40,186

State Data

	Min	Q1	Mean	Median	Q3	Max	N	Range Avg Min	Range Avg Max
IL	15,912	17,909	24,034	20,353	30,160	39,520	4	22,880	52,000
MI	27,040	27,040	27,706	27,706	28,371	28,371	2	23,629	28,371
PA	20,176	20,176	20,176	20,176	20,176	20,176	1	.	.

Degree Required Data

	Min	Q1	Mean	Median	Q3	Max	N	Range Avg Min	Range Avg Max
High School	15,912	20,176	22,460	20,800	27,040	28,371	5	23,629	28,371
Associate's	19,906	19,906	19,906	19,906	19,906	19,906	1	.	.
Bachelor's	39,520	39,520	39,520	39,520	39,520	39,520	1	22,880	52,000
Master's	.	.	.	.	.	.	.	.	.
Doctoral	.	.	.	.	.	.	.	.	.

SERIALS PROCESSING ASSISTANT - CONTINUED
Medium Public Library
(Serving a population of 25,000 to 99,999)
Regional Data

	Min	Q1	Mean	Median	Q3	Max	N	Range Avg Min	Range Avg Max
North Atlantic	28,216	30,332	35,077	34,850	39,822	42,390	4	30,118	37,253
Great Lakes & Plains	16,661	22,381	27,813	23,379	35,764	42,266	9	21,559	31,725
West & Southwest	24,170	24,170	24,170	24,170	24,170	24,170	1	19,906	24,170
ALL REGIONS	16,661	22,828	29,628	29,510	36,786	42,390	14	23,768	32,225

State Data

	Min	Q1	Mean	Median	Q3	Max	N	Range Avg Min	Range Avg Max
CA	24,170	24,170	24,170	24,170	24,170	24,170	1	19,906	24,170
CT	32,448	32,448	37,364	37,253	42,390	42,390	3	30,118	37,253
IL	23,379	30,805	33,800	35,764	36,786	42,266	5	27,102	41,402
IN	22,381	22,381	22,605	22,605	22,828	22,828	2	.	.
KS	16,661	16,661	16,661	16,661	16,661	16,661	1	15,392	21,216
NY	28,216	28,216	28,216	28,216	28,216	28,216	1	.	.
OH	19,448	19,448	19,448	19,448	19,448	19,448	1	16,640	22,880

Degree Required Data

	Min	Q1	Mean	Median	Q3	Max	N	Range Avg Min	Range Avg Max
High School	16,661	22,381	28,287	24,170	37,253	42,266	7	24,827	32,431
Associate's	19,448	19,448	28,117	28,117	36,786	36,786	2	16,640	22,880
Bachelor's	30,805	30,805	36,598	36,598	42,390	42,390	2	25,605	40,539
Master's	.	.	.	.	.	.	.	.	.
Doctoral	.	.	.	.	.	.	.	.	.

SERIALS PROCESSING ASSISTANT - CONTINUED
Large Public Library
(Serving a population of 100,000 to 499,999)
Regional Data

	Min	Q1	Mean	Median	Q3	Max	N	Range Avg Min	Range Avg Max
North Atlantic	25,085	25,709	31,959	29,464	38,210	43,826	4	22,901	28,621
Great Lakes & Plains	19,245	23,514	29,819	31,257	35,241	39,279	8	22,495	27,872
Southeast	16,625	20,171	26,859	24,841	32,619	42,989	8	18,918	27,997
West & Southwest	16,556	21,195	27,757	27,277	34,828	35,880	11	21,466	29,873
ALL REGIONS	16,556	22,004	28,600	27,677	34,283	43,826	31	21,305	28,972

State Data

	Min	Q1	Mean	Median	Q3	Max	N	Range Avg Min	Range Avg Max
AZ	35,880	35,880	35,880	35,880	35,880	35,880	1		
CA	26,770	26,770	31,034	31,138	35,196	35,196	3	23,286	28,964
CO	34,828	34,828	34,828	34,828	34,828	34,828	1		
FL	19,771	19,771	19,771	19,771	19,771	19,771	1		
IL	24,024	24,024	24,024	24,024	24,024	24,024	1		
IN	19,245	19,245	19,245	19,245	19,245	19,245	1		
LA	20,571	20,571	20,571	20,571	20,571	20,571	1	19,573	27,685
MA	43,826	43,826	43,826	43,826	43,826	43,826	1		
MD	25,085	25,085	25,085	25,085	25,085	25,085	1		
MI	31,418	31,418	31,418	31,418	31,418	31,418	1		
MN	39,279	39,279	39,279	39,279	39,279	39,279	1		
MO	23,005	23,005	23,005	23,005	23,005	23,005	1	16,952	24,648
MS	16,625	16,625	16,625	16,625	16,625	16,625	1		
NC	22,004	22,004	22,004	22,004	22,004	22,004	1	18,262	28,309
NM	27,277	27,277	27,277	27,277	27,277	27,277	1		
NY	32,594	32,594	32,594	32,594	32,594	32,594	1		
OR	21,195	21,195	21,195	21,195	21,195	21,195	1	21,195	27,934
PA	26,333	26,333	26,333	26,333	26,333	26,333	1	22,901	28,621
TN	27,677	27,677	27,677	27,677	27,677	27,677	1		
TX	16,556	16,556	18,574	18,574	20,592	20,592	2	17,472	31,491
VA	30,955	30,955	36,076	34,283	42,989	42,989	3		
WA	25,626	25,626	27,947	27,947	30,268	30,268	2	22,090	32,011
WI	31,096	31,096	33,860	32,157	38,326	38,326	3	28,038	31,096

Degree Required Data

	Min	Q1	Mean	Median	Q3	Max	N	Range Avg Min	Range Avg Max
High School	16,556	20,592	26,824	26,198	31,418	39,279	22	20,479	28,861
Associate's	21,195	23,764	31,599	31,106	39,435	42,989	4	22,048	28,278
Bachelor's	27,677	27,677	35,444	34,828	43,826	43,826	3		
Master's									
Doctoral									

SERIALS PROCESSING ASSISTANT - CONTINUED
Very Large Public Library
(Serving a population of 500,000 or more)
Regional Data

	Min	Q1	Mean	Median	Q3	Max	N	Range Avg Min	Range Avg Max
North Atlantic	20,800	23,975	26,182	27,149	28,389	29,628	4	16,640	22,880
Great Lakes & Plains	20,770	28,267	30,297	31,125	32,331	44,257	29	25,266	34,245
Southeast	23,441	28,161	32,338	31,309	31,928	47,882	6	33,331	55,551
West & Southwest	29,875	33,654	35,821	33,696	41,392	43,656	7	27,344	35,751
ALL REGIONS	20,770	28,205	31,046	31,125	33,010	47,882	46	25,713	35,039

State Data

	Min	Q1	Mean	Median	Q3	Max	N	Range Avg Min	Range Avg Max
AZ	34,819	34,819	34,819	34,819	34,819	34,819	1	24,024	34,819
CA	43,656	43,656	43,656	43,656	43,656	43,656	1	.	.
FL	28,161	28,161	30,045	30,045	31,928	31,928	2	.	.
GA	23,441	23,441	28,686	30,999	31,619	31,619	3	.	.
MD	20,800	23,975	26,182	27,149	28,389	29,628	4	16,640	22,880
MI	31,125	31,125	31,344	31,125	31,125	32,331	11	.	.
MO	20,770	20,770	20,893	20,893	21,017	21,017	2	.	.
OH	24,981	26,832	28,497	28,267	29,474	33,939	11	22,381	33,509
OR	33,654	33,654	36,234	33,654	41,392	41,392	3	29,467	36,234
TX	29,875	29,875	31,786	31,786	33,696	33,696	2	24,294	35,235
VA	47,882	47,882	47,882	47,882	47,882	47,882	1	33,331	55,551
WI	33,010	33,010	35,716	33,010	35,296	44,257	5	31,038	35,718

Degree Required Data

	Min	Q1	Mean	Median	Q3	Max	N	Range Avg Min	Range Avg Max
High School	20,770	30,500	31,763	31,125	33,654	47,882	32	28,020	35,853
Associate's	41,392	41,392	41,392	41,392	41,392	41,392	1	33,654	41,392
Bachelor's	.	.	.	.	.	.		.	.
Master's	.	.	.	.	.	.		.	.
Doctoral	.	.	.	.	.	.		.	.

SERIALS PROCESSING ASSISTANT - CONTINUED
ALL PUBLIC LIBRARIES
Regional Data

	Min	Q1	Mean	Median	Q3	Max	N	Range Avg Min	Range Avg Max
North Atlantic	20,176	26,333	30,234	28,216	32,594	43,826	13	24,944	31,502
Great Lakes & Plains	15,912	24,502	29,212	30,950	32,331	44,257	52	24,206	33,769
Southeast	16,625	22,004	29,208	29,558	31,928	47,882	14	23,722	37,181
West & Southwest	16,556	24,898	29,852	30,703	34,824	43,656	20	23,296	30,758
ALL REGIONS	15,912	24,170	29,475	30,268	33,010	47,882	99	23,982	32,937

State Data

	Min	Q1	Mean	Median	Q3	Max	N	Range Avg Min	Range Avg Max
AZ	34,819	34,819	35,350	35,350	35,880	35,880	2	24,024	34,819
CA	24,170	26,770	32,186	31,138	35,196	43,656	5	22,159	27,366
CO	16,806	16,806	25,817	25,817	34,828	34,828	2	15,600	16,806
CT	32,448	32,448	37,364	37,253	42,390	42,390	3	30,118	37,253
FL	19,771	19,771	26,620	28,161	31,928	31,928	3	.	.
GA	23,441	23,441	28,686	30,999	31,619	31,619	3	.	.
IL	15,912	20,800	28,916	27,414	36,786	42,266	10	25,695	44,935
IN	19,245	19,245	21,485	22,381	22,828	22,828	3	.	.
KS	16,661	16,661	16,661	16,661	16,661	16,661	1	15,392	21,216
LA	20,571	20,571	20,571	20,571	20,571	20,571	1	19,573	27,685
MA	43,826	43,826	43,826	43,826	43,826	43,826	1	.	.
MD	20,800	25,085	25,962	27,149	27,149	29,628	5	16,640	22,880
MI	27,040	31,125	30,830	31,125	31,125	32,331	14	23,629	28,371
MN	39,279	39,279	39,279	39,279	39,279	39,279	1	.	.
MO	20,770	20,770	21,597	21,017	23,005	23,005	3	16,952	24,648
MS	16,625	16,625	16,625	16,625	16,625	16,625	1	.	.
NC	22,004	22,004	22,004	22,004	22,004	22,004	1	18,262	28,309
NM	27,277	27,277	27,277	27,277	27,277	27,277	1	.	.
NY	28,216	28,216	30,405	30,405	32,594	32,594	2	.	.
OH	19,448	26,686	27,743	28,236	29,474	33,939	12	21,859	32,543
OR	21,195	27,425	32,474	33,654	37,523	41,392	4	27,399	34,159
PA	20,176	20,176	23,254	23,254	26,333	26,333	2	22,901	28,621
TN	27,677	27,677	27,677	27,677	27,677	27,677	1	.	.
TX	16,556	18,574	25,180	25,234	31,786	33,696	4	20,883	33,363
VA	30,955	32,619	39,027	38,636	45,436	47,882	4	33,331	55,551
WA	25,626	25,626	27,947	27,947	30,268	30,268	2	22,090	32,011
WI	31,096	32,583	35,020	33,010	36,811	44,257	8	30,538	34,947

Degree Required Data

	Min	Q1	Mean	Median	Q3	Max	N	Range Avg Min	Range Avg Max
High School	15,912	22,828	28,861	31,096	33,010	47,882	67	24,598	32,150
Associate's	19,448	20,550	30,491	31,106	39,089	42,989	8	23,598	30,207
Bachelor's	27,677	30,805	36,508	37,174	42,390	43,826	6	24,242	46,270
Master's	.	.	.	.	.	.	.	.	.
Doctoral	.	.	.	.	.	.	.	.	.

COLLECTION DEVELOPMENT/MANAGEMENT

Analyzes community and library data to determine areas of the collection which need updating. Selects materials to update the collection. Performs related work as required.

Small Public Library
(Serving a population of 10,000 to 25,000)
Regional Data

	Min	Q1	Mean	Median	Q3	Max	N	Range Avg Min	Range Avg Max
Great Lakes & Plains	24,960	24,960	26,000	26,000	27,040	27,040	2	24,960	31,200
West & Southwest	44,096	44,096	44,096	44,096	44,096	44,096	1	.	.
ALL REGIONS	24,960	24,960	32,032	27,040	44,096	44,096	3	24,960	31,200

State Data

	Min	Q1	Mean	Median	Q3	Max	N	Range Avg Min	Range Avg Max
IL	27,040	27,040	27,040	27,040	27,040	27,040	1	24,960	31,200
MI	24,960	24,960	24,960	24,960	24,960	24,960	1	.	.
NM	44,096	44,096	44,096	44,096	44,096	44,096	1	.	.

Degree Required Data

	Min	Q1	Mean	Median	Q3	Max	N	Range Avg Min	Range Avg Max
High School	24,960	24,960	24,960	24,960	24,960	24,960	1	.	.
Associate's	.	.	.	.	.	.		.	.
Bachelor's	44,096	44,096	44,096	44,096	44,096	44,096	1	.	.
Master's	27,040	27,040	27,040	27,040	27,040	27,040	1	24,960	31,200
Doctoral	.	.	.	.	.	.		.	.

COLLECTION DEVELOPMENT/MANAGEMENT - CONTINUED
Medium Public Library
(Serving a population of 25,000 to 99,999)
Regional Data

	Min	Q1	Mean	Median	Q3	Max	N	Range Avg Min	Range Avg Max
North Atlantic	27,000	27,000	27,000	27,000	27,000	27,000	1	.	.
Great Lakes & Plains	21,861	21,861	22,838	22,838	23,816	23,816	2	.	.
Southeast	20,197	20,197	26,598	26,598	33,000	33,000	2	13,520	22,880
ALL REGIONS	20,197	21,861	25,175	23,816	27,000	33,000	5	13,520	22,880

State Data

	Min	Q1	Mean	Median	Q3	Max	N	Range Avg Min	Range Avg Max
AR	20,197	20,197	20,197	20,197	20,197	20,197	1	13,520	22,880
MI	23,816	23,816	23,816	23,816	23,816	23,816	1	.	.
OH	21,861	21,861	21,861	21,861	21,861	21,861	1	.	.
PA	27,000	27,000	27,000	27,000	27,000	27,000	1	.	.
TN	33,000	33,000	33,000	33,000	33,000	33,000	1	.	.

Degree Required Data

	Min	Q1	Mean	Median	Q3	Max	N	Range Avg Min	Range Avg Max
High School									
Associate's									
Bachelor's	21,861	21,861	24,226	23,816	27,000	27,000	3		
Master's	33,000	33,000	33,000	33,000	33,000	33,000	1		
Doctoral									

COLLECTION DEVELOPMENT/MANAGEMENT - CONTINUED
Large Public Library
(Serving a population of 100,000 to 499,999)
Regional Data

	Min	Q1	Mean	Median	Q3	Max	N	Range Avg Min	Range Avg Max
North Atlantic	16,640	33,520	35,757	38,465	43,727	43,727	6	22,963	34,341
Great Lakes & Plains	13,728	14,664	25,028	15,600	35,391	55,182	4	18,980	31,200
Southeast	35,482	35,482	36,960	36,960	38,438	38,438	2	37,024	51,293
West & Southwest	101,920	101,920	101,920	101,920	101,920	101,920	1	72,800	101,920
ALL REGIONS	13,728	16,640	37,730	35,482	43,727	101,920	13	28,959	43,337

State Data

	Min	Q1	Mean	Median	Q3	Max	N	Range Avg Min	Range Avg Max
CA	101,920	101,920	101,920	101,920	101,920	101,920	1	72,800	101,920
FL	35,482	35,482	35,482	35,482	35,482	35,482	1		
LA	38,438	38,438	38,438	38,438	38,438	38,438	1	37,024	51,293
MD	33,520	34,798	39,581	42,131	43,727	43,727	5	29,286	43,722
NE	13,728	13,728	14,976	15,600	15,600	15,600	3	11,440	18,720
OH	55,182	55,182	55,182	55,182	55,182	55,182	1	41,600	68,640
PA	16,640	16,640	16,640	16,640	16,640	16,640	1	16,640	24,960

Degree Required Data

	Min	Q1	Mean	Median	Q3	Max	N	Range Avg Min	Range Avg Max
High School									
Associate's	16,640	16,640	16,640	16,640	16,640	16,640	1	16,640	24,960
Bachelor's	33,520	35,140	40,876	40,285	43,727	55,182	8	35,970	54,551
Master's	101,920	101,920	101,920	101,920	101,920	101,920	1	72,800	101,920
Doctoral									

COLLECTION DEVELOPMENT/MANAGEMENT - CONTINUED
Very Large Public Library
(Serving a population of 500,000 or more)
Regional Data

	Min	Q1	Mean	Median	Q3	Max	N	Range Avg Min	Range Avg Max
North Atlantic	35,360	42,065	57,393	54,939	70,542	86,655	10	31,200	41,600
Great Lakes & Plains	63,796	63,796	63,796	63,796	63,796	63,796	1	.	.
Southeast	32,373	32,373	41,361	36,294	55,416	55,416	3	.	.
West & Southwest	41,392	41,392	61,802	63,143	80,870	80,870	3	43,909	61,131
ALL REGIONS	32,373	41,600	55,718	55,416	67,938	86,655	17	37,554	51,366

State Data

	Min	Q1	Mean	Median	Q3	Max	N	Range Avg Min	Range Avg Max
AZ	80,870	80,870	80,870	80,870	80,870	80,870	1	54,163	80,870
CA	63,143	63,143	63,143	63,143	63,143	63,143	1	.	.
FL	32,373	32,373	34,334	34,334	36,294	36,294	2	.	.
MD	35,360	35,360	39,675	41,600	42,065	42,065	3	31,200	41,600
NC	55,416	55,416	55,416	55,416	55,416	55,416	1	.	.
NJ	49,350	49,945	64,986	67,938	70,542	86,655	7	.	.
OH	63,796	63,796	63,796	63,796	63,796	63,796	1	.	.
OR	41,392	41,392	41,392	41,392	41,392	41,392	1	33,654	41,392

Degree Required Data

	Min	Q1	Mean	Median	Q3	Max	N	Range Avg Min	Range Avg Max
High School	42,065	42,065	42,065	42,065	42,065	42,065	1	.	.
Associate's	41,392	41,392	41,392	41,392	41,392	41,392	1	33,654	41,392
Bachelor's	35,360	35,360	44,125	41,600	55,416	55,416	3	31,200	41,600
Master's	63,143	63,143	69,270	63,796	80,870	80,870	3	54,163	80,870
Doctoral	.	.	.	.	.	.		.	.

COLLECTION DEVELOPMENT/MANAGEMENT - CONTINUED
ALL PUBLIC LIBRARIES
Regional Data

	Min	Q1	Mean	Median	Q3	Max	N	Range Avg Min	Range Avg Max
North Atlantic	16,640	35,360	47,969	43,727	59,933	86,655	17	27,082	37,970
Great Lakes & Plains	13,728	15,600	29,065	23,816	27,040	63,796	9	20,176	31,200
Southeast	20,197	32,373	35,886	35,482	38,438	55,416	7	25,272	37,086
West & Southwest	41,392	44,096	66,284	63,143	80,870	101,920	5	53,539	74,727
ALL REGIONS	13,728	27,040	43,676	41,496	55,416	101,920	38	30,026	43,303

State Data

	Min	Q1	Mean	Median	Q3	Max	N	Range Avg Min	Range Avg Max
AR	20,197	20,197	20,197	20,197	20,197	20,197	1	13,520	22,880
AZ	80,870	80,870	80,870	80,870	80,870	80,870	1	54,163	80,870
CA	63,143	63,143	82,532	82,532	101,920	101,920	2	72,800	101,920
FL	32,373	32,373	34,716	35,482	36,294	36,294	3	.	.
IL	27,040	27,040	27,040	27,040	27,040	27,040	1	24,960	31,200
LA	38,438	38,438	38,438	38,438	38,438	38,438	1	37,024	51,293
MD	33,520	35,079	39,616	41,833	42,929	43,727	8	30,562	42,307
MI	23,816	23,816	24,388	24,388	24,960	24,960	2	.	.
NC	55,416	55,416	55,416	55,416	55,416	55,416	1	.	.
NE	13,728	13,728	14,976	15,600	15,600	15,600	3	11,440	18,720
NJ	49,350	49,945	64,986	67,938	70,542	86,655	7	.	.
NM	44,096	44,096	44,096	44,096	44,096	44,096	1	.	.
OH	21,861	21,861	46,946	55,182	63,796	63,796	3	41,600	68,640
OR	41,392	41,392	41,392	41,392	41,392	41,392	1	33,654	41,392
PA	16,640	16,640	21,820	21,820	27,000	27,000	2	16,640	24,960
TN	33,000	33,000	33,000	33,000	33,000	33,000	1	.	.

Degree Required Data

	Min	Q1	Mean	Median	Q3	Max	N	Range Avg Min	Range Avg Max
High School	24,960	24,960	33,513	33,513	42,065	42,065	2	.	.
Associate's	16,640	16,640	29,016	29,016	41,392	41,392	2	25,147	33,176
Bachelor's	21,861	33,520	38,410	38,438	43,727	55,416	15	34,062	49,371
Master's	27,040	33,000	61,628	63,469	80,870	101,920	6	50,641	71,330
Doctoral	.	.	.	.	.	.	.	.	.

INTER-LIBRARY LOAN ASSISTANT

Coordinates materials loaned through the inter-library loan system for patrons, other libraries and institutions. Searches databases and the Internet for inter-library loan requests utilizing ISBN, ISSN and citation numbers. Determines best sources for materials.

Very Small Public Library
(Serving a population of less than 10,000)
Regional Data

	Min	Q1	Mean	Median	Q3	Max	N	Range Avg Min	Range Avg Max
North Atlantic	20,800	20,800	26,905	26,905	33,010	33,010	2	.	.
Great Lakes & Plains	14,789	18,720	21,296	19,760	24,960	29,786	6	19,562	29,099
West & Southwest	16,224	16,224	25,265	17,139	42,432	42,432	3	20,134	25,265
ALL REGIONS	14,789	17,139	23,398	20,800	29,786	42,432	11	19,906	26,799

State Data

	Min	Q1	Mean	Median	Q3	Max	N	Range Avg Min	Range Avg Max
CO	16,224	16,224	25,265	17,139	42,432	42,432	3	20,134	25,265
CT	20,800	20,800	20,800	20,800	20,800	20,800	1	.	.
IA	29,786	29,786	29,786	29,786	29,786	29,786	1	24,565	33,238
IL	18,720	18,720	18,720	18,720	18,720	18,720	2	14,560	24,960
KS	14,789	14,789	14,789	14,789	14,789	14,789	1	.	.
PA	33,010	33,010	33,010	33,010	33,010	33,010	1	.	.
SD	20,800	20,800	20,800	20,800	20,800	20,800	1	.	.
WI	24,960	24,960	24,960	24,960	24,960	24,960	1	.	.

Degree Required Data

	Min	Q1	Mean	Median	Q3	Max	N	Range Avg Min	Range Avg Max
High School	14,789	16,224	20,345	18,720	24,960	29,786	7	17,737	22,890
Associate's	18,720	18,720	18,720	18,720	18,720	18,720	1	.	.
Bachelor's	33,010	33,010	37,721	37,721	42,432	42,432	2	28,579	42,432
Master's	.	.	.	.	.	.		.	.
Doctoral	.	.	.	.	.	.		.	.

INTER-LIBRARY LOAN ASSISTANT - CONTINUED
Small Public Library
(Serving a population of 10,000 to 25,000)
Regional Data

	Min	Q1	Mean	Median	Q3	Max	N	Range Avg Min	Range Avg Max
North Atlantic	25,750	26,957	36,550	40,103	43,597	46,343	5	37,211	56,389
Great Lakes & Plains	14,560	18,824	23,257	21,053	25,511	41,600	12	22,880	52,000
Southeast	19,885	19,885	20,442	20,442	21,000	21,000	2	16,224	18,304
West & Southwest	20,800	20,800	30,160	30,160	39,520	39,520	2	24,960	32,240
ALL REGIONS	14,560	19,788	26,811	23,608	31,200	46,343	21	25,247	38,235

State Data

	Min	Q1	Mean	Median	Q3	Max	N	Range Avg Min	Range Avg Max
CO	20,800	20,800	20,800	20,800	20,800	20,800	1	20,800	20,800
GA	21,000	21,000	21,000	21,000	21,000	21,000	1	.	.
IA	18,221	18,221	18,221	18,221	18,221	18,221	1	.	.
IL	19,427	23,608	28,380	26,062	31,200	41,600	5	22,880	52,000
KS	14,560	14,560	16,068	16,068	17,576	17,576	2	.	.
LA	19,885	19,885	19,885	19,885	19,885	19,885	1	16,224	18,304
MI	19,760	19,760	22,360	22,360	24,960	24,960	2	.	.
NH	43,597	43,597	43,597	43,597	43,597	43,597	1	37,211	56,389
NJ	40,103	40,103	43,223	43,223	46,343	46,343	2	.	.
NM	39,520	39,520	39,520	39,520	39,520	39,520	1	29,120	43,680
OH	19,788	19,788	21,053	21,053	22,318	22,318	2	.	.
PA	25,750	25,750	26,354	26,354	26,957	26,957	2	.	.

Degree Required Data

	Min	Q1	Mean	Median	Q3	Max	N	Range Avg Min	Range Avg Max
High School	14,560	18,990	25,478	22,980	29,078	46,343	12	22,672	30,992
Associate's	19,427	19,427	30,514	30,514	41,600	41,600	2	22,880	52,000
Bachelor's	20,800	21,559	31,705	31,211	41,850	43,597	4	29,006	38,594
Master's	.	.	.	.	.	.	.	.	.
Doctoral	.	.	.	.	.	.	.	.	.

INTER-LIBRARY LOAN ASSISTANT - CONTINUED
Medium Public Library
(Serving a population of 25,000 to 99,999)
Regional Data

	Min	Q1	Mean	Median	Q3	Max	N	Range Avg Min	Range Avg Max
North Atlantic	12,480	21,663	29,149	27,269	36,674	60,160	12	25,820	31,353
Great Lakes & Plains	18,720	23,275	27,716	25,594	31,823	40,368	20	23,016	31,732
Southeast	12,480	13,572	16,975	15,813	20,378	23,795	4	12,480	12,480
West & Southwest	12,480	15,226	25,432	25,532	35,686	38,091	8	18,537	27,535
ALL REGIONS	12,480	21,424	26,715	25,168	32,819	60,160	44	21,654	29,433

State Data

	Min	Q1	Mean	Median	Q3	Max	N	Range Avg Min	Range Avg Max
AR	23,795	23,795	23,795	23,795	23,795	23,795	1	.	.
CA	15,891	15,891	21,258	21,258	26,624	26,624	2	18,782	26,458
CO	24,440	24,440	33,541	38,091	38,091	38,091	3	18,720	31,200
CT	28,954	28,954	33,405	33,405	37,856	37,856	2	27,976	28,954
IA	32,571	32,571	32,571	32,571	32,571	32,571	1	.	.
ID	33,280	33,280	33,280	33,280	33,280	33,280	1	24,960	39,520
IL	20,800	24,960	29,094	27,179	33,067	40,368	11	25,896	37,361
IN	23,566	23,566	23,566	23,566	23,566	23,566	1	.	.
KS	22,984	22,984	22,984	22,984	22,984	22,984	1	16,661	22,984
LA	12,480	12,480	12,480	12,480	12,480	12,480	1	12,480	12,480
MA	20,446	20,446	21,663	21,663	22,880	22,880	2	19,864	22,880
ME	37,523	37,523	37,523	37,523	37,523	37,523	1	29,619	42,224
MI	22,048	22,048	23,182	23,182	24,315	24,315	2	20,446	24,315
MN	39,018	39,018	39,018	39,018	39,018	39,018	1	.	.
MO	25,958	25,958	25,958	25,958	25,958	25,958	1	.	.
MS	14,664	14,664	14,664	14,664	14,664	14,664	1	.	.
ND	25,106	25,106	25,106	25,106	25,106	25,106	1	21,840	32,760
NE	18,720	18,720	18,720	18,720	18,720	18,720	1	18,720	18,720
NJ	29,516	29,516	29,516	29,516	29,516	29,516	1	.	.
NY	60,160	60,160	60,160	60,160	60,160	60,160	1	.	.
PA	12,480	15,683	22,490	22,880	25,584	35,824	5	.	.
TX	12,480	12,480	13,520	13,520	14,560	14,560	2	11,440	14,040
VA	16,961	16,961	16,961	16,961	16,961	16,961	1	.	.

Degree Required Data

	Min	Q1	Mean	Median	Q3	Max	N	Range Avg Min	Range Avg Max
High School	12,480	15,891	26,788	26,624	32,571	60,160	17	20,779	27,590
Associate's	20,446	22,880	27,811	24,960	35,824	40,368	13	20,311	26,416
Bachelor's	16,961	24,950	28,250	26,343	34,299	37,856	8	25,698	36,156
Master's	.	.	.	.	.	.		.	.
Doctoral	.	.	.	.	.	.		.	.

INTER-LIBRARY LOAN ASSISTANT - CONTINUED
Large Public Library
(Serving a population of 100,000 to 499,999)
Regional Data

	Min	Q1	Mean	Median	Q3	Max	N	Range Avg Min	Range Avg Max
North Atlantic	16,640	27,217	29,170	29,024	33,004	37,669	20	20,898	32,022
Great Lakes & Plains	15,725	24,367	27,155	26,052	31,512	38,776	32	21,942	32,253
Southeast	17,052	24,932	28,829	27,040	32,157	44,910	11	23,140	34,408
West & Southwest	16,557	20,977	28,074	27,113	34,091	44,046	24	22,368	30,344
ALL REGIONS	15,725	24,086	28,084	27,331	32,781	44,910	87	22,032	31,750

State Data

	Min	Q1	Mean	Median	Q3	Max	N	Range Avg Min	Range Avg Max
AZ	32,323	32,323	32,323	32,323	32,323	32,323	1	.	.
CA	26,770	26,894	31,296	27,331	37,107	38,376	5	26,508	33,725
CO	32,323	32,323	38,185	38,185	44,046	44,046	2	20,405	30,597
FL	24,939	24,939	28,045	27,040	32,157	32,157	3	23,026	33,394
IL	24,086	24,864	28,596	27,238	31,928	36,223	6	25,522	30,666
IN	28,253	28,253	28,253	28,253	28,253	28,253	1	.	.
KS	21,632	22,329	25,649	25,823	27,238	32,781	8	21,632	36,067
LA	27,165	27,165	27,165	27,165	27,165	27,165	1	23,629	33,405
MA	24,170	27,622	26,932	27,622	27,622	27,622	5	.	.
MD	21,154	22,630	29,531	30,426	35,774	37,669	5	21,154	31,699
MI	24,981	24,981	31,311	31,024	37,078	38,776	6	19,802	24,981
MN	15,725	15,725	26,510	26,205	37,600	37,600	3	.	.
MO	16,952	16,952	20,800	20,800	24,648	24,648	2	17,555	25,522
MS	17,052	17,052	21,114	21,114	25,176	25,176	2	.	.
NC	22,880	22,880	25,985	24,932	30,144	30,144	3	22,880	37,440
NJ	32,270	32,270	32,929	32,929	33,588	33,588	2	.	.
NM	22,277	22,277	22,277	22,277	22,277	22,277	1	.	.
NY	32,594	32,594	33,787	33,787	34,980	34,980	2	29,183	33,831
OH	18,720	20,634	24,658	23,878	28,683	32,157	4	20,218	30,326
OK	18,782	18,782	20,065	20,654	20,758	20,758	3	17,950	23,296
OR	21,195	21,195	28,796	28,796	36,396	36,396	2	21,195	27,934
PA	16,640	27,040	27,943	28,985	33,004	33,004	6	18,699	31,730
TX	16,557	17,472	22,350	20,509	24,149	34,902	6	17,014	28,756
VA	40,726	40,726	42,818	42,818	44,910	44,910	2	.	.
WA	29,016	30,909	33,611	33,041	36,313	39,346	4	24,502	33,537
WI	25,230	25,230	28,163	28,163	31,096	31,096	2	28,038	31,096

Degree Required Data

	Min	Q1	Mean	Median	Q3	Max	N	Range Avg Min	Range Avg Max
High School	15,725	22,755	27,087	26,905	32,042	40,726	52	22,498	31,923
Associate's	18,782	21,632	27,567	27,040	32,323	39,346	19	20,285	30,712
Bachelor's	24,932	27,165	33,927	33,114	38,776	44,910	9	23,629	33,405
Master's	.	.	.	.	.	.	.	.	.
Doctoral	.	.	.	.	.	.	.	.	.

INTER-LIBRARY LOAN ASSISTANT - CONTINUED
Very Large Public Library
(Serving a population of 500,000 or more)
Regional Data

	Min	Q1	Mean	Median	Q3	Max	N	Range Avg Min	Range Avg Max
North Atlantic	22,880	22,880	24,236	22,880	25,593	28,305	4	16,640	22,880
Great Lakes & Plains	18,533	28,454	33,216	30,958	38,474	49,662	5	30,566	33,467
Southeast	19,995	26,840	33,656	30,657	41,178	50,573	11	30,521	50,868
West & Southwest	23,754	30,549	36,088	34,221	41,392	50,097	18	29,615	38,600
ALL REGIONS	18,533	28,305	33,758	32,198	41,392	50,573	38	27,414	36,544

State Data

	Min	Q1	Mean	Median	Q3	Max	N	Range Avg Min	Range Avg Max
AZ	42,141	42,141	42,141	42,141	42,141	42,141	2	28,850	42,141
CA	30,549	30,549	37,469	31,762	50,097	50,097	3	24,961	31,155
CO	32,992	32,992	37,188	34,722	43,851	43,851	3	.	.
FL	19,995	26,394	30,686	30,009	34,439	43,810	8	.	.
GA	32,969	32,969	32,969	32,969	32,969	32,969	1	.	.
MD	22,880	22,880	24,236	22,880	25,593	28,305	4	16,640	22,880
MO	18,533	18,533	24,746	24,746	30,958	30,958	2	.	.
OH	28,454	28,454	39,058	39,058	49,662	49,662	2	27,810	28,454
OR	41,392	41,392	41,392	41,392	41,392	41,392	4	33,654	41,392
TX	23,754	28,073	29,293	28,787	32,635	33,720	6	24,294	35,235
VA	41,178	41,178	45,876	45,876	50,573	50,573	2	30,521	50,868
WI	38,474	38,474	38,474	38,474	38,474	38,474	1	33,322	38,480

Degree Required Data

	Min	Q1	Mean	Median	Q3	Max	N	Range Avg Min	Range Avg Max
High School	22,880	22,880	31,205	29,427	32,969	50,573	10	22,983	33,241
Associate's	18,533	36,175	37,418	41,392	41,766	42,141	8	32,053	41,642
Bachelor's	28,454	32,992	38,070	34,722	43,851	50,097	9	30,566	33,467
Master's	38,222	38,222	38,222	38,222	38,222	38,222	1	.	.
Doctoral	.	.	.	.	.	.	.	.	.

INTER-LIBRARY LOAN ASSISTANT - CONTINUED
ALL PUBLIC LIBRARIES
Regional Data

	Min	Q1	Mean	Median	Q3	Max	N	Range Avg Min	Range Avg Max
North Atlantic	12,480	22,880	29,458	27,622	33,588	60,160	43	22,206	31,660
Great Lakes & Plains	14,560	22,069	26,616	25,230	31,075	49,662	75	22,687	32,614
Southeast	12,480	21,940	28,433	26,940	32,563	50,573	28	22,788	33,769
West & Southwest	12,480	21,507	30,235	31,762	38,091	50,097	55	23,678	31,780
ALL REGIONS	12,480	22,630	28,468	27,165	33,067	60,160	201	23,006	32,241

State Data

	Min	Q1	Mean	Median	Q3	Max	N	Range Avg Min	Range Avg Max
AR	23,795	23,795	23,795	23,795	23,795	23,795	1	.	.
AZ	32,323	32,323	38,868	42,141	42,141	42,141	3	28,850	42,141
CA	15,891	26,770	31,140	28,940	37,107	50,097	10	24,447	31,539
CO	16,224	22,620	32,096	33,857	40,262	44,046	12	20,055	26,399
CT	20,800	20,800	29,203	28,954	37,856	37,856	3	27,976	28,954
FL	19,995	25,949	29,966	29,504	32,157	43,810	11	23,026	33,394
GA	21,000	21,000	26,985	26,985	32,969	32,969	2	.	.
IA	18,221	18,221	26,859	29,786	32,571	32,571	3	24,565	33,238
ID	33,280	33,280	33,280	33,280	33,280	33,280	1	24,960	39,520
IL	18,720	23,847	27,956	26,416	31,564	41,600	24	24,348	35,576
IN	23,566	23,566	25,910	25,910	28,253	28,253	2	.	.
KS	14,560	19,604	22,925	22,786	26,354	32,781	12	21,080	34,614
LA	12,480	12,480	19,843	19,885	27,165	27,165	3	17,444	21,396
MA	20,446	22,880	25,427	27,622	27,622	27,622	7	19,864	22,880
MD	21,154	22,880	27,178	22,880	30,426	37,669	9	18,445	26,408
ME	37,523	37,523	37,523	37,523	37,523	37,523	1	29,619	42,224
MI	19,760	24,315	27,895	24,981	33,114	38,776	10	20,124	24,648
MN	15,725	20,965	29,637	31,903	38,309	39,018	4	.	.
MO	16,952	18,533	23,410	24,648	25,958	30,958	5	17,555	25,522
MS	14,664	14,664	18,964	17,052	25,176	25,176	3	.	.
NC	22,880	22,880	25,985	24,932	30,144	30,144	3	22,880	37,440
ND	25,106	25,106	25,106	25,106	25,106	25,106	1	21,840	32,760
NE	18,720	18,720	18,720	18,720	18,720	18,720	1	18,720	18,720
NH	43,597	43,597	43,597	43,597	43,597	43,597	1	37,211	56,389
NJ	29,516	32,270	36,364	33,588	40,103	46,343	5	.	.
NM	22,277	22,277	30,899	30,899	39,520	39,520	2	29,120	43,680
NY	32,594	32,594	42,578	34,980	60,160	60,160	3	29,183	33,831
OH	18,720	21,053	27,357	23,878	30,306	49,662	8	22,748	29,702
OK	18,782	18,782	20,065	20,654	20,758	20,758	3	17,950	23,296
OR	21,195	36,396	37,193	41,392	41,392	41,392	6	31,163	38,700
PA	12,480	22,880	26,130	26,998	33,004	35,824	14	18,699	31,730
SD	20,800	20,800	20,800	20,800	20,800	20,800	1	.	.
TX	12,480	17,472	24,064	23,951	28,787	34,902	14	17,441	26,697
VA	16,961	40,726	38,870	41,178	44,910	50,573	5	30,521	50,868
WA	29,016	30,909	33,611	33,041	36,313	39,346	4	24,502	33,537
WI	24,960	25,095	29,940	28,163	34,785	38,474	4	30,680	34,788

Degree Required Data

	Min	Q1	Mean	Median	Q3	Max	N	Range Avg Min	Range Avg Max
High School	12,480	21,154	26,777	26,155	31,762	60,160	98	21,857	30,511
Associate's	18,533	22,069	29,405	27,040	38,091	42,141	43	23,339	33,615
Bachelor's	16,961	26,343	33,632	33,062	39,439	50,097	32	27,414	36,458
Master's	38,222	38,222	38,222	38,222	38,222	38,222	1	.	.
Doctoral								.	.

DRIVER

Drives a library vehicle to pick-up and deliver library material between libraries, systems and branches. Determines sequence of loading for delivery purposes. Performs basic maintenance on vehicle. Informs supervisor when additional vehicle maintenance is necessary.

Medium Public Library
(Serving a population of 25,000 to 99,999)
Regional Data

	Min	Q1	Mean	Median	Q3	Max	N	Range Avg Min	Range Avg Max
North Atlantic	30,576	30,576	30,576	30,576	30,576	30,576	1	22,755	32,448
Great Lakes & Plains	19,840	19,840	21,266	21,266	22,693	22,693	2	.	.
ALL REGIONS	19,840	19,840	24,370	22,693	30,576	30,576	3	22,755	32,448

State Data

	Min	Q1	Mean	Median	Q3	Max	N	Range Avg Min	Range Avg Max
IN	22,693	22,693	22,693	22,693	22,693	22,693	1	.	.
ME	30,576	30,576	30,576	30,576	30,576	30,576	1	22,755	32,448
MI	19,840	19,840	19,840	19,840	19,840	19,840	1	.	.

Degree Required Data

	Min	Q1	Mean	Median	Q3	Max	N	Range Avg Min	Range Avg Max
High School	19,840	19,840	24,370	22,693	30,576	30,576	3	22,755	32,448
Associate's								.	.
Bachelor's								.	.
Master's								.	.
Doctoral								.	.

DRIVER - CONTINUED
Large Public Library
(Serving a population of 100,000 to 499,999)
Regional Data

	Min	Q1	Mean	Median	Q3	Max	N	Range Avg Min	Range Avg Max
North Atlantic	21,858	24,523	27,483	26,767	30,038	35,922	14	21,928	30,300
Great Lakes & Plains	18,117	23,130	25,629	25,251	27,533	38,079	33	21,439	29,501
Southeast	17,576	19,760	22,698	22,583	24,223	33,280	17	19,906	27,851
West & Southwest	14,706	18,355	24,981	24,960	30,690	36,171	24	22,156	29,422
ALL REGIONS	14,706	21,859	25,181	24,960	28,621	38,079	88	21,566	29,375

State Data

	Min	Q1	Mean	Median	Q3	Max	N	Range Avg Min	Range Avg Max
CA	16,644	23,005	27,372	26,917	32,332	36,171	10	24,833	30,139
CO	24,960	24,960	24,960	24,960	24,960	24,960	1	22,422	34,133
FL	17,576	17,576	18,304	17,576	19,760	19,760	3	17,576	25,501
IL	21,070	21,070	21,070	21,070	21,070	21,070	2	.	.
IN	19,237	19,237	19,237	19,237	19,237	19,237	1	.	.
KS	28,517	28,818	32,110	31,876	35,402	36,171	4	26,395	43,992
LA	21,861	21,861	21,861	21,861	21,861	21,861	1	18,387	25,979
MD	21,858	22,116	24,250	24,558	25,700	27,019	5	21,154	31,699
MI	23,067	23,067	26,326	26,978	28,933	28,933	3	23,057	28,413
MN	27,040	27,040	33,070	34,091	38,079	38,079	3	.	.
MO	22,339	23,130	24,385	25,251	25,251	26,395	14	20,855	26,297
MS	26,330	26,330	26,330	26,330	26,330	26,330	1	.	.
NC	18,952	19,886	23,936	21,756	27,986	33,280	4	20,384	32,490
NE	27,533	27,533	27,533	27,533	27,533	27,533	2	20,203	27,533
NJ	30,038	30,038	31,246	31,246	32,453	32,453	2	.	.
NM	16,640	16,640	16,640	16,640	16,640	16,640	1	.	.
NY	26,514	26,514	26,514	26,514	26,514	26,514	1	.	.
OH	18,117	18,117	20,904	18,117	26,478	26,478	3	17,306	27,165
OR	17,829	17,829	17,829	17,829	17,829	17,829	1	15,600	18,595
PA	23,644	24,523	29,084	28,621	33,175	35,922	6	22,187	29,834
SC	22,583	22,583	23,657	23,716	24,671	24,671	3	.	.
TN	20,800	20,800	20,800	20,800	20,800	20,800	1	.	.
TX	14,706	16,680	18,867	18,355	20,082	25,022	6	16,708	25,095
VA	18,012	20,404	23,812	23,510	27,221	30,218	4	22,797	22,797
WA	27,602	29,723	30,639	30,493	32,690	32,690	5	24,378	35,318
WI	18,574	18,574	18,574	18,574	18,574	18,574	1	.	.

Degree Required Data

	Min	Q1	Mean	Median	Q3	Max	N	Range Avg Min	Range Avg Max
High School	14,706	21,070	24,755	24,614	27,533	38,079	78	21,319	29,259
Associate's	.	.	.	.	.	.	.	.	.
Bachelor's	.	.	.	.	.	.	.	.	.
Master's	.	.	.	.	.	.	.	.	.
Doctoral	.	.	.	.	.	.	.	.	.

DRIVER - CONTINUED
Very Large Public Library
(Serving a population of 500,000 or more)
Regional Data

	Min	Q1	Mean	Median	Q3	Max	N	Range Avg Min	Range Avg Max
North Atlantic	24,648	25,971	28,535	26,894	28,306	41,316	23	.	.
Great Lakes & Plains	22,069	27,953	32,509	31,158	39,677	42,769	47	26,821	30,929
Southeast	19,032	19,995	23,590	23,202	25,968	33,289	13	19,032	34,195
West & Southwest	19,234	26,973	29,935	29,722	33,654	41,376	42	25,629	32,673
ALL REGIONS	19,032	25,971	29,986	28,787	33,672	42,769	125	26,055	31,872

State Data

	Min	Q1	Mean	Median	Q3	Max	N	Range Avg Min	Range Avg Max
AZ	22,152	27,747	30,683	32,240	34,445	34,445	8	24,950	33,862
CA	23,571	27,702	31,497	30,285	33,672	41,376	15	24,761	30,066
CO	26,973	26,973	29,003	26,973	33,062	33,062	3		
FL	19,032	19,043	20,970	19,519	23,202	25,504	6	19,032	34,195
GA	20,784	20,784	21,796	20,784	23,820	23,820	3		
IN	24,451	26,043	27,012	27,275	28,361	28,932	5		
MD	25,971	25,971	31,533	28,014	39,427	41,316	9		
MI	29,272	29,712	30,288	30,151	30,864	31,577	4		
MO	23,059	23,163	24,153	23,262	23,329	27,953	5		
NC	25,968	26,806	28,867	28,106	30,929	33,289	4		
NJ	24,648	26,125	26,609	26,582	26,957	28,808	14		
OH	22,069	29,744	34,275	35,863	39,880	42,093	30	24,967	29,060
OR	29,016	30,784	32,913	34,164	34,674	34,674	6	28,184	34,674
TX	19,234	22,901	25,274	26,208	27,040	31,117	7	22,672	32,011
UT	22,032	22,032	25,992	26,784	29,160	29,160	3		
WI	38,573	38,573	40,898	41,350	42,769	42,769	3	38,563	42,765

Degree Required Data

	Min	Q1	Mean	Median	Q3	Max	N	Range Avg Min	Range Avg Max
High School	19,234	26,973	31,538	31,158	37,972	42,769	81	26,585	32,193
Associate's									
Bachelor's	25,968	26,806	28,867	28,106	30,929	33,289	4		
Master's									
Doctoral									

DRIVER - CONTINUED
ALL PUBLIC LIBRARIES
Regional Data

	Min	Q1	Mean	Median	Q3	Max	N	Range Avg Min	Range Avg Max
North Atlantic	21,858	25,971	28,201	26,926	28,621	41,316	38	22,094	30,730
Great Lakes & Plains	18,117	23,329	29,466	28,439	34,632	42,769	82	23,958	30,169
Southeast	17,576	19,760	23,085	22,638	25,504	33,289	30	19,760	28,909
West & Southwest	14,706	23,571	28,134	28,787	32,690	41,376	66	24,153	31,291
ALL REGIONS	14,706	23,232	27,950	27,030	31,772	42,769	216	23,685	30,579

State Data

	Min	Q1	Mean	Median	Q3	Max	N	Range Avg Min	Range Avg Max
AZ	22,152	27,747	30,683	32,240	34,445	34,445	8	24,950	33,862
CA	16,644	24,960	29,847	30,285	33,637	41,376	25	24,797	30,103
CO	24,960	25,967	27,992	26,973	30,018	33,062	4	22,422	34,133
FL	17,576	19,032	20,081	19,043	19,995	25,504	9	18,304	29,848
GA	20,784	20,784	21,796	20,784	23,820	23,820	3	.	.
IL	21,070	21,070	21,070	21,070	21,070	21,070	2	.	.
IN	19,237	22,693	25,285	26,043	28,361	28,932	7	.	.
KS	28,517	28,818	32,110	31,876	35,402	36,171	4	26,395	43,992
LA	21,861	21,861	21,861	21,861	21,861	21,861	1	18,387	25,979
MD	21,858	25,700	28,932	26,495	28,306	41,316	14	21,154	31,699
ME	30,576	30,576	30,576	30,576	30,576	30,576	1	22,755	32,448
MI	19,840	25,022	27,496	29,103	30,151	31,577	8	23,057	28,413
MN	27,040	27,040	33,070	34,091	38,079	38,079	3	.	.
MO	22,339	23,130	24,324	23,329	25,251	27,953	19	20,855	26,297
MS	26,330	26,330	26,330	26,330	26,330	26,330	1	.	.
NC	18,952	21,756	26,402	26,806	30,924	33,289	8	20,384	32,490
NE	27,533	27,533	27,533	27,533	27,533	27,533	2	20,203	27,533
NJ	24,648	26,125	27,188	26,853	27,983	32,453	16	.	.
NM	16,640	16,640	16,640	16,640	16,640	16,640	1	.	.
NY	26,514	26,514	26,514	26,514	26,514	26,514	1	.	.
OH	18,117	29,099	33,059	32,594	39,880	42,093	33	23,922	28,801
OR	17,829	29,016	30,758	33,654	34,674	34,674	7	26,386	32,377
PA	23,644	24,523	29,084	28,621	33,175	35,922	6	22,187	29,834
SC	22,583	22,583	23,657	23,716	24,671	24,671	3	.	.
TN	20,800	20,800	20,800	20,800	20,800	20,800	1	.	.
TX	14,706	18,741	22,317	22,901	26,208	31,117	13	17,900	26,478
UT	22,032	22,032	25,992	26,784	29,160	29,160	3	.	.
VA	18,012	20,404	23,812	23,510	27,221	30,218	4	22,797	22,797
WA	27,602	29,723	30,639	30,493	32,690	32,690	5	24,378	35,318
WI	18,574	28,574	35,317	39,962	42,060	42,769	4	38,563	42,765

Degree Required Data

	Min	Q1	Mean	Median	Q3	Max	N	Range Avg Min	Range Avg Max
High School	14,706	23,130	28,140	27,404	33,062	42,769	162	23,628	30,574
Associate's	.	.	.	.	.	.		.	.
Bachelor's	25,968	26,806	28,867	28,106	30,929	33,289	4	.	.
Master's	.	.	.	.	.	.		.	.
Doctoral	.	.	.	.	.	.		.	.

INFORMATION TECHNOLOGY (IT) MANAGER

Manages day-to-day IT operations including systems analysis, programming, and computer and auxiliary operations. Directs the development and maintenance of systems. Determines and recommends department budgets and analyzes controllable expenditures. May plan and coordinate the evaluation and effectiveness of existing data processing applications and the feasibility and potential value of new applications. May assist staff and patrons with troubleshooting equipment or software problems.

Very Small Public Library
(Serving a population of less than 10,000)
Regional Data

	Min	Q1	Mean	Median	Q3	Max	N	Range Avg Min	Range Avg Max
Great Lakes & Plains	22,880	22,880	31,440	31,440	40,000	40,000	2	.	.
ALL REGIONS	22,880	22,880	31,440	31,440	40,000	40,000	2	.	.

State Data

	Min	Q1	Mean	Median	Q3	Max	N	Range Avg Min	Range Avg Max
KS	40,000	40,000	40,000	40,000	40,000	40,000	1	.	.
MI	22,880	22,880	22,880	22,880	22,880	22,880	1	.	.

Degree Required Data

	Min	Q1	Mean	Median	Q3	Max	N	Range Avg Min	Range Avg Max
High School	22,880	22,880	22,880	22,880	22,880	22,880	1	.	.
Associate's	.	.	.	.	.	.	.	.	.
Bachelor's	40,000	40,000	40,000	40,000	40,000	40,000	1	.	.
Master's	.	.	.	.	.	.	.	.	.
Doctoral	.	.	.	.	.	.	.	.	.

INFORMATION TECHNOLOGY (IT) MANAGER - CONTINUED
Small Public Library
(Serving a population of 10,000 to 25,000)
Regional Data

	Min	Q1	Mean	Median	Q3	Max	N	Range Avg Min	Range Avg Max
North Atlantic	44,876	44,876	44,876	44,876	44,876	44,876	1	.	.
Great Lakes & Plains	16,640	19,427	32,545	29,120	45,531	59,294	7	28,676	48,166
Southeast	12,480	12,480	12,480	12,480	12,480	12,480	1	.	.
West & Southwest	37,500	37,500	38,650	38,650	39,800	39,800	2	.	.
ALL REGIONS	12,480	19,427	32,952	31,574	44,876	59,294	11	28,676	48,166

State Data

	Min	Q1	Mean	Median	Q3	Max	N	Range Avg Min	Range Avg Max
AZ	39,800	39,800	39,800	39,800	39,800	39,800	1	.	.
CO	37,500	37,500	37,500	37,500	37,500	37,500	1	.	.
GA	12,480	12,480	12,480	12,480	12,480	12,480	1	.	.
IA	26,229	26,229	26,229	26,229	26,229	26,229	1	.	.
IL	16,640	16,640	37,967	37,967	59,294	59,294	2	39,520	81,120
IN	19,427	19,427	19,427	19,427	19,427	19,427	1	18,720	30,160
MI	29,120	29,120	30,347	30,347	31,574	31,574	2	27,789	33,218
NJ	44,876	44,876	44,876	44,876	44,876	44,876	1	.	.
OH	45,531	45,531	45,531	45,531	45,531	45,531	1	.	.

Degree Required Data

	Min	Q1	Mean	Median	Q3	Max	N	Range Avg Min	Range Avg Max
High School	16,640	19,427	26,852	29,120	31,574	37,500	5	23,254	31,689
Associate's	26,229	26,229	26,229	26,229	26,229	26,229	1	.	.
Bachelor's	12,480	39,800	40,396	44,876	45,531	59,294	5	39,520	81,120
Master's	.	.	.	.	.	.	.	.	.
Doctoral	.	.	.	.	.	.	.	.	.

INFORMATION TECHNOLOGY (IT) MANAGER - CONTINUED
Medium Public Library
(Serving a population of 25,000 to 99,999)
Regional Data

	Min	Q1	Mean	Median	Q3	Max	N	Range Avg Min	Range Avg Max
North Atlantic	21,961	33,862	44,037	35,121	44,533	93,624	6	30,992	42,120
Great Lakes & Plains	27,248	35,006	49,463	47,965	63,655	76,606	11	42,457	57,524
Southeast	34,953	34,953	43,809	41,600	54,875	54,875	3	31,200	62,400
West & Southwest	26,000	42,224	47,420	49,920	53,916	65,042	5	49,213	65,010
ALL REGIONS	21,961	34,953	47,074	42,224	56,514	93,624	25	41,434	58,018

State Data

	Min	Q1	Mean	Median	Q3	Max	N	Range Avg Min	Range Avg Max
AR	41,600	41,600	41,600	41,600	41,600	41,600	1	31,200	62,400
CA	53,916	53,916	59,479	59,479	65,042	65,042	2	58,906	71,781
CT	93,624	93,624	93,624	93,624	93,624	93,624	1	.	.
ID	42,224	42,224	46,072	46,072	49,920	49,920	2	39,520	58,240
IL	75,504	75,504	76,055	76,055	76,606	76,606	2	54,298	80,735
IN	27,248	27,248	40,254	37,000	56,514	56,514	3	27,248	27,248
KS	38,875	38,875	38,875	38,875	38,875	38,875	1	33,904	47,445
LA	34,953	34,953	34,953	34,953	34,953	34,953	1	.	.
MA	36,067	36,067	40,300	40,300	44,533	44,533	2	.	.
ME	33,862	33,862	33,862	33,862	33,862	33,862	1	30,992	42,120
MN	63,655	63,655	63,655	63,655	63,655	63,655	1	.	.
OH	28,205	28,205	40,241	35,006	57,511	57,511	3	.	.
PA	21,961	21,961	28,068	28,068	34,175	34,175	2	.	.
TN	54,875	54,875	54,875	54,875	54,875	54,875	1	.	.
TX	26,000	26,000	26,000	26,000	26,000	26,000	1	.	.
WI	47,965	47,965	47,965	47,965	47,965	47,965	1	42,536	51,459

Degree Required Data

	Min	Q1	Mean	Median	Q3	Max	N	Range Avg Min	Range Avg Max
High School	53,916	53,916	73,770	73,770	93,624	93,624	2	.	.
Associate's	21,961	23,980	35,385	31,034	46,789	57,511	4	.	.
Bachelor's	27,248	34,564	47,458	43,378	60,084	76,606	16	44,210	60,143
Master's	38,875	38,875	43,420	43,420	47,965	47,965	2	38,220	49,452
Doctoral	.	.	.	.	.	.		.	.

INFORMATION TECHNOLOGY (IT) MANAGER - CONTINUED
Large Public Library
(Serving a population of 100,000 to 499,999)
Regional Data

	Min	Q1	Mean	Median	Q3	Max	N	Range Avg Min	Range Avg Max
North Atlantic	24,000	52,581	64,363	68,447	75,868	88,504	12	43,430	68,952
Great Lakes & Plains	41,870	45,867	54,560	54,300	63,918	67,548	11	45,162	69,883
Southeast	26,412	34,949	55,314	44,040	86,985	95,455	6	43,451	65,166
West & Southwest	28,371	35,880	53,215	46,200	72,357	85,280	17	47,204	66,192
ALL REGIONS	24,000	42,765	56,719	54,390	71,822	95,455	46	45,997	67,461

State Data

	Min	Q1	Mean	Median	Q3	Max	N	Range Avg Min	Range Avg Max
AL	42,765	42,765	42,765	42,765	42,765	42,765	1	43,451	65,166
CA	35,796	38,700	63,792	72,357	84,760	85,280	7	61,984	85,876
CO	43,992	43,992	52,729	52,729	61,466	61,466	2	39,666	55,162
FL	45,316	45,316	45,316	45,316	45,316	45,316	1	.	.
IL	44,012	44,012	51,128	52,692	56,680	56,680	3	39,042	55,120
KS	63,918	63,918	63,918	63,918	63,918	63,918	1	49,005	81,682
MA	46,946	46,946	46,946	46,946	46,946	46,946	1	.	.
MD	47,727	66,976	70,613	72,888	75,878	87,318	6	.	.
MI	45,867	45,867	50,083	50,083	54,300	54,300	2	.	.
MO	64,563	64,563	66,056	66,056	67,548	67,548	2	51,002	74,090
MS	26,412	26,412	26,412	26,412	26,412	26,412	1	.	.
NM	34,403	34,403	43,945	43,945	53,487	53,487	2	52,021	71,282
OH	49,747	49,747	54,357	54,357	58,968	58,968	2	41,600	68,640
OR	28,371	28,371	28,371	28,371	28,371	28,371	1	28,371	37,461
PA	24,000	57,436	60,347	59,974	71,822	88,504	5	43,430	68,952
TX	31,179	31,179	35,351	35,880	38,995	38,995	3	24,419	41,808
VA	34,949	34,949	72,463	86,985	95,455	95,455	3	.	.
WA	54,480	54,480	65,166	65,166	75,852	75,852	2	.	.
WI	41,870	41,870	41,870	41,870	41,870	41,870	1	.	.

Degree Required Data

	Min	Q1	Mean	Median	Q3	Max	N	Range Avg Min	Range Avg Max
High School	26,412	26,412	55,363	52,692	86,985	86,985	3	.	.
Associate's	24,000	31,179	40,522	35,373	41,870	85,280	10	44,403	59,998
Bachelor's	38,700	45,867	59,569	56,680	69,919	95,455	25	40,940	61,022
Master's	57,436	63,918	69,814	68,460	75,852	84,760	6	49,988	77,371
Doctoral	.	.	.	.	.	.	.	.	.

INFORMATION TECHNOLOGY (IT) MANAGER - CONTINUED
Very Large Public Library
(Serving a population of 500,000 or more)
Regional Data

	Min	Q1	Mean	Median	Q3	Max	N	Range Avg Min	Range Avg Max
North Atlantic	70,455	70,455	78,094	76,911	86,917	86,917	3	.	.
Great Lakes & Plains	66,518	82,900	99,356	100,109	115,811	130,686	4	54,205	78,000
Southeast	38,172	53,358	65,715	64,248	81,496	92,456	7	.	.
West & Southwest	49,358	58,614	71,580	69,094	82,239	111,306	18	57,797	72,560
ALL REGIONS	38,172	58,653	74,379	73,088	87,337	130,686	32	57,438	73,104

State Data

	Min	Q1	Mean	Median	Q3	Max	N	Range Avg Min	Range Avg Max
AZ	58,614	58,614	69,742	69,742	80,870	80,870	2	61,058	95,399
CA	49,358	49,358	71,576	69,094	84,997	111,306	12	56,865	66,035
CO	77,391	77,391	77,391	77,391	77,391	77,391	1	.	.
FL	38,172	45,765	65,038	64,762	84,311	92,456	4	.	.
GA	54,107	54,107	59,177	59,177	64,248	64,248	2	.	.
IN	100,936	100,936	100,936	100,936	100,936	100,936	1	.	.
MD	70,455	70,455	78,686	78,686	86,917	86,917	2	.	.
MI	99,282	99,282	99,282	99,282	99,282	99,282	1	.	.
NC	81,496	81,496	81,496	81,496	81,496	81,496	1	.	.
NJ	76,911	76,911	76,911	76,911	76,911	76,911	1	.	.
OH	66,518	66,518	98,602	98,602	130,686	130,686	2	54,205	78,000
TX	58,692	58,692	74,596	74,596	90,501	90,501	2	.	.
UT	63,456	63,456	63,456	63,456	63,456	63,456	1	.	.

Degree Required Data

	Min	Q1	Mean	Median	Q3	Max	N	Range Avg Min	Range Avg Max
High School	49,358	49,358	53,414	49,358	49,358	69,638	5	40,934	49,358
Associate's	.	.	.	.	.	.		.	.
Bachelor's	53,358	65,383	79,673	77,151	89,128	130,686	24	68,440	88,935
Master's	99,282	99,282	99,282	99,282	99,282	99,282	1	.	.
Doctoral	.	.	.	.	.	.		.	.

INFORMATION TECHNOLOGY (IT) MANAGER - CONTINUED
ALL PUBLIC LIBRARIES
Regional Data

	Min	Q1	Mean	Median	Q3	Max	N	Range Avg Min	Range Avg Max
North Atlantic	21,961	44,533	59,806	63,475	75,878	93,624	22	37,211	55,536
Great Lakes & Plains	16,640	35,006	52,353	49,747	63,918	130,686	35	41,013	60,742
Southeast	12,480	38,172	55,047	53,358	76,165	95,455	17	37,326	63,783
West & Southwest	26,000	42,224	59,702	56,547	75,852	111,306	42	52,724	69,245
ALL REGIONS	12,480	38,935	56,822	54,204	73,931	130,686	116	46,608	64,991

State Data

	Min	Q1	Mean	Median	Q3	Max	N	Range Avg Min	Range Avg Max
AL	42,765	42,765	42,765	42,765	42,765	42,765	1	43,451	65,166
AR	41,600	41,600	41,600	41,600	41,600	41,600	1	31,200	62,400
AZ	39,800	39,800	59,762	58,614	80,870	80,870	3	61,058	95,399
CA	35,796	49,358	67,829	68,549	83,450	111,306	21	58,447	71,968
CO	37,500	40,746	55,087	52,729	69,429	77,391	4	39,666	55,162
CT	93,624	93,624	93,624	93,624	93,624	93,624	1	.	.
FL	38,172	45,316	61,093	53,358	76,165	92,456	5	.	.
GA	12,480	12,480	43,612	54,107	64,248	64,248	3	.	.
IA	26,229	26,229	26,229	26,229	26,229	26,229	1	.	.
ID	42,224	42,224	46,072	46,072	49,920	49,920	2	39,520	58,240
IL	16,640	44,012	54,490	56,680	75,504	76,606	7	46,790	74,428
IN	19,427	27,248	48,225	37,000	56,514	100,936	5	22,984	28,704
KS	38,875	38,875	47,598	40,000	63,918	63,918	3	41,454	64,563
LA	34,953	34,953	34,953	34,953	34,953	34,953	1	.	.
MA	36,067	36,067	42,515	44,533	46,946	46,946	3	.	.
MD	47,727	68,447	72,631	73,157	81,398	87,318	8	.	.
ME	33,862	33,862	33,862	33,862	33,862	33,862	1	30,992	42,120
MI	22,880	29,120	47,171	38,721	54,300	99,282	6	27,789	33,218
MN	63,655	63,655	63,655	63,655	63,655	63,655	1	.	.
MO	64,563	64,563	66,056	66,056	67,548	67,548	2	51,002	74,090
MS	26,412	26,412	26,412	26,412	26,412	26,412	1	.	.
NC	81,496	81,496	81,496	81,496	81,496	81,496	1	.	.
NJ	44,876	44,876	60,893	60,893	76,911	76,911	2	.	.
NM	34,403	34,403	43,945	43,945	53,487	53,487	2	52,021	71,282
OH	28,205	40,269	59,021	53,629	62,743	130,686	8	47,902	73,320
OR	28,371	28,371	28,371	28,371	28,371	28,371	1	28,371	37,461
PA	21,961	24,000	51,125	57,436	71,822	88,504	7	43,430	68,952
TN	54,875	54,875	54,875	54,875	54,875	54,875	1	.	.
TX	26,000	31,179	46,875	37,438	58,692	90,501	6	24,419	41,808
UT	63,456	63,456	63,456	63,456	63,456	63,456	1	.	.
VA	34,949	34,949	72,463	86,985	95,455	95,455	3	.	.
WA	54,480	54,480	65,166	65,166	75,852	75,852	2	.	.
WI	41,870	41,870	44,917	44,917	47,965	47,965	2	42,536	51,459

Degree Required Data

	Min	Q1	Mean	Median	Q3	Max	N	Range Avg Min	Range Avg Max
High School	16,640	27,766	46,115	49,358	53,304	93,624	16	35,041	43,469
Associate's	21,961	26,229	38,199	34,949	41,870	85,280	15	44,403	59,998
Bachelor's	12,480	44,876	62,010	59,294	76,165	130,686	71	51,716	71,746
Master's	38,875	57,436	67,223	64,563	75,852	99,282	9	46,065	68,065
Doctoral	.	.	.	.	.	.	.	.	.

SYSTEMS ADMINISTRATOR

Manages day-to-day IT operations including systems analysis, programming, and computer and auxiliary operations. Directs the development and maintenance of systems. Determines and recommends department budgets and analyzes controllable expenditures. May plan and coordinate the evaluation and effectiveness of existing data processing applications and the feasibility and potential value of new applications. May assist staff and patrons with troubleshooting equipment or software problems.

Very Small Public Library
(Serving a population of less than 10,000)
Regional Data

	Min	Q1	Mean	Median	Q3	Max	N	Range Avg Min	Range Avg Max
North Atlantic	17,659	17,659	17,659	17,659	17,659	17,659	1	.	.
Great Lakes & Plains	29,120	29,120	37,708	37,708	46,295	46,295	2	14,872	29,120
West & Southwest	23,772	23,772	39,966	39,966	56,160	56,160	2	39,083	56,680
ALL REGIONS	17,659	23,772	34,601	29,120	46,295	56,160	5	26,978	42,900

State Data

	Min	Q1	Mean	Median	Q3	Max	N	Range Avg Min	Range Avg Max
AZ	23,772	23,772	23,772	23,772	23,772	23,772	1	.	.
CO	56,160	56,160	56,160	56,160	56,160	56,160	1	39,083	56,680
MO	46,295	46,295	46,295	46,295	46,295	46,295	1	.	.
NY	17,659	17,659	17,659	17,659	17,659	17,659	1	.	.
OH	29,120	29,120	29,120	29,120	29,120	29,120	1	14,872	29,120

Degree Required Data

	Min	Q1	Mean	Median	Q3	Max	N	Range Avg Min	Range Avg Max
High School	17,659	17,659	23,390	23,390	29,120	29,120	2	14,872	29,120
Associate's	.	.	.	.	.	.	.	.	.
Bachelor's	46,295	46,295	51,228	51,228	56,160	56,160	2	39,083	56,680
Master's	.	.	.	.	.	.	.	.	.
Doctoral	.	.	.	.	.	.	.	.	.

SYSTEMS ADMINISTRATOR - CONTINUED
Small Public Library
(Serving a population of 10,000 to 25,000)
Regional Data

	Min	Q1	Mean	Median	Q3	Max	N	Range Avg Min	Range Avg Max
Great Lakes & Plains	21,133	27,934	31,946	31,200	34,869	44,475	9	21,840	38,480
Southeast	27,602	27,602	27,602	27,602	27,602	27,602	1	23,816	25,896
West & Southwest	58,240	58,240	58,240	58,240	58,240	58,240	1	43,680	64,480
ALL REGIONS	21,133	27,602	33,942	31,200	37,440	58,240	11	25,809	40,716

State Data

	Min	Q1	Mean	Median	Q3	Max	N	Range Avg Min	Range Avg Max
IL	37,440	37,440	37,440	37,440	37,440	37,440	1	22,880	52,000
IN	31,200	31,200	37,838	37,838	44,475	44,475	2	24,960	39,520
KS	26,607	26,607	30,738	30,738	34,869	34,869	2	20,800	33,280
LA	27,602	27,602	27,602	27,602	27,602	27,602	1	23,816	25,896
MI	29,120	29,120	29,120	29,120	29,120	29,120	1	.	.
MO	21,133	21,133	21,133	21,133	21,133	21,133	1	18,720	29,120
NM	58,240	58,240	58,240	58,240	58,240	58,240	1	43,680	64,480
OH	27,934	27,934	27,934	27,934	27,934	27,934	1	.	.
WI	34,739	34,739	34,739	34,739	34,739	34,739	1	.	.

Degree Required Data

	Min	Q1	Mean	Median	Q3	Max	N	Range Avg Min	Range Avg Max
High School	27,934	27,934	28,527	28,527	29,120	29,120	2	.	.
Associate's	26,607	26,607	30,673	30,673	34,739	34,739	2	20,800	33,280
Bachelor's	21,133	27,602	36,423	34,869	44,475	58,240	7	26,811	42,203
Master's	.	.	.	.	.	.		.	.
Doctoral	.	.	.	.	.	.		.	.

SYSTEMS ADMINISTRATOR - CONTINUED
Medium Public Library
(Serving a population of 25,000 to 99,999)
Regional Data

	Min	Q1	Mean	Median	Q3	Max	N	Range Avg Min	Range Avg Max
North Atlantic	38,522	38,917	54,406	48,494	75,714	76,295	6	32,032	48,672
Great Lakes & Plains	17,139	27,976	42,961	42,130	56,019	75,555	18	27,734	43,488
Southeast	19,240	21,216	26,901	28,800	32,240	33,008	5	25,168	42,598
West & Southwest	42,224	42,224	45,718	45,718	49,213	49,213	2	31,200	49,920
ALL REGIONS	17,139	28,800	42,763	38,917	56,019	76,295	31	28,525	44,814

State Data

	Min	Q1	Mean	Median	Q3	Max	N	Range Avg Min	Range Avg Max
CA	49,213	49,213	49,213	49,213	49,213	49,213	1	31,200	49,920
CT	38,522	38,719	48,428	39,738	58,137	75,714	4	32,032	48,672
GA	19,240	19,240	19,240	19,240	19,240	19,240	1	.	.
IA	17,139	17,139	33,980	33,980	50,821	50,821	2	.	.
ID	42,224	42,224	42,224	42,224	42,224	42,224	1	.	.
IL	26,874	35,776	50,619	51,181	63,149	75,555	6	31,304	48,589
IN	67,600	67,600	67,600	67,600	67,600	67,600	1	.	.
KS	31,595	31,595	31,595	31,595	31,595	31,595	1	27,248	38,126
MI	31,200	31,200	31,200	31,200	31,200	31,200	1	21,570	31,200
MN	60,919	60,919	60,919	60,919	60,919	60,919	1	.	.
MS	21,216	21,216	25,008	25,008	28,800	28,800	2	.	.
NY	56,427	56,427	66,361	66,361	76,295	76,295	2	.	.
OH	18,733	27,914	35,050	32,947	47,840	49,920	6	23,920	42,110
TN	32,240	32,240	32,240	32,240	32,240	32,240	1	25,168	42,598
VA	33,008	33,008	33,008	33,008	33,008	33,008	1	.	.

Degree Required Data

	Min	Q1	Mean	Median	Q3	Max	N	Range Avg Min	Range Avg Max
High School	17,139	21,216	36,570	33,218	38,917	75,714	6	29,675	50,121
Associate's	18,733	27,976	41,829	33,008	56,019	75,555	11	26,411	41,246
Bachelor's	31,595	37,918	47,166	44,283	50,821	76,295	10	31,517	47,804
Master's	19,240	19,240	43,420	43,420	67,600	67,600	2	.	.
Doctoral	.	.	.	.	.	.	.	.	.

SYSTEMS ADMINISTRATOR - CONTINUED
Large Public Library
(Serving a population of 100,000 to 499,999)
Regional Data

	Min	Q1	Mean	Median	Q3	Max	N	Range Avg Min	Range Avg Max
North Atlantic	24,000	36,990	44,637	45,767	50,209	61,638	18	31,647	43,566
Great Lakes & Plains	26,516	37,918	42,655	44,328	48,853	59,711	27	32,921	49,850
Southeast	29,661	37,868	44,608	44,755	51,979	61,445	17	33,342	40,997
West & Southwest	23,379	35,796	47,940	49,294	56,659	69,180	21	43,168	57,537
ALL REGIONS	23,379	37,215	44,822	45,513	52,125	69,180	83	35,172	50,221

State Data

	Min	Q1	Mean	Median	Q3	Max	N	Range Avg Min	Range Avg Max
AZ	52,125	52,125	52,135	52,135	52,146	52,146	2		
CA	34,248	35,796	49,976	46,176	64,480	69,180	5	51,106	62,088
CO	46,150	46,150	50,701	49,294	56,659	56,659	3	44,491	73,424
FL	32,635	34,361	39,593	41,225	44,232	45,513	5		
GA	29,661	29,661	40,944	40,944	52,228	52,228	2	29,661	30,701
IL	44,328	44,378	46,061	45,531	47,743	48,853	4	33,134	46,779
IN	26,516	26,516	27,434	27,434	28,352	28,352	2		
KS	37,918	37,960	43,597	39,000	44,762	58,344	5	33,476	55,794
LA	38,875	38,875	38,875	38,875	38,875	38,875	1	37,024	51,293
MA	39,458	39,458	39,458	39,458	39,458	39,458	1		
MD	47,189	49,649	53,269	51,937	57,262	61,638	6		
MI	27,040	36,909	39,013	38,720	43,701	48,693	5		
MN	47,590	47,590	52,767	51,000	59,711	59,711	3		
MO	31,346	31,346	34,944	34,944	38,542	38,542	2	27,456	39,894
NC	37,215	37,215	37,215	37,215	37,215	37,215	1		
NE	51,393	51,393	52,509	52,509	53,624	53,624	2	42,292	54,002
NJ	31,200	31,200	33,987	33,987	36,774	36,774	2		
NM	31,200	31,200	31,200	31,200	31,200	31,200	1		
NY	42,273	42,273	42,273	42,273	42,273	42,273	1		
OH	29,848	29,848	38,820	39,499	47,112	47,112	3	27,414	43,867
PA	24,000	35,717	41,770	44,242	48,610	53,019	8	31,647	43,566
SC	45,749	45,749	45,749	45,749	45,749	45,749	1		
TN	37,868	37,868	41,311	41,311	44,755	44,755	2		
TX	23,379	31,212	38,749	39,166	45,947	53,622	6	23,379	33,925
VA	50,668	51,979	54,804	53,637	56,291	61,445	5		
WA	56,160	58,187	59,200	60,214	60,214	60,214	4	45,760	56,160
WI	49,866	49,866	49,866	49,866	49,866	49,866	1		

Degree Required Data

	Min	Q1	Mean	Median	Q3	Max	N	Range Avg Min	Range Avg Max
High School	26,516	36,990	46,022	50,038	51,979	56,160	10	36,046	48,547
Associate's	23,379	31,200	40,573	43,701	47,189	64,480	15	36,816	49,913
Bachelor's	28,352	37,939	45,729	46,049	53,631	61,638	48	34,276	50,520
Master's	44,288	45,513	51,323	46,634	51,000	69,180	5	33,134	46,779
Doctoral									

SYSTEMS ADMINISTRATOR - CONTINUED
Very Large Public Library
(Serving a population of 500,000 or more)
Regional Data

	Min	Q1	Mean	Median	Q3	Max	N	Range Avg Min	Range Avg Max
North Atlantic	37,143	43,082	48,519	45,187	56,043	64,888	9		
Great Lakes & Plains	38,178	47,612	62,714	59,125	70,346	115,173	14	55,775	79,050
Southeast	39,656	43,044	55,951	56,800	66,622	79,269	10	53,228	88,713
West & Southwest	49,668	63,579	67,327	68,302	70,096	89,336	17	57,384	74,868
ALL REGIONS	37,143	47,612	60,375	60,494	68,302	115,173	50	56,615	77,271

State Data

	Min	Q1	Mean	Median	Q3	Max	N	Range Avg Min	Range Avg Max
AZ	49,858	49,858	67,382	67,382	84,906	84,906	2	56,410	87,578
CA	51,916	65,052	67,930	68,302	68,994	89,336	11	58,462	71,018
CO	58,584	58,584	58,584	58,584	58,584	58,584	1	.	.
FL	39,656	52,052	60,453	64,666	66,622	79,269	5	.	.
GA	42,069	42,069	42,719	43,044	43,044	43,044	3	.	.
IN	76,621	76,621	76,621	76,621	76,621	76,621	1	.	.
MD	56,043	56,043	59,047	56,209	64,888	64,888	3	.	.
MI	47,154	47,154	47,459	47,612	47,612	47,612	3	.	.
MO	38,178	38,178	38,178	38,178	38,178	38,178	1	.	.
NJ	37,143	42,952	43,255	43,082	45,187	48,083	6	.	.
OH	57,369	58,096	68,803	62,074	68,769	115,173	8	49,254	70,886
TX	49,668	49,668	64,073	64,073	78,478	78,478	2	50,710	80,246
UT	75,840	75,840	75,840	75,840	75,840	75,840	1	.	.
VA	61,549	61,549	64,543	64,543	67,537	67,537	2	53,228	88,713
WI	70,393	70,393	70,393	70,393	70,393	70,393	1	62,296	87,214

Degree Required Data

	Min	Q1	Mean	Median	Q3	Max	N	Range Avg Min	Range Avg Max
High School	47,154	47,612	53,897	49,764	61,549	67,537	6	53,228	88,713
Associate's	57,369	58,812	64,985	64,666	70,346	79,269	9	62,296	87,214
Bachelor's	37,143	43,082	59,742	56,209	68,994	115,173	27	57,078	78,989
Master's	38,178	38,178	38,178	38,178	38,178	38,178	1	.	.
Doctoral	.	.	.	.	.	.	.	.	.

SYSTEMS ADMINISTRATOR - CONTINUED
ALL PUBLIC LIBRARIES
Regional Data

	Min	Q1	Mean	Median	Q3	Max	N	Range Avg Min	Range Avg Max
North Atlantic	17,659	38,917	46,595	44,767	53,664	76,295	34	31,840	46,119
Great Lakes & Plains	17,139	31,595	45,227	44,618	53,624	115,173	70	30,844	47,753
Southeast	19,240	34,361	44,847	43,044	52,228	79,269	33	37,021	54,652
West & Southwest	23,379	46,150	55,370	56,160	68,302	89,336	43	50,580	67,490
ALL REGIONS	17,139	37,179	47,839	46,873	57,375	115,173	180	38,143	54,944

State Data

	Min	Q1	Mean	Median	Q3	Max	N	Range Avg Min	Range Avg Max
AZ	23,772	49,858	52,561	52,125	52,146	84,906	5	56,410	87,578
CA	34,248	51,916	61,549	65,052	68,302	89,336	17	54,646	67,476
CO	46,150	49,294	53,369	56,160	56,659	58,584	5	41,787	65,052
CT	38,522	38,719	48,428	39,738	58,137	75,714	4	32,032	48,672
FL	32,635	39,656	50,023	44,873	64,666	79,269	10	.	.
GA	19,240	29,661	38,214	42,557	43,044	52,228	6	29,661	30,701
IA	17,139	17,139	33,980	33,980	50,821	50,821	2	.	.
ID	42,224	42,224	42,224	42,224	42,224	42,224	1	.	.
IL	26,874	37,440	47,763	46,342	56,019	75,555	11	30,624	48,559
IN	26,516	28,352	45,794	37,838	67,600	76,621	6	24,960	39,520
KS	26,607	33,232	38,882	37,939	41,881	58,344	8	30,775	50,054
LA	27,602	27,602	33,238	33,238	38,875	38,875	2	30,420	38,594
MA	39,458	39,458	39,458	39,458	39,458	39,458	1	.	.
MD	47,189	50,209	55,195	56,043	57,262	64,888	9	.	.
MI	27,040	31,200	39,776	41,210	47,612	48,693	10	21,570	31,200
MN	47,590	49,295	54,805	55,356	60,315	60,919	4	.	.
MO	21,133	31,346	35,099	38,178	38,542	46,295	5	24,544	36,303
MS	21,216	21,216	25,008	25,008	28,800	28,800	2	.	.
NC	37,215	37,215	37,215	37,215	37,215	37,215	1	.	.
NE	51,393	51,393	52,509	52,509	53,624	53,624	2	42,292	54,002
NJ	31,200	36,958	40,938	43,017	44,135	48,083	8	.	.
NM	31,200	31,200	44,720	44,720	58,240	58,240	2	43,680	64,480
NY	17,659	29,966	48,164	49,350	66,361	76,295	4	.	.
OH	18,733	29,120	49,170	47,840	59,439	115,173	19	27,799	45,327
PA	24,000	35,717	41,770	44,242	48,610	53,019	8	31,647	43,566
SC	45,749	45,749	45,749	45,749	45,749	45,749	1	.	.
TN	32,240	32,240	38,288	37,868	44,755	44,755	3	25,168	42,598
TX	23,379	32,628	45,080	45,118	51,645	78,478	8	37,045	57,086
UT	75,840	75,840	75,840	75,840	75,840	75,840	1	.	.
VA	33,008	51,324	54,514	54,964	61,497	67,537	8	53,228	88,713
WA	56,160	58,187	59,200	60,214	60,214	60,214	4	45,760	56,160
WI	34,739	34,739	51,666	49,866	70,393	70,393	3	62,296	87,214

Degree Required Data

	Min	Q1	Mean	Median	Q3	Max	N	Range Avg Min	Range Avg Max
High School	17,139	29,120	42,571	47,383	51,916	75,714	26	35,306	56,750
Associate's	18,733	32,240	46,349	44,755	58,812	79,269	37	33,243	48,358
Bachelor's	21,133	38,720	49,331	47,351	57,262	115,173	94	37,903	55,301
Master's	19,240	41,233	47,704	46,073	59,300	69,180	8	33,134	46,779
Doctoral	.	.	.	.	.	.	.	.	.

WEB CONTENT ADMINISTRATOR

Develops, provides, and authorizes website content to increase traffic, support and promote services, and gain content visibility.
Manages and performs website editorial activities including gathering and researching information that enhances the value of the site.
May oversee data control technicians and writers dedicated to website.

Very Small Public Library
(Serving a population of less than 10,000)
Regional Data

	Min	Q1	Mean	Median	Q3	Max	N	Range Avg Min	Range Avg Max
Great Lakes & Plains	20,800	20,800	20,800	20,800	20,800	20,800	1	20,384	24,544
ALL REGIONS	20,800	20,800	20,800	20,800	20,800	20,800	1	20,384	24,544

State Data

	Min	Q1	Mean	Median	Q3	Max	N	Range Avg Min	Range Avg Max
IL	20,800	20,800	20,800	20,800	20,800	20,800	1	20,384	24,544

Degree Required Data

	Min	Q1	Mean	Median	Q3	Max	N	Range Avg Min	Range Avg Max
High School	.	.	.	.	.	.	.	.	.
Associate's									
Bachelor's									
Master's									
Doctoral									

WEB CONTENT ADMINISTRATOR - CONTINUED
Small Public Library
(Serving a population of 10,000 to 25,000)
Regional Data

	Min	Q1	Mean	Median	Q3	Max	N	Range Avg Min	Range Avg Max
North Atlantic	41,600	41,600	41,600	41,600	41,600	41,600	1	.	.
ALL REGIONS	41,600	41,600	41,600	41,600	41,600	41,600	1	.	.

State Data

	Min	Q1	Mean	Median	Q3	Max	N	Range Avg Min	Range Avg Max
ME	41,600	41,600	41,600	41,600	41,600	41,600	1	.	.

Degree Required Data

	Min	Q1	Mean	Median	Q3	Max	N	Range Avg Min	Range Avg Max
High School	41,600	41,600	41,600	41,600	41,600	41,600	1	.	.
Associate's									
Bachelor's									
Master's									
Doctoral									

WEB CONTENT ADMINISTRATOR - CONTINUED
Medium Public Library
(Serving a population of 25,000 to 99,999)
Regional Data

	Min	Q1	Mean	Median	Q3	Max	N	Range Avg Min	Range Avg Max
Great Lakes & Plains	41,600	41,600	44,793	44,793	47,986	47,986	2	38,376	58,802
ALL REGIONS	41,600	41,600	44,793	44,793	47,986	47,986	2	38,376	58,802

State Data

	Min	Q1	Mean	Median	Q3	Max	N	Range Avg Min	Range Avg Max
IL	47,986	47,986	47,986	47,986	47,986	47,986	1	38,376	58,802
OH	41,600	41,600	41,600	41,600	41,600	41,600	1	.	.

Degree Required Data

	Min	Q1	Mean	Median	Q3	Max	N	Range Avg Min	Range Avg Max
High School	.	.	.	.	.	.		.	.
Associate's	.	.	.	.	.	.		.	.
Bachelor's	41,600	41,600	44,793	44,793	47,986	47,986	2	38,376	58,802
Master's	.	.	.	.	.	.		.	.
Doctoral	.	.	.	.	.	.		.	.

WEB CONTENT ADMINISTRATOR - CONTINUED
Large Public Library
(Serving a population of 100,000 to 499,999)
Regional Data

	Min	Q1	Mean	Median	Q3	Max	N	Range Avg Min	Range Avg Max
Great Lakes & Plains	17,971	26,395	45,912	48,005	67,548	67,548	6	20,946	29,515
Southeast	36,110	36,110	56,934	56,934	77,757	77,757	2	.	.
West & Southwest	32,677	32,677	32,677	32,677	32,677	32,677	1	24,482	36,733
ALL REGIONS	17,971	32,677	46,891	36,110	67,548	77,757	9	22,124	31,921

State Data

	Min	Q1	Mean	Median	Q3	Max	N	Range Avg Min	Range Avg Max
CO	32,677	32,677	32,677	32,677	32,677	32,677	1	24,482	36,733
IL	35,950	35,950	35,950	35,950	35,950	35,950	1	.	.
IN	17,971	17,971	17,971	17,971	17,971	17,971	1	17,971	24,274
MO	26,395	43,228	55,388	63,804	67,548	67,548	4	23,920	34,757
VA	36,110	36,110	56,934	56,934	77,757	77,757	2	.	.

Degree Required Data

	Min	Q1	Mean	Median	Q3	Max	N	Range Avg Min	Range Avg Max
High School	17,971	17,971	26,961	26,961	35,950	35,950	2	17,971	24,274
Associate's	36,110	36,110	36,110	36,110	36,110	36,110	1	.	.
Bachelor's	26,395	32,677	55,331	63,804	67,548	77,757	6	24,201	35,745
Master's	.	.	.	.	.	.		.	.
Doctoral	.	.	.	.	.	.		.	.

WEB CONTENT ADMINISTRATOR - CONTINUED
Very Large Public Library
(Serving a population of 500,000 or more)
Regional Data

	Min	Q1	Mean	Median	Q3	Max	N	Range Avg Min	Range Avg Max
North Atlantic	50,175	50,175	50,217	50,217	50,259	50,259	2		
Great Lakes & Plains	28,411	44,803	44,578	44,803	47,082	57,788	5	44,803	64,501
Southeast	30,418	31,874	40,835	35,400	49,795	62,121	4	32,360	53,932
West & Southwest	64,542	64,617	70,545	66,366	76,473	84,906	4	56,950	77,865
ALL REGIONS	28,411	37,470	51,256	50,175	64,542	84,906	15	42,941	63,790

State Data

	Min	Q1	Mean	Median	Q3	Max	N	Range Avg Min	Range Avg Max
AZ	84,906	84,906	84,906	84,906	84,906	84,906	1	59,862	89,274
CA	64,691	64,691	66,366	66,366	68,040	68,040	2		
IN	47,082	47,082	47,082	47,082	47,082	47,082	1		
MD	50,175	50,175	50,217	50,217	50,259	50,259	2		
MO	28,411	28,411	28,411	28,411	28,411	28,411	1		
NC	62,121	62,121	62,121	62,121	62,121	62,121	1		
OH	44,803	44,803	49,132	44,803	57,788	57,788	3	44,803	64,501
OR	64,542	64,542	64,542	64,542	64,542	64,542	1	54,038	66,456
VA	30,418	30,418	33,739	33,331	37,470	37,470	3	32,360	53,932

Degree Required Data

	Min	Q1	Mean	Median	Q3	Max	N	Range Avg Min	Range Avg Max
High School	30,418	31,874	37,848	35,400	43,822	50,175	4	32,360	53,932
Associate's	28,411	28,411	46,551	46,551	64,691	64,691	2		
Bachelor's	44,803	47,531	59,658	59,955	66,291	84,906	8	50,877	71,183
Master's	47,082	47,082	47,082	47,082	47,082	47,082	1		
Doctoral									

WEB CONTENT ADMINISTRATOR - CONTINUED
ALL PUBLIC LIBRARIES
Regional Data

	Min	Q1	Mean	Median	Q3	Max	N	Range Avg Min	Range Avg Max
North Atlantic	41,600	41,600	47,345	50,175	50,259	50,259	3		
Great Lakes & Plains	17,971	28,411	43,482	44,803	57,788	67,548	14	31,710	45,230
Southeast	30,418	33,331	46,201	36,790	62,121	77,757	6	32,360	53,932
West & Southwest	32,677	64,542	62,971	64,691	68,040	84,906	5	46,127	64,154
ALL REGIONS	17,971	34,640	47,959	45,943	63,332	84,906	28	35,477	52,136

State Data

	Min	Q1	Mean	Median	Q3	Max	N	Range Avg Min	Range Avg Max
AZ	84,906	84,906	84,906	84,906	84,906	84,906	1	59,862	89,274
CA	64,691	64,691	66,366	66,366	68,040	68,040	2	.	.
CO	32,677	32,677	32,677	32,677	32,677	32,677	1	24,482	36,733
IL	20,800	20,800	34,912	35,950	47,986	47,986	3	29,380	41,673
IN	17,971	17,971	32,527	32,527	47,082	47,082	2	17,971	24,274
MD	50,175	50,175	50,217	50,217	50,259	50,259	2	.	.
ME	41,600	41,600	41,600	41,600	41,600	41,600	1	.	.
MO	26,395	28,411	49,992	60,060	67,548	67,548	5	23,920	34,757
NC	62,121	62,121	62,121	62,121	62,121	62,121	1	.	.
OH	41,600	43,202	47,249	44,803	51,296	57,788	4	44,803	64,501
OR	64,542	64,542	64,542	64,542	64,542	64,542	1	54,038	66,456
VA	30,418	33,331	43,017	36,110	37,470	77,757	5	32,360	53,932

Degree Required Data

	Min	Q1	Mean	Median	Q3	Max	N	Range Avg Min	Range Avg Max
High School	17,971	30,418	35,273	35,950	41,600	50,175	7	28,762	46,518
Associate's	28,411	28,411	43,071	36,110	64,691	64,691	3	.	.
Bachelor's	26,395	44,803	56,177	58,924	67,548	84,906	16	41,469	59,289
Master's	47,082	47,082	47,082	47,082	47,082	47,082	1	.	.
Doctoral	.	.	.	.	.	.		.	.

WEBMASTER

Responsible for the library's Internet and or Intranet technical functions. Maps the flow of the site, creates general graphics, provides specifications to the web authors, developers, and outside vendors for the development of databases, interactive applets, and custom graphics. Supervises development efforts including content, design and production, site maintenance and updating. Acts as a liaison between the site and users.

Very Small Public Library
(Serving a population of less than 10,000)
Regional Data

	Min	Q1	Mean	Median	Q3	Max	N	Range Avg Min	Range Avg Max
West & Southwest	37,440	37,440	37,440	37,440	37,440	37,440	1	31,928	46,322
ALL REGIONS	37,440	37,440	37,440	37,440	37,440	37,440	1	31,928	46,322

State Data

	Min	Q1	Mean	Median	Q3	Max	N	Range Avg Min	Range Avg Max
CO	37,440	37,440	37,440	37,440	37,440	37,440	1	31,928	46,322

Degree Required Data

	Min	Q1	Mean	Median	Q3	Max	N	Range Avg Min	Range Avg Max
High School									
Associate's									
Bachelor's	37,440	37,440	37,440	37,440	37,440	37,440	1	31,928	46,322
Master's									
Doctoral									

WEBMASTER - CONTINUED
Small Public Library
(Serving a population of 10,000 to 25,000)
Regional Data

	Min	Q1	Mean	Median	Q3	Max	N	Range Avg Min	Range Avg Max
Great Lakes & Plains	25,000	25,000	33,300	33,300	41,600	41,600	2	22,880	52,000
ALL REGIONS	25,000	25,000	33,300	33,300	41,600	41,600	2	22,880	52,000

State Data

	Min	Q1	Mean	Median	Q3	Max	N	Range Avg Min	Range Avg Max
IL	25,000	25,000	33,300	33,300	41,600	41,600	2	22,880	52,000

Degree Required Data

	Min	Q1	Mean	Median	Q3	Max	N	Range Avg Min	Range Avg Max
High School									
Associate's									
Bachelor's	41,600	41,600	41,600	41,600	41,600	41,600	1	22,880	52,000
Master's									
Doctoral									

WEBMASTER - CONTINUED
Medium Public Library
(Serving a population of 25,000 to 99,999)
Regional Data

	Min	Q1	Mean	Median	Q3	Max	N	Range Avg Min	Range Avg Max
Great Lakes & Plains	24,731	34,195	37,080	37,099	40,227	49,130	6	35,062	56,583
ALL REGIONS	24,731	34,195	37,080	37,099	40,227	49,130	6	35,062	56,583

State Data

	Min	Q1	Mean	Median	Q3	Max	N	Range Avg Min	Range Avg Max
IL	37,199	37,199	38,713	38,713	40,227	40,227	2	38,397	54,392
IN	34,195	34,195	35,598	35,598	37,000	37,000	2		
OH	24,731	24,731	36,930	36,930	49,130	49,130	2	33,394	57,678

Degree Required Data

	Min	Q1	Mean	Median	Q3	Max	N	Range Avg Min	Range Avg Max
High School	24,731	24,731	24,731	24,731	24,731	24,731	1	20,259	37,752
Associate's	.	.	.	.	.	.		.	.
Bachelor's	34,195	37,000	39,550	37,199	40,227	49,130	5	42,463	65,998
Master's	.	.	.	.	.	.		.	.
Doctoral	.	.	.	.	.	.		.	.

WEBMASTER - CONTINUED
Large Public Library
(Serving a population of 100,000 to 499,999)
Regional Data

	Min	Q1	Mean	Median	Q3	Max	N	Range Avg Min	Range Avg Max
North Atlantic	31,788	33,718	43,219	43,764	49,137	60,729	8	33,238	52,379
Great Lakes & Plains	26,750	35,950	41,005	42,390	44,359	55,578	5	37,960	60,070
Southeast	30,430	33,197	47,029	39,929	53,349	77,617	9	30,493	41,558
West & Southwest	33,862	44,693	51,805	50,648	64,480	66,498	6	47,809	61,188
ALL REGIONS	26,750	34,371	45,888	44,526	53,403	77,617	28	39,736	56,359

State Data

	Min	Q1	Mean	Median	Q3	Max	N	Range Avg Min	Range Avg Max
CA	53,456	53,456	61,478	64,480	66,498	66,498	3	49,878	63,558
CO	44,693	44,693	44,693	44,693	44,693	44,693	1	.	.
FL	31,762	31,762	35,846	35,846	39,929	39,929	2	.	.
IL	35,950	35,950	35,950	35,950	35,950	35,950	1	.	.
IN	26,750	26,750	26,750	26,750	26,750	26,750	1	.	.
KS	55,578	55,578	55,578	55,578	55,578	55,578	1	37,586	62,650
LA	33,197	33,197	33,197	33,197	33,197	33,197	1	30,493	41,558
MD	34,880	34,880	47,338	46,406	60,729	60,729	3	.	.
MI	44,359	44,359	44,359	44,359	44,359	44,359	1	.	.
NJ	51,868	51,868	51,868	51,868	51,868	51,868	1	.	.
NY	42,066	42,066	43,764	43,764	45,462	45,462	2	36,149	41,906
OH	42,390	42,390	42,390	42,390	42,390	42,390	1	38,334	57,491
PA	31,788	31,788	32,172	32,172	32,556	32,556	2	31,782	57,616
SC	39,531	39,531	39,531	39,531	39,531	39,531	1	.	.
TX	33,862	33,862	33,862	33,862	33,862	33,862	1	.	.
VA	30,430	48,567	55,769	53,349	68,881	77,617	5	.	.
WA	47,840	47,840	47,840	47,840	47,840	47,840	1	41,600	54,080

Degree Required Data

	Min	Q1	Mean	Median	Q3	Max	N	Range Avg Min	Range Avg Max
High School	35,950	39,929	45,357	42,066	44,359	64,480	5	47,195	56,313
Associate's	31,788	32,556	52,126	50,958	68,881	77,617	6	31,782	57,616
Bachelor's	26,750	34,371	43,144	43,542	49,854	60,729	12	37,003	53,945
Master's	30,430	30,430	31,096	31,096	31,762	31,762	2	.	.
Doctoral	.	.	.	.	.	.		.	.

WEBMASTER - CONTINUED
Very Large Public Library
(Serving a population of 500,000 or more)
Regional Data

	Min	Q1	Mean	Median	Q3	Max	N	Range Avg Min	Range Avg Max
North Atlantic	48,402	48,402	53,614	53,614	58,825	58,825	2		
Great Lakes & Plains	42,149	42,149	49,356	49,356	56,564	56,564	2		
Southeast	38,834	38,834	50,144	53,107	58,492	58,492	3		
West & Southwest	47,190	50,064	56,876	57,668	59,883	69,576	5	53,841	80,496
ALL REGIONS	38,834	47,796	53,396	54,836	58,659	69,576	12	53,841	80,496

State Data

	Min	Q1	Mean	Median	Q3	Max	N	Range Avg Min	Range Avg Max
AZ	69,576	69,576	69,576	69,576	69,576	69,576	1	56,971	84,906
CA	57,668	57,668	57,668	57,668	57,668	57,668	1		
FL	38,834	38,834	48,663	48,663	58,492	58,492	2		
IN	56,564	56,564	56,564	56,564	56,564	56,564	1		
MD	48,402	48,402	53,614	53,614	58,825	58,825	2		
MO	42,149	42,149	42,149	42,149	42,149	42,149	1		
NC	53,107	53,107	53,107	53,107	53,107	53,107	1		
TX	47,190	47,190	53,537	53,537	59,883	59,883	2	50,710	76,086
UT	50,064	50,064	50,064	50,064	50,064	50,064	1		

Degree Required Data

	Min	Q1	Mean	Median	Q3	Max	N	Range Avg Min	Range Avg Max
High School	47,190	47,190	54,914	57,668	59,883	59,883	3	50,710	76,086
Associate's									
Bachelor's	38,834	45,275	53,244	54,836	58,659	69,576	8	56,971	84,906
Master's									
Doctoral									

WEBMASTER - CONTINUED
ALL PUBLIC LIBRARIES
Regional Data

	Min	Q1	Mean	Median	Q3	Max	N	Range Avg Min	Range Avg Max
North Atlantic	31,788	34,880	45,298	45,934	51,868	60,729	10	33,238	52,379
Great Lakes & Plains	24,731	34,195	39,521	40,227	44,359	56,564	15	33,998	56,982
Southeast	30,430	36,015	47,808	44,248	55,921	77,617	12	30,493	41,558
West & Southwest	33,862	45,942	52,721	51,760	62,182	69,576	12	47,264	64,581
ALL REGIONS	24,731	37,000	45,962	44,693	53,456	77,617	49	39,120	58,391

State Data

	Min	Q1	Mean	Median	Q3	Max	N	Range Avg Min	Range Avg Max
AZ	69,576	69,576	69,576	69,576	69,576	69,576	1	56,971	84,906
CA	53,456	55,562	60,525	61,074	65,489	66,498	4	49,878	63,558
CO	37,440	37,440	41,067	41,067	44,693	44,693	2	31,928	46,322
FL	31,762	35,298	42,254	39,381	49,211	58,492	4	.	.
IL	25,000	35,950	35,995	37,199	40,227	41,600	5	30,638	53,196
IN	26,750	30,473	38,627	35,598	46,782	56,564	4	.	.
KS	55,578	55,578	55,578	55,578	55,578	55,578	1	37,586	62,650
LA	33,197	33,197	33,197	33,197	33,197	33,197	1	30,493	41,558
MD	34,880	46,406	49,848	48,402	58,825	60,729	5	.	.
MI	44,359	44,359	44,359	44,359	44,359	44,359	1	.	.
MO	42,149	42,149	42,149	42,149	42,149	42,149	1	.	.
NC	53,107	53,107	53,107	53,107	53,107	53,107	1	.	.
NJ	51,868	51,868	51,868	51,868	51,868	51,868	1	.	.
NY	42,066	42,066	43,764	43,764	45,462	45,462	2	36,149	41,906
OH	24,731	24,731	38,750	42,390	49,130	49,130	3	35,041	57,616
PA	31,788	31,788	32,172	32,172	32,556	32,556	2	31,782	57,616
SC	39,531	39,531	39,531	39,531	39,531	39,531	1	.	.
TX	33,862	33,862	46,979	47,190	59,883	59,883	3	50,710	76,086
UT	50,064	50,064	50,064	50,064	50,064	50,064	1	.	.
VA	30,430	48,567	55,769	53,349	68,881	77,617	5	.	.
WA	47,840	47,840	47,840	47,840	47,840	47,840	1	41,600	54,080

Degree Required Data

	Min	Q1	Mean	Median	Q3	Max	N	Range Avg Min	Range Avg Max
High School	24,731	39,929	46,251	44,359	57,668	64,480	9	41,340	56,616
Associate's	31,788	32,556	52,126	50,958	68,881	77,617	6	31,782	57,616
Bachelor's	26,750	37,199	45,202	42,390	53,107	69,576	27	38,302	59,000
Master's	30,430	30,430	31,096	31,096	31,762	31,762	2	.	.
Doctoral	.	.	.	.	.	.		.	.

COMPUTER LAB ASSISTANT

Monitors the operation of adult and/or youth computer labs. Assists patrons with questions and problem resolution. Enforces computer lab rules. May assist with installation, operation and configuring of personal computer hardware and software. Investigates reoccurring problems and recommends course of action to supervisor. May perform back-up operations and print reports.

Small Public Library
(Serving a population of 10,000 to 25,000)
Regional Data

	Min	Q1	Mean	Median	Q3	Max	N	Range Avg Min	Range Avg Max
North Atlantic	19,344	19,344	19,344	19,344	19,344	19,344	1	.	.
Great Lakes & Plains	16,869	17,222	19,277	18,720	18,720	24,855	5	17,680	27,040
Southeast	14,873	14,873	14,873	14,873	14,873	14,873	1	.	.
West & Southwest	20,800	20,800	20,800	20,800	20,800	20,800	1	20,800	20,800
ALL REGIONS	14,873	17,045	18,925	18,720	20,072	24,855	8	18,200	26,000

State Data

	Min	Q1	Mean	Median	Q3	Max	N	Range Avg Min	Range Avg Max
CO	20,800	20,800	20,800	20,800	20,800	20,800	1	20,800	20,800
IL	17,222	17,971	19,879	18,720	21,788	24,855	4	18,200	29,120
IN	16,869	16,869	16,869	16,869	16,869	16,869	1	15,600	18,720
MS	14,873	14,873	14,873	14,873	14,873	14,873	1	.	.
PA	19,344	19,344	19,344	19,344	19,344	19,344	1	.	.

Degree Required Data

	Min	Q1	Mean	Median	Q3	Max	N	Range Avg Min	Range Avg Max
High School	14,873	16,796	18,278	18,720	19,760	20,800	4	19,413	27,733
Associate's	17,222	17,222	21,038	21,038	24,855	24,855	2	17,680	27,040
Bachelor's	.	.	.	.	.	.	.	.	.
Master's	.	.	.	.	.	.	.	.	.
Doctoral	.	.	.	.	.	.	.	.	.

COMPUTER LAB ASSISTANT - CONTINUED
Medium Public Library
(Serving a population of 25,000 to 99,999)
Regional Data

	Min	Q1	Mean	Median	Q3	Max	N	Range Avg Min	Range Avg Max
North Atlantic	14,040	14,851	20,080	15,579	22,500	47,269	20	15,538	31,415
Great Lakes & Plains	17,202	19,042	22,823	19,968	24,866	39,770	16	21,339	29,413
Southeast	33,000	33,000	33,000	33,000	33,000	33,000	1	.	.
West & Southwest	20,883	20,883	20,883	20,883	20,883	20,883	1	19,906	24,170
ALL REGIONS	14,040	15,579	21,597	19,427	24,960	47,269	38	18,379	30,196

State Data

	Min	Q1	Mean	Median	Q3	Max	N	Range Avg Min	Range Avg Max
CA	20,883	20,883	20,883	20,883	20,883	20,883	1	19,906	24,170
CT	24,960	24,960	24,960	24,960	24,960	24,960	1	.	.
IL	18,990	18,990	20,766	19,906	20,550	28,565	9	19,068	27,898
IN	19,094	19,552	23,448	21,112	27,344	32,473	4	.	.
MN	39,770	39,770	39,770	39,770	39,770	39,770	1	37,877	48,339
NY	14,040	14,851	19,812	15,298	16,307	47,269	18	15,538	31,415
OH	27,518	27,518	27,518	27,518	27,518	27,518	1	27,518	33,571
PA	20,040	20,040	20,040	20,040	20,040	20,040	1	.	.
TN	33,000	33,000	33,000	33,000	33,000	33,000	1	.	.
WI	17,202	17,202	17,202	17,202	17,202	17,202	1	16,786	18,450

Degree Required Data

	Min	Q1	Mean	Median	Q3	Max	N	Range Avg Min	Range Avg Max
High School	14,040	14,851	20,058	16,307	20,883	47,269	25	17,755	31,616
Associate's	20,040	20,040	25,375	27,518	28,565	28,565	3	27,518	33,571
Bachelor's	24,960	24,960	24,960	24,960	24,960	24,960	1	.	.
Master's	33,000	33,000	33,000	33,000	33,000	33,000	1	.	.
Doctoral	.	.	.	.	.	.	.	.	.

COMPUTER LAB ASSISTANT - CONTINUED
Large Public Library
(Serving a population of 100,000 to 499,999)
Regional Data

	Min	Q1	Mean	Median	Q3	Max	N	Range Avg Min	Range Avg Max
North Atlantic	24,538	25,694	31,368	27,581	31,788	46,619	9	34,372	51,906
Great Lakes & Plains	10,712	11,939	22,732	25,854	28,874	44,512	49	17,520	21,552
Southeast	20,363	20,800	26,519	26,780	29,917	35,568	12	25,861	34,736
West & Southwest	14,560	16,578	23,888	24,534	27,686	46,321	20	25,903	35,825
ALL REGIONS	10,712	20,134	24,358	25,774	29,074	46,619	90	20,312	26,235

State Data

	Min	Q1	Mean	Median	Q3	Max	N	Range Avg Min	Range Avg Max
AL	26,520	26,520	29,661	29,661	32,802	32,802	2	26,978	40,456
CA	24,960	24,960	32,080	24,960	46,321	46,321	3	24,960	31,200
CO	14,560	15,122	15,500	15,413	15,891	16,515	5	.	.
GA	27,040	27,040	31,304	31,304	35,568	35,568	2	.	.
IL	22,667	25,854	27,699	27,774	29,074	36,160	27	23,995	29,167
IN	15,205	15,205	15,205	15,205	15,205	15,205	1	14,851	18,554
MD	24,538	24,538	26,397	25,694	25,694	31,519	5	.	.
MI	10,712	10,712	13,151	11,024	11,648	28,018	15	11,595	12,236
MO	20,134	20,134	20,134	20,134	20,134	20,134	2	19,469	28,288
NC	20,363	20,363	21,668	20,675	22,974	24,960	4	21,424	34,570
NM	16,640	16,900	20,420	19,562	23,941	25,917	4	.	.
NY	27,581	27,581	37,100	37,100	46,619	46,619	2	.	.
OH	22,069	22,672	28,314	23,338	33,956	44,512	4	27,491	41,226
PA	31,788	31,788	38,067	38,067	44,346	44,346	2	34,372	51,906
TX	17,927	24,534	27,793	27,686	32,975	34,029	8	27,789	45,074
VA	20,612	24,897	27,407	29,182	29,917	30,651	4	29,182	29,182

Degree Required Data

	Min	Q1	Mean	Median	Q3	Max	N	Range Avg Min	Range Avg Max
High School	14,560	22,667	24,997	25,854	28,874	35,568	51	22,845	28,118
Associate's	20,134	22,069	27,928	25,917	31,788	46,321	13	24,636	34,752
Bachelor's	24,378	27,789	34,894	33,051	44,346	46,619	9	31,408	45,935
Master's	.	.	.	.	.	.		.	.
Doctoral	.	.	.	.	.	.		.	.

COMPUTER LAB ASSISTANT - CONTINUED
Very Large Public Library
(Serving a population of 500,000 or more)
Regional Data

	Min	Q1	Mean	Median	Q3	Max	N	Range Avg Min	Range Avg Max
North Atlantic	37,414	37,414	37,414	37,414	37,414	37,414	1		
Great Lakes & Plains	24,480	40,461	64,232	70,824	74,373	90,402	72		
Southeast	23,282	29,141	35,299	31,282	33,063	66,190	43		
West & Southwest	14,832	29,370	42,362	45,417	52,312	68,120	16	39,298	54,944
ALL REGIONS	14,832	30,618	51,953	47,360	74,373	90,402	132	39,298	54,944

State Data

	Min	Q1	Mean	Median	Q3	Max	N	Range Avg Min	Range Avg Max
AZ	51,085	53,539	58,814	56,285	65,042	68,120	5	48,693	71,386
CA	22,424	25,024	34,648	29,063	47,362	49,368	5	27,936	33,959
FL	23,282	29,141	35,300	31,075	32,698	66,190	41		
GA	33,063	33,063	35,294	35,294	37,525	37,525	2		
IN	24,480	24,480	24,480	24,480	24,480	24,480	1		
MD	37,414	37,414	37,414	37,414	37,414	37,414	1		
MI	30,468	31,973	33,102	33,100	34,985	34,985	6		
MO	24,971	26,020	30,972	30,429	34,896	43,149	11		
OH	37,773	70,824	75,202	74,373	78,078	90,402	54		
TX	14,832	29,676	35,081	36,398	43,472	49,712	6	37,773	56,680

Degree Required Data

	Min	Q1	Mean	Median	Q3	Max	N	Range Avg Min	Range Avg Max
High School	14,832	29,141	30,850	30,618	31,845	53,879	46	27,561	36,288
Associate's	32,008	43,935	51,087	52,312	58,430	68,120	10	48,693	71,386
Bachelor's	24,971	70,824	67,258	74,373	78,078	90,402	66		
Master's									
Doctoral									

COMPUTER LAB ASSISTANT - CONTINUED
ALL PUBLIC LIBRARIES
Regional Data

	Min	Q1	Mean	Median	Q3	Max	N	Range Avg Min	Range Avg Max
North Atlantic	14,040	14,851	23,893	20,040	31,519	47,269	31	18,228	34,342
Great Lakes & Plains	10,712	23,275	43,663	29,930	70,824	90,402	142	18,493	24,141
Southeast	14,873	29,141	33,052	30,618	32,802	66,190	57	25,861	34,736
West & Southwest	14,560	20,800	31,507	26,750	43,472	68,120	38	34,093	46,792
ALL REGIONS	10,712	22,545	37,396	29,177	47,314	90,402	268	21,967	31,054

State Data

	Min	Q1	Mean	Median	Q3	Max	N	Range Avg Min	Range Avg Max
AL	26,520	26,520	29,661	29,661	32,802	32,802	2	26,978	40,456
AZ	51,085	53,539	58,814	56,285	65,042	68,120	5	48,693	71,386
CA	20,883	24,960	32,263	25,024	46,321	49,368	9	25,938	31,772
CO	14,560	15,122	16,383	15,652	16,515	20,800	6	20,800	20,800
CT	24,960	24,960	24,960	24,960	24,960	24,960	1	.	.
FL	23,282	29,141	35,300	31,075	32,698	66,190	41	.	.
GA	27,040	30,052	33,299	34,316	36,547	37,525	4	.	.
IL	17,222	20,883	25,357	25,854	28,874	36,160	40	20,866	28,650
IN	15,205	16,869	21,478	20,010	24,480	32,473	7	15,226	18,637
MD	24,538	24,538	28,233	25,694	31,519	37,414	6	.	.
MI	10,712	10,712	18,851	11,648	30,468	34,985	21	11,595	12,236
MN	39,770	39,770	39,770	39,770	39,770	39,770	1	37,877	48,339
MO	20,134	25,920	29,305	29,173	30,535	43,149	13	19,469	28,288
MS	14,873	14,873	14,873	14,873	14,873	14,873	1	.	.
NC	20,363	20,363	21,668	20,675	22,974	24,960	4	21,424	34,570
NM	16,640	16,900	20,420	19,562	23,941	25,917	4	.	.
NY	14,040	14,851	21,540	15,579	27,716	47,269	20	15,538	31,415
OH	22,069	70,824	71,215	74,373	78,078	90,402	59	27,498	39,312
PA	19,344	19,692	28,879	25,914	38,067	44,346	4	34,372	51,906
TN	33,000	33,000	33,000	33,000	33,000	33,000	1	.	.
TX	14,832	24,690	30,917	30,842	34,029	49,712	14	32,781	50,877
VA	20,612	24,897	27,407	29,182	29,917	30,651	4	29,182	29,182
WI	17,202	17,202	17,202	17,202	17,202	17,202	1	16,786	18,450

Degree Required Data

	Min	Q1	Mean	Median	Q3	Max	N	Range Avg Min	Range Avg Max
High School	14,040	20,363	25,941	27,551	30,472	53,879	126	20,679	30,646
Associate's	17,222	24,045	35,433	30,610	47,844	68,120	28	31,063	44,550
Bachelor's	24,378	40,461	62,869	70,824	74,373	90,402	76	31,408	45,935
Master's	33,000	33,000	33,000	33,000	33,000	33,000	1	.	.
Doctoral	.	.	.	.	.	.	.	.	.

ADMINISTRATIVE ASSISTANT (SECRETARY)

Performs secretarial duties for a department and its staff. Takes and transcribes dictation, and prepares correspondence. Operates word processing equipment as required. Composes correspondence from written materials provided. Maintains personal files and department records. Arranges and schedules meetings and appointments. Takes, screens, and places telephone calls, and acts as Receptionist as needed. Compiles standard reports with data that is provided.

Very Small Public Library
(Serving a population of less than 10,000)
Regional Data

	Min	Q1	Mean	Median	Q3	Max	N	Range Avg Min	Range Avg Max
North Atlantic	27,165	27,165	33,883	33,883	40,601	40,601	2	33,405	37,794
Great Lakes & Plains	13,520	13,520	19,244	19,244	24,968	24,968	2		
Southeast	10,712	10,712	20,384	20,384	30,056	30,056	2	10,712	15,600
West & Southwest	38,251	38,251	38,251	38,251	38,251	38,251	1	31,928	46,322
ALL REGIONS	10,712	13,520	26,468	27,165	38,251	40,601	7	25,348	33,238

State Data

	Min	Q1	Mean	Median	Q3	Max	N	Range Avg Min	Range Avg Max
AL	30,056	30,056	30,056	30,056	30,056	30,056	1		
CO	38,251	38,251	38,251	38,251	38,251	38,251	1	31,928	46,322
IA	24,968	24,968	24,968	24,968	24,968	24,968	1		
IL	13,520	13,520	13,520	13,520	13,520	13,520	1		
KY	10,712	10,712	10,712	10,712	10,712	10,712	1	10,712	15,600
MA	27,165	27,165	27,165	27,165	27,165	27,165	1	33,405	37,794
NJ	40,601	40,601	40,601	40,601	40,601	40,601	1		

Degree Required Data

	Min	Q1	Mean	Median	Q3	Max	N	Range Avg Min	Range Avg Max
High School	10,712	10,712	25,657	25,657	40,601	40,601	2	10,712	15,600
Associate's	30,056	30,056	30,056	30,056	30,056	30,056	1		
Bachelor's	27,165	27,165	32,708	32,708	38,251	38,251	2	32,666	42,058
Master's									
Doctoral									

ADMINISTRATIVE ASSISTANT (SECRETARY) - CONTINUED
Small Public Library
(Serving a population of 10,000 to 25,000)
Regional Data

	Min	Q1	Mean	Median	Q3	Max	N	Range Avg Min	Range Avg Max
North Atlantic	22,880	23,504	32,386	27,040	37,648	50,857	5	22,152	31,886
Great Lakes & Plains	17,000	19,448	29,242	27,040	41,600	45,760	11	24,487	37,762
West & Southwest	20,800	20,800	20,800	20,800	20,800	20,800	1	20,800	20,800
ALL REGIONS	17,000	21,171	29,670	27,040	37,648	50,857	17	23,293	33,660

State Data

	Min	Q1	Mean	Median	Q3	Max	N	Range Avg Min	Range Avg Max
CO	20,800	20,800	20,800	20,800	20,800	20,800	1	20,800	20,800
IL	17,000	20,980	32,330	33,280	43,680	45,760	4	31,200	54,080
IN	19,448	19,448	19,448	19,448	19,448	19,448	1	.	.
KS	21,171	21,171	28,015	28,015	34,859	34,859	2	16,640	27,040
MA	23,504	23,504	29,397	27,040	37,648	37,648	3	23,504	30,493
MI	27,040	27,040	27,040	27,040	27,040	27,040	1	.	.
MN	42,848	42,848	42,848	42,848	42,848	42,848	1	32,053	42,848
NJ	50,857	50,857	50,857	50,857	50,857	50,857	1	.	.
OH	18,054	18,054	23,487	23,487	28,920	28,920	2	18,054	27,082
PA	22,880	22,880	22,880	22,880	22,880	22,880	1	20,800	33,280

Degree Required Data

	Min	Q1	Mean	Median	Q3	Max	N	Range Avg Min	Range Avg Max
High School	19,448	24,232	28,926	27,040	33,284	42,848	8	27,778	36,670
Associate's	17,000	21,171	32,078	34,859	41,600	45,760	5	23,920	40,560
Bachelor's	18,054	19,427	28,148	21,840	36,869	50,857	4	19,885	27,054
Master's	.	.	.	.	.	.		.	.
Doctoral	.	.	.	.	.	.		.	.

ADMINISTRATIVE ASSISTANT (SECRETARY) - CONTINUED
Medium Public Library
(Serving a population of 25,000 to 99,999)
Regional Data

	Min	Q1	Mean	Median	Q3	Max	N	Range Avg Min	Range Avg Max
North Atlantic	19,760	32,072	42,920	43,283	57,314	68,240	23	24,346	32,718
Great Lakes & Plains	20,259	27,186	32,669	31,928	36,774	51,417	27	26,040	39,097
Southeast	18,866	21,000	27,813	30,618	33,000	38,161	7	18,138	14,238
West & Southwest	18,720	25,230	39,224	38,232	49,712	64,210	15	35,483	45,234
ALL REGIONS	18,720	25,740	36,837	34,287	45,781	68,240	72	28,698	38,650

State Data

	Min	Q1	Mean	Median	Q3	Max	N	Range Avg Min	Range Avg Max
AR	30,618	30,618	30,618	30,618	30,618	30,618	1		
CA	18,720	38,232	45,928	47,039	56,722	64,210	10	41,294	50,520
CO	26,000	26,000	26,000	26,000	26,000	26,000	1	18,720	31,200
CT	45,573	46,114	52,575	48,361	59,946	62,880	5		
IA	45,198	45,198	45,198	45,198	45,198	45,198	1		
ID	23,920	23,920	27,560	27,560	31,200	31,200	2	23,525	33,748
IL	20,280	27,456	32,354	31,138	35,214	50,856	10	25,471	39,744
IN	29,453	32,560	37,195	34,172	41,395	51,417	6		
LA	18,866	18,866	18,866	18,866	18,866	18,866	1	18,138	26,395
MA	43,283	43,283	43,283	43,283	43,283	43,283	1	29,120	43,680
MI	40,560	40,560	40,560	40,560	40,560	40,560	1	37,586	40,560
MO	22,963	22,963	22,963	22,963	22,963	22,963	1		
MS	21,000	21,000	21,000	21,000	21,000	21,000	1		2,080
NC	31,735	31,735	31,735	31,735	31,735	31,735	1		
NJ	21,424	32,072	44,208	49,049	50,254	68,240	5	17,139	22,859
NY	22,495	22,984	43,102	37,430	59,696	66,594	7		
OH	20,259	21,112	28,994	29,765	36,288	36,774	6	24,440	38,527
PA	19,760	21,216	29,078	27,456	36,940	41,640	4	18,720	22,402
RI	41,933	41,933	41,933	41,933	41,933	41,933	1	32,406	41,933
SC	38,161	38,161	38,161	38,161	38,161	38,161	1		
TN	21,310	21,310	27,155	27,155	33,000	33,000	2		
TX	22,734	22,734	23,982	23,982	25,230	25,230	2		
WI	25,480	25,480	26,333	26,333	27,186	27,186	2	26,021	34,091

Degree Required Data

	Min	Q1	Mean	Median	Q3	Max	N	Range Avg Min	Range Avg Max
High School	18,720	25,230	37,840	35,618	48,361	68,240	50	28,214	39,743
Associate's	19,760	27,186	36,026	34,663	38,161	64,210	10	33,359	45,419
Bachelor's	29,453	30,618	37,141	36,940	42,780	46,114	6		
Master's	33,000	33,000	33,000	33,000	33,000	33,000	1		
Doctoral									

ADMINISTRATIVE ASSISTANT (SECRETARY) - CONTINUED
Large Public Library
(Serving a population of 100,000 to 499,999)
Regional Data

	Min	Q1	Mean	Median	Q3	Max	N	Range Avg Min	Range Avg Max
North Atlantic	28,122	35,564	41,492	39,458	43,191	68,008	17	29,737	43,325
Great Lakes & Plains	20,987	29,536	32,679	30,798	34,996	45,198	24	25,680	35,979
Southeast	21,798	24,400	30,126	29,120	33,966	44,958	25	23,407	32,788
West & Southwest	20,322	28,912	37,311	36,234	46,010	62,400	31	32,126	44,622
ALL REGIONS	20,322	28,475	35,046	33,387	40,400	68,008	97	27,089	37,936

State Data

	Min	Q1	Mean	Median	Q3	Max	N	Range Avg Min	Range Avg Max
AL	28,142	28,142	28,142	28,142	28,142	28,142	1	26,978	33,717
AZ	42,162	42,162	42,162	42,162	42,162	42,162	1	.	.
CA	24,684	36,015	44,524	45,271	53,332	62,400	12	37,211	50,090
CO	31,762	31,762	33,796	32,677	36,949	36,949	3	22,526	34,070
FL	21,798	23,129	27,860	24,440	30,493	44,958	8	22,367	32,441
IL	33,613	33,613	38,501	36,691	45,198	45,198	3	29,723	41,974
IN	30,395	30,395	30,395	30,395	30,395	30,395	1	.	.
KS	28,475	30,878	32,937	33,935	34,996	35,402	4	24,014	40,030
LA	22,194	22,194	28,080	28,080	33,966	33,966	2	22,194	31,366
MA	39,458	39,458	39,458	39,458	39,458	39,458	1	.	.
MD	33,467	34,414	37,212	35,564	35,564	47,054	5	.	.
MI	23,046	27,622	29,070	30,094	31,200	33,387	5	23,993	33,696
MN	33,694	33,694	33,694	33,694	33,694	33,694	1	.	.
MO	29,536	29,536	29,536	29,536	29,536	29,536	5	24,294	29,536
MS	24,400	24,400	24,400	24,400	24,400	24,400	1	.	.
NC	29,120	29,120	33,280	33,280	37,440	37,440	2	22,880	37,440
NE	43,085	43,085	43,085	43,085	43,085	43,085	1	32,302	43,085
NJ	43,191	43,191	43,992	43,992	44,793	44,793	2	.	.
NM	28,205	28,205	28,205	28,205	28,205	28,205	1	.	.
NY	36,928	38,181	49,473	40,313	63,937	68,008	5	30,790	35,689
OH	20,987	20,987	30,910	27,230	44,512	44,512	3	18,366	27,560
OR	47,136	47,136	47,136	47,136	47,136	47,136	1	.	.
PA	28,122	30,531	36,125	37,001	41,720	42,377	4	28,683	50,960
SC	30,791	30,791	30,791	30,791	30,791	30,791	1	.	.
TN	23,703	23,703	29,840	29,840	35,977	35,977	2	.	.
TX	20,322	22,547	28,164	28,912	31,720	40,400	9	21,736	40,102
VA	26,437	28,757	33,066	32,958	36,434	41,800	8	26,437	26,437
WA	27,943	32,692	37,499	38,004	42,306	46,044	4	31,200	37,440
WI	44,117	44,117	44,117	44,117	44,117	44,117	1	35,256	45,885

Degree Required Data

	Min	Q1	Mean	Median	Q3	Max	N	Range Avg Min	Range Avg Max
High School	20,322	28,059	33,672	32,926	38,334	62,400	71	26,591	36,270
Associate's	23,026	29,887	34,072	33,280	38,568	46,044	15	26,437	41,288
Bachelor's	28,142	32,546	37,377	38,203	42,208	44,958	4	26,978	33,717
Master's	.	.	.	.	.	.	.	.	.
Doctoral	.	.	.	.	.	.	.	.	.

ADMINISTRATIVE ASSISTANT (SECRETARY) - CONTINUED
Very Large Public Library
(Serving a population of 500,000 or more)
Regional Data

	Min	Q1	Mean	Median	Q3	Max	N	Range Avg Min	Range Avg Max
North Atlantic	29,746	29,748	38,085	35,843	47,088	50,016	16	.	.
Great Lakes & Plains	22,866	35,318	40,690	39,763	44,257	65,753	37	33,057	46,209
Southeast	23,067	30,860	37,572	36,245	42,395	76,108	42	25,957	43,262
West & Southwest	27,804	35,799	44,224	40,477	53,378	58,136	22	38,714	49,522
ALL REGIONS	22,866	33,802	39,879	38,237	45,295	76,108	117	31,106	45,672

State Data

	Min	Q1	Mean	Median	Q3	Max	N	Range Avg Min	Range Avg Max
AZ	34,549	34,549	36,109	36,109	37,669	37,669	2	29,099	44,158
CA	39,984	50,648	52,553	53,378	54,956	58,136	11	43,910	53,290
CO	34,656	34,656	36,410	36,410	38,163	38,163	2	.	.
FL	33,802	36,048	44,977	39,899	57,148	76,108	14	.	.
GA	30,860	30,860	35,455	37,649	37,856	37,856	3	.	.
IN	31,974	34,159	36,079	35,597	38,303	40,543	8	.	.
MD	29,746	29,748	37,819	36,135	45,986	48,312	13	.	.
MI	34,055	35,236	39,408	36,827	44,300	49,200	6	.	.
MO	22,866	22,866	23,054	23,054	23,242	23,242	2	.	.
NC	32,000	32,000	39,593	39,593	47,185	47,185	2	.	.
NJ	32,153	32,153	39,240	35,551	50,016	50,016	3	.	.
OH	32,302	39,763	44,975	42,184	52,687	65,753	19	32,089	47,419
OR	39,560	39,560	39,883	39,883	40,206	40,206	2	32,656	40,206
TX	27,804	31,070	34,672	35,067	38,273	40,747	4	32,614	48,942
UT	31,366	31,366	31,366	31,366	31,366	31,366	1	28,538	39,998
VA	23,067	26,389	33,165	32,967	40,166	47,688	23	25,957	43,262
WI	35,544	35,544	39,900	39,900	44,257	44,257	2	36,930	41,371

Degree Required Data

	Min	Q1	Mean	Median	Q3	Max	N	Range Avg Min	Range Avg Max
High School	22,866	32,302	38,667	37,649	44,126	76,108	89	28,166	44,156
Associate's	39,560	39,560	39,883	39,883	40,206	40,206	2	32,656	40,206
Bachelor's	32,000	34,656	38,092	36,981	40,747	47,185	6	32,614	48,942
Master's	.	.	.	.	.	.	.	.	.
Doctoral	.	.	.	.	.	.	.	.	.

ADMINISTRATIVE ASSISTANT (SECRETARY) - CONTINUED
ALL PUBLIC LIBRARIES
Regional Data

	Min	Q1	Mean	Median	Q3	Max	N	Range Avg Min	Range Avg Max
North Atlantic	19,760	31,864	40,184	39,458	48,190	68,240	63	26,063	35,454
Great Lakes & Plains	13,520	29,120	34,971	34,590	41,392	65,753	101	27,334	39,450
Southeast	10,712	27,031	33,772	32,983	38,248	76,108	76	24,604	38,120
West & Southwest	18,720	31,366	39,671	38,242	49,712	64,210	70	35,203	45,985
ALL REGIONS	10,712	29,536	36,798	35,547	43,191	76,108	310	28,725	40,629

State Data

	Min	Q1	Mean	Median	Q3	Max	N	Range Avg Min	Range Avg Max
AL	28,142	28,142	29,099	29,099	30,056	30,056	2	26,978	33,717
AR	30,618	30,618	30,618	30,618	30,618	30,618	1	.	.
AZ	34,549	34,549	38,126	37,669	42,162	42,162	3	29,099	44,158
CA	18,720	41,400	47,626	50,648	54,956	64,210	33	41,124	51,453
CO	20,800	28,881	32,407	33,666	37,556	38,251	8	23,300	33,292
CT	45,573	46,114	52,575	48,361	59,946	62,880	5	.	.
FL	21,798	28,059	38,753	36,245	44,958	76,108	22	22,367	32,441
GA	30,860	30,860	35,455	37,649	37,856	37,856	3	.	.
IA	24,968	24,968	35,083	35,083	45,198	45,198	2	.	.
ID	23,920	23,920	27,560	27,560	31,200	31,200	2	23,525	33,748
IL	13,520	24,960	32,327	32,771	41,392	50,856	18	26,657	41,311
IN	19,448	32,267	35,103	34,823	38,303	51,417	16	.	.
KS	21,171	28,475	31,296	33,935	34,859	35,402	6	22,539	37,432
KY	10,712	10,712	10,712	10,712	10,712	10,712	1	10,712	15,600
LA	18,866	18,866	25,009	22,194	33,966	33,966	3	20,842	29,709
MA	23,504	27,040	33,016	32,406	39,458	43,283	6	28,676	37,322
MD	29,746	29,748	37,650	35,564	45,986	48,312	18	.	.
MI	23,046	30,094	34,569	34,055	37,746	49,200	13	28,524	35,984
MN	33,694	33,694	38,271	38,271	42,848	42,848	2	32,053	42,848
MO	22,866	23,103	27,094	29,536	29,536	29,536	8	24,294	29,536
MS	21,000	21,000	22,700	22,700	24,400	24,400	2	.	2,080
NC	29,120	31,735	35,496	32,000	37,440	47,185	5	22,880	37,440
NE	43,085	43,085	43,085	43,085	43,085	43,085	1	32,302	43,085
NJ	21,424	33,852	43,183	43,992	50,135	68,240	12	17,139	22,859
NM	28,205	28,205	28,205	28,205	28,205	28,205	1	.	.
NY	22,495	36,065	45,757	39,247	61,817	68,008	12	30,790	35,689
OH	18,054	30,410	38,940	39,902	44,512	65,753	30	27,921	42,007
OR	39,560	39,560	42,301	40,206	47,136	47,136	3	32,656	40,206
PA	19,760	22,880	31,521	32,240	41,063	42,377	9	22,734	35,547
RI	41,933	41,933	41,933	41,933	41,933	41,933	1	32,406	41,933
SC	30,791	30,791	34,476	34,476	38,161	38,161	2	.	.
TN	21,310	22,507	28,498	28,352	34,489	35,977	4	.	.
TX	20,322	22,734	29,342	28,912	34,336	40,747	15	27,175	44,522
UT	31,366	31,366	31,366	31,366	31,366	31,366	1	28,538	39,998
VA	23,067	27,626	33,140	32,967	38,334	47,688	31	25,977	42,561
WA	27,943	32,692	37,499	38,004	42,306	46,044	4	31,200	37,440
WI	25,480	27,186	35,317	35,544	44,117	44,257	5	33,784	40,680

Degree Required Data

	Min	Q1	Mean	Median	Q3	Max	N	Range Avg Min	Range Avg Max
High School	10,712	29,120	36,394	35,245	42,621	76,108	220	27,460	40,006
Associate's	17,000	29,887	34,592	34,590	39,560	64,210	33	29,190	42,682
Bachelor's	18,054	29,453	35,405	36,374	41,640	50,857	22	26,368	35,419
Master's	33,000	33,000	33,000	33,000	33,000	33,000	1	.	.
Doctoral	.	.	.	.	.	.		.	.

RECEPTIONIST

Operates multiple line telephone console or PBX switchboard and greets visitors. Receives incoming calls, secures identity of callers, and connects to proper parties. Takes and relays messages. Places outgoing calls. Announces and directs calls to proper party. Registers individuals and issues visitor badges. Maintains required records. Performs a wide variety of clerical duties as time permits, such as word processing, record posting and maintenance.

Small Public Library
(Serving a population of 10,000 to 25,000)
Regional Data

	Min	Q1	Mean	Median	Q3	Max	N	Range Avg Min	Range Avg Max
Great Lakes & Plains	16,640	18,720	20,280	20,800	21,840	22,880	4	18,720	31,200
ALL REGIONS	16,640	18,720	20,280	20,800	21,840	22,880	4	18,720	31,200

State Data

	Min	Q1	Mean	Median	Q3	Max	N	Range Avg Min	Range Avg Max
IL	16,640	18,720	20,280	20,800	21,840	22,880	4	18,720	31,200

Degree Required Data

	Min	Q1	Mean	Median	Q3	Max	N	Range Avg Min	Range Avg Max
High School	16,640	18,720	20,280	20,800	21,840	22,880	4	18,720	31,200
Associate's	.	.	.	.	.	.		.	.
Bachelor's	.	.	.	.	.	.		.	.
Master's	.	.	.	.	.	.		.	.
Doctoral	.	.	.	.	.	.		.	.

RECEPTIONIST - CONTINUED
Medium Public Library
(Serving a population of 25,000 to 99,999)
Regional Data

	Min	Q1	Mean	Median	Q3	Max	N	Range Avg Min	Range Avg Max
North Atlantic	15,995	15,995	31,463	28,371	50,023	50,023	3	23,754	33,862
Great Lakes & Plains	18,970	19,552	23,385	21,362	29,370	33,426	11	20,488	35,046
West & Southwest	18,720	22,360	32,883	36,300	41,808	41,808	6	30,467	39,156
ALL REGIONS	15,995	19,739	27,446	22,911	34,767	50,023	20	23,572	36,136

State Data

	Min	Q1	Mean	Median	Q3	Max	N	Range Avg Min	Range Avg Max
CA	36,109	36,109	39,908	41,808	41,808	41,808	3	34,382	41,808
CO	22,360	22,360	22,360	22,360	22,360	22,360	1	18,720	31,200
IL	18,970	19,552	23,385	21,362	29,370	33,426	11	20,488	35,046
ME	28,371	28,371	28,371	28,371	28,371	28,371	1	23,754	33,862
NY	50,023	50,023	50,023	50,023	50,023	50,023	1	.	.
PA	15,995	15,995	15,995	15,995	15,995	15,995	1	.	.
TX	18,720	18,720	27,606	27,606	36,492	36,492	2	.	.

Degree Required Data

	Min	Q1	Mean	Median	Q3	Max	N	Range Avg Min	Range Avg Max
High School	15,995	19,354	25,427	21,362	30,046	50,023	16	20,815	34,927
Associate's	.	.	.	.	.	.		.	.
Bachelor's	.	.	.	.	.	.		.	.
Master's	.	.	.	.	.	.		.	.
Doctoral	.	.	.	.	.	.		.	.

RECEPTIONIST - CONTINUED
Large Public Library
(Serving a population of 100,000 to 499,999)
Regional Data

	Min	Q1	Mean	Median	Q3	Max	N	Range Avg Min	Range Avg Max
North Atlantic	19,740	23,754	27,992	26,762	28,233	52,666	11	21,954	30,235
Great Lakes & Plains	20,814	23,046	26,265	25,698	29,328	35,100	14	22,357	32,076
Southeast	16,224	17,347	26,846	25,495	30,987	50,888	8	18,850	25,137
West & Southwest	18,865	26,770	32,472	33,207	41,600	41,615	10	24,490	30,921
ALL REGIONS	16,224	23,754	28,258	26,762	31,025	52,666	43	22,139	30,216

State Data

	Min	Q1	Mean	Median	Q3	Max	N	Range Avg Min	Range Avg Max
AL	16,224	16,224	16,973	16,557	18,138	18,138	3	16,744	25,126
CA	26,770	32,178	36,336	36,338	41,615	41,615	7	26,901	33,523
GA	31,200	31,200	31,200	31,200	31,200	31,200	1	.	.
IL	20,842	20,888	23,431	23,268	25,973	26,347	4	23,587	29,224
KS	24,544	24,544	26,166	25,750	28,205	28,205	3	21,632	36,067
MD	19,740	22,454	28,131	26,693	27,176	52,666	8	21,154	31,699
MI	23,046	23,046	24,346	24,346	25,646	25,646	2	23,046	28,808
MN	31,025	31,025	33,063	33,063	35,100	35,100	2	.	.
NC	30,773	30,773	30,773	30,773	30,773	30,773	1	.	.
NE	30,524	30,524	30,524	30,524	30,524	30,524	1	24,831	33,844
NY	28,233	28,233	28,494	28,494	28,755	28,755	2	23,556	27,306
OH	20,814	20,814	25,071	25,071	29,328	29,328	2	17,680	30,160
OR	18,865	18,865	18,865	18,865	18,865	18,865	1	18,866	24,918
PA	25,875	25,875	25,875	25,875	25,875	25,875	1	.	.
TX	24,460	24,460	24,460	24,460	24,460	24,460	1	.	.
VA	25,168	25,168	33,959	25,821	50,888	50,888	3	25,168	25,168
WA	27,040	27,040	27,040	27,040	27,040	27,040	1	22,880	29,120

Degree Required Data

	Min	Q1	Mean	Median	Q3	Max	N	Range Avg Min	Range Avg Max
High School	16,224	24,460	28,651	26,766	31,025	52,666	38	22,084	30,392
Associate's	18,865	18,865	22,256	22,256	25,646	25,646	2	18,866	24,918
Bachelor's									
Master's									
Doctoral									

RECEPTIONIST - CONTINUED
Very Large Public Library
(Serving a population of 500,000 or more)
Regional Data

	Min	Q1	Mean	Median	Q3	Max	N	Range Avg Min	Range Avg Max
North Atlantic	22,859	25,459	27,554	28,475	29,536	31,114	7		
Great Lakes & Plains	22,347	23,525	30,638	32,647	35,114	39,558	5	27,317	33,973
Southeast	21,660	21,660	27,795	26,770	35,466	35,827	7	23,067	38,445
West & Southwest	20,966	26,208	34,806	31,737	39,021	72,436	25	29,666	40,742
ALL REGIONS	20,966	24,856	32,063	29,162	35,290	72,436	44	29,120	39,838

State Data

	Min	Q1	Mean	Median	Q3	Max	N	Range Avg Min	Range Avg Max
AZ	20,966	24,253	27,726	27,394	31,990	36,525	11	21,730	34,823
CA	31,737	37,973	48,785	46,280	58,799	72,436	8	43,104	52,323
CO	32,361	32,361	32,361	32,361	32,361	32,361	1		
FL	21,660	21,660	23,363	21,660	26,770	26,770	3		
GA	26,094	26,094	26,590	26,590	27,086	27,086	2		
MD	29,536	29,536	30,062	29,536	31,114	31,114	3		
MO	22,347	22,347	22,347	22,347	22,347	22,347	1		
NC	35,466	35,466	35,466	35,466	35,466	35,466	1		
NJ	22,859	24,159	25,672	25,678	27,186	28,475	4		
OH	23,525	23,525	31,542	31,542	39,558	39,558	2	23,005	33,072
OR	30,784	30,784	34,902	34,902	39,021	39,021	2	29,536	36,338
TX	23,150	23,150	24,241	23,366	26,208	26,208	3	23,150	33,592
VA	35,827	35,827	35,827	35,827	35,827	35,827	1	23,067	38,445
WI	32,647	32,647	33,881	33,881	35,114	35,114	2	29,474	34,424

Degree Required Data

	Min	Q1	Mean	Median	Q3	Max	N	Range Avg Min	Range Avg Max
High School	20,966	24,253	29,909	29,162	32,974	48,412	32	25,131	36,112
Associate's									
Bachelor's	35,466	35,466	45,553	45,553	55,640	55,640	2	45,786	55,640
Master's									
Doctoral									

RECEPTIONIST - CONTINUED
ALL PUBLIC LIBRARIES
Regional Data

	Min	Q1	Mean	Median	Q3	Max	N	Range Avg Min	Range Avg Max
North Atlantic	15,995	25,459	28,342	27,020	28,755	52,666	21	22,404	31,142
Great Lakes & Plains	16,640	20,814	25,272	23,494	29,370	39,558	34	21,698	33,233
Southeast	16,224	21,660	27,289	26,094	31,200	50,888	15	19,693	27,798
West & Southwest	18,720	26,208	33,955	32,178	41,600	72,436	41	28,910	38,894
ALL REGIONS	15,995	22,859	29,333	27,020	32,647	72,436	111	24,966	35,331

State Data

	Min	Q1	Mean	Median	Q3	Max	N	Range Avg Min	Range Avg Max
AL	16,224	16,224	16,973	16,557	18,138	18,138	3	16,744	25,126
AZ	20,966	24,253	27,726	27,394	31,990	36,525	11	21,730	34,823
CA	26,770	34,237	42,464	41,615	44,148	72,436	18	37,352	45,558
CO	22,360	22,360	27,361	27,361	32,361	32,361	2	18,720	31,200
FL	21,660	21,660	23,363	21,660	26,770	26,770	3	.	.
GA	26,094	26,094	28,127	27,086	31,200	31,200	3	.	.
IL	16,640	19,926	22,741	20,935	25,600	33,426	19	20,627	32,993
KS	24,544	24,544	26,166	25,750	28,205	28,205	3	21,632	36,067
MD	19,740	23,754	28,658	27,020	29,536	52,666	11	21,154	31,699
ME	28,371	28,371	28,371	28,371	28,371	28,371	1	23,754	33,862
MI	23,046	23,046	24,346	24,346	25,646	25,646	2	23,046	28,808
MN	31,025	31,025	33,063	33,063	35,100	35,100	2	.	.
MO	22,347	22,347	22,347	22,347	22,347	22,347	1	.	.
NC	30,773	30,773	33,120	33,120	35,466	35,466	2	.	.
NE	30,524	30,524	30,524	30,524	30,524	30,524	1	24,831	33,844
NJ	22,859	24,159	25,672	25,678	27,186	28,475	4	.	.
NY	28,233	28,233	35,670	28,755	50,023	50,023	3	23,556	27,306
OH	20,814	22,169	28,306	26,426	34,443	39,558	4	20,342	31,616
OR	18,865	18,865	29,557	30,784	39,021	39,021	3	25,979	32,531
PA	15,995	15,995	20,935	20,935	25,875	25,875	2	.	.
TX	18,720	23,150	25,399	23,913	26,208	36,492	6	23,150	33,592
VA	25,168	25,495	34,426	30,824	43,358	50,888	4	24,117	31,806
WA	27,040	27,040	27,040	27,040	27,040	27,040	1	22,880	29,120
WI	32,647	32,647	33,881	33,881	35,114	35,114	2	29,474	34,424

Degree Required Data

	Min	Q1	Mean	Median	Q3	Max	N	Range Avg Min	Range Avg Max
High School	15,995	22,347	28,153	26,766	31,737	52,666	90	22,740	33,467
Associate's	18,865	18,865	22,256	22,256	25,646	25,646	2	18,866	24,918
Bachelor's	35,466	35,466	45,553	45,553	55,640	55,640	2	45,786	55,640
Master's	.	.	.	.	.	.		.	.
Doctoral	.	.	.	.	.	.		.	.

OFFICE MANAGER

Assumes direct responsibility for dictation, filing, mail, communications, and printing departments. Implements and follows through on general office policies. Confers with other departments regarding the purchasing of office equipment, systems, and procedures affecting more than one department, and the hiring and transferring of employees and office salary structure. Prepares payroll tax returns and performs payroll accounting for organization as required. Maintains retention schedule for library records.

Very Small Public Library
(Serving a population of less than 10,000)
Regional Data

	Min	Q1	Mean	Median	Q3	Max	N	Range Avg Min	Range Avg Max
Great Lakes & Plains	23,504	23,504	25,792	25,792	28,080	28,080	2	20,800	28,080
West & Southwest	11,520	11,520	11,520	11,520	11,520	11,520	1		
ALL REGIONS	11,520	11,520	21,035	23,504	28,080	28,080	3	20,800	28,080

State Data

	Min	Q1	Mean	Median	Q3	Max	N	Range Avg Min	Range Avg Max
IN	28,080	28,080	28,080	28,080	28,080	28,080	1	20,800	28,080
KS	23,504	23,504	23,504	23,504	23,504	23,504	1		
TX	11,520	11,520	11,520	11,520	11,520	11,520	1		

Degree Required Data

	Min	Q1	Mean	Median	Q3	Max	N	Range Avg Min	Range Avg Max
High School	11,520	11,520	17,512	17,512	23,504	23,504	2		
Associate's	28,080	28,080	28,080	28,080	28,080	28,080	1	20,800	28,080
Bachelor's									
Master's									
Doctoral									

OFFICE MANAGER - CONTINUED
Small Public Library
(Serving a population of 10,000 to 25,000)
Regional Data

	Min	Q1	Mean	Median	Q3	Max	N	Range Avg Min	Range Avg Max
North Atlantic	27,664	37,714	45,618	42,869	50,544	69,301	5	39,062	59,218
Great Lakes & Plains	23,608	28,392	34,138	31,200	42,037	45,760	9	29,619	40,040
Southeast	20,634	20,634	20,634	20,634	20,634	20,634	1	17,264	19,344
West & Southwest	35,360	35,360	35,360	35,360	35,360	35,360	1	29,120	41,600
ALL REGIONS	20,634	28,063	36,958	35,493	43,277	69,301	16	29,193	40,045

State Data

	Min	Q1	Mean	Median	Q3	Max	N	Range Avg Min	Range Avg Max
IL	23,608	23,608	27,514	27,733	31,200	31,200	3	27,040	37,440
IN	28,392	28,392	28,392	28,392	28,392	28,392	1	.	.
KS	35,625	35,625	35,625	35,625	35,625	35,625	1	24,960	41,600
LA	20,634	20,634	20,634	20,634	20,634	20,634	1	17,264	19,344
MA	42,869	42,869	42,869	42,869	42,869	42,869	1	.	.
MI	29,203	29,203	37,482	37,482	45,760	45,760	2	32,282	39,562
MN	42,037	42,037	42,037	42,037	42,037	42,037	1	31,533	42,037
NH	50,544	50,544	50,544	50,544	50,544	50,544	1	39,062	59,218
NJ	37,714	37,714	53,508	53,508	69,301	69,301	2	.	.
NM	35,360	35,360	35,360	35,360	35,360	35,360	1	29,120	41,600
RI	27,664	27,664	27,664	27,664	27,664	27,664	1	.	.
WI	43,685	43,685	43,685	43,685	43,685	43,685	1	.	.

Degree Required Data

	Min	Q1	Mean	Median	Q3	Max	N	Range Avg Min	Range Avg Max
High School	20,634	27,664	31,967	31,876	37,714	42,037	6	25,972	34,327
Associate's	23,608	26,406	31,720	30,202	37,034	42,869	4	28,122	33,322
Bachelor's	27,733	35,625	45,441	44,723	50,544	69,301	6	33,127	50,246
Master's	.	.	.	.	.	.	.	.	.
Doctoral	.	.	.	.	.	.	.	.	.

OFFICE MANAGER - CONTINUED
Medium Public Library
(Serving a population of 25,000 to 99,999)
Regional Data

	Min	Q1	Mean	Median	Q3	Max	N	Range Avg Min	Range Avg Max
North Atlantic	25,709	27,671	38,624	37,104	49,577	54,579	4	44,096	54,579
Great Lakes & Plains	31,200	33,600	46,716	53,123	59,077	60,777	7	35,187	53,810
Southeast	20,197	33,000	33,381	33,200	38,161	42,347	5	14,560	24,960
West & Southwest	33,280	33,280	33,280	33,280	33,280	33,280	1	33,280	37,440
ALL REGIONS	20,197	33,000	40,099	34,445	53,123	60,777	17	32,916	46,401

State Data

	Min	Q1	Mean	Median	Q3	Max	N	Range Avg Min	Range Avg Max
AR	20,197	20,197	20,197	20,197	20,197	20,197	1	14,560	24,960
CT	44,574	44,574	49,577	49,577	54,579	54,579	2	44,096	54,579
IA	33,600	33,600	33,600	33,600	33,600	33,600	1	.	.
IL	31,200	31,200	48,921	54,787	60,777	60,777	3	38,085	56,264
KS	34,445	34,445	34,445	34,445	34,445	34,445	1	27,248	38,126
MN	59,077	59,077	59,077	59,077	59,077	59,077	1	.	.
MS	42,347	42,347	42,347	42,347	42,347	42,347	1	.	.
NJ	25,709	25,709	25,709	25,709	25,709	25,709	1	.	.
OH	53,123	53,123	53,123	53,123	53,123	53,123	1	40,227	67,038
PA	29,634	29,634	29,634	29,634	29,634	29,634	1	.	.
SC	38,161	38,161	38,161	38,161	38,161	38,161	1	.	.
TN	33,000	33,000	33,100	33,100	33,200	33,200	2	.	.
TX	33,280	33,280	33,280	33,280	33,280	33,280	1	33,280	37,440

Degree Required Data

	Min	Q1	Mean	Median	Q3	Max	N	Range Avg Min	Range Avg Max
High School	25,709	27,671	40,813	41,379	53,955	54,787	4	39,156	61,651
Associate's	31,200	33,200	38,317	34,445	38,161	54,579	5	35,672	46,353
Bachelor's	33,280	33,600	45,609	43,461	59,077	60,777	6	33,280	37,440
Master's	33,000	33,000	33,000	33,000	33,000	33,000	1	.	.
Doctoral									

OFFICE MANAGER - CONTINUED
Large Public Library
(Serving a population of 100,000 to 499,999)
Regional Data

	Min	Q1	Mean	Median	Q3	Max	N	Range Avg Min	Range Avg Max
North Atlantic	37,335	37,335	45,207	40,523	57,761	57,761	3	.	.
Great Lakes & Plains	38,430	39,957	46,541	47,362	53,655	54,075	7	36,712	56,441
Southeast	21,900	28,848	37,038	35,121	42,631	56,121	10	23,629	33,405
West & Southwest	25,230	26,853	35,496	35,370	39,615	50,536	6	24,170	31,647
ALL REGIONS	21,900	30,035	40,183	40,081	49,960	57,761	26	29,078	41,916

State Data

	Min	Q1	Mean	Median	Q3	Max	N	Range Avg Min	Range Avg Max
CA	35,796	35,796	35,796	35,796	35,796	35,796	1		
GA	50,544	50,544	50,544	50,544	50,544	50,544	1		
IL	42,347	42,347	48,211	48,211	54,075	54,075	2		
KS	39,957	39,957	39,957	39,957	39,957	39,957	1	28,995	48,318
LA	30,035	30,035	30,035	30,035	30,035	30,035	1	23,629	33,405
MD	37,335	37,335	45,207	40,523	57,761	57,761	3		
MN	53,655	53,655	53,655	53,655	53,655	53,655	1		
MO	47,362	47,362	47,362	47,362	47,362	47,362	1	44,429	64,563
MS	21,900	21,900	32,266	32,266	42,631	42,631	2		
NC	28,109	28,478	32,235	29,238	35,993	42,357	4		
OH	38,430	38,430	44,195	44,195	49,960	49,960	2		
OK	26,853	26,853	26,853	26,853	26,853	26,853	1	23,109	29,973
OR	25,230	25,230	25,230	25,230	25,230	25,230	1	25,230	33,322
TX	34,944	34,944	41,698	39,615	50,536	50,536	3		
VA	40,206	40,206	48,164	48,164	56,121	56,121	2		

Degree Required Data

	Min	Q1	Mean	Median	Q3	Max	N	Range Avg Min	Range Avg Max
High School	26,853	30,035	42,424	43,940	53,655	56,121	6	23,369	31,689
Associate's	25,230	29,628	37,336	37,706	42,347	54,075	10	25,230	33,322
Bachelor's	28,109	39,957	43,884	42,631	49,960	57,761	9	36,712	56,441
Master's	.	.	.	.	.	.	.	.	.
Doctoral	.	.	.	.	.	.	.	.	.

OFFICE MANAGER - CONTINUED
Very Large Public Library
(Serving a population of 500,000 or more)
Regional Data

	Min	Q1	Mean	Median	Q3	Max	N	Range Avg Min	Range Avg Max
North Atlantic	32,526	32,526	38,447	32,526	44,368	56,210	4		
Great Lakes & Plains	47,023	59,468	57,038	59,567	59,567	59,567	5	42,474	59,467
Southeast	56,220	56,220	61,368	61,368	66,515	66,515	2		
West & Southwest	59,100	59,100	60,815	60,164	63,180	63,180	3	51,974	63,180
ALL REGIONS	32,526	47,023	53,154	59,284	59,567	66,515	14	48,807	61,942

State Data

	Min	Q1	Mean	Median	Q3	Max	N	Range Avg Min	Range Avg Max
CA	59,100	59,100	60,815	60,164	63,180	63,180	3	51,974	63,180
FL	56,220	56,220	61,368	61,368	66,515	66,515	2		
MD	32,526	32,526	38,447	32,526	44,368	56,210	4		
OH	47,023	53,295	56,431	59,567	59,567	59,567	4		
WI	59,468	59,468	59,468	59,468	59,468	59,468	1	42,474	59,467

Degree Required Data

	Min	Q1	Mean	Median	Q3	Max	N	Range Avg Min	Range Avg Max
High School	32,526	32,526	48,735	56,210	59,567	59,567	9		
Associate's									
Bachelor's	59,468	59,816	62,332	61,672	64,848	66,515	4	48,807	61,942
Master's									
Doctoral									

OFFICE MANAGER - CONTINUED
ALL PUBLIC LIBRARIES
Regional Data

	Min	Q1	Mean	Median	Q3	Max	N	Range Avg Min	Range Avg Max
North Atlantic	25,709	32,526	42,000	39,119	52,562	69,301	16	41,579	56,898
Great Lakes & Plains	23,504	31,200	43,227	43,016	54,075	60,777	30	32,529	46,838
Southeast	20,197	28,848	37,814	35,681	42,631	66,515	18	18,484	25,903
West & Southwest	11,520	30,066	39,632	35,578	54,818	63,180	12	35,781	44,782
ALL REGIONS	11,520	30,618	41,119	39,786	53,389	69,301	76	32,333	44,446

State Data

	Min	Q1	Mean	Median	Q3	Max	N	Range Avg Min	Range Avg Max
AR	20,197	20,197	20,197	20,197	20,197	20,197	1	14,560	24,960
CA	35,796	47,448	54,560	59,632	61,672	63,180	4	51,974	63,180
CT	44,574	44,574	49,577	49,577	54,579	54,579	2	44,096	54,579
FL	56,220	56,220	61,368	61,368	66,515	66,515	2	.	.
GA	50,544	50,544	50,544	50,544	50,544	50,544	1	.	.
IA	33,600	33,600	33,600	33,600	33,600	33,600	1	.	.
IL	23,608	29,467	40,716	36,773	54,431	60,777	8	32,562	46,852
IN	28,080	28,080	28,236	28,236	28,392	28,392	2	20,800	28,080
KS	23,504	28,974	33,383	35,035	37,791	39,957	4	27,068	42,682
LA	20,634	20,634	25,334	25,334	30,035	30,035	2	20,446	26,374
MA	42,869	42,869	42,869	42,869	42,869	42,869	1	.	.
MD	32,526	32,526	41,344	37,335	56,210	57,761	7	.	.
MI	29,203	29,203	37,482	37,482	45,760	45,760	2	32,282	39,562
MN	42,037	42,037	51,590	53,655	59,077	59,077	3	31,533	42,037
MO	47,362	47,362	47,362	47,362	47,362	47,362	1	44,429	64,563
MS	21,900	21,900	35,626	42,347	42,631	42,631	3	.	.
NC	28,109	28,478	32,235	29,238	35,993	42,357	4	.	.
NH	50,544	50,544	50,544	50,544	50,544	50,544	1	39,062	59,218
NJ	25,709	25,709	44,241	37,714	69,301	69,301	3	.	.
NM	35,360	35,360	35,360	35,360	35,360	35,360	1	29,120	41,600
OH	38,430	47,023	52,462	53,123	59,567	59,567	7	40,227	67,038
OK	26,853	26,853	26,853	26,853	26,853	26,853	1	23,109	29,973
OR	25,230	25,230	25,230	25,230	25,230	25,230	1	25,230	33,322
PA	29,634	29,634	29,634	29,634	29,634	29,634	1	.	.
RI	27,664	27,664	27,664	27,664	27,664	27,664	1	.	.
SC	38,161	38,161	38,161	38,161	38,161	38,161	1	.	.
TN	33,000	33,000	33,100	33,100	33,200	33,200	2	.	.
TX	11,520	33,280	33,979	34,944	39,615	50,536	5	33,280	37,440
VA	40,206	40,206	48,164	48,164	56,121	56,121	2	.	.
WI	43,685	43,685	51,577	51,577	59,468	59,468	2	42,474	59,467

Degree Required Data

	Min	Q1	Mean	Median	Q3	Max	N	Range Avg Min	Range Avg Max
High School	11,520	28,392	40,120	37,335	54,787	59,567	27	28,995	41,380
Associate's	23,608	29,416	35,995	34,694	41,435	54,579	20	28,936	36,792
Bachelor's	27,733	39,957	47,623	45,760	59,077	69,301	25	39,168	54,098
Master's	33,000	33,000	33,000	33,000	33,000	33,000	1	.	.
Doctoral	.	.	.	.	.	.	.	.	.

PUBLIC RELATIONS OFFICER

Promotes and administers public relations policies and programs such as special events, news articles, and audio and visual communication media. Maintains relations with newspaper, radio and TV media, community groups and agencies, school districts and Board of Trustees.

Very Small Public Library
(Serving a population of less than 10,000)
Regional Data

	Min	Q1	Mean	Median	Q3	Max	N	Range Avg Min	Range Avg Max
Great Lakes & Plains	26,545	26,545	26,545	26,545	26,545	26,545	1		
West & Southwest	39,000	39,000	39,000	39,000	39,000	39,000	1	31,928	46,322
ALL REGIONS	26,545	26,545	32,773	32,773	39,000	39,000	2	31,928	46,322

State Data

	Min	Q1	Mean	Median	Q3	Max	N	Range Avg Min	Range Avg Max
CO	39,000	39,000	39,000	39,000	39,000	39,000	1	31,928	46,322
OH	26,545	26,545	26,545	26,545	26,545	26,545	1		

Degree Required Data

	Min	Q1	Mean	Median	Q3	Max	N	Range Avg Min	Range Avg Max
High School									
Associate's									
Bachelor's	39,000	39,000	39,000	39,000	39,000	39,000	1	31,928	46,322
Master's									
Doctoral									

PUBLIC RELATIONS OFFICER - CONTINUED
Small Public Library
(Serving a population of 10,000 to 25,000)
Regional Data

	Min	Q1	Mean	Median	Q3	Max	N	Range Avg Min	Range Avg Max
Great Lakes & Plains	27,507	27,507	38,289	37,440	49,920	49,920	3	24,267	42,293
West & Southwest	39,520	39,520	39,520	39,520	39,520	39,520	1	33,280	47,840
ALL REGIONS	27,507	32,474	38,597	38,480	44,720	49,920	4	26,520	43,680

State Data

	Min	Q1	Mean	Median	Q3	Max	N	Range Avg Min	Range Avg Max
IL	49,920	49,920	49,920	49,920	49,920	49,920	1	22,880	52,000
KS	27,507	27,507	27,507	27,507	27,507	27,507	1	18,720	31,200
MI	37,440	37,440	37,440	37,440	37,440	37,440	1	31,200	43,680
NM	39,520	39,520	39,520	39,520	39,520	39,520	1	33,280	47,840

Degree Required Data

	Min	Q1	Mean	Median	Q3	Max	N	Range Avg Min	Range Avg Max
High School	39,520	39,520	39,520	39,520	39,520	39,520	1	33,280	47,840
Associate's	27,507	27,507	27,507	27,507	27,507	27,507	1	18,720	31,200
Bachelor's	37,440	37,440	43,680	43,680	49,920	49,920	2	27,040	47,840
Master's	.	.	.	.	.	.		.	.
Doctoral	.	.	.	.	.	.		.	.

PUBLIC RELATIONS OFFICER - CONTINUED
Medium Public Library
(Serving a population of 25,000 to 99,999)
Regional Data

	Min	Q1	Mean	Median	Q3	Max	N	Range Avg Min	Range Avg Max
North Atlantic	21,088	23,275	47,371	41,902	72,800	89,406	7	.	.
Great Lakes & Plains	21,070	31,200	42,856	38,158	57,436	72,301	15	37,318	54,057
Southeast	22,000	22,000	26,119	24,173	32,184	32,184	3	.	.
West & Southwest	44,803	44,803	44,803	44,803	44,803	44,803	1	37,523	46,134
ALL REGIONS	21,070	29,120	42,215	35,709	52,753	89,406	26	37,338	53,265

State Data

	Min	Q1	Mean	Median	Q3	Max	N	Range Avg Min	Range Avg Max
CT	89,406	89,406	89,406	89,406	89,406	89,406	1	.	.
DE	31,158	31,158	31,158	31,158	31,158	31,158	1	.	.
IL	29,120	31,200	45,714	39,915	69,056	72,301	7	37,495	53,796
IN	33,176	33,176	33,176	33,176	33,176	33,176	1	.	.
KS	21,070	21,070	21,070	21,070	21,070	21,070	1	21,070	29,058
LA	24,173	24,173	28,179	28,179	32,184	32,184	2	.	.
MN	57,436	57,436	57,436	57,436	57,436	57,436	1	.	.
NY	41,902	41,902	46,934	46,934	51,966	51,966	2	.	.
OH	25,632	32,085	42,233	33,259	52,753	67,434	5	44,907	67,340
PA	23,275	23,275	48,038	48,038	72,800	72,800	2	.	.
RI	21,088	21,088	21,088	21,088	21,088	21,088	1	.	.
TN	22,000	22,000	22,000	22,000	22,000	22,000	1	.	.
WY	44,803	44,803	44,803	44,803	44,803	44,803	1	37,523	46,134

Degree Required Data

	Min	Q1	Mean	Median	Q3	Max	N	Range Avg Min	Range Avg Max
High School	51,966	51,966	70,686	70,686	89,406	89,406	2	.	.
Associate's	21,070	21,070	21,070	21,070	21,070	21,070	1	21,070	29,058
Bachelor's	21,088	31,158	41,488	33,259	52,753	72,800	21	39,146	55,954
Master's	22,000	22,000	22,000	22,000	22,000	22,000	1	.	.
Doctoral	.	.	.	.	.	.		.	.

PUBLIC RELATIONS OFFICER - CONTINUED
Large Public Library
(Serving a population of 100,000 to 499,999)
Regional Data

	Min	Q1	Mean	Median	Q3	Max	N	Range Avg Min	Range Avg Max
North Atlantic	31,500	40,551	50,142	50,432	59,787	68,100	8	.	.
Great Lakes & Plains	30,160	37,128	46,401	46,114	58,240	61,776	15	36,923	55,129
Southeast	26,000	32,178	37,680	33,280	43,950	58,144	11	31,942	44,838
West & Southwest	23,650	37,428	47,667	48,028	57,101	83,428	12	37,554	57,169
ALL REGIONS	23,650	34,000	45,297	44,295	55,754	83,428	46	36,226	53,964

State Data

	Min	Q1	Mean	Median	Q3	Max	N	Range Avg Min	Range Avg Max
AL	33,280	33,280	33,280	33,280	33,280	33,280	1	32,635	40,810
CA	44,640	51,544	61,839	59,644	72,134	83,428	4	46,384	68,869
CO	39,000	39,000	45,916	45,916	52,832	52,832	2	36,546	57,855
FL	32,205	32,205	36,291	32,718	43,950	43,950	3	.	.
GA	26,000	26,000	26,000	26,000	26,000	26,000	1	.	.
IL	47,528	48,153	53,601	53,571	59,049	59,733	4	36,858	52,042
KS	58,115	58,115	58,115	58,115	58,115	58,115	1	37,586	62,650
LA	32,178	32,178	32,178	32,178	32,178	32,178	1	31,990	43,784
MD	31,500	32,389	46,088	42,969	59,787	66,913	4	.	.
MI	34,000	35,886	43,637	39,386	51,388	61,776	4	.	.
MN	30,160	30,160	30,160	30,160	30,160	30,160	1	.	.
MO	58,240	58,240	58,240	58,240	58,240	58,240	1	44,429	64,563
NC	37,440	37,440	39,168	39,168	40,896	40,896	2	31,200	49,920
NJ	47,824	47,824	47,824	47,824	47,824	47,824	1	.	.
NM	35,857	35,857	35,857	35,857	35,857	35,857	1	35,838	49,109
NY	48,687	48,687	50,432	50,432	52,177	52,177	2	.	.
OH	37,128	37,128	41,711	41,891	46,114	46,114	3	36,254	57,075
PA	68,100	68,100	68,100	68,100	68,100	68,100	1	.	.
SC	31,485	31,485	31,485	31,485	31,485	31,485	1	.	.
TN	46,187	46,187	46,187	46,187	46,187	46,187	1	.	.
TX	23,650	23,650	29,929	24,814	41,323	41,323	3	23,629	40,456
VA	58,144	58,144	58,144	58,144	58,144	58,144	1	.	.
WA	51,415	51,415	53,584	53,584	55,754	55,754	2	.	.
WI	35,422	35,422	35,422	35,422	35,422	35,422	1	30,826	35,422

Degree Required Data

	Min	Q1	Mean	Median	Q3	Max	N	Range Avg Min	Range Avg Max
High School	23,650	23,650	27,285	26,000	32,205	32,205	3	.	.
Associate's	24,814	24,814	34,727	34,727	44,640	44,640	2	23,629	40,456
Bachelor's	30,160	35,857	46,735	46,150	55,754	83,428	38	36,199	53,345
Master's									
Doctoral									

PUBLIC RELATIONS OFFICER - CONTINUED
Very Large Public Library
(Serving a population of 500,000 or more)
Regional Data

	Min	Q1	Mean	Median	Q3	Max	N	Range Avg Min	Range Avg Max
North Atlantic	25,463	33,311	44,075	41,287	45,238	75,075	5	.	.
Great Lakes & Plains	42,154	46,680	81,039	86,419	100,185	124,380	6	65,603	94,370
Southeast	43,512	54,502	61,911	57,084	73,345	85,259	9	41,127	68,545
West & Southwest	32,952	41,175	51,239	52,900	61,568	72,800	9	47,698	64,158
ALL REGIONS	25,463	42,113	59,181	54,622	73,345	124,380	29	48,379	69,727

State Data

	Min	Q1	Mean	Median	Q3	Max	N	Range Avg Min	Range Avg Max
CA	41,175	41,794	54,801	52,615	67,808	72,800	4	55,929	67,808
CO	52,900	52,900	52,900	52,900	52,900	52,900	1	.	.
FL	56,797	56,797	66,380	57,084	85,259	85,259	3	.	.
GA	43,512	43,512	53,251	54,502	61,740	61,740	3	.	.
IN	100,185	100,185	100,185	100,185	100,185	100,185	1	.	.
MD	45,238	45,238	60,157	60,157	75,075	75,075	2	.	.
MI	46,680	46,680	46,680	46,680	46,680	46,680	1	.	.
MO	42,154	42,154	42,154	42,154	42,154	42,154	1	.	.
NC	77,604	77,604	77,604	77,604	77,604	77,604	1	.	.
NJ	25,463	25,463	33,354	33,311	41,287	41,287	3	.	.
OH	78,468	78,468	99,073	94,370	124,380	124,380	3	65,603	94,370
OR	54,622	54,622	54,622	54,622	54,622	54,622	1	.	.
TX	39,907	39,907	50,738	50,738	61,568	61,568	2	45,989	74,714
UT	32,952	32,952	32,952	32,952	32,952	32,952	1	32,947	46,301
VA	47,355	47,355	60,350	60,350	73,345	73,345	2	41,127	68,545

Degree Required Data

	Min	Q1	Mean	Median	Q3	Max	N	Range Avg Min	Range Avg Max
High School	47,355	47,355	60,350	60,350	73,345	73,345	2	41,127	68,545
Associate's	42,413	42,413	42,963	42,963	43,512	43,512	2	.	.
Bachelor's	39,907	49,069	66,142	61,654	78,036	124,380	20	55,862	76,175
Master's	46,680	46,680	46,680	46,680	46,680	46,680	1	.	.
Doctoral	.	.	.	.	.	.		.	.

PUBLIC RELATIONS OFFICER - CONTINUED
ALL PUBLIC LIBRARIES
Regional Data

	Min	Q1	Mean	Median	Q3	Max	N	Range Avg Min	Range Avg Max
North Atlantic	21,088	32,389	47,655	46,531	59,787	89,406	20	.	.
Great Lakes & Plains	21,070	33,630	49,163	42,023	58,303	124,380	40	36,636	54,683
Southeast	22,000	32,184	45,654	43,512	57,084	85,259	23	35,616	54,321
West & Southwest	23,650	39,260	48,187	44,722	57,101	83,428	24	39,912	56,918
ALL REGIONS	21,070	33,278	47,908	43,950	58,144	124,380	107	37,622	55,400

State Data

	Min	Q1	Mean	Median	Q3	Max	N	Range Avg Min	Range Avg Max
AL	33,280	33,280	33,280	33,280	33,280	33,280	1	32,635	40,810
CA	41,175	43,527	58,320	59,644	67,808	83,428	8	51,156	68,338
CO	39,000	39,000	45,933	45,916	52,866	52,900	4	35,006	54,011
CT	89,406	89,406	89,406	89,406	89,406	89,406	1		
DE	31,158	31,158	31,158	31,158	31,158	31,158	1		
FL	32,205	32,718	51,336	50,374	57,084	85,259	6		
GA	26,000	34,756	46,439	49,007	58,121	61,740	4		
IL	29,120	39,037	48,693	48,153	59,049	72,301	12	35,589	53,352
IN	33,176	33,176	66,681	66,681	100,185	100,185	2		
KS	21,070	21,070	35,564	27,507	58,115	58,115	3	25,792	40,969
LA	24,173	24,173	29,512	32,178	32,184	32,184	3	31,990	43,784
MD	31,500	33,278	50,777	48,949	66,913	75,075	6		
MI	34,000	37,440	43,111	39,386	46,680	61,776	6	31,200	43,680
MN	30,160	30,160	43,798	43,798	57,436	57,436	2		
MO	42,154	42,154	50,197	50,197	58,240	58,240	2	44,429	64,563
NC	37,440	37,440	51,980	40,896	77,604	77,604	3	31,200	49,920
NJ	25,463	29,387	36,971	37,299	44,555	47,824	4		
NM	35,857	35,857	37,688	37,688	39,520	39,520	2	34,559	48,474
NY	41,902	45,294	48,683	50,326	52,071	52,177	4		
OH	25,632	32,672	55,005	44,002	72,951	124,380	12	44,030	66,713
OR	54,622	54,622	54,622	54,622	54,622	54,622	1		
PA	23,275	23,275	54,725	68,100	72,800	72,800	3		
RI	21,088	21,088	21,088	21,088	21,088	21,088	1		
SC	31,485	31,485	31,485	31,485	31,485	31,485	1		
TN	22,000	22,000	34,094	34,094	46,187	46,187	2		
TX	23,650	24,814	38,253	39,907	41,323	61,568	5	34,809	57,585
UT	32,952	32,952	32,952	32,952	32,952	32,952	1	32,947	46,301
VA	47,355	47,355	59,615	58,144	73,345	73,345	3	41,127	68,545
WA	51,415	51,415	53,584	53,584	55,754	55,754	2		
WI	35,422	35,422	35,422	35,422	35,422	35,422	1	30,826	35,422
WY	44,803	44,803	44,803	44,803	44,803	44,803	1	37,523	46,134

Degree Required Data

	Min	Q1	Mean	Median	Q3	Max	N	Range Avg Min	Range Avg Max
High School	23,650	29,103	47,931	43,438	62,656	89,406	8	38,512	61,644
Associate's	21,070	24,814	33,993	34,960	43,512	44,640	6	21,140	33,571
Bachelor's	21,088	35,857	49,956	46,150	58,365	124,380	82	39,148	56,801
Master's	22,000	22,000	34,340	34,340	46,680	46,680	2		
Doctoral									

GRAPHIC ARTIST

Designs unique, original materials based on aesthetic trends. Plans layout and creates materials such as brochures, manuals, advertisements, reports, newsletters and forms using a variety of desktop publishing software. Researches and recommends the purchase of related software and hardware. Organizes and implements desktop publishing and operating methods and procedures.

Small Public Library
(Serving a population of 10,000 to 25,000)
Regional Data

	Min	Q1	Mean	Median	Q3	Max	N	Range Avg Min	Range Avg Max
North Atlantic	54,286	54,286	54,286	54,286	54,286	54,286	1	.	.
Great Lakes & Plains	27,040	27,040	36,400	32,240	45,760	54,080	4	31,200	66,560
ALL REGIONS	27,040	27,040	39,977	37,440	54,080	54,286	5	31,200	66,560

State Data

	Min	Q1	Mean	Median	Q3	Max	N	Range Avg Min	Range Avg Max
IL	27,040	27,040	36,400	32,240	45,760	54,080	4	31,200	66,560
NY	54,286	54,286	54,286	54,286	54,286	54,286	1	.	.

Degree Required Data

	Min	Q1	Mean	Median	Q3	Max	N	Range Avg Min	Range Avg Max
High School	54,286	54,286	54,286	54,286	54,286	54,286	1	.	.
Associate's	27,040	27,040	30,507	27,040	37,440	37,440	3	22,880	52,000
Bachelor's	54,080	54,080	54,080	54,080	54,080	54,080	1	39,520	81,120
Master's	.	.	.	.	.	.		.	
Doctoral	.	.	.	.	.	.		.	

GRAPHIC ARTIST - CONTINUED
Medium Public Library
(Serving a population of 25,000 to 99,999)
Regional Data

	Min	Q1	Mean	Median	Q3	Max	N	Range Avg Min	Range Avg Max
North Atlantic	28,023	29,786	36,837	38,517	39,811	48,048	5	36,858	48,402
Great Lakes & Plains	15,395	32,000	35,853	37,817	41,309	45,074	14	27,747	45,041
West & Southwest	42,804	42,804	42,804	42,804	42,804	42,804	1	.	.
ALL REGIONS	15,395	31,694	36,447	38,191	41,731	48,048	20	29,772	45,788

State Data

	Min	Q1	Mean	Median	Q3	Max	N	Range Avg Min	Range Avg Max
CA	42,804	42,804	42,804	42,804	42,804	42,804	1	.	.
CT	48,048	48,048	48,048	48,048	48,048	48,048	1	44,096	54,579
IA	37,768	37,768	37,768	37,768	37,768	37,768	1	.	.
IL	31,387	37,440	39,633	41,215	42,153	44,387	6	27,572	44,208
IN	32,000	32,000	35,013	32,032	41,008	41,008	3	.	.
ME	39,811	39,811	39,811	39,811	39,811	39,811	1	29,619	42,224
MI	15,395	15,395	15,395	15,395	15,395	15,395	1	.	.
MN	37,866	37,866	37,866	37,866	37,866	37,866	1	.	.
NY	28,023	28,023	33,270	33,270	38,517	38,517	2	.	.
OH	23,005	23,005	34,039	34,039	45,074	45,074	2	28,184	47,122
PA	29,786	29,786	29,786	29,786	29,786	29,786	1	.	.

Degree Required Data

	Min	Q1	Mean	Median	Q3	Max	N	Range Avg Min	Range Avg Max
High School	23,005	27,502	34,081	35,258	40,660	42,804	4	20,259	37,752
Associate's	29,786	31,387	37,763	37,440	42,153	48,048	5	30,105	46,509
Bachelor's	15,395	37,768	37,577	40,410	41,309	45,074	10	31,475	46,962
Master's	.	.	.	.	.	.		.	.
Doctoral	.	.	.	.	.	.		.	.

GRAPHIC ARTIST - CONTINUED
Large Public Library
(Serving a population of 100,000 to 499,999)
Regional Data

	Min	Q1	Mean	Median	Q3	Max	N	Range Avg Min	Range Avg Max
North Atlantic	24,688	30,285	37,393	37,197	42,489	52,669	10	29,286	43,722
Great Lakes & Plains	20,331	30,152	33,473	32,097	39,728	48,442	18	25,357	36,128
Southeast	26,496	30,205	35,475	36,110	39,936	43,892	7	27,206	41,434
West & Southwest	30,381	38,393	44,568	45,307	51,706	55,349	8	36,261	48,623
ALL REGIONS	20,331	30,381	36,775	36,123	42,994	55,349	43	28,185	39,994

State Data

	Min	Q1	Mean	Median	Q3	Max	N	Range Avg Min	Range Avg Max
CA	44,640	44,640	49,995	49,995	55,349	55,349	2	.	.
CO	48,693	48,693	48,693	48,693	48,693	48,693	1	39,666	55,162
FL	26,496	26,496	33,216	33,216	39,936	39,936	2	27,206	41,434
IL	31,040	31,467	36,345	35,674	41,224	42,994	4	24,960	29,120
IN	32,300	32,300	40,371	40,371	48,442	48,442	2	.	.
KS	39,728	39,728	39,978	39,978	40,227	40,227	2	28,995	48,318
MD	24,688	28,620	31,597	30,285	36,123	38,272	5	29,286	43,722
MI	31,179	31,179	32,408	31,418	34,626	34,626	3	.	.
MN	43,500	43,500	43,500	43,500	43,500	43,500	1	.	.
MO	22,339	22,339	28,548	28,548	34,757	34,757	2	23,982	34,840
NE	30,152	30,152	30,152	30,152	30,152	30,152	1	29,343	37,471
NJ	42,489	42,489	47,579	47,579	52,669	52,669	2	.	.
NM	45,973	45,973	45,973	45,973	45,973	45,973	1	35,838	49,109
NY	42,160	42,160	43,725	43,725	45,290	45,290	2	.	.
OH	20,331	20,331	22,821	23,026	25,106	25,106	3	21,497	31,564
PA	33,334	33,334	33,334	33,334	33,334	33,334	1	.	.
SC	30,205	30,205	30,205	30,205	30,205	30,205	1	.	.
TX	30,381	30,381	30,381	30,381	30,381	30,381	1	.	.
VA	32,753	34,432	37,921	37,520	41,411	43,892	4	.	.
WA	37,440	37,440	43,835	39,346	54,720	54,720	3	33,280	41,600

Degree Required Data

	Min	Q1	Mean	Median	Q3	Max	N	Range Avg Min	Range Avg Max
High School	20,331	30,152	33,367	31,655	37,440	52,669	10	27,950	35,749
Associate's	23,026	33,334	39,141	39,346	44,640	54,720	9	30,576	43,670
Bachelor's	22,339	31,179	37,641	38,601	42,994	55,349	22	28,624	43,267
Master's	.	.	.	.	.	.		.	.
Doctoral	.	.	.	.	.	.		.	.

GRAPHIC ARTIST - CONTINUED
Very Large Public Library
(Serving a population of 500,000 or more)
Regional Data

	Min	Q1	Mean	Median	Q3	Max	N	Range Avg Min	Range Avg Max
North Atlantic	27,747	32,553	37,724	38,254	41,131	48,402	6	.	.
Great Lakes & Plains	30,597	36,418	40,923	39,333	41,633	57,495	9	30,597	44,054
Southeast	33,629	38,558	45,863	49,504	50,843	60,749	9	30,521	50,868
West & Southwest	32,242	40,300	44,666	45,072	50,232	57,006	11	35,250	46,213
ALL REGIONS	27,747	36,418	42,821	41,131	50,049	60,749	35	32,908	46,496

State Data

	Min	Q1	Mean	Median	Q3	Max	N	Range Avg Min	Range Avg Max
CA	32,922	44,700	46,284	46,423	50,232	57,006	6	34,180	41,577
CO	40,300	40,300	40,300	40,300	40,300	40,300	1	.	.
FL	33,629	38,558	46,657	49,504	50,843	60,749	5	.	.
GA	39,888	39,888	39,888	39,888	39,888	39,888	1	.	.
IN	41,633	41,633	41,633	41,633	41,633	41,633	1	.	.
MD	39,837	39,837	44,120	44,120	48,402	48,402	2	.	.
MI	36,870	36,870	36,870	36,870	36,870	36,870	1	.	.
MO	36,418	36,418	36,418	36,418	36,418	36,418	1	.	.
NC	50,049	50,049	50,049	50,049	50,049	50,049	1	.	.
NJ	27,747	30,150	34,526	34,612	38,901	41,131	4	.	.
OH	30,597	32,032	42,232	39,535	54,195	57,495	6	30,597	44,054
OR	47,986	47,986	47,986	47,986	47,986	47,986	1	39,021	47,986
TX	32,242	32,242	37,181	37,181	42,120	42,120	2	32,614	48,942
UT	50,976	50,976	50,976	50,976	50,976	50,976	1	36,254	50,981
VA	34,000	34,000	44,775	44,775	55,551	55,551	2	30,521	50,868

Degree Required Data

	Min	Q1	Mean	Median	Q3	Max	N	Range Avg Min	Range Avg Max
High School	32,242	34,000	43,542	45,072	50,843	55,551	5	30,521	50,868
Associate's	39,888	40,300	48,694	47,986	57,006	60,749	7	40,206	49,109
Bachelor's	30,597	38,101	43,561	41,877	49,777	57,495	16	32,132	46,417
Master's	.	.	.	.	.	.	.	.	.
Doctoral	.	.	.	.	.	.	.	.	.

GRAPHIC ARTIST - CONTINUED
ALL PUBLIC LIBRARIES
Regional Data

	Min	Q1	Mean	Median	Q3	Max	N	Range Avg Min	Range Avg Max
North Atlantic	24,688	30,285	38,125	38,394	42,489	54,286	22	33,072	46,062
Great Lakes & Plains	15,395	31,179	35,964	36,870	41,122	57,495	45	27,459	43,130
Southeast	26,496	33,815	41,318	39,409	49,777	60,749	16	29,416	47,723
West & Southwest	30,381	39,823	44,534	44,886	49,462	57,006	20	35,629	47,117
ALL REGIONS	15,395	32,032	38,921	39,333	44,700	60,749	103	30,061	44,724

State Data

	Min	Q1	Mean	Median	Q3	Max	N	Range Avg Min	Range Avg Max
CA	32,922	44,640	46,722	45,072	50,232	57,006	9	34,180	41,577
CO	40,300	40,300	44,496	44,496	48,693	48,693	2	39,666	55,162
CT	48,048	48,048	48,048	48,048	48,048	48,048	1	44,096	54,579
FL	26,496	33,629	42,816	39,936	50,843	60,749	7	27,206	41,434
GA	39,888	39,888	39,888	39,888	39,888	39,888	1	.	.
IA	37,768	37,768	37,768	37,768	37,768	37,768	1	.	.
IL	27,040	31,387	37,770	38,447	42,153	54,080	14	27,798	45,822
IN	32,000	32,032	37,903	36,654	41,633	48,442	6	.	.
KS	39,728	39,728	39,978	39,978	40,227	40,227	2	28,995	48,318
MD	24,688	28,620	35,175	36,123	39,837	48,402	7	29,286	43,722
ME	39,811	39,811	39,811	39,811	39,811	39,811	1	29,619	42,224
MI	15,395	31,179	29,897	31,418	34,626	36,870	5	.	.
MN	37,866	37,866	40,683	40,683	43,500	43,500	2	.	.
MO	22,339	22,339	31,171	34,757	36,418	36,418	3	23,982	34,840
NC	50,049	50,049	50,049	50,049	50,049	50,049	1	.	.
NE	30,152	30,152	30,152	30,152	30,152	30,152	1	29,343	37,471
NJ	27,747	32,553	38,877	38,901	42,489	52,669	6	.	.
NM	45,973	45,973	45,973	45,973	45,973	45,973	1	35,838	49,109
NY	28,023	38,517	41,655	42,160	45,290	54,286	5	.	.
OH	20,331	23,026	35,448	32,032	45,074	57,495	11	27,307	41,362
OR	47,986	47,986	47,986	47,986	47,986	47,986	1	39,021	47,986
PA	29,786	29,786	31,560	31,560	33,334	33,334	2	.	.
SC	30,205	30,205	30,205	30,205	30,205	30,205	1	.	.
TX	30,381	30,381	34,914	32,242	42,120	42,120	3	32,614	48,942
UT	50,976	50,976	50,976	50,976	50,976	50,976	1	36,254	50,981
VA	32,753	34,000	40,206	37,520	43,892	55,551	6	30,521	50,868
WA	37,440	37,440	43,835	39,346	54,720	54,720	3	33,280	41,600

Degree Required Data

	Min	Q1	Mean	Median	Q3	Max	N	Range Avg Min	Range Avg Max
High School	20,331	31,229	37,100	33,150	43,938	55,551	20	27,631	39,779
Associate's	23,026	32,361	40,561	40,094	48,017	60,749	24	31,845	47,135
Bachelor's	15,395	36,110	39,896	39,811	45,074	57,495	49	30,995	47,271
Master's	.	.	.	.	.	.	.	.	.
Doctoral	.	.	.	.	.	.	.	.	.

VOLUNTEER COORDINATOR

Coordinates all volunteers and volunteer programs. Assesses volunteer needs. Recruits, screens and places volunteers. Works with staff ensure proper orientation given and evaluation of performance. May develop and coordinate volunteer recognition programs.

Very Small Public Library
(Serving a population of less than 10,000)
Regional Data

	Min	Q1	Mean	Median	Q3	Max	N	Range Avg Min	Range Avg Max
Great Lakes & Plains	16,120	16,120	16,120	16,120	16,120	16,120	1	.	.
ALL REGIONS	16,120	16,120	16,120	16,120	16,120	16,120	1	.	.

State Data

	Min	Q1	Mean	Median	Q3	Max	N	Range Avg Min	Range Avg Max
IA	16,120	16,120	16,120	16,120	16,120	16,120	1	.	.

Degree Required Data

	Min	Q1	Mean	Median	Q3	Max	N	Range Avg Min	Range Avg Max
High School	16,120	16,120	16,120	16,120	16,120	16,120	1	.	.
Associate's	.	.	.	.	.	.		.	.
Bachelor's	.	.	.	.	.	.		.	.
Master's	.	.	.	.	.	.		.	.
Doctoral	.	.	.	.	.	.		.	.

VOLUNTEER COORDINATOR - CONTINUED
Small Public Library
(Serving a population of 10,000 to 25,000)
Regional Data

	Min	Q1	Mean	Median	Q3	Max	N	Range Avg Min	Range Avg Max
Great Lakes & Plains	24,960	24,960	30,160	30,160	35,360	35,360	2	29,120	39,520
West & Southwest	32,971	32,971	33,094	33,094	33,217	33,217	2	28,974	37,627
ALL REGIONS	24,960	28,965	31,627	33,094	34,289	35,360	4	29,047	38,574

State Data

	Min	Q1	Mean	Median	Q3	Max	N	Range Avg Min	Range Avg Max
AZ	33,217	33,217	33,217	33,217	33,217	33,217	1	.	.
MI	24,960	24,960	30,160	30,160	35,360	35,360	2	29,120	39,520
OR	32,971	32,971	32,971	32,971	32,971	32,971	1	28,974	37,627

Degree Required Data

	Min	Q1	Mean	Median	Q3	Max	N	Range Avg Min	Range Avg Max
High School	24,960	24,960	31,097	32,971	35,360	35,360	3	29,047	38,574
Associate's									
Bachelor's	33,217	33,217	33,217	33,217	33,217	33,217	1		
Master's									
Doctoral									

VOLUNTEER COORDINATOR - CONTINUED
Medium Public Library
(Serving a population of 25,000 to 99,999)
Regional Data

	Min	Q1	Mean	Median	Q3	Max	N	Range Avg Min	Range Avg Max
North Atlantic	36,130	36,130	36,130	36,130	36,130	36,130	1		
Great Lakes & Plains	22,880	25,334	34,635	35,308	44,491	44,491	6	31,262	39,534
Southeast	25,334	25,334	25,334	25,334	25,334	25,334	1		
West & Southwest	53,308	53,308	55,264	55,264	57,221	57,221	2	47,070	57,221
ALL REGIONS	22,880	25,334	37,981	38,373	44,491	57,221	10	35,214	43,956

State Data

	Min	Q1	Mean	Median	Q3	Max	N	Range Avg Min	Range Avg Max
AR	25,334	25,334	25,334	25,334	25,334	25,334	1		
CA	57,221	57,221	57,221	57,221	57,221	57,221	1	47,070	57,221
IA	40,616	40,616	40,616	40,616	40,616	40,616	1		
IL	22,880	22,880	22,880	22,880	22,880	22,880	1		
MN	44,491	44,491	44,491	44,491	44,491	44,491	2	34,861	35,131
OH	25,334	25,334	27,667	27,667	30,000	30,000	2	24,066	48,339
PA	36,130	36,130	36,130	36,130	36,130	36,130	1		
TX	53,308	53,308	53,308	53,308	53,308	53,308	1		

Degree Required Data

	Min	Q1	Mean	Median	Q3	Max	N	Range Avg Min	Range Avg Max
High School	25,334	25,334	25,334	25,334	25,334	25,334	2	24,066	48,339
Associate's									
Bachelor's	22,880	33,065	41,142	42,554	48,900	57,221	8	38,931	42,494
Master's									
Doctoral									

VOLUNTEER COORDINATOR - CONTINUED
Large Public Library
(Serving a population of 100,000 to 499,999)
Regional Data

	Min	Q1	Mean	Median	Q3	Max	N	Range Avg Min	Range Avg Max
North Atlantic	31,533	34,611	38,636	38,501	42,660	46,009	4	34,382	53,196
Great Lakes & Plains	15,829	15,829	36,601	42,192	51,783	51,783	3	15,829	23,005
Southeast	24,960	24,960	27,105	27,030	29,325	29,325	3	.	.
West & Southwest	17,867	27,456	36,033	40,139	43,035	50,440	13	30,056	40,930
ALL REGIONS	15,829	27,030	35,395	38,228	43,035	51,783	23	29,359	41,756

State Data

	Min	Q1	Mean	Median	Q3	Max	N	Range Avg Min	Range Avg Max
CA	38,228	38,228	44,664	45,323	50,440	50,440	3	40,113	49,691
CO	27,456	27,456	33,797	33,797	40,139	40,139	2	24,482	36,733
FL	27,030	27,030	27,030	27,030	27,030	27,030	1	.	.
IL	51,783	51,783	51,783	51,783	51,783	51,783	1	.	.
MA	31,533	31,533	31,533	31,533	31,533	31,533	1	.	.
MD	37,690	37,690	37,690	37,690	37,690	37,690	1	29,286	43,722
MO	15,829	15,829	29,010	29,010	42,192	42,192	2	15,829	23,005
OR	21,195	21,195	31,430	31,430	41,664	41,664	2	21,195	27,934
PA	39,312	39,312	42,660	42,660	46,009	46,009	2	39,478	62,670
SC	29,325	29,325	29,325	29,325	29,325	29,325	1	.	.
TN	24,960	24,960	24,960	24,960	24,960	24,960	1	.	.
TX	17,867	21,715	29,255	28,059	36,795	43,035	4	24,378	40,602
WA	40,920	40,920	43,482	43,482	46,044	46,044	2	.	.

Degree Required Data

	Min	Q1	Mean	Median	Q3	Max	N	Range Avg Min	Range Avg Max
High School	15,829	27,030	32,902	31,533	39,312	50,440	9	32,018	40,796
Associate's	21,195	21,195	31,058	31,058	40,920	40,920	2	21,195	27,934
Bachelor's	24,960	28,390	37,988	40,901	44,522	51,783	12	29,406	45,932
Master's	.	.	.	.	.	.	.	.	.
Doctoral	.	.	.	.	.	.	.	.	.

VOLUNTEER COORDINATOR - CONTINUED
Very Large Public Library
(Serving a population of 500,000 or more)
Regional Data

	Min	Q1	Mean	Median	Q3	Max	N	Range Avg Min	Range Avg Max
North Atlantic	41,287	41,287	41,287	41,287	41,287	41,287	1	.	.
Great Lakes & Plains	46,671	47,223	51,011	49,389	54,798	58,594	4	40,726	58,594
Southeast	30,840	38,854	46,486	44,445	48,299	69,994	5	41,996	69,994
West & Southwest	36,400	38,958	51,719	52,971	64,480	64,536	4	29,692	42,546
ALL REGIONS	30,840	41,287	48,903	47,223	58,594	69,994	14	35,527	53,420

State Data

	Min	Q1	Mean	Median	Q3	Max	N	Range Avg Min	Range Avg Max
CA	41,517	41,517	56,826	64,425	64,536	64,536	3	32,552	41,517
FL	30,840	30,840	34,847	34,847	38,854	38,854	2	.	.
GA	44,445	44,445	44,445	44,445	44,445	44,445	1	.	.
IN	47,775	47,775	47,775	47,775	47,775	47,775	1	.	.
MO	46,671	46,671	46,671	46,671	46,671	46,671	1	.	.
NC	48,299	48,299	48,299	48,299	48,299	48,299	1	.	.
NJ	41,287	41,287	41,287	41,287	41,287	41,287	1	.	.
OH	51,003	51,003	54,798	54,798	58,594	58,594	2	40,726	58,594
TX	36,400	36,400	36,400	36,400	36,400	36,400	1	26,832	43,576
VA	69,994	69,994	69,994	69,994	69,994	69,994	1	41,996	69,994

Degree Required Data

	Min	Q1	Mean	Median	Q3	Max	N	Range Avg Min	Range Avg Max
High School	38,854	38,854	51,639	51,639	64,425	64,425	2	.	.
Associate's	69,994	69,994	69,994	69,994	69,994	69,994	1	41,996	69,994
Bachelor's	36,400	44,445	48,804	47,775	51,003	64,536	9	33,370	47,895
Master's	.	.	.	.	.	.		.	.
Doctoral	.	.	.	.	.	.		.	.

VOLUNTEER COORDINATOR - CONTINUED
ALL PUBLIC LIBRARIES
Regional Data

	Min	Q1	Mean	Median	Q3	Max	N	Range Avg Min	Range Avg Max
North Atlantic	31,533	36,130	38,660	38,501	41,287	46,009	6	34,382	53,196
Great Lakes & Plains	15,829	25,147	37,381	41,404	47,223	58,594	16	29,910	39,953
Southeast	24,960	27,030	37,676	30,840	44,445	69,994	9	41,996	69,994
West & Southwest	17,867	32,971	40,573	40,920	46,044	64,536	21	31,745	42,732
ALL REGIONS	15,829	29,662	38,869	39,725	46,026	69,994	52	31,996	44,483

State Data

	Min	Q1	Mean	Median	Q3	Max	N	Range Avg Min	Range Avg Max
AR	25,334	25,334	25,334	25,334	25,334	25,334	1		
AZ	33,217	33,217	33,217	33,217	33,217	33,217	1		
CA	38,228	41,517	51,670	50,440	64,425	64,536	7	39,962	49,530
CO	27,456	27,456	33,797	33,797	40,139	40,139	2	24,482	36,733
FL	27,030	27,030	32,241	30,840	38,854	38,854	3		
GA	44,445	44,445	44,445	44,445	44,445	44,445	1		
IA	16,120	16,120	28,368	28,368	40,616	40,616	2		
IL	22,880	22,880	37,332	37,332	51,783	51,783	2		
IN	47,775	47,775	47,775	47,775	47,775	47,775	1		
MA	31,533	31,533	31,533	31,533	31,533	31,533	1		
MD	37,690	37,690	37,690	37,690	37,690	37,690	1	29,286	43,722
MI	24,960	24,960	30,160	30,160	35,360	35,360	2	29,120	39,520
MN	44,491	44,491	44,491	44,491	44,491	44,491	2	34,861	35,131
MO	15,829	15,829	34,897	42,192	46,671	46,671	3	15,829	23,005
NC	48,299	48,299	48,299	48,299	48,299	48,299	1		
NJ	41,287	41,287	41,287	41,287	41,287	41,287	1		
OH	25,334	27,667	41,233	40,502	54,798	58,594	4	32,396	53,466
OR	21,195	21,195	31,943	32,971	41,664	41,664	3	25,085	32,781
PA	36,130	36,130	40,484	39,312	46,009	46,009	3	39,478	62,670
SC	29,325	29,325	29,325	29,325	29,325	29,325	1		
TN	24,960	24,960	24,960	24,960	24,960	24,960	1		
TX	17,867	25,563	34,455	33,478	43,035	53,308	6	25,605	42,089
VA	69,994	69,994	69,994	69,994	69,994	69,994	1	41,996	69,994
WA	40,920	40,920	43,482	43,482	46,044	46,044	2		

Degree Required Data

	Min	Q1	Mean	Median	Q3	Max	N	Range Avg Min	Range Avg Max
High School	15,829	25,334	32,910	31,533	38,854	64,425	17	29,702	41,312
Associate's	21,195	21,195	44,036	40,920	69,994	69,994	3	31,596	48,964
Bachelor's	22,880	36,130	41,915	42,614	47,775	64,536	30	33,453	45,490
Master's									
Doctoral									

SENIOR ACCOUNTANT

Oversees clerical activities in connection with payables, debits, or credits. Prepares work sheets, analyzes to verify accuracy, prepares monthly journal entries, statements, monthly balance sheet, monthly statements, profit and loss, subsidiary, and other analyses and statements, following prescribed procedures.

Very Small Public Library
(Serving a population of less than 10,000)
Regional Data

	Min	Q1	Mean	Median	Q3	Max	N	Range Avg Min	Range Avg Max
Great Lakes & Plains	35,760	35,760	35,760	35,760	35,760	35,760	1		
West & Southwest	39,000	39,000	44,884	44,884	50,768	50,768	2		
ALL REGIONS	35,760	35,760	41,843	39,000	50,768	50,768	3		

State Data

	Min	Q1	Mean	Median	Q3	Max	N	Range Avg Min	Range Avg Max
CO	50,768	50,768	50,768	50,768	50,768	50,768	1	.	.
OH	35,760	35,760	35,760	35,760	35,760	35,760	1	.	.
TX	39,000	39,000	39,000	39,000	39,000	39,000	1	.	.

Degree Required Data

	Min	Q1	Mean	Median	Q3	Max	N	Range Avg Min	Range Avg Max
High School	.	.	.	.	.	.			
Associate's	35,760	35,760	35,760	35,760	35,760	35,760	1	.	.
Bachelor's	50,768	50,768	50,768	50,768	50,768	50,768	1	.	.
Master's	.	.	.	.	.	.			
Doctoral	.	.	.	.	.	.			

SENIOR ACCOUNTANT - CONTINUED
Small Public Library
(Serving a population of 10,000 to 25,000)
Regional Data

	Min	Q1	Mean	Median	Q3	Max	N	Range Avg Min	Range Avg Max
Great Lakes & Plains	37,398	37,398	37,398	37,398	37,398	37,398	1	.	.
West & Southwest	43,680	43,680	43,680	43,680	43,680	43,680	1	33,280	49,920
ALL REGIONS	37,398	37,398	40,539	40,539	43,680	43,680	2	33,280	49,920

State Data

	Min	Q1	Mean	Median	Q3	Max	N	Range Avg Min	Range Avg Max
NM	43,680	43,680	43,680	43,680	43,680	43,680	1	33,280	49,920
OH	37,398	37,398	37,398	37,398	37,398	37,398	1	.	.

Degree Required Data

	Min	Q1	Mean	Median	Q3	Max	N	Range Avg Min	Range Avg Max
High School	43,680	43,680	43,680	43,680	43,680	43,680	1	33,280	49,920
Associate's	.	.	.	.	.	.			
Bachelor's	37,398	37,398	37,398	37,398	37,398	37,398	1	.	.
Master's	.	.	.	.	.	.			
Doctoral	.	.	.	.	.	.			

SENIOR ACCOUNTANT - CONTINUED
Medium Public Library
(Serving a population of 25,000 to 99,999)
Regional Data

	Min	Q1	Mean	Median	Q3	Max	N	Range Avg Min	Range Avg Max
North Atlantic	30,285	52,851	61,817	57,355	81,704	91,354	6		
Great Lakes & Plains	29,120	37,680	43,464	44,294	48,990	56,909	12	38,251	55,091
Southeast	33,000	33,000	34,709	34,709	36,417	36,417	2		
West & Southwest	41,600	41,600	41,600	41,600	41,600	41,600	1	31,200	41,600
ALL REGIONS	29,120	36,417	47,785	46,966	52,851	91,354	21	37,076	52,842

State Data

	Min	Q1	Mean	Median	Q3	Max	N	Range Avg Min	Range Avg Max
CA	41,600	41,600	41,600	41,600	41,600	41,600	1	31,200	41,600
CT	81,704	81,704	86,529	86,529	91,354	91,354	2		
IL	35,360	42,068	47,991	49,847	53,914	56,909	4	43,833	65,957
IN	46,966	46,966	48,085	48,085	49,204	49,204	2		
LA	36,417	36,417	36,417	36,417	36,417	36,417	1		
ME	59,155	59,155	59,155	59,155	59,155	59,155	1		
NE	29,120	29,120	29,120	29,120	29,120	29,120	1	22,880	31,200
NY	52,851	52,851	54,203	54,203	55,554	55,554	2		
OH	33,485	40,000	40,863	41,101	41,621	48,110	5	36,878	46,384
PA	30,285	30,285	30,285	30,285	30,285	30,285	1		
TN	33,000	33,000	33,000	33,000	33,000	33,000	1		

Degree Required Data

	Min	Q1	Mean	Median	Q3	Max	N	Range Avg Min	Range Avg Max
High School	29,120	41,621	51,441	49,204	55,554	81,704	5	29,879	38,792
Associate's	33,485	33,485	38,728	41,101	41,600	41,600	3	31,200	41,600
Bachelor's	35,360	40,000	50,535	48,110	50,918	91,354	9	43,833	65,957
Master's	33,000	33,000	46,078	46,078	59,155	59,155	2		
Doctoral									

SENIOR ACCOUNTANT - CONTINUED
Large Public Library
(Serving a population of 100,000 to 499,999)
Regional Data

	Min	Q1	Mean	Median	Q3	Max	N	Range Avg Min	Range Avg Max
North Atlantic	28,919	56,222	59,663	68,738	69,680	74,755	5	24,854	28,806
Great Lakes & Plains	41,829	51,409	55,290	55,182	58,729	70,400	12	42,580	63,996
Southeast	20,800	43,786	47,243	50,241	56,540	64,849	5	19,219	30,410
West & Southwest	38,568	52,183	62,559	63,356	76,816	81,078	6	52,797	70,526
ALL REGIONS	20,800	50,820	56,192	55,910	67,618	81,078	28	41,537	59,077

State Data

	Min	Q1	Mean	Median	Q3	Max	N	Range Avg Min	Range Avg Max
AL	20,800	20,800	20,800	20,800	20,800	20,800	1	19,219	30,410
CA	52,183	52,183	66,586	66,498	81,078	81,078	3	52,797	70,526
IL	51,418	51,418	61,052	61,339	70,400	70,400	3	40,539	57,242
IN	43,739	43,739	43,739	43,739	43,739	43,739	1	.	.
MA	56,222	56,222	56,222	56,222	56,222	56,222	1	.	.
MD	68,738	68,738	68,738	68,738	68,738	68,738	1	.	.
MI	51,400	51,400	60,103	60,103	68,806	68,806	2	.	.
MN	41,829	41,829	41,829	41,829	41,829	41,829	1	.	.
NE	52,368	52,368	52,368	52,368	52,368	52,368	1	39,262	52,368
NJ	69,680	69,680	69,680	69,680	69,680	69,680	1	.	.
NY	28,919	28,919	28,919	28,919	28,919	28,919	1	24,854	28,806
OH	55,016	55,016	55,494	55,349	56,118	56,118	3	44,366	70,124
PA	74,755	74,755	74,755	74,755	74,755	74,755	1	.	.
SC	56,540	56,540	56,540	56,540	56,540	56,540	1	.	.
VA	43,786	43,786	52,959	50,241	64,849	64,849	3	.	.
WA	38,568	38,568	58,533	60,214	76,816	76,816	3	.	.
WI	55,702	55,702	55,702	55,702	55,702	55,702	1	.	.

Degree Required Data

	Min	Q1	Mean	Median	Q3	Max	N	Range Avg Min	Range Avg Max
High School	28,919	28,919	38,815	43,739	43,786	43,786	3	24,854	28,806
Associate's	56,118	56,118	56,118	56,118	56,118	56,118	1	41,538	67,787
Bachelor's	20,800	51,418	58,014	56,222	68,806	81,078	23	42,431	61,098
Master's	.	.	.	.	.	.	.	.	.
Doctoral	.	.	.	.	.	.	.	.	.

SENIOR ACCOUNTANT - CONTINUED
Very Large Public Library
(Serving a population of 500,000 or more)
Regional Data

	Min	Q1	Mean	Median	Q3	Max	N	Range Avg Min	Range Avg Max
North Atlantic	53,490	53,490	70,802	71,997	86,918	86,918	3	.	.
Great Lakes & Plains	48,629	60,321	70,710	75,006	81,100	84,200	4	52,822	75,005
Southeast	33,656	58,842	65,400	65,529	82,776	86,070	6	49,726	82,878
West & Southwest	51,803	56,000	60,332	58,094	62,962	74,932	9	50,038	72,194
ALL REGIONS	33,656	56,000	65,029	62,951	74,932	86,918	22	50,656	75,568

State Data

	Min	Q1	Mean	Median	Q3	Max	N	Range Avg Min	Range Avg Max
AZ	54,163	54,163	58,562	58,562	62,962	62,962	2	42,619	63,638
CA	51,803	57,070	63,441	63,514	69,812	74,932	4	61,646	74,932
CO	56,000	56,000	56,000	56,000	56,000	56,000	1	.	.
FL	33,656	33,656	58,216	58,216	82,776	82,776	2	.	.
GA	58,842	58,842	60,891	60,891	62,940	62,940	2	.	.
IN	48,629	48,629	48,629	48,629	48,629	48,629	1	.	.
MD	53,490	53,490	70,204	70,204	86,918	86,918	2	.	.
NJ	71,997	71,997	71,997	71,997	71,997	71,997	1	.	.
OH	78,000	78,000	81,100	81,100	84,200	84,200	2	54,205	78,000
TX	58,094	58,094	58,094	58,094	58,094	58,094	1	53,269	86,570
UT	58,008	58,008	58,008	58,008	58,008	58,008	1	.	.
VA	68,118	68,118	77,094	77,094	86,070	86,070	2	49,726	82,878
WI	72,013	72,013	72,013	72,013	72,013	72,013	1	51,438	72,010

Degree Required Data

	Min	Q1	Mean	Median	Q3	Max	N	Range Avg Min	Range Avg Max
High School	68,118	68,118	77,094	77,094	86,070	86,070	2	49,726	82,878
Associate's	.	.	.	.	.	.	.	.	.
Bachelor's	48,629	55,082	64,235	62,639	73,472	86,918	16	50,966	73,131
Master's	58,842	58,842	71,521	71,521	84,200	84,200	2	.	.
Doctoral	.	.	.	.	.	.	.	.	.

SENIOR ACCOUNTANT - CONTINUED
ALL PUBLIC LIBRARIES
Regional Data

	Min	Q1	Mean	Median	Q3	Max	N	Range Avg Min	Range Avg Max
North Atlantic	28,919	53,490	62,973	63,947	74,755	91,354	14	24,854	28,806
Great Lakes & Plains	29,120	41,621	51,368	50,061	56,118	84,200	30	42,483	62,120
Southeast	20,800	36,417	53,695	56,540	64,849	86,070	13	39,557	65,388
West & Southwest	38,568	50,768	57,547	58,008	64,691	81,078	19	47,003	65,764
ALL REGIONS	20,800	43,710	55,449	55,182	65,673	91,354	76	43,054	62,492

State Data

	Min	Q1	Mean	Median	Q3	Max	N	Range Avg Min	Range Avg Max
AL	20,800	20,800	20,800	20,800	20,800	20,800	1	19,219	30,410
AZ	54,163	54,163	58,562	58,562	62,962	62,962	2	42,619	63,638
CA	41,600	51,993	61,890	63,514	70,715	81,078	8	50,248	65,622
CO	50,768	50,768	53,384	53,384	56,000	56,000	2	.	.
CT	81,704	81,704	86,529	86,529	91,354	91,354	2	.	.
FL	33,656	33,656	58,216	58,216	82,776	82,776	2	.	.
GA	58,842	58,842	60,891	60,891	62,940	62,940	2	.	.
IL	35,360	48,776	53,589	51,418	61,339	70,400	7	43,009	63,778
IN	43,739	45,353	47,135	47,798	48,917	49,204	4	.	.
LA	36,417	36,417	36,417	36,417	36,417	36,417	1	.	.
MA	56,222	56,222	56,222	56,222	56,222	56,222	1	.	.
MD	53,490	53,490	69,715	68,738	86,918	86,918	3	.	.
ME	59,155	59,155	59,155	59,155	59,155	59,155	1	.	.
MI	51,400	51,400	60,103	60,103	68,806	68,806	2	.	.
MN	41,829	41,829	41,829	41,829	41,829	41,829	1	.	.
NE	29,120	29,120	40,744	40,744	52,368	52,368	2	31,071	41,784
NJ	69,680	69,680	70,838	70,838	71,997	71,997	2	.	.
NM	43,680	43,680	43,680	43,680	43,680	43,680	1	33,280	49,920
NY	28,919	28,919	45,775	52,851	55,554	55,554	3	24,854	28,806
OH	33,485	38,699	50,513	44,866	55,734	84,200	12	44,836	66,951
PA	30,285	30,285	52,520	52,520	74,755	74,755	2	.	.
SC	56,540	56,540	56,540	56,540	56,540	56,540	1	.	.
TN	33,000	33,000	33,000	33,000	33,000	33,000	1	.	.
TX	39,000	39,000	48,547	48,547	58,094	58,094	2	53,269	86,570
UT	58,008	58,008	58,008	58,008	58,008	58,008	1	.	.
VA	43,786	50,241	62,613	64,849	68,118	86,070	5	49,726	82,878
WA	38,568	38,568	58,533	60,214	76,816	76,816	3	.	.
WI	55,702	55,702	63,857	63,857	72,013	72,013	2	51,438	72,010

Degree Required Data

	Min	Q1	Mean	Median	Q3	Max	N	Range Avg Min	Range Avg Max
High School	28,919	41,621	51,956	43,786	68,118	86,070	11	36,224	53,678
Associate's	33,485	35,760	41,613	41,101	41,600	56,118	5	36,369	54,694
Bachelor's	20,800	50,768	58,101	56,111	68,738	91,354	50	45,894	66,521
Master's	33,000	45,921	58,799	58,999	71,677	84,200	4	.	.
Doctoral	.	.	.	.	.	.		.	.

ACCOUNTANT

Computes and prepares reports and analyses as requested by organization personnel. Calculates and checks work sheets prior to closing general ledger. Posts, balances, and reconciles general ledger accounts. Prepares profit and loss statement and balance sheets, and compute required financial statements and statistical reports as directed. Computes, checks, and files tax returns.

Very Small Public Library
(Serving a population of less than 10,000)
Regional Data

	Min	Q1	Mean	Median	Q3	Max	N	Range Avg Min	Range Avg Max
Great Lakes & Plains	15,600	15,600	20,263	20,263	24,926	24,926	2	.	.
ALL REGIONS	15,600	15,600	20,263	20,263	24,926	24,926	2	.	.

State Data

	Min	Q1	Mean	Median	Q3	Max	N	Range Avg Min	Range Avg Max
IL	15,600	15,600	15,600	15,600	15,600	15,600	1	.	.
OH	24,926	24,926	24,926	24,926	24,926	24,926	1	.	.

Degree Required Data

	Min	Q1	Mean	Median	Q3	Max	N	Range Avg Min	Range Avg Max
High School	24,926	24,926	24,926	24,926	24,926	24,926	1	.	.
Associate's	.	.	.	.	.	.		.	.
Bachelor's	15,600	15,600	15,600	15,600	15,600	15,600	1	.	.
Master's	.	.	.	.	.	.		.	.
Doctoral	.	.	.	.	.	.		.	.

ACCOUNTANT - CONTINUED
Small Public Library
(Serving a population of 10,000 to 25,000)
Regional Data

	Min	Q1	Mean	Median	Q3	Max	N	Range Avg Min	Range Avg Max
North Atlantic	53,283	53,283	53,283	53,283	53,283	53,283	1	.	.
Great Lakes & Plains	30,118	30,118	30,118	30,118	30,118	30,118	1	.	.
ALL REGIONS	30,118	30,118	41,701	41,701	53,283	53,283	2	.	.

State Data

	Min	Q1	Mean	Median	Q3	Max	N	Range Avg Min	Range Avg Max
NY	53,283	53,283	53,283	53,283	53,283	53,283	1	.	.
OH	30,118	30,118	30,118	30,118	30,118	30,118	1	.	.

Degree Required Data

	Min	Q1	Mean	Median	Q3	Max	N	Range Avg Min	Range Avg Max
High School	30,118	30,118	30,118	30,118	30,118	30,118	1	.	.
Associate's	.	.	.	.	.	.		.	.
Bachelor's	53,283	53,283	53,283	53,283	53,283	53,283	1	.	.
Master's	.	.	.	.	.	.		.	.
Doctoral	.	.	.	.	.	.		.	.

ACCOUNTANT - CONTINUED
Medium Public Library
(Serving a population of 25,000 to 99,999)
Regional Data

	Min	Q1	Mean	Median	Q3	Max	N	Range Avg Min	Range Avg Max
North Atlantic	33,280	33,280	62,317	62,317	91,354	91,354	2	.	.
Great Lakes & Plains	39,042	39,042	42,276	42,276	45,510	45,510	2	37,918	59,342
Southeast	25,450	25,450	29,225	29,225	33,000	33,000	2	.	.
ALL REGIONS	25,450	33,000	44,606	36,161	45,510	91,354	6	37,918	59,342

State Data

	Min	Q1	Mean	Median	Q3	Max	N	Range Avg Min	Range Avg Max
CT	91,354	91,354	91,354	91,354	91,354	91,354	1	.	.
NY	33,280	33,280	33,280	33,280	33,280	33,280	1	.	.
OH	39,042	39,042	42,276	42,276	45,510	45,510	2	37,918	59,342
TN	33,000	33,000	33,000	33,000	33,000	33,000	1	.	.
VA	25,450	25,450	25,450	25,450	25,450	25,450	1	.	.

Degree Required Data

	Min	Q1	Mean	Median	Q3	Max	N	Range Avg Min	Range Avg Max
High School	.	.	.	.	.	.		.	.
Associate's	39,042	39,042	39,042	39,042	39,042	39,042	1	.	.
Bachelor's	25,450	25,450	54,105	45,510	91,354	91,354	3	37,918	59,342
Master's	33,000	33,000	33,000	33,000	33,000	33,000	1	.	.
Doctoral	.	.	.	.	.	.		.	.

ACCOUNTANT - CONTINUED
Large Public Library
(Serving a population of 100,000 to 499,999)
Regional Data

	Min	Q1	Mean	Median	Q3	Max	N	Range Avg Min	Range Avg Max
North Atlantic	43,285	43,285	43,285	43,285	43,285	43,285	1	39,520	49,920
Great Lakes & Plains	19,840	20,053	33,640	36,574	43,389	45,411	6	29,120	33,280
Southeast	41,627	41,627	46,032	45,926	50,544	50,544	3	.	.
West & Southwest	44,450	47,528	50,899	51,427	54,271	56,293	4	36,369	47,528
ALL REGIONS	19,840	38,649	41,916	43,919	50,544	56,293	14	35,344	44,564

State Data

	Min	Q1	Mean	Median	Q3	Max	N	Range Avg Min	Range Avg Max
CA	44,450	44,450	49,101	50,606	52,248	52,248	3	36,369	47,528
CO	56,293	56,293	56,293	56,293	56,293	56,293	1	.	.
FL	45,926	45,926	45,926	45,926	45,926	45,926	1	.	.
GA	50,544	50,544	50,544	50,544	50,544	50,544	1	.	.
IL	20,053	20,053	20,053	20,053	20,053	20,053	1	29,120	33,280
MI	34,500	34,500	38,945	38,945	43,389	43,389	2	.	.
OH	19,840	19,840	29,244	29,244	38,649	38,649	2	.	.
PA	43,285	43,285	43,285	43,285	43,285	43,285	1	39,520	49,920
VA	41,627	41,627	41,627	41,627	41,627	41,627	1	.	.
WI	45,411	45,411	45,411	45,411	45,411	45,411	1	.	.

Degree Required Data

	Min	Q1	Mean	Median	Q3	Max	N	Range Avg Min	Range Avg Max
High School	19,840	41,627	40,162	43,389	45,411	50,544	5	.	.
Associate's	20,053	20,053	32,613	34,500	43,285	43,285	3	34,320	41,600
Bachelor's	38,649	42,287	48,279	49,087	54,271	56,293	4	.	.
Master's	.	.	.	.	.	.		.	.
Doctoral	.	.	.	.	.	.		.	.

ACCOUNTANT - CONTINUED
Very Large Public Library
(Serving a population of 500,000 or more)
Regional Data

	Min	Q1	Mean	Median	Q3	Max	N	Range Avg Min	Range Avg Max
North Atlantic	46,111	46,111	46,111	46,111	46,111	46,111	1	.	.
Great Lakes & Plains	31,347	38,509	52,558	54,990	66,607	68,904	4	.	.
Southeast	26,597	30,418	38,729	36,610	47,272	55,494	13	29,784	49,639
West & Southwest	41,175	51,620	60,261	63,378	68,902	73,112	4	48,963	73,112
ALL REGIONS	26,597	32,350	45,493	43,968	55,494	73,112	22	32,181	52,573

State Data

	Min	Q1	Mean	Median	Q3	Max	N	Range Avg Min	Range Avg Max
AZ	73,112	73,112	73,112	73,112	73,112	73,112	1	48,963	73,112
CA	41,175	41,175	55,977	62,064	64,691	64,691	3	.	.
FL	26,597	26,783	32,897	31,789	39,011	41,413	4	.	.
GA	42,264	42,264	42,264	42,264	42,264	42,264	1	.	.
IN	31,347	31,347	31,347	31,347	31,347	31,347	1	.	.
MD	46,111	46,111	46,111	46,111	46,111	46,111	1	.	.
MI	45,671	45,671	45,671	45,671	45,671	45,671	1	.	.
MO	64,309	64,309	64,309	64,309	64,309	64,309	1	.	.
NC	53,237	53,237	53,237	53,237	53,237	53,237	1	.	.
OH	68,904	68,904	68,904	68,904	68,904	68,904	1	.	.
VA	30,344	30,418	39,483	32,737	47,767	55,494	7	29,784	49,639

Degree Required Data

	Min	Q1	Mean	Median	Q3	Max	N	Range Avg Min	Range Avg Max
High School	30,344	31,384	40,257	39,204	47,520	55,494	8	29,784	49,639
Associate's	31,347	31,347	31,347	31,347	31,347	31,347	1	.	.
Bachelor's	36,610	41,413	53,990	53,237	64,691	73,112	11	48,963	73,112
Master's	.	.	.	.	.	.	.	.	.
Doctoral	.	.	.	.	.	.	.	.	.

ACCOUNTANT - CONTINUED
ALL PUBLIC LIBRARIES
Regional Data

	Min	Q1	Mean	Median	Q3	Max	N	Range Avg Min	Range Avg Max
North Atlantic	33,280	43,285	53,463	46,111	53,283	91,354	5	39,520	49,920
Great Lakes & Plains	15,600	24,926	37,818	38,649	45,510	68,904	15	33,519	46,311
Southeast	25,450	30,418	38,890	39,011	47,272	55,494	18	29,784	49,639
West & Southwest	41,175	47,528	55,580	54,271	63,378	73,112	8	40,567	56,056
ALL REGIONS	15,600	32,350	43,027	42,774	50,606	91,354	46	33,596	50,629

State Data

	Min	Q1	Mean	Median	Q3	Max	N	Range Avg Min	Range Avg Max
AZ	73,112	73,112	73,112	73,112	73,112	73,112	1	48,963	73,112
CA	41,175	44,450	52,539	51,427	62,064	64,691	6	36,369	47,528
CO	56,293	56,293	56,293	56,293	56,293	56,293	1	.	.
CT	91,354	91,354	91,354	91,354	91,354	91,354	1	.	.
FL	26,597	26,969	35,503	36,610	41,413	45,926	5	.	.
GA	42,264	42,264	46,404	46,404	50,544	50,544	2	.	.
IL	15,600	15,600	17,827	17,827	20,053	20,053	2	29,120	33,280
IN	31,347	31,347	31,347	31,347	31,347	31,347	1	.	.
MD	46,111	46,111	46,111	46,111	46,111	46,111	1	.	.
MI	34,500	34,500	41,187	43,389	45,671	45,671	3	.	.
MO	64,309	64,309	64,309	64,309	64,309	64,309	1	.	.
NC	53,237	53,237	53,237	53,237	53,237	53,237	1	.	.
NY	33,280	33,280	43,282	43,282	53,283	53,283	2	.	.
OH	19,840	24,926	38,141	38,649	45,510	68,904	7	37,918	59,342
PA	43,285	43,285	43,285	43,285	43,285	43,285	1	39,520	49,920
TN	33,000	33,000	33,000	33,000	33,000	33,000	1	.	.
VA	25,450	30,418	38,162	32,737	47,272	55,494	9	29,784	49,639
WI	45,411	45,411	45,411	45,411	45,411	45,411	1	.	.

Degree Required Data

	Min	Q1	Mean	Median	Q3	Max	N	Range Avg Min	Range Avg Max
High School	19,840	30,344	38,527	41,627	47,272	55,494	15	29,784	49,639
Associate's	20,053	31,347	33,645	34,500	39,042	43,285	5	34,320	41,600
Bachelor's	15,600	41,294	50,910	49,180	63,187	91,354	20	43,441	66,227
Master's	33,000	33,000	33,000	33,000	33,000	33,000	1	.	.
Doctoral	.	.	.	.	.	.	.	.	.

BOOKKEEPER

Performs diversified duties in maintaining accounting records. Verifies credits and deductions. Checks allocation of charges on bills payable. Maintains and balances petty cash account. Pays minor expenses, prepares daily cash balance figures, and weekly transaction report. Checks employee expense accounts. Prepares monthly receipts and disbursement summaries, takes trial balances, locates discrepancies, and reconciles bank statements. Compiles special reports. Analyzes facts to determine action to be taken, within the limits of standard practice.

Very Small Public Library
(Serving a population of less than 10,000)
Regional Data

	Min	Q1	Mean	Median	Q3	Max	N	Range Avg Min	Range Avg Max
North Atlantic	34,840	34,840	34,840	34,840	34,840	34,840	1	24,960	35,360
Great Lakes & Plains	18,928	18,928	18,928	18,928	18,928	18,928	1	14,560	20,800
ALL REGIONS	18,928	18,928	26,884	26,884	34,840	34,840	2	19,760	28,080

State Data

	Min	Q1	Mean	Median	Q3	Max	N	Range Avg Min	Range Avg Max
IN	18,928	18,928	18,928	18,928	18,928	18,928	1	14,560	20,800
NJ	34,840	34,840	34,840	34,840	34,840	34,840	1	24,960	35,360

Degree Required Data

	Min	Q1	Mean	Median	Q3	Max	N	Range Avg Min	Range Avg Max
High School	18,928	18,928	26,884	26,884	34,840	34,840	2	19,760	28,080
Associate's	.	.	.	.	.	.	.	.	.
Bachelor's	.	.	.	.	.	.	.	.	.
Master's	.	.	.	.	.	.	.	.	.
Doctoral	.	.	.	.	.	.	.	.	.

BOOKKEEPER - CONTINUED
Small Public Library
(Serving a population of 10,000 to 25,000)
Regional Data

	Min	Q1	Mean	Median	Q3	Max	N	Range Avg Min	Range Avg Max
North Atlantic	22,360	33,252	39,650	42,058	46,459	51,302	8	25,764	36,705
Great Lakes & Plains	16,120	22,253	30,127	27,747	39,568	45,760	8	22,360	35,100
Southeast	18,571	18,571	20,752	20,752	22,932	22,932	2		
West & Southwest	38,800	38,800	38,800	38,800	38,800	38,800	1		
ALL REGIONS	16,120	22,932	33,606	36,920	42,515	51,302	19	23,819	35,788

State Data

	Min	Q1	Mean	Median	Q3	Max	N	Range Avg Min	Range Avg Max
AZ	38,800	38,800	38,800	38,800	38,800	38,800	1	.	.
IL	16,120	18,720	27,612	24,284	36,504	45,760	4	27,040	41,600
IN	28,246	28,246	32,583	32,583	36,920	36,920	2	18,720	30,160
KS	23,185	23,185	23,185	23,185	23,185	23,185	1	16,640	27,040
NC	18,571	18,571	20,752	20,752	22,932	22,932	2	.	.
NJ	40,000	40,000	47,193	50,278	51,302	51,302	3	.	.
NY	26,504	26,504	36,915	41,600	42,640	42,640	3	41,600	42,640
OH	42,216	42,216	42,216	42,216	42,216	42,216	1	.	.
PA	22,360	22,360	22,360	22,360	22,360	22,360	1	10,712	24,960
RI	42,515	42,515	42,515	42,515	42,515	42,515	1	24,981	42,515

Degree Required Data

	Min	Q1	Mean	Median	Q3	Max	N	Range Avg Min	Range Avg Max
High School	16,120	22,360	28,050	26,876	36,920	41,600	10	17,437	28,080
Associate's	23,185	23,185	37,244	37,244	51,302	51,302	2	16,640	27,040
Bachelor's	38,800	42,515	43,999	42,640	45,760	50,278	5	32,594	46,412
Master's	.	.	.	.	.	.	.	.	.
Doctoral	.	.	.	.	.	.	.	.	.

BOOKKEEPER - CONTINUED
Medium Public Library
(Serving a population of 25,000 to 99,999)
Regional Data

	Min	Q1	Mean	Median	Q3	Max	N	Range Avg Min	Range Avg Max
North Atlantic	13,789	21,500	40,791	35,821	52,137	87,399	11	.	.
Great Lakes & Plains	23,275	27,248	34,238	33,500	37,440	54,350	11	27,149	35,984
Southeast	18,720	25,961	27,013	28,080	29,303	33,000	5	.	.
West & Southwest	27,581	27,581	29,754	29,754	31,928	31,928	2	26,458	34,622
ALL REGIONS	13,789	26,686	35,169	31,928	37,053	87,399	29	26,919	35,530

State Data

	Min	Q1	Mean	Median	Q3	Max	N	Range Avg Min	Range Avg Max
CA	27,581	27,581	27,581	27,581	27,581	27,581	1	26,312	31,990
CT	75,714	75,714	75,714	75,714	75,714	75,714	1	.	.
ID	31,928	31,928	31,928	31,928	31,928	31,928	1	26,603	37,253
IL	34,274	34,801	42,236	40,159	49,670	54,350	4	31,990	50,648
IN	23,275	23,275	27,821	26,686	33,500	33,500	3	23,275	32,469
LA	25,961	25,961	25,961	25,961	25,961	25,961	1	.	.
MA	19,906	19,906	33,930	37,053	44,831	44,831	3	.	.
MI	27,248	27,248	27,248	27,248	27,248	27,248	1	25,813	27,248
MS	28,080	28,080	28,692	28,692	29,303	29,303	2	.	.
NJ	35,348	35,348	61,373	61,373	87,399	87,399	2	.	.
NY	35,821	35,821	43,979	43,979	52,137	52,137	2	.	.
OH	28,954	28,954	32,323	30,576	37,440	37,440	3	27,518	33,571
PA	13,789	13,789	20,166	21,500	25,209	25,209	3	.	.
TN	33,000	33,000	33,000	33,000	33,000	33,000	1	.	.
WV	18,720	18,720	18,720	18,720	18,720	18,720	1	.	.

Degree Required Data

	Min	Q1	Mean	Median	Q3	Max	N	Range Avg Min	Range Avg Max
High School	25,209	29,128	46,438	36,394	63,926	87,399	8	27,518	33,571
Associate's	19,906	23,275	30,337	27,581	35,328	54,350	9	27,193	38,369
Bachelor's	18,720	26,686	31,525	31,928	34,274	44,990	7	26,603	37,253
Master's	33,000	33,000	33,000	33,000	33,000	33,000	1	.	.
Doctoral	.	.	.	.	.	.	.	.	.

BOOKKEEPER - CONTINUED
Large Public Library
(Serving a population of 100,000 to 499,999)
Regional Data

	Min	Q1	Mean	Median	Q3	Max	N	Range Avg Min	Range Avg Max
North Atlantic	31,200	31,949	36,819	39,125	40,209	41,613	5	31,200	41,600
Great Lakes & Plains	22,559	26,664	35,163	33,583	36,909	68,334	14	28,649	43,437
Southeast	21,844	25,168	31,293	30,912	37,589	39,774	15	29,450	38,955
ALL REGIONS	21,844	26,999	33,699	33,166	37,898	68,334	34	29,390	40,418

State Data

	Min	Q1	Mean	Median	Q3	Max	N	Range Avg Min	Range Avg Max
AL	38,480	38,480	38,480	38,480	38,480	38,480	1	36,774	44,886
FL	24,211	25,605	31,674	32,294	37,743	37,898	4	26,437	39,478
GA	32,781	32,781	32,781	32,781	32,781	32,781	1	32,781	33,821
IL	25,854	26,259	34,989	30,140	43,720	53,823	4	.	.
IN	24,250	24,250	24,250	24,250	24,250	24,250	1	.	.
KS	39,125	39,125	39,125	39,125	39,125	39,125	1	26,395	43,992
LA	33,592	33,592	33,592	33,592	33,592	33,592	1	33,592	46,176
MD	39,125	39,125	39,667	39,667	40,209	40,209	2	.	.
MI	36,909	36,909	52,622	52,622	68,334	68,334	2	.	.
MN	28,371	28,371	31,186	31,186	34,000	34,000	2	.	.
MS	21,844	21,844	21,844	21,844	21,844	21,844	1	.	.
NC	24,223	24,223	29,944	28,169	37,440	37,440	3	24,960	43,680
NY	41,613	41,613	41,613	41,613	41,613	41,613	1	.	.
OH	22,559	22,559	25,642	25,642	28,725	28,725	2	26,000	42,640
PA	31,200	31,200	31,574	31,574	31,949	31,949	2	31,200	41,600
SC	30,912	30,912	30,912	30,912	30,912	30,912	1	.	.
TN	30,319	30,319	30,319	30,319	30,319	30,319	1	.	.
VA	25,168	25,168	32,471	32,471	39,774	39,774	2	25,168	25,168
WI	33,550	33,550	35,027	35,027	36,504	36,504	2	33,550	43,680

Degree Required Data

	Min	Q1	Mean	Median	Q3	Max	N	Range Avg Min	Range Avg Max
High School	22,559	25,511	31,180	30,615	37,960	39,774	12	28,967	37,911
Associate's	21,844	28,725	35,311	33,550	37,589	68,334	17	29,549	41,358
Bachelor's	24,223	26,297	32,428	32,640	38,559	40,209	4	.	.
Master's	.	.	.	.	.	.		.	.
Doctoral	.	.	.	.	.	.		.	.

BOOKKEEPER - CONTINUED
Very Large Public Library
(Serving a population of 500,000 or more)
Regional Data

	Min	Q1	Mean	Median	Q3	Max	N	Range Avg Min	Range Avg Max
North Atlantic	36,164	36,789	38,171	37,816	39,553	40,887	4	.	.
Great Lakes & Plains	33,316	37,516	42,352	43,754	47,187	48,582	4	35,266	39,218
Southeast	25,433	27,088	33,729	32,263	38,649	48,401	8	33,331	55,551
West & Southwest	30,347	31,331	36,712	34,251	40,612	50,960	8	29,033	39,208
ALL REGIONS	25,433	31,331	36,901	36,531	41,301	50,960	24	30,896	41,026

State Data

	Min	Q1	Mean	Median	Q3	Max	N	Range Avg Min	Range Avg Max
AZ	30,347	30,347	37,284	37,284	44,221	44,221	2	30,347	44,221
CA	30,549	31,331	37,499	34,244	43,668	50,960	4	27,976	34,153
GA	25,433	27,088	30,852	27,648	36,686	40,612	6	.	.
MD	36,164	36,164	36,789	36,789	37,414	37,414	2	.	.
NC	36,319	36,319	36,319	36,319	36,319	36,319	1	.	.
NJ	38,218	38,218	39,553	39,553	40,887	40,887	2	.	.
OH	45,793	45,793	47,187	47,187	48,582	48,582	2	.	.
TX	32,126	32,126	34,565	34,565	37,003	37,003	2	29,578	44,346
VA	48,401	48,401	48,401	48,401	48,401	48,401	1	33,331	55,551
WI	33,316	33,316	37,516	37,516	41,715	41,715	2	35,266	39,218

Degree Required Data

	Min	Q1	Mean	Median	Q3	Max	N	Range Avg Min	Range Avg Max
High School	25,433	32,112	37,776	36,376	45,793	50,960	15	31,299	39,408
Associate's	30,347	30,347	37,284	37,284	44,221	44,221	2	30,347	44,221
Bachelor's	36,319	36,319	36,319	36,319	36,319	36,319	1	.	.
Master's	.	.	.	.	.	.	.	.	.
Doctoral	.	.	.	.	.	.	.	.	.

BOOKKEEPER - CONTINUED
ALL PUBLIC LIBRARIES
Regional Data

	Min	Q1	Mean	Median	Q3	Max	N	Range Avg Min	Range Avg Max
North Atlantic	13,789	31,949	39,225	38,218	42,515	87,399	29	26,691	37,415
Great Lakes & Plains	16,120	26,686	34,165	33,525	39,125	68,334	38	26,363	36,706
Southeast	18,571	25,433	30,527	28,755	36,686	48,401	30	29,935	41,030
West & Southwest	27,581	30,549	35,637	32,126	38,800	50,960	11	28,389	38,061
ALL REGIONS	13,789	27,088	34,663	33,571	39,450	87,399	108	27,689	38,105

State Data

	Min	Q1	Mean	Median	Q3	Max	N	Range Avg Min	Range Avg Max
AL	38,480	38,480	38,480	38,480	38,480	38,480	1	36,774	44,886
AZ	30,347	30,347	37,789	38,800	44,221	44,221	3	30,347	44,221
CA	27,581	30,549	35,516	32,112	36,376	50,960	5	27,560	33,613
CT	75,714	75,714	75,714	75,714	75,714	75,714	1	.	.
FL	24,211	25,605	31,674	32,294	37,743	37,898	4	26,437	39,478
GA	25,433	27,088	31,128	28,207	36,686	40,612	7	32,781	33,821
ID	31,928	31,928	31,928	31,928	31,928	31,928	1	26,603	37,253
IL	16,120	26,259	34,946	33,945	45,375	54,350	12	28,690	44,616
IN	18,928	23,275	27,401	26,686	33,500	36,920	7	18,852	27,810
KS	23,185	23,185	31,155	31,155	39,125	39,125	2	21,518	35,516
LA	25,961	25,961	29,777	29,777	33,592	33,592	2	33,592	46,176
MA	19,906	19,906	33,930	37,053	44,831	44,831	3	.	.
MD	36,164	36,789	38,228	38,270	39,667	40,209	4	.	.
MI	27,248	27,248	44,164	36,909	68,334	68,334	3	25,813	27,248
MN	28,371	28,371	31,186	31,186	34,000	34,000	2	.	.
MS	21,844	21,844	26,409	28,080	29,303	29,303	3	.	.
NC	18,571	22,932	27,942	26,196	36,319	37,440	6	24,960	43,680
NJ	34,840	36,783	47,284	40,443	50,790	87,399	8	24,960	35,360
NY	26,504	35,821	40,052	41,606	42,640	52,137	6	41,600	42,640
OH	22,559	28,839	35,606	34,008	44,005	48,582	8	26,759	38,106
PA	13,789	21,500	24,334	23,785	31,200	31,949	6	20,956	33,280
RI	42,515	42,515	42,515	42,515	42,515	42,515	1	24,981	42,515
SC	30,912	30,912	30,912	30,912	30,912	30,912	1	.	.
TN	30,319	30,319	31,659	31,659	33,000	33,000	2	.	.
TX	32,126	32,126	34,565	34,565	37,003	37,003	2	29,578	44,346
VA	25,168	25,168	37,781	39,774	48,401	48,401	3	29,249	40,359
WI	33,316	33,433	36,271	35,027	39,109	41,715	4	34,694	40,706
WV	18,720	18,720	18,720	18,720	18,720	18,720	1	.	.

Degree Required Data

	Min	Q1	Mean	Median	Q3	Max	N	Range Avg Min	Range Avg Max
High School	16,120	26,504	35,034	33,316	39,774	87,399	47	26,270	34,944
Associate's	19,906	26,999	34,079	32,365	37,589	68,334	30	28,236	40,104
Bachelor's	18,720	30,576	35,688	36,319	42,515	50,278	17	31,096	44,122
Master's	33,000	33,000	33,000	33,000	33,000	33,000	1	.	.
Doctoral	.	.	.	.	.	.		.	.

PAYROLL ADMINISTRATOR

Makes a variety of computations on employee overtime, shift premium, and various payroll deductions, following standard procedures, to prepare payroll. Summarizes and reconciles payroll sheets. Investigates and resolves payroll problems, responding to employee requests. Maintains and updates data base records. Generates federal and state tax documents. Prepares special payroll analysis reports.

Small Public Library
(Serving a population of 10,000 to 25,000)
Regional Data

	Min	Q1	Mean	Median	Q3	Max	N	Range Avg Min	Range Avg Max
Great Lakes & Plains	24,960	24,960	29,280	29,280	33,600	33,600	2	24,960	39,520
ALL REGIONS	24,960	24,960	29,280	29,280	33,600	33,600	2	24,960	39,520

State Data

	Min	Q1	Mean	Median	Q3	Max	N	Range Avg Min	Range Avg Max
IN	24,960	24,960	24,960	24,960	24,960	24,960	1	24,960	39,520
OH	33,600	33,600	33,600	33,600	33,600	33,600	1	.	.

Degree Required Data

	Min	Q1	Mean	Median	Q3	Max	N	Range Avg Min	Range Avg Max
High School	33,600	33,600	33,600	33,600	33,600	33,600	1	.	.
Associate's	24,960	24,960	24,960	24,960	24,960	24,960	1	24,960	39,520
Bachelor's	.	.	.	.	.	.		.	.
Master's	.	.	.	.	.	.		.	.
Doctoral	.	.	.	.	.	.		.	.

PAYROLL ADMINISTRATOR - CONTINUED
Medium Public Library
(Serving a population of 25,000 to 99,999)
Regional Data

	Min	Q1	Mean	Median	Q3	Max	N	Range Avg Min	Range Avg Max
North Atlantic	39,333	41,954	49,390	47,944	56,826	62,338	4	.	.
Great Lakes & Plains	21,715	21,715	26,031	26,031	30,347	30,347	2	19,386	33,051
Southeast	33,000	33,000	33,000	33,000	33,000	33,000	1	.	.
ALL REGIONS	21,715	30,347	40,374	39,333	51,314	62,338	7	19,386	33,051

State Data

	Min	Q1	Mean	Median	Q3	Max	N	Range Avg Min	Range Avg Max
CT	44,574	44,574	52,742	51,314	62,338	62,338	3	.	.
IL	30,347	30,347	30,347	30,347	30,347	30,347	1	18,512	28,350
ME	39,333	39,333	39,333	39,333	39,333	39,333	1	.	.
OH	21,715	21,715	21,715	21,715	21,715	21,715	1	20,259	37,752
TN	33,000	33,000	33,000	33,000	33,000	33,000	1	.	.

Degree Required Data

	Min	Q1	Mean	Median	Q3	Max	N	Range Avg Min	Range Avg Max
High School	21,715	26,031	41,429	40,830	56,826	62,338	4	19,386	33,051
Associate's									
Bachelor's	39,333	39,333	41,954	41,954	44,574	44,574	2		
Master's	33,000	33,000	33,000	33,000	33,000	33,000	1		
Doctoral									

PAYROLL ADMINISTRATOR - CONTINUED
Large Public Library
(Serving a population of 100,000 to 499,999)
Regional Data

	Min	Q1	Mean	Median	Q3	Max	N	Range Avg Min	Range Avg Max
North Atlantic	20,725	31,990	39,585	38,181	55,390	55,848	7	34,542	45,067
Great Lakes & Plains	24,648	27,238	34,862	33,781	43,186	45,841	8	25,220	37,304
Southeast	23,168	24,032	31,764	35,768	37,516	38,334	5		
West & Southwest	23,291	33,550	36,613	37,608	39,291	49,920	9	28,492	37,253
ALL REGIONS	20,725	29,723	36,011	35,768	40,310	55,848	29	28,630	39,076

State Data

	Min	Q1	Mean	Median	Q3	Max	N	Range Avg Min	Range Avg Max
CA	24,419	28,985	35,360	33,550	41,735	49,920	4	29,494	37,383
CO	39,291	39,291	39,291	39,291	39,291	39,291	1	24,482	36,733
FL	24,032	24,032	24,032	24,032	24,032	24,032	1		
IL	29,723	29,723	29,723	29,723	29,723	29,723	1	29,723	41,974
KS	34,861	34,861	34,861	34,861	34,861	34,861	1	26,395	43,992
MD	20,725	20,725	36,923	34,653	55,390	55,390	3	41,288	61,922
MI	44,359	44,359	44,359	44,359	44,359	44,359	1		
MO	24,648	24,648	24,648	24,648	24,648	24,648	1	23,920	34,757
MS	23,168	23,168	23,168	23,168	23,168	23,168	1		
NE	32,702	32,702	32,702	32,702	32,702	32,702	1	23,993	32,702
NY	31,990	31,990	36,827	38,181	40,310	40,310	3	31,169	36,639
OH	24,752	24,752	33,382	33,382	42,012	42,012	2	22,069	33,093
PA	55,848	55,848	55,848	55,848	55,848	55,848	1		
SC	37,516	37,516	37,516	37,516	37,516	37,516	1		
TX	23,291	23,291	30,834	30,834	38,376	38,376	2		
VA	35,768	35,768	37,051	37,051	38,334	38,334	2		
WA	37,608	37,608	43,561	43,561	49,513	49,513	2		
WI	45,841	45,841	45,841	45,841	45,841	45,841	1		

Degree Required Data

	Min	Q1	Mean	Median	Q3	Max	N	Range Avg Min	Range Avg Max
High School	20,725	31,990	37,844	38,334	45,841	55,848	13	31,115	39,575
Associate's	23,168	34,861	34,702	36,642	37,608	39,291	6	25,438	40,362
Bachelor's	24,648	33,330	41,602	43,186	49,875	55,390	4	32,604	48,339
Master's									
Doctoral									

PAYROLL ADMINISTRATOR - CONTINUED
Very Large Public Library
(Serving a population of 500,000 or more)
Regional Data

	Min	Q1	Mean	Median	Q3	Max	N	Range Avg Min	Range Avg Max
North Atlantic	22,859	22,859	28,453	25,558	34,047	39,837	4		
Great Lakes & Plains	33,051	47,676	48,512	52,725	53,290	55,821	5	32,417	47,445
Southeast	28,067	37,057	47,288	43,355	46,039	85,859	6		
West & Southwest	28,912	31,600	41,939	40,186	49,812	65,702	11	35,315	46,850
ALL REGIONS	22,859	31,600	42,363	40,186	49,812	85,859	26	34,671	46,982

State Data

	Min	Q1	Mean	Median	Q3	Max	N	Range Avg Min	Range Avg Max
AZ	28,912	28,912	28,912	28,912	28,912	28,912	1	27,706	40,851
CA	40,186	40,186	48,104	44,999	52,554	65,702	6	38,474	46,565
CO	31,600	31,600	31,600	31,600	31,600	31,600	1		
FL	28,067	28,067	35,659	37,057	41,853	41,853	3		
GA	44,856	44,856	45,448	45,448	46,039	46,039	2		
IN	52,725	52,725	52,725	52,725	52,725	52,725	1		
MD	39,837	39,837	39,837	39,837	39,837	39,837	1		
MI	47,676	47,676	47,676	47,676	47,676	47,676	1		
NC	85,859	85,859	85,859	85,859	85,859	85,859	1		
NJ	22,859	22,859	24,659	22,859	28,257	28,257	3		
OH	33,051	33,051	47,387	53,290	55,821	55,821	3	32,417	47,445
TX	31,195	31,195	37,916	37,916	44,637	44,637	2	39,686	64,480
UT	36,358	36,358	36,358	36,358	36,358	36,358	1	25,917	36,358

Degree Required Data

	Min	Q1	Mean	Median	Q3	Max	N	Range Avg Min	Range Avg Max
High School	28,912	35,516	43,664	46,858	51,183	53,290	8	32,365	47,070
Associate's	31,600	32,326	43,299	42,888	54,273	55,821	4	27,810	41,600
Bachelor's	41,853	44,637	56,581	44,856	65,702	85,859	5	46,870	65,091
Master's									
Doctoral									

PAYROLL ADMINISTRATOR - CONTINUED
ALL PUBLIC LIBRARIES
Regional Data

	Min	Q1	Mean	Median	Q3	Max	N	Range Avg Min	Range Avg Max
North Atlantic	20,725	28,257	39,231	39,333	51,314	62,338	15	34,542	45,067
Great Lakes & Plains	21,715	29,723	37,181	33,600	45,841	55,821	17	25,466	38,703
Southeast	23,168	30,533	39,629	37,286	43,355	85,859	12		
West & Southwest	23,291	32,575	39,542	38,834	47,075	65,702	20	32,472	42,851
ALL REGIONS	20,725	30,771	38,859	37,894	45,348	85,859	64	29,918	41,458

State Data

	Min	Q1	Mean	Median	Q3	Max	N	Range Avg Min	Range Avg Max
AZ	28,912	28,912	28,912	28,912	28,912	28,912	1	27,706	40,851
CA	24,419	33,550	43,006	40,186	49,920	65,702	10	33,984	41,974
CO	31,600	31,600	35,446	35,446	39,291	39,291	2	24,482	36,733
CT	44,574	44,574	52,742	51,314	62,338	62,338	3	.	.
FL	24,032	26,049	32,752	32,562	39,455	41,853	4	.	.
GA	44,856	44,856	45,448	45,448	46,039	46,039	2	.	.
IL	29,723	29,723	30,035	30,035	30,347	30,347	2	24,118	35,162
IN	24,960	24,960	38,843	38,843	52,725	52,725	2	24,960	39,520
KS	34,861	34,861	34,861	34,861	34,861	34,861	1	26,395	43,992
MD	20,725	27,689	37,651	37,245	47,614	55,390	4	41,288	61,922
ME	39,333	39,333	39,333	39,333	39,333	39,333	1	.	.
MI	44,359	44,359	46,018	46,018	47,676	47,676	2	.	.
MO	24,648	24,648	24,648	24,648	24,648	24,648	1	23,920	34,757
MS	23,168	23,168	23,168	23,168	23,168	23,168	1	.	.
NC	85,859	85,859	85,859	85,859	85,859	85,859	1	.	.
NE	32,702	32,702	32,702	32,702	32,702	32,702	1	23,993	32,702
NJ	22,859	22,859	24,659	22,859	28,257	28,257	3	.	.
NY	31,990	31,990	36,827	38,181	40,310	40,310	3	31,169	36,639
OH	21,715	24,752	37,749	33,600	53,290	55,821	7	26,790	41,434
PA	55,848	55,848	55,848	55,848	55,848	55,848	1	.	.
SC	37,516	37,516	37,516	37,516	37,516	37,516	1	.	.
TN	33,000	33,000	33,000	33,000	33,000	33,000	1	.	.
TX	23,291	27,243	34,375	34,785	41,506	44,637	4	39,686	64,480
UT	36,358	36,358	36,358	36,358	36,358	36,358	1	25,917	36,358
VA	35,768	35,768	37,051	37,051	38,334	38,334	2	.	.
WA	37,608	37,608	43,561	43,561	49,513	49,513	2	.	.
WI	45,841	45,841	45,841	45,841	45,841	45,841	1	.	.

Degree Required Data

	Min	Q1	Mean	Median	Q3	Max	N	Range Avg Min	Range Avg Max
High School	20,725	31,195	40,023	39,107	49,812	62,338	26	28,786	39,791
Associate's	23,168	31,600	36,943	35,768	39,291	55,821	11	25,912	40,461
Bachelor's	24,648	41,853	48,475	44,574	55,390	85,859	11	39,737	56,715
Master's	33,000	33,000	33,000	33,000	33,000	33,000	1	.	.
Doctoral	.	.	.	.	.	.	.	.	.

HUMAN RESOURCES MANAGER

General responsibility for all personnel activities, such as employment, training, wage and salary administration, safety and working conditions, employee counseling, and personnel records. Investigates, advises, and prepares policies affecting personnel, and consults and advises on interpretation and administration. Conducts union contract negotiations as required. Advises management on interpretation of policy.

Very Small Public Library
(Serving a population of less than 10,000)
Regional Data

	Min	Q1	Mean	Median	Q3	Max	N	Range Avg Min	Range Avg Max
Great Lakes & Plains	37,440	37,440	37,440	37,440	37,440	37,440	1	.	.
ALL REGIONS	37,440	37,440	37,440	37,440	37,440	37,440	1	.	.

State Data

	Min	Q1	Mean	Median	Q3	Max	N	Range Avg Min	Range Avg Max
MI	37,440	37,440	37,440	37,440	37,440	37,440	1	.	.

Degree Required Data

	Min	Q1	Mean	Median	Q3	Max	N	Range Avg Min	Range Avg Max
High School	.	.	.	.	.	.		.	.
Associate's	.	.	.	.	.	.		.	.
Bachelor's	37,440	37,440	37,440	37,440	37,440	37,440	1	.	.
Master's	.	.	.	.	.	.		.	.
Doctoral	.	.	.	.	.	.		.	.

HUMAN RESOURCES MANAGER - CONTINUED
Small Public Library
(Serving a population of 10,000 to 25,000)
Regional Data

	Min	Q1	Mean	Median	Q3	Max	N	Range Avg Min	Range Avg Max
Great Lakes & Plains	45,760	45,760	45,760	45,760	45,760	45,760	1	31,200	54,080
ALL REGIONS	45,760	45,760	45,760	45,760	45,760	45,760	1	31,200	54,080

State Data

	Min	Q1	Mean	Median	Q3	Max	N	Range Avg Min	Range Avg Max
IL	45,760	45,760	45,760	45,760	45,760	45,760	1	31,200	54,080

Degree Required Data

	Min	Q1	Mean	Median	Q3	Max	N	Range Avg Min	Range Avg Max
High School	.	.	.	.	.	.		.	.
Associate's	.	.	.	.	.	.		.	.
Bachelor's	45,760	45,760	45,760	45,760	45,760	45,760	1	31,200	54,080
Master's	.	.	.	.	.	.		.	.
Doctoral	.	.	.	.	.	.		.	.

HUMAN RESOURCES MANAGER - CONTINUED
Medium Public Library
(Serving a population of 25,000 to 99,999)
Regional Data

	Min	Q1	Mean	Median	Q3	Max	N	Range Avg Min	Range Avg Max
North Atlantic	44,103	45,714	75,847	56,139	91,354	141,924	5	.	.
Great Lakes & Plains	35,422	41,400	53,644	51,117	67,250	78,624	10	41,317	70,308
Southeast	33,000	33,000	33,850	33,850	34,700	34,700	2	.	.
ALL REGIONS	33,000	41,400	57,845	50,213	67,250	141,924	17	41,317	70,308

State Data

	Min	Q1	Mean	Median	Q3	Max	N	Range Avg Min	Range Avg Max
CT	91,354	91,354	91,354	91,354	91,354	91,354	1	.	.
GA	34,700	34,700	34,700	34,700	34,700	34,700	1	.	.
IL	37,440	43,827	58,943	59,853	74,058	78,624	4	44,734	72,294
IN	48,500	48,500	50,260	50,260	52,020	52,020	2	.	.
ME	56,139	56,139	56,139	56,139	56,139	56,139	1	.	.
NY	45,714	45,714	93,819	93,819	141,924	141,924	2	.	.
OH	35,422	38,411	50,037	48,738	61,663	67,250	4	36,192	67,330
PA	44,103	44,103	44,103	44,103	44,103	44,103	1	.	.
TN	33,000	33,000	33,000	33,000	33,000	33,000	1	.	.

Degree Required Data

	Min	Q1	Mean	Median	Q3	Max	N	Range Avg Min	Range Avg Max
High School	.	.	.	.	.	.	.	.	.
Associate's	35,422	39,763	68,367	48,062	96,972	141,924	4	28,080	60,819
Bachelor's	37,440	41,400	59,254	50,213	78,624	91,354	7	37,492	64,698
Master's	33,000	33,850	48,333	45,420	62,816	69,493	4	59,218	87,485
Doctoral	.	.	.	.	.	.	.	.	.

HUMAN RESOURCES MANAGER - CONTINUED
Large Public Library
(Serving a population of 100,000 to 499,999)
Regional Data

	Min	Q1	Mean	Median	Q3	Max	N	Range Avg Min	Range Avg Max
North Atlantic	43,285	52,371	59,266	56,222	60,686	83,767	5	41,600	49,920
Great Lakes & Plains	38,430	48,734	54,813	54,205	60,050	84,406	13	43,443	62,949
Southeast	40,747	44,123	54,124	50,261	57,030	89,419	8	.	.
West & Southwest	26,936	30,680	46,791	45,282	55,754	76,816	6	30,680	45,900
ALL REGIONS	26,936	43,822	53,832	51,686	60,368	89,419	32	38,153	54,827

State Data

	Min	Q1	Mean	Median	Q3	Max	N	Range Avg Min	Range Avg Max
CA	48,755	48,755	48,755	48,755	48,755	48,755	1	37,710	56,555
CO	41,808	41,808	41,808	41,808	41,808	41,808	1	32,635	48,963
FL	45,725	45,725	45,725	45,725	45,725	45,725	1	.	.
IL	48,734	48,734	49,088	49,088	49,442	49,442	2	36,483	51,522
KS	61,630	61,630	61,630	61,630	61,630	61,630	1	42,931	71,552
MA	56,222	56,222	56,222	56,222	56,222	56,222	1	.	.
MD	83,767	83,767	83,767	83,767	83,767	83,767	1	.	.
MI	44,359	44,359	61,088	54,500	84,406	84,406	3	67,538	84,406
MN	51,000	51,000	51,000	51,000	51,000	51,000	1	.	.
MO	58,531	58,531	63,040	63,040	67,548	67,548	2	.	.
MS	40,747	40,747	40,747	40,747	40,747	40,747	1	.	.
NY	52,371	52,371	56,529	56,529	60,686	60,686	2	.	.
OH	38,430	39,079	48,103	46,966	57,127	60,050	4	35,131	53,633
OK	30,680	30,680	30,680	30,680	30,680	30,680	1	27,955	36,275
PA	43,285	43,285	43,285	43,285	43,285	43,285	1	41,600	49,920
SC	49,891	49,891	49,891	49,891	49,891	49,891	1	.	.
TN	42,520	42,520	42,520	42,520	42,520	42,520	1	.	.
TX	26,936	26,936	26,936	26,936	26,936	26,936	1	24,419	41,808
VA	50,631	51,861	63,528	57,030	75,194	89,419	4	.	.
WA	55,754	55,754	66,285	66,285	76,816	76,816	2	.	.

Degree Required Data

	Min	Q1	Mean	Median	Q3	Max	N	Range Avg Min	Range Avg Max
High School	26,936	28,808	40,335	40,656	51,861	53,091	4	26,187	39,042
Associate's	43,285	43,285	43,285	43,285	43,285	43,285	1	41,600	49,920
Bachelor's	38,430	45,042	54,227	53,288	60,368	83,767	20	36,851	54,219
Master's	51,000	56,315	71,614	73,018	86,913	89,419	4	55,234	77,979
Doctoral	.	.	.	.	.	.		.	.

HUMAN RESOURCES MANAGER - CONTINUED
Very Large Public Library
(Serving a population of 500,000 or more)
Regional Data

	Min	Q1	Mean	Median	Q3	Max	N	Range Avg Min	Range Avg Max
North Atlantic	86,655	86,655	86,803	86,837	86,917	86,917	3	.	.
Great Lakes & Plains	72,013	73,361	84,893	77,330	94,370	124,380	7	58,521	83,190
Southeast	64,190	69,552	81,027	87,992	88,345	95,056	5	.	.
West & Southwest	55,670	61,812	74,656	67,101	96,278	103,982	11	56,650	80,815
ALL REGIONS	55,670	67,101	80,039	76,321	88,345	124,380	26	57,184	81,494

State Data

	Min	Q1	Mean	Median	Q3	Max	N	Range Avg Min	Range Avg Max
AZ	59,862	59,862	61,610	61,610	63,357	63,357	2	50,669	80,756
CA	62,816	75,312	87,678	96,278	100,000	103,982	5	65,601	80,067
CO	55,670	55,670	55,670	55,670	55,670	55,670	1	.	.
FL	69,552	69,552	84,318	88,345	95,056	95,056	3	.	.
GA	87,992	87,992	87,992	87,992	87,992	87,992	1	.	.
IN	77,330	77,330	77,330	77,330	77,330	77,330	1	.	.
MD	86,837	86,837	86,877	86,877	86,917	86,917	2	.	.
MI	78,799	78,799	78,799	78,799	78,799	78,799	1	.	.
MO	74,000	74,000	74,000	74,000	74,000	74,000	1	.	.
NC	64,190	64,190	64,190	64,190	64,190	64,190	1	.	.
NJ	86,655	86,655	86,655	86,655	86,655	86,655	1	.	.
OH	73,361	73,361	97,370	94,370	124,380	124,380	3	65,603	94,370
TX	61,812	61,812	64,456	64,456	67,101	67,101	2	50,710	82,430
UT	75,024	75,024	75,024	75,024	75,024	75,024	1	.	.
WI	72,013	72,013	72,013	72,013	72,013	72,013	1	51,438	72,010

Degree Required Data

	Min	Q1	Mean	Median	Q3	Max	N	Range Avg Min	Range Avg Max
High School	.	.	.	.	.	.		.	.
Associate's	.	.	.	.	.	.		.	.
Bachelor's	55,670	63,357	76,335	73,361	88,345	103,982	17	57,184	81,494
Master's	74,000	75,024	89,587	86,917	100,000	124,380	7	.	.
Doctoral	.	.	.	.	.	.		.	.

HUMAN RESOURCES MANAGER - CONTINUED
ALL PUBLIC LIBRARIES
Regional Data

	Min	Q1	Mean	Median	Q3	Max	N	Range Avg Min	Range Avg Max
North Atlantic	43,285	52,371	71,998	60,686	86,837	141,924	13	41,600	49,920
Great Lakes & Plains	35,422	47,130	60,202	55,288	72,687	124,380	32	44,003	68,211
Southeast	33,000	42,520	60,389	53,091	87,992	95,056	15	.	.
West & Southwest	26,936	55,670	64,821	62,816	75,312	103,982	17	45,108	65,298
ALL REGIONS	26,936	48,500	63,250	59,862	76,816	141,924	77	44,331	66,276

State Data

	Min	Q1	Mean	Median	Q3	Max	N	Range Avg Min	Range Avg Max
AZ	59,862	59,862	61,610	61,610	63,357	63,357	2	50,669	80,756
CA	48,755	62,816	81,191	85,795	100,000	103,982	6	56,304	72,230
CO	41,808	41,808	48,739	48,739	55,670	55,670	2	32,635	48,963
CT	91,354	91,354	91,354	91,354	91,354	91,354	1	.	.
FL	45,725	57,639	74,670	78,949	91,701	95,056	4	.	.
GA	34,700	34,700	61,346	61,346	87,992	87,992	2	.	.
IL	37,440	45,760	54,244	49,442	69,493	78,624	7	40,377	64,497
IN	48,500	48,500	59,283	52,020	77,330	77,330	3	.	.
KS	61,630	61,630	61,630	61,630	61,630	61,630	1	42,931	71,552
MA	56,222	56,222	56,222	56,222	56,222	56,222	1	.	.
MD	83,767	83,767	85,840	86,837	86,917	86,917	3	.	.
ME	56,139	56,139	56,139	56,139	56,139	56,139	1	.	.
MI	37,440	44,359	59,901	54,500	78,799	84,406	5	67,538	84,406
MN	51,000	51,000	51,000	51,000	51,000	51,000	1	.	.
MO	58,531	58,531	66,693	67,548	74,000	74,000	3	.	.
MS	40,747	40,747	40,747	40,747	40,747	40,747	1	.	.
NC	64,190	64,190	64,190	64,190	64,190	64,190	1	.	.
NJ	86,655	86,655	86,655	86,655	86,655	86,655	1	.	.
NY	45,714	49,043	75,174	56,529	101,305	141,924	4	.	.
OH	35,422	39,728	62,243	56,077	73,361	124,380	11	41,650	67,259
OK	30,680	30,680	30,680	30,680	30,680	30,680	1	27,955	36,275
PA	43,285	43,285	43,694	43,694	44,103	44,103	2	41,600	49,920
SC	49,891	49,891	49,891	49,891	49,891	49,891	1	.	.
TN	33,000	33,000	37,760	37,760	42,520	42,520	2	.	.
TX	26,936	26,936	51,950	61,812	67,101	67,101	3	37,565	62,119
UT	75,024	75,024	75,024	75,024	75,024	75,024	1	.	.
VA	50,631	51,861	63,528	57,030	75,194	89,419	4	.	.
WA	55,754	55,754	66,285	66,285	76,816	76,816	2	.	.
WI	72,013	72,013	72,013	72,013	72,013	72,013	1	51,438	72,010

Degree Required Data

	Min	Q1	Mean	Median	Q3	Max	N	Range Avg Min	Range Avg Max
High School	26,936	28,808	40,335	40,656	51,861	53,091	4	26,187	39,042
Associate's	35,422	43,285	63,351	44,103	52,020	141,924	5	34,840	55,370
Bachelor's	37,440	48,734	62,613	60,368	75,312	103,982	46	47,464	70,507
Master's	33,000	56,139	73,793	75,024	87,992	124,380	15	56,562	81,148
Doctoral	.	.	.	.	.	.	.	.	.

HUMAN RESOURCES ASSISTANT

Organizes and maintains records, and files government reports as scheduled. Maintains employment statistical data and prepares related reports. Assists in employment activities involving interviewing, verifying qualifications, and checking references. Assists in administering employee benefit programs. Responds to employee inquiries on matters related to library programs and activities.

Medium Public Library
(Serving a population of 25,000 to 99,999)
Regional Data

	Min	Q1	Mean	Median	Q3	Max	N	Range Avg Min	Range Avg Max
North Atlantic	44,574	44,574	44,574	44,574	44,574	44,574	1	.	.
Great Lakes & Plains	27,040	27,040	34,714	34,923	42,180	42,180	3	31,470	46,488
Southeast	33,000	33,000	33,000	33,000	33,000	33,000	1	.	.
ALL REGIONS	27,040	33,000	36,344	34,923	42,180	44,574	5	31,470	46,488

State Data

	Min	Q1	Mean	Median	Q3	Max	N	Range Avg Min	Range Avg Max
CT	44,574	44,574	44,574	44,574	44,574	44,574	1	.	.
IL	34,923	34,923	34,923	34,923	34,923	34,923	1	31,470	46,488
IN	42,180	42,180	42,180	42,180	42,180	42,180	1	.	.
OH	27,040	27,040	27,040	27,040	27,040	27,040	1	.	.
TN	33,000	33,000	33,000	33,000	33,000	33,000	1	.	.

Degree Required Data

	Min	Q1	Mean	Median	Q3	Max	N	Range Avg Min	Range Avg Max
High School	27,040	27,040	34,714	34,923	42,180	42,180	3	31,470	46,488
Associate's	.	.	.	.	.	.		.	.
Bachelor's	44,574	44,574	44,574	44,574	44,574	44,574	1		
Master's	33,000	33,000	33,000	33,000	33,000	33,000	1		
Doctoral	.	.	.	.	.	.		.	.

HUMAN RESOURCES ASSISTANT - CONTINUED
Large Public Library
(Serving a population of 100,000 to 499,999)
Regional Data

	Min	Q1	Mean	Median	Q3	Max	N	Range Avg Min	Range Avg Max
North Atlantic	32,689	35,844	39,218	40,275	42,591	43,633	4	.	.
Great Lakes & Plains	21,466	25,854	32,193	29,099	37,343	47,861	12	22,796	33,697
Southeast	20,758	20,758	24,038	23,732	27,623	27,623	3	19,573	27,685
West & Southwest	28,013	28,013	35,671	31,200	47,800	47,800	3	31,200	37,440
ALL REGIONS	20,758	25,854	32,832	30,472	38,999	47,861	22	23,660	33,318

State Data

	Min	Q1	Mean	Median	Q3	Max	N	Range Avg Min	Range Avg Max
IL	25,854	25,854	25,854	25,854	25,854	25,854	2	.	.
IN	25,463	25,463	25,463	25,463	25,463	25,463	1	.	.
KS	26,000	26,000	26,000	26,000	26,000	26,000	1	21,632	36,067
LA	20,758	20,758	20,758	20,758	20,758	20,758	1	19,573	27,685
MD	32,689	32,689	38,441	38,999	43,633	43,633	3	.	.
MI	29,744	29,744	36,892	33,779	47,154	47,154	3	.	.
MO	21,466	21,466	21,466	21,466	21,466	21,466	1	21,466	30,285
NE	36,256	36,256	36,256	36,256	36,256	36,256	1	26,601	36,256
OH	28,454	28,454	38,249	38,430	47,861	47,861	3	21,486	32,178
PA	41,550	41,550	41,550	41,550	41,550	41,550	1	.	.
SC	27,623	27,623	27,623	27,623	27,623	27,623	1	.	.
TX	28,013	28,013	28,013	28,013	28,013	28,013	1	.	.
VA	23,732	23,732	23,732	23,732	23,732	23,732	1	.	.
WA	31,200	31,200	39,500	39,500	47,800	47,800	2	31,200	37,440

Degree Required Data

	Min	Q1	Mean	Median	Q3	Max	N	Range Avg Min	Range Avg Max
High School	20,758	25,854	30,376	27,872	36,256	43,633	10	24,751	34,362
Associate's	21,466	24,545	31,336	28,039	38,127	47,800	4	21,476	31,231
Bachelor's	23,732	30,351	36,651	36,105	44,352	47,861	8	.	.
Master's	.	.	.	.	.	.	.	.	.
Doctoral	.	.	.	.	.	.	.	.	.

HUMAN RESOURCES ASSISTANT - CONTINUED
Very Large Public Library
(Serving a population of 500,000 or more)
Regional Data

	Min	Q1	Mean	Median	Q3	Max	N	Range Avg Min	Range Avg Max
North Atlantic	20,800	25,965	31,911	29,565	40,471	43,305	10	16,640	22,880
Great Lakes & Plains	27,810	31,956	38,180	35,206	44,120	57,829	11	31,696	46,377
Southeast	30,741	32,762	39,091	36,934	45,308	51,982	8	31,874	53,123
West & Southwest	38,605	40,227	58,204	57,962	69,628	81,432	9	48,504	61,779
ALL REGIONS	20,800	31,956	41,465	37,981	48,464	81,432	38	37,439	51,871

State Data

	Min	Q1	Mean	Median	Q3	Max	N	Range Avg Min	Range Avg Max
AZ	40,227	40,227	40,227	40,227	40,227	40,227	1	31,346	46,613
CA	57,962	69,628	71,242	69,628	77,558	81,432	5	57,161	69,368
FL	30,741	33,626	39,056	36,934	44,486	51,616	4	.	.
GA	30,860	30,860	30,860	30,860	30,860	30,860	1	.	.
IN	44,120	44,120	44,120	44,120	44,120	44,120	1	.	.
MD	20,800	32,526	34,186	34,060	40,471	43,071	5	16,640	22,880
MI	30,999	30,999	35,017	35,017	39,035	39,035	2	.	.
MO	31,956	31,956	33,581	33,581	35,206	35,206	2	.	.
NC	34,664	34,664	34,664	34,664	34,664	34,664	1	.	.
NJ	25,959	25,965	29,637	26,354	26,603	43,305	5	.	.
OH	27,810	32,594	36,167	34,694	37,274	48,464	5	28,979	42,973
TX	38,605	38,605	43,698	43,698	48,792	48,792	2	31,034	46,592
UT	40,008	40,008	40,008	40,008	40,008	40,008	1	.	.
VA	39,000	39,000	45,491	45,491	51,982	51,982	2	31,874	53,123
WI	57,829	57,829	57,829	57,829	57,829	57,829	1	45,282	63,398

Degree Required Data

	Min	Q1	Mean	Median	Q3	Max	N	Range Avg Min	Range Avg Max
High School	20,800	32,526	37,360	37,357	40,227	51,982	11	29,078	44,841
Associate's	27,810	30,202	33,093	33,644	35,984	37,274	4	27,810	41,600
Bachelor's	30,860	35,206	46,716	43,188	57,829	77,558	14	47,659	62,182
Master's	.	.	.	.	.	.	.	.	.
Doctoral	.	.	.	.	.	.	.	.	.

HUMAN RESOURCES ASSISTANT - CONTINUED
ALL PUBLIC LIBRARIES
Regional Data

	Min	Q1	Mean	Median	Q3	Max	N	Range Avg Min	Range Avg Max
North Atlantic	20,800	26,354	34,704	34,060	43,071	44,574	15	16,640	22,880
Great Lakes & Plains	21,466	27,810	35,017	34,237	39,035	57,829	26	28,439	41,776
Southeast	20,758	29,182	34,820	33,832	38,178	51,982	12	27,774	44,644
West & Southwest	28,013	39,306	52,571	48,296	69,628	81,432	12	46,032	58,302
ALL REGIONS	20,758	28,454	38,149	35,206	43,305	81,432	65	33,410	46,567

State Data

	Min	Q1	Mean	Median	Q3	Max	N	Range Avg Min	Range Avg Max
AZ	40,227	40,227	40,227	40,227	40,227	40,227	1	31,346	46,613
CA	57,962	69,628	71,242	69,628	77,558	81,432	5	57,161	69,368
CT	44,574	44,574	44,574	44,574	44,574	44,574	1	.	.
FL	30,741	33,626	39,056	36,934	44,486	51,616	4	.	.
GA	30,860	30,860	30,860	30,860	30,860	30,860	1	.	.
IL	25,854	25,854	28,877	25,854	34,923	34,923	3	31,470	46,488
IN	25,463	25,463	37,254	42,180	44,120	44,120	3	.	.
KS	26,000	26,000	26,000	26,000	26,000	26,000	1	21,632	36,067
LA	20,758	20,758	20,758	20,758	20,758	20,758	1	19,573	27,685
MD	20,800	32,608	35,781	36,530	41,771	43,633	8	16,640	22,880
MI	29,744	30,999	36,142	33,779	39,035	47,154	5	.	.
MO	21,466	21,466	29,542	31,956	35,206	35,206	3	21,466	30,285
NC	34,664	34,664	34,664	34,664	34,664	34,664	1	.	.
NE	36,256	36,256	36,256	36,256	36,256	36,256	1	26,601	36,256
NJ	25,959	25,965	29,637	26,354	26,603	43,305	5	.	.
OH	27,040	28,454	35,847	34,694	38,430	48,464	9	27,730	41,174
PA	41,550	41,550	41,550	41,550	41,550	41,550	1	.	.
SC	27,623	27,623	27,623	27,623	27,623	27,623	1	.	.
TN	33,000	33,000	33,000	33,000	33,000	33,000	1	.	.
TX	28,013	28,013	38,470	38,605	48,792	48,792	3	31,034	46,592
UT	40,008	40,008	40,008	40,008	40,008	40,008	1	.	.
VA	23,732	23,732	38,238	39,000	51,982	51,982	3	31,874	53,123
WA	31,200	31,200	39,500	39,500	47,800	47,800	2	31,200	37,440
WI	57,829	57,829	57,829	57,829	57,829	57,829	1	45,282	63,398

Degree Required Data

	Min	Q1	Mean	Median	Q3	Max	N	Range Avg Min	Range Avg Max
High School	20,758	26,520	34,119	34,492	39,018	51,982	24	27,586	40,814
Associate's	21,466	27,717	32,214	30,524	35,984	47,800	8	25,698	38,144
Bachelor's	23,732	33,779	43,122	41,550	47,861	77,558	23	47,659	62,182
Master's	33,000	33,000	33,000	33,000	33,000	33,000	1	.	.
Doctoral	.	.	.	.	.	.	.	.	.

FACILITY ENGINEERING MANAGER (MAINTENANCE)

Responsible for grounds, buildings, and building equipment. Supervises the installation, maintenance, and repair of: electrical, gas, air, and water installations; fire sprinklers; the operation of building equipment and facilities; janitorial services; and the maintenance of grounds. Works with outside contractors and architects on building construction as necessary. Plans, lays out, and assigns work, involving diagnosing and remedying difficult problems. Reports defective equipment and recommends the replacement of obsolete or damaged equipment when estimates of repair costs are excessive. Expedites building repairs in construction to avoid production delays. Performs normal supervisory functions in a department with seldom more than 10 persons.

Very Small Public Library
(Serving a population of less than 10,000)
Regional Data

	Min	Q1	Mean	Median	Q3	Max	N	Range Avg Min	Range Avg Max
West & Southwest	48,402	48,402	48,402	48,402	48,402	48,402	1	31,928	48,402
ALL REGIONS	48,402	48,402	48,402	48,402	48,402	48,402	1	31,928	48,402

State Data

	Min	Q1	Mean	Median	Q3	Max	N	Range Avg Min	Range Avg Max
CO	48,402	48,402	48,402	48,402	48,402	48,402	1	31,928	48,402

Degree Required Data

	Min	Q1	Mean	Median	Q3	Max	N	Range Avg Min	Range Avg Max
High School	48,402	48,402	48,402	48,402	48,402	48,402	1	31,928	48,402
Associate's	.	.	.	.	.	.		.	.
Bachelor's	.	.	.	.	.	.		.	.
Master's	.	.	.	.	.	.		.	.
Doctoral	.	.	.	.	.	.		.	.

FACILITY ENGINEERING MANAGER (MAINTENANCE) - CONTINUED
Small Public Library
(Serving a population of 10,000 to 25,000)
Regional Data

	Min	Q1	Mean	Median	Q3	Max	N	Range Avg Min	Range Avg Max
North Atlantic	26,649	26,649	39,876	39,876	53,102	53,102	2	.	.
Great Lakes & Plains	22,506	25,718	35,219	30,065	44,720	58,240	4	28,080	54,080
ALL REGIONS	22,506	26,649	36,771	30,065	53,102	58,240	6	28,080	54,080

State Data

	Min	Q1	Mean	Median	Q3	Max	N	Range Avg Min	Range Avg Max
IL	58,240	58,240	58,240	58,240	58,240	58,240	1	39,520	81,120
KS	22,506	22,506	22,506	22,506	22,506	22,506	1	16,640	27,040
MA	53,102	53,102	53,102	53,102	53,102	53,102	1	.	.
NY	26,649	26,649	26,649	26,649	26,649	26,649	1	.	.
OH	28,930	28,930	28,930	28,930	28,930	28,930	1	.	.
WI	31,200	31,200	31,200	31,200	31,200	31,200	1	.	.

Degree Required Data

	Min	Q1	Mean	Median	Q3	Max	N	Range Avg Min	Range Avg Max
High School	22,506	24,578	33,364	28,925	42,151	53,102	4	16,640	27,040
Associate's	58,240	58,240	58,240	58,240	58,240	58,240	1	39,520	81,120
Bachelor's									
Master's									
Doctoral									

FACILITY ENGINEERING MANAGER (MAINTENANCE) - CONTINUED
Medium Public Library
(Serving a population of 25,000 to 99,999)
Regional Data

	Min	Q1	Mean	Median	Q3	Max	N	Range Avg Min	Range Avg Max
North Atlantic	23,109	33,882	48,764	44,129	59,114	97,178	12	34,242	43,170
Great Lakes & Plains	23,171	34,000	44,123	41,142	49,150	73,154	21	35,915	53,308
Southeast	29,355	29,355	29,355	29,355	29,355	29,355	1		
West & Southwest	20,692	20,692	41,270	50,244	52,874	52,874	3	45,614	56,098
ALL REGIONS	20,692	33,862	44,997	42,806	50,244	97,178	37	36,116	50,791

State Data

	Min	Q1	Mean	Median	Q3	Max	N	Range Avg Min	Range Avg Max
CA	50,244	50,244	50,244	50,244	50,244	50,244	1		
CT	64,872	64,872	64,872	64,872	64,872	64,872	1		
IL	29,224	39,520	54,351	60,549	70,998	73,154	7	41,400	62,358
IN	34,000	34,000	37,000	37,000	40,000	40,000	2		
KS	24,960	24,960	24,960	24,960	24,960	24,960	1	21,070	29,058
MA	33,902	33,902	42,344	44,131	49,000	49,000	3	35,325	42,827
ME	33,862	33,862	33,862	33,862	33,862	33,862	1	30,992	44,200
MI	23,171	23,171	23,171	23,171	23,171	23,171	1		
MN	47,923	47,923	47,923	47,923	47,923	47,923	1		
MO	49,587	49,587	49,587	49,587	49,587	49,587	1		
NJ	25,294	25,294	61,236	61,236	97,178	97,178	2		
NY	39,098	41,612	53,454	48,741	65,296	77,234	4		
OH	29,682	31,774	40,836	43,243	47,923	49,150	6	32,739	49,733
PA	23,109	23,109	23,109	23,109	23,109	23,109	1		
TN	29,355	29,355	29,355	29,355	29,355	29,355	1		
TX	20,692	20,692	20,692	20,692	20,692	20,692	1		
WI	40,317	40,317	40,730	40,730	41,142	41,142	2	32,864	43,035
WY	52,874	52,874	52,874	52,874	52,874	52,874	1	45,614	56,098

Degree Required Data

	Min	Q1	Mean	Median	Q3	Max	N	Range Avg Min	Range Avg Max
High School	20,692	29,355	42,585	39,707	49,150	97,178	22	33,332	47,507
Associate's	29,224	35,647	44,978	44,533	49,622	70,998	8	34,762	47,393
Bachelor's	40,000	49,587	55,233	52,874	60,549	73,154	5	45,344	64,078
Master's									
Doctoral									

FACILITY ENGINEERING MANAGER (MAINTENANCE) - CONTINUED
Large Public Library
(Serving a population of 100,000 to 499,999)
Regional Data

	Min	Q1	Mean	Median	Q3	Max	N	Range Avg Min	Range Avg Max
North Atlantic	16,640	32,854	44,850	44,310	58,261	67,218	9	25,917	46,030
Great Lakes & Plains	32,272	45,699	52,160	54,674	57,466	67,413	16	40,016	60,062
Southeast	26,000	35,000	44,152	42,010	52,163	70,231	10	49,005	66,248
West & Southwest	19,310	23,570	37,242	35,522	52,343	55,754	8	29,468	38,964
ALL REGIONS	16,640	35,000	45,992	46,786	56,324	70,231	43	35,716	51,677

State Data

	Min	Q1	Mean	Median	Q3	Max	N	Range Avg Min	Range Avg Max
CA	50,606	50,606	50,606	50,606	50,606	50,606	1	36,171	50,606
FL	45,277	45,277	48,720	48,720	52,163	52,163	2	.	.
GA	35,000	35,000	35,000	35,000	35,000	35,000	1	.	.
IL	49,216	52,907	58,303	58,291	63,700	67,413	4	39,042	55,120
IN	46,786	46,786	46,786	46,786	46,786	46,786	1	.	.
KS	44,470	44,470	51,241	51,241	58,011	58,011	2	37,690	62,816
LA	50,003	50,003	50,003	50,003	50,003	50,003	1	49,005	66,248
MA	58,261	58,261	58,261	58,261	58,261	58,261	1	.	.
MD	31,693	31,693	49,456	49,456	67,218	67,218	2	.	.
MI	32,272	37,636	41,667	44,266	45,699	45,867	4	.	.
MN	62,815	62,815	62,815	62,815	62,815	62,815	1	.	.
MO	54,350	54,350	54,350	54,350	54,350	54,350	1	44,429	64,563
MS	26,000	26,000	26,000	26,000	26,000	26,000	1	.	.
NE	54,997	54,997	54,997	54,997	54,997	54,997	1	41,232	54,997
NM	19,310	19,310	25,006	25,904	29,806	29,806	3	20,051	25,584
NY	48,676	48,676	54,622	54,622	60,567	60,567	2	.	.
OH	56,324	56,324	56,324	56,324	56,324	56,324	1	.	.
PA	16,640	24,747	34,309	38,142	43,870	44,310	4	25,917	46,030
SC	37,033	37,033	37,033	37,033	37,033	37,033	1	.	.
TN	38,743	38,743	38,743	38,743	38,743	38,743	1	.	.
TX	21,237	21,237	31,238	31,238	41,239	41,239	2	.	.
VA	30,952	30,952	52,435	56,121	70,231	70,231	3	.	.
WA	54,080	54,080	54,917	54,917	55,754	55,754	2	41,600	54,080
WI	56,921	56,921	56,921	56,921	56,921	56,921	1	.	.

Degree Required Data

	Min	Q1	Mean	Median	Q3	Max	N	Range Avg Min	Range Avg Max
High School	16,640	29,806	42,348	43,430	56,921	67,413	23	20,051	25,584
Associate's	32,854	37,033	42,907	40,872	49,216	56,597	6	32,479	50,575
Bachelor's	44,470	46,786	52,273	54,350	56,324	59,986	9	42,009	62,288
Master's	52,163	52,163	61,197	61,197	70,231	70,231	2	.	.
Doctoral	.	.	.	.	.	.		.	.

FACILITY ENGINEERING MANAGER (MAINTENANCE) - CONTINUED
Very Large Public Library
(Serving a population of 500,000 or more)
Regional Data

	Min	Q1	Mean	Median	Q3	Max	N	Range Avg Min	Range Avg Max
North Atlantic	64,888	64,888	72,369	65,563	86,655	86,655	3		
Great Lakes & Plains	56,056	74,826	78,049	74,995	85,173	99,195	5	72,155	103,813
Southeast	24,998	29,332	41,790	37,665	56,002	62,064	15	40,126	66,877
West & Southwest	53,250	57,892	70,635	67,364	75,525	110,268	8	55,099	77,178
ALL REGIONS	24,998	37,665	58,041	58,693	72,634	110,268	31	55,620	81,262

State Data

	Min	Q1	Mean	Median	Q3	Max	N	Range Avg Min	Range Avg Max
CA	53,250	62,801	75,332	71,926	78,416	110,268	5	59,488	71,926
CO	60,775	60,775	60,775	60,775	60,775	60,775	1		
FL	24,998	29,332	39,800	35,285	48,341	62,064	13		
IN	85,173	85,173	85,173	85,173	85,173	85,173	1		
MD	64,888	64,888	65,226	65,226	65,563	65,563	2		
MI	74,995	74,995	74,995	74,995	74,995	74,995	1		
NC	56,002	56,002	56,002	56,002	56,002	56,002	1		
NJ	86,655	86,655	86,655	86,655	86,655	86,655	1		
OH	56,056	56,056	76,692	74,826	99,195	99,195	3	72,155	103,813
TX	72,634	72,634	72,634	72,634	72,634	72,634	1	50,710	82,430
UT	55,008	55,008	55,008	55,008	55,008	55,008	1		
VA	53,455	53,455	53,455	53,455	53,455	53,455	1	40,126	66,877

Degree Required Data

	Min	Q1	Mean	Median	Q3	Max	N	Range Avg Min	Range Avg Max
High School	53,250	53,455	62,056	62,621	65,563	74,826	6	40,126	66,877
Associate's	62,801	62,801	62,801	62,801	62,801	62,801	1		
Bachelor's	56,002	58,416	76,887	73,814	92,184	110,268	8	61,433	93,122
Master's									
Doctoral									

FACILITY ENGINEERING MANAGER (MAINTENANCE) - CONTINUED
ALL PUBLIC LIBRARIES
Regional Data

	Min	Q1	Mean	Median	Q3	Max	N	Range Avg Min	Range Avg Max
North Atlantic	16,640	33,862	49,449	46,493	64,872	97,178	26	32,577	43,742
Great Lakes & Plains	22,506	40,000	49,832	47,923	58,240	99,195	46	38,197	58,076
Southeast	24,998	29,355	42,220	38,204	53,455	70,231	26	44,565	66,562
West & Southwest	19,310	35,522	51,761	53,062	61,788	110,268	20	38,202	51,839
ALL REGIONS	16,640	33,862	48,397	48,132	58,261	110,268	118	37,733	54,907

State Data

	Min	Q1	Mean	Median	Q3	Max	N	Range Avg Min	Range Avg Max
CA	50,244	50,606	68,216	62,801	78,416	110,268	7	47,830	61,266
CO	48,402	48,402	54,588	54,588	60,775	60,775	2	31,928	48,402
CT	64,872	64,872	64,872	64,872	64,872	64,872	1	.	.
FL	24,998	29,332	40,989	37,665	52,163	62,064	15	.	.
GA	35,000	35,000	35,000	35,000	35,000	35,000	1	.	.
IL	29,224	44,836	55,993	59,113	66,987	73,154	12	40,795	64,005
IN	34,000	37,000	51,490	43,393	65,979	85,173	4	.	.
KS	22,506	23,733	37,487	34,715	51,241	58,011	4	28,272	45,432
LA	50,003	50,003	50,003	50,003	50,003	50,003	1	49,005	66,248
MA	33,902	44,131	47,679	49,000	53,102	58,261	5	35,325	42,827
MD	31,693	48,291	57,341	65,226	66,391	67,218	4	.	.
ME	33,862	33,862	33,862	33,862	33,862	33,862	1	30,992	44,200
MI	23,171	32,272	44,139	44,266	45,867	74,995	6	.	.
MN	47,923	47,923	55,369	55,369	62,815	62,815	2	.	.
MO	49,587	49,587	51,969	51,969	54,350	54,350	2	44,429	64,563
MS	26,000	26,000	26,000	26,000	26,000	26,000	1	.	.
NC	56,002	56,002	56,002	56,002	56,002	56,002	1	.	.
NE	54,997	54,997	54,997	54,997	54,997	54,997	1	41,232	54,997
NJ	25,294	25,294	69,709	86,655	97,178	97,178	3	.	.
NM	19,310	19,310	25,006	25,904	29,806	29,806	3	20,051	25,584
NY	26,649	39,098	49,958	48,676	60,567	77,234	7	.	.
OH	28,930	31,774	50,941	47,923	56,324	99,195	11	42,593	63,253
PA	16,640	23,109	32,069	32,854	43,430	44,310	5	25,917	46,030
SC	37,033	37,033	37,033	37,033	37,033	37,033	1	.	.
TN	29,355	29,355	34,049	34,049	38,743	38,743	2	.	.
TX	20,692	20,964	38,950	31,238	56,936	72,634	4	50,710	82,430
UT	55,008	55,008	55,008	55,008	55,008	55,008	1	.	.
VA	30,952	42,203	52,690	54,788	63,176	70,231	4	40,126	66,877
WA	54,080	54,080	54,917	54,917	55,754	55,754	2	41,600	54,080
WI	31,200	35,758	42,395	40,730	49,032	56,921	4	32,864	43,035
WY	52,874	52,874	52,874	52,874	52,874	52,874	1	45,614	56,098

Degree Required Data

	Min	Q1	Mean	Median	Q3	Max	N	Range Avg Min	Range Avg Max
High School	16,640	29,744	44,019	43,118	56,521	97,178	56	30,419	44,119
Associate's	29,224	37,888	46,144	45,462	53,420	70,998	16	34,789	53,120
Bachelor's	40,000	50,003	61,896	56,190	72,634	110,268	22	46,894	68,992
Master's	52,163	52,163	61,197	61,197	70,231	70,231	2	.	.
Doctoral	.	.	.	.	.	.		.	.

BUILDING MAINTENANCE

Performs routine and preventive maintenance as directed. Performs various repairs requiring general knowledge of carpentry, plumbing, HVAC, and electrical and mechanical repair. Operates lawn mowing and snow blowing equipment. Arranges meeting rooms for special events.

Very Small Public Library
(Serving a population of less than 10,000)
Regional Data

	Min	Q1	Mean	Median	Q3	Max	N	Range Avg Min	Range Avg Max
North Atlantic	23,442	23,442	23,442	23,442	23,442	23,442	1	.	.
Great Lakes & Plains	16,640	16,640	21,721	17,982	27,583	33,500	6	.	.
Southeast	18,824	18,824	18,824	18,824	18,824	18,824	1	.	.
ALL REGIONS	16,640	16,942	21,574	18,772	25,512	33,500	8	.	.

State Data

	Min	Q1	Mean	Median	Q3	Max	N	Range Avg Min	Range Avg Max
IA	16,640	16,640	20,489	17,243	27,583	27,583	3	.	.
IL	18,720	18,720	18,720	18,720	18,720	18,720	1	.	.
KS	33,500	33,500	33,500	33,500	33,500	33,500	1	.	.
NJ	23,442	23,442	23,442	23,442	23,442	23,442	1	.	.
OH	16,640	16,640	16,640	16,640	16,640	16,640	1	.	.
WV	18,824	18,824	18,824	18,824	18,824	18,824	1	.	.

Degree Required Data

	Min	Q1	Mean	Median	Q3	Max	N	Range Avg Min	Range Avg Max
High School	17,243	18,720	23,219	21,133	27,583	33,500	6	.	.
Associate's	.	.	.	.	.	.	.	.	.
Bachelor's	.	.	.	.	.	.	.	.	.
Master's	.	.	.	.	.	.	.	.	.
Doctoral	.	.	.	.	.	.	.	.	.

BUILDING MAINTENANCE - CONTINUED
Small Public Library
(Serving a population of 10,000 to 25,000)
Regional Data

	Min	Q1	Mean	Median	Q3	Max	N	Range Avg Min	Range Avg Max
North Atlantic	22,318	26,208	29,490	30,160	33,280	35,485	5	21,840	38,480
Great Lakes & Plains	15,662	24,232	27,785	25,085	31,200	44,063	13	20,816	29,916
Southeast	18,720	18,720	18,720	18,720	18,720	18,720	1	15,600	18,720
ALL REGIONS	15,662	22,880	27,756	26,208	31,554	44,063	19	20,528	30,455

State Data

	Min	Q1	Mean	Median	Q3	Max	N	Range Avg Min	Range Avg Max
IL	15,662	24,596	29,420	26,821	36,400	44,063	8	21,216	32,032
KY	18,720	18,720	18,720	18,720	18,720	18,720	1	15,600	18,720
MA	35,485	35,485	35,485	35,485	35,485	35,485	1	.	.
ME	26,208	26,208	26,208	26,208	26,208	26,208	1	.	.
MI	25,085	25,085	25,085	25,085	25,085	25,085	1	25,085	25,085
ND	25,000	25,000	25,000	25,000	25,000	25,000	1	.	.
NJ	30,160	30,160	31,720	31,720	33,280	33,280	2	21,840	38,480
OH	21,320	21,320	25,251	22,880	31,554	31,554	3	17,680	27,040
RI	22,318	22,318	22,318	22,318	22,318	22,318	1	.	.

Degree Required Data

	Min	Q1	Mean	Median	Q3	Max	N	Range Avg Min	Range Avg Max
High School	15,662	22,880	27,756	26,208	31,554	44,063	19	20,528	30,455
Associate's	.	.	.	.	.	.		.	.
Bachelor's	.	.	.	.	.	.		.	.
Master's	.	.	.	.	.	.		.	.
Doctoral	.	.	.	.	.	.		.	.

BUILDING MAINTENANCE - CONTINUED
Medium Public Library
(Serving a population of 25,000 to 99,999)
Regional Data

	Min	Q1	Mean	Median	Q3	Max	N	Range Avg Min	Range Avg Max
North Atlantic	11,232	24,461	38,190	39,027	55,771	83,736	28	27,366	33,765
Great Lakes & Plains	18,720	23,483	30,935	27,019	37,885	59,511	19	22,840	31,625
Southeast	17,659	18,817	20,802	19,510	20,770	27,252	5	17,285	22,797
West & Southwest	23,400	23,400	29,692	29,692	35,984	35,984	2	24,138	33,592
ALL REGIONS	11,232	22,880	33,712	29,156	42,640	83,736	54	23,728	31,583

State Data

	Min	Q1	Mean	Median	Q3	Max	N	Range Avg Min	Range Avg Max
CA	35,984	35,984	35,984	35,984	35,984	35,984	1	29,557	35,984
CO	23,400	23,400	23,400	23,400	23,400	23,400	1	18,720	31,200
CT	46,363	46,363	52,803	52,803	59,243	59,243	2	.	.
IA	19,219	19,219	27,698	30,596	33,280	33,280	3	29,120	33,280
IL	18,720	18,720	26,101	25,625	27,477	41,870	7	21,457	33,858
IN	22,880	22,880	28,083	23,483	37,885	37,885	3	20,062	24,222
LA	17,659	18,238	19,189	19,164	20,140	20,770	4	17,285	22,797
MA	31,769	35,644	37,721	39,520	39,798	40,075	4	37,440	39,520
ME	25,605	25,605	25,605	25,605	25,605	25,605	1	22,755	32,448
MN	45,708	45,708	45,708	45,708	45,708	45,708	1	.	.
NC	27,252	27,252	27,252	27,252	27,252	27,252	1	.	.
ND	33,010	33,010	33,010	33,010	33,010	33,010	1	24,107	36,150
NJ	55,542	55,542	69,639	69,639	83,736	83,736	2	.	.
NY	22,672	29,869	42,589	42,640	56,200	59,556	13	22,187	30,368
OH	25,085	25,085	43,991	47,378	59,511	59,511	3	24,586	26,624
PA	11,232	13,333	15,715	14,675	16,204	24,171	6	.	.
WI	27,019	27,019	27,019	27,019	27,019	27,019	1	26,021	34,091

Degree Required Data

	Min	Q1	Mean	Median	Q3	Max	N	Range Avg Min	Range Avg Max
High School	13,333	22,880	35,394	31,182	46,363	83,736	38	22,838	31,795
Associate's	25,625	25,625	29,452	29,452	33,280	33,280	2	29,120	33,280
Bachelor's	40,075	40,075	40,075	40,075	40,075	40,075	1	.	.
Master's	.	.	.	.	.	.		.	.
Doctoral	.	.	.	.	.	.		.	.

BUILDING MAINTENANCE - CONTINUED
Large Public Library
(Serving a population of 100,000 to 499,999)
Regional Data

	Min	Q1	Mean	Median	Q3	Max	N	Range Avg Min	Range Avg Max
North Atlantic	20,950	30,576	35,619	35,076	35,922	81,873	17	25,486	33,498
Great Lakes & Plains	15,829	26,374	32,602	31,221	38,794	48,256	36	25,646	35,323
Southeast	16,832	22,420	27,164	28,382	31,926	36,472	15	22,682	33,124
West & Southwest	16,058	20,051	28,437	27,935	34,653	42,578	11	26,745	36,762
ALL REGIONS	15,829	25,230	31,639	31,325	35,980	81,873	79	25,619	35,242

State Data

	Min	Q1	Mean	Median	Q3	Max	N	Range Avg Min	Range Avg Max
AL	29,515	29,515	29,515	29,515	29,515	29,515	1	24,523	36,774
CA	21,944	21,944	32,261	32,261	42,578	42,578	2	26,042	32,261
CO	32,302	32,302	32,302	32,302	32,302	32,302	1	20,405	30,597
FL	28,382	31,619	32,714	32,685	34,439	36,472	6	.	.
GA	22,880	22,880	22,880	22,880	22,880	22,880	1	.	.
IL	20,227	24,024	29,858	26,667	37,572	44,563	11	25,743	31,089
IN	24,251	24,251	24,251	24,251	24,251	24,251	1	.	.
KS	28,413	31,117	32,847	31,325	34,632	38,750	5	25,530	42,553
LA	20,946	20,946	20,946	20,946	20,946	20,946	1	20,842	29,474
MA	36,171	36,171	36,171	36,171	36,171	36,171	1	.	.
MD	20,950	20,950	24,005	24,005	27,059	27,059	2	.	.
MI	23,067	23,067	27,747	28,018	32,157	32,157	3	23,067	28,018
MN	35,980	35,980	35,980	35,980	35,980	35,980	1	.	.
MO	15,829	21,050	25,168	27,279	29,286	30,285	4	20,545	28,579
MS	16,832	16,832	16,832	16,832	16,832	16,832	1	.	.
NE	33,844	33,844	36,341	36,341	38,838	38,838	2	28,496	38,838
NJ	34,826	34,826	34,826	34,826	34,826	34,826	1	.	.
NY	32,190	33,633	47,192	37,353	60,751	81,873	4	27,661	32,062
OH	25,168	27,279	34,975	33,249	42,671	48,235	4	26,208	37,534
PA	24,478	30,576	33,083	35,922	35,922	36,215	9	24,398	34,216
SC	30,558	30,558	30,558	30,558	30,558	30,558	1	.	.
TN	22,420	22,420	24,145	23,416	26,600	26,600	3	.	.
TX	16,058	16,723	23,527	23,673	27,935	33,102	6	.	.
VA	18,012	18,012	18,012	18,012	18,012	18,012	1	.	.
WA	34,653	34,653	37,409	37,409	40,165	40,165	2	30,618	44,346
WI	41,815	42,994	44,853	43,659	47,539	48,256	5	40,685	42,994

Degree Required Data

	Min	Q1	Mean	Median	Q3	Max	N	Range Avg Min	Range Avg Max
High School	15,829	24,854	30,481	30,567	35,922	48,256	68	25,515	34,222
Associate's	34,632	34,653	38,553	38,750	40,165	44,563	5	29,806	46,332
Bachelor's	.	.	.	.	.	.		.	.
Master's	.	.	.	.	.	.		.	.
Doctoral	.	.	.	.	.	.		.	.

BUILDING MAINTENANCE - CONTINUED
Very Large Public Library
(Serving a population of 500,000 or more)
Regional Data

	Min	Q1	Mean	Median	Q3	Max	N	Range Avg Min	Range Avg Max
North Atlantic	25,971	28,571	34,549	32,526	40,545	48,190	17	16,640	22,880
Great Lakes & Plains	28,633	35,049	44,058	42,105	52,354	65,753	72	34,053	45,886
Southeast	24,229	31,955	39,250	39,214	46,349	56,592	10	.	.
West & Southwest	24,696	27,936	41,542	38,147	62,348	75,868	27	36,334	44,780
ALL REGIONS	24,229	33,342	41,854	40,362	48,075	75,868	126	33,871	45,022

State Data

	Min	Q1	Mean	Median	Q3	Max	N	Range Avg Min	Range Avg Max
CA	38,147	38,147	55,337	62,348	62,348	75,868	11	39,631	47,577
CO	36,587	36,650	41,283	40,235	45,917	48,075	4	.	.
FL	40,062	43,206	48,360	48,393	53,515	56,592	4	.	.
GA	42,264	42,264	42,264	42,264	42,264	42,264	1	.	.
MD	25,971	28,306	34,555	31,114	43,998	48,190	9	16,640	22,880
MI	32,395	35,029	43,693	44,432	52,367	54,416	17	.	.
MO	28,633	30,149	35,202	36,306	39,481	41,109	8	.	.
NC	24,229	28,429	31,359	31,955	33,818	38,366	5	.	.
NJ	28,571	28,571	34,542	34,035	40,362	41,829	8	.	.
OH	29,390	35,069	44,959	41,883	54,579	65,753	38	29,542	43,553
TX	28,954	28,954	28,954	28,954	28,954	28,954	1	23,150	33,592
UT	24,696	25,368	28,985	27,936	30,744	39,168	11	.	.
WI	37,392	42,796	48,816	44,905	52,341	65,518	9	43,077	50,553

Degree Required Data

	Min	Q1	Mean	Median	Q3	Max	N	Range Avg Min	Range Avg Max
High School	25,971	34,590	42,715	41,883	48,190	65,753	86	33,077	44,669
Associate's	42,264	42,264	45,170	45,170	48,075	48,075	2	.	.
Bachelor's	24,229	31,955	48,262	62,348	62,348	62,348	11	.	.
Master's	.	.	.	.	.	.		.	.
Doctoral	.	.	.	.	.	.		.	.

BUILDING MAINTENANCE - CONTINUED
ALL PUBLIC LIBRARIES
Regional Data

	Min	Q1	Mean	Median	Q3	Max	N	Range Avg Min	Range Avg Max
North Atlantic	11,232	27,563	35,780	34,823	40,362	83,736	68	25,081	33,577
Great Lakes & Plains	15,662	27,583	37,158	35,528	44,054	65,753	146	27,929	38,240
Southeast	16,832	20,858	29,422	28,406	34,129	56,592	32	19,107	26,112
West & Southwest	16,058	27,471	37,346	35,318	43,168	75,868	40	30,306	39,575
ALL REGIONS	11,232	27,040	35,991	34,515	42,796	83,736	286	27,421	37,214

State Data

	Min	Q1	Mean	Median	Q3	Max	N	Range Avg Min	Range Avg Max
AL	29,515	29,515	29,515	29,515	29,515	29,515	1	24,523	36,774
CA	21,944	38,147	50,658	53,331	62,348	75,868	14	34,309	41,545
CO	23,400	32,302	36,806	36,650	43,758	48,075	6	19,562	30,898
CT	46,363	46,363	52,803	52,803	59,243	59,243	2	.	.
FL	28,382	31,926	38,972	35,456	46,349	56,592	10	.	.
GA	22,880	22,880	32,572	32,572	42,264	42,264	2	.	.
IA	16,640	17,243	24,094	23,401	30,596	33,280	6	29,120	33,280
IL	15,662	23,920	28,342	26,478	35,556	44,563	27	22,989	32,249
IN	22,880	23,182	27,125	23,867	31,068	37,885	4	20,062	24,222
KS	28,413	31,117	32,956	32,412	34,632	38,750	6	25,530	42,553
KY	18,720	18,720	18,720	18,720	18,720	18,720	1	15,600	18,720
LA	17,659	18,817	19,540	19,510	20,770	20,946	5	18,470	25,022
MA	31,769	35,485	37,090	37,846	39,520	40,075	6	37,440	39,520
MD	20,950	27,059	32,637	29,120	43,998	48,190	11	16,640	22,880
ME	25,605	25,605	25,906	25,906	26,208	26,208	2	22,755	32,448
MI	23,067	33,869	40,529	37,614	52,162	54,416	21	24,076	26,551
MN	35,980	35,980	40,844	40,844	45,708	45,708	2	.	.
MO	15,829	28,460	31,857	30,351	37,967	41,109	12	20,545	28,579
MS	16,832	16,832	16,832	16,832	16,832	16,832	1	.	.
NC	24,229	27,252	30,675	30,192	33,818	38,366	6	.	.
ND	25,000	25,000	29,005	29,005	33,010	33,010	2	24,107	36,150
NE	33,844	33,844	36,341	36,341	38,838	38,838	2	28,496	38,838
NJ	23,442	28,571	38,380	34,053	40,545	83,736	14	21,840	38,480
NY	22,672	32,190	43,672	39,629	56,200	81,873	17	23,555	30,791
OH	16,640	34,054	42,300	41,883	48,235	65,753	49	27,861	40,592
PA	11,232	15,851	26,136	27,976	35,922	36,215	15	24,398	34,216
RI	22,318	22,318	22,318	22,318	22,318	22,318	1	.	.
SC	30,558	30,558	30,558	30,558	30,558	30,558	1	.	.
TN	22,420	22,420	24,145	23,416	26,600	26,600	3	.	.
TX	16,058	16,723	24,302	27,294	28,954	33,102	7	23,150	33,592
UT	24,696	25,368	28,985	27,936	30,744	39,168	11	.	.
VA	18,012	18,012	18,012	18,012	18,012	18,012	1	.	.
WA	34,653	34,653	37,409	37,409	40,165	40,165	2	30,618	44,346
WI	27,019	42,796	46,042	43,659	52,021	65,518	15	41,309	48,369
WV	18,824	18,824	18,824	18,824	18,824	18,824	1	.	.

Degree Required Data

	Min	Q1	Mean	Median	Q3	Max	N	Range Avg Min	Range Avg Max
High School	13,333	27,040	35,751	34,381	42,994	83,736	217	27,136	37,097
Associate's	25,625	34,632	38,001	38,750	42,264	48,075	9	29,669	43,722
Bachelor's	24,229	32,887	47,580	51,212	62,348	62,348	12	.	.
Master's	.	.	.	.	.	.	.	.	.
Doctoral	.	.	.	.	.	.	.	.	.

JANITORIAL CLEANER

Cleans assigned areas using power equipment as needed. Cleans drinking fountains, offices partition windows, washrooms, toilets and lavatories. Replenishes supplies.

Very Small Public Library
(Serving a population of less than 10,000)
Regional Data

	Min	Q1	Mean	Median	Q3	Max	N	Range Avg Min	Range Avg Max
North Atlantic	10,920	21,944	27,110	28,021	30,763	42,989	6	22,547	29,754
Great Lakes & Plains	14,560	16,640	22,536	18,667	25,147	40,320	19	15,834	22,381
West & Southwest	12,938	13,000	23,691	26,707	28,891	37,710	7	21,746	28,721
ALL REGIONS	10,920	16,942	23,646	21,663	28,891	42,989	32	19,909	26,780

State Data

	Min	Q1	Mean	Median	Q3	Max	N	Range Avg Min	Range Avg Max
CO	12,938	26,707	27,028	28,891	28,891	37,710	5	23,953	31,782
CT	30,763	30,763	30,763	30,763	30,763	30,763	1	.	.
IA	16,640	16,640	20,828	17,243	28,600	28,600	3	.	.
IL	14,560	18,373	26,395	18,720	40,000	40,320	5	14,560	20,800
IN	14,560	14,560	16,622	16,640	18,667	18,667	3	.	.
KS	16,390	16,390	20,525	20,525	24,660	24,660	2	.	.
MA	21,944	21,944	25,972	25,972	30,000	30,000	2	21,944	29,016
MI	17,511	17,511	21,236	21,236	24,960	24,960	2	15,246	20,696
MN	21,382	21,382	23,265	23,265	25,147	25,147	2	16,890	25,147
NH	26,042	26,042	26,042	26,042	26,042	26,042	1	23,150	30,493
NM	13,000	13,000	13,000	13,000	13,000	13,000	1	10,712	13,416
NY	42,989	42,989	42,989	42,989	42,989	42,989	1	.	.
PA	10,920	10,920	10,920	10,920	10,920	10,920	1	.	.
TX	17,698	17,698	17,698	17,698	17,698	17,698	1	.	.
WI	18,450	18,450	26,905	26,905	35,360	35,360	2	16,640	22,880

Degree Required Data

	Min	Q1	Mean	Median	Q3	Max	N	Range Avg Min	Range Avg Max
High School	10,920	17,511	25,038	24,960	30,000	42,989	25	20,184	26,928
Associate's	.	.	.	.	.	.	.	.	.
Bachelor's	.	.	.	.	.	.	.	.	.
Master's	.	.	.	.	.	.	.	.	.
Doctoral	.	.	.	.	.	.	.	.	.

JANITORIAL CLEANER - CONTINUED
Small Public Library
(Serving a population of 10,000 to 25,000)
Regional Data

	Min	Q1	Mean	Median	Q3	Max	N	Range Avg Min	Range Avg Max
North Atlantic	12,480	20,363	25,365	23,771	32,323	38,667	15	21,081	27,680
Great Lakes & Plains	15,600	18,346	24,337	21,798	27,830	43,200	21	18,539	26,248
Southeast	15,080	15,226	17,087	17,119	18,949	19,032	4	14,352	16,432
West & Southwest	26,984	26,984	29,492	29,492	32,000	32,000	2	.	.
ALL REGIONS	12,480	18,720	24,259	21,819	29,557	43,200	42	18,651	25,379

State Data

	Min	Q1	Mean	Median	Q3	Max	N	Range Avg Min	Range Avg Max
AZ	26,984	26,984	26,984	26,984	26,984	26,984	1	.	.
IL	17,784	17,784	27,208	21,840	42,000	42,000	3	20,800	27,040
IN	18,720	18,720	19,760	19,760	20,800	20,800	2	18,720	24,960
KS	16,429	16,429	17,211	17,211	17,992	17,992	2	14,560	18,720
LA	15,080	15,080	16,973	16,973	18,866	18,866	2	14,352	16,432
MA	27,040	28,298	31,101	30,940	33,904	35,485	4	23,504	30,493
ME	22,880	22,880	22,880	22,880	22,880	22,880	1	.	.
MI	21,798	27,040	27,660	27,830	30,430	31,200	5	23,559	29,598
MS	15,372	15,372	15,372	15,372	15,372	15,372	1	.	.
NH	32,427	32,427	32,427	32,427	32,427	32,427	1	24,502	35,152
NJ	38,667	38,667	38,667	38,667	38,667	38,667	1	.	.
NM	32,000	32,000	32,000	32,000	32,000	32,000	1	.	.
NY	23,771	23,771	25,863	25,863	27,955	27,955	2	.	.
OH	15,600	16,973	23,727	19,230	29,307	43,200	8	13,971	26,000
PA	12,480	13,936	17,212	17,784	20,488	20,800	4	20,800	20,800
RI	20,363	20,363	20,758	20,758	21,154	21,154	2	15,517	24,274
VA	19,032	19,032	19,032	19,032	19,032	19,032	1	.	.
WI	27,394	27,394	27,394	27,394	27,394	27,394	1	.	.

Degree Required Data

	Min	Q1	Mean	Median	Q3	Max	N	Range Avg Min	Range Avg Max
High School	15,080	18,720	24,128	21,819	27,955	42,000	34	18,635	25,955
Associate's	.	.	.	.	.	.	.	.	.
Bachelor's	.	.	.	.	.	.	.	.	.
Master's	.	.	.	.	.	.	.	.	.
Doctoral	.	.	.	.	.	.	.	.	.

JANITORIAL CLEANER - CONTINUED
Medium Public Library
(Serving a population of 25,000 to 99,999)
Regional Data

	Min	Q1	Mean	Median	Q3	Max	N	Range Avg Min	Range Avg Max
North Atlantic	11,231	24,590	31,779	29,587	37,440	52,263	43	24,347	32,970
Great Lakes & Plains	10,712	20,516	24,284	21,694	29,598	44,782	49	21,116	28,968
Southeast	11,024	13,485	15,419	14,042	16,474	24,960	13	14,560	31,200
West & Southwest	16,453	17,287	20,263	19,448	23,618	24,939	12	19,025	25,695
ALL REGIONS	10,712	19,386	25,641	23,629	30,930	52,263	117	21,781	29,863

State Data

	Min	Q1	Mean	Median	Q3	Max	N	Range Avg Min	Range Avg Max
AR	24,960	24,960	24,960	24,960	24,960	24,960	1	14,560	31,200
CA	16,453	16,453	17,313	16,869	18,616	18,616	3	16,453	21,050
CO	20,280	20,280	22,610	22,610	24,939	24,939	2	18,720	31,200
CT	40,272	49,895	47,970	49,895	49,895	49,895	5		
IA	24,480	24,480	24,480	24,480	24,480	24,480	1		
ID	22,880	22,880	22,880	22,880	22,880	22,880	1	20,800	31,200
IL	18,720	20,800	27,999	26,822	33,634	44,782	18	25,447	38,128
IN	18,720	20,904	22,964	21,736	25,730	29,598	9	19,926	20,966
KS	19,469	19,469	19,469	19,469	19,469	19,469	1	17,285	23,878
MA	27,414	29,586	31,992	32,376	34,890	38,149	11	30,368	32,032
ME	24,149	24,149	24,513	24,513	24,877	24,877	2	22,755	32,448
MI	10,712	15,756	19,027	21,549	22,298	22,298	4	17,633	19,027
MN	20,717	20,779	25,395	21,154	30,010	38,555	4		
MO	19,427	19,427	22,783	20,259	28,662	28,662	3		
MS	11,024	12,480	12,676	12,834	13,520	13,520	5		
NC	18,624	18,624	18,624	18,624	18,624	18,624	1		
ND	20,592	20,592	20,592	20,592	20,592	20,592	1	16,640	24,960
NJ	33,295	33,961	39,877	37,017	47,555	47,555	5		
NY	18,200	24,232	27,311	25,958	27,560	52,263	13	21,122	34,211
OH	14,560	15,350	19,291	18,637	19,781	30,160	7	15,971	19,915
PA	11,231	12,060	16,014	14,972	19,968	22,880	4	14,664	19,198
RI	33,218	33,218	35,748	33,218	40,810	40,810	3	28,274	35,748
SC	16,474	16,474	16,474	16,474	16,474	16,474	1		
TN	17,653	17,653	17,653	17,653	17,653	17,653	1		
TX	16,515	16,515	17,308	17,705	17,705	17,705	3	16,515	24,773
VA	14,042	14,042	15,293	15,656	16,180	16,180	3		
WI	33,638	33,638	33,638	33,638	33,638	33,638	1		
WV	13,485	13,485	13,485	13,485	13,485	13,485	1		
WY	23,275	23,275	23,733	23,962	23,962	23,962	3	21,944	26,978

Degree Required Data

	Min	Q1	Mean	Median	Q3	Max	N	Range Avg Min	Range Avg Max
High School	12,834	19,427	26,852	24,149	33,218	52,263	91	22,666	30,346
Associate's	.	.	.	.	.	.	.	.	.
Bachelor's	.	.	.	.	.	.	.	.	.
Master's	.	.	.	.	.	.	.	.	.
Doctoral	.	.	.	.	.	.	.	.	.

JANITORIAL CLEANER - CONTINUED
Large Public Library
(Serving a population of 100,000 to 499,999)
Regional Data

	Min	Q1	Mean	Median	Q3	Max	N	Range Avg Min	Range Avg Max
North Atlantic	16,432	23,907	29,538	28,586	32,136	56,374	42	24,753	31,565
Great Lakes & Plains	14,851	20,396	24,517	23,639	26,811	43,049	46	23,366	30,139
Southeast	14,560	16,973	20,451	19,173	20,800	39,504	18	14,664	21,050
West & Southwest	16,058	16,640	18,099	17,514	18,242	23,571	11	15,288	22,443
ALL REGIONS	14,560	19,448	25,091	23,400	29,550	56,374	117	21,877	28,615

State Data

	Min	Q1	Mean	Median	Q3	Max	N	Range Avg Min	Range Avg Max
AL	14,664	15,413	18,044	17,888	20,675	21,736	4	14,576	21,850
CO	17,514	17,514	17,690	17,690	17,867	17,867	2	15,288	22,443
GA	14,560	14,560	18,027	16,640	22,880	22,880	3	.	.
IL	17,181	18,408	23,122	20,396	28,559	29,744	7	.	.
IN	21,927	21,927	22,032	22,032	22,136	22,136	2	.	.
KS	21,632	22,464	24,362	24,357	24,835	30,514	12	21,632	36,067
LA	19,448	19,448	19,448	19,448	19,448	19,448	1	16,224	22,922
MA	27,622	27,622	29,858	30,430	31,520	31,520	3	.	.
MD	16,432	21,153	23,107	21,859	26,246	30,037	9	.	.
MI	22,298	22,298	24,086	24,981	24,981	24,981	3	19,802	24,981
MO	16,952	16,952	18,210	18,210	19,469	19,469	2	15,829	23,005
MS	16,973	16,973	17,725	17,306	18,898	18,898	3	.	.
NC	32,136	32,136	32,136	32,136	32,136	32,136	1	.	.
NM	16,640	16,640	16,640	16,640	16,640	16,640	1	.	.
NY	21,887	26,770	32,955	31,200	35,398	56,374	21	26,078	32,953
OH	14,851	18,138	21,476	21,330	25,667	29,182	14	16,900	24,679
PA	19,635	24,045	27,891	25,043	35,922	35,922	9	20,114	26,707
TN	17,264	17,930	19,519	20,800	20,800	20,800	5	14,061	18,512
TX	16,058	16,266	17,963	17,098	18,242	23,571	7	.	.
VA	39,504	39,504	39,504	39,504	39,504	39,504	1	.	.
WA	21,329	21,329	21,329	21,329	21,329	21,329	1	.	.
WI	21,257	34,983	36,699	39,278	42,349	43,049	6	40,019	42,349

Degree Required Data

	Min	Q1	Mean	Median	Q3	Max	N	Range Avg Min	Range Avg Max
High School	14,560	17,930	24,146	21,893	29,550	43,049	79	21,829	27,233
Associate's									
Bachelor's									
Master's									
Doctoral									

JANITORIAL CLEANER - CONTINUED
Very Large Public Library
(Serving a population of 500,000 or more)
Regional Data

	Min	Q1	Mean	Median	Q3	Max	N	Range Avg Min	Range Avg Max
North Atlantic	23,614	24,441	29,612	27,098	33,197	48,190	17		
Great Lakes & Plains	18,179	25,568	31,145	33,526	36,766	44,054	165	26,918	34,788
Southeast	20,376	23,566	25,378	25,002	26,883	35,430	29		
West & Southwest	19,224	24,756	35,755	42,276	44,356	58,136	60	34,254	41,922
ALL REGIONS	18,179	24,569	31,452	29,945	37,287	58,136	271	29,574	37,371

State Data

	Min	Q1	Mean	Median	Q3	Max	N	Range Avg Min	Range Avg Max
CA	26,702	42,276	42,761	44,356	44,356	58,136	39	36,705	44,483
FL	21,897	24,149	24,913	25,002	25,293	28,226	11		
GA	20,376	20,886	25,545	24,549	28,049	35,430	16		
MD	23,614	24,441	29,612	27,098	33,197	48,190	17		
MI	23,570	28,569	27,819	28,569	28,569	28,569	20		
MO	18,179	18,898	21,653	21,216	24,253	25,646	39	18,179	27,269
NC	26,305	26,305	26,594	26,594	26,883	26,883	2		
OH	22,526	32,836	34,855	36,201	37,287	44,054	77	25,096	36,247
TX	24,253	24,253	26,783	27,726	28,371	28,371	3	24,294	35,235
UT	19,224	20,088	22,073	21,816	24,720	24,794	18	18,595	24,814
WI	33,526	34,954	36,352	36,766	37,453	37,956	29	33,562	37,478

Degree Required Data

	Min	Q1	Mean	Median	Q3	Max	N	Range Avg Min	Range Avg Max
High School	20,376	27,820	31,763	31,272	36,400	48,190	128	25,069	36,213
Associate's									
Bachelor's	26,305	26,305	26,594	26,594	26,883	26,883	2		
Master's									
Doctoral									

JANITORIAL CLEANER - CONTINUED
ALL PUBLIC LIBRARIES
Regional Data

	Min	Q1	Mean	Median	Q3	Max	N	Range Avg Min	Range Avg Max
North Atlantic	10,920	24,045	29,705	27,622	33,295	56,374	123	24,134	31,768
Great Lakes & Plains	10,712	21,063	27,986	27,872	36,201	44,782	300	24,320	32,060
Southeast	11,024	16,806	21,451	20,800	25,088	39,504	64	14,591	21,141
West & Southwest	12,938	20,088	30,570	26,704	44,356	58,136	92	30,016	37,444
ALL REGIONS	10,712	20,862	28,039	26,702	35,360	58,136	579	25,289	32,882

State Data

	Min	Q1	Mean	Median	Q3	Max	N	Range Avg Min	Range Avg Max
AL	14,664	15,413	18,044	17,888	20,675	21,736	4	14,576	21,850
AR	24,960	24,960	24,960	24,960	24,960	24,960	1	14,560	31,200
AZ	26,984	26,984	26,984	26,984	26,984	26,984	1	.	.
CA	16,453	40,300	40,943	44,356	44,356	58,136	42	35,147	42,681
CO	12,938	17,867	23,971	24,939	28,891	37,710	9	21,133	29,375
CT	30,763	40,272	45,102	49,895	49,895	49,895	6	.	.
FL	21,897	24,149	24,913	25,002	25,293	28,226	11	.	.
GA	14,560	20,376	24,358	24,036	27,914	35,430	19	.	.
IA	16,640	16,942	21,741	20,862	26,540	28,600	4	.	.
ID	22,880	22,880	22,880	22,880	22,880	22,880	1	20,800	31,200
IL	14,560	20,396	26,649	22,880	33,363	44,782	33	24,476	36,352
IN	14,560	18,720	21,258	21,018	22,373	29,598	16	19,323	22,963
KS	16,390	21,632	22,781	23,400	24,773	30,514	17	17,826	26,222
LA	15,080	15,080	17,798	18,866	19,448	19,448	3	14,976	18,595
MA	21,944	28,590	30,892	30,369	32,376	38,149	20	28,184	31,381
MD	16,432	23,614	27,360	25,739	29,945	48,190	26	.	.
ME	22,880	22,880	23,969	24,149	24,877	24,877	3	22,755	32,448
MI	10,712	24,569	26,045	28,569	28,569	31,200	34	19,584	23,398
MN	20,717	20,842	24,685	21,424	25,147	38,555	6	16,890	25,147
MO	16,952	18,916	21,573	20,980	24,242	28,662	44	17,918	26,795
MS	11,024	12,834	14,658	13,520	16,973	18,898	9	.	.
NC	18,624	22,465	25,987	26,594	29,510	32,136	4	.	.
ND	20,592	20,592	20,592	20,592	20,592	20,592	1	16,640	24,960
NH	26,042	26,042	29,234	29,234	32,427	32,427	2	23,826	32,822
NJ	33,295	33,961	39,675	37,842	47,555	47,555	6	.	.
NM	13,000	13,000	20,547	16,640	32,000	32,000	3	10,712	13,416
NY	18,200	24,253	30,860	27,560	32,136	56,374	37	24,139	33,445
OH	14,560	27,082	31,221	34,638	37,287	44,054	106	22,324	32,145
PA	10,920	15,392	21,936	20,800	25,043	35,922	18	19,320	24,471
RI	20,363	21,154	29,752	33,218	33,218	40,810	5	25,085	32,880
SC	16,474	16,474	16,474	16,474	16,474	16,474	1	.	.
TN	17,264	17,653	19,208	19,365	20,800	20,800	6	14,061	18,512
TX	16,058	16,723	19,694	17,705	23,571	28,371	14	20,405	30,004
UT	19,224	20,088	22,073	21,816	24,720	24,794	18	18,595	24,814
VA	14,042	15,656	20,883	16,180	19,032	39,504	5	.	.
WA	21,329	21,329	21,329	21,329	21,329	21,329	1	.	.
WI	18,450	34,954	35,622	36,766	37,453	43,049	39	33,437	37,326
WV	13,485	13,485	13,485	13,485	13,485	13,485	1	.	.
WY	23,275	23,275	23,733	23,962	23,962	23,962	3	21,944	26,978

Degree Required Data

	Min	Q1	Mean	Median	Q3	Max	N	Range Avg Min	Range Avg Max
High School	10,920	20,800	27,628	27,706	34,008	52,263	357	22,415	30,299
Associate's	.	.	.	.	.	.	.	.	.
Bachelor's	26,305	26,305	26,594	26,594	26,883	26,883	2	.	.
Master's	.	.	.	.	.	.	.	.	.
Doctoral	.	.	.	.	.	.	.	.	.

SECURITY (DISCIPLINE MONITOR)

Makes regular watch rounds of premises outside of scheduled working hours, where frequency of trips and stations is prescribed. Checks buildings, equipment and materials for leaks, fires, unauthorized individuals and other conditions. Ensures that all entrances and windows are secured, and that elevator and fire doors are closed. Makes written report of all irregularities or unusual circumstances.

Small Public Library
(Serving a population of 10,000 to 25,000)
Regional Data

	Min	Q1	Mean	Median	Q3	Max	N	Range Avg Min	Range Avg Max
North Atlantic	26,749	26,749	26,749	26,749	26,749	26,749	1	20,800	31,200
Great Lakes & Plains	21,200	23,080	26,100	27,040	29,120	29,120	4	20,800	33,280
ALL REGIONS	21,200	24,960	26,230	26,749	29,120	29,120	5	20,800	32,760

State Data

	Min	Q1	Mean	Median	Q3	Max	N	Range Avg Min	Range Avg Max
IL	21,200	23,080	26,100	27,040	29,120	29,120	4	20,800	33,280
NH	26,749	26,749	26,749	26,749	26,749	26,749	1	20,800	31,200

Degree Required Data

	Min	Q1	Mean	Median	Q3	Max	N	Range Avg Min	Range Avg Max
High School	21,200	23,080	26,100	27,040	29,120	29,120	4	20,800	33,280
Associate's	.	.	.	.	.	.	.	.	.
Bachelor's	26,749	26,749	26,749	26,749	26,749	26,749	1	20,800	31,200
Master's	.	.	.	.	.	.	.	.	.
Doctoral	.	.	.	.	.	.	.	.	.

SECURITY (DISCIPLINE MONITOR) - CONTINUED
Medium Public Library
(Serving a population of 25,000 to 99,999)
Regional Data

	Min	Q1	Mean	Median	Q3	Max	N	Range Avg Min	Range Avg Max
North Atlantic	19,677	21,559	30,116	27,352	40,290	42,848	8	21,493	31,429
Great Lakes & Plains	15,163	21,258	25,304	24,710	31,200	36,358	23	21,840	37,765
Southeast	12,584	12,584	18,061	16,640	24,960	24,960	3	.	.
West & Southwest	31,720	31,720	33,969	32,531	33,301	49,176	11	30,950	38,626
ALL REGIONS	12,584	22,194	27,795	29,598	32,531	49,176	45	24,458	36,900

State Data

	Min	Q1	Mean	Median	Q3	Max	N	Range Avg Min	Range Avg Max
CA	31,720	31,720	33,969	32,531	33,301	49,176	11	30,950	38,626
GA	24,960	24,960	24,960	24,960	24,960	24,960	1		
IL	18,720	22,194	26,268	25,422	30,572	36,358	18	23,367	40,887
MA	19,677	19,677	19,677	19,677	19,677	19,677	2	19,677	21,840
ME	23,442	23,442	23,442	23,442	23,442	23,442	2	22,755	32,448
MS	12,584	12,584	14,612	14,612	16,640	16,640	2		
NY	31,262	31,262	35,121	35,121	38,979	38,979	2	22,048	39,998
OH	15,163	15,350	21,836	16,266	31,200	31,200	5	14,206	22,152
PA	41,600	41,600	42,224	42,224	42,848	42,848	2		

Degree Required Data

	Min	Q1	Mean	Median	Q3	Max	N	Range Avg Min	Range Avg Max
High School	12,584	22,194	27,905	30,085	32,531	49,176	40	24,938	37,697
Associate's	24,960	24,960	24,960	24,960	24,960	24,960	1		
Bachelor's									
Master's									
Doctoral									

SECURITY (DISCIPLINE MONITOR) - CONTINUED
Large Public Library
(Serving a population of 100,000 to 499,999)
Regional Data

	Min	Q1	Mean	Median	Q3	Max	N	Range Avg Min	Range Avg Max
North Atlantic	15,600	15,600	18,312	19,232	20,104	20,104	3	17,361	25,709
Great Lakes & Plains	18,158	21,118	26,824	26,778	29,827	40,107	18	25,688	36,134
Southeast	20,800	20,800	28,641	26,552	36,942	42,024	11	21,980	35,095
West & Southwest	15,454	20,800	23,566	22,693	26,520	31,200	22	20,189	26,212
ALL REGIONS	15,454	20,800	25,394	24,101	28,080	42,024	54	21,921	30,510

State Data

	Min	Q1	Mean	Median	Q3	Max	N	Range Avg Min	Range Avg Max
CA	20,800	20,800	22,869	21,944	24,170	30,160	11	19,760	24,459
CO	22,506	22,506	24,676	23,982	27,539	27,539	3	21,764	32,642
IL	19,032	19,508	25,111	24,032	28,000	40,107	9	27,040	31,893
IN	35,734	35,734	35,734	35,734	35,734	35,734	1	26,229	38,043
KS	28,080	28,080	30,373	28,954	32,666	35,506	4	26,395	43,992
MO	18,158	18,158	18,158	18,158	18,158	18,158	1	16,952	24,648
NC	20,800	20,800	25,658	23,296	26,552	39,206	6	21,980	35,095
NM	25,480	26,000	27,560	26,780	29,120	31,200	4		
OH	22,302	22,302	29,876	29,876	37,449	37,449	2		
PA	15,600	15,600	18,312	19,232	20,104	20,104	3	17,361	25,709
SC	26,442	27,110	29,769	27,846	32,428	36,942	4		
TX	15,454	15,922	20,660	18,470	25,397	30,243	4		
VA	42,024	42,024	42,024	42,024	42,024	42,024	1		
WI	21,693	21,693	21,693	21,693	21,693	21,693	1	26,998	26,998

Degree Required Data

	Min	Q1	Mean	Median	Q3	Max	N	Range Avg Min	Range Avg Max
High School	15,454	20,800	24,311	21,944	28,000	42,024	42	21,805	29,902
Associate's	22,506	25,480	28,522	26,536	31,200	39,206	10	22,110	33,911
Bachelor's	27,539	27,539	32,494	32,494	37,449	37,449	2	24,482	36,733
Master's	.	.	.	.	.	.	.	.	.
Doctoral	.	.	.	.	.	.	.	.	.

SECURITY (DISCIPLINE MONITOR) - CONTINUED
Very Large Public Library
(Serving a population of 500,000 or more)
Regional Data

	Min	Q1	Mean	Median	Q3	Max	N	Range Avg Min	Range Avg Max
North Atlantic	23,712	24,939	34,006	26,125	47,923	47,923	13	.	.
Great Lakes & Plains	24,898	25,397	32,354	31,543	38,210	44,207	66	25,967	34,113
Southeast	23,352	26,877	29,574	30,437	33,049	35,621	17	.	.
West & Southwest	22,901	27,664	30,487	28,850	31,928	40,248	39	27,555	40,119
ALL REGIONS	22,901	26,125	31,624	30,347	36,525	47,923	135	26,640	36,657

State Data

	Min	Q1	Mean	Median	Q3	Max	N	Range Avg Min	Range Avg Max
AZ	27,227	27,664	30,860	28,850	31,928	40,248	35	27,664	40,248
FL	26,252	27,294	30,507	30,670	33,049	34,391	12	.	.
GA	23,352	24,036	27,335	24,996	28,668	35,621	5	.	.
MD	47,923	47,923	47,923	47,923	47,923	47,923	5	.	.
NJ	23,712	24,627	25,308	25,490	26,083	26,353	8	.	.
OH	24,898	25,397	32,354	31,543	38,210	44,207	66	25,967	34,113
TX	22,901	23,317	27,222	26,884	31,127	32,219	4	23,754	35,610

Degree Required Data

	Min	Q1	Mean	Median	Q3	Max	N	Range Avg Min	Range Avg Max
High School	23,352	26,832	31,630	30,347	36,525	44,207	107	26,640	36,657
Associate's	.	.	.	.	.	.	.	.	.
Bachelor's	.	.	.	.	.	.	.	.	.
Master's	.	.	.	.	.	.	.	.	.
Doctoral	.	.	.	.	.	.	.	.	.

SECURITY (DISCIPLINE MONITOR) - CONTINUED
ALL PUBLIC LIBRARIES
Regional Data

	Min	Q1	Mean	Median	Q3	Max	N	Range Avg Min	Range Avg Max
North Atlantic	15,600	23,442	30,588	26,042	41,600	47,923	25	20,184	29,690
Great Lakes & Plains	15,163	24,898	29,771	28,454	35,714	44,207	111	24,810	35,156
Southeast	12,584	24,960	28,129	27,377	33,049	42,024	31	21,980	35,095
West & Southwest	15,454	26,000	28,904	28,850	31,824	49,176	72	26,402	36,625
ALL REGIONS	12,584	24,898	29,383	28,392	33,049	49,176	239	25,057	35,372

State Data

	Min	Q1	Mean	Median	Q3	Max	N	Range Avg Min	Range Avg Max
AZ	27,227	27,664	30,860	28,850	31,928	40,248	35	27,664	40,248
CA	20,800	21,944	28,419	30,940	32,531	49,176	22	25,089	31,205
CO	22,506	22,506	24,676	23,982	27,539	27,539	3	21,764	32,642
FL	26,252	27,294	30,507	30,670	33,049	34,391	12	.	.
GA	23,352	24,036	26,939	24,978	28,668	35,621	6	.	.
IL	18,720	21,258	25,910	24,960	29,598	40,107	31	23,525	38,516
IN	35,734	35,734	35,734	35,734	35,734	35,734	1	26,229	38,043
KS	28,080	28,080	30,373	28,954	32,666	35,506	4	26,395	43,992
MA	19,677	19,677	19,677	19,677	19,677	19,677	2	19,677	21,840
MD	47,923	47,923	47,923	47,923	47,923	47,923	5	.	.
ME	23,442	23,442	23,442	23,442	23,442	23,442	2	22,755	32,448
MO	18,158	18,158	18,158	18,158	18,158	18,158	1	16,952	24,648
MS	12,584	12,584	14,612	14,612	16,640	16,640	2	.	.
NC	20,800	20,800	25,658	23,296	26,552	39,206	6	21,980	35,095
NH	26,749	26,749	26,749	26,749	26,749	26,749	1	20,800	31,200
NJ	23,712	24,627	25,308	25,490	26,083	26,353	8	.	.
NM	25,480	26,000	27,560	26,780	29,120	31,200	4	.	.
NY	31,262	31,262	35,121	35,121	38,979	38,979	2	22,048	39,998
OH	15,163	25,355	31,566	31,200	37,449	44,207	73	25,289	33,423
PA	15,600	19,232	27,877	20,104	41,600	42,848	5	17,361	25,709
SC	26,442	27,110	29,769	27,846	32,428	36,942	4	.	.
TX	15,454	18,470	23,941	23,317	30,139	32,219	8	23,754	35,610
VA	42,024	42,024	42,024	42,024	42,024	42,024	1	.	.
WI	21,693	21,693	21,693	21,693	21,693	21,693	1	26,998	26,998

Degree Required Data

	Min	Q1	Mean	Median	Q3	Max	N	Range Avg Min	Range Avg Max
High School	12,584	24,898	29,151	28,454	33,283	49,176	193	25,267	35,544
Associate's	22,506	24,960	28,198	26,520	31,200	39,206	11	22,110	33,911
Bachelor's	26,749	26,749	30,579	27,539	37,449	37,449	3	22,641	33,966
Master's	.	.	.	.	.	.	.	.	.
Doctoral	.	.	.	.	.	.	.	.	.

DEVELOPMENT MANAGER

Manages and may participate in all aspects of library's annual fund development program. Identifies potential donors and maintains donor database. Responsible for maintaining budgets of delegated programs and may supervise staff.

Very Small Public Library
(Serving a population of less than 10,000)
Regional Data

	Min	Q1	Mean	Median	Q3	Max	N	Range Avg Min	Range Avg Max
Great Lakes & Plains	32,000	32,000	32,000	32,000	32,000	32,000	1	.	.
ALL REGIONS	32,000	32,000	32,000	32,000	32,000	32,000	1	.	.

State Data

	Min	Q1	Mean	Median	Q3	Max	N	Range Avg Min	Range Avg Max
KS	32,000	32,000	32,000	32,000	32,000	32,000	1	.	.

Degree Required Data

	Min	Q1	Mean	Median	Q3	Max	N	Range Avg Min	Range Avg Max
High School	32,000	32,000	32,000	32,000	32,000	32,000	1	.	.
Associate's	.	.	.	.	.	.	.	.	.
Bachelor's	.	.	.	.	.	.	.	.	.
Master's	.	.	.	.	.	.	.	.	.
Doctoral	.	.	.	.	.	.	.	.	.

DEVELOPMENT MANAGER - CONTINUED
Small Public Library
(Serving a population of 10,000 to 25,000)
Regional Data

	Min	Q1	Mean	Median	Q3	Max	N	Range Avg Min	Range Avg Max
North Atlantic	31,200	31,200	31,200	31,200	31,200	31,200	1	.	.
ALL REGIONS	31,200	31,200	31,200	31,200	31,200	31,200	1	.	.

State Data

	Min	Q1	Mean	Median	Q3	Max	N	Range Avg Min	Range Avg Max
ME	31,200	31,200	31,200	31,200	31,200	31,200	1	.	.

Degree Required Data

	Min	Q1	Mean	Median	Q3	Max	N	Range Avg Min	Range Avg Max
High School	.	.	.	.	.	.	.	.	.
Associate's	.	.	.	.	.	.	.	.	.
Bachelor's	31,200	31,200	31,200	31,200	31,200	31,200	1	.	.
Master's	.	.	.	.	.	.	.	.	.
Doctoral	.	.	.	.	.	.	.	.	.

DEVELOPMENT MANAGER - CONTINUED
Medium Public Library
(Serving a population of 25,000 to 99,999)
Regional Data

	Min	Q1	Mean	Median	Q3	Max	N	Range Avg Min	Range Avg Max
North Atlantic	46,634	46,634	57,668	57,668	68,702	68,702	2	41,434	59,072
Great Lakes & Plains	44,574	44,574	64,626	64,626	84,677	84,677	2	55,266	84,677
West & Southwest	36,000	36,000	43,122	43,122	50,244	50,244	2	.	.
ALL REGIONS	36,000	44,574	55,139	48,439	68,702	84,677	6	48,350	71,874

State Data

	Min	Q1	Mean	Median	Q3	Max	N	Range Avg Min	Range Avg Max
CA	50,244	50,244	50,244	50,244	50,244	50,244	1	.	.
CO	36,000	36,000	36,000	36,000	36,000	36,000	1	.	.
IL	84,677	84,677	84,677	84,677	84,677	84,677	1	55,266	84,677
ME	46,634	46,634	46,634	46,634	46,634	46,634	1	41,434	59,072
MN	44,574	44,574	44,574	44,574	44,574	44,574	1	.	.
PA	68,702	68,702	68,702	68,702	68,702	68,702	1	.	.

Degree Required Data

	Min	Q1	Mean	Median	Q3	Max	N	Range Avg Min	Range Avg Max
High School	68,702	68,702	68,702	68,702	68,702	68,702	1	.	.
Associate's	.	.	.	.	.	.		.	.
Bachelor's	44,574	44,574	47,151	46,634	50,244	50,244	3	41,434	59,072
Master's	84,677	84,677	84,677	84,677	84,677	84,677	1	55,266	84,677
Doctoral	.	.	.	.	.	.		.	.

DEVELOPMENT MANAGER - CONTINUED
Large Public Library
(Serving a population of 100,000 to 499,999)
Regional Data

	Min	Q1	Mean	Median	Q3	Max	N	Range Avg Min	Range Avg Max
North Atlantic	24,000	45,647	58,492	56,945	73,129	94,286	6	.	.
Great Lakes & Plains	45,448	45,448	56,767	57,304	67,548	67,548	3	37,222	57,346
Southeast	24,960	24,960	24,960	24,960	24,960	24,960	1	.	.
West & Southwest	56,472	56,472	78,293	78,293	100,113	100,113	2	43,846	70,366
ALL REGIONS	24,000	45,547	58,566	56,888	70,339	100,113	12	39,430	61,686

State Data

	Min	Q1	Mean	Median	Q3	Max	N	Range Avg Min	Range Avg Max
CA	100,113	100,113	100,113	100,113	100,113	100,113	1	.	.
CO	56,472	56,472	56,472	56,472	56,472	56,472	1	43,846	70,366
GA	24,960	24,960	24,960	24,960	24,960	24,960	1	.	.
IL	45,448	45,448	45,448	45,448	45,448	45,448	1	36,858	52,042
KS	57,304	57,304	57,304	57,304	57,304	57,304	1	37,586	62,650
MD	45,647	45,647	45,647	45,647	45,647	45,647	1	.	.
MO	67,548	67,548	67,548	67,548	67,548	67,548	1	.	.
NJ	60,557	60,557	60,557	60,557	60,557	60,557	1	.	.
NY	73,129	73,129	73,129	73,129	73,129	73,129	1	.	.
PA	24,000	24,000	57,207	53,333	94,286	94,286	3	.	.

Degree Required Data

	Min	Q1	Mean	Median	Q3	Max	N	Range Avg Min	Range Avg Max
High School	24,960	24,960	24,960	24,960	24,960	24,960	1	.	.
Associate's	.	.	.	.	.	.		.	.
Bachelor's	24,000	45,647	57,917	57,304	67,548	94,286	9	37,222	57,346
Master's	56,472	56,472	78,293	78,293	100,113	100,113	2	43,846	70,366
Doctoral	.	.	.	.	.	.		.	.

DEVELOPMENT MANAGER - CONTINUED
Very Large Public Library
(Serving a population of 500,000 or more)
Regional Data

	Min	Q1	Mean	Median	Q3	Max	N	Range Avg Min	Range Avg Max
North Atlantic	75,075	75,075	75,075	75,075	75,075	75,075	1	.	.
Great Lakes & Plains	66,587	66,587	69,601	70,350	71,864	71,864	3	65,603	94,370
Southeast	55,685	87,011	93,358	100,848	102,627	120,619	5	.	.
West & Southwest	75,660	75,660	88,055	82,763	105,742	105,742	3	62,270	75,660
ALL REGIONS	55,685	71,107	84,569	79,212	101,737	120,619	12	63,937	85,015

State Data

	Min	Q1	Mean	Median	Q3	Max	N	Range Avg Min	Range Avg Max
CA	75,660	75,660	88,055	82,763	105,742	105,742	3	62,270	75,660
FL	87,011	87,011	103,419	102,627	120,619	120,619	3	.	.
MD	75,075	75,075	75,075	75,075	75,075	75,075	1	.	.
MO	70,350	70,350	70,350	70,350	70,350	70,350	1	.	.
NC	55,685	55,685	55,685	55,685	55,685	55,685	1	.	.
OH	66,587	66,587	69,226	69,226	71,864	71,864	2	65,603	94,370
VA	100,848	100,848	100,848	100,848	100,848	100,848	1	.	.

Degree Required Data

	Min	Q1	Mean	Median	Q3	Max	N	Range Avg Min	Range Avg Max
High School	100,848	100,848	100,848	100,848	100,848	100,848	1	.	.
Associate's	.	.	.	.	.	.		.	.
Bachelor's	55,685	71,864	84,541	75,660	102,627	120,619	9	63,937	85,015
Master's	70,350	70,350	70,350	70,350	70,350	70,350	1	.	.
Doctoral	.	.	.	.	.	.		.	.

DEVELOPMENT MANAGER - CONTINUED
ALL PUBLIC LIBRARIES
Regional Data

	Min	Q1	Mean	Median	Q3	Max	N	Range Avg Min	Range Avg Max
North Atlantic	24,000	45,647	57,256	56,945	73,129	94,286	10	41,434	59,072
Great Lakes & Plains	32,000	45,448	60,039	66,587	70,350	84,677	9	48,828	73,434
Southeast	24,960	55,685	81,958	93,929	102,627	120,619	6	.	.
West & Southwest	36,000	50,244	72,428	75,660	100,113	105,742	7	53,058	73,013
ALL REGIONS	24,000	46,140	65,989	67,068	83,720	120,619	32	48,980	71,262

State Data

	Min	Q1	Mean	Median	Q3	Max	N	Range Avg Min	Range Avg Max
CA	50,244	75,660	82,904	82,763	100,113	105,742	5	62,270	75,660
CO	36,000	36,000	46,236	46,236	56,472	56,472	2	43,846	70,366
FL	87,011	87,011	103,419	102,627	120,619	120,619	3	.	.
GA	24,960	24,960	24,960	24,960	24,960	24,960	1		
IL	45,448	45,448	65,062	65,062	84,677	84,677	2	46,062	68,359
KS	32,000	32,000	44,652	44,652	57,304	57,304	2	37,586	62,650
MD	45,647	45,647	60,361	60,361	75,075	75,075	2	.	.
ME	31,200	31,200	38,917	38,917	46,634	46,634	2	41,434	59,072
MN	44,574	44,574	44,574	44,574	44,574	44,574	1		
MO	67,548	67,548	68,949	68,949	70,350	70,350	2	.	.
NC	55,685	55,685	55,685	55,685	55,685	55,685	1		
NJ	60,557	60,557	60,557	60,557	60,557	60,557	1		
NY	73,129	73,129	73,129	73,129	73,129	73,129	1		
OH	66,587	66,587	69,226	69,226	71,864	71,864	2	65,603	94,370
PA	24,000	38,667	60,081	61,018	81,494	94,286	4	.	.
VA	100,848	100,848	100,848	100,848	100,848	100,848	1		

Degree Required Data

	Min	Q1	Mean	Median	Q3	Max	N	Range Avg Min	Range Avg Max
High School	24,960	28,480	56,628	50,351	84,775	100,848	4	.	.
Associate's	.	.	.	.	.	.		.	.
Bachelor's	24,000	46,634	66,126	63,572	75,660	120,619	22	48,750	68,759
Master's	56,472	63,411	77,903	77,513	92,395	100,113	4	49,556	77,522
Doctoral	.	.	.	.	.	.		.	.

GRANT PROPOSAL WRITER

Researches and investigates grant opportunities. Prepares grant proposals in accordance with funder's giving policies, guidelines, and criteria.

Large Public Library
(Serving a population of 100,000 to 499,999)
Regional Data

	Min	Q1	Mean	Median	Q3	Max	N	Range Avg Min	Range Avg Max
North Atlantic	21,800	21,800	31,745	35,877	37,559	37,559	3	.	.
Southeast	34,244	34,244	34,244	34,244	34,244	34,244	1	.	.
West & Southwest	46,224	46,224	73,169	73,169	100,113	100,113	2	.	.
ALL REGIONS	21,800	34,244	45,970	36,718	46,224	100,113	6	.	.

State Data

	Min	Q1	Mean	Median	Q3	Max	N	Range Avg Min	Range Avg Max
CA	46,224	46,224	73,169	73,169	100,113	100,113	2	.	.
MD	37,559	37,559	37,559	37,559	37,559	37,559	1	.	.
NJ	35,877	35,877	35,877	35,877	35,877	35,877	1	.	.
PA	21,800	21,800	21,800	21,800	21,800	21,800	1	.	.
TN	34,244	34,244	34,244	34,244	34,244	34,244	1	.	.

Degree Required Data

	Min	Q1	Mean	Median	Q3	Max	N	Range Avg Min	Range Avg Max
High School	.	.	.	.	.	.		.	.
Associate's	.	.	.	.	.	.		.	.
Bachelor's	21,800	34,244	35,141	35,877	37,559	46,224	5	.	.
Master's	100,113	100,113	100,113	100,113	100,113	100,113	1	.	.
Doctoral	.	.	.	.	.	.		.	.

GRANT PROPOSAL WRITER - CONTINUED
Very Large Public Library
(Serving a population of 500,000 or more)
Regional Data

	Min	Q1	Mean	Median	Q3	Max	N	Range Avg Min	Range Avg Max
North Atlantic	36,135	36,135	36,135	36,135	36,135	36,135	1	.	.
Great Lakes & Plains	32,760	32,760	47,773	47,773	62,785	62,785	2	.	.
Southeast	56,046	56,046	72,303	64,115	96,748	96,748	3	.	.
West & Southwest	73,112	73,112	73,112	73,112	73,112	73,112	1	48,963	73,112
ALL REGIONS	32,760	36,135	60,243	62,785	73,112	96,748	7	48,963	73,112

State Data

	Min	Q1	Mean	Median	Q3	Max	N	Range Avg Min	Range Avg Max
AZ	73,112	73,112	73,112	73,112	73,112	73,112	1	48,963	73,112
FL	96,748	96,748	96,748	96,748	96,748	96,748	1	.	.
GA	56,046	56,046	56,046	56,046	56,046	56,046	1	.	.
IN	32,760	32,760	32,760	32,760	32,760	32,760	1	.	.
MD	36,135	36,135	36,135	36,135	36,135	36,135	1	.	.
MI	62,785	62,785	62,785	62,785	62,785	62,785	1	.	.
NC	64,115	64,115	64,115	64,115	64,115	64,115	1	.	.

Degree Required Data

	Min	Q1	Mean	Median	Q3	Max	N	Range Avg Min	Range Avg Max
High School	.	.	.	.	.	.		.	.
Associate's	.	.	.	.	.	.		.	.
Bachelor's	32,760	36,135	58,098	59,416	64,115	96,748	6	.	.
Master's	73,112	73,112	73,112	73,112	73,112	73,112	1	48,963	73,112
Doctoral	.	.	.	.	.	.		.	.

GRANT PROPOSAL WRITER - CONTINUED
ALL PUBLIC LIBRARIES
Regional Data

	Min	Q1	Mean	Median	Q3	Max	N	Range Avg Min	Range Avg Max
North Atlantic	21,800	28,839	32,843	36,006	36,847	37,559	4	.	.
Great Lakes & Plains	32,760	32,760	47,773	47,773	62,785	62,785	2	.	.
Southeast	34,244	45,145	62,788	60,081	80,432	96,748	4	.	.
West & Southwest	46,224	46,224	73,150	73,112	100,113	100,113	3	48,963	73,112
ALL REGIONS	21,800	35,877	53,655	46,224	64,115	100,113	13	48,963	73,112

State Data

	Min	Q1	Mean	Median	Q3	Max	N	Range Avg Min	Range Avg Max
AZ	73,112	73,112	73,112	73,112	73,112	73,112	1	48,963	73,112
CA	46,224	46,224	73,169	73,169	100,113	100,113	2	.	.
FL	96,748	96,748	96,748	96,748	96,748	96,748	1	.	.
GA	56,046	56,046	56,046	56,046	56,046	56,046	1	.	.
IN	32,760	32,760	32,760	32,760	32,760	32,760	1	.	.
MD	36,135	36,135	36,847	36,847	37,559	37,559	2	.	.
MI	62,785	62,785	62,785	62,785	62,785	62,785	1	.	.
NC	64,115	64,115	64,115	64,115	64,115	64,115	1	.	.
NJ	35,877	35,877	35,877	35,877	35,877	35,877	1	.	.
PA	21,800	21,800	21,800	21,800	21,800	21,800	1	.	.
TN	34,244	34,244	34,244	34,244	34,244	34,244	1	.	.

Degree Required Data

	Min	Q1	Mean	Median	Q3	Max	N	Range Avg Min	Range Avg Max
High School	.	.	.	.	.	.		.	.
Associate's									
Bachelor's	21,800	34,244	47,663	37,559	62,785	96,748	11	.	.
Master's	73,112	73,112	86,613	86,613	100,113	100,113	2	48,963	73,112
Doctoral	.	.	.	.	.	.		.	.

ASSOCIATE LIBRARIAN OF ADULT SERVICES (NON-MLS DEGREED)

Provides assistance to patrons including topical research and material location. Assists patrons with the use of library resources and equipment. Screens the collection for outdated or unused materials following established guidelines. May perform managerial and administrative duties. Provides access to materials, services and programs intended to meet the needs of the adult users of a public library.

Two-Year College
Regional Data

	Min	Q1	Mean	Median	Q3	Max	N	Range Avg Min	Range Avg Max
North Atlantic	29,120	29,120	35,060	29,560	41,000	52,000	4	.	.
Great Lakes & Plains	15,273	16,000	25,873	22,187	38,000	38,000	10	.	.
Southeast	16,105	31,200	39,538	32,000	52,099	66,286	5	.	.
West & Southwest	18,000	18,000	24,157	20,155	34,315	34,315	3	18,304	20,155
ALL REGIONS	15,273	17,493	30,415	29,560	38,000	66,286	22	18,304	20,155

State Data

	Min	Q1	Mean	Median	Q3	Max	N	Range Avg Min	Range Avg Max
AL	32,000	32,000	49,143	49,143	66,286	66,286	2	.	.
AR	16,105	16,105	16,105	16,105	16,105	16,105	1	.	.
FL	31,200	31,200	31,200	31,200	31,200	31,200	1	.	.
IL	35,800	35,800	35,800	35,800	35,800	35,800	1	.	.
KS	15,273	15,787	16,409	16,000	17,493	17,493	5	.	.
MA	52,000	52,000	52,000	52,000	52,000	52,000	1	.	.
MN	26,880	26,880	26,880	26,880	26,880	26,880	1	.	.
MO	38,000	38,000	38,000	38,000	38,000	38,000	3	.	.
MT	20,155	20,155	20,155	20,155	20,155	20,155	1	18,304	20,155
NM	18,000	18,000	18,000	18,000	18,000	18,000	1	.	.
OR	34,315	34,315	34,315	34,315	34,315	34,315	1	.	.
PA	29,120	29,120	29,413	29,120	30,000	30,000	3	.	.
WV	52,099	52,099	52,099	52,099	52,099	52,099	1	.	.

Degree Level Data

	Min	Q1	Mean	Median	Q3	Max	N	Range Avg Min	Range Avg Max
High School	15,273	15,273	16,185	15,787	17,493	17,493	3	.	.
Associates	16,000	16,105	20,915	18,000	20,155	34,315	5	18,304	20,155
Bachelors	30,000	30,600	36,300	31,600	42,000	52,000	4	.	.
Masters	26,880	29,120	39,615	35,800	52,099	66,286	7	.	.
Doctoral									

ASSOCIATE LIBRARIAN OF ADULT SERVICES (NON-MLS DEGREED) - CONTINUED
Four-Year College
Regional Data

	Min	Q1	Mean	Median	Q3	Max	N	Range Avg Min	Range Avg Max
North Atlantic	34,500	34,500	34,500	34,500	34,500	34,500	1		
Great Lakes & Plains	20,800	25,520	28,891	28,968	30,200	40,955	8	30,472	44,928
Southeast	17,659	17,659	20,552	17,659	20,707	40,364	12		
West & Southwest	17,555	18,408	26,727	22,031	32,982	47,316	10	17,472	29,099
ALL REGIONS	17,555	17,659	25,146	21,703	30,077	47,316	31	20,072	32,265

State Data

	Min	Q1	Mean	Median	Q3	Max	N	Range Avg Min	Range Avg Max
CO	47,316	47,316	47,316	47,316	47,316	47,316	1		
FL	19,532	19,532	19,532	19,532	19,532	19,532	1		
IA	30,323	30,323	30,323	30,323	30,323	30,323	1		
IL	29,536	29,536	29,806	29,806	30,077	30,077	2		
KY	17,659	17,659	17,659	17,659	17,659	17,659	7		
LA	21,413	21,413	21,558	21,558	21,703	21,703	2		
ME	34,500	34,500	34,500	34,500	34,500	34,500	1		
MN	40,955	40,955	40,955	40,955	40,955	40,955	1	30,472	44,928
MO	24,000	24,000	24,000	24,000	24,000	24,000	1		
OH	20,800	20,800	24,600	24,600	28,400	28,400	2		
SC	40,364	40,364	40,364	40,364	40,364	40,364	1		
TN	20,000	20,000	20,000	20,000	20,000	20,000	1		
TX	39,999	39,999	39,999	39,999	39,999	39,999	1		
UT	17,555	18,117	22,494	21,702	24,889	32,982	8	17,472	29,099
WI	27,040	27,040	27,040	27,040	27,040	27,040	1		

Degree Required Data

	Min	Q1	Mean	Median	Q3	Max	N	Range Avg Min	Range Avg Max
High School	17,659	17,659	26,485	17,659	40,955	47,316	6	30,472	44,928
Associate's	27,040	27,040	28,558	28,558	30,077	30,077	2		
Bachelor's	17,555	18,408	23,795	21,558	28,400	40,364	22	17,472	29,099
Master's	39,999	39,999	39,999	39,999	39,999	39,999	1		
Doctoral									

ASSOCIATE LIBRARIAN OF ADULT SERVICES (NON-MLS DEGREED) - CONTINUED
University
(Includes ARL Data)
Regional Data

	Min	Q1	Mean	Median	Q3	Max	N	Range Avg Min	Range Avg Max
North Atlantic	19,776	25,488	32,474	34,220	39,460	41,680	4		
Great Lakes & Plains	32,714	41,113	43,875	45,790	45,790	55,752	11		
Southeast	18,096	22,507	27,699	26,541	30,911	52,582	58		
West & Southwest	24,909	25,872	36,553	35,520	43,020	54,696	7		
ALL REGIONS	18,096	23,937	30,937	30,072	36,703	55,752	80		

State Data

	Min	Q1	Mean	Median	Q3	Max	N	Range Avg Min	Range Avg Max
AL	39,920	39,920	39,920	39,920	39,920	39,920	1	.	.
CO	43,020	43,020	43,020	43,020	43,020	43,020	1	.	.
DC	37,240	37,240	37,240	37,240	37,240	37,240	1	.	.
FL	24,373	24,373	24,478	24,478	24,583	24,583	2	.	.
GA	30,639	30,639	35,135	35,135	39,631	39,631	2	.	.
IA	41,113	45,665	46,180	45,790	45,790	55,752	9	.	.
LA	18,096	19,843	25,722	23,650	31,602	38,840	19	.	.
MA	41,680	41,680	41,680	41,680	41,680	41,680	1	.	.
MO	34,287	34,287	34,287	34,287	34,287	34,287	1	.	.
MT	30,568	30,568	30,568	30,568	30,568	30,568	1	.	.
NC	20,155	22,507	26,541	25,262	30,280	44,160	22	.	.
NY	31,200	31,200	31,200	31,200	31,200	31,200	1	.	.
PA	19,776	19,776	19,776	19,776	19,776	19,776	1	.	.
SC	24,770	25,145	31,231	30,290	33,726	52,582	12	.	.
SD	32,714	32,714	32,714	32,714	32,714	32,714	1	.	.
TX	24,909	24,909	28,767	25,872	35,520	35,520	3	.	.
WA	41,283	41,283	47,990	47,990	54,696	54,696	2	.	.

Degree Required Data

	Min	Q1	Mean	Median	Q3	Max	N	Range Avg Min	Range Avg Max
High School	18,096	21,763	28,578	25,257	31,200	45,790	50	.	.
Associate's	.	.	.	.	.	.		.	.
Bachelor's	19,776	27,103	33,967	31,121	39,236	55,752	20	.	.
Master's	30,139	30,676	36,171	33,726	38,923	52,582	8	.	.
Doctoral	.	.	.	.	.	.		.	.

ASSOCIATE LIBRARIAN OF ADULT SERVICES (NON-MLS DEGREED) - CONTINUED
ALL ACADEMIC LIBRARIES
Regional Data

	Min	Q1	Mean	Median	Q3	Max	N	Range Avg Min	Range Avg Max
North Atlantic	19,776	29,120	33,848	31,200	37,240	52,000	9	.	.
Great Lakes & Plains	15,273	26,880	33,534	34,287	44,141	55,752	29	30,472	44,928
Southeast	16,105	20,717	27,345	24,770	31,056	66,286	75	.	.
West & Southwest	17,555	20,764	29,780	26,810	37,760	54,696	20	17,638	27,310
ALL REGIONS	15,273	21,372	29,501	28,426	34,500	66,286	133	19,777	30,247

State Data

	Min	Q1	Mean	Median	Q3	Max	N	Range Avg Min	Range Avg Max
AL	32,000	32,000	46,069	39,920	66,286	66,286	3		
AR	16,105	16,105	16,105	16,105	16,105	16,105	1		
CO	43,020	43,020	45,168	45,168	47,316	47,316	2		
DC	37,240	37,240	37,240	37,240	37,240	37,240	1		
FL	19,532	21,953	24,922	24,478	27,892	31,200	4		
GA	30,639	30,639	35,135	35,135	39,631	39,631	2		
IA	30,323	44,141	44,594	45,790	45,790	55,752	10		
IL	29,536	29,536	31,804	30,077	35,800	35,800	3		
KS	15,273	15,787	16,409	16,000	17,493	17,493	5		
KY	17,659	17,659	17,659	17,659	17,659	17,659	7		
LA	18,096	20,717	25,325	22,006	30,005	38,840	21		
MA	41,680	41,680	46,840	46,840	52,000	52,000	2		
ME	34,500	34,500	34,500	34,500	34,500	34,500	1		
MN	26,880	26,880	33,918	33,918	40,955	40,955	2	30,472	44,928
MO	24,000	34,287	34,457	38,000	38,000	38,000	5		
MT	20,155	20,155	25,362	25,362	30,568	30,568	2	18,304	20,155
NC	20,155	22,507	26,541	25,262	30,280	44,160	22		
NM	18,000	18,000	18,000	18,000	18,000	18,000	1		
NY	31,200	31,200	31,200	31,200	31,200	31,200	1		
OH	20,800	20,800	24,600	24,600	28,400	28,400	2		
OR	34,315	34,315	34,315	34,315	34,315	34,315	1		
PA	19,776	24,448	27,004	29,120	29,560	30,000	4		
SC	24,770	25,520	31,933	30,441	34,108	52,582	13		
SD	32,714	32,714	32,714	32,714	32,714	32,714	1		
TN	20,000	20,000	20,000	20,000	20,000	20,000	1		
TX	24,909	25,391	31,575	30,696	37,760	39,999	4		
UT	17,555	18,117	22,494	21,702	24,889	32,982	8	17,472	29,099
WA	41,283	41,283	47,990	47,990	54,696	54,696	2		
WI	27,040	27,040	27,040	27,040	27,040	27,040	1		
WV	52,099	52,099	52,099	52,099	52,099	52,099	1		

Degree Required Data

	Min	Q1	Mean	Median	Q3	Max	N	Range Avg Min	Range Avg Max
High School	15,273	20,699	27,735	24,583	31,200	47,316	59	30,472	44,928
Associate's	16,000	16,105	23,099	20,155	30,077	34,315	7	18,304	20,155
Bachelor's	17,555	21,413	29,305	28,700	32,982	55,752	46	17,472	29,099
Master's	26,880	30,290	37,917	34,954	40,840	66,286	16		
Doctoral									

ASSOCIATE LIBRARIAN OF ARCHIVES AND SPECIAL COLLECTIONS (NON-MLS DEGREED)

Provides assistance to patrons including topical research and material location. Assists patrons with the use of library resources and equipment. Screens the collection for outdated or unused materials following established guidelines. May perform managerial and administrative duties. Manages and maintains collection; identifies and appraises records, authenticates, describes and documents, facilitates access and use, preserves and conserves, and exhibits collection.

Four-Year College
Regional Data

	Min	Q1	Mean	Median	Q3	Max	N	Range Avg Min	Range Avg Max
North Atlantic	38,811	38,811	43,557	43,557	48,302	48,302	2	.	.
Southeast	21,549	21,549	26,774	26,774	32,000	32,000	2	.	.
West & Southwest	48,000	48,000	48,000	48,000	48,000	48,000	1	.	.
ALL REGIONS	21,549	32,000	37,732	38,811	48,000	48,302	5	.	.

State Data

	Min	Q1	Mean	Median	Q3	Max	N	Range Avg Min	Range Avg Max
CO	48,000	48,000	48,000	48,000	48,000	48,000	1	.	.
GA	21,549	21,549	21,549	21,549	21,549	21,549	1	.	.
MD	48,302	48,302	48,302	48,302	48,302	48,302	1	.	.
NY	38,811	38,811	38,811	38,811	38,811	38,811	1	.	.
WV	32,000	32,000	32,000	32,000	32,000	32,000	1	.	.

Degree Required Data

	Min	Q1	Mean	Median	Q3	Max	N	Range Avg Min	Range Avg Max
High School	21,549	21,549	34,774	34,774	48,000	48,000	2	.	.
Associate's	.	.	.	.	.			.	.
Bachelor's	32,000	32,000	35,406	35,406	38,811	38,811	2	.	.
Master's	48,302	48,302	48,302	48,302	48,302	48,302	1	.	.
Doctoral	.	.	.	.	.			.	.

ASSOCIATE LIBRARIAN OF ARCHIVES AND SPECIAL COLLECTIONS (NON-MLS DEGREED) - CONTINUED
University
(Includes ARL Data)
Regional Data

	Min	Q1	Mean	Median	Q3	Max	N	Range Avg Min	Range Avg Max
North Atlantic	29,531	45,197	45,625	47,543	52,100	55,745	9	.	.
Great Lakes & Plains	24,000	28,600	41,830	36,145	42,811	95,526	8	.	.
Southeast	19,727	25,476	31,539	29,584	35,566	52,053	16	.	.
West & Southwest	29,330	36,552	54,496	53,291	58,628	104,000	7	.	.
ALL REGIONS	19,727	29,109	40,784	36,342	48,769	104,000	40	.	.

State Data

	Min	Q1	Mean	Median	Q3	Max	N	Range Avg Min	Range Avg Max
AR	26,182	26,182	26,182	26,182	26,182	26,182	1	.	.
AZ	53,291	53,291	54,088	54,088	54,885	54,885	2	.	.
CA	104,000	104,000	104,000	104,000	104,000	104,000	1	.	.
CO	36,552	36,552	40,668	40,668	44,784	44,784	2	.	.
DC	29,531	29,531	29,531	29,531	29,531	29,531	1	.	.
FL	34,188	34,188	35,160	35,160	36,132	36,132	2	.	.
GA	19,727	19,727	33,134	33,134	46,540	46,540	2	.	.
IA	38,002	38,002	38,065	38,065	38,127	38,127	2	.	.
IL	24,000	24,000	55,674	47,495	95,526	95,526	3	.	.
LA	19,812	19,812	35,933	35,933	52,053	52,053	2	.	.
MA	49,996	49,996	51,048	51,048	52,100	52,100	2	.	.
MD	45,197	45,197	50,471	50,471	55,745	55,745	4	.	.
MO	34,287	34,287	34,287	34,287	34,287	34,287	1	.	.
NC	28,888	29,584	33,255	32,640	36,925	38,850	4	.	.
NE	26,000	26,000	26,000	26,000	26,000	26,000	1	.	.
NY	29,571	29,571	38,557	38,557	47,543	47,543	2	.	.
OH	31,200	31,200	31,200	31,200	31,200	31,200	1	.	.
SC	24,770	24,770	27,393	28,141	28,239	31,046	5	.	.
TX	29,330	29,330	29,330	29,330	29,330	29,330	1	.	.
WA	58,628	58,628	58,628	58,628	58,628	58,628	1	.	.

Degree Required Data

	Min	Q1	Mean	Median	Q3	Max	N	Range Avg Min	Range Avg Max
High School	24,770	28,190	35,252	32,234	38,065	55,745	12	.	.
Associate's	19,727	19,727	19,727	19,727	19,727	19,727	1	.	.
Bachelor's	19,812	26,182	33,182	29,551	38,850	49,996	10	.	.
Master's	24,000	31,200	49,644	46,540	54,885	104,000	11	.	.
Doctoral	47,495	47,495	65,025	52,053	95,526	95,526	3	.	.

ASSOCIATE LIBRARIAN OF ARCHIVES AND SPECIAL COLLECTIONS (NON-MLS DEGREED) - CONTINUED
ALL ACADEMIC LIBRARIES
Regional Data

	Min	Q1	Mean	Median	Q3	Max	N	Range Avg Min	Range Avg Max
North Atlantic	29,531	38,811	45,249	47,543	52,100	55,745	11	.	.
Great Lakes & Plains	24,000	28,600	41,830	36,145	42,811	95,526	8	.	.
Southeast	19,727	24,770	31,009	29,584	35,000	52,053	18	.	.
West & Southwest	29,330	40,668	53,684	50,646	56,757	104,000	8	.	.
ALL REGIONS	19,727	29,330	40,445	36,552	48,000	104,000	45	.	.

State Data

	Min	Q1	Mean	Median	Q3	Max	N	Range Avg Min	Range Avg Max
AR	26,182	26,182	26,182	26,182	26,182	26,182	1	.	.
AZ	53,291	53,291	54,088	54,088	54,885	54,885	2	.	.
CA	104,000	104,000	104,000	104,000	104,000	104,000	1	.	.
CO	36,552	36,552	43,112	44,784	48,000	48,000	3	.	.
DC	29,531	29,531	29,531	29,531	29,531	29,531	1	.	.
FL	34,188	34,188	35,160	35,160	36,132	36,132	2	.	.
GA	19,727	19,727	29,272	21,549	46,540	46,540	3	.	.
IA	38,002	38,002	38,065	38,065	38,127	38,127	2	.	.
IL	24,000	24,000	55,674	47,495	95,526	95,526	3	.	.
LA	19,812	19,812	35,933	35,933	52,053	52,053	2	.	.
MA	49,996	49,996	51,048	51,048	52,100	52,100	2	.	.
MD	45,197	45,197	50,037	48,302	55,745	55,745	5	.	.
MO	34,287	34,287	34,287	34,287	34,287	34,287	1	.	.
NC	28,888	29,584	33,255	32,640	36,925	38,850	4	.	.
NE	26,000	26,000	26,000	26,000	26,000	26,000	1	.	.
NY	29,571	29,571	38,642	38,811	47,543	47,543	3	.	.
OH	31,200	31,200	31,200	31,200	31,200	31,200	1	.	.
SC	24,770	24,770	27,393	28,141	28,239	31,046	5	.	.
TX	29,330	29,330	29,330	29,330	29,330	29,330	1	.	.
WA	58,628	58,628	58,628	58,628	58,628	58,628	1	.	.
WV	32,000	32,000	32,000	32,000	32,000	32,000	1	.	.

Degree Required Data

	Min	Q1	Mean	Median	Q3	Max	N	Range Avg Min	Range Avg Max
High School	21,549	28,141	35,184	32,234	38,127	55,745	14	.	.
Associate's	19,727	19,727	19,727	19,727	19,727	19,727	1	.	.
Bachelor's	19,812	27,756	33,552	30,786	38,831	49,996	12	.	.
Master's	24,000	38,198	49,532	47,421	54,088	104,000	12	.	.
Doctoral	47,495	47,495	65,025	52,053	95,526	95,526	3	.	.

ASSOCIATE LIBRARIAN OF CHILDREN'S SERVICES/YOUNG ADULT SERVICES (NON-MLS DEGREED)

Provides assistance to patrons including topical research and material location. Assists patrons with the use of library resources and equipment. Screens the collection for outdated or unused materials following established guidelines. May perform managerial and administrative duties. Provides services intended for children and youth through twelfth grade; develops collection, provides homework and readers advisory services, and develops age appropriate programs.

University
(Includes ARL Data)
Regional Data

	Min	Q1	Mean	Median	Q3	Max	N	Range Avg Min	Range Avg Max
North Atlantic	28,286	28,286	28,286	28,286	28,286	28,286	3	.	.
Great Lakes & Plains	34,287	34,287	34,287	34,287	34,287	34,287	1	.	.
ALL REGIONS	28,286	28,286	29,786	28,286	31,286	34,287	4	.	.

State Data

	Min	Q1	Mean	Median	Q3	Max	N	Range Avg Min	Range Avg Max
DC	28,286	28,286	28,286	28,286	28,286	28,286	3	.	.
MO	34,287	34,287	34,287	34,287	34,287	34,287	1	.	.

Degree Required Data

	Min	Q1	Mean	Median	Q3	Max	N	Range Avg Min	Range Avg Max
High School	.	.	.	.	.	.		.	.
Associate's	.	.	.	.	.	.		.	.
Bachelor's	28,286	28,286	28,286	28,286	28,286	28,286	3	.	.
Master's	.	.	.	.	.	.		.	.
Doctoral	.	.	.	.	.	.		.	.

ASSOCIATE LIBRARIAN OF CHILDREN'S SERVICES/YOUNG ADULT SERVICES (NON-MLS DEGREED) - CONTINUED
ALL ACADEMIC LIBRARIES
Regional Data

	Min	Q1	Mean	Median	Q3	Max	N	Range Avg Min	Range Avg Max
North Atlantic	28,286	28,286	28,286	28,286	28,286	28,286	3	.	.
Great Lakes & Plains	34,287	34,287	34,287	34,287	34,287	34,287	1	.	.
ALL REGIONS	28,286	28,286	29,786	28,286	31,286	34,287	4	.	.

State Data

	Min	Q1	Mean	Median	Q3	Max	N	Range Avg Min	Range Avg Max
DC	28,286	28,286	28,286	28,286	28,286	28,286	3	.	.
MO	34,287	34,287	34,287	34,287	34,287	34,287	1	.	.

Degree Required Data

	Min	Q1	Mean	Median	Q3	Max	N	Range Avg Min	Range Avg Max
High School	.	.	.	.	.	.		.	.
Associate's	.	.	.	.	.	.		.	.
Bachelor's	28,286	28,286	28,286	28,286	28,286	28,286	3	.	.
Master's	.	.	.	.	.	.		.	.
Doctoral	.	.	.	.	.	.		.	.

ASSOCIATE LIBRARIAN OF GOVERNMENT DOCUMENTS (NON-MLS DEGREED)

Provides assistance to patrons including topical research and material location. Assists patrons with the use of library resources and equipment. Screens the collection for outdated or unused materials following established guidelines. May perform managerial and administrative duties. Provides access to publications of the U. S. federal government such as transcripts of hearings and text of bills, resolutions, statutes, reports, charters, treaties, periodicals and statistics.

Two-Year College
Regional Data

	Min	Q1	Mean	Median	Q3	Max	N	Range Avg Min	Range Avg Max
Great Lakes & Plains	33,333	33,333	33,333	33,333	33,333	33,333	1	.	.
ALL REGIONS	33,333	33,333	33,333	33,333	33,333	33,333	1	.	.

State Data

	Min	Q1	Mean	Median	Q3	Max	N	Range Avg Min	Range Avg Max
KS	33,333	33,333	33,333	33,333	33,333	33,333	1	.	.

Degree Required Data

	Min	Q1	Mean	Median	Q3	Max	N	Range Avg Min	Range Avg Max
High School	.	.	.	.	.	.		.	.
Associate's	.	.	.	.	.	.		.	.
Bachelor's	33,333	33,333	33,333	33,333	33,333	33,333	1	.	.
Master's	.	.	.	.	.	.		.	.
Doctoral	.	.	.	.	.	.		.	.

ASSOCIATE LIBRARIAN OF GOVERNMENT DOCUMENTS (NON-MLS DEGREED) - CONTINUED
Four-Year College
Regional Data

	Min	Q1	Mean	Median	Q3	Max	N	Range Avg Min	Range Avg Max
North Atlantic	38,857	38,857	38,857	38,857	38,857	38,857	1	.	.
Great Lakes & Plains	21,840	21,840	21,840	21,840	21,840	21,840	1	17,680	26,000
Southeast	35,382	35,382	36,358	36,358	37,333	37,333	2	.	.
West & Southwest	17,500	17,500	17,500	17,500	17,500	17,500	1	.	.
ALL REGIONS	17,500	21,840	30,183	35,382	37,333	38,857	5	17,680	26,000

State Data

	Min	Q1	Mean	Median	Q3	Max	N	Range Avg Min	Range Avg Max
PA	38,857	38,857	38,857	38,857	38,857	38,857	1	.	.
SD	21,840	21,840	21,840	21,840	21,840	21,840	1	17,680	26,000
TX	17,500	17,500	17,500	17,500	17,500	17,500	1	.	.
WV	35,382	35,382	36,358	36,358	37,333	37,333	2	.	.

Degree Required Data

	Min	Q1	Mean	Median	Q3	Max	N	Range Avg Min	Range Avg Max
High School	17,500	17,500	27,417	27,417	37,333	37,333	2	.	.
Associate's	35,382	35,382	35,382	35,382	35,382	35,382	1	.	.
Bachelor's	21,840	21,840	30,349	30,349	38,857	38,857	2	17,680	26,000
Master's	.	.	.	.	.	.	.	.	.
Doctoral	.	.	.	.	.	.	.	.	.

ASSOCIATE LIBRARIAN OF GOVERNMENT DOCUMENTS (NON-MLS DEGREED) - CONTINUED
University
(Includes ARL Data)
Regional Data

	Min	Q1	Mean	Median	Q3	Max	N	Range Avg Min	Range Avg Max
North Atlantic	34,417	34,417	42,206	42,206	49,996	49,996	2	.	.
Great Lakes & Plains	21,342	26,511	30,139	32,463	33,767	34,287	4	.	.
Southeast	21,690	23,388	28,219	27,737	33,051	35,713	4	.	.
West & Southwest	26,324	41,736	42,074	47,436	47,436	47,436	5	.	.
ALL REGIONS	21,342	26,324	35,214	34,287	47,436	49,996	15	.	.

State Data

	Min	Q1	Mean	Median	Q3	Max	N	Range Avg Min	Range Avg Max
CO	41,736	44,586	46,011	47,436	47,436	47,436	4	.	.
DC	34,417	34,417	34,417	34,417	34,417	34,417	1	.	.
GA	21,690	21,690	21,690	21,690	21,690	21,690	1	.	.
IL	31,680	31,680	31,680	31,680	31,680	31,680	1	.	.
LA	25,086	25,086	25,086	25,086	25,086	25,086	1	.	.
MA	49,996	49,996	49,996	49,996	49,996	49,996	1	.	.
MO	34,287	34,287	34,287	34,287	34,287	34,287	1	.	.
NE	33,246	33,246	33,246	33,246	33,246	33,246	1	.	.
NM	26,324	26,324	26,324	26,324	26,324	26,324	1	.	.
OH	21,342	21,342	21,342	21,342	21,342	21,342	1	.	.
SC	35,713	35,713	35,713	35,713	35,713	35,713	1	.	.
VA	30,389	30,389	30,389	30,389	30,389	30,389	1	.	.

Degree Required Data

	Min	Q1	Mean	Median	Q3	Max	N	Range Avg Min	Range Avg Max
High School	31,680	31,680	31,680	31,680	31,680	31,680	1	.	.
Associate's	21,342	21,342	21,516	21,516	21,690	21,690	2	.	.
Bachelor's	25,086	26,324	33,654	32,403	35,713	49,996	6	.	.
Master's	.	.	.	.	.	.	.	.	.
Doctoral	.	.	.	.	.	.	.	.	.

ASSOCIATE LIBRARIAN OF GOVERNMENT DOCUMENTS (NON-MLS DEGREED) - CONTINUED
ALL ACADEMIC LIBRARIES
Regional Data

	Min	Q1	Mean	Median	Q3	Max	N	Range Avg Min	Range Avg Max
North Atlantic	34,417	34,417	41,090	38,857	49,996	49,996	3		
Great Lakes & Plains	21,342	21,840	29,288	32,463	33,333	34,287	6	17,680	26,000
Southeast	21,690	25,086	30,932	32,886	35,713	37,333	6		
West & Southwest	17,500	26,324	37,978	44,586	47,436	47,436	6		
ALL REGIONS	17,500	26,324	33,927	34,287	38,857	49,996	21	17,680	26,000

State Data

	Min	Q1	Mean	Median	Q3	Max	N	Range Avg Min	Range Avg Max
CO	41,736	44,586	46,011	47,436	47,436	47,436	4		
DC	34,417	34,417	34,417	34,417	34,417	34,417	1		
GA	21,690	21,690	21,690	21,690	21,690	21,690	1		
IL	31,680	31,680	31,680	31,680	31,680	31,680	1		
KS	33,333	33,333	33,333	33,333	33,333	33,333	1		
LA	25,086	25,086	25,086	25,086	25,086	25,086	1		
MA	49,996	49,996	49,996	49,996	49,996	49,996	1		
MO	34,287	34,287	34,287	34,287	34,287	34,287	1		
NE	33,246	33,246	33,246	33,246	33,246	33,246	1		
NM	26,324	26,324	26,324	26,324	26,324	26,324	1		
OH	21,342	21,342	21,342	21,342	21,342	21,342	1		
PA	38,857	38,857	38,857	38,857	38,857	38,857	1		
SC	35,713	35,713	35,713	35,713	35,713	35,713	1		
SD	21,840	21,840	21,840	21,840	21,840	21,840	1	17,680	26,000
TX	17,500	17,500	17,500	17,500	17,500	17,500	1		
VA	30,389	30,389	30,389	30,389	30,389	30,389	1		
WV	35,382	35,382	36,358	36,358	37,333	37,333	2		

Degree Required Data

	Min	Q1	Mean	Median	Q3	Max	N	Range Avg Min	Range Avg Max
High School	17,500	17,500	28,838	31,680	37,333	37,333	3		
Associate's	21,342	21,342	26,138	21,690	35,382	35,382	3		
Bachelor's	21,840	26,324	32,884	33,333	35,713	49,996	9	17,680	26,000
Master's									
Doctoral									

ASSOCIATE LIBRARIAN OF INSTRUCTIONAL SERVICE/LITERACY (NON-MLS DEGREED)

Provides assistance to patrons including topical research and material location. Assists patrons with the use of library resources and equipment. Screens the collection for outdated or unused materials following established guidelines. May perform managerial and administrative duties. Advances learning, teaching and research with respect to information literacy in higher education; assists patrons to develop the ability to read and write.

Two-Year College
Regional Data

	Min	Q1	Mean	Median	Q3	Max	N	Range Avg Min	Range Avg Max
Great Lakes & Plains	31,250	31,250	31,250	31,250	31,250	31,250	1	.	.
Southeast	20,800	20,800	20,800	20,800	20,800	20,800	1	.	.
West & Southwest	23,590	23,590	23,590	23,590	23,590	23,590	1	.	.
ALL REGIONS	20,800	20,800	25,213	23,590	31,250	31,250	3	.	.

State Data

	Min	Q1	Mean	Median	Q3	Max	N	Range Avg Min	Range Avg Max
FL	20,800	20,800	20,800	20,800	20,800	20,800	1	.	.
IA	31,250	31,250	31,250	31,250	31,250	31,250	1	.	.
TX	23,590	23,590	23,590	23,590	23,590	23,590	1	.	.

Degree Required Data

	Min	Q1	Mean	Median	Q3	Max	N	Range Avg Min	Range Avg Max
High School	.	.	.	.	.	.		.	.
Associate's	31,250	31,250	31,250	31,250	31,250	31,250	1	.	.
Bachelor's	20,800	20,800	20,800	20,800	20,800	20,800	1	.	.
Master's	.	.	.	.	.	.		.	.
Doctoral	.	.	.	.	.	.		.	.

ASSOCIATE LIBRARIAN OF INSTRUCTIONAL SERVICE/LITERACY (NON-MLS DEGREED) - CONTINUED
Four-Year College
Regional Data

	Min	Q1	Mean	Median	Q3	Max	N	Range Avg Min	Range Avg Max
Southeast	24,000	24,000	24,000	24,000	24,000	24,000	1	.	.
ALL REGIONS	24,000	24,000	24,000	24,000	24,000	24,000	1	.	.

State Data

	Min	Q1	Mean	Median	Q3	Max	N	Range Avg Min	Range Avg Max
AL	24,000	24,000	24,000	24,000	24,000	24,000	1	.	.

Degree Required Data

	Min	Q1	Mean	Median	Q3	Max	N	Range Avg Min	Range Avg Max
High School	.	.	.	.	.	.		.	.
Associate's	.	.	.	.	.	.		.	.
Bachelor's	24,000	24,000	24,000	24,000	24,000	24,000	1	.	.
Master's	.	.	.	.	.	.		.	.
Doctoral	.	.	.	.	.	.		.	.

ASSOCIATE LIBRARIAN OF INSTRUCTIONAL SERVICE/LITERACY (NON-MLS DEGREED) - CONTINUED
University
(Includes ARL Data)
Regional Data

	Min	Q1	Mean	Median	Q3	Max	N	Range Avg Min	Range Avg Max
North Atlantic	34,417	34,417	34,417	34,417	34,417	34,417	2	.	.
Great Lakes & Plains	25,437	28,080	29,833	28,080	33,280	34,287	5	.	.
Southeast	42,667	42,667	49,357	51,733	53,671	53,671	3	.	.
West & Southwest	38,824	38,824	43,130	43,130	47,436	47,436	2	.	.
ALL REGIONS	25,437	30,680	37,694	34,417	45,051	53,671	12	.	.

State Data

	Min	Q1	Mean	Median	Q3	Max	N	Range Avg Min	Range Avg Max
CO	47,436	47,436	47,436	47,436	47,436	47,436	1	.	.
DC	34,417	34,417	34,417	34,417	34,417	34,417	2	.	.
IL	33,280	33,280	33,280	33,280	33,280	33,280	1	.	.
IN	28,080	28,080	28,080	28,080	28,080	28,080	2	.	.
LA	42,667	42,667	42,667	42,667	42,667	42,667	1	.	.
MO	34,287	34,287	34,287	34,287	34,287	34,287	1	.	.
NC	53,671	53,671	53,671	53,671	53,671	53,671	1	.	.
NE	25,437	25,437	25,437	25,437	25,437	25,437	1	.	.
TN	51,733	51,733	51,733	51,733	51,733	51,733	1	.	.
TX	38,824	38,824	38,824	38,824	38,824	38,824	1	.	.

Degree Required Data

	Min	Q1	Mean	Median	Q3	Max	N	Range Avg Min	Range Avg Max
High School	.	.	.	.	.	.		.	.
Associate's	.	.	.	.	.	.		.	.
Bachelor's	25,437	28,080	34,526	33,849	36,621	53,671	8	.	.
Master's	42,667	42,667	47,200	47,200	51,733	51,733	2	.	.
Doctoral	.	.	.	.	.	.		.	.

ASSOCIATE LIBRARIAN OF INSTRUCTIONAL SERVICE/LITERACY (NON-MLS DEGREED) - CONTINUED
ALL ACADEMIC LIBRARIES
Regional Data

	Min	Q1	Mean	Median	Q3	Max	N	Range Avg Min	Range Avg Max
North Atlantic	34,417	34,417	34,417	34,417	34,417	34,417	2	.	.
Great Lakes & Plains	25,437	28,080	30,069	29,665	33,280	34,287	6	.	.
Southeast	20,800	24,000	38,574	42,667	51,733	53,671	5	.	.
West & Southwest	23,590	23,590	36,617	38,824	47,436	47,436	3	.	.
ALL REGIONS	20,800	26,759	34,498	33,784	40,745	53,671	16	.	.

State Data

	Min	Q1	Mean	Median	Q3	Max	N	Range Avg Min	Range Avg Max
AL	24,000	24,000	24,000	24,000	24,000	24,000	1	.	.
CO	47,436	47,436	47,436	47,436	47,436	47,436	1	.	.
DC	34,417	34,417	34,417	34,417	34,417	34,417	2	.	.
FL	20,800	20,800	20,800	20,800	20,800	20,800	1	.	.
IA	31,250	31,250	31,250	31,250	31,250	31,250	1	.	.
IL	33,280	33,280	33,280	33,280	33,280	33,280	1	.	.
IN	28,080	28,080	28,080	28,080	28,080	28,080	2	.	.
LA	42,667	42,667	42,667	42,667	42,667	42,667	1	.	.
MO	34,287	34,287	34,287	34,287	34,287	34,287	1	.	.
NC	53,671	53,671	53,671	53,671	53,671	53,671	1	.	.
NE	25,437	25,437	25,437	25,437	25,437	25,437	1	.	.
TN	51,733	51,733	51,733	51,733	51,733	51,733	1	.	.
TX	23,590	23,590	31,207	31,207	38,824	38,824	2	.	.

Degree Required Data

	Min	Q1	Mean	Median	Q3	Max	N	Range Avg Min	Range Avg Max
High School	.	.	.	.	.	.		.	.
Associate's	31,250	31,250	31,250	31,250	31,250	31,250	1	.	.
Bachelor's	20,800	25,437	32,101	30,680	34,417	53,671	10	.	.
Master's	42,667	42,667	47,200	47,200	51,733	51,733	2	.	.
Doctoral	.	.	.	.	.	.		.	.

ASSOCIATE LIBRARIAN OF REFERENCE/INFORMATION SERVICES (NON-MLS DEGREED)

Provides assistance to patrons including topical research and material location. Assists patrons with the use of library resources and equipment. Screens the collection for outdated or unused materials following established guidelines. May perform managerial and administrative duties. Assists patrons with questions; instructs in the selection and use of appropriate tools and techniques for finding information; conducts searches for materials; contributes to reference collection development.

Two-Year College
Regional Data

	Min	Q1	Mean	Median	Q3	Max	N	Range Avg Min	Range Avg Max
Great Lakes & Plains	17,000	24,396	35,908	33,207	47,420	60,217	4	.	.
Southeast	20,800	24,615	28,697	26,040	28,030	44,000	5	.	.
ALL REGIONS	17,000	24,615	31,902	28,030	34,623	60,217	9	.	.

State Data

	Min	Q1	Mean	Median	Q3	Max	N	Range Avg Min	Range Avg Max
AL	26,040	26,040	32,690	28,030	44,000	44,000	3	.	.
FL	20,800	20,800	20,800	20,800	20,800	20,800	1	.	.
IA	60,217	60,217	60,217	60,217	60,217	60,217	1	.	.
KS	17,000	17,000	17,000	17,000	17,000	17,000	1	.	.
NC	24,615	24,615	24,615	24,615	24,615	24,615	1	.	.
ND	31,792	31,792	33,207	33,207	34,623	34,623	2	.	.

Degree Required Data

	Min	Q1	Mean	Median	Q3	Max	N	Range Avg Min	Range Avg Max
High School	.	.	.	.	.	.		.	.
Associate's	17,000	17,000	20,808	20,808	24,615	24,615	2	.	.
Bachelor's	20,800	24,415	28,811	29,911	33,207	34,623	4	.	.
Master's	26,040	26,040	43,419	44,000	60,217	60,217	3	.	.
Doctoral	.	.	.	.	.	.		.	.

ASSOCIATE LIBRARIAN OF REFERENCE/INFORMATION SERVICES (NON-MLS DEGREED) - CONTINUED
Four-Year College
Regional Data

	Min	Q1	Mean	Median	Q3	Max	N	Range Avg Min	Range Avg Max
North Atlantic	27,429	41,600	46,800	46,901	55,226	62,744	6	.	.
Great Lakes & Plains	17,680	18,720	21,708	21,476	24,000	26,894	6	17,680	26,693
Southeast	20,000	20,267	28,699	28,690	32,260	42,290	6	.	.
West & Southwest	28,000	28,000	29,456	29,456	30,912	30,912	2	.	.
ALL REGIONS	17,680	21,476	32,108	28,286	41,945	62,744	20	17,680	26,693

State Data

	Min	Q1	Mean	Median	Q3	Max	N	Range Avg Min	Range Avg Max
AL	20,000	20,000	20,000	20,000	20,000	20,000	1		
CO	30,912	30,912	30,912	30,912	30,912	30,912	1		
GA	28,808	28,808	30,534	30,534	32,260	32,260	2		
KY	42,290	42,290	42,290	42,290	42,290	42,290	1		
MA	41,600	41,600	41,600	41,600	41,600	41,600	1		
MD	46,900	46,900	52,182	46,901	62,744	62,744	3		
MO	24,000	24,000	24,000	24,000	24,000	24,000	1		
NC	20,267	20,267	20,267	20,267	20,267	20,267	1		
OH	18,720	18,720	19,760	19,760	20,800	20,800	2		
PA	27,429	27,429	41,327	41,327	55,226	55,226	2		
SC	28,571	28,571	28,571	28,571	28,571	28,571	1		
SD	17,680	17,680	22,242	22,152	26,894	26,894	3	17,680	26,693
TX	28,000	28,000	28,000	28,000	28,000	28,000	1		

Degree Required Data

	Min	Q1	Mean	Median	Q3	Max	N	Range Avg Min	Range Avg Max
High School	20,267	20,267	20,267	20,267	20,267	20,267	1		
Associate's									
Bachelor's	17,680	20,800	28,244	26,894	30,912	55,226	13	17,680	26,693
Master's	28,000	28,571	42,453	44,250	46,901	62,744	6		
Doctoral									

ASSOCIATE LIBRARIAN OF REFERENCE/INFORMATION SERVICES (NON-MLS DEGREED) - CONTINUED
University
(Includes ARL Data)
Regional Data

	Min	Q1	Mean	Median	Q3	Max	N	Range Avg Min	Range Avg Max
North Atlantic	28,145	31,807	40,975	43,252	48,034	53,724	16		
Great Lakes & Plains	20,000	28,080	31,456	28,080	32,477	56,000	29	27,248	42,328
Southeast	23,085	27,483	32,410	33,427	35,855	42,667	8		
West & Southwest	18,415	29,126	38,548	40,068	44,220	69,816	19	34,757	39,104
ALL REGIONS	18,415	28,080	35,549	32,633	43,452	69,816	72	31,002	40,716

State Data

	Min	Q1	Mean	Median	Q3	Max	N	Range Avg Min	Range Avg Max
CA	38,110	38,110	38,110	38,110	38,110	38,110	1		
CO	29,126	41,088	44,294	43,452	46,116	69,816	12		
DC	29,531	29,531	32,101	29,531	37,240	37,240	3		
GA	23,085	23,085	23,085	23,085	23,085	23,085	1		
IA	45,790	45,790	46,131	46,131	46,471	46,471	2		
IL	24,960	24,960	31,680	31,680	38,400	38,400	2		
IN	20,000	28,080	30,715	28,080	29,390	56,000	17		
LA	34,343	34,343	34,343	34,343	34,343	34,343	1		
MA	32,756	40,395	44,700	48,034	49,005	49,975	4		
MD	44,502	44,502	49,113	49,113	53,724	53,724	4		
MO	34,287	34,287	34,287	34,287	34,287	34,287	1		
NC	35,810	35,810	35,810	35,810	35,810	35,810	1		
ND	30,227	30,227	31,352	31,352	32,477	32,477	2		
NE	23,078	23,078	24,665	24,960	25,958	25,958	3		
NM	25,071	25,071	25,698	25,698	26,324	26,324	2		
OH	20,987	20,987	31,739	31,739	42,491	42,491	2	27,248	42,328
OR	34,757	34,757	34,757	34,757	34,757	34,757	1	34,757	39,104
PA	28,145	30,857	36,809	35,147	42,001	47,894	5		
SC	28,239	28,239	28,239	28,239	28,239	28,239	1		
TN	26,726	26,726	34,697	34,697	42,667	42,667	2		
TX	18,415	18,415	25,542	27,732	30,480	30,480	3		
VA	32,510	32,510	34,206	34,206	35,901	35,901	2		

Degree Required Data

	Min	Q1	Mean	Median	Q3	Max	N	Range Avg Min	Range Avg Max
High School	23,078	29,000	37,286	33,951	47,894	56,000	18	27,248	42,328
Associate's	18,415	18,415	18,415	18,415	18,415	18,415	1		
Bachelor's	20,000	27,732	30,195	28,080	32,510	46,471	34	34,757	39,104
Master's	38,400	42,667	46,253	44,502	53,724	53,724	6		
Doctoral									

ASSOCIATE LIBRARIAN OF REFERENCE/INFORMATION SERVICES (NON-MLS DEGREED) - CONTINUED
ALL ACADEMIC LIBRARIES
Regional Data

	Min	Q1	Mean	Median	Q3	Max	N	Range Avg Min	Range Avg Max
North Atlantic	27,429	32,756	42,564	44,502	48,034	62,744	22		
Great Lakes & Plains	17,000	24,960	30,413	28,080	32,477	60,217	39	20,072	30,602
Southeast	20,000	24,615	30,261	28,571	35,810	44,000	19		
West & Southwest	18,415	29,126	37,682	38,110	43,872	69,816	21	34,757	39,104
ALL REGIONS	17,000	28,000	34,543	30,912	42,667	69,816	101	23,009	32,302

State Data

	Min	Q1	Mean	Median	Q3	Max	N	Range Avg Min	Range Avg Max
AL	20,000	23,020	29,518	27,035	36,015	44,000	4		
CA	38,110	38,110	38,110	38,110	38,110	38,110	1		
CO	29,126	40,068	43,265	43,032	45,864	69,816	13		
DC	29,531	29,531	32,101	29,531	37,240	37,240	3		
FL	20,800	20,800	20,800	20,800	20,800	20,800	1		
GA	23,085	23,085	28,051	28,808	32,260	32,260	3		
IA	45,790	45,790	50,826	46,471	60,217	60,217	3		
IL	24,960	24,960	31,680	31,680	38,400	38,400	2		
IN	20,000	28,080	30,715	28,080	29,390	56,000	17		
KS	17,000	17,000	17,000	17,000	17,000	17,000	1		
KY	42,290	42,290	42,290	42,290	42,290	42,290	1		
LA	34,343	34,343	34,343	34,343	34,343	34,343	1		
MA	32,756	41,600	44,080	48,034	48,034	49,975	5		
MD	44,502	44,502	50,428	46,901	53,724	62,744	7		
MO	24,000	24,000	29,144	29,144	34,287	34,287	2		
NC	20,267	20,267	26,897	24,615	35,810	35,810	3		
ND	30,227	31,010	32,280	32,135	33,550	34,623	4		
NE	23,078	23,078	24,665	24,960	25,958	25,958	3		
NM	25,071	25,071	25,698	25,698	26,324	26,324	2		
OH	18,720	19,760	25,750	20,894	31,739	42,491	4	27,248	42,328
OR	34,757	34,757	34,757	34,757	34,757	34,757	1	34,757	39,104
PA	27,429	28,145	38,100	35,147	47,894	55,226	7		
SC	28,239	28,239	28,405	28,405	28,571	28,571	2		
SD	17,680	17,680	22,242	22,152	26,894	26,894	3	17,680	26,693
TN	26,726	26,726	34,697	34,697	42,667	42,667	2		
TX	18,415	23,074	26,157	27,866	29,240	30,480	4		
VA	32,510	32,510	34,206	34,206	35,901	35,901	2		

Degree Required Data

	Min	Q1	Mean	Median	Q3	Max	N	Range Avg Min	Range Avg Max
High School	20,267	28,239	36,390	32,756	47,894	56,000	19	27,248	42,328
Associate's	17,000	17,000	20,010	18,415	24,615	24,615	3		
Bachelor's	17,680	25,958	29,589	28,080	32,477	55,226	51	21,949	29,796
Master's	26,040	38,400	44,166	44,502	53,724	62,744	15		
Doctoral	.	.	.	.	.	.	.	.	.

ASSOCIATE LIBRARIAN OF OUTREACH/BOOKMOBILE (NON-MLS DEGREED)

Provides assistance to patrons including topical research and material location. Assists patrons with the use of library resources and equipment. Screens the collection for outdated or unused materials following established guidelines. May perform managerial and administrative duties. Provides services and programs to homebound, disabled, institutionalized or other underserved patrons.

University
(Includes ARL Data)
Regional Data

	Min	Q1	Mean	Median	Q3	Max	N	Range Avg Min	Range Avg Max
North Atlantic	40,063	40,063	40,063	40,063	40,063	40,063	2	.	.
Great Lakes & Plains	34,267	34,267	34,267	34,267	34,267	34,267	1	.	.
Southeast	41,647	41,647	41,647	41,647	41,647	41,647	1	.	.
ALL REGIONS	34,267	37,165	39,010	40,063	40,855	41,647	4	.	.

State Data

	Min	Q1	Mean	Median	Q3	Max	N	Range Avg Min	Range Avg Max
DC	40,063	40,063	40,063	40,063	40,063	40,063	2	.	.
LA	41,647	41,647	41,647	41,647	41,647	41,647	1	.	.
MO	34,267	34,267	34,267	34,267	34,267	34,267	1	.	.

Degree Required Data

	Min	Q1	Mean	Median	Q3	Max	N	Range Avg Min	Range Avg Max
High School	.	.	.	.	.	.		.	.
Associate's	.	.	.	.	.	.		.	.
Bachelor's	40,063	40,063	40,591	40,063	41,647	41,647	3	.	.
Master's	.	.	.	.	.	.		.	.
Doctoral	.	.	.	.	.	.		.	.

ASSOCIATE LIBRARIAN OF OUTREACH/BOOKMOBILE (NON-MLS DEGREED) - CONTINUED
ALL ACADEMIC LIBRARIES
Regional Data

	Min	Q1	Mean	Median	Q3	Max	N	Range Avg Min	Range Avg Max
North Atlantic	40,063	40,063	40,063	40,063	40,063	40,063	2	.	.
Great Lakes & Plains	34,267	34,267	34,267	34,267	34,267	34,267	1	.	.
Southeast	41,647	41,647	41,647	41,647	41,647	41,647	1	.	.
ALL REGIONS	34,267	37,165	39,010	40,063	40,855	41,647	4	.	.

State Data

	Min	Q1	Mean	Median	Q3	Max	N	Range Avg Min	Range Avg Max
DC	40,063	40,063	40,063	40,063	40,063	40,063	2	.	.
LA	41,647	41,647	41,647	41,647	41,647	41,647	1	.	.
MO	34,267	34,267	34,267	34,267	34,267	34,267	1	.	.

Degree Required Data

	Min	Q1	Mean	Median	Q3	Max	N	Range Avg Min	Range Avg Max
High School	.	.	.	.	.	.	.	.	.
Associate's	.	.	.	.	.	.	.	.	.
Bachelor's	40,063	40,063	40,591	40,063	41,647	41,647	3	.	.
Master's	.	.	.	.	.	.	.	.	.
Doctoral	.	.	.	.	.	.	.	.	.

ASSOCIATE LIBRARIAN OF MEDIA SERVICES (NON-MLS DEGREED)

Provides assistance to patrons including topical research and material location. Assists patrons with the use of library resources and equipment. Screens the collection for outdated or unused materials following established guidelines. May perform managerial and administrative duties. Develops and manages non-print library materials such as files, video recordings, audio recordings, CD-ROMs, computer software, etc.

Two-Year College
Regional Data

	Min	Q1	Mean	Median	Q3	Max	N	Range Avg Min	Range Avg Max
Southeast	22,880	22,880	22,880	22,880	22,880	22,880	1	.	.
West & Southwest	25,641	25,641	25,641	25,641	25,641	25,641	1	.	.
ALL REGIONS	22,880	22,880	24,261	24,261	25,641	25,641	2	.	.

State Data

	Min	Q1	Mean	Median	Q3	Max	N	Range Avg Min	Range Avg Max
FL	22,880	22,880	22,880	22,880	22,880	22,880	1		.
TX	25,641	25,641	25,641	25,641	25,641	25,641	1		.

Degree Required Data

	Min	Q1	Mean	Median	Q3	Max	N	Range Avg Min	Range Avg Max
High School	.	.	.	.	.	.	.	.	.
Associate's	.	.	.	.	.	.	.	.	.
Bachelor's	22,880	22,880	22,880	22,880	22,880	22,880	1	.	.
Master's	.	.	.	.	.	.	.	.	.
Doctoral	.	.	.	.	.	.	.	.	.

ASSOCIATE LIBRARIAN OF MEDIA SERVICES (NON-MLS DEGREED) - CONTINUED
Four-Year College
Regional Data

	Min	Q1	Mean	Median	Q3	Max	N	Range Avg Min	Range Avg Max
North Atlantic	45,835	45,835	45,835	45,835	45,835	45,835	1	.	.
Great Lakes & Plains	20,800	20,800	22,880	21,840	26,000	26,000	3	17,680	26,000
West & Southwest	47,316	47,316	47,316	47,316	47,316	47,316	1	.	.
ALL REGIONS	20,800	21,840	32,358	26,000	45,835	47,316	5	17,680	26,000

State Data

	Min	Q1	Mean	Median	Q3	Max	N	Range Avg Min	Range Avg Max
CO	47,316	47,316	47,316	47,316	47,316	47,316	1	.	.
IL	20,800	20,800	23,400	23,400	26,000	26,000	2	.	.
MA	45,835	45,835	45,835	45,835	45,835	45,835	1	.	.
SD	21,840	21,840	21,840	21,840	21,840	21,840	1	17,680	26,000

Degree Required Data

	Min	Q1	Mean	Median	Q3	Max	N	Range Avg Min	Range Avg Max
High School	20,800	20,800	34,058	34,058	47,316	47,316	2	.	.
Associate's	.	.	.	.	.	.			
Bachelor's	21,840	21,840	21,840	21,840	21,840	21,840	1	17,680	26,000
Master's	45,835	45,835	45,835	45,835	45,835	45,835	1	.	.
Doctoral	.	.	.	.	.	.			

ASSOCIATE LIBRARIAN OF MEDIA SERVICES (NON-MLS DEGREED) - CONTINUED
University
(Includes ARL Data)
Regional Data

	Min	Q1	Mean	Median	Q3	Max	N	Range Avg Min	Range Avg Max
North Atlantic	27,429	27,429	39,494	27,429	46,629	82,618	7	.	.
Great Lakes & Plains	24,702	29,725	36,143	36,637	43,091	45,790	7	.	.
Southeast	21,377	29,557	35,742	32,780	38,847	70,485	15	.	.
West & Southwest	45,988	45,988	49,088	49,088	52,188	52,188	2	.	.
ALL REGIONS	21,377	29,124	37,541	35,707	43,091	82,618	31	.	.

State Data

	Min	Q1	Mean	Median	Q3	Max	N	Range Avg Min	Range Avg Max
CO	52,188	52,188	52,188	52,188	52,188	52,188	1	.	.
DC	27,429	27,429	27,429	27,429	27,429	27,429	4	.	.
FL	29,631	29,631	29,631	29,631	29,631	29,631	1	.	.
IA	45,790	45,790	45,790	45,790	45,790	45,790	1	.	.
IL	38,771	38,771	38,771	38,771	38,771	38,771	1	.	.
LA	36,743	36,743	53,614	53,614	70,485	70,485	2	.	.
MN	36,637	36,637	39,864	39,864	43,091	43,091	2	.	.
MO	34,287	34,287	34,287	34,287	34,287	34,287	1	.	.
NC	32,780	32,780	32,780	32,780	32,780	32,780	1	.	.
NE	29,725	29,725	29,725	29,725	29,725	29,725	1	.	.
NY	37,500	37,500	55,582	46,629	82,618	82,618	3	.	.
OH	24,702	24,702	24,702	24,702	24,702	24,702	1	.	.
SC	21,377	29,311	33,621	33,152	39,079	44,506	8	.	.
TN	29,124	29,124	29,124	29,124	29,124	29,124	1	.	.
VA	29,557	29,557	34,202	34,202	38,847	38,847	2	.	.
WA	45,988	45,988	45,988	45,988	45,988	45,988	1	.	.

Degree Required Data

	Min	Q1	Mean	Median	Q3	Max	N	Range Avg Min	Range Avg Max
High School	21,377	27,166	33,282	34,243	38,136	45,790	8		
Associate's	27,429	27,429	27,768	27,429	27,429	29,124	5		
Bachelor's	28,484	30,597	37,451	36,743	43,091	46,629	9		
Master's	30,139	38,823	50,903	41,676	70,485	82,618	6		
Doctoral									

ASSOCIATE LIBRARIAN OF MEDIA SERVICES (NON-MLS DEGREED) - CONTINUED
ALL ACADEMIC LIBRARIES
Regional Data

	Min	Q1	Mean	Median	Q3	Max	N	Range Avg Min	Range Avg Max
North Atlantic	27,429	27,429	40,287	32,464	46,232	82,618	8		
Great Lakes & Plains	20,800	24,702	32,164	32,006	38,771	45,790	10	17,680	26,000
Southeast	21,377	29,340	34,938	31,689	38,835	70,485	16		
West & Southwest	25,641	35,815	42,783	46,652	49,752	52,188	4		
ALL REGIONS	20,800	27,429	36,160	33,534	43,091	82,618	38	17,680	26,000

State Data

	Min	Q1	Mean	Median	Q3	Max	N	Range Avg Min	Range Avg Max
CO	47,316	47,316	49,752	49,752	52,188	52,188	2		
DC	27,429	27,429	27,429	27,429	27,429	27,429	4		
FL	22,880	22,880	26,256	26,256	29,631	29,631	2		
IA	45,790	45,790	45,790	45,790	45,790	45,790	1		
IL	20,800	20,800	28,524	26,000	38,771	38,771	3		
LA	36,743	36,743	53,614	53,614	70,485	70,485	2		
MA	45,835	45,835	45,835	45,835	45,835	45,835	1		
MN	36,637	36,637	39,864	39,864	43,091	43,091	2		
MO	34,287	34,287	34,287	34,287	34,287	34,287	1		
NC	32,780	32,780	32,780	32,780	32,780	32,780	1		
NE	29,725	29,725	29,725	29,725	29,725	29,725	1		
NY	37,500	37,500	55,582	46,629	82,618	82,618	3		
OH	24,702	24,702	24,702	24,702	24,702	24,702	1		
SC	21,377	29,311	33,621	33,152	39,079	44,506	8		
SD	21,840	21,840	21,840	21,840	21,840	21,840	1	17,680	26,000
TN	29,124	29,124	29,124	29,124	29,124	29,124	1		
TX	25,641	25,641	25,641	25,641	25,641	25,641	1		
VA	29,557	29,557	34,202	34,202	38,847	38,847	2		
WA	45,988	45,988	45,988	45,988	45,988	45,988	1		

Degree Required Data

	Min	Q1	Mean	Median	Q3	Max	N	Range Avg Min	Range Avg Max
High School	20,800	24,702	33,437	34,243	38,771	47,316	10		
Associate's	27,429	27,429	27,768	27,429	27,429	29,124	5		
Bachelor's	21,840	28,484	34,707	36,637	43,091	46,629	11	17,680	26,000
Master's	30,139	38,823	50,179	44,506	70,485	82,618	7		
Doctoral									

ASSOCIATE LIBRARIAN OF TECHNICAL ASSISTANCE (NON-MLS DEGREED)

Provides assistance to patrons including topical research and material location. Assists patrons with the use of library resources and equipment. Screens the collection for outdated or unused materials following established guidelines. May perform managerial and administrative duties. Acquires, organizes (bibliographic control), physically processes and maintains library collections.

Two-Year College
Regional Data

	Min	Q1	Mean	Median	Q3	Max	N	Range Avg Min	Range Avg Max
Great Lakes & Plains	27,206	27,206	27,965	27,965	28,725	28,725	2	21,902	34,362
Southeast	24,276	24,276	25,402	25,263	26,667	26,667	3	.	.
West & Southwest	25,641	25,641	34,932	26,154	53,000	53,000	3	.	.
ALL REGIONS	24,276	25,452	29,616	26,410	27,965	53,000	8	21,902	34,362

State Data

	Min	Q1	Mean	Median	Q3	Max	N	Range Avg Min	Range Avg Max
AL	24,276	24,276	24,770	24,770	25,263	25,263	2	.	.
MI	27,206	27,206	27,206	27,206	27,206	27,206	1	.	.
NC	26,667	26,667	26,667	26,667	26,667	26,667	1	.	.
OH	28,725	28,725	28,725	28,725	28,725	28,725	1	21,902	34,362
TX	25,641	25,641	34,932	26,154	53,000	53,000	3	.	.

Degree Required Data

	Min	Q1	Mean	Median	Q3	Max	N	Range Avg Min	Range Avg Max
High School	25,263	25,263	26,994	26,994	28,725	28,725	2	21,902	34,362
Associate's	26,667	26,667	26,936	26,936	27,206	27,206	2	.	.
Bachelor's	24,276	24,276	24,276	24,276	24,276	24,276	1	.	.
Master's	53,000	53,000	53,000	53,000	53,000	53,000	1	.	.
Doctoral	.	.	.	.	.	.		.	.

ASSOCIATE LIBRARIAN OF TECHNICAL ASSISTANCE (NON-MLS DEGREED) - CONTINUED
Four-Year College
Regional Data

	Min	Q1	Mean	Median	Q3	Max	N	Range Avg Min	Range Avg Max
North Atlantic	23,400	28,340	40,427	36,502	52,514	65,304	4	22,360	24,024
Great Lakes & Plains	17,680	17,680	27,231	23,965	37,336	40,955	7	21,944	32,309
Southeast	13,998	13,998	20,952	20,000	27,518	33,280	7	.	.
West & Southwest	18,200	18,200	32,758	32,758	47,316	47,316	2	.	.
ALL REGIONS	13,998	17,940	28,225	23,683	35,308	65,304	20	22,048	30,238

State Data

	Min	Q1	Mean	Median	Q3	Max	N	Range Avg Min	Range Avg Max
AL	20,000	20,000	20,000	20,000	20,000	20,000	1		
CO	47,316	47,316	47,316	47,316	47,316	47,316	1		
GA	27,518	27,518	27,518	27,518	27,518	27,518	1		
IL	37,336	37,336	37,336	37,336	37,336	37,336	1		
KY	20,800	20,800	27,040	27,040	33,280	33,280	2		
MA	33,280	33,280	33,280	33,280	33,280	33,280	1		
MD	65,304	65,304	65,304	65,304	65,304	65,304	1		
MN	40,955	40,955	40,955	40,955	40,955	40,955	1	30,472	44,928
MO	23,965	23,965	23,965	23,965	23,965	23,965	1		
NC	17,067	17,067	17,067	17,067	17,067	17,067	1		
ND	23,004	23,004	26,502	26,502	30,000	30,000	2		
PA	39,723	39,723	39,723	39,723	39,723	39,723	1		
SD	17,680	17,680	17,680	17,680	17,680	17,680	2	17,680	26,000
TX	18,200	18,200	18,200	18,200	18,200	18,200	1		
VT	23,400	23,400	23,400	23,400	23,400	23,400	1	22,360	24,024
WV	13,998	13,998	13,998	13,998	13,998	13,998	2		

Degree Required Data

	Min	Q1	Mean	Median	Q3	Max	N	Range Avg Min	Range Avg Max
High School	13,998	15,533	25,702	19,500	37,118	47,316	8	30,472	44,928
Associate's	20,000	23,400	26,444	23,965	27,518	37,336	5	22,360	24,024
Bachelor's	17,680	17,680	26,895	26,502	33,280	39,723	6	17,680	26,000
Master's	65,304	65,304	65,304	65,304	65,304	65,304	1		
Doctoral									

ASSOCIATE LIBRARIAN OF TECHNICAL ASSISTANCE (NON-MLS DEGREED) - CONTINUED
University
(Includes ARL Data)
Regional Data

	Min	Q1	Mean	Median	Q3	Max	N	Range Avg Min	Range Avg Max
North Atlantic	23,400	29,410	39,379	43,472	49,975	49,975	13		
Great Lakes & Plains	19,018	30,903	36,675	34,917	42,496	54,766	20		
Southeast	24,702	28,000	32,721	32,900	34,850	49,747	27		
West & Southwest	26,100	29,783	37,427	35,904	47,436	50,484	15		
ALL REGIONS	19,018	29,410	35,871	33,779	43,098	54,766	75		

State Data

	Min	Q1	Mean	Median	Q3	Max	N	Range Avg Min	Range Avg Max
AL	39,920	39,920	39,920	39,920	39,920	39,920	1	.	.
AR	27,548	27,548	30,309	30,309	33,069	33,069	2	.	.
CO	31,258	35,904	41,387	42,144	47,436	50,484	9	.	.
CT	44,055	44,055	44,055	44,055	44,055	44,055	1	.	.
DC	28,571	28,571	28,571	28,571	28,571	28,571	2	.	.
FL	24,702	25,879	28,600	28,201	31,321	33,296	4	.	.
GA	28,101	28,101	28,101	28,101	28,101	28,101	1	.	.
IA	44,433	44,433	44,433	44,433	44,433	44,433	1	.	.
IL	29,714	33,768	38,464	35,929	41,894	54,766	13	.	.
IN	28,080	28,080	28,080	28,080	28,080	28,080	1	.	.
LA	28,000	28,000	28,000	28,000	28,000	28,000	1	.	.
MA	43,472	49,975	48,892	49,975	49,975	49,975	6	.	.
MO	34,287	34,287	34,287	34,287	34,287	34,287	2	.	.
MT	33,795	33,795	33,795	33,795	33,795	33,795	1	.	.
NC	25,886	28,000	31,102	32,900	32,935	35,329	13	.	.
ND	30,262	30,262	30,262	30,262	30,262	30,262	1	.	.
NE	43,098	43,098	43,098	43,098	43,098	43,098	1	.	.
NM	27,930	27,930	28,857	28,857	29,783	29,783	2	.	.
NY	23,400	23,400	28,080	29,410	31,429	31,429	3	.	.
OH	19,018	19,018	19,018	19,018	19,018	19,018	1	.	.
OR	26,100	26,100	26,100	26,100	26,100	26,100	1	.	.
PA	33,143	33,143	33,143	33,143	33,143	33,143	1	.	.
SC	48,574	48,574	49,161	49,161	49,747	49,747	2	.	.
TN	32,004	32,004	36,600	38,424	39,372	39,372	3	.	.
TX	26,670	26,670	26,670	26,670	26,670	26,670	1	.	.
WA	44,644	44,644	44,644	44,644	44,644	44,644	1	.	.

Degree Required Data

	Min	Q1	Mean	Median	Q3	Max	N	Range Avg Min	Range Avg Max
High School	19,018	29,378	36,464	33,538	43,970	54,766	32	.	.
Associate's	28,000	28,000	28,000	28,000	28,000	28,000	2	.	.
Bachelor's	23,400	28,571	33,093	32,004	35,929	44,644	25	.	.
Master's	30,606	37,331	43,246	46,315	49,161	49,747	4	.	.
Doctoral								.	.

ASSOCIATE LIBRARIAN OF TECHNICAL ASSISTANCE (NON-MLS DEGREED) - CONTINUED
ALL ACADEMIC LIBRARIES
Regional Data

	Min	Q1	Mean	Median	Q3	Max	N	Range Avg Min	Range Avg Max
North Atlantic	23,400	29,410	39,626	39,723	49,975	65,304	17	22,360	24,024
Great Lakes & Plains	17,680	28,725	33,795	34,287	40,955	54,766	29	21,934	32,822
Southeast	13,998	26,637	29,901	29,346	33,280	49,747	37	.	.
West & Southwest	18,200	27,300	36,586	34,852	47,376	53,000	20	.	.
ALL REGIONS	13,998	27,206	33,900	32,935	40,955	65,304	103	22,019	31,063

State Data

	Min	Q1	Mean	Median	Q3	Max	N	Range Avg Min	Range Avg Max
AL	20,000	22,138	27,365	24,770	32,592	39,920	4		
AR	27,548	27,548	30,309	30,309	33,069	33,069	2		
CO	31,258	35,904	41,980	44,730	47,436	50,484	10		
CT	44,055	44,055	44,055	44,055	44,055	44,055	1		
DC	28,571	28,571	28,571	28,571	28,571	28,571	2		
FL	24,702	25,879	28,600	28,201	31,321	33,296	4		
GA	27,518	27,518	27,810	27,810	28,101	28,101	2		
IA	44,433	44,433	44,433	44,433	44,433	44,433	1		
IL	29,714	33,768	38,383	36,317	41,894	54,766	14		
IN	28,080	28,080	28,080	28,080	28,080	28,080	1		
KY	20,800	20,800	27,040	27,040	33,280	33,280	2		
LA	28,000	28,000	28,000	28,000	28,000	28,000	1		
MA	33,280	43,472	46,661	49,975	49,975	49,975	7		
MD	65,304	65,304	65,304	65,304	65,304	65,304	1		
MI	27,206	27,206	27,206	27,206	27,206	27,206	1		
MN	40,955	40,955	40,955	40,955	40,955	40,955	1	30,472	44,928
MO	23,965	23,965	30,846	34,287	34,287	34,287	3		
MT	33,795	33,795	33,795	33,795	33,795	33,795	1		
NC	17,067	26,637	29,870	31,352	32,935	35,329	15		
ND	23,004	23,004	27,755	30,000	30,262	30,262	3		
NE	43,098	43,098	43,098	43,098	43,098	43,098	1		
NM	27,930	27,930	28,857	28,857	29,783	29,783	2		
NY	23,400	23,400	28,080	29,410	31,429	31,429	3		
OH	19,018	19,018	23,871	23,871	28,725	28,725	2	21,902	34,362
OR	26,100	26,100	26,100	26,100	26,100	26,100	1		
PA	33,143	33,143	36,433	36,433	39,723	39,723	2		
SC	48,574	48,574	49,161	49,161	49,747	49,747	2		
SD	17,680	17,680	17,680	17,680	17,680	17,680	2	17,680	26,000
TN	32,004	32,004	36,600	38,424	39,372	39,372	3		
TX	18,200	25,641	29,933	26,154	26,670	53,000	5		
VT	23,400	23,400	23,400	23,400	23,400	23,400	1	22,360	24,024
WA	44,644	44,644	44,644	44,644	44,644	44,644	1		
WV	13,998	13,998	13,998	13,998	13,998	13,998	2		

Degree Required Data

	Min	Q1	Mean	Median	Q3	Max	N	Range Avg Min	Range Avg Max
High School	13,998	26,637	33,963	32,935	41,894	54,766	42	26,187	39,645
Associate's	20,000	23,965	26,899	27,206	28,000	37,336	9	22,360	24,024
Bachelor's	17,680	28,005	31,656	31,314	35,586	44,644	32	17,680	26,000
Master's	30,606	44,055	48,548	49,161	53,000	65,304	6		
Doctoral									

LIBRARY TECHNICAL ASSISTANT OF ADULT SERVICES

Provides basic assistance to patrons referring patrons to Librarian for professional assistance. Locates materials and information for patrons. May complete routine copy cataloging. Assists with special programming. Provides access to materials, services and programs intended to meet the needs of the adult users of a public library.

Two-Year College
Regional Data

	Min	Q1	Mean	Median	Q3	Max	N	Range Avg Min	Range Avg Max
North Atlantic	26,241	26,241	26,241	26,241	26,241	26,241	1	.	.
Great Lakes & Plains	31,946	31,946	31,946	31,946	31,946	31,946	1	.	.
Southeast	16,515	19,000	27,993	23,230	40,938	46,159	10	.	.
West & Southwest	20,155	20,155	24,706	24,706	29,256	29,256	2	18,304	20,155
ALL REGIONS	16,515	19,619	27,680	24,910	31,946	46,159	14	18,304	20,155

State Data

	Min	Q1	Mean	Median	Q3	Max	N	Range Avg Min	Range Avg Max
AL	19,000	19,000	19,000	19,000	19,000	19,000	1	.	.
CA	29,256	29,256	29,256	29,256	29,256	29,256	1	.	.
FL	16,515	17,198	19,224	18,750	21,250	22,880	4	.	.
IL	31,946	31,946	31,946	31,946	31,946	31,946	1	.	.
MD	26,241	26,241	26,241	26,241	26,241	26,241	1	.	.
MT	20,155	20,155	20,155	20,155	20,155	20,155	1	18,304	20,155
WV	23,579	31,292	36,807	40,938	42,065	46,159	5	.	.

Degree Required Data

	Min	Q1	Mean	Median	Q3	Max	N	Range Avg Min	Range Avg Max
High School	16,515	17,880	23,003	22,880	29,256	31,292	7	.	.
Associate's	19,000	20,155	32,358	31,946	42,065	46,159	7	18,304	20,155
Bachelor's	.	.	.	.	.	.	.	.	.
Master's	.	.	.	.	.	.	.	.	.
Doctoral	.	.	.	.	.	.	.	.	.

LIBRARY TECHNICAL ASSISTANT OF ADULT SERVICES - CONTINUED
Four-Year College
Regional Data

	Min	Q1	Mean	Median	Q3	Max	N	Range Avg Min	Range Avg Max
North Atlantic	21,598	21,598	25,274	25,771	28,454	28,454	3	.	.
Great Lakes & Plains	20,800	20,800	22,890	22,890	24,981	24,981	2	.	.
Southeast	14,500	17,659	20,379	19,830	23,140	28,213	12	.	.
West & Southwest	39,384	39,384	39,384	39,384	39,384	39,384	1	.	.
ALL REGIONS	14,500	17,659	22,530	22,440	24,981	39,384	18	.	.

State Data

	Min	Q1	Mean	Median	Q3	Max	N	Range Avg Min	Range Avg Max
CO	39,384	39,384	39,384	39,384	39,384	39,384	1	.	.
IL	20,800	20,800	20,800	20,800	20,800	20,800	1	.	.
KY	14,500	17,659	19,434	17,659	22,880	24,960	10	.	.
ME	28,454	28,454	28,454	28,454	28,454	28,454	1	.	.
OH	24,981	24,981	24,981	24,981	24,981	24,981	1	.	.
PA	21,598	21,598	23,685	23,685	25,771	25,771	2	.	.
SC	28,213	28,213	28,213	28,213	28,213	28,213	1	.	.
TN	22,000	22,000	22,000	22,000	22,000	22,000	1	.	.

Degree Required Data

	Min	Q1	Mean	Median	Q3	Max	N	Range Avg Min	Range Avg Max
High School	14,500	15,080	20,847	17,659	20,800	39,384	6	.	.
Associate's	24,981	24,981	24,981	24,981	24,981	24,981	1	.	.
Bachelor's	17,659	21,598	23,013	22,880	25,771	28,454	9	.	.
Master's								.	.
Doctoral								.	.

LIBRARY TECHNICAL ASSISTANT OF ADULT SERVICES - CONTINUED
University
(Includes ARL Data)
Regional Data

	Min	Q1	Mean	Median	Q3	Max	N	Range Avg Min	Range Avg Max
North Atlantic	29,531	29,531	29,801	29,531	29,742	30,940	6	.	.
Great Lakes & Plains	19,130	28,919	36,743	39,004	41,948	55,038	31	.	.
Southeast	19,386	20,010	23,118	22,169	25,520	32,335	14	.	.
West & Southwest	20,239	28,524	33,339	33,072	40,524	45,516	13	.	.
ALL REGIONS	19,130	25,484	32,420	30,956	39,784	55,038	64	.	.

State Data

	Min	Q1	Mean	Median	Q3	Max	N	Range Avg Min	Range Avg Max
CO	30,972	33,072	37,737	36,396	43,704	45,516	9	.	.
CT	29,742	29,742	30,341	30,341	30,940	30,940	2	.	.
DC	29,531	29,531	29,531	29,531	29,531	29,531	4	.	.
FL	19,386	19,968	21,553	21,016	22,316	26,863	10	.	.
GA	24,478	24,478	25,133	25,133	25,788	25,788	2	.	.
IA	25,328	34,055	39,046	41,071	45,790	47,698	18	.	.
IN	30,992	30,992	30,992	30,992	30,992	30,992	1	.	.
MN	25,448	29,583	37,098	39,004	39,291	55,038	9	.	.
MO	19,130	19,130	19,130	19,130	19,130	19,130	1	.	.
MT	22,198	22,198	22,198	22,198	22,198	22,198	1	.	.
NC	32,335	32,335	32,335	32,335	32,335	32,335	1	.	.
SC	25,520	25,520	25,520	25,520	25,520	25,520	1	.	.
SD	25,719	25,719	26,100	26,100	26,481	26,481	2	.	.
TX	20,239	20,239	21,524	21,524	22,809	22,809	2	.	.
WA	28,524	28,524	28,524	28,524	28,524	28,524	1	.	.

Degree Required Data

	Min	Q1	Mean	Median	Q3	Max	N	Range Avg Min	Range Avg Max
High School	19,386	22,022	27,727	25,484	29,583	55,038	26	.	.
Associate's	25,788	25,788	29,061	29,061	32,335	32,335	2	.	.
Bachelor's	24,478	29,531	29,285	29,531	30,341	30,992	8	.	.
Master's	.	.	.	.	.	.		.	.
Doctoral	.	.	.	.	.	.		.	.

LIBRARY TECHNICAL ASSISTANT OF ADULT SERVICES - CONTINUED
ALL ACADEMIC LIBRARIES
Regional Data

	Min	Q1	Mean	Median	Q3	Max	N	Range Avg Min	Range Avg Max
North Atlantic	21,598	26,241	28,087	29,531	29,531	30,940	10	.	.
Great Lakes & Plains	19,130	27,666	35,787	38,712	41,948	55,038	34	.	.
Southeast	14,500	19,193	23,559	22,169	25,240	46,159	36	.	.
West & Southwest	20,155	25,667	32,638	32,436	39,954	45,516	16	18,304	20,155
ALL REGIONS	14,500	22,257	29,875	28,489	39,004	55,038	96	18,304	20,155

State Data

	Min	Q1	Mean	Median	Q3	Max	N	Range Avg Min	Range Avg Max
AL	19,000	19,000	19,000	19,000	19,000	19,000	1	.	.
CA	29,256	29,256	29,256	29,256	29,256	29,256	1	.	.
CO	30,972	33,072	37,902	37,890	43,704	45,516	10	.	.
CT	29,742	29,742	30,341	30,341	30,940	30,940	2	.	.
DC	29,531	29,531	29,531	29,531	29,531	29,531	4	.	.
FL	16,515	19,619	20,888	20,010	22,316	26,863	14	.	.
GA	24,478	24,478	25,133	25,133	25,788	25,788	2	.	.
IA	25,328	34,055	39,046	41,071	45,790	47,698	18	.	.
IL	20,800	20,800	26,373	26,373	31,946	31,946	2	.	.
IN	30,992	30,992	30,992	30,992	30,992	30,992	1	.	.
KY	14,500	17,659	19,434	17,659	22,880	24,960	10	.	.
MD	26,241	26,241	26,241	26,241	26,241	26,241	1	.	.
ME	28,454	28,454	28,454	28,454	28,454	28,454	1	.	.
MN	25,448	29,583	37,098	39,004	39,291	55,038	9	.	.
MO	19,130	19,130	19,130	19,130	19,130	19,130	1	.	.
MT	20,155	20,155	21,177	21,177	22,198	22,198	2	18,304	20,155
NC	32,335	32,335	32,335	32,335	32,335	32,335	1	.	.
OH	24,981	24,981	24,981	24,981	24,981	24,981	1	.	.
PA	21,598	21,598	23,685	23,685	25,771	25,771	2	.	.
SC	25,520	25,520	26,867	26,867	28,213	28,213	2	.	.
SD	25,719	25,719	26,100	26,100	26,481	26,481	2	.	.
TN	22,000	22,000	22,000	22,000	22,000	22,000	1	.	.
TX	20,239	20,239	21,524	21,524	22,809	22,809	2	.	.
WA	28,524	28,524	28,524	28,524	28,524	28,524	1	.	.
WV	23,579	31,292	36,807	40,938	42,065	46,159	5	.	.

Degree Required Data

	Min	Q1	Mean	Median	Q3	Max	N	Range Avg Min	Range Avg Max
High School	14,500	19,968	25,821	22,880	29,256	55,038	39	.	.
Associate's	19,000	24,981	30,961	29,094	40,938	46,159	10	18,304	20,155
Bachelor's	17,659	22,880	25,964	28,213	29,531	30,992	17	.	.
Master's	.	.	.	.	.	.		.	.
Doctoral	.	.	.	.	.	.		.	.

LIBRARY TECHNICAL ASSISTANT OF ARCHIVES AND SPECIAL COLLECTIONS

Provides basic assistance to patrons referring patrons to Librarian for professional assistance. Locates materials and information for patrons. May complete routine copy cataloging. Assists with special programming. Manages and maintains collection; identifies and appraises records, authenticates, describes and documents, facilitates access and use, preserves and conserves, and exhibits collection.

Two-Year College
Regional Data

	Min	Q1	Mean	Median	Q3	Max	N	Range Avg Min	Range Avg Max
Southeast	16,105	16,105	18,806	18,806	21,507	21,507	2	.	.
ALL REGIONS	16,105	16,105	18,806	18,806	21,507	21,507	2	.	.

State Data

	Min	Q1	Mean	Median	Q3	Max	N	Range Avg Min	Range Avg Max
AR	16,105	16,105	16,105	16,105	16,105	16,105	1	.	.
FL	21,507	21,507	21,507	21,507	21,507	21,507	1	.	.

Degree Required Data

	Min	Q1	Mean	Median	Q3	Max	N	Range Avg Min	Range Avg Max
High School	21,507	21,507	21,507	21,507	21,507	21,507	1	.	.
Associate's	16,105	16,105	16,105	16,105	16,105	16,105	1	.	.
Bachelor's	.	.	.	.	.	.		.	.
Master's	.	.	.	.	.	.		.	.
Doctoral	.	.	.	.	.	.		.	.

LIBRARY TECHNICAL ASSISTANT OF ARCHIVES AND SPECIAL COLLECTIONS - CONTINUED
Four-Year College
Regional Data

	Min	Q1	Mean	Median	Q3	Max	N	Range Avg Min	Range Avg Max
North Atlantic	26,182	26,556	29,297	28,784	32,038	33,438	4	.	.
Great Lakes & Plains	25,719	25,719	25,719	25,719	25,719	25,719	1	.	.
Southeast	17,659	19,860	26,733	27,385	33,607	34,504	4	.	.
ALL REGIONS	17,659	25,719	27,760	26,930	32,710	34,504	9	.	.

State Data

	Min	Q1	Mean	Median	Q3	Max	N	Range Avg Min	Range Avg Max
GA	34,504	34,504	34,504	34,504	34,504	34,504	1	.	.
KY	17,659	17,659	19,860	19,860	22,060	22,060	2	.	.
ME	26,182	26,182	30,086	30,638	33,438	33,438	3	.	.
PA	26,930	26,930	26,930	26,930	26,930	26,930	1	.	.
SD	25,719	25,719	25,719	25,719	25,719	25,719	1	.	.
WV	32,710	32,710	32,710	32,710	32,710	32,710	1	.	.

Degree Required Data

	Min	Q1	Mean	Median	Q3	Max	N	Range Avg Min	Range Avg Max
High School	32,710	32,710	32,710	32,710	32,710	32,710	1	.	.
Associate's	.	.	.	.	.	.		.	.
Bachelor's	17,659	23,890	27,141	26,556	32,038	34,504	8	.	.
Master's	.	.	.	.	.	.		.	.
Doctoral	.	.	.	.	.	.		.	.

LIBRARY TECHNICAL ASSISTANT OF ARCHIVES AND SPECIAL COLLECTIONS - CONTINUED
University
(Includes ARL Data)
Regional Data

	Min	Q1	Mean	Median	Q3	Max	N	Range Avg Min	Range Avg Max
North Atlantic	21,570	24,242	34,411	36,067	43,074	43,437	7	20,800	22,880
Great Lakes & Plains	20,800	23,148	29,692	24,260	38,646	45,790	17	24,232	39,118
Southeast	17,306	24,000	30,407	29,872	33,240	84,074	35	21,944	38,334
West & Southwest	17,268	28,689	34,225	34,032	40,008	53,826	27	.	.
ALL REGIONS	17,268	24,000	31,790	31,096	37,080	84,074	86	22,897	36,150

State Data

	Min	Q1	Mean	Median	Q3	Max	N	Range Avg Min	Range Avg Max
AL	32,156	32,156	32,156	32,156	32,156	32,156	1	.	.
AR	17,306	17,318	24,528	24,576	29,450	33,945	6	.	.
AZ	32,737	33,004	36,761	34,335	40,285	48,535	7	.	.
CA	34,032	36,792	39,071	39,780	41,351	42,693	4	.	.
CO	31,200	37,080	41,100	38,496	47,436	51,288	5	.	.
CT	43,074	43,074	43,074	43,074	43,074	43,074	1	.	.
DC	33,904	34,986	37,998	37,326	41,010	43,437	4	.	.
FL	19,490	19,745	25,827	24,936	31,909	33,946	4	.	.
GA	24,859	24,859	24,859	24,859	24,859	24,859	1	.	.
IA	23,198	26,048	34,959	35,423	43,869	45,790	4	.	.
IL	20,800	22,537	29,770	29,817	37,003	38,646	4	22,922	42,702
IN	22,069	22,069	22,464	22,443	22,880	22,880	3	20,800	24,960
KY	31,319	31,319	31,319	31,319	31,319	31,319	1	.	.
LA	24,000	24,000	44,025	24,000	84,074	84,074	3	.	.
MN	39,004	39,004	39,004	39,004	39,004	39,004	1	.	.
NC	26,037	30,405	32,913	32,935	35,810	41,600	14	.	.
ND	24,260	24,260	24,260	24,260	24,260	24,260	2	.	.
NE	23,148	23,148	23,148	23,148	23,148	23,148	1	.	.
NY	21,570	21,570	22,906	22,906	24,242	24,242	2	20,800	22,880
OH	44,516	44,516	44,516	44,516	44,516	44,516	1	28,974	49,691
SD	23,271	23,271	23,271	23,271	23,271	23,271	1	.	.
TN	21,036	23,691	26,516	25,189	29,424	33,240	5	21,944	38,334
TX	17,268	17,268	21,993	20,900	27,812	27,812	3	.	.
UT	19,375	19,375	29,774	28,689	37,690	53,826	7	.	.
WA	30,564	30,564	30,564	30,564	30,564	30,564	1	.	.

Degree Required Data

	Min	Q1	Mean	Median	Q3	Max	N	Range Avg Min	Range Avg Max
High School	17,268	21,036	27,927	27,812	32,935	44,516	41	23,416	37,310
Associate's	22,880	24,260	27,899	24,260	32,737	35,360	5	21,861	33,831
Bachelor's	20,000	29,450	35,593	33,946	39,552	84,074	31	.	.
Master's	.	.	.	.	.	.	.	.	.
Doctoral	.	.	.	.	.	.	.	.	.

LIBRARY TECHNICAL ASSISTANT OF ARCHIVES AND SPECIAL COLLECTIONS - CONTINUED
ALL ACADEMIC LIBRARIES
Regional Data

	Min	Q1	Mean	Median	Q3	Max	N	Range Avg Min	Range Avg Max
North Atlantic	21,570	26,182	32,551	33,438	38,584	43,437	11	20,800	22,880
Great Lakes & Plains	20,800	23,148	29,471	24,267	38,646	45,790	18	24,232	39,118
Southeast	16,105	23,691	29,483	29,450	32,954	84,074	41	21,944	38,334
West & Southwest	17,268	28,689	34,225	34,032	40,008	53,826	27	.	.
ALL REGIONS	16,105	24,000	31,149	30,564	35,810	84,074	97	22,897	36,150

State Data

	Min	Q1	Mean	Median	Q3	Max	N	Range Avg Min	Range Avg Max
AL	32,156	32,156	32,156	32,156	32,156	32,156	1	.	.
AR	16,105	17,306	23,325	20,000	29,450	33,945	7	.	.
AZ	32,737	33,004	36,761	34,335	40,285	48,535	7	.	.
CA	34,032	36,792	39,071	39,780	41,351	42,693	4	.	.
CO	31,200	37,080	41,100	38,496	47,436	51,288	5	.	.
CT	43,074	43,074	43,074	43,074	43,074	43,074	1	.	.
DC	33,904	34,986	37,998	37,326	41,010	43,437	4	.	.
FL	19,490	20,000	24,963	21,507	29,872	33,946	5	.	.
GA	24,859	24,859	29,682	29,682	34,504	34,504	2	.	.
IA	23,198	26,048	34,959	35,423	43,869	45,790	4	.	.
IL	20,800	22,537	29,770	29,817	37,003	38,646	4	22,922	42,702
IN	22,069	22,069	22,464	22,443	22,880	22,880	3	20,800	24,960
KY	17,659	17,659	23,680	22,060	31,319	31,319	3	.	.
LA	24,000	24,000	44,025	24,000	84,074	84,074	3	.	.
ME	26,182	26,182	30,086	30,638	33,438	33,438	3	.	.
MN	39,004	39,004	39,004	39,004	39,004	39,004	1	.	.
NC	26,037	30,405	32,913	32,935	35,810	41,600	14	.	.
ND	24,260	24,260	24,260	24,260	24,260	24,260	2	.	.
NE	23,148	23,148	23,148	23,148	23,148	23,148	1	.	.
NY	21,570	21,570	22,906	22,906	24,242	24,242	2	20,800	22,880
OH	44,516	44,516	44,516	44,516	44,516	44,516	1	28,974	49,691
PA	26,930	26,930	26,930	26,930	26,930	26,930	1	.	.
SD	23,271	23,271	24,495	24,495	25,719	25,719	2	.	.
TN	21,036	23,691	26,516	25,189	29,424	33,240	5	21,944	38,334
TX	17,268	17,268	21,993	20,900	27,812	27,812	3	.	.
UT	19,375	19,375	29,774	28,689	37,690	53,826	7	.	.
WA	30,564	30,564	30,564	30,564	30,564	30,564	1	.	.
WV	32,710	32,710	32,710	32,710	32,710	32,710	1	.	.

Degree Required Data

	Min	Q1	Mean	Median	Q3	Max	N	Range Avg Min	Range Avg Max
High School	17,268	21,036	27,889	27,812	32,935	44,516	43	23,416	37,310
Associate's	16,105	22,880	25,934	24,260	32,737	35,360	6	21,861	33,831
Bachelor's	17,659	26,182	33,859	33,438	37,690	84,074	39	.	.
Master's	.	.	.	.	.	.	.	.	.
Doctoral	.	.	.	.	.	.	.	.	.

LIBRARY TECHNICAL ASSISTANT OF CHILDREN'S SERVICES/YOUNG ADULT SERVICES

Provides basic assistance to patrons referring patrons to Librarian for professional assistance. Locates materials and information for patrons. May complete routine copy cataloging. Assists with special programming. Provides services intended for children and youths through twelfth grade; develops collection, provides homework and reader's advisory services, and develops age appropriate programs.

Four-Year College
Regional Data

	Min	Q1	Mean	Median	Q3	Max	N	Range Avg Min	Range Avg Max
Southeast	27,159	27,159	27,159	27,159	27,159	27,159	1	.	.
ALL REGIONS	27,159	27,159	27,159	27,159	27,159	27,159	1	.	.

State Data

	Min	Q1	Mean	Median	Q3	Max	N	Range Avg Min	Range Avg Max
WV	27,159	27,159	27,159	27,159	27,159	27,159	1	.	.

Degree Required Data

	Min	Q1	Mean	Median	Q3	Max	N	Range Avg Min	Range Avg Max
High School	27,159	27,159	27,159	27,159	27,159	27,159	1	.	.
Associate's								.	.
Bachelor's								.	.
Master's								.	.
Doctoral								.	.

LIBRARY TECHNICAL ASSISTANT OF CHILDREN'S SERVICES/YOUNG ADULT SERVICES - CONTINUED
University
(Includes ARL Data)
Regional Data

	Min	Q1	Mean	Median	Q3	Max	N	Range Avg Min	Range Avg Max
North Atlantic	21,570	29,531	33,543	29,531	39,760	47,322	5	20,800	22,880
Great Lakes & Plains	19,130	19,130	19,130	19,130	19,130	19,130	1	.	.
Southeast	27,000	27,000	27,000	27,000	27,000	27,000	1	.	.
West & Southwest	21,600	21,600	21,600	21,600	21,600	21,600	1	.	.
ALL REGIONS	19,130	21,585	29,431	28,266	34,646	47,322	8	20,800	22,880

State Data

	Min	Q1	Mean	Median	Q3	Max	N	Range Avg Min	Range Avg Max
AR	27,000	27,000	27,000	27,000	27,000	27,000	1	.	.
CT	47,322	47,322	47,322	47,322	47,322	47,322	1	.	.
DC	29,531	29,531	29,531	29,531	29,531	29,531	2	.	.
MA	39,760	39,760	39,760	39,760	39,760	39,760	1	.	.
MO	19,130	19,130	19,130	19,130	19,130	19,130	1	.	.
NY	21,570	21,570	21,570	21,570	21,570	21,570	1	20,800	22,880
WY	21,600	21,600	21,600	21,600	21,600	21,600	1	.	.

Degree Required Data

	Min	Q1	Mean	Median	Q3	Max	N	Range Avg Min	Range Avg Max
High School	21,570	21,570	34,446	34,446	47,322	47,322	2	20,800	22,880
Associate's	.	.	.	.	.	.	.	.	.
Bachelor's	19,130	27,000	28,991	29,531	29,531	39,760	5	.	.
Master's	.	.	.	.	.	.	.	.	.
Doctoral	.	.	.	.	.	.	.	.	.

LIBRARY TECHNICAL ASSISTANT OF CHILDREN'S SERVICES/YOUNG ADULT SERVICES - CONTINUED
ALL ACADEMIC LIBRARIES
Regional Data

	Min	Q1	Mean	Median	Q3	Max	N	Range Avg Min	Range Avg Max
North Atlantic	21,570	29,531	33,543	29,531	39,760	47,322	5	20,800	22,880
Great Lakes & Plains	19,130	19,130	19,130	19,130	19,130	19,130	1	.	.
Southeast	27,000	27,000	27,080	27,080	27,159	27,159	2	.	.
West & Southwest	21,600	21,600	21,600	21,600	21,600	21,600	1	.	.
ALL REGIONS	19,130	21,600	29,178	27,159	29,531	47,322	9	20,800	22,880

State Data

	Min	Q1	Mean	Median	Q3	Max	N	Range Avg Min	Range Avg Max
AR	27,000	27,000	27,000	27,000	27,000	27,000	1	.	.
CT	47,322	47,322	47,322	47,322	47,322	47,322	1	.	.
DC	29,531	29,531	29,531	29,531	29,531	29,531	2	.	.
MA	39,760	39,760	39,760	39,760	39,760	39,760	1	.	.
MO	19,130	19,130	19,130	19,130	19,130	19,130	1	.	.
NY	21,570	21,570	21,570	21,570	21,570	21,570	1	20,800	22,880
WV	27,159	27,159	27,159	27,159	27,159	27,159	1	.	.
WY	21,600	21,600	21,600	21,600	21,600	21,600	1	.	.

Degree Required Data

	Min	Q1	Mean	Median	Q3	Max	N	Range Avg Min	Range Avg Max
High School	21,570	21,570	32,017	27,159	47,322	47,322	3	20,800	22,880
Associate's	.	.	.	.	.	.	.	.	.
Bachelor's	19,130	27,000	28,991	29,531	29,531	39,760	5	.	.
Master's	.	.	.	.	.	.	.	.	.
Doctoral	.	.	.	.	.	.	.	.	.

LIBRARY TECHNICAL ASSISTANT OF GOVERNMENT DOCUMENTS

Provides basic assistance to patrons referring patrons to Librarian for professional assistance. Locates materials and information for patrons. May complete routine copy cataloging. Assists with special programming. Provides access to publications of the U. S. federal government such as transcripts of hearings and text of bills, resolutions, statutes, reports, charters, treaties, periodicals and statistics.

Two-Year College
Regional Data

	Min	Q1	Mean	Median	Q3	Max	N	Range Avg Min	Range Avg Max
West & Southwest	36,341	36,341	36,341	36,341	36,341	36,341	1	.	.
ALL REGIONS	36,341	36,341	36,341	36,341	36,341	36,341	1	.	.

State Data

	Min	Q1	Mean	Median	Q3	Max	N	Range Avg Min	Range Avg Max
TX	36,341	36,341	36,341	36,341	36,341	36,341	1	.	.

Degree Required Data

	Min	Q1	Mean	Median	Q3	Max	N	Range Avg Min	Range Avg Max
High School	.	.	.	.	.	.		.	.
Associate's	36,341	36,341	36,341	36,341	36,341	36,341	1	.	.
Bachelor's	.	.	.	.	.	.		.	.
Master's	.	.	.	.	.	.		.	.
Doctoral	.	.	.	.	.	.		.	.

LIBRARY TECHNICAL ASSISTANT OF GOVERNMENT DOCUMENTS - CONTINUED
Four-Year College
Regional Data

	Min	Q1	Mean	Median	Q3	Max	N	Range Avg Min	Range Avg Max
West & Southwest	33,804	33,804	40,326	40,326	46,848	46,848	2	.	.
ALL REGIONS	33,804	33,804	40,326	40,326	46,848	46,848	2	.	.

State Data

	Min	Q1	Mean	Median	Q3	Max	N	Range Avg Min	Range Avg Max
CO	33,804	33,804	40,326	40,326	46,848	46,848	2	.	.

Degree Required Data

	Min	Q1	Mean	Median	Q3	Max	N	Range Avg Min	Range Avg Max
High School	33,804	33,804	40,326	40,326	46,848	46,848	2	.	.
Associate's	.	.	.	.	.	.		.	.
Bachelor's	.	.	.	.	.	.		.	.
Master's	.	.	.	.	.	.		.	.
Doctoral	.	.	.	.	.	.		.	.

LIBRARY TECHNICAL ASSISTANT OF GOVERNMENT DOCUMENTS - CONTINUED
University
(Includes ARL Data)
Regional Data

	Min	Q1	Mean	Median	Q3	Max	N	Range Avg Min	Range Avg Max
North Atlantic	21,570	28,706	33,278	32,168	39,229	44,451	8	20,800	22,880
Great Lakes & Plains	16,899	22,838	29,933	27,945	38,420	41,948	14	26,603	39,582
Southeast	18,696	23,105	26,544	26,158	30,387	34,702	16	20,363	35,589
West & Southwest	14,200	18,984	28,027	27,088	35,430	47,016	8	.	.
ALL REGIONS	14,200	22,838	29,005	28,664	34,702	47,016	46	22,589	32,684

State Data

	Min	Q1	Mean	Median	Q3	Max	N	Range Avg Min	Range Avg Max
AL	30,742	30,742	30,742	30,742	30,742	30,742	1	.	.
AR	19,403	19,814	24,598	22,143	29,382	34,702	4	.	.
CA	39,216	39,216	43,116	43,116	47,016	47,016	2	.	.
CT	44,451	44,451	44,451	44,451	44,451	44,451	1	.	.
DC	34,278	34,278	37,579	37,524	40,934	40,934	3	.	.
FL	22,149	24,262	27,539	27,822	30,817	32,365	4	.	.
GA	28,623	28,623	28,623	28,623	28,623	28,623	1	.	.
IA	38,420	38,420	40,184	40,184	41,948	41,948	2	.	.
IL	37,170	37,170	37,212	37,212	37,253	37,253	2	.	.
IN	22,838	22,838	26,242	27,934	27,955	27,955	3	.	.
MD	28,706	28,706	28,706	28,706	28,706	28,706	2	.	.
MN	39,004	39,004	39,004	39,004	39,004	39,004	1	.	.
NC	25,941	25,941	27,987	27,987	30,032	30,032	2	.	.
ND	16,899	16,899	19,984	19,640	23,412	23,412	3	.	.
NE	21,135	21,135	21,135	21,135	21,135	21,135	1	.	.
NY	21,570	21,570	21,570	21,570	21,570	21,570	1	20,800	22,880
OH	39,735	39,735	39,735	39,735	39,735	39,735	1	26,603	39,582
OK	14,200	14,200	14,200	14,200	14,200	14,200	1	.	.
PA	30,058	30,058	30,058	30,058	30,058	30,058	1	.	.
SC	24,661	24,661	25,202	25,202	25,742	25,742	2	.	.
SD	25,719	25,719	25,719	25,719	25,719	25,719	1	.	.
TN	18,696	18,696	25,208	25,208	31,720	31,720	2	20,363	35,589
TX	17,268	18,984	25,124	25,792	31,264	31,643	4	.	.
WY	23,292	23,292	23,292	23,292	23,292	23,292	1	.	.

Degree Required Data

	Min	Q1	Mean	Median	Q3	Max	N	Range Avg Min	Range Avg Max
High School	14,200	22,149	27,763	28,330	31,643	44,451	26	22,589	32,684
Associate's	16,899	18,270	21,971	21,526	25,673	27,934	4	.	.
Bachelor's	20,700	25,941	32,790	32,365	39,216	47,016	11	.	.
Master's	.	.	.	.	.	.	.	.	.
Doctoral	.	.	.	.	.	.	.	.	.

LIBRARY TECHNICAL ASSISTANT OF GOVERNMENT DOCUMENTS - CONTINUED
ALL ACADEMIC LIBRARIES
Regional Data

	Min	Q1	Mean	Median	Q3	Max	N	Range Avg Min	Range Avg Max
North Atlantic	21,570	28,706	33,278	32,168	39,229	44,451	8	20,800	22,880
Great Lakes & Plains	16,899	22,838	29,933	27,945	38,420	41,948	14	26,603	39,582
Southeast	18,696	23,105	26,544	26,158	30,387	34,702	16	20,363	35,589
West & Southwest	14,200	20,700	31,019	31,643	39,216	47,016	11		.
ALL REGIONS	14,200	23,292	29,616	28,706	36,341	47,016	49	22,589	32,684

State Data

	Min	Q1	Mean	Median	Q3	Max	N	Range Avg Min	Range Avg Max
AL	30,742	30,742	30,742	30,742	30,742	30,742	1		.
AR	19,403	19,814	24,598	22,143	29,382	34,702	4		.
CA	39,216	39,216	43,116	43,116	47,016	47,016	2		.
CO	33,804	33,804	40,326	40,326	46,848	46,848	2		.
CT	44,451	44,451	44,451	44,451	44,451	44,451	1		.
DC	34,278	34,278	37,579	37,524	40,934	40,934	3		.
FL	22,149	24,262	27,539	27,822	30,817	32,365	4		.
GA	28,623	28,623	28,623	28,623	28,623	28,623	1		.
IA	38,420	38,420	40,184	40,184	41,948	41,948	2		.
IL	37,170	37,170	37,212	37,212	37,253	37,253	2		.
IN	22,838	22,838	26,242	27,934	27,955	27,955	3		.
MD	28,706	28,706	28,706	28,706	28,706	28,706	2		.
MN	39,004	39,004	39,004	39,004	39,004	39,004	1		.
NC	25,941	25,941	27,987	27,987	30,032	30,032	2		.
ND	16,899	16,899	19,984	19,640	23,412	23,412	3		.
NE	21,135	21,135	21,135	21,135	21,135	21,135	1		.
NY	21,570	21,570	21,570	21,570	21,570	21,570	1	20,800	22,880
OH	39,735	39,735	39,735	39,735	39,735	39,735	1	26,603	39,582
OK	14,200	14,200	14,200	14,200	14,200	14,200	1		.
PA	30,058	30,058	30,058	30,058	30,058	30,058	1		.
SC	24,661	24,661	25,202	25,202	25,742	25,742	2		.
SD	25,719	25,719	25,719	25,719	25,719	25,719	1		.
TN	18,696	18,696	25,208	25,208	31,720	31,720	2	20,363	35,589
TX	17,268	20,700	27,367	30,884	31,643	36,341	5		.
WY	23,292	23,292	23,292	23,292	23,292	23,292	1		.

Degree Required Data

	Min	Q1	Mean	Median	Q3	Max	N	Range Avg Min	Range Avg Max
High School	14,200	22,494	28,660	28,706	32,762	46,848	28	22,589	32,684
Associate's	16,899	19,640	24,845	23,412	27,934	36,341	5		.
Bachelor's	20,700	25,941	32,790	32,365	39,216	47,016	11		.
Master's	.	.	.	.	.	.	.		.
Doctoral	.	.	.	.	.	.	.		.

LIBRARY TECHNICAL ASSISTANT OF INSTRUCTIONAL SERVICES/LITERACY

Provides basic assistance to patrons referring patrons to Librarian for professional assistance. Locates materials and information for patrons. May complete routine copy cataloging. Assists with special programming. Advances learning, teaching and research with respect to information literacy in higher education; assists patrons to develop the ability to read and write.

Two-Year College
Regional Data

	Min	Q1	Mean	Median	Q3	Max	N	Range Avg Min	Range Avg Max
North Atlantic	60,382	60,382	60,382	60,382	60,382	60,382	1	.	.
Great Lakes & Plains	20,800	20,800	20,800	20,800	20,800	20,800	1	16,640	22,880
Southeast	15,371	17,798	20,937	20,856	24,077	26,667	4	.	.
West & Southwest	23,590	23,590	23,590	23,590	23,590	23,590	1	.	.
ALL REGIONS	15,371	20,225	26,932	21,486	26,667	60,382	7	16,640	22,880

State Data

	Min	Q1	Mean	Median	Q3	Max	N	Range Avg Min	Range Avg Max
AR	20,225	20,225	20,225	20,225	20,225	20,225	1	.	.
FL	15,371	15,371	18,429	18,429	21,486	21,486	2	.	.
IA	20,800	20,800	20,800	20,800	20,800	20,800	1	16,640	22,880
MA	60,382	60,382	60,382	60,382	60,382	60,382	1	.	.
NC	26,667	26,667	26,667	26,667	26,667	26,667	1	.	.
TX	23,590	23,590	23,590	23,590	23,590	23,590	1	.	.

Degree Required Data

	Min	Q1	Mean	Median	Q3	Max	N	Range Avg Min	Range Avg Max
High School	15,371	15,371	18,429	18,429	21,486	21,486	2	.	.
Associate's	20,225	20,225	20,513	20,513	20,800	20,800	2	16,640	22,880
Bachelor's	60,382	60,382	60,382	60,382	60,382	60,382	1	.	.
Master's	.	.	.	.	.	.		.	.
Doctoral	.	.	.	.	.	.		.	.

LIBRARY TECHNICAL ASSISTANT OF INSTRUCTIONAL SERVICES/LITERACY - CONTINUED
Four-Year College
Regional Data

	Min	Q1	Mean	Median	Q3	Max	N	Range Avg Min	Range Avg Max
West & Southwest	47,316	47,316	47,316	47,316	47,316	47,316	1	.	.
ALL REGIONS	47,316	47,316	47,316	47,316	47,316	47,316	1	.	.

State Data

	Min	Q1	Mean	Median	Q3	Max	N	Range Avg Min	Range Avg Max
CO	47,316	47,316	47,316	47,316	47,316	47,316	1	.	.

Degree Required Data

	Min	Q1	Mean	Median	Q3	Max	N	Range Avg Min	Range Avg Max
High School	47,316	47,316	47,316	47,316	47,316	47,316	1	.	.
Associate's	.	.	.	.	.	.		.	.
Bachelor's	.	.	.	.	.	.		.	.
Master's	.	.	.	.	.	.		.	.
Doctoral	.	.	.	.	.	.		.	.

LIBRARY TECHNICAL ASSISTANT OF INSTRUCTIONAL SERVICES/LITERACY - CONTINUED
University
(Includes ARL Data)
Regional Data

	Min	Q1	Mean	Median	Q3	Max	N	Range Avg Min	Range Avg Max
North Atlantic	27,429	27,429	28,480	28,480	29,531	29,531	4	.	.
Great Lakes & Plains	23,344	23,344	30,172	30,172	37,000	37,000	2	.	.
Southeast	26,340	26,340	26,340	26,340	26,340	26,340	1	.	.
West & Southwest	42,936	42,936	43,020	43,020	43,104	43,104	2	.	.
ALL REGIONS	23,344	27,429	31,849	29,531	37,000	43,104	9	.	.

State Data

	Min	Q1	Mean	Median	Q3	Max	N	Range Avg Min	Range Avg Max
CO	42,936	42,936	42,936	42,936	42,936	42,936	1	.	.
DC	27,429	27,429	28,480	28,480	29,531	29,531	4	.	.
MN	37,000	37,000	37,000	37,000	37,000	37,000	1	.	.
NE	23,344	23,344	23,344	23,344	23,344	23,344	1	.	.
OR	43,104	43,104	43,104	43,104	43,104	43,104	1	.	.
TN	26,340	26,340	26,340	26,340	26,340	26,340	1	.	.

Degree Required Data

	Min	Q1	Mean	Median	Q3	Max	N	Range Avg Min	Range Avg Max
High School	.	.	.	.	.	.		.	.
Associate's	27,429	27,429	27,429	27,429	27,429	27,429	2	.	.
Bachelor's	26,340	27,936	30,601	29,531	33,266	37,000	4	.	.
Master's	.	.	.	.	.	.		.	.
Doctoral	.	.	.	.	.	.		.	.

LIBRARY TECHNICAL ASSISTANT OF INSTRUCTIONAL SERVICES/LITERACY - CONTINUED
ALL ACADEMIC LIBRARIES
Regional Data

	Min	Q1	Mean	Median	Q3	Max	N	Range Avg Min	Range Avg Max
North Atlantic	27,429	27,429	34,860	29,531	29,531	60,382	5	.	.
Great Lakes & Plains	20,800	20,800	27,048	23,344	37,000	37,000	3	16,640	22,880
Southeast	15,371	20,225	22,018	21,486	26,340	26,667	5	.	.
West & Southwest	23,590	33,263	39,236	43,020	45,210	47,316	4	.	.
ALL REGIONS	15,371	23,344	30,734	27,429	37,000	60,382	17	16,640	22,880

State Data

	Min	Q1	Mean	Median	Q3	Max	N	Range Avg Min	Range Avg Max
AR	20,225	20,225	20,225	20,225	20,225	20,225	1	.	.
CO	42,936	42,936	45,126	45,126	47,316	47,316	2	.	.
DC	27,429	27,429	28,480	28,480	29,531	29,531	4	.	.
FL	15,371	15,371	18,429	18,429	21,486	21,486	2	.	.
IA	20,800	20,800	20,800	20,800	20,800	20,800	1	16,640	22,880
MA	60,382	60,382	60,382	60,382	60,382	60,382	1	.	.
MN	37,000	37,000	37,000	37,000	37,000	37,000	1	.	.
NC	26,667	26,667	26,667	26,667	26,667	26,667	1	.	.
NE	23,344	23,344	23,344	23,344	23,344	23,344	1	.	.
OR	43,104	43,104	43,104	43,104	43,104	43,104	1	.	.
TN	26,340	26,340	26,340	26,340	26,340	26,340	1	.	.
TX	23,590	23,590	23,590	23,590	23,590	23,590	1	.	.

Degree Required Data

	Min	Q1	Mean	Median	Q3	Max	N	Range Avg Min	Range Avg Max
High School	15,371	15,371	28,058	21,486	47,316	47,316	3	.	.
Associate's	20,225	20,513	23,971	24,114	27,429	27,429	4	16,640	22,880
Bachelor's	26,340	29,531	36,557	29,531	37,000	60,382	5	.	.
Master's	.	.	.	.	.	.			
Doctoral	.	.	.	.	.	.			

LIBRARY TECHNICAL ASSISTANT OF REFERENCE/INFORMATION SERVICES

Provides basic assistance to patrons referring patrons to Librarian for professional assistance. Locates materials and information for patrons. May complete routine copy cataloging. Assists with special programming. Assists patrons with questions; instructs in the selection and use of appropriate tools and techniques for finding information; conducts searches for materials; contributes to reference collection development.

Two-Year College
Regional Data

	Min	Q1	Mean	Median	Q3	Max	N	Range Avg Min	Range Avg Max
Great Lakes & Plains	18,061	18,061	18,061	18,061	18,061	18,061	1	.	.
Southeast	14,560	18,990	22,291	22,526	24,533	30,920	15	14,560	14,560
West & Southwest	26,667	26,667	34,966	36,492	41,741	41,741	3	.	.
ALL REGIONS	14,560	18,990	24,070	22,526	26,667	41,741	19	14,560	14,560

State Data

	Min	Q1	Mean	Median	Q3	Max	N	Range Avg Min	Range Avg Max
CA	36,492	36,492	39,116	39,116	41,741	41,741	2	.	.
FL	15,600	18,990	21,413	22,526	22,526	26,362	11	.	.
IL	18,061	18,061	18,061	18,061	18,061	18,061	1	.	.
KY	14,560	14,560	14,560	14,560	14,560	14,560	1	14,560	14,560
NC	24,533	24,533	26,667	26,667	28,800	28,800	2	.	.
TX	26,667	26,667	26,667	26,667	26,667	26,667	1	.	.
VA	30,920	30,920	30,920	30,920	30,920	30,920	1	.	.

Degree Required Data

	Min	Q1	Mean	Median	Q3	Max	N	Range Avg Min	Range Avg Max
High School	14,560	18,543	20,405	22,006	22,526	22,526	8	14,560	14,560
Associate's	18,061	18,990	26,746	25,448	32,646	41,741	8	.	.
Bachelor's	30,920	30,920	30,920	30,920	30,920	30,920	1	.	.
Master's	.	.	.	.	.	.	.	.	.
Doctoral	.	.	.	.	.	.	.	.	.

LIBRARY TECHNICAL ASSISTANT OF REFERENCE/INFORMATION SERVICES - CONTINUED
Four-Year College
Regional Data

	Min	Q1	Mean	Median	Q3	Max	N	Range Avg Min	Range Avg Max
North Atlantic	24,502	30,821	38,784	38,764	46,747	53,105	4		.
Great Lakes & Plains	20,696	21,320	34,958	37,905	43,893	48,026	6		.
Southeast	23,920	23,920	27,440	23,920	34,481	34,481	3		.
West & Southwest	16,333	16,333	34,680	40,392	47,316	47,316	3		.
ALL REGIONS	16,333	23,920	34,453	36,701	42,143	53,105	16		.

State Data

	Min	Q1	Mean	Median	Q3	Max	N	Range Avg Min	Range Avg Max
CO	40,392	40,392	43,854	43,854	47,316	47,316	2		.
KY	23,920	23,920	23,920	23,920	23,920	23,920	2		.
ME	24,502	24,502	24,502	24,502	24,502	24,502	1		.
MN	36,262	37,905	41,932	41,721	45,960	48,026	4		.
OH	20,696	20,696	21,008	21,008	21,320	21,320	2		.
PA	37,140	37,140	43,545	40,389	53,105	53,105	3		.
TX	16,333	16,333	16,333	16,333	16,333	16,333	1		.
WV	34,481	34,481	34,481	34,481	34,481	34,481	1		.

Degree Required Data

	Min	Q1	Mean	Median	Q3	Max	N	Range Avg Min	Range Avg Max
High School	16,333	20,696	29,211	21,320	40,392	47,316	5		.
Associate's	34,481	35,811	41,279	38,764	46,747	53,105	4		.
Bachelor's	23,920	23,920	34,296	36,262	43,893	48,026	7		.
Master's	.	.	.	.	.	.	.	.	.
Doctoral	.	.	.	.	.	.	.	.	.

LIBRARY TECHNICAL ASSISTANT OF REFERENCE/INFORMATION SERVICES - CONTINUED
University
(Includes ARL Data)
Regional Data

	Min	Q1	Mean	Median	Q3	Max	N	Range Avg Min	Range Avg Max
North Atlantic	23,472	30,286	34,153	33,021	38,755	49,996	68	.	.
Great Lakes & Plains	17,352	23,344	31,009	30,805	37,668	53,926	61	25,584	36,878
Southeast	18,990	23,898	26,562	26,255	28,633	38,297	104	20,815	36,385
West & Southwest	14,200	24,920	30,048	30,038	35,653	47,436	63	.	.
ALL REGIONS	14,200	24,961	29,964	28,806	34,465	53,926	296	21,411	36,447

State Data

	Min	Q1	Mean	Median	Q3	Max	N	Range Avg Min	Range Avg Max
AL	21,965	22,547	26,989	27,990	29,620	32,822	5	.	.
AR	19,552	22,346	24,995	26,174	26,861	29,394	12	.	.
AZ	24,912	28,210	31,461	31,619	34,439	40,562	30	.	.
CA	39,945	39,945	39,945	39,945	39,945	39,945	1	.	.
CO	27,000	30,600	37,488	38,304	43,284	47,436	6	.	.
DC	28,286	28,286	33,905	28,286	45,143	45,143	3	.	.
FL	19,000	20,000	23,192	22,022	25,187	29,244	13	.	.
IA	31,341	37,438	39,346	40,549	41,948	45,790	20	.	.
IL	26,062	31,013	37,103	34,956	41,702	53,926	6	.	.
IN	20,280	22,318	25,363	23,920	28,600	33,987	31	.	.
LA	21,060	21,060	24,006	24,006	26,951	26,951	2	.	.
MA	31,838	31,838	37,419	33,225	44,394	49,996	6	.	.
MD	25,975	30,449	34,127	33,537	38,755	42,258	56	.	.
MO	17,352	17,352	17,352	17,352	17,352	17,352	1	.	.
NC	22,426	25,077	27,710	26,950	29,888	38,297	52	.	.
NE	23,344	23,344	23,344	23,344	23,344	23,344	1	.	.
OH	37,020	37,020	37,020	37,020	37,020	37,020	1	25,584	36,878
OK	14,200	14,200	14,200	14,200	14,200	14,200	1	.	.
OR	22,476	22,476	28,180	26,100	35,964	35,964	3	.	.
PA	23,472	23,472	28,338	28,439	33,103	33,103	3	.	.
SC	27,468	27,468	30,948	28,610	36,765	36,765	3	.	.
SD	18,051	18,051	18,051	18,051	18,051	18,051	1	.	.
TN	18,990	22,452	25,049	24,086	27,498	36,060	14	20,815	36,385
TX	18,024	21,212	24,474	23,813	24,941	38,558	14	.	.
UT	36,799	36,799	36,799	36,799	36,799	36,799	1	.	.
VA	29,500	29,500	31,187	31,100	32,960	32,960	3	.	.
WA	36,948	36,948	36,948	36,948	36,948	36,948	1	.	.
WY	21,600	23,256	28,196	26,622	35,004	36,072	6	.	.

Degree Required Data

	Min	Q1	Mean	Median	Q3	Max	N	Range Avg Min	Range Avg Max
High School	14,200	24,141	29,287	28,113	33,574	44,394	211	19,685	32,843
Associate's	21,060	25,404	27,841	27,924	29,958	33,388	16	.	.
Bachelor's	19,552	27,548	31,811	31,100	36,060	53,926	49	24,287	42,453
Master's	.	.	.	.	.	.	.	.	.
Doctoral	.	.	.	.	.	.	.	.	.

LIBRARY TECHNICAL ASSISTANT OF REFERENCE/INFORMATION SERVICES - CONTINUED
ALL ACADEMIC LIBRARIES
Regional Data

	Min	Q1	Mean	Median	Q3	Max	N	Range Avg Min	Range Avg Max
North Atlantic	23,472	30,286	34,410	33,062	39,003	53,105	72	.	.
Great Lakes & Plains	17,352	23,234	31,167	30,909	38,608	53,926	68	25,584	36,878
Southeast	14,560	22,547	26,058	26,174	28,330	38,297	122	20,033	33,657
West & Southwest	14,200	24,941	30,463	30,038	36,072	47,436	69	.	.
ALL REGIONS	14,200	24,350	29,843	28,439	34,726	53,926	331	20,650	34,015

State Data

	Min	Q1	Mean	Median	Q3	Max	N	Range Avg Min	Range Avg Max
AL	21,965	22,547	26,989	27,990	29,620	32,822	5	.	.
AR	19,552	22,346	24,995	26,174	26,861	29,394	12	.	.
AZ	24,912	28,210	31,461	31,619	34,439	40,562	30	.	.
CA	36,492	36,492	39,393	39,945	41,741	41,741	3	.	.
CO	27,000	33,588	39,080	40,212	45,300	47,436	8	.	.
DC	28,286	28,286	33,905	28,286	45,143	45,143	3	.	.
FL	15,600	19,946	22,377	22,274	25,031	29,244	24	.	.
IA	31,341	37,438	39,346	40,549	41,948	45,790	20	.	.
IL	18,061	26,062	34,383	32,742	41,702	53,926	7	.	.
IN	20,280	22,318	25,363	23,920	28,600	33,987	31	.	.
KY	14,560	14,560	20,800	23,920	23,920	23,920	3	14,560	14,560
LA	21,060	21,060	24,006	24,006	26,951	26,951	2	.	.
MA	31,838	31,838	37,419	33,225	44,394	49,996	6	.	.
MD	25,975	30,449	34,127	33,537	38,755	42,258	56	.	.
ME	24,502	24,502	24,502	24,502	24,502	24,502	1	.	.
MN	36,262	37,905	41,932	41,721	45,960	48,026	4	.	.
MO	17,352	17,352	17,352	17,352	17,352	17,352	1	.	.
NC	22,426	24,850	27,672	26,950	29,536	38,297	54	.	.
NE	23,344	23,344	23,344	23,344	23,344	23,344	1	.	.
OH	20,696	20,696	26,345	21,320	37,020	37,020	3	25,584	36,878
OK	14,200	14,200	14,200	14,200	14,200	14,200	1	.	.
OR	22,476	22,476	28,180	26,100	35,964	35,964	3	.	.
PA	23,472	28,439	35,941	35,121	40,389	53,105	6	.	.
SC	27,468	27,468	30,948	28,610	36,765	36,765	3	.	.
SD	18,051	18,051	18,051	18,051	18,051	18,051	1	.	.
TN	18,990	22,452	25,049	24,086	27,498	36,060	14	20,815	36,385
TX	16,333	20,548	24,102	23,813	25,551	38,558	16	.	.
UT	36,799	36,799	36,799	36,799	36,799	36,799	1	.	.
VA	29,500	30,210	31,120	31,010	32,030	32,960	4	.	.
WA	36,948	36,948	36,948	36,948	36,948	36,948	1	.	.
WV	34,481	34,481	34,481	34,481	34,481	34,481	1	.	.
WY	21,600	23,256	28,196	26,622	35,004	36,072	6	.	.

Degree Required Data

	Min	Q1	Mean	Median	Q3	Max	N	Range Avg Min	Range Avg Max
High School	14,200	23,719	28,968	27,948	33,224	47,316	224	18,831	29,796
Associate's	18,061	25,192	29,448	28,067	32,722	53,105	28	.	.
Bachelor's	19,552	27,498	32,101	31,100	36,245	53,926	57	24,287	42,453
Master's	.	.	.	.	.	.	.	.	.
Doctoral	.	.	.	.	.	.	.	.	.

LIBRARY TECHNICAL ASSISTANT OF OUTREACH/BOOKMOBILE

Provides basic assistance to patrons referring patrons to Librarian for professional assistance. Locates materials and information for patrons. May complete routine copy cataloging. Assists with special programming. Provides services and programs to homebound, disabled, institutionalized or other underserved patrons.

University
(Includes ARL Data)
Regional Data

	Min	Q1	Mean	Median	Q3	Max	N	Range Avg Min	Range Avg Max
North Atlantic	32,000	32,000	32,000	32,000	32,000	32,000	1	.	.
Great Lakes & Plains	19,552	19,552	19,552	19,552	19,552	19,552	1	.	.
Southeast	25,127	25,127	25,127	25,127	25,127	25,127	1	.	.
ALL REGIONS	19,552	19,552	25,560	25,127	32,000	32,000	3	.	.

State Data

	Min	Q1	Mean	Median	Q3	Max	N	Range Avg Min	Range Avg Max
DC	32,000	32,000	32,000	32,000	32,000	32,000	1	.	.
LA	25,127	25,127	25,127	25,127	25,127	25,127	1	.	.
NE	19,552	19,552	19,552	19,552	19,552	19,552	1	.	.

Degree Required Data

	Min	Q1	Mean	Median	Q3	Max	N	Range Avg Min	Range Avg Max
High School	19,552	19,552	19,552	19,552	19,552	19,552	1	.	.
Associate's	.	.	.	.	.	.	.	.	.
Bachelor's	25,127	25,127	28,564	28,564	32,000	32,000	2	.	.
Master's	.	.	.	.	.	.	.	.	.
Doctoral	.	.	.	.	.	.	.	.	.

LIBRARY TECHNICAL ASSISTANT OF OUTREACH/BOOKMOBILE - CONTINUED
ALL ACADEMIC LIBRARIES
Regional Data

	Min	Q1	Mean	Median	Q3	Max	N	Range Avg Min	Range Avg Max
North Atlantic	32,000	32,000	32,000	32,000	32,000	32,000	1	.	.
Great Lakes & Plains	19,552	19,552	19,552	19,552	19,552	19,552	1	.	.
Southeast	25,127	25,127	25,127	25,127	25,127	25,127	1	.	.
ALL REGIONS	19,552	19,552	25,560	25,127	32,000	32,000	3	.	.

State Data

	Min	Q1	Mean	Median	Q3	Max	N	Range Avg Min	Range Avg Max
DC	32,000	32,000	32,000	32,000	32,000	32,000	1	.	.
LA	25,127	25,127	25,127	25,127	25,127	25,127	1	.	.
NE	19,552	19,552	19,552	19,552	19,552	19,552	1	.	.

Degree Required Data

	Min	Q1	Mean	Median	Q3	Max	N	Range Avg Min	Range Avg Max
High School	19,552	19,552	19,552	19,552	19,552	19,552	1	.	.
Associate's	.	.	.	.	.	.		.	.
Bachelor's	25,127	25,127	28,564	28,564	32,000	32,000	2	.	.
Master's	.	.	.	.	.	.		.	.
Doctoral	.	.	.	.	.	.		.	.

LIBRARY TECHNICAL ASSISTANT OF MEDIA SERVICES

Provides basic assistance to patrons referring patrons to Librarian for professional assistance. Locates materials and information for patrons. May complete routine copy cataloging. Assists with special programming.Develops and manages non-print library materials such as files, video recordings, audio recordings, CD-ROMs, computer software, etc.

**Two-Year College
Regional Data**

	Min	Q1	Mean	Median	Q3	Max	N	Range Avg Min	Range Avg Max
Great Lakes & Plains	17,493	17,493	17,493	17,493	17,493	17,493	1	.	.
Southeast	24,693	24,693	24,693	24,693	24,693	24,693	1	.	.
ALL REGIONS	17,493	17,493	21,093	21,093	24,693	24,693	2	.	.

State Data

	Min	Q1	Mean	Median	Q3	Max	N	Range Avg Min	Range Avg Max
FL	24,693	24,693	24,693	24,693	24,693	24,693	1	.	.
KS	17,493	17,493	17,493	17,493	17,493	17,493	1	.	.

Degree Required Data

	Min	Q1	Mean	Median	Q3	Max	N	Range Avg Min	Range Avg Max
High School	17,493	17,493	21,093	21,093	24,693	24,693	2	.	.
Associate's	.	.	.	.	.	.		.	.
Bachelor's	.	.	.	.	.	.		.	.
Master's	.	.	.	.	.	.		.	.
Doctoral	.	.	.	.	.	.		.	.

LIBRARY TECHNICAL ASSISTANT OF MEDIA SERVICES - CONTINUED
Four-Year College
Regional Data

	Min	Q1	Mean	Median	Q3	Max	N	Range Avg Min	Range Avg Max
North Atlantic	20,722	30,056	32,449	32,033	36,689	42,746	5	.	.
Great Lakes & Plains	27,787	27,787	28,453	28,453	29,120	29,120	2	.	.
Southeast	17,659	17,659	17,659	17,659	17,659	17,659	1	.	.
West & Southwest	38,196	38,196	39,865	39,384	42,016	42,016	3	.	.
ALL REGIONS	17,659	27,787	32,401	32,033	39,384	42,746	11	.	.

State Data

	Min	Q1	Mean	Median	Q3	Max	N	Range Avg Min	Range Avg Max
CO	38,196	38,196	38,790	38,790	39,384	39,384	2	.	.
IA	27,787	27,787	27,787	27,787	27,787	27,787	1	.	.
IL	29,120	29,120	29,120	29,120	29,120	29,120	1	.	.
KY	17,659	17,659	17,659	17,659	17,659	17,659	1	.	.
MD	36,689	36,689	39,718	39,718	42,746	42,746	2	.	.
ME	32,033	32,033	32,033	32,033	32,033	32,033	1	.	.
PA	20,722	20,722	25,389	25,389	30,056	30,056	2	.	.
TX	42,016	42,016	42,016	42,016	42,016	42,016	1	.	.

Degree Required Data

	Min	Q1	Mean	Median	Q3	Max	N	Range Avg Min	Range Avg Max
High School	38,196	38,196	39,865	39,384	42,016	42,016	3	.	.
Associate's	20,722	20,722	27,292	29,120	32,033	32,033	3	.	.
Bachelor's	17,659	22,723	29,562	28,921	36,401	42,746	4	.	.
Master's									
Doctoral									

LIBRARY TECHNICAL ASSISTANT OF MEDIA SERVICES - CONTINUED
University
(Includes ARL Data)
Regional Data

	Min	Q1	Mean	Median	Q3	Max	N	Range Avg Min	Range Avg Max
North Atlantic	19,199	22,494	33,735	38,607	41,571	49,975	12	.	.
Great Lakes & Plains	19,130	24,928	31,909	30,135	38,618	46,025	16	28,101	42,723
Southeast	21,320	23,560	27,281	26,323	30,671	38,847	28	.	.
West & Southwest	14,200	32,028	35,757	37,077	45,336	50,760	11	.	.
ALL REGIONS	14,200	23,960	30,934	28,721	37,704	50,760	67	28,101	42,723

State Data

	Min	Q1	Mean	Median	Q3	Max	N	Range Avg Min	Range Avg Max
AL	21,320	21,320	23,663	24,835	24,835	24,835	3		
AR	23,428	23,428	23,428	23,428	23,428	23,428	1		
CA	32,081	32,081	39,278	37,704	48,048	48,048	3		
CO	45,336	45,336	48,048	48,048	50,760	50,760	2		
DC	19,199	19,199	28,228	21,451	44,034	44,034	3		
FL	22,146	22,580	25,206	24,754	27,832	29,169	4		
GA	34,531	34,531	34,531	34,531	34,531	34,531	1		
IA	26,476	26,476	34,362	34,306	38,816	45,790	6		
IL	37,440	37,440	37,440	37,440	37,440	37,440	1	32,323	51,709
IN	21,736	21,736	25,907	25,907	30,077	30,077	2		
KY	35,324	35,324	35,324	35,324	35,324	35,324	1		
LA	33,040	33,040	33,040	33,040	33,040	33,040	1		
MA	49,975	49,975	49,975	49,975	49,975	49,975	1		
MD	40,652	40,652	41,111	41,111	41,571	41,571	4		
MI	46,025	46,025	46,025	46,025	46,025	46,025	1		
MO	19,130	19,130	19,130	19,130	19,130	19,130	1		
NC	24,187	26,150	27,543	26,835	28,721	32,533	6		
NE	24,147	24,147	24,147	24,147	24,147	24,147	1		
NY	21,343	21,343	23,050	23,536	24,272	24,272	3		
OH	23,650	23,650	33,371	37,020	39,442	39,442	3	25,990	38,230
OK	14,200	14,200	14,200	14,200	14,200	14,200	1		
PA	36,561	36,561	36,561	36,561	36,561	36,561	1		
SC	22,319	22,765	23,603	23,262	24,441	25,567	4		
SD	25,709	25,709	25,709	25,709	25,709	25,709	1		
TN	23,691	24,440	26,803	26,496	27,216	32,172	5		
TX	23,960	23,960	23,960	23,960	23,960	23,960	1		
UT	37,077	37,077	38,110	38,110	39,142	39,142	2		
VA	33,197	33,197	36,022	36,022	38,847	38,847	2		
WA	32,028	32,028	32,028	32,028	32,028	32,028	1		
WY	32,988	32,988	32,988	32,988	32,988	32,988	1		

Degree Required Data

	Min	Q1	Mean	Median	Q3	Max	N	Range Avg Min	Range Avg Max
High School	14,200	23,314	27,733	25,567	29,169	49,975	29	25,990	38,230
Associate's	21,343	23,536	29,995	29,402	37,440	38,847	6	32,323	51,709
Bachelor's	19,130	24,440	32,840	33,040	40,652	48,048	21		
Master's									
Doctoral									

LIBRARY TECHNICAL ASSISTANT OF MEDIA SERVICES - CONTINUED
ALL ACADEMIC LIBRARIES
Regional Data

	Min	Q1	Mean	Median	Q3	Max	N	Range Avg Min	Range Avg Max
North Atlantic	19,199	23,536	33,357	36,561	41,571	49,975	17	.	.
Great Lakes & Plains	17,493	24,147	30,787	29,120	38,419	46,025	19	28,101	42,723
Southeast	17,659	23,428	26,874	25,858	29,169	38,847	30	.	.
West & Southwest	14,200	32,081	36,637	37,950	42,016	50,760	14	.	.
ALL REGIONS	14,200	24,054	30,889	29,145	37,950	50,760	80	28,101	42,723

State Data

	Min	Q1	Mean	Median	Q3	Max	N	Range Avg Min	Range Avg Max
AL	21,320	21,320	23,663	24,835	24,835	24,835	3	.	.
AR	23,428	23,428	23,428	23,428	23,428	23,428	1	.	.
CA	32,081	32,081	39,278	37,704	48,048	48,048	3	.	.
CO	38,196	38,790	43,419	42,360	48,048	50,760	4	.	.
DC	19,199	19,199	28,228	21,451	44,034	44,034	3	.	.
FL	22,146	23,013	25,103	24,693	26,495	29,169	5	.	.
GA	34,531	34,531	34,531	34,531	34,531	34,531	1	.	.
IA	26,476	26,476	33,422	30,192	38,816	45,790	7	.	.
IL	29,120	29,120	33,280	33,280	37,440	37,440	2	32,323	51,709
IN	21,736	21,736	25,907	25,907	30,077	30,077	2	.	.
KS	17,493	17,493	17,493	17,493	17,493	17,493	1	.	.
KY	17,659	17,659	26,491	26,491	35,324	35,324	2	.	.
LA	33,040	33,040	33,040	33,040	33,040	33,040	1	.	.
MA	49,975	49,975	49,975	49,975	49,975	49,975	1	.	.
MD	36,689	40,652	40,647	41,111	41,571	42,746	6	.	.
ME	32,033	32,033	32,033	32,033	32,033	32,033	1	.	.
MI	46,025	46,025	46,025	46,025	46,025	46,025	1	.	.
MO	19,130	19,130	19,130	19,130	19,130	19,130	1	.	.
NC	24,187	26,150	27,543	26,835	28,721	32,533	6	.	.
NE	24,147	24,147	24,147	24,147	24,147	24,147	1	.	.
NY	21,343	21,343	23,050	23,536	24,272	24,272	3	.	.
OH	23,650	23,650	33,371	37,020	39,442	39,442	3	25,990	38,230
OK	14,200	14,200	14,200	14,200	14,200	14,200	1	.	.
PA	20,722	20,722	29,113	30,056	36,561	36,561	3	.	.
SC	22,319	22,765	23,603	23,262	24,441	25,567	4	.	.
SD	25,709	25,709	25,709	25,709	25,709	25,709	1	.	.
TN	23,691	24,440	26,803	26,496	27,216	32,172	5	.	.
TX	23,960	23,960	32,988	32,988	42,016	42,016	2	.	.
UT	37,077	37,077	38,110	38,110	39,142	39,142	2	.	.
VA	33,197	33,197	36,022	36,022	38,847	38,847	2	.	.
WA	32,028	32,028	32,028	32,028	32,028	32,028	1	.	.
WY	32,988	32,988	32,988	32,988	32,988	32,988	1	.	.

Degree Required Data

	Min	Q1	Mean	Median	Q3	Max	N	Range Avg Min	Range Avg Max
High School	14,200	23,314	28,413	25,858	32,028	49,975	34	25,990	38,230
Associate's	20,722	23,536	29,094	29,120	34,531	38,847	9	32,323	51,709
Bachelor's	17,659	24,440	32,316	32,533	40,652	48,048	25	.	.
Master's	.	.	.	.	.	.		.	.
Doctoral	.	.	.	.	.	.		.	.

LIBRARY TECHNICAL ASSISTANT OF ACQUISITIONS

Provides basic assistance to patrons referring patrons to Librarian for professional assistance. Locates materials and information for patrons. May complete routine copy cataloging. Assists with special programming. Selects, orders, and receives new materials and maintains accurate records of such transactions.

Two-Year College
Regional Data

	Min	Q1	Mean	Median	Q3	Max	N	Range Avg Min	Range Avg Max
North Atlantic	36,447	36,447	36,447	36,447	36,447	36,447	1	.	.
Great Lakes & Plains	22,000	25,319	30,036	28,230	33,065	46,819	7	.	.
Southeast	23,467	24,693	25,307	24,693	24,693	28,987	5	.	.
West & Southwest	35,256	35,256	35,256	35,256	35,256	35,256	1	.	.
ALL REGIONS	22,000	24,693	29,178	26,820	33,065	46,819	14	.	.

State Data

	Min	Q1	Mean	Median	Q3	Max	N	Range Avg Min	Range Avg Max
FL	24,693	24,693	24,693	24,693	24,693	24,693	3	.	.
HI	35,256	35,256	35,256	35,256	35,256	35,256	1	.	.
IA	29,411	29,411	29,411	29,411	29,411	29,411	1	.	.
IL	25,319	25,319	28,871	28,230	33,065	33,065	3	.	.
MD	36,447	36,447	36,447	36,447	36,447	36,447	1	.	.
MI	22,000	22,000	22,000	22,000	22,000	22,000	1	.	.
MN	46,819	46,819	46,819	46,819	46,819	46,819	1	.	.
ND	25,409	25,409	25,409	25,409	25,409	25,409	1	.	.
TN	23,467	23,467	23,467	23,467	23,467	23,467	1	.	.
VA	28,987	28,987	28,987	28,987	28,987	28,987	1	.	.

Degree Required Data

	Min	Q1	Mean	Median	Q3	Max	N	Range Avg Min	Range Avg Max
High School	24,693	24,693	30,126	25,319	35,256	46,819	7	.	.
Associate's	23,467	25,409	29,267	28,609	33,065	36,447	6	.	.
Bachelor's	.	.	.	.	.	.		.	.
Master's	.	.	.	.	.	.		.	.
Doctoral	.	.	.	.	.	.		.	.

LIBRARY TECHNICAL ASSISTANT OF ACQUISITIONS - CONTINUED
Four-Year College
Regional Data

	Min	Q1	Mean	Median	Q3	Max	N	Range Avg Min	Range Avg Max
North Atlantic	21,010	30,323	35,629	34,286	40,160	55,411	13	33,509	56,971
Great Lakes & Plains	23,000	25,719	32,135	30,773	39,250	45,905	11	27,248	38,480
Southeast	17,659	22,429	25,534	25,843	28,696	31,803	12	.	.
West & Southwest	17,600	18,720	28,074	29,499	34,728	38,400	6	.	.
ALL REGIONS	17,600	24,128	30,750	29,768	34,728	55,411	42	32,614	54,330

State Data

	Min	Q1	Mean	Median	Q3	Max	N	Range Avg Min	Range Avg Max
CA	18,720	18,720	28,560	28,560	38,400	38,400	2	.	.
CO	34,728	34,728	34,728	34,728	34,728	34,728	1	.	.
GA	26,354	26,354	28,898	28,538	31,803	31,803	3	.	.
IA	30,773	30,773	30,773	30,773	30,773	30,773	1	.	.
IL	26,312	26,312	32,947	33,280	39,250	39,250	3	.	.
KY	17,659	17,659	22,220	23,400	25,600	25,600	3	.	.
MA	31,200	31,200	31,200	31,200	31,200	31,200	1	.	.
MD	30,323	30,323	30,323	30,323	30,323	30,323	1	.	.
ME	40,160	40,160	40,160	40,160	40,160	40,160	1	.	.
MN	32,302	32,302	41,073	45,013	45,905	45,905	3	27,248	38,480
MO	27,807	27,807	27,807	27,807	27,807	27,807	1	.	.
NC	22,000	22,000	22,000	22,000	22,000	22,000	1	.	.
ND	23,000	23,000	23,000	23,000	23,000	23,000	1	.	.
NY	29,890	29,890	29,890	29,890	29,890	29,890	1	.	.
OH	24,128	24,128	24,128	24,128	24,128	24,128	1	.	.
PA	21,010	33,966	36,845	37,440	41,496	55,411	9	33,509	56,971
SC	22,857	22,857	25,855	25,855	28,853	28,853	2	.	.
SD	25,719	25,719	25,719	25,719	25,719	25,719	1	.	.
TN	22,000	22,000	22,000	22,000	22,000	22,000	1	.	.
TX	17,600	17,600	17,600	17,600	17,600	17,600	1	.	.
UT	29,353	29,353	29,499	29,499	29,645	29,645	2	.	.
VA	26,085	26,085	26,085	26,085	26,085	26,085	1	.	.
WV	31,253	31,253	31,253	31,253	31,253	31,253	1	.	.

Degree Required Data

	Min	Q1	Mean	Median	Q3	Max	N	Range Avg Min	Range Avg Max
High School	17,600	20,258	24,941	25,220	28,122	34,728	8	.	.
Associate's	18,720	19,865	22,384	21,505	24,904	27,807	4	.	.
Bachelor's	22,000	28,853	33,760	31,803	38,400	55,411	29	32,614	54,330
Master's	.	.	.	.	.	.	.	.	.
Doctoral	.	.	.	.	.	.	.	.	.

LIBRARY TECHNICAL ASSISTANT OF ACQUISITIONS - CONTINUED
University
(Includes ARL Data)
Regional Data

	Min	Q1	Mean	Median	Q3	Max	N	Range Avg Min	Range Avg Max
North Atlantic	17,117	30,118	33,340	32,697	36,842	56,521	35	27,040	41,600
Great Lakes & Plains	19,115	25,005	31,355	29,435	36,978	45,790	54	29,796	43,534
Southeast	16,910	24,463	27,356	27,003	30,454	41,354	100	21,944	38,334
West & Southwest	18,773	25,436	30,229	29,979	34,320	47,436	38	.	.
ALL REGIONS	16,910	24,990	29,711	29,307	33,324	56,521	227	27,144	41,751

State Data

	Min	Q1	Mean	Median	Q3	Max	N	Range Avg Min	Range Avg Max
AL	16,910	21,924	24,299	25,708	27,705	28,642	9		
AR	19,554	23,422	25,938	23,428	29,042	34,244	5		
AZ	25,405	29,528	31,444	30,171	34,008	39,640	10		
CA	27,768	27,768	33,609	29,547	43,512	43,512	3		
CO	30,000	31,824	35,988	33,324	39,180	47,436	9		
CT	56,521	56,521	56,521	56,521	56,521	56,521	1		
DC	19,533	19,533	32,501	32,501	45,469	45,469	2		
FL	17,715	22,817	25,878	25,263	28,330	32,843	14		
GA	21,542	24,422	26,270	27,635	28,118	28,267	4		
IA	30,213	38,419	40,052	41,948	41,948	45,790	10		
IL	26,541	27,830	32,479	29,692	35,360	45,760	6	34,216	50,190
IN	19,115	22,475	26,744	25,501	31,005	34,798	20		
KY	30,129	30,129	32,131	32,131	34,132	34,132	2		
LA	25,794	25,897	31,098	28,621	36,298	41,354	4		
MA	31,986	36,962	40,900	41,093	46,204	48,256	5	27,040	41,600
MD	17,117	29,848	31,284	31,031	35,139	36,842	24		
MI	35,661	35,661	35,661	35,661	35,661	35,661	1		
MN	26,790	33,280	37,118	37,991	42,890	43,763	6		
NC	22,426	25,193	28,397	27,931	32,034	38,297	38		
ND	20,908	20,908	20,908	20,908	20,908	20,908	1		
NE	24,386	24,386	25,725	25,725	27,063	27,063	2		
NY	33,800	33,800	33,800	33,800	33,800	33,800	1		
OH	25,902	26,295	30,358	28,541	35,851	37,020	6	25,376	36,878
OR	27,960	27,960	27,960	27,960	27,960	27,960	1		
PA	20,281	20,281	28,123	28,123	35,966	35,966	2		
SC	20,359	22,319	23,503	23,211	24,960	25,567	7		
SD	24,990	24,990	24,998	24,998	25,005	25,005	2		
TN	22,843	24,895	27,811	26,820	30,924	34,152	11	21,944	38,334
TX	18,773	19,688	21,518	21,666	22,417	25,830	8		
UT	25,436	25,436	30,395	30,395	35,353	35,353	2		
VA	22,880	28,150	30,288	30,352	33,322	36,672	6		
WY	23,568	26,328	29,726	30,024	34,320	34,392	5		

Degree Required Data

	Min	Q1	Mean	Median	Q3	Max	N	Range Avg Min	Range Avg Max
High School	16,910	24,485	28,582	27,748	31,986	56,521	159	23,660	37,606
Associate's	20,908	26,541	30,682	30,129	33,669	39,640	23	.	.
Bachelor's	19,533	26,726	31,319	30,770	35,360	45,760	23	30,628	45,895
Master's	.	.	.	.	.	.		.	.
Doctoral	.	.	.	.	.	.		.	.

LIBRARY TECHNICAL ASSISTANT OF ACQUISITIONS - CONTINUED
ALL ACADEMIC LIBRARIES
Regional Data

	Min	Q1	Mean	Median	Q3	Max	N	Range Avg Min	Range Avg Max
North Atlantic	17,117	30,118	34,010	33,800	36,842	56,521	49	32,585	54,775
Great Lakes & Plains	19,115	25,364	31,346	29,359	36,415	46,819	72	28,947	41,850
Southeast	16,910	23,467	27,082	26,637	30,129	41,354	117	21,944	38,334
West & Southwest	17,600	25,436	30,053	29,958	34,392	47,436	45	.	.
ALL REGIONS	16,910	24,950	29,839	29,307	33,800	56,521	283	30,625	49,755

State Data

	Min	Q1	Mean	Median	Q3	Max	N	Range Avg Min	Range Avg Max
AL	16,910	21,924	24,299	25,708	27,705	28,642	9		
AR	19,554	23,422	25,938	23,428	29,042	34,244	5		
AZ	25,405	29,528	31,444	30,171	34,008	39,640	10		
CA	18,720	27,768	31,589	29,547	38,400	43,512	5		
CO	30,000	31,824	35,862	34,026	39,180	47,436	10		
CT	56,521	56,521	56,521	56,521	56,521	56,521	1		
DC	19,533	19,533	32,501	32,501	45,469	45,469	2		
FL	17,715	22,940	25,669	24,819	28,036	32,843	17		
GA	21,542	26,354	27,396	27,968	28,538	31,803	7		
HI	35,256	35,256	35,256	35,256	35,256	35,256	1		
IA	29,411	31,892	38,392	40,727	41,948	45,790	12		
IL	25,319	27,186	31,694	29,692	34,320	45,760	12	34,216	50,190
IN	19,115	22,475	26,744	25,501	31,005	34,798	20		
KY	17,659	23,400	26,184	25,600	30,129	34,132	5		
LA	25,794	25,897	31,098	28,621	36,298	41,354	4		
MA	31,200	31,986	39,283	39,027	46,204	48,256	6	27,040	41,600
MD	17,117	30,118	31,446	31,031	35,787	36,842	26		
ME	40,160	40,160	40,160	40,160	40,160	40,160	1		
MI	22,000	22,000	28,831	28,831	35,661	35,661	2		
MN	26,790	33,280	39,274	40,947	45,013	46,819	10	27,248	38,480
MO	27,807	27,807	27,807	27,807	27,807	27,807	1		
NC	22,000	24,950	28,233	27,748	32,034	38,297	39		
ND	20,908	20,908	23,106	23,000	25,409	25,409	3		
NE	24,386	24,386	25,725	25,725	27,063	27,063	2		
NY	29,890	29,890	31,845	31,845	33,800	33,800	2		
OH	24,128	25,902	29,468	27,520	35,851	37,020	7	25,376	36,878
OR	27,960	27,960	27,960	27,960	27,960	27,960	1		
PA	20,281	22,630	35,259	35,966	41,496	55,411	11	33,509	56,971
SC	20,359	22,857	24,026	23,211	24,960	28,853	9		
SD	24,990	24,990	25,238	25,005	25,719	25,719	3		
TN	22,000	24,440	27,029	26,726	29,916	34,152	13	21,944	38,334
TX	17,600	19,140	21,083	21,404	22,213	25,830	9		
UT	25,436	27,395	29,947	29,499	32,499	35,353	4		
VA	22,880	27,118	29,600	29,461	32,046	36,672	8		
WV	31,253	31,253	31,253	31,253	31,253	31,253	1		
WY	23,568	26,328	29,726	30,024	34,320	34,392	5		

Degree Required Data

	Min	Q1	Mean	Median	Q3	Max	N	Range Avg Min	Range Avg Max
High School	16,910	24,485	28,476	27,411	31,560	56,521	174	23,660	37,606
Associate's	18,720	26,104	29,419	29,934	33,157	39,640	33		
Bachelor's	19,533	28,059	32,680	31,248	37,201	55,411	52	32,173	52,455
Master's									
Doctoral									

LIBRARY TECHNICAL ASSISTANT OF CATALOGING

Provides basic assistance to patrons referring patrons to Librarian for professional assistance. Locates materials and information for patrons. May complete routine copy cataloging. Assists with special programming. Prepares bibliographic records to represent the items acquired by the library, including bibliographic description, subject analysis, and classification.

Two-Year College
Regional Data

	Min	Q1	Mean	Median	Q3	Max	N	Range Avg Min	Range Avg Max
North Atlantic	36,447	36,447	36,447	36,447	36,447	36,447	1	.	.
Great Lakes & Plains	23,400	23,400	34,979	40,569	40,967	40,967	3	.	.
Southeast	17,998	23,317	23,934	24,690	24,690	28,974	5	23,847	43,264
West & Southwest	22,485	22,485	29,488	29,488	36,492	36,492	2	21,174	22,485
ALL REGIONS	17,998	23,317	29,093	24,690	36,492	40,967	11	22,956	36,338

State Data

	Min	Q1	Mean	Median	Q3	Max	N	Range Avg Min	Range Avg Max
AR	17,998	17,998	17,998	17,998	17,998	17,998	1	.	.
CA	36,492	36,492	36,492	36,492	36,492	36,492	1	.	.
FL	24,690	24,690	24,690	24,690	24,690	24,690	2	.	.
IL	23,400	23,400	31,985	31,985	40,569	40,569	2	.	.
LA	23,317	23,317	23,317	23,317	23,317	23,317	1	18,720	27,040
MD	36,447	36,447	36,447	36,447	36,447	36,447	1	.	.
MN	40,967	40,967	40,967	40,967	40,967	40,967	1	.	.
OR	22,485	22,485	22,485	22,485	22,485	22,485	1	21,174	22,485
VA	28,974	28,974	28,974	28,974	28,974	28,974	1	28,974	59,488

Degree Required Data

	Min	Q1	Mean	Median	Q3	Max	N	Range Avg Min	Range Avg Max
High School	22,485	23,317	27,230	24,690	24,690	40,967	5	19,947	24,762
Associate's	17,998	27,222	32,876	36,469	38,531	40,569	4	.	.
Bachelor's	23,400	23,400	26,187	26,187	28,974	28,974	2	28,974	59,488
Master's	.	.	.	.	.	.		.	.
Doctoral	.	.	.	.	.	.		.	.

LIBRARY TECHNICAL ASSISTANT OF CATALOGING - CONTINUED
Four-Year College
Regional Data

	Min	Q1	Mean	Median	Q3	Max	N	Range Avg Min	Range Avg Max
North Atlantic	19,000	29,245	29,824	31,159	31,897	36,483	6	.	.
Great Lakes & Plains	26,270	29,120	35,617	32,261	42,734	51,303	7	.	.
Southeast	21,840	23,467	26,466	25,936	27,943	37,080	9	.	.
West & Southwest	22,000	26,520	31,947	30,533	39,384	39,384	7	.	.
ALL REGIONS	19,000	26,270	30,693	29,120	36,483	51,303	29	.	.

State Data

	Min	Q1	Mean	Median	Q3	Max	N	Range Avg Min	Range Avg Max
CA	26,520	26,520	26,520	26,520	26,520	26,520	1	.	.
CO	38,412	38,412	39,060	39,384	39,384	39,384	3	.	.
GA	21,965	21,965	28,996	27,943	37,080	37,080	3	.	.
IL	29,120	29,120	29,120	29,120	29,120	29,120	2	.	.
KY	21,840	21,840	24,476	23,467	28,121	28,121	3	.	.
MD	31,897	31,897	31,897	31,897	31,897	31,897	1	.	.
ME	36,483	36,483	36,483	36,483	36,483	36,483	1	.	.
MN	38,513	38,513	44,184	42,734	51,303	51,303	3	.	.
NC	26,667	26,667	26,667	26,667	26,667	26,667	1	.	.
NY	29,245	29,245	30,521	31,159	31,159	31,159	3	.	.
OH	26,270	26,270	29,266	29,266	32,261	32,261	2	.	.
OK	22,000	22,000	22,000	22,000	22,000	22,000	1	.	.
PA	19,000	19,000	19,000	19,000	19,000	19,000	1	.	.
SC	25,173	25,173	25,173	25,173	25,173	25,173	1	.	.
UT	27,397	27,397	28,965	28,965	30,533	30,533	2	.	.
VA	25,936	25,936	25,936	25,936	25,936	25,936	1	.	.

Degree Required Data

	Min	Q1	Mean	Median	Q3	Max	N	Range Avg Min	Range Avg Max
High School	21,965	26,270	30,260	31,159	32,261	39,384	11	.	.
Associate's	.	.	.	.	.	.	.	.	.
Bachelor's	19,000	25,936	31,124	29,120	37,080	51,303	17	.	.
Master's	.	.	.	.	.	.	.	.	.
Doctoral	.	.	.	.	.	.	.	.	.

LIBRARY TECHNICAL ASSISTANT OF CATALOGING - CONTINUED
University
(Includes ARL Data)
Regional Data

	Min	Q1	Mean	Median	Q3	Max	N	Range Avg Min	Range Avg Max
North Atlantic	18,319	31,393	34,688	37,794	39,270	44,394	13	.	.
Great Lakes & Plains	16,898	29,907	35,403	37,020	41,948	55,038	46	26,312	39,603
Southeast	16,910	24,675	27,564	27,126	30,454	46,853	77	23,629	41,309
West & Southwest	16,500	26,447	32,662	33,268	40,356	45,485	21	.	.
ALL REGIONS	16,500	26,042	31,132	30,097	37,020	55,038	157	24,970	40,456

State Data

	Min	Q1	Mean	Median	Q3	Max	N	Range Avg Min	Range Avg Max
AL	16,910	16,910	24,297	27,165	31,010	32,970	7	.	.
AR	17,222	20,679	25,665	24,947	30,097	37,426	11	.	.
AZ	35,456	35,456	37,598	36,494	40,844	40,844	3	.	.
CA	31,212	33,268	39,610	42,036	44,784	45,485	7	.	.
CO	30,012	30,012	35,184	35,184	40,356	40,356	2	.	.
DC	18,319	18,319	28,057	28,057	37,794	37,794	2	.	.
FL	17,270	22,833	25,426	25,039	27,040	37,335	22	.	.
GA	27,713	27,713	27,713	27,713	27,713	27,713	1	.	.
IA	28,919	33,284	38,576	41,948	41,948	41,948	21	.	.
IL	23,982	34,195	35,831	35,807	40,456	44,736	6	.	.
IN	24,107	25,334	33,792	34,590	42,037	42,890	5	.	.
LA	27,019	27,019	29,974	29,974	32,930	32,930	2	.	.
MA	29,231	31,689	36,664	38,882	39,270	44,394	8	.	.
MN	30,337	30,337	41,460	39,004	55,038	55,038	3	.	.
NC	24,544	26,637	29,819	29,887	32,653	34,782	23	.	.
ND	16,898	16,898	16,898	16,898	16,898	16,898	1	.	.
NE	20,904	21,202	22,906	21,712	24,610	27,295	4	.	.
OH	29,432	29,907	35,174	37,020	37,020	42,491	5	26,312	39,603
OK	22,000	22,000	22,000	22,000	22,000	22,000	1	.	.
OR	32,748	32,748	32,748	32,748	32,748	32,748	1	.	.
PA	23,544	23,544	33,842	35,981	42,002	42,002	3	.	.
SD	25,719	25,719	25,719	25,719	25,719	25,719	1	.	.
TN	26,042	26,726	28,935	29,472	29,765	31,704	7	23,629	41,309
TX	16,500	20,750	21,931	21,000	24,960	26,447	5	.	.
UT	26,615	26,615	30,529	30,529	34,443	34,443	2	.	.
VA	26,857	27,708	33,653	30,452	39,599	46,853	4	.	.

Degree Required Data

	Min	Q1	Mean	Median	Q3	Max	N	Range Avg Min	Range Avg Max
High School	16,500	24,960	30,542	29,966	34,782	55,038	110	26,312	39,603
Associate's	16,898	23,982	30,714	30,546	35,456	46,853	6	.	.
Bachelor's	18,319	26,857	31,181	29,508	34,443	45,485	34	23,629	41,309
Master's	.	.	.	.	.	.	.	.	.
Doctoral	.	.	.	.	.	.	.	.	.

LIBRARY TECHNICAL ASSISTANT OF CATALOGING - CONTINUED
ALL ACADEMIC LIBRARIES
Regional Data

	Min	Q1	Mean	Median	Q3	Max	N	Range Avg Min	Range Avg Max
North Atlantic	18,319	30,202	33,317	33,983	38,882	44,394	20	.	.
Great Lakes & Plains	16,898	29,276	35,407	37,020	41,948	55,038	56	26,312	39,603
Southeast	16,910	24,408	27,256	26,919	30,097	46,853	91	23,738	42,286
West & Southwest	16,500	26,447	32,283	33,008	39,384	45,485	30	21,174	22,485
ALL REGIONS	16,500	25,719	30,954	29,907	36,972	55,038	197	24,107	38,691

State Data

	Min	Q1	Mean	Median	Q3	Max	N	Range Avg Min	Range Avg Max
AL	16,910	16,910	24,297	27,165	31,010	32,970	7	.	.
AR	17,222	20,116	25,026	24,504	28,612	37,426	12	.	.
AZ	35,456	35,456	37,598	36,494	40,844	40,844	3	.	.
CA	26,520	33,268	37,809	36,972	43,512	45,485	9	.	.
CO	30,012	38,412	37,510	39,384	39,384	40,356	5	.	.
DC	18,319	18,319	28,057	28,057	37,794	37,794	2	.	.
FL	17,270	22,833	25,364	24,710	26,980	37,335	24	.	.
GA	21,965	24,839	28,675	27,828	32,512	37,080	4	.	.
IA	28,919	33,284	38,576	41,948	41,948	41,948	21	.	.
IL	23,400	29,120	33,719	34,320	40,456	44,736	10	.	.
IN	24,107	25,334	33,792	34,590	42,037	42,890	5	.	.
KY	21,840	21,840	24,476	23,467	28,121	28,121	3	.	.
LA	23,317	23,317	27,755	27,019	32,930	32,930	3	18,720	27,040
MA	29,231	31,689	36,664	38,882	39,270	44,394	8	.	.
MD	31,897	31,897	34,172	34,172	36,447	36,447	2	.	.
ME	36,483	36,483	36,483	36,483	36,483	36,483	1	.	.
MN	30,337	38,513	42,557	40,967	51,303	55,038	7	.	.
NC	24,544	26,652	29,687	29,712	32,593	34,782	24	.	.
ND	16,898	16,898	16,898	16,898	16,898	16,898	1	.	.
NE	20,904	21,202	22,906	21,712	24,610	27,295	4	.	.
NY	29,245	29,245	30,521	31,159	31,159	31,159	3	.	.
OH	26,270	29,432	33,486	32,261	37,020	42,491	7	26,312	39,603
OK	22,000	22,000	22,000	22,000	22,000	22,000	2	.	.
OR	22,485	22,485	27,616	27,616	32,748	32,748	2	21,174	22,485
PA	19,000	21,272	30,132	29,762	38,991	42,002	4	.	.
SC	25,173	25,173	25,173	25,173	25,173	25,173	1	.	.
SD	25,719	25,719	25,719	25,719	25,719	25,719	1	.	.
TN	26,042	26,726	28,935	29,472	29,765	31,704	7	23,629	41,309
TX	16,500	20,750	21,931	21,000	24,960	26,447	5	.	.
UT	26,615	27,006	29,747	28,965	32,488	34,443	4	.	.
VA	25,936	26,857	31,587	28,767	32,344	46,853	6	28,974	59,488

Degree Required Data

	Min	Q1	Mean	Median	Q3	Max	N	Range Avg Min	Range Avg Max
High School	16,500	24,731	30,386	29,913	34,768	55,038	126	23,130	32,183
Associate's	16,898	23,982	31,579	33,995	36,492	46,853	10	.	.
Bachelor's	18,319	26,520	30,974	29,231	36,483	51,303	53	25,411	47,369
Master's	.	.	.	.	.	.	.	.	.
Doctoral	.	.	.	.	.	.	.	.	.

ADULT SERVICES CLERK

Performs routine duties requiring the use of a variety of forms, reports or procedures. Provides basic patron assistance: sets up computer stations, locates materials, provides information. Maintains departmental or area records. Performs miscellaneous clerical duties such as filing, typing, sorting or photocopying. Provides access to materials, services and programs intended to meet the needs of the adult users of a public library.

Two-Year College
Regional Data

	Min	Q1	Mean	Median	Q3	Max	N	Range Avg Min	Range Avg Max
Great Lakes & Plains	18,200	18,700	20,660	20,780	22,620	22,880	4	.	.
Southeast	15,600	15,600	20,432	20,432	25,263	25,263	2	13,520	15,600
ALL REGIONS	15,600	18,200	20,584	20,780	22,880	25,263	6	13,520	15,600

State Data

	Min	Q1	Mean	Median	Q3	Max	N	Range Avg Min	Range Avg Max
AL	25,263	25,263	25,263	25,263	25,263	25,263	1	.	.
FL	15,600	15,600	15,600	15,600	15,600	15,600	1	13,520	15,600
IL	18,200	18,200	21,147	22,360	22,880	22,880	3	.	.
MN	19,200	19,200	19,200	19,200	19,200	19,200	1	.	.

Degree Required Data

	Min	Q1	Mean	Median	Q3	Max	N	Range Avg Min	Range Avg Max
High School	15,600	15,600	20,432	20,432	25,263	25,263	2	13,520	15,600
Associate's	18,200	18,200	21,147	22,360	22,880	22,880	3	.	.
Bachelor's	19,200	19,200	19,200	19,200	19,200	19,200	1	.	.
Master's	.	.	.	.	.	.		.	.
Doctoral	.	.	.	.	.	.		.	.

ADULT SERVICES CLERK - CONTINUED
Four-Year College
Regional Data

	Min	Q1	Mean	Median	Q3	Max	N	Range Avg Min	Range Avg Max
North Atlantic	20,800	20,800	20,800	20,800	20,800	20,800	2	.	.
Great Lakes & Plains	23,000	23,000	23,000	23,000	23,000	23,000	1	.	.
Southeast	11,440	11,440	12,198	11,440	11,440	22,360	24	22,360	22,360
West & Southwest	16,744	16,744	17,631	17,264	17,264	34,368	31	13,416	19,344
ALL REGIONS	11,440	11,440	15,585	16,744	17,264	34,368	58	13,705	19,441

State Data

	Min	Q1	Mean	Median	Q3	Max	N	Range Avg Min	Range Avg Max
CO	34,368	34,368	34,368	34,368	34,368	34,368	1	.	.
IL	23,000	23,000	23,000	23,000	23,000	23,000	1	.	.
KY	11,440	11,440	11,757	11,440	11,440	18,720	23	.	.
PA	20,800	20,800	20,800	20,800	20,800	20,800	2	.	.
SC	22,360	22,360	22,360	22,360	22,360	22,360	1	22,360	22,360
UT	16,744	16,744	17,073	17,264	17,264	17,264	30	13,416	19,344

Degree Required Data

	Min	Q1	Mean	Median	Q3	Max	N	Range Avg Min	Range Avg Max
High School	11,440	11,440	15,455	16,744	17,264	34,368	57	13,705	19,441
Associate's	.	.	.	.	.	.	.	.	.
Bachelor's	23,000	23,000	23,000	23,000	23,000	23,000	1	.	.
Master's	.	.	.	.	.	.	.	.	.
Doctoral	.	.	.	.	.	.	.	.	.

ADULT SERVICES CLERK - CONTINUED
University
(Includes ARL Data)
Regional Data

	Min	Q1	Mean	Median	Q3	Max	N	Range Avg Min	Range Avg Max
Great Lakes & Plains	20,800	20,800	23,145	22,800	25,834	25,834	3	.	.
Southeast	25,005	25,005	32,159	33,303	38,168	38,168	3	.	.
West & Southwest	16,947	16,947	16,947	16,947	16,947	16,947	1	.	.
ALL REGIONS	16,947	20,800	26,122	25,005	33,303	38,168	7	.	.

State Data

	Min	Q1	Mean	Median	Q3	Max	N	Range Avg Min	Range Avg Max
IL	20,800	20,800	23,145	22,800	25,834	25,834	3	.	.
NC	33,303	33,303	33,303	33,303	33,303	33,303	1	.	.
TX	16,947	16,947	16,947	16,947	16,947	16,947	1	.	.
VA	25,005	25,005	31,587	31,587	38,168	38,168	2	.	.

Degree Required Data

	Min	Q1	Mean	Median	Q3	Max	N	Range Avg Min	Range Avg Max
High School	16,947	16,947	20,182	20,800	22,800	22,800	3	.	.
Associate's	25,005	25,420	30,578	29,569	35,736	38,168	4	.	.
Bachelor's	.	.	.	.	.	.	.	.	.
Master's	.	.	.	.	.	.	.	.	.
Doctoral	.	.	.	.	.	.	.	.	.

ADULT SERVICES CLERK - CONTINUED
ALL ACADEMIC LIBRARIES
Regional Data

	Min	Q1	Mean	Median	Q3	Max	N	Range Avg Min	Range Avg Max
North Atlantic	20,800	20,800	20,800	20,800	20,800	20,800	2	.	.
Great Lakes & Plains	18,200	20,000	21,884	22,580	22,940	25,834	8	.	.
Southeast	11,440	11,440	14,831	11,440	11,440	38,168	29	17,940	18,980
West & Southwest	16,744	16,744	17,610	17,264	17,264	34,368	32	13,416	19,344
ALL REGIONS	11,440	11,440	17,046	17,264	17,264	38,168	71	13,699	19,321

State Data

	Min	Q1	Mean	Median	Q3	Max	N	Range Avg Min	Range Avg Max
AL	25,263	25,263	25,263	25,263	25,263	25,263	1	.	.
CO	34,368	34,368	34,368	34,368	34,368	34,368	1	.	.
FL	15,600	15,600	15,600	15,600	15,600	15,600	1	13,520	15,600
IL	18,200	20,800	22,268	22,800	23,000	25,834	7	.	.
KY	11,440	11,440	11,757	11,440	11,440	18,720	23	.	.
MN	19,200	19,200	19,200	19,200	19,200	19,200	1	.	.
NC	33,303	33,303	33,303	33,303	33,303	33,303	1	.	.
PA	20,800	20,800	20,800	20,800	20,800	20,800	2	.	.
SC	22,360	22,360	22,360	22,360	22,360	22,360	1	22,360	22,360
TX	16,947	16,947	16,947	16,947	16,947	16,947	1	.	.
UT	16,744	16,744	17,073	17,264	17,264	17,264	30	13,416	19,344
VA	25,005	25,005	31,587	31,587	38,168	38,168	2	.	.

Degree Required Data

	Min	Q1	Mean	Median	Q3	Max	N	Range Avg Min	Range Avg Max
High School	11,440	11,440	15,844	16,744	17,264	34,368	62	13,699	19,321
Associate's	18,200	22,360	26,536	25,005	33,303	38,168	7	.	.
Bachelor's	19,200	19,200	21,100	21,100	23,000	23,000	2	.	.
Master's	.	.	.	.	.	.		.	.
Doctoral	.	.	.	.	.	.		.	.

ARCHIVES AND SPECIAL COLLECTIONS CLERK

Performs routine duties requiring the use of a variety of forms, reports or procedures. Provides basic patron assistance: sets up computer stations, locates materials, provides information. Maintains departmental or area records. Performs miscellaneous clerical duties such as filing, typing, sorting or photocopying. Manages and maintains collection; identifies and appraises records, authenticates, describes and documents, facilitates access and use, preserves and conserves, and exhibits collection.

Four-Year College
Regional Data

	Min	Q1	Mean	Median	Q3	Max	N	Range Avg Min	Range Avg Max
Great Lakes & Plains	20,480	20,480	20,480	20,480	20,480	20,480	1	.	.
West & Southwest	34,006	34,006	34,006	34,006	34,006	34,006	1	.	.
ALL REGIONS	20,480	20,480	27,243	27,243	34,006	34,006	2	.	.

State Data

	Min	Q1	Mean	Median	Q3	Max	N	Range Avg Min	Range Avg Max
CO	34,006	34,006	34,006	34,006	34,006	34,006	1	.	.
SD	20,480	20,480	20,480	20,480	20,480	20,480	1	.	.

Degree Required Data

	Min	Q1	Mean	Median	Q3	Max	N	Range Avg Min	Range Avg Max
High School	20,480	20,480	27,243	27,243	34,006	34,006	2	.	.
Associate's	.	.	.	.	.	.	.	.	.
Bachelor's	.	.	.	.	.	.	.	.	.
Master's	.	.	.	.	.	.	.	.	.
Doctoral	.	.	.	.	.	.	.	.	.

ARCHIVES AND SPECIAL COLLECTIONS CLERK - CONTINUED
University
(Includes ARL Data)
Regional Data

	Min	Q1	Mean	Median	Q3	Max	N	Range Avg Min	Range Avg Max
North Atlantic	17,680	35,029	39,254	42,618	48,000	49,975	7	.	.
Great Lakes & Plains	25,622	25,622	29,313	29,576	32,740	32,740	3	.	.
Southeast	17,318	19,554	22,953	21,151	23,514	37,867	8	.	.
West & Southwest	13,374	15,600	24,741	21,526	31,462	52,687	43	.	.
ALL REGIONS	13,374	19,376	26,397	23,526	33,263	52,687	61	.	.

State Data

	Min	Q1	Mean	Median	Q3	Max	N	Range Avg Min	Range Avg Max
AL	21,507	21,507	23,514	23,514	25,520	25,520	2	.	.
AR	17,318	17,318	18,809	19,554	19,554	19,554	3	.	.
FL	21,003	21,003	21,003	21,003	21,003	21,003	1	.	.
IA	32,740	32,740	32,740	32,740	32,740	32,740	1	.	.
IN	29,576	29,576	29,576	29,576	29,576	29,576	1	.	.
MA	49,975	49,975	49,975	49,975	49,975	49,975	1	.	.
MD	42,618	42,618	42,618	42,618	42,618	42,618	2	.	.
NC	21,298	21,298	21,298	21,298	21,298	21,298	1	.	.
NY	17,680	26,354	34,891	36,943	43,429	48,000	4	.	.
TX	14,124	18,477	23,999	26,176	29,521	29,521	4	.	.
UT	13,374	15,600	24,817	21,400	31,700	52,687	39	.	.
VA	37,867	37,867	37,867	37,867	37,867	37,867	1	.	.
WI	25,622	25,622	25,622	25,622	25,622	25,622	1	.	.

Degree Required Data

	Min	Q1	Mean	Median	Q3	Max	N	Range Avg Min	Range Avg Max
High School	13,374	15,600	22,526	20,592	23,888	49,975	41	.	.
Associate's	29,576	29,576	29,576	29,576	29,576	29,576	1	.	.
Bachelor's	17,680	29,521	35,081	34,132	40,000	52,687	18	.	.
Master's	.	.	.	.	.	.		.	.
Doctoral	.	.	.	.	.	.		.	.

ARCHIVES AND SPECIAL COLLECTIONS CLERK - CONTINUED
ALL ACADEMIC LIBRARIES
Regional Data

	Min	Q1	Mean	Median	Q3	Max	N	Range Avg Min	Range Avg Max
North Atlantic	17,680	35,029	39,254	42,618	48,000	49,975	7	.	.
Great Lakes & Plains	20,480	23,051	27,105	27,599	31,158	32,740	4	.	.
Southeast	17,318	19,554	22,953	21,151	23,514	37,867	8	.	.
West & Southwest	13,374	15,600	24,952	22,178	31,581	52,687	44	.	.
ALL REGIONS	13,374	19,376	26,424	23,526	34,006	52,687	63	.	.

State Data

	Min	Q1	Mean	Median	Q3	Max	N	Range Avg Min	Range Avg Max
AL	21,507	21,507	23,514	23,514	25,520	25,520	2	.	.
AR	17,318	17,318	18,809	19,554	19,554	19,554	3	.	.
CO	34,006	34,006	34,006	34,006	34,006	34,006	1	.	.
FL	21,003	21,003	21,003	21,003	21,003	21,003	1	.	.
IA	32,740	32,740	32,740	32,740	32,740	32,740	1	.	.
IN	29,576	29,576	29,576	29,576	29,576	29,576	1	.	.
MA	49,975	49,975	49,975	49,975	49,975	49,975	1	.	.
MD	42,618	42,618	42,618	42,618	42,618	42,618	2	.	.
NC	21,298	21,298	21,298	21,298	21,298	21,298	1	.	.
NY	17,680	26,354	34,891	36,943	43,429	48,000	4	.	.
SD	20,480	20,480	20,480	20,480	20,480	20,480	1	.	.
TX	14,124	18,477	23,999	26,176	29,521	29,521	4	.	.
UT	13,374	15,600	24,817	21,400	31,700	52,687	39	.	.
VA	37,867	37,867	37,867	37,867	37,867	37,867	1	.	.
WI	25,622	25,622	25,622	25,622	25,622	25,622	1	.	.

Degree Required Data

	Min	Q1	Mean	Median	Q3	Max	N	Range Avg Min	Range Avg Max
High School	13,374	15,600	22,745	20,592	24,400	49,975	43	.	.
Associate's	29,576	29,576	29,576	29,576	29,576	29,576	1	.	.
Bachelor's	17,680	29,521	35,081	34,132	40,000	52,687	18	.	.
Master's	.	.	.	.	.	.		.	.
Doctoral	.	.	.	.	.	.		.	.

CHILDREN'S SERVICES/YOUNG ADULT SERVICES CLERK

Performs routine duties requiring the use of a variety of forms, reports or procedures. Provides basic patron assistance: sets up computer stations, locates materials, provides information. Maintains departmental or area records. Performs miscellaneous clerical duties such as filing, typing, sorting or photocopying. Provides services intended for children and youths through twelfth grade; develops collection, provides homework and reader's advisory services, and develops age appropriate programs.

University
(Includes ARL Data)
Regional Data

	Min	Q1	Mean	Median	Q3	Max	N	Range Avg Min	Range Avg Max
North Atlantic	29,714	29,714	35,890	32,240	45,714	45,714	3	27,040	47,840
Great Lakes & Plains	20,800	20,800	20,800	20,800	20,800	20,800	1	.	.
West & Southwest	20,895	20,895	20,895	20,895	20,895	20,895	1	.	.
ALL REGIONS	20,800	20,895	29,873	29,714	32,240	45,714	5	27,040	47,840

State Data

	Min	Q1	Mean	Median	Q3	Max	N	Range Avg Min	Range Avg Max
CT	32,240	32,240	32,240	32,240	32,240	32,240	1	27,040	47,840
IL	20,800	20,800	20,800	20,800	20,800	20,800	1	.	.
NY	29,714	29,714	37,714	37,714	45,714	45,714	2	.	.
TX	20,895	20,895	20,895	20,895	20,895	20,895	1	.	.

Degree Required Data

	Min	Q1	Mean	Median	Q3	Max	N	Range Avg Min	Range Avg Max
High School	20,800	20,895	29,873	29,714	32,240	45,714	5	27,040	47,840
Associate's	.	.	.	.	.	.	.	.	.
Bachelor's	.	.	.	.	.	.	.	.	.
Master's	.	.	.	.	.	.	.	.	.
Doctoral	.	.	.	.	.	.	.	.	.

CHILDREN'S SERVICES/YOUNG ADULT SERVICES CLERK - CONTINUED
ALL ACADEMIC LIBRARIES
Regional Data

	Min	Q1	Mean	Median	Q3	Max	N	Range Avg Min	Range Avg Max
North Atlantic	29,714	29,714	35,890	32,240	45,714	45,714	3	27,040	47,840
Great Lakes & Plains	20,800	20,800	20,800	20,800	20,800	20,800	1	.	.
West & Southwest	20,895	20,895	20,895	20,895	20,895	20,895	1	.	.
ALL REGIONS	20,800	20,895	29,873	29,714	32,240	45,714	5	27,040	47,840

State Data

	Min	Q1	Mean	Median	Q3	Max	N	Range Avg Min	Range Avg Max
CT	32,240	32,240	32,240	32,240	32,240	32,240	1	27,040	47,840
IL	20,800	20,800	20,800	20,800	20,800	20,800	1	.	.
NY	29,714	29,714	37,714	37,714	45,714	45,714	2	.	.
TX	20,895	20,895	20,895	20,895	20,895	20,895	1	.	.

Degree Required Data

	Min	Q1	Mean	Median	Q3	Max	N	Range Avg Min	Range Avg Max
High School	20,800	20,895	29,873	29,714	32,240	45,714	5	27,040	47,840
Associate's	.	.	.	.	.	.		.	.
Bachelor's	.	.	.	.	.	.		.	.
Master's	.	.	.	.	.	.		.	.
Doctoral	.	.	.	.	.	.		.	.

GOVERNMENT DOCUMENTS CLERK

Performs routine duties requiring the use of a variety of forms, reports or procedures. Provides basic patron assistance: sets up computer stations, locates materials, provides information. Maintains departmental or area records. Performs miscellaneous clerical duties such as filing, typing, sorting or photocopying. Provides access to publications of the U. S. federal government such as transcripts of hearings and text of bills, resolutions, statutes, reports, charters, treaties, periodicals and statistics.

**Four-Year College
Regional Data**

	Min	Q1	Mean	Median	Q3	Max	N	Range Avg Min	Range Avg Max
North Atlantic	26,543	26,543	26,543	26,543	26,543	26,543	1	.	.
Southeast	28,093	28,093	28,093	28,093	28,093	28,093	1	.	.
ALL REGIONS	26,543	26,543	27,318	27,318	28,093	28,093	2	.	.

State Data

	Min	Q1	Mean	Median	Q3	Max	N	Range Avg Min	Range Avg Max
ME	26,543	26,543	26,543	26,543	26,543	26,543	1	.	.
WV	28,093	28,093	28,093	28,093	28,093	28,093	1	.	.

Degree Required Data

	Min	Q1	Mean	Median	Q3	Max	N	Range Avg Min	Range Avg Max
High School	26,543	26,543	27,318	27,318	28,093	28,093	2	.	.
Associate's	.	.	.	.	.	.		.	.
Bachelor's	.	.	.	.	.	.		.	.
Master's	.	.	.	.	.	.		.	.
Doctoral	.	.	.	.	.	.		.	.

GOVERNMENT DOCUMENTS CLERK - CONTINUED
University
(Includes ARL Data)
Regional Data

	Min	Q1	Mean	Median	Q3	Max	N	Range Avg Min	Range Avg Max
North Atlantic	24,960	24,960	31,706	34,286	35,871	35,871	3	.	.
Great Lakes & Plains	17,060	17,060	23,421	26,004	27,200	27,200	3	.	.
Southeast	13,980	15,160	16,928	17,222	19,032	19,247	5	.	.
West & Southwest	14,560	14,560	18,332	14,566	23,548	27,066	11	.	.
ALL REGIONS	13,980	14,560	20,531	18,127	26,004	35,871	22	.	.

State Data

	Min	Q1	Mean	Median	Q3	Max	N	Range Avg Min	Range Avg Max
AL	19,032	19,032	19,032	19,032	19,032	19,032	1	.	.
AR	17,222	17,222	17,222	17,222	17,222	17,222	1	.	.
GA	13,980	13,980	16,129	15,160	19,247	19,247	3	.	.
IN	17,060	17,060	17,060	17,060	17,060	17,060	1	.	.
MA	35,871	35,871	35,871	35,871	35,871	35,871	1	.	.
MD	24,960	24,960	24,960	24,960	24,960	24,960	1	.	.
ND	27,200	27,200	27,200	27,200	27,200	27,200	1	.	.
NY	34,286	34,286	34,286	34,286	34,286	34,286	1	.	.
TX	22,009	22,009	24,340	24,340	26,670	26,670	2	.	.
UT	14,560	14,560	16,997	14,560	14,996	27,066	9	.	.
WI	26,004	26,004	26,004	26,004	26,004	26,004	1	.	.

Degree Required Data

	Min	Q1	Mean	Median	Q3	Max	N	Range Avg Min	Range Avg Max
High School	13,980	14,560	19,699	16,110	23,548	35,871	18	.	.
Associate's	26,670	26,670	26,670	26,670	26,670	26,670	1	.	.
Bachelor's	17,222	17,222	22,211	22,211	27,200	27,200	2	.	.
Master's	.	.	.	.	.	.		.	.
Doctoral	.	.	.	.	.	.		.	.

GOVERNMENT DOCUMENTS CLERK - CONTINUED
ALL ACADEMIC LIBRARIES
Regional Data

	Min	Q1	Mean	Median	Q3	Max	N	Range Avg Min	Range Avg Max
North Atlantic	24,960	25,752	30,415	30,414	35,078	35,871	4	.	.
Great Lakes & Plains	17,060	17,060	23,421	26,004	27,200	27,200	3	.	.
Southeast	13,980	15,160	18,789	18,127	19,247	28,093	6	.	.
West & Southwest	14,560	14,560	18,332	14,566	23,548	27,066	11	.	.
ALL REGIONS	13,980	14,563	21,096	19,139	26,607	35,871	24	.	.

State Data

	Min	Q1	Mean	Median	Q3	Max	N	Range Avg Min	Range Avg Max
AL	19,032	19,032	19,032	19,032	19,032	19,032	1	.	.
AR	17,222	17,222	17,222	17,222	17,222	17,222	1	.	.
GA	13,980	13,980	16,129	15,160	19,247	19,247	3	.	.
IN	17,060	17,060	17,060	17,060	17,060	17,060	1	.	.
MA	35,871	35,871	35,871	35,871	35,871	35,871	1	.	.
MD	24,960	24,960	24,960	24,960	24,960	24,960	1	.	.
ME	26,543	26,543	26,543	26,543	26,543	26,543	1	.	.
ND	27,200	27,200	27,200	27,200	27,200	27,200	1	.	.
NY	34,286	34,286	34,286	34,286	34,286	34,286	1	.	.
TX	22,009	22,009	24,340	24,340	26,670	26,670	2	.	.
UT	14,560	14,560	16,997	14,560	14,996	27,066	9	.	.
WI	26,004	26,004	26,004	26,004	26,004	26,004	1	.	.
WV	28,093	28,093	28,093	28,093	28,093	28,093	1	.	.

Degree Required Data

	Min	Q1	Mean	Median	Q3	Max	N	Range Avg Min	Range Avg Max
High School	13,980	14,560	20,461	18,046	25,752	35,871	20	.	.
Associate's	26,670	26,670	26,670	26,670	26,670	26,670	1	.	.
Bachelor's	17,222	17,222	22,211	22,211	27,200	27,200	2	.	.
Master's	.	.	.	.	.	.		.	.
Doctoral	.	.	.	.	.	.		.	.

INSTRUCTIONAL SERVICES/LITERACY CLERK

Performs routine duties requiring the use of a variety of forms, reports or procedures. Provides basic patron assistance: sets up computer stations, locates materials, provides information. Maintains departmental or area records. Performs miscellaneous clerical duties such as filing, typing, sorting or photocopying. Advances learning, teaching and research with respect to information literacy in higher education; assists patrons to develop the ability to read and write.

University
(Includes ARL Data)
Regional Data

	Min	Q1	Mean	Median	Q3	Max	N	Range Avg Min	Range Avg Max
Great Lakes & Plains	26,125	26,125	26,125	26,125	26,125	26,125	1	.	.
ALL REGIONS	26,125	26,125	26,125	26,125	26,125	26,125	1	.	.

State Data

	Min	Q1	Mean	Median	Q3	Max	N	Range Avg Min	Range Avg Max
IL	26,125	26,125	26,125	26,125	26,125	26,125	1	.	.

Degree Required Data

	Min	Q1	Mean	Median	Q3	Max	N	Range Avg Min	Range Avg Max
High School									
Associate's									
Bachelor's	26,125	26,125	26,125	26,125	26,125	26,125	1		
Master's									
Doctoral									

INSTRUCTIONAL SERVICES/LITERACY CLERK - CONTINUED
ALL ACADEMIC LIBRARIES
Regional Data

	Min	Q1	Mean	Median	Q3	Max	N	Range Avg Min	Range Avg Max
Great Lakes & Plains	26,125	26,125	26,125	26,125	26,125	26,125	1		
ALL REGIONS	26,125	26,125	26,125	26,125	26,125	26,125	1		

State Data

	Min	Q1	Mean	Median	Q3	Max	N	Range Avg Min	Range Avg Max
IL	26,125	26,125	26,125	26,125	26,125	26,125	1		

Degree Required Data

	Min	Q1	Mean	Median	Q3	Max	N	Range Avg Min	Range Avg Max
High School									
Associate's									
Bachelor's	26,125	26,125	26,125	26,125	26,125	26,125	1		
Master's									
Doctoral									

REFERENCE/INFORMATION SERVICES CLERK

Performs routine duties requiring the use of a variety of forms, reports or procedures. Provides basic patron assistance: sets up computer stations, locates materials, provides information. Maintains departmental or area records. Performs miscellaneous clerical duties such as filing, typing, sorting or photocopying. Assists patrons with questions; instructs in the selection and use of appropriate tools and techniques for finding information; conducts searches for materials; contributes to reference collection development.

Two-Year College
Regional Data

	Min	Q1	Mean	Median	Q3	Max	N	Range Avg Min	Range Avg Max
Southeast	13,520	22,194	23,301	22,194	26,499	32,100	5	22,173	45,531
ALL REGIONS	13,520	22,194	23,301	22,194	26,499	32,100	5	22,173	45,531

State Data

	Min	Q1	Mean	Median	Q3	Max	N	Range Avg Min	Range Avg Max
AL	32,100	32,100	32,100	32,100	32,100	32,100	1		
FL	13,520	13,520	13,520	13,520	13,520	13,520	1		
VA	22,194	22,194	23,629	22,194	26,499	26,499	3	22,173	45,531

Degree Required Data

	Min	Q1	Mean	Median	Q3	Max	N	Range Avg Min	Range Avg Max
High School	13,520	13,520	22,810	22,810	32,100	32,100	2	.	.
Associate's	22,194	22,194	23,629	22,194	26,499	26,499	3	22,173	45,531
Bachelor's	.	.	.	.	.	.		.	.
Master's	.	.	.	.	.	.		.	.
Doctoral	.	.	.	.	.	.		.	.

REFERENCE/INFORMATION SERVICES CLERK - CONTINUED
Four-Year College
Regional Data

	Min	Q1	Mean	Median	Q3	Max	N	Range Avg Min	Range Avg Max
North Atlantic	20,800	20,800	20,800	20,800	20,800	20,800	1	.	.
Southeast	22,880	22,880	23,040	23,040	23,200	23,200	2	.	.
West & Southwest	27,143	27,143	27,143	27,143	27,143	27,143	1	.	.
ALL REGIONS	20,800	21,840	23,506	23,040	25,172	27,143	4	.	.

State Data

	Min	Q1	Mean	Median	Q3	Max	N	Range Avg Min	Range Avg Max
CO	27,143	27,143	27,143	27,143	27,143	27,143	1	.	.
KY	22,880	22,880	22,880	22,880	22,880	22,880	1	.	.
PA	20,800	20,800	20,800	20,800	20,800	20,800	1	.	.
VA	23,200	23,200	23,200	23,200	23,200	23,200	1	.	.

Degree Required Data

	Min	Q1	Mean	Median	Q3	Max	N	Range Avg Min	Range Avg Max
High School	27,143	27,143	27,143	27,143	27,143	27,143	1	.	.
Associate's	.	.	.	.	.	.		.	.
Bachelor's	20,800	20,800	22,000	22,000	23,200	23,200	2	.	.
Master's	.	.	.	.	.	.		.	.
Doctoral	.	.	.	.	.	.		.	.

REFERENCE/INFORMATION SERVICES CLERK - CONTINUED
University
(Includes ARL Data)
Regional Data

	Min	Q1	Mean	Median	Q3	Max	N	Range Avg Min	Range Avg Max
North Atlantic	19,776	20,191	29,708	30,857	34,286	43,429	5	.	.
Great Lakes & Plains	19,064	20,800	25,180	24,960	27,040	35,360	11	24,759	39,051
Southeast	14,581	16,106	22,306	23,691	25,486	32,000	15	21,417	37,419
West & Southwest	14,560	15,331	17,731	16,017	19,137	31,212	71	.	.
ALL REGIONS	14,560	15,600	19,794	17,733	23,276	43,429	102	23,923	38,643

State Data

	Min	Q1	Mean	Median	Q3	Max	N	Range Avg Min	Range Avg Max
AR	15,353	15,353	16,617	15,730	17,881	19,655	4	.	.
CA	31,212	31,212	31,212	31,212	31,212	31,212	1	.	.
IL	20,800	22,880	25,792	26,000	27,040	35,360	10	24,759	39,051
LA	14,581	14,581	14,581	14,581	14,581	14,581	1	.	.
NE	19,064	19,064	19,064	19,064	19,064	19,064	1	.	.
NY	30,857	30,857	36,190	34,286	43,429	43,429	3	.	.
PA	19,776	19,776	19,983	19,983	20,191	20,191	2	.	.
TN	23,483	23,691	24,423	24,804	24,948	25,189	5	21,417	37,419
TX	20,104	22,512	24,909	24,963	27,305	29,605	4	.	.
UT	14,560	15,183	17,092	15,600	18,408	27,082	66	.	.
VA	18,720	25,486	26,284	25,576	29,640	32,000	5	.	.

Degree Required Data

	Min	Q1	Mean	Median	Q3	Max	N	Range Avg Min	Range Avg Max
High School	14,560	15,600	18,643	16,328	20,632	43,429	85	21,112	32,510
Associate's	20,191	22,880	25,212	24,960	27,040	32,000	9	24,274	39,887
Bachelor's	18,720	21,734	25,933	25,337	29,623	35,360	8	26,035	42,286
Master's	.	.	.	.	.	.		.	.
Doctoral	.	.	.	.	.	.		.	.

REFERENCE/INFORMATION SERVICES CLERK - CONTINUED
ALL ACADEMIC LIBRARIES
Regional Data

	Min	Q1	Mean	Median	Q3	Max	N	Range Avg Min	Range Avg Max
North Atlantic	19,776	20,191	28,223	25,829	34,286	43,429	6	.	.
Great Lakes & Plains	19,064	20,800	25,180	24,960	27,040	35,360	11	24,759	39,051
Southeast	13,520	18,720	22,599	23,342	25,486	32,100	22	21,795	41,475
West & Southwest	14,560	15,465	17,862	16,017	19,137	31,212	72	.	.
ALL REGIONS	13,520	15,600	20,086	18,720	23,483	43,429	111	23,573	40,021

State Data

	Min	Q1	Mean	Median	Q3	Max	N	Range Avg Min	Range Avg Max
AL	32,100	32,100	32,100	32,100	32,100	32,100	1	.	.
AR	15,353	15,353	16,617	15,730	17,881	19,655	4	.	.
CA	31,212	31,212	31,212	31,212	31,212	31,212	1	.	.
CO	27,143	27,143	27,143	27,143	27,143	27,143	1	.	.
FL	13,520	13,520	13,520	13,520	13,520	13,520	1	.	.
IL	20,800	22,880	25,792	26,000	27,040	35,360	10	24,759	39,051
KY	22,880	22,880	22,880	22,880	22,880	22,880	1	.	.
LA	14,581	14,581	14,581	14,581	14,581	14,581	1	.	.
NE	19,064	19,064	19,064	19,064	19,064	19,064	1	.	.
NY	30,857	30,857	36,190	34,286	43,429	43,429	3	.	.
PA	19,776	19,776	20,256	20,191	20,800	20,800	3	.	.
TN	23,483	23,691	24,423	24,804	24,948	25,189	5	21,417	37,419
TX	20,104	22,512	24,909	24,963	27,305	29,605	4	.	.
UT	14,560	15,183	17,092	15,600	18,408	27,082	66	.	.
VA	18,720	22,194	25,056	25,486	26,499	32,000	9	22,173	45,531

Degree Required Data

	Min	Q1	Mean	Median	Q3	Max	N	Range Avg Min	Range Avg Max
High School	13,520	15,477	18,834	16,328	20,852	43,429	88	21,112	32,510
Associate's	20,191	22,194	24,816	23,920	27,040	32,000	12	23,573	41,769
Bachelor's	18,720	20,800	25,147	24,440	29,605	35,360	10	26,035	42,286
Master's	.	.	.	.	.	.		.	.
Doctoral	.	.	.	.	.	.		.	.

OUTREACH/BOOKMOBILE CLERK

Performs routine duties requiring the use of a variety of forms, reports or procedures. Provides basic patron assistance: sets up computer stations, locates materials, provides information. Maintains departmental or area records. Performs miscellaneous clerical duties such as filing, typing, sorting or photocopying. Provides services and programs to homebound, disabled, institutionalized or other underserved patrons.

University
(Includes ARL Data)
Regional Data

	Min	Q1	Mean	Median	Q3	Max	N	Range Avg Min	Range Avg Max
Southeast	16,690	16,690	16,690	16,690	16,690	16,690	1	.	.
ALL REGIONS	16,690	16,690	16,690	16,690	16,690	16,690	1	.	.

State Data

	Min	Q1	Mean	Median	Q3	Max	N	Range Avg Min	Range Avg Max
GA	16,690	16,690	16,690	16,690	16,690	16,690	1	.	.

Degree Required Data

	Min	Q1	Mean	Median	Q3	Max	N	Range Avg Min	Range Avg Max
High School	16,690	16,690	16,690	16,690	16,690	16,690	1	.	.
Associate's	.	.	.	.	.	.		.	.
Bachelor's	.	.	.	.	.	.		.	.
Master's	.	.	.	.	.	.		.	.
Doctoral	.	.	.	.	.	.		.	.

OUTREACH/BOOKMOBILE CLERK - CONTINUED
ALL ACADEMIC LIBRARIES
Regional Data

	Min	Q1	Mean	Median	Q3	Max	N	Range Avg Min	Range Avg Max
Southeast	16,690	16,690	16,690	16,690	16,690	16,690	1	.	.
ALL REGIONS	16,690	16,690	16,690	16,690	16,690	16,690	1	.	.

State Data

	Min	Q1	Mean	Median	Q3	Max	N	Range Avg Min	Range Avg Max
GA	16,690	16,690	16,690	16,690	16,690	16,690	1	.	.

Degree Required Data

	Min	Q1	Mean	Median	Q3	Max	N	Range Avg Min	Range Avg Max
High School	16,690	16,690	16,690	16,690	16,690	16,690	1	.	.
Associate's	.	.	.	.	.	.		.	.
Bachelor's	.	.	.	.	.	.		.	.
Master's	.	.	.	.	.	.		.	.
Doctoral	.	.	.	.	.	.		.	.

MEDIA SERVICES CLERK

Performs routine duties requiring the use of a variety of forms, reports or procedures. Provides basic patron assistance: sets up computer stations, locates materials, provides information. Maintains departmental or area records. Performs miscellaneous clerical duties such as filing, typing, sorting or photocopying.Develops and manages non-print library materials such as files, video recordings, audio recordings, CD-ROMs, computer software, etc.

Two-Year College
Regional Data

	Min	Q1	Mean	Median	Q3	Max	N	Range Avg Min	Range Avg Max
Great Lakes & Plains	20,800	20,800	20,800	20,800	20,800	20,800	1	16,640	24,960
Southeast	30,504	30,504	30,504	30,504	30,504	30,504	1	.	.
West & Southwest	20,722	23,714	32,683	32,084	41,050	42,494	7	.	.
ALL REGIONS	20,722	23,714	31,121	30,504	40,581	42,494	9	16,640	24,960

State Data

	Min	Q1	Mean	Median	Q3	Max	N	Range Avg Min	Range Avg Max
AL	30,504	30,504	30,504	30,504	30,504	30,504	1	.	.
IA	20,800	20,800	20,800	20,800	20,800	20,800	1	16,640	24,960
TX	20,722	23,714	32,683	32,084	41,050	42,494	7	.	.

Degree Required Data

	Min	Q1	Mean	Median	Q3	Max	N	Range Avg Min	Range Avg Max
High School	30,504	30,504	30,504	30,504	30,504	30,504	1	.	.
Associate's	20,722	22,257	31,198	30,111	40,816	42,494	8	16,640	24,960
Bachelor's	.	.	.	.	.	.		.	.
Master's	.	.	.	.	.	.		.	.
Doctoral	.	.	.	.	.	.		.	.

MEDIA SERVICES CLERK - CONTINUED
Four-Year College
Regional Data

	Min	Q1	Mean	Median	Q3	Max	N	Range Avg Min	Range Avg Max
North Atlantic	20,800	20,800	22,641	22,641	24,483	24,483	2	.	.
Great Lakes & Plains	20,883	20,883	20,883	20,883	20,883	20,883	1	.	.
West & Southwest	31,516	31,516	33,248	33,248	34,980	34,980	2	.	.
ALL REGIONS	20,800	20,883	26,532	24,483	31,516	34,980	5	.	.

State Data

	Min	Q1	Mean	Median	Q3	Max	N	Range Avg Min	Range Avg Max
CO	31,516	31,516	33,248	33,248	34,980	34,980	2	.	.
MD	20,800	20,800	20,800	20,800	20,800	20,800	1	.	.
ME	24,483	24,483	24,483	24,483	24,483	24,483	1	.	.
OH	20,883	20,883	20,883	20,883	20,883	20,883	1	.	.

Degree Required Data

	Min	Q1	Mean	Median	Q3	Max	N	Range Avg Min	Range Avg Max
High School	20,800	20,883	26,532	24,483	31,516	34,980	5	.	.
Associate's	.	.	.	.	.	.		.	.
Bachelor's	.	.	.	.	.	.		.	.
Master's	.	.	.	.	.	.		.	.
Doctoral	.	.	.	.	.	.		.	.

MEDIA SERVICES CLERK - CONTINUED
University
(Includes ARL Data)
Regional Data

	Min	Q1	Mean	Median	Q3	Max	N	Range Avg Min	Range Avg Max
North Atlantic	16,536	28,954	34,097	37,524	41,822	48,517	9	.	.
Great Lakes & Plains	19,868	20,480	25,575	25,043	30,670	32,346	4	.	.
Southeast	17,981	20,717	22,895	22,318	24,740	31,068	13	17,562	30,708
West & Southwest	18,396	18,396	26,353	24,964	35,700	35,700	3	.	.
ALL REGIONS	16,536	20,717	27,099	24,740	32,346	48,517	29	17,562	30,708

State Data

	Min	Q1	Mean	Median	Q3	Max	N	Range Avg Min	Range Avg Max
DC	37,524	37,524	37,524	37,524	37,524	37,524	1	.	.
FL	21,012	21,012	21,012	21,012	21,012	21,012	1	.	.
GA	17,981	17,981	17,981	17,981	17,981	17,981	1	.	.
IL	32,346	32,346	32,346	32,346	32,346	32,346	1	.	.
LA	28,225	28,225	28,225	28,225	28,225	28,225	1	.	.
MA	28,954	28,954	36,682	39,270	41,822	41,822	3	.	.
MI	28,995	28,995	28,995	28,995	28,995	28,995	1	.	.
NY	34,286	34,286	42,077	43,429	48,517	48,517	3	.	.
OH	21,091	21,091	21,091	21,091	21,091	21,091	1	.	.
OR	35,700	35,700	35,700	35,700	35,700	35,700	1	.	.
PA	16,536	16,536	16,536	16,536	16,536	16,536	2	.	.
SD	19,868	19,868	19,868	19,868	19,868	19,868	1	.	.
TN	18,420	20,717	22,853	22,318	22,788	31,068	9	17,562	30,708
TX	18,396	18,396	21,680	21,680	24,964	24,964	2	.	.
VA	24,740	24,740	24,740	24,740	24,740	24,740	1	.	.

Degree Required Data

	Min	Q1	Mean	Median	Q3	Max	N	Range Avg Min	Range Avg Max
High School	16,536	19,868	26,549	22,714	32,346	48,517	23	17,562	30,708
Associate's	24,740	24,740	24,740	24,740	24,740	24,740	1	.	.
Bachelor's	17,981	23,103	28,700	29,647	34,296	37,524	4	.	.
Master's									
Doctoral									

MEDIA SERVICES CLERK - CONTINUED
ALL ACADEMIC LIBRARIES
Regional Data

	Min	Q1	Mean	Median	Q3	Max	N	Range Avg Min	Range Avg Max
North Atlantic	16,536	20,800	32,014	34,286	41,822	48,517	11	.	.
Great Lakes & Plains	19,868	20,800	23,997	20,987	28,995	32,346	6	16,640	24,960
Southeast	17,981	20,717	23,439	22,516	27,684	31,068	14	17,562	30,708
West & Southwest	18,396	24,339	31,195	31,800	38,141	42,494	12	.	.
ALL REGIONS	16,536	20,800	27,875	24,964	34,286	48,517	43	17,332	29,271

State Data

	Min	Q1	Mean	Median	Q3	Max	N	Range Avg Min	Range Avg Max
AL	30,504	30,504	30,504	30,504	30,504	30,504	1	.	.
CO	31,516	31,516	33,248	33,248	34,980	34,980	2	.	.
DC	37,524	37,524	37,524	37,524	37,524	37,524	1	.	.
FL	21,012	21,012	21,012	21,012	21,012	21,012	1	.	.
GA	17,981	17,981	17,981	17,981	17,981	17,981	1	.	.
IA	20,800	20,800	20,800	20,800	20,800	20,800	1	16,640	24,960
IL	32,346	32,346	32,346	32,346	32,346	32,346	1	.	.
LA	28,225	28,225	28,225	28,225	28,225	28,225	1	.	.
MA	28,954	28,954	36,682	39,270	41,822	41,822	3	.	.
MD	20,800	20,800	20,800	20,800	20,800	20,800	1	.	.
ME	24,483	24,483	24,483	24,483	24,483	24,483	1	.	.
MI	28,995	28,995	28,995	28,995	28,995	28,995	1	.	.
NY	34,286	34,286	42,077	43,429	48,517	48,517	3	.	.
OH	20,883	20,883	20,987	20,987	21,091	21,091	2	.	.
OR	35,700	35,700	35,700	35,700	35,700	35,700	1	.	.
PA	16,536	16,536	16,536	16,536	16,536	16,536	2	.	.
SD	19,868	19,868	19,868	19,868	19,868	19,868	1	.	.
TN	18,420	20,717	22,853	22,318	22,788	31,068	9	17,562	30,708
TX	18,396	23,714	30,238	28,138	40,581	42,494	9	.	.
VA	24,740	24,740	24,740	24,740	24,740	24,740	1	.	.

Degree Required Data

	Min	Q1	Mean	Median	Q3	Max	N	Range Avg Min	Range Avg Max
High School	16,536	20,800	26,683	22,788	31,516	48,517	29	17,562	30,708
Associate's	20,722	23,714	30,480	28,138	40,581	42,494	9	16,640	24,960
Bachelor's	17,981	23,103	28,700	29,647	34,296	37,524	4	.	.
Master's	.	.	.	.	.	.	.	.	.
Doctoral	.	.	.	.	.	.	.	.	.

ACQUISITIONS CLERK

Performs routine duties requiring the use of a variety of forms, reports or procedures. Provides basic patron assistance: sets up computer stations, locates materials, provides information. Maintains departmental or area records. Performs miscellaneous clerical duties such as filing, typing, sorting or photocopying. Orders and receives new materials; works with collections staff to determine most appropriate sources; checks shipments to ensure correct quantity, material and quality.

Two-Year College
Regional Data

	Min	Q1	Mean	Median	Q3	Max	N	Range Avg Min	Range Avg Max
North Atlantic	20,571	20,571	20,571	20,571	20,571	20,571	1	.	.
Great Lakes & Plains	17,453	17,453	18,086	18,086	18,720	18,720	2	.	.
Southeast	23,585	23,585	23,585	23,585	23,585	23,585	1	.	.
West & Southwest	30,463	30,463	30,463	30,463	30,463	30,463	1	.	.
ALL REGIONS	17,453	18,720	22,158	20,571	23,585	30,463	5	.	.

State Data

	Min	Q1	Mean	Median	Q3	Max	N	Range Avg Min	Range Avg Max
FL	23,585	23,585	23,585	23,585	23,585	23,585	1	.	.
IL	17,453	17,453	18,086	18,086	18,720	18,720	2	.	.
MD	20,571	20,571	20,571	20,571	20,571	20,571	1	.	.
TX	30,463	30,463	30,463	30,463	30,463	30,463	1	.	.

Degree Required Data

	Min	Q1	Mean	Median	Q3	Max	N	Range Avg Min	Range Avg Max
High School	17,453	17,453	18,086	18,086	18,720	18,720	2	.	.
Associate's	20,571	20,571	25,517	25,517	30,463	30,463	2	.	.
Bachelor's	23,585	23,585	23,585	23,585	23,585	23,585	1	.	.
Master's	.	.	.	.	.	.		.	.
Doctoral	.	.	.	.	.	.		.	.

ACQUISITIONS CLERK - CONTINUED
Four-Year College
Regional Data

	Min	Q1	Mean	Median	Q3	Max	N	Range Avg Min	Range Avg Max
North Atlantic	32,500	32,500	33,758	34,093	34,682	34,682	3	.	.
Great Lakes & Plains	20,800	21,840	28,257	23,837	34,674	44,554	4	44,554	44,554
Southeast	20,675	20,738	23,644	23,451	26,551	27,000	4	20,800	24,960
West & Southwest	24,977	27,923	33,170	28,074	39,775	45,102	5	.	.
ALL REGIONS	20,675	23,837	29,671	27,462	34,387	45,102	16	32,677	34,757

State Data

	Min	Q1	Mean	Median	Q3	Max	N	Range Avg Min	Range Avg Max
AL	27,000	27,000	27,000	27,000	27,000	27,000	1	.	.
CO	39,775	39,775	42,438	42,438	45,102	45,102	2	.	.
IA	44,554	44,554	44,554	44,554	44,554	44,554	1	44,554	44,554
ME	34,093	34,093	34,093	34,093	34,093	34,093	1	.	.
MN	22,880	22,880	22,880	22,880	22,880	22,880	1	.	.
ND	20,800	20,800	20,800	20,800	20,800	20,800	1	.	.
NY	34,682	34,682	34,682	34,682	34,682	34,682	1	.	.
OH	24,794	24,794	24,794	24,794	24,794	24,794	1	.	.
OR	27,923	27,923	27,999	27,999	28,074	28,074	2	.	.
PA	32,500	32,500	32,500	32,500	32,500	32,500	1	.	.
SC	20,800	20,800	20,800	20,800	20,800	20,800	1	20,800	24,960
TN	20,675	20,675	20,675	20,675	20,675	20,675	1	.	.
TX	24,977	24,977	24,977	24,977	24,977	24,977	1	.	.
WV	26,102	26,102	26,102	26,102	26,102	26,102	1	.	.

Degree Required Data

	Min	Q1	Mean	Median	Q3	Max	N	Range Avg Min	Range Avg Max
High School	20,800	24,977	31,217	30,287	34,682	44,554	10	32,677	34,757
Associate's	26,102	26,102	35,602	35,602	45,102	45,102	2	.	.
Bachelor's	20,675	20,738	22,839	21,840	24,940	27,000	4	.	.
Master's	.	.	.	.	.	.	.	.	.
Doctoral	.	.	.	.	.	.	.	.	.

ACQUISITIONS CLERK - CONTINUED
University
(Includes ARL Data)
Regional Data

	Min	Q1	Mean	Median	Q3	Max	N	Range Avg Min	Range Avg Max
North Atlantic	23,608	35,206	38,844	38,618	40,269	63,240	33	19,760	29,682
Great Lakes & Plains	18,720	20,218	25,616	22,360	31,550	38,420	35	22,922	42,702
Southeast	14,060	18,641	23,460	23,071	27,591	32,779	19	.	.
West & Southwest	14,200	19,992	22,884	21,902	24,901	34,020	17	.	.
ALL REGIONS	14,060	21,164	28,973	28,211	35,613	63,240	104	21,868	38,362

State Data

	Min	Q1	Mean	Median	Q3	Max	N	Range Avg Min	Range Avg Max
AL	15,017	15,017	15,017	15,017	15,017	15,017	1	.	.
AR	17,318	17,318	23,001	23,001	28,683	28,683	2	.	.
CA	34,020	34,020	34,020	34,020	34,020	34,020	1	.	.
DC	30,597	37,814	37,269	38,397	39,270	40,269	5	.	.
GA	14,060	14,201	18,429	16,492	22,658	26,674	4	.	.
IA	31,550	31,550	34,237	32,740	38,420	38,420	3	.	.
IL	22,880	26,029	29,277	30,352	31,980	34,611	8	22,922	42,702
IN	19,115	19,802	21,202	20,259	21,486	32,843	18	.	.
LA	24,000	24,000	24,000	24,000	24,000	24,000	1	.	.
MA	29,675	38,278	42,440	39,270	44,153	63,240	16	.	.
MD	23,608	26,216	33,199	34,503	40,181	40,181	4	19,760	29,682
MI	18,720	18,720	27,146	28,995	33,722	33,722	3	.	.
NC	25,850	25,850	25,850	25,850	25,850	25,850	1	.	.
ND	23,146	23,146	29,749	29,749	36,352	36,352	2	.	.
NY	28,571	32,811	36,691	38,526	40,571	41,143	4	.	.
OK	14,200	14,200	14,200	14,200	14,200	14,200	1	.	.
PA	30,481	30,481	33,251	33,251	36,020	36,020	2	.	.
RI	35,206	35,206	35,206	35,206	35,206	35,206	2	.	.
SC	22,352	22,352	25,212	23,071	27,859	32,779	8	.	.
TX	17,772	18,030	22,239	22,327	24,017	31,390	8	.	.
UT	20,925	20,925	21,410	21,402	21,902	21,902	3	.	.
VA	27,591	27,591	29,727	29,727	31,863	31,863	2	.	.
WA	27,851	27,851	29,208	29,208	30,564	30,564	2	.	.
WI	37,062	37,062	37,062	37,062	37,062	37,062	1	.	.
WY	19,992	19,992	20,124	20,124	20,256	20,256	2	.	.

Degree Required Data

	Min	Q1	Mean	Median	Q3	Max	N	Range Avg Min	Range Avg Max
High School	14,060	20,239	25,478	22,975	30,955	41,143	68	19,760	29,682
Associate's	18,720	31,200	38,239	36,609	43,400	63,240	18	22,922	42,702
Bachelor's	24,000	27,679	34,229	37,083	39,726	40,269	12	.	.
Master's	41,835	41,835	41,835	41,835	41,835	41,835	1	.	.
Doctoral	.	.	.	.	.	.		.	.

ACQUISITIONS CLERK - CONTINUED
ALL ACADEMIC LIBRARIES
Regional Data

	Min	Q1	Mean	Median	Q3	Max	N	Range Avg Min	Range Avg Max
North Atlantic	20,571	34,093	37,938	38,397	40,181	63,240	37	19,760	29,682
Great Lakes & Plains	17,453	20,218	25,506	22,360	31,346	44,554	41	30,132	43,319
Southeast	14,060	20,738	23,496	23,328	26,899	32,779	24	20,800	24,960
West & Southwest	14,200	20,256	25,449	23,133	30,463	45,102	23	.	.
ALL REGIONS	14,060	20,925	28,790	27,591	34,682	63,240	125	26,191	36,920

State Data

	Min	Q1	Mean	Median	Q3	Max	N	Range Avg Min	Range Avg Max
AL	15,017	15,017	21,009	21,009	27,000	27,000	2		
AR	17,318	17,318	23,001	23,001	28,683	28,683	2		
CA	34,020	34,020	34,020	34,020	34,020	34,020	1		
CO	39,775	39,775	42,438	42,438	45,102	45,102	2		
DC	30,597	37,814	37,269	38,397	39,270	40,269	5		
FL	23,585	23,585	23,585	23,585	23,585	23,585	1		
GA	14,060	14,201	18,429	16,492	22,658	26,674	4		
IA	31,550	32,145	36,816	35,580	41,487	44,554	4	44,554	44,554
IL	17,453	22,880	27,039	28,301	31,346	34,611	10	22,922	42,702
IN	19,115	19,802	21,202	20,259	21,486	32,843	18		
LA	24,000	24,000	24,000	24,000	24,000	24,000	1		
MA	29,675	38,278	42,440	39,270	44,153	63,240	16		
MD	20,571	23,608	30,673	28,824	40,181	40,181	5	19,760	29,682
ME	34,093	34,093	34,093	34,093	34,093	34,093	1		
MI	18,720	18,720	27,146	28,995	33,722	33,722	3		
MN	22,880	22,880	22,880	22,880	22,880	22,880	1		
NC	25,850	25,850	25,850	25,850	25,850	25,850	1		
ND	20,800	20,800	26,766	23,146	36,352	36,352	3		
NY	28,571	34,682	36,289	37,051	40,000	41,143	5		
OH	24,794	24,794	24,794	24,794	24,794	24,794	1		
OK	14,200	14,200	14,200	14,200	14,200	14,200	1		
OR	27,923	27,923	27,999	27,999	28,074	28,074	2		
PA	30,481	30,481	33,000	32,500	36,020	36,020	3		
RI	35,206	35,206	35,206	35,206	35,206	35,206	2		
SC	20,800	22,352	24,722	23,071	26,799	32,779	9	20,800	24,960
TN	20,675	20,675	20,675	20,675	20,675	20,675	1		
TX	17,772	18,030	23,335	22,818	24,977	31,390	10		
UT	20,925	20,925	21,410	21,402	21,902	21,902	3		
VA	27,591	27,591	29,727	29,727	31,863	31,863	2		
WA	27,851	27,851	29,208	29,208	30,564	30,564	2		
WI	37,062	37,062	37,062	37,062	37,062	37,062	1		
WV	26,102	26,102	26,102	26,102	26,102	26,102	1		
WY	19,992	19,992	20,124	20,124	20,256	20,256	2		

Degree Required Data

	Min	Q1	Mean	Median	Q3	Max	N	Range Avg Min	Range Avg Max
High School	14,060	20,259	26,010	23,371	31,700	44,554	80	28,371	33,065
Associate's	18,720	30,463	36,842	35,206	43,400	63,240	22	22,922	42,702
Bachelor's	20,675	24,000	30,923	28,683	38,397	40,269	17		
Master's	41,835	41,835	41,835	41,835	41,835	41,835	1		
Doctoral									

CIRCULATION CLERK

Performs routine duties requiring the use of a variety of forms, reports or procedures. Provides basic patron assistance: sets up computer stations, locates materials, provides information. Maintains departmental or area records. Performs miscellaneous clerical duties such as filing, typing, sorting or photocopying. Checks in and out materials; inspects materials for damage, verifies due date and calculates fine; assists patrons with basic informational questions; sorts materials and prepares for reshelving; issues and updates identification cards according to established procedures.

Two-Year College
Regional Data

	Min	Q1	Mean	Median	Q3	Max	N	Range Avg Min	Range Avg Max
North Atlantic	31,227	31,227	31,227	31,227	31,227	31,227	1		
Great Lakes & Plains	12,480	13,520	17,853	14,498	18,720	42,136	29	13,520	16,536
Southeast	11,200	15,787	22,183	24,708	26,935	30,504	12	17,846	30,566
West & Southwest	15,040	15,234	22,570	17,371	29,832	36,660	18	16,640	17,680
ALL REGIONS	11,200	13,728	20,357	16,640	26,438	42,136	60	14,841	18,576

State Data

	Min	Q1	Mean	Median	Q3	Max	N	Range Avg Min	Range Avg Max
AL	26,532	26,532	28,124	27,337	30,504	30,504	3		
CA	34,982	34,982	34,982	34,982	34,982	34,982	1		
FL	15,600	15,600	22,160	22,516	28,363	28,363	3	13,520	15,600
GA	15,974	15,974	15,974	15,974	15,974	15,974	1		
HI	24,792	25,812	29,610	28,494	33,408	36,660	4		
IA	21,000	21,000	22,943	23,078	24,752	24,752	3		
IL	12,480	13,728	15,247	14,529	17,046	18,720	12		
MD	31,227	31,227	31,227	31,227	31,227	31,227	1		
MI	22,180	22,180	28,468	28,468	34,755	34,755	2		
MN	31,675	31,675	36,906	36,906	42,136	42,136	2		
OH	13,520	13,520	13,520	13,520	13,520	13,520	10	13,520	16,536
OR	16,640	16,640	16,640	16,640	16,640	16,640	4	16,640	17,680
TN	23,467	23,467	23,467	23,467	23,467	23,467	1		
TX	15,040	15,040	20,698	15,234	26,377	36,579	9		
VA	26,499	26,499	26,499	26,499	26,499	26,499	1	22,173	45,531
WV	11,200	11,200	16,469	12,259	25,949	25,949	3		

Degree Required Data

	Min	Q1	Mean	Median	Q3	Max	N	Range Avg Min	Range Avg Max
High School	11,200	13,520	18,709	16,640	23,078	42,136	43	14,352	16,779
Associate's	15,974	23,467	27,347	27,850	31,227	36,579	10	22,173	45,531
Bachelor's	26,377	26,377	26,377	26,377	26,377	26,377	1		
Master's									
Doctoral									

CIRCULATION CLERK - CONTINUED
Four-Year College
Regional Data

	Min	Q1	Mean	Median	Q3	Max	N	Range Avg Min	Range Avg Max
North Atlantic	16,640	16,640	27,208	25,522	33,218	59,591	37	21,460	28,163
Great Lakes & Plains	10,800	19,469	23,303	22,907	27,040	35,443	26	27,900	42,044
Southeast	14,560	21,238	25,567	22,933	28,180	47,543	13	17,680	19,760
West & Southwest	16,400	29,762	29,629	30,227	32,484	40,326	14	.	.
ALL REGIONS	10,800	19,000	26,220	25,368	30,589	59,591	90	22,079	29,470

State Data

	Min	Q1	Mean	Median	Q3	Max	N	Range Avg Min	Range Avg Max
AL	20,322	20,322	20,322	20,322	20,322	20,322	1	.	.
CA	30,160	30,160	30,160	30,160	30,160	30,160	1	.	.
CO	29,892	30,294	32,953	32,352	34,020	40,326	9	.	.
DE	16,640	16,640	16,640	16,640	16,640	16,640	10	16,640	16,640
GA	26,993	26,993	26,993	26,993	26,993	26,993	1	.	.
IA	29,920	29,920	29,920	29,920	29,920	29,920	1	.	.
IL	18,720	20,800	21,849	21,840	22,933	24,960	6	.	.
MA	31,200	31,200	34,320	34,320	37,440	37,440	2	.	.
MD	31,111	31,111	45,351	45,351	59,591	59,591	2	.	.
ME	24,209	25,236	25,795	25,843	26,520	27,117	6	.	.
MI	10,800	14,304	19,877	19,504	25,450	29,700	4	.	.
MN	25,501	27,050	30,789	31,106	34,528	35,443	4	31,564	47,632
MO	16,640	16,640	21,290	16,640	30,589	30,589	3	.	.
NC	14,560	14,560	31,051	31,051	47,543	47,543	2	14,560	14,560
ND	18,000	18,000	20,760	20,760	23,520	23,520	2	.	.
NY	18,387	28,321	32,344	31,960	35,654	47,779	6	.	.
OH	19,469	19,469	21,512	19,916	23,556	26,749	4	.	.
OK	18,500	18,500	18,500	18,500	18,500	18,500	1	.	.
OR	23,400	23,400	23,400	23,400	23,400	23,400	1	.	.
PA	16,800	19,000	30,354	29,572	40,269	45,579	10	33,509	56,971
SC	20,800	21,826	23,122	22,893	24,419	25,904	4	20,800	24,960
SD	23,733	23,733	23,733	23,733	23,733	23,733	1	20,571	30,867
TX	16,400	16,400	23,081	23,081	29,762	29,762	2	.	.
VA	28,180	28,180	28,180	28,180	28,180	28,180	1	.	.
VT	28,587	28,587	28,587	28,587	28,587	28,587	1	.	.
WI	27,040	27,040	27,040	27,040	27,040	27,040	1	.	.
WV	21,238	22,066	25,572	25,830	29,078	29,389	4	.	.

Degree Required Data

	Min	Q1	Mean	Median	Q3	Max	N	Range Avg Min	Range Avg Max
High School	10,800	16,640	24,672	23,400	30,160	59,591	51	18,166	20,390
Associate's	18,387	20,800	26,414	24,960	27,040	47,543	9	.	.
Bachelor's	16,800	22,467	29,195	28,988	35,698	45,579	28	33,338	55,644
Master's									
Doctoral									

CIRCULATION CLERK - CONTINUED
University
(Includes ARL Data)
Regional Data

	Min	Q1	Mean	Median	Q3	Max	N	Range Avg Min	Range Avg Max
North Atlantic	15,358	27,948	32,368	31,735	38,234	56,521	102	23,962	34,436
Great Lakes & Plains	16,898	22,109	26,512	26,004	29,363	43,680	75	24,886	42,940
Southeast	14,248	19,781	23,342	22,817	25,736	54,164	159	18,020	31,498
West & Southwest	14,200	17,496	22,175	20,800	26,604	41,000	71	.	.
ALL REGIONS	14,200	20,547	25,985	24,358	30,564	56,521	407	22,635	36,340

State Data

	Min	Q1	Mean	Median	Q3	Max	N	Range Avg Min	Range Avg Max
AL	26,560	26,842	28,116	27,135	29,390	31,635	4		
AR	15,142	15,353	18,398	17,318	20,200	26,824	17		
CA	24,945	24,945	31,357	31,357	37,768	37,768	2		
CO	27,451	27,451	28,726	28,726	30,000	30,000	2		
CT	31,200	31,200	39,168	38,933	41,691	56,521	7	24,267	40,907
DC	15,819	29,744	29,931	32,022	33,634	42,162	10		
FL	19,200	19,200	22,225	22,149	22,817	33,322	25		
GA	14,248	14,342	17,097	15,009	19,399	24,688	18		
IA	26,476	27,071	31,406	29,556	36,551	38,420	8		
IL	18,720	22,880	27,921	27,069	30,223	43,680	20	24,804	43,950
IN	19,115	20,925	22,678	23,433	24,349	25,574	10		
LA	22,661	22,960	27,763	24,376	32,628	36,431	7		
MA	27,040	35,388	38,485	38,527	39,271	54,734	25	27,040	41,600
MD	22,235	29,403	31,786	31,619	36,041	39,064	26	19,760	31,200
MI	20,300	25,827	26,324	26,100	28,288	30,936	9		
MN	39,004	39,004	39,004	39,004	39,004	39,004	1		
MO	19,130	19,130	19,130	19,130	19,130	19,130	1		
NC	22,426	23,073	26,931	25,072	28,113	54,164	33		
ND	16,898	16,898	22,132	23,008	26,490	26,490	3		
NE	18,595	20,199	22,279	20,970	21,272	31,666	6		
NM	19,943	19,943	19,943	19,943	19,943	19,943	1		
NY	15,358	22,144	28,609	29,947	34,286	41,143	30	25,147	27,040
OH	17,160	22,494	27,627	27,564	34,880	36,269	12	25,376	36,878
OK	14,200	14,200	14,200	14,200	14,200	14,200	2		
OR	26,100	26,100	27,030	27,030	27,960	27,960	2		
PA	18,720	18,797	20,309	19,887	21,821	22,741	4	18,720	18,720
SC	20,359	22,319	23,006	22,443	24,157	27,892	19		
SD	21,038	21,038	21,574	21,574	22,109	22,109	2		
TN	19,572	20,622	22,681	21,798	24,154	31,616	20	18,020	31,498
TX	16,944	18,324	20,722	20,216	22,924	29,273	30		
UT	14,872	14,872	19,587	14,872	21,500	41,000	23		
VA	18,720	21,911	28,061	29,935	31,999	40,170	16		
WA	26,604	26,604	31,056	31,296	33,588	36,948	6		
WI	20,790	20,790	27,397	26,004	35,398	35,398	3		
WY	27,828	27,828	31,120	29,100	36,432	36,432	3		

Degree Required Data

	Min	Q1	Mean	Median	Q3	Max	N	Range Avg Min	Range Avg Max
High School	14,200	20,218	25,328	23,654	29,794	56,521	305	20,398	33,209
Associate's	15,358	22,070	27,017	24,349	30,000	54,734	25	22,922	42,702
Bachelor's	15,819	22,880	28,780	27,384	33,634	52,755	51	29,432	44,463
Master's	49,996	49,996	49,996	49,996	49,996	49,996	1	.	.
Doctoral	.	.	.	.	.	.		.	.

CIRCULATION CLERK - CONTINUED
ALL ACADEMIC LIBRARIES
Regional Data

	Min	Q1	Mean	Median	Q3	Max	N	Range Avg Min	Range Avg Max
North Atlantic	15,358	24,594	30,996	31,130	37,173	59,591	140	22,439	30,618
Great Lakes & Plains	10,800	18,845	23,939	23,043	28,877	43,680	130	19,655	29,604
Southeast	11,200	19,929	23,424	22,887	26,546	54,164	184	17,917	28,964
West & Southwest	14,200	16,944	23,257	21,500	29,762	41,000	103	16,640	17,680
ALL REGIONS	10,800	19,375	25,416	24,000	30,160	59,591	557	20,262	29,064

State Data

	Min	Q1	Mean	Median	Q3	Max	N	Range Avg Min	Range Avg Max
AL	20,322	26,546	27,145	27,135	28,921	31,635	8		
AR	15,142	15,353	18,398	17,318	20,200	26,824	17		
CA	24,945	27,553	31,964	32,571	36,375	37,768	4		
CO	27,451	29,916	32,185	31,345	34,020	40,326	11		
CT	31,200	31,200	39,168	38,933	41,691	56,521	7	24,267	40,907
DC	15,819	29,744	29,931	32,022	33,634	42,162	10		
DE	16,640	16,640	16,640	16,640	16,640	16,640	10	16,640	16,640
FL	15,600	19,200	22,218	22,149	22,825	33,322	28	13,520	15,600
GA	14,248	14,342	17,535	15,446	19,687	26,993	20		
HI	24,792	25,812	29,610	28,494	33,408	36,660	4		
IA	21,000	25,614	29,167	28,293	32,437	38,420	12		
IL	12,480	17,453	22,960	22,880	27,098	43,680	38	24,804	43,950
IN	19,115	20,925	22,678	23,433	24,349	25,574	10		
LA	22,661	22,960	27,763	24,376	32,628	36,431	7		
MA	27,040	31,850	38,177	38,494	39,271	54,734	27	27,040	41,600
MD	22,235	29,403	32,702	31,619	36,041	59,591	29	19,760	31,200
ME	24,209	25,236	25,795	25,843	26,520	27,117	6		
MI	10,800	21,200	24,890	26,100	29,216	34,755	15		
MN	25,501	28,600	33,710	33,613	39,004	42,136	7	31,564	47,632
MO	16,640	16,640	20,750	17,885	24,860	30,589	4		
NC	14,560	23,073	27,167	25,072	28,642	54,164	35	14,560	14,560
ND	16,898	18,000	21,583	23,008	23,520	26,490	5		
NE	18,595	20,199	22,279	20,970	21,272	31,666	6		
NM	19,943	19,943	19,943	19,943	19,943	19,943	1		
NY	15,358	22,934	29,232	30,095	34,286	47,779	36	25,147	27,040
OH	13,520	13,520	21,261	19,469	26,749	36,269	26	14,598	18,385
OK	14,200	14,200	15,633	14,200	18,500	18,500	3		
OR	16,640	16,640	20,574	16,640	26,100	27,960	7	16,640	17,680
PA	16,800	19,000	27,484	22,371	37,440	45,579	14	30,551	49,321
SC	20,359	22,319	23,026	22,852	24,157	27,892	23	20,800	24,960
SD	21,038	21,038	22,293	22,109	23,733	23,733	3	20,571	30,867
TN	19,572	20,736	22,718	21,986	23,806	31,616	21	18,020	31,498
TX	15,040	18,024	20,832	19,168	22,934	36,579	41		
UT	14,872	14,872	19,587	14,872	21,500	41,000	23		
VA	18,720	22,279	27,980	29,025	31,730	40,170	18	22,173	45,531
VT	28,587	28,587	28,587	28,587	28,587	28,587	1		
WA	26,604	26,604	31,056	31,296	33,588	36,948	6		
WI	20,790	23,397	27,308	26,522	31,219	35,398	4		
WV	11,200	12,259	21,671	22,894	28,767	29,389	7		
WY	27,828	27,828	31,120	29,100	36,432	36,432	3		

Degree Required Data

	Min	Q1	Mean	Median	Q3	Max	N	Range Avg Min	Range Avg Max
High School	10,800	18,720	24,531	23,073	29,403	59,591	399	17,405	22,882
Associate's	15,358	22,293	26,969	25,267	29,935	54,734	44	22,797	43,174
Bachelor's	15,819	22,907	28,895	28,383	34,143	52,755	80	31,873	51,451
Master's	49,996	49,996	49,996	49,996	49,996	49,996	1		
Doctoral									

ACCOUNTING (PAYABLES) CLERK

Performs routine duties requiring the use of a variety of forms, reports or procedures. Provides basic patron assistance: sets up computer stations, locates materials, provides information. Maintains departmental or area records. Performs miscellaneous clerical duties such as filing, typing, sorting or photocopying. Checks in and out materials; inspects materials for damage, verifies due date and calculates fine; assists patrons with basic informational questions; sorts materials and prepares for reshelving; issues and updates identification cards according to established procedures.

Two-Year College
Regional Data

	Min	Q1	Mean	Median	Q3	Max	N	Range Avg Min	Range Avg Max
Great Lakes & Plains	42,136	42,136	42,136	42,136	42,136	42,136	1	.	.
Southeast	23,566	23,566	23,566	23,566	23,566	23,566	1	.	.
West & Southwest	27,000	27,000	27,568	27,568	28,136	28,136	2	.	.
ALL REGIONS	23,566	25,283	30,210	27,568	35,136	42,136	4	.	.

State Data

	Min	Q1	Mean	Median	Q3	Max	N	Range Avg Min	Range Avg Max
FL	23,566	23,566	23,566	23,566	23,566	23,566	1	.	.
MN	42,136	42,136	42,136	42,136	42,136	42,136	1	.	.
TX	27,000	27,000	27,568	27,568	28,136	28,136	2	.	.

Degree Required Data

	Min	Q1	Mean	Median	Q3	Max	N	Range Avg Min	Range Avg Max
High School	27,000	27,000	34,568	34,568	42,136	42,136	2	.	.
Associate's	23,566	23,566	25,851	25,851	28,136	28,136	2	.	.
Bachelor's	.	.	.	.	.	.		.	.
Master's	.	.	.	.	.	.		.	.
Doctoral	.	.	.	.	.	.		.	.

ACCOUNTING (PAYABLES) CLERK - CONTINUED
Four-Year College
Regional Data

	Min	Q1	Mean	Median	Q3	Max	N	Range Avg Min	Range Avg Max
North Atlantic	30,661	30,661	35,144	35,144	39,628	39,628	2	.	.
Southeast	22,194	22,194	22,194	22,194	22,194	22,194	1	.	.
West & Southwest	32,760	32,760	37,713	37,713	42,667	42,667	2	.	.
ALL REGIONS	22,194	30,661	33,582	32,760	39,628	42,667	5	.	.

State Data

	Min	Q1	Mean	Median	Q3	Max	N	Range Avg Min	Range Avg Max
CA	32,760	32,760	37,713	37,713	42,667	42,667	2	.	.
MD	30,661	30,661	30,661	30,661	30,661	30,661	1	.	.
NY	39,628	39,628	39,628	39,628	39,628	39,628	1	.	.
TN	22,194	22,194	22,194	22,194	22,194	22,194	1	.	.

Degree Required Data

	Min	Q1	Mean	Median	Q3	Max	N	Range Avg Min	Range Avg Max
High School	30,661	30,661	37,652	39,628	42,667	42,667	3	.	.
Associate's	22,194	22,194	22,194	22,194	22,194	22,194	1	.	.
Bachelor's	32,760	32,760	32,760	32,760	32,760	32,760	1	.	.
Master's	.	.	.	.	.	.		.	.
Doctoral	.	.	.	.	.	.		.	.

ACCOUNTING (PAYABLES) CLERK - CONTINUED
University
(Includes ARL Data)
Regional Data

	Min	Q1	Mean	Median	Q3	Max	N	Range Avg Min	Range Avg Max
North Atlantic	20,164	26,400	35,943	36,102	38,735	64,121	10	22,360	33,176
Great Lakes & Plains	20,800	22,157	30,631	26,915	37,014	50,668	9	26,603	39,582
Southeast	18,019	21,409	25,928	26,484	30,419	32,544	12	.	.
West & Southwest	14,560	21,608	25,507	24,919	30,000	41,616	10	.	.
ALL REGIONS	14,560	22,296	29,300	26,915	33,238	64,121	41	24,482	36,379

State Data

	Min	Q1	Mean	Median	Q3	Max	N	Range Avg Min	Range Avg Max
AL	30,056	30,056	30,056	30,056	30,056	30,056	1	.	.
AR	18,019	18,019	20,966	20,522	24,356	24,356	3	.	.
CA	41,616	41,616	41,616	41,616	41,616	41,616	1	.	.
DC	33,238	33,238	33,238	33,238	33,238	33,238	1	.	.
GA	24,855	24,855	24,855	24,855	24,855	24,855	1	.	.
IL	26,270	26,270	28,506	28,506	30,742	30,742	2	.	.
IN	20,800	21,466	30,129	24,523	38,792	50,668	4	.	.
MA	38,735	38,735	40,120	40,120	41,505	41,505	2	.	.
MD	25,459	25,459	32,554	36,102	36,102	36,102	3	22,360	33,176
NC	28,113	28,194	29,616	29,528	31,038	31,294	4	.	.
ND	22,157	22,157	22,157	22,157	22,157	22,157	1	.	.
NE	37,014	37,014	37,014	37,014	37,014	37,014	1	.	.
NY	20,164	23,282	37,071	32,000	50,861	64,121	4	.	.
OH	38,983	38,983	38,983	38,983	38,983	38,983	1	26,603	39,582
OR	30,768	30,768	30,768	30,768	30,768	30,768	1	.	.
TN	20,028	20,028	24,956	22,296	32,544	32,544	3	.	.
TX	16,947	21,608	23,021	23,954	25,580	26,081	6	.	.
UT	14,560	14,560	22,280	22,280	30,000	30,000	2	.	.

Degree Required Data

	Min	Q1	Mean	Median	Q3	Max	N	Range Avg Min	Range Avg Max
High School	14,560	21,204	27,026	25,925	30,419	50,668	28	24,482	36,379
Associate's	22,157	23,650	31,857	33,238	38,735	41,505	5	.	.
Bachelor's	24,356	25,219	30,660	31,091	36,102	36,102	4	.	.
Master's	.	.	.	.	.	.		.	.
Doctoral	.	.	.	.	.	.		.	.

ACCOUNTING (PAYABLES) CLERK - CONTINUED
ALL ACADEMIC LIBRARIES
Regional Data

	Min	Q1	Mean	Median	Q3	Max	N	Range Avg Min	Range Avg Max
North Atlantic	20,164	28,531	35,810	36,102	39,181	64,121	12	22,360	33,176
Great Lakes & Plains	20,800	22,157	31,782	28,829	38,983	50,668	10	26,603	39,582
Southeast	18,019	22,194	25,493	24,606	30,056	32,544	14	.	.
West & Southwest	14,560	23,650	27,545	26,541	30,768	42,667	14	.	.
ALL REGIONS	14,560	23,566	29,801	28,125	36,102	64,121	50	24,482	36,379

State Data

	Min	Q1	Mean	Median	Q3	Max	N	Range Avg Min	Range Avg Max
AL	30,056	30,056	30,056	30,056	30,056	30,056	1	.	.
AR	18,019	18,019	20,966	20,522	24,356	24,356	3	.	.
CA	32,760	32,760	39,014	41,616	42,667	42,667	3	.	.
DC	33,238	33,238	33,238	33,238	33,238	33,238	1	.	.
FL	23,566	23,566	23,566	23,566	23,566	23,566	1	.	.
GA	24,855	24,855	24,855	24,855	24,855	24,855	1	.	.
IL	26,270	26,270	28,506	28,506	30,742	30,742	2	.	.
IN	20,800	21,466	30,129	24,523	38,792	50,668	4	.	.
MA	38,735	38,735	40,120	40,120	41,505	41,505	2	.	.
MD	25,459	28,060	32,081	33,381	36,102	36,102	4	22,360	33,176
MN	42,136	42,136	42,136	42,136	42,136	42,136	1	.	.
NC	28,113	28,194	29,616	29,528	31,038	31,294	4	.	.
ND	22,157	22,157	22,157	22,157	22,157	22,157	1	.	.
NE	37,014	37,014	37,014	37,014	37,014	37,014	1	.	.
NY	20,164	26,400	37,583	37,600	39,628	64,121	5	.	.
OH	38,983	38,983	38,983	38,983	38,983	38,983	1	26,603	39,582
OR	30,768	30,768	30,768	30,768	30,768	30,768	1	.	.
TN	20,028	21,111	24,265	22,245	27,420	32,544	4	.	.
TX	16,947	22,629	24,157	24,919	26,541	28,136	8	.	.
UT	14,560	14,560	22,280	22,280	30,000	30,000	2	.	.

Degree Required Data

	Min	Q1	Mean	Median	Q3	Max	N	Range Avg Min	Range Avg Max
High School	14,560	22,131	28,449	26,915	31,294	50,668	33	24,482	36,379
Associate's	22,157	22,880	29,148	25,893	35,987	41,505	8	.	.
Bachelor's	24,356	26,081	31,080	32,760	36,102	36,102	5	.	.
Master's	.	.	.	.	.	.		.	.
Doctoral	.	.	.	.	.	.		.	.

SHELVER/PAGE

Moves and unloads carts. Shelves materials in appropriate locations. Shelf-reads assigned areas and straightens collection as needed. Removes out-of-place materials for reshelving.

Two-Year College
Regional Data

	Min	Q1	Mean	Median	Q3	Max	N	Range Avg Min	Range Avg Max
Great Lakes & Plains	21,067	21,067	21,067	21,067	21,067	21,067	1	.	.
West & Southwest	10,800	10,800	11,687	10,800	10,800	16,120	6	16,120	16,120
ALL REGIONS	10,800	10,800	13,027	10,800	16,120	21,067	7	16,120	16,120

State Data

	Min	Q1	Mean	Median	Q3	Max	N	Range Avg Min	Range Avg Max
CA	16,120	16,120	16,120	16,120	16,120	16,120	1	16,120	16,120
IA	21,067	21,067	21,067	21,067	21,067	21,067	1	.	.
TX	10,800	10,800	10,800	10,800	10,800	10,800	5	.	.

Degree Required Data

	Min	Q1	Mean	Median	Q3	Max	N	Range Avg Min	Range Avg Max
High School	10,800	10,800	13,027	10,800	16,120	21,067	7	16,120	16,120
Associate's	.	.	.	.	.	.		.	.
Bachelor's	.	.	.	.	.	.		.	.
Master's	.	.	.	.	.	.		.	.
Doctoral	.	.	.	.	.	.		.	.

SHELVER/PAGE - CONTINUED
Four-Year College
Regional Data

	Min	Q1	Mean	Median	Q3	Max	N	Range Avg Min	Range Avg Max
North Atlantic	14,560	14,560	14,560	14,560	14,560	14,560	1	14,560	16,640
West & Southwest	14,560	15,340	24,275	24,086	33,210	34,368	4	16,120	16,120
ALL REGIONS	14,560	14,560	22,332	16,120	32,052	34,368	5	15,340	16,380

State Data

	Min	Q1	Mean	Median	Q3	Max	N	Range Avg Min	Range Avg Max
AK	16,120	16,120	16,120	16,120	16,120	16,120	1	16,120	16,120
CA	14,560	14,560	14,560	14,560	14,560	14,560	1	.	.
CO	32,052	32,052	33,210	33,210	34,368	34,368	2	.	.
NY	14,560	14,560	14,560	14,560	14,560	14,560	1	14,560	16,640

Degree Required Data

	Min	Q1	Mean	Median	Q3	Max	N	Range Avg Min	Range Avg Max
High School	14,560	14,560	22,332	16,120	32,052	34,368	5	15,340	16,380
Associate's	.	.	.	.	.	.		.	.
Bachelor's	.	.	.	.	.	.		.	.
Master's	.	.	.	.	.	.		.	.
Doctoral	.	.	.	.	.	.		.	.

SHELVER/PAGE - CONTINUED
University
(Includes ARL Data)
Regional Data

	Min	Q1	Mean	Median	Q3	Max	N	Range Avg Min	Range Avg Max
North Atlantic	26,286	27,286	28,369	27,948	27,948	35,429	10	22,880	37,440
Great Lakes & Plains	17,060	23,234	28,350	27,727	31,221	41,600	13	26,603	39,582
Southeast	12,792	12,792	15,033	13,832	15,600	29,817	148	18,886	33,030
West & Southwest	14,560	14,820	20,595	18,585	25,502	34,940	12	.	.
ALL REGIONS	12,792	13,312	17,072	14,352	19,200	41,600	183	22,790	36,684

State Data

	Min	Q1	Mean	Median	Q3	Max	N	Range Avg Min	Range Avg Max
CT	27,040	27,040	27,040	27,040	27,040	27,040	1	22,880	37,440
FL	12,792	12,792	14,416	13,832	14,560	19,200	139	.	.
IL	22,339	25,126	28,925	27,997	31,221	41,600	10	.	.
IN	17,060	17,060	19,783	19,783	22,506	22,506	2	.	.
MD	27,286	27,286	27,727	27,948	27,948	27,948	6	.	.
NC	28,163	28,163	28,990	28,990	29,817	29,817	2	.	.
NY	26,286	26,286	30,095	28,571	35,429	35,429	3	.	.
OH	39,735	39,735	39,735	39,735	39,735	39,735	1	26,603	39,582
SC	22,352	22,352	22,794	22,619	23,412	23,412	3	.	.
TN	21,072	21,102	23,670	22,980	26,238	27,648	4	18,886	33,030
UT	14,560	14,768	20,236	15,080	26,463	34,940	11	.	.
WY	24,540	24,540	24,540	24,540	24,540	24,540	1	.	.

Degree Required Data

	Min	Q1	Mean	Median	Q3	Max	N	Range Avg Min	Range Avg Max
High School	12,792	13,312	16,871	14,352	17,680	41,600	179	22,790	36,684
Associate's	29,817	29,817	29,817	29,817	29,817	29,817	1	.	.
Bachelor's	27,648	27,648	27,648	27,648	27,648	27,648	1	.	.
Master's	.	.	.	.	.	.	.	.	.
Doctoral	.	.	.	.	.	.	.	.	.

SHELVER/PAGE - CONTINUED
ALL ACADEMIC LIBRARIES
Regional Data

	Min	Q1	Mean	Median	Q3	Max	N	Range Avg Min	Range Avg Max
North Atlantic	14,560	27,040	27,114	27,948	27,948	35,429	11	18,720	27,040
Great Lakes & Plains	17,060	22,506	27,830	27,457	31,221	41,600	14	26,603	39,582
Southeast	12,792	12,792	15,033	13,832	15,600	29,817	148	18,886	33,030
West & Southwest	10,800	14,560	18,834	14,976	24,540	34,940	22	16,120	16,120
ALL REGIONS	10,800	13,312	17,062	14,560	19,200	41,600	195	19,195	26,489

State Data

	Min	Q1	Mean	Median	Q3	Max	N	Range Avg Min	Range Avg Max
AK	16,120	16,120	16,120	16,120	16,120	16,120	1	16,120	16,120
CA	14,560	14,560	15,340	15,340	16,120	16,120	2	16,120	16,120
CO	32,052	32,052	33,210	33,210	34,368	34,368	2	.	.
CT	27,040	27,040	27,040	27,040	27,040	27,040	1	22,880	37,440
FL	12,792	12,792	14,416	13,832	14,560	19,200	139	.	.
IA	21,067	21,067	21,067	21,067	21,067	21,067	1	.	.
IL	22,339	25,126	28,925	27,997	31,221	41,600	10	.	.
IN	17,060	17,060	19,783	19,783	22,506	22,506	2	.	.
MD	27,286	27,286	27,727	27,948	27,948	27,948	6	.	.
NC	28,163	28,163	28,990	28,990	29,817	29,817	2	.	.
NY	14,560	20,423	26,211	27,429	32,000	35,429	4	14,560	16,640
OH	39,735	39,735	39,735	39,735	39,735	39,735	1	26,603	39,582
SC	22,352	22,352	22,794	22,619	23,412	23,412	3	.	.
TN	21,072	21,102	23,670	22,980	26,238	27,648	4	18,886	33,030
TX	10,800	10,800	10,800	10,800	10,800	10,800	5	.	.
UT	14,560	14,768	20,236	15,080	26,463	34,940	11	.	.
WY	24,540	24,540	24,540	24,540	24,540	24,540	1	.	.

Degree Required Data

	Min	Q1	Mean	Median	Q3	Max	N	Range Avg Min	Range Avg Max
High School	10,800	13,312	16,873	14,352	17,680	41,600	191	19,195	26,489
Associate's	29,817	29,817	29,817	29,817	29,817	29,817	1	.	.
Bachelor's	27,648	27,648	27,648	27,648	27,648	27,648	1	.	.
Master's	.	.	.	.	.	.	.	.	.
Doctoral	.	.	.	.	.	.	.	.	.

BOOKMOBILE DRIVER

Loads and unloads materials. Drives to and from specified locations. Assists patrons with material selection. Checks in and out materials.

University
(Includes ARL Data)
Regional Data

	Min	Q1	Mean	Median	Q3	Max	N	Range Avg Min	Range Avg Max
Southeast	20,613	20,613	21,753	21,965	22,680	22,680	3	17,534	30,638
ALL REGIONS	20,613	20,613	21,753	21,965	22,680	22,680	3	17,534	30,638

State Data

	Min	Q1	Mean	Median	Q3	Max	N	Range Avg Min	Range Avg Max
TN	20,613	20,613	21,753	21,965	22,680	22,680	3	17,534	30,638

Degree Required Data

	Min	Q1	Mean	Median	Q3	Max	N	Range Avg Min	Range Avg Max
High School	20,613	20,613	21,753	21,965	22,680	22,680	3	17,534	30,638
Associate's	.	.	.	.	.	.	.	.	.
Bachelor's	.	.	.	.	.	.	.	.	.
Master's	.	.	.	.	.	.	.	.	.
Doctoral	.	.	.	.	.	.	.	.	.

BOOKMOBILE DRIVER - CONTINUED
ALL ACADEMIC LIBRARIES
Regional Data

	Min	Q1	Mean	Median	Q3	Max	N	Range Avg Min	Range Avg Max
Southeast	20,613	20,613	21,753	21,965	22,680	22,680	3	17,534	30,638
ALL REGIONS	20,613	20,613	21,753	21,965	22,680	22,680	3	17,534	30,638

State Data

	Min	Q1	Mean	Median	Q3	Max	N	Range Avg Min	Range Avg Max
TN	20,613	20,613	21,753	21,965	22,680	22,680	3	17,534	30,638

Degree Required Data

	Min	Q1	Mean	Median	Q3	Max	N	Range Avg Min	Range Avg Max
High School	20,613	20,613	21,753	21,965	22,680	22,680	3	17,534	30,638
Associate's	.	.	.	.	.	.	.	.	.
Bachelor's	.	.	.	.	.	.	.	.	.
Master's	.	.	.	.	.	.	.	.	.
Doctoral	.	.	.	.	.	.	.	.	.

COPY CATALOGER

Performs copy cataloging for print and non-print materials using OCLC, AACRII, MARC, DDC and local consortium standards. Edits previously cataloged materials. Serves a resource for other library personnel concerning cataloging rules and practices.

Two-Year College
Regional Data

	Min	Q1	Mean	Median	Q3	Max	N	Range Avg Min	Range Avg Max
Southeast	16,515	17,653	21,240	21,507	26,040	26,667	7	.	.
West & Southwest	24,157	24,157	30,838	30,156	38,200	38,200	3	.	.
ALL REGIONS	16,515	18,792	24,119	22,832	26,667	38,200	10	.	.

State Data

	Min	Q1	Mean	Median	Q3	Max	N	Range Avg Min	Range Avg Max
AL	26,040	26,040	26,040	26,040	26,040	26,040	1	.	.
AR	17,653	17,653	17,653	17,653	17,653	17,653	1	.	.
FL	16,515	17,654	19,580	20,150	21,507	21,507	4	.	.
HI	30,156	30,156	30,156	30,156	30,156	30,156	1	.	.
TN	26,667	26,667	26,667	26,667	26,667	26,667	1	.	.
TX	24,157	24,157	31,179	31,179	38,200	38,200	2	.	.

Degree Required Data

	Min	Q1	Mean	Median	Q3	Max	N	Range Avg Min	Range Avg Max
High School	16,515	16,515	21,821	18,792	30,156	30,156	3	.	.
Associate's	17,653	21,507	24,949	22,832	26,667	38,200	6	.	.
Bachelor's									
Master's	26,040	26,040	26,040	26,040	26,040	26,040	1	.	.
Doctoral									

COPY CATALOGER - CONTINUED
Four-Year College
Regional Data

	Min	Q1	Mean	Median	Q3	Max	N	Range Avg Min	Range Avg Max
North Atlantic	21,320	24,660	33,187	32,249	41,715	46,932	4	.	.
Great Lakes & Plains	28,704	28,704	31,373	31,907	33,509	33,509	3	27,248	38,480
Southeast	18,360	24,643	29,200	30,149	35,619	37,228	5	.	.
West & Southwest	24,977	27,232	34,622	32,095	44,712	46,620	6	.	.
ALL REGIONS	18,360	27,232	32,256	31,028	36,497	46,932	18	27,248	38,480

State Data

	Min	Q1	Mean	Median	Q3	Max	N	Range Avg Min	Range Avg Max
AL	18,360	18,360	18,360	18,360	18,360	18,360	1	.	.
CA	36,267	36,267	36,267	36,267	36,267	36,267	1	.	.
CO	44,712	44,712	45,666	45,666	46,620	46,620	2	.	.
ME	36,497	36,497	36,497	36,497	36,497	36,497	1	.	.
MN	33,509	33,509	33,509	33,509	33,509	33,509	1	27,248	38,480
NY	21,320	21,320	34,126	34,126	46,932	46,932	2	.	.
OH	28,704	28,704	30,306	30,306	31,907	31,907	2	.	.
OR	27,232	27,232	27,578	27,578	27,923	27,923	2	.	.
PA	28,000	28,000	28,000	28,000	28,000	28,000	1	.	.
SC	35,619	35,619	35,619	35,619	35,619	35,619	1	.	.
TX	24,977	24,977	24,977	24,977	24,977	24,977	1	.	.
WV	24,643	24,643	30,673	30,149	37,228	37,228	3	.	.

Degree Required Data

	Min	Q1	Mean	Median	Q3	Max	N	Range Avg Min	Range Avg Max
High School	18,360	24,643	30,540	27,923	36,497	46,620	11	27,248	38,480
Associate's	37,228	37,228	37,228	37,228	37,228	37,228	1	.	.
Bachelor's	28,000	28,352	31,219	30,306	34,087	36,267	4	.	.
Master's	46,932	46,932	46,932	46,932	46,932	46,932	1	.	.
Doctoral	.	.	.	.	.	.		.	.

COPY CATALOGER - CONTINUED
University
(Includes ARL Data)
Regional Data

	Min	Q1	Mean	Median	Q3	Max	N	Range Avg Min	Range Avg Max
North Atlantic	15,091	27,948	33,101	33,927	38,774	58,217	48	23,920	23,920
Great Lakes & Plains	18,720	28,621	35,202	34,682	41,948	52,835	55	31,120	44,712
Southeast	18,019	24,661	28,792	28,113	31,232	46,853	54	.	.
West & Southwest	18,143	25,560	30,576	30,610	35,055	43,680	51	.	.
ALL REGIONS	15,091	26,556	31,919	30,571	37,142	58,217	208	30,160	41,940

State Data

	Min	Q1	Mean	Median	Q3	Max	N	Range Avg Min	Range Avg Max
AL	24,525	24,525	26,115	26,115	27,705	27,705	2	.	.
AR	18,019	18,019	18,019	18,019	18,019	18,019	1	.	.
CA	27,768	28,958	33,705	34,226	38,452	38,600	4	.	.
CO	30,600	30,972	35,632	36,840	37,932	43,680	10	.	.
CT	47,332	47,332	54,589	58,217	58,217	58,217	3	.	.
DC	15,091	17,086	22,048	19,195	23,198	34,417	9	.	.
GA	20,146	20,146	22,001	22,001	23,855	23,855	2	.	.
IA	34,682	41,948	44,388	45,790	45,790	52,835	18	.	.
IL	18,720	27,144	32,861	33,280	37,440	47,840	19	31,120	44,712
IN	25,667	25,667	29,035	28,751	30,698	36,379	8	.	.
KY	27,123	27,457	30,368	30,130	33,279	34,091	4	.	.
LA	19,503	21,751	23,376	24,000	25,000	26,000	4	.	.
MA	44,394	44,394	44,394	44,394	44,394	44,394	1	.	.
MD	25,663	29,403	33,178	33,614	38,543	40,000	26	.	.
MI	27,019	27,019	27,019	27,019	27,019	27,019	2	.	.
MT	18,143	18,143	18,143	18,143	18,143	18,143	1	.	.
NC	23,073	26,260	28,909	28,353	30,843	38,297	24	.	.
ND	20,908	20,908	24,037	21,051	30,153	30,153	3	.	.
NE	29,110	29,110	29,110	29,110	29,110	29,110	1	.	.
NY	22,880	29,380	35,656	35,429	37,804	57,143	8	23,920	23,920
OH	34,663	34,663	34,663	34,663	34,663	34,663	1	.	.
OR	22,476	22,476	22,476	22,476	22,476	22,476	1	.	.
PA	34,407	34,407	34,407	34,407	34,407	34,407	1	.	.
SC	23,211	24,661	29,451	28,115	30,542	43,322	10	.	.
SD	25,714	25,714	25,714	25,714	25,714	25,714	1	.	.
TN	21,228	21,228	25,760	25,760	30,292	30,292	2	.	.
TX	23,163	28,990	31,371	30,610	36,891	38,796	11	.	.
UT	21,402	21,402	25,303	22,148	29,132	35,055	11	.	.
VA	28,559	31,917	37,141	37,800	40,576	46,853	5	.	.
WA	32,028	32,028	34,553	33,588	34,368	40,752	5	.	.
WI	31,727	31,727	32,434	32,434	33,141	33,141	2	.	.
WY	21,312	25,902	28,932	29,718	32,268	34,368	8	.	.

Degree Required Data

	Min	Q1	Mean	Median	Q3	Max	N	Range Avg Min	Range Avg Max
High School	18,019	25,667	31,332	29,403	35,328	58,217	113	.	.
Associate's	20,908	24,960	28,776	28,990	31,200	38,670	11	26,166	35,947
Bachelor's	15,091	27,123	31,653	33,614	37,739	47,840	47	34,216	50,190
Master's	.	.	.	.	.	.	.	.	.
Doctoral	.	.	.	.	.	.	.	.	.

COPY CATALOGER - CONTINUED
ALL ACADEMIC LIBRARIES
Regional Data

	Min	Q1	Mean	Median	Q3	Max	N	Range Avg Min	Range Avg Max
North Atlantic	15,091	27,948	33,108	33,927	38,774	58,217	52	23,920	23,920
Great Lakes & Plains	18,720	28,704	35,004	34,086	41,948	52,835	58	30,843	44,267
Southeast	16,515	24,450	28,022	27,952	30,542	46,853	66	.	.
West & Southwest	18,143	26,396	30,994	30,605	36,277	46,620	60	.	.
ALL REGIONS	15,091	25,857	31,614	30,454	36,438	58,217	236	29,978	41,724

State Data

	Min	Q1	Mean	Median	Q3	Max	N	Range Avg Min	Range Avg Max
AL	18,360	21,443	24,158	25,283	26,873	27,705	4	.	.
AR	17,653	17,653	17,836	17,836	18,019	18,019	2	.	.
CA	27,768	30,147	34,217	36,267	38,304	38,600	5	.	.
CO	30,600	30,972	37,304	37,608	41,868	46,620	12	.	.
CT	47,332	47,332	54,589	58,217	58,217	58,217	3	.	.
DC	15,091	17,086	22,048	19,195	23,198	34,417	9	.	.
FL	16,515	17,654	19,580	20,150	21,507	21,507	4	.	.
GA	20,146	20,146	22,001	22,001	23,855	23,855	2	.	.
HI	30,156	30,156	30,156	30,156	30,156	30,156	1	.	.
IA	34,682	41,948	44,388	45,790	45,790	52,835	18	.	.
IL	18,720	27,144	32,861	33,280	37,440	47,840	19	31,120	44,712
IN	25,667	25,667	29,035	28,751	30,698	36,379	8	.	.
KY	27,123	27,457	30,368	30,130	33,279	34,091	4	.	.
LA	19,503	21,751	23,376	24,000	25,000	26,000	4	.	.
MA	44,394	44,394	44,394	44,394	44,394	44,394	1	.	.
MD	25,663	29,403	33,178	33,614	38,543	40,000	26	.	.
ME	36,497	36,497	36,497	36,497	36,497	36,497	1	.	.
MI	27,019	27,019	27,019	27,019	27,019	27,019	2	.	.
MN	33,509	33,509	33,509	33,509	33,509	33,509	1	27,248	38,480
MT	18,143	18,143	18,143	18,143	18,143	18,143	1	.	.
NC	23,073	26,260	28,909	28,353	30,843	38,297	24	.	.
ND	20,908	20,908	24,037	21,051	30,153	30,153	3	.	.
NE	29,110	29,110	29,110	29,110	29,110	29,110	1	.	.
NY	21,320	24,960	35,350	35,429	40,000	57,143	10	23,920	23,920
OH	28,704	28,704	31,758	31,907	34,663	34,663	3	.	.
OR	22,476	22,476	25,877	27,232	27,923	27,923	3	.	.
PA	28,000	28,000	31,204	31,204	34,407	34,407	2	.	.
SC	23,211	24,661	30,012	28,630	35,619	43,322	11	.	.
SD	25,714	25,714	25,714	25,714	25,714	25,714	1	.	.
TN	21,228	21,228	26,062	26,667	30,292	30,292	3	.	.
TX	23,163	25,560	30,887	30,109	36,891	38,796	14	.	.
UT	21,402	21,402	25,303	22,148	29,132	35,055	11	.	.
VA	28,559	31,917	37,141	37,800	40,576	46,853	5	.	.
WA	32,028	32,028	34,553	33,588	34,368	40,752	5	.	.
WI	31,727	31,727	32,434	32,434	33,141	33,141	2	.	.
WV	24,643	24,643	30,673	30,149	37,228	37,228	3	.	.
WY	21,312	25,902	28,932	29,718	32,268	34,368	8	.	.

Degree Required Data

	Min	Q1	Mean	Median	Q3	Max	N	Range Avg Min	Range Avg Max
High School	16,515	25,663	31,039	29,363	35,328	58,217	127	27,248	38,480
Associate's	17,653	21,507	27,970	27,415	31,200	38,670	18	26,166	35,947
Bachelor's	15,091	28,000	31,619	33,280	37,440	47,840	51	34,216	50,190
Master's	26,040	26,040	36,486	36,486	46,932	46,932	2	.	.
Doctoral									

BOOK REPAIRER

Checks the condition of the materials and determines the most suitable method of repairing. Recreates packaging, labels and barcodes.

Two-Year College
Regional Data

	Min	Q1	Mean	Median	Q3	Max	N	Range Avg Min	Range Avg Max
West & Southwest	18,720	18,720	18,720	18,720	18,720	18,720	1	16,640	18,720
ALL REGIONS	18,720	18,720	18,720	18,720	18,720	18,720	1	16,640	18,720

State Data

	Min	Q1	Mean	Median	Q3	Max	N	Range Avg Min	Range Avg Max
OR	18,720	18,720	18,720	18,720	18,720	18,720	1	16,640	18,720

Degree Required Data

	Min	Q1	Mean	Median	Q3	Max	N	Range Avg Min	Range Avg Max
High School	18,720	18,720	18,720	18,720	18,720	18,720	1	16,640	18,720
Associate's									
Bachelor's									
Master's									
Doctoral									

BOOK REPAIRER - CONTINUED
Four-Year College
Regional Data

	Min	Q1	Mean	Median	Q3	Max	N	Range Avg Min	Range Avg Max
North Atlantic	34,311	34,311	34,311	34,311	34,311	34,311	1	.	.
ALL REGIONS	34,311	34,311	34,311	34,311	34,311	34,311	1	.	.

State Data

	Min	Q1	Mean	Median	Q3	Max	N	Range Avg Min	Range Avg Max
ME	34,311	34,311	34,311	34,311	34,311	34,311	1	.	.

Degree Required Data

	Min	Q1	Mean	Median	Q3	Max	N	Range Avg Min	Range Avg Max
High School	34,311	34,311	34,311	34,311	34,311	34,311	1	.	.
Associate's	.	.	.	.	.	.		.	.
Bachelor's	.	.	.	.	.	.		.	.
Master's	.	.	.	.	.	.		.	.
Doctoral	.	.	.	.	.	.		.	.

BOOK REPAIRER - CONTINUED
University
(Includes ARL Data)
Regional Data

	Min	Q1	Mean	Median	Q3	Max	N	Range Avg Min	Range Avg Max
North Atlantic	28,571	38,822	37,742	38,822	40,990	41,505	5	.	.
Great Lakes & Plains	22,601	27,040	35,047	31,391	45,790	45,790	11	26,978	34,258
Southeast	18,019	19,584	24,449	25,016	26,125	32,935	6	.	.
West & Southwest	14,560	16,640	20,178	18,303	19,509	44,136	29	.	.
ALL REGIONS	14,560	18,019	25,610	22,601	32,935	45,790	51	26,978	34,258

State Data

	Min	Q1	Mean	Median	Q3	Max	N	Range Avg Min	Range Avg Max
AL	26,125	26,125	26,125	26,125	26,125	26,125	1	.	.
AR	18,019	18,019	18,802	18,802	19,584	19,584	2	.	.
CO	44,136	44,136	44,136	44,136	44,136	44,136	1	.	.
IA	30,192	41,948	41,910	43,869	45,790	45,790	6	.	.
IL	27,040	27,040	29,215	29,215	31,391	31,391	2	26,978	34,258
IN	28,912	28,912	28,912	28,912	28,912	28,912	1	.	.
LA	25,082	25,082	25,082	25,082	25,082	25,082	1	.	.
MA	40,990	40,990	41,247	41,247	41,505	41,505	2	.	.
MD	38,822	38,822	38,822	38,822	38,822	38,822	2	.	.
NC	24,950	24,950	28,943	28,943	32,935	32,935	2	.	.
ND	24,118	24,118	24,118	24,118	24,118	24,118	1	.	.
NE	22,601	22,601	22,601	22,601	22,601	22,601	1	.	.
NY	28,571	28,571	28,571	28,571	28,571	28,571	1	.	.
TX	20,290	20,290	24,490	24,490	28,690	28,690	2	.	.
UT	14,560	16,017	18,766	18,097	18,366	38,059	25	.	.
WY	22,908	22,908	22,908	22,908	22,908	22,908	1	.	.

Degree Required Data

	Min	Q1	Mean	Median	Q3	Max	N	Range Avg Min	Range Avg Max
High School	14,560	16,806	23,843	19,442	28,912	45,790	34	.	.
Associate's	24,118	24,118	25,579	25,579	27,040	27,040	2	26,978	34,258
Bachelor's	25,082	25,082	34,242	38,822	38,822	38,822	3	.	.
Master's	.	.	.	.	.	.		.	.
Doctoral	.	.	.	.	.	.		.	.

BOOK REPAIRER - CONTINUED
ALL ACADEMIC LIBRARIES
Regional Data

	Min	Q1	Mean	Median	Q3	Max	N	Range Avg Min	Range Avg Max
North Atlantic	28,571	34,311	37,170	38,822	40,990	41,505	6		
Great Lakes & Plains	22,601	27,040	35,047	31,391	45,790	45,790	11	26,978	34,258
Southeast	18,019	19,584	24,449	25,016	26,125	32,935	6		
West & Southwest	14,560	16,640	20,130	18,303	19,509	44,136	30	16,640	18,720
ALL REGIONS	14,560	18,097	25,644	22,601	32,935	45,790	53	21,809	26,489

State Data

	Min	Q1	Mean	Median	Q3	Max	N	Range Avg Min	Range Avg Max
AL	26,125	26,125	26,125	26,125	26,125	26,125	1		
AR	18,019	18,019	18,802	18,802	19,584	19,584	2		
CO	44,136	44,136	44,136	44,136	44,136	44,136	1		
IA	30,192	41,948	41,910	43,869	45,790	45,790	6		
IL	27,040	27,040	29,215	29,215	31,391	31,391	2	26,978	34,258
IN	28,912	28,912	28,912	28,912	28,912	28,912	1		
LA	25,082	25,082	25,082	25,082	25,082	25,082	1		
MA	40,990	40,990	41,247	41,247	41,505	41,505	2		
MD	38,822	38,822	38,822	38,822	38,822	38,822	2		
ME	34,311	34,311	34,311	34,311	34,311	34,311	1		
NC	24,950	24,950	28,943	28,943	32,935	32,935	2		
ND	24,118	24,118	24,118	24,118	24,118	24,118	1		
NE	22,601	22,601	22,601	22,601	22,601	22,601	1		
NY	28,571	28,571	28,571	28,571	28,571	28,571	1		
OR	18,720	18,720	18,720	18,720	18,720	18,720	1	16,640	18,720
TX	20,290	20,290	24,490	24,490	28,690	28,690	2		
UT	14,560	16,017	18,766	18,097	18,366	38,059	25		
WY	22,908	22,908	22,908	22,908	22,908	22,908	1		

Degree Required Data

	Min	Q1	Mean	Median	Q3	Max	N	Range Avg Min	Range Avg Max
High School	14,560	16,983	23,991	19,442	30,151	45,790	36	16,640	18,720
Associate's	24,118	24,118	25,579	25,579	27,040	27,040	2	26,978	34,258
Bachelor's	25,082	25,082	34,242	38,822	38,822	38,822	3		
Master's									
Doctoral									

PROCESSING ASSISTANT

Prepares materials for placement throughout the library. Prepares spines, labels and barcodes. May send materials to outside bindery for processing. May perform simple repairs as needed. Transfers processed materials to appropriate department.

Two-Year College
Regional Data

	Min	Q1	Mean	Median	Q3	Max	N	Range Avg Min	Range Avg Max
Great Lakes & Plains	15,273	15,273	15,273	15,273	15,273	15,273	1	.	.
Southeast	15,325	15,325	17,350	17,350	19,375	19,375	2	.	.
ALL REGIONS	15,273	15,273	16,658	15,325	19,375	19,375	3	.	.

State Data

	Min	Q1	Mean	Median	Q3	Max	N	Range Avg Min	Range Avg Max
AL	15,325	15,325	15,325	15,325	15,325	15,325	1	.	.
GA	19,375	19,375	19,375	19,375	19,375	19,375	1	.	.
KS	15,273	15,273	15,273	15,273	15,273	15,273	1	.	.

Degree Required Data

	Min	Q1	Mean	Median	Q3	Max	N	Range Avg Min	Range Avg Max
High School	15,273	15,273	17,324	17,324	19,375	19,375	2	.	.
Associate's	15,325	15,325	15,325	15,325	15,325	15,325	1	.	.
Bachelor's	.	.	.	.	.	.		.	.
Master's	.	.	.	.	.	.		.	.
Doctoral	.	.	.	.	.	.		.	.

PROCESSING ASSISTANT - CONTINUED
Four-Year College
Regional Data

	Min	Q1	Mean	Median	Q3	Max	N	Range Avg Min	Range Avg Max
North Atlantic	21,091	22,360	28,544	28,922	34,311	35,654	6	21,289	30,545
Great Lakes & Plains	15,600	15,600	19,614	19,614	23,629	23,629	2	.	.
Southeast	15,600	15,600	20,878	21,129	25,904	25,904	3	.	.
West & Southwest	32,988	32,988	33,736	33,852	34,368	34,368	3	.	.
ALL REGIONS	15,600	21,129	26,738	26,191	33,852	35,654	14	21,289	30,545

State Data

	Min	Q1	Mean	Median	Q3	Max	N	Range Avg Min	Range Avg Max
CO	32,988	32,988	33,736	33,852	34,368	34,368	3		
IL	15,600	15,600	15,600	15,600	15,600	15,600	1		
ME	31,366	31,366	32,839	32,839	34,311	34,311	2		
NY	26,478	26,478	31,066	31,066	35,654	35,654	2		
OH	23,629	23,629	23,629	23,629	23,629	23,629	1		
PA	21,091	21,091	21,091	21,091	21,091	21,091	1	22,298	37,898
SC	15,600	15,600	20,752	20,752	25,904	25,904	2		
VT	22,360	22,360	22,360	22,360	22,360	22,360	1	20,280	23,192
WV	21,129	21,129	21,129	21,129	21,129	21,129	1		

Degree Required Data

	Min	Q1	Mean	Median	Q3	Max	N	Range Avg Min	Range Avg Max
High School	15,600	21,744	27,925	28,922	34,082	35,654	12	21,289	30,545
Associate's	15,600	15,600	19,614	19,614	23,629	23,629	2		
Bachelor's									
Master's									
Doctoral									

PROCESSING ASSISTANT - CONTINUED
University
(Includes ARL Data)
Regional Data

	Min	Q1	Mean	Median	Q3	Max	N	Range Avg Min	Range Avg Max
North Atlantic	20,929	25,712	30,763	29,628	35,407	49,996	16		
Great Lakes & Plains	17,600	19,698	28,831	27,436	32,198	80,000	25	20,353	31,434
Southeast	16,398	19,200	23,827	24,280	27,039	35,936	41	24,638	43,066
West & Southwest	16,947	21,276	26,399	25,011	29,952	40,128	18		
ALL REGIONS	16,398	19,874	26,651	26,042	29,332	80,000	100	21,781	35,311

State Data

	Min	Q1	Mean	Median	Q3	Max	N	Range Avg Min	Range Avg Max
AL	19,510	19,510	22,495	22,495	25,480	25,480	2	.	.
AR	18,019	18,019	18,019	18,019	18,019	18,019	1	.	.
AZ	27,192	27,192	30,056	29,528	33,447	33,447	3	.	.
CA	27,768	27,768	27,768	27,768	27,768	27,768	1	.	.
CO	17,550	26,859	33,449	38,058	40,038	40,128	4	.	.
DC	26,083	26,083	28,714	28,714	31,346	31,346	2	.	.
FL	19,200	19,200	19,595	19,200	19,200	23,085	12	.	.
GA	16,398	16,398	19,654	19,654	22,910	22,910	2	.	.
IA	27,436	27,666	32,940	33,011	38,419	39,797	7	.	.
IL	17,600	18,720	25,250	27,430	29,120	31,200	6	22,204	36,837
IN	19,698	19,698	20,429	20,429	21,160	21,160	2	.	.
KY	25,667	25,667	25,667	25,667	25,667	25,667	1	.	.
LA	24,000	24,000	25,000	25,000	26,000	26,000	2	.	.
MA	49,996	49,996	49,996	49,996	49,996	49,996	1	.	.
MD	25,342	25,804	30,328	28,193	34,852	39,585	8	.	.
MN	24,158	24,158	27,730	26,834	32,198	32,198	3	.	.
NC	23,073	24,844	26,956	27,118	27,416	33,770	10	.	.
ND	18,412	18,412	18,498	18,498	18,583	18,583	2	.	.
NE	18,512	18,512	19,323	19,323	20,134	20,134	2	.	.
NY	20,929	20,929	28,042	29,137	34,060	34,060	3	.	.
OH	39,735	39,735	59,868	59,868	80,000	80,000	2	18,502	26,031
OR	21,276	21,276	21,276	21,276	21,276	21,276	1	.	.
PA	21,282	21,282	29,018	29,018	36,754	36,754	2	.	.
SC	26,528	27,327	29,669	27,949	32,324	35,936	6	.	.
SD	19,278	19,278	19,278	19,278	19,278	19,278	1	.	.
TN	21,258	22,905	24,142	24,611	25,379	26,088	4	24,638	43,066
TX	16,947	18,384	20,833	21,276	23,570	23,630	7	.	.
UT	26,392	26,392	26,392	26,392	26,392	26,392	1	.	.
VA	19,664	19,664	19,664	19,664	19,664	19,664	1	.	.
WY	29,952	29,952	29,952	29,952	29,952	29,952	1	.	.

Degree Required Data

	Min	Q1	Mean	Median	Q3	Max	N	Range Avg Min	Range Avg Max
High School	16,398	19,200	25,363	24,611	27,416	80,000	70	21,553	33,833
Associate's	18,412	23,570	27,516	29,120	31,346	33,447	7	22,922	42,702
Bachelor's	22,910	26,000	29,997	27,826	35,936	39,585	11	.	.
Master's	.	.	.	.	.	.		.	.
Doctoral	.	.	.	.	.	.		.	.

PROCESSING ASSISTANT - CONTINUED
ALL ACADEMIC LIBRARIES
Regional Data

	Min	Q1	Mean	Median	Q3	Max	N	Range Avg Min	Range Avg Max
North Atlantic	20,929	25,342	30,158	29,628	34,311	49,996	22	21,289	30,545
Great Lakes & Plains	15,273	18,999	27,689	26,966	31,699	80,000	28	20,353	31,434
Southeast	15,325	19,200	23,353	23,543	26,528	35,936	46	24,638	43,066
West & Southwest	16,947	21,276	27,447	27,192	33,447	40,128	21	.	.
ALL REGIONS	15,273	19,698	26,405	25,904	29,952	80,000	117	21,658	34,120

State Data

	Min	Q1	Mean	Median	Q3	Max	N	Range Avg Min	Range Avg Max
AL	15,325	15,325	20,105	19,510	25,480	25,480	3	.	.
AR	18,019	18,019	18,019	18,019	18,019	18,019	1	.	.
AZ	27,192	27,192	30,056	29,528	33,447	33,447	3	.	.
CA	27,768	27,768	27,768	27,768	27,768	27,768	1	.	.
CO	17,550	32,988	33,572	34,368	39,948	40,128	7	.	.
DC	26,083	26,083	28,714	28,714	31,346	31,346	2	.	.
FL	19,200	19,200	19,595	19,200	19,200	23,085	12	.	.
GA	16,398	16,398	19,561	19,375	22,910	22,910	3	.	.
IA	27,436	27,666	32,940	33,011	38,419	39,797	7	.	.
IL	15,600	17,600	23,872	27,098	29,120	31,200	7	22,204	36,837
IN	19,698	19,698	20,429	20,429	21,160	21,160	2	.	.
KS	15,273	15,273	15,273	15,273	15,273	15,273	1	.	.
KY	25,667	25,667	25,667	25,667	25,667	25,667	1	.	.
LA	24,000	24,000	25,000	25,000	26,000	26,000	2	.	.
MA	49,996	49,996	49,996	49,996	49,996	49,996	1	.	.
MD	25,342	25,804	30,328	28,193	34,852	39,585	8	.	.
ME	31,366	31,366	32,839	32,839	34,311	34,311	2	.	.
MN	24,158	24,158	27,730	26,834	32,198	32,198	3	.	.
NC	23,073	24,844	26,956	27,118	27,416	33,770	10	.	.
ND	18,412	18,412	18,498	18,498	18,583	18,583	2	.	.
NE	18,512	18,512	19,323	19,323	20,134	20,134	2	.	.
NY	20,929	26,478	29,252	29,137	34,060	35,654	5	.	.
OH	23,629	23,629	47,788	39,735	80,000	80,000	3	18,502	26,031
OR	21,276	21,276	21,276	21,276	21,276	21,276	1	.	.
PA	21,091	21,091	26,376	21,282	36,754	36,754	3	22,298	37,898
SC	15,600	26,216	27,440	27,577	30,198	35,936	8	.	.
SD	19,278	19,278	19,278	19,278	19,278	19,278	1	.	.
TN	21,258	22,905	24,142	24,611	25,379	26,088	4	24,638	43,066
TX	16,947	18,384	20,833	21,276	23,570	23,630	7	.	.
UT	26,392	26,392	26,392	26,392	26,392	26,392	1	.	.
VA	19,664	19,664	19,664	19,664	19,664	19,664	1	.	.
VT	22,360	22,360	22,360	22,360	22,360	22,360	1	20,280	23,192
WV	21,129	21,129	21,129	21,129	21,129	21,129	1	.	.
WY	29,952	29,952	29,952	29,952	29,952	29,952	1	.	.

Degree Required Data

	Min	Q1	Mean	Median	Q3	Max	N	Range Avg Min	Range Avg Max
High School	15,273	19,239	25,538	24,756	27,766	80,000	84	21,477	32,894
Associate's	15,325	18,412	24,717	25,410	29,528	33,447	10	22,922	42,702
Bachelor's	22,910	26,000	29,997	27,826	35,936	39,585	11	.	.
Master's	.	.	.	.	.	.	.	.	.
Doctoral	.	.	.	.	.	.	.	.	.

SERIALS PROCESSING ASSISTANT

Orders, receives and prepares library subscriptions. Updates online systems to reflect holdings, locations and identity. Monitors subscription status, processes invoices and renewals, and resolves issues with vendors as needed.

Two-Year College
Regional Data

	Min	Q1	Mean	Median	Q3	Max	N	Range Avg Min	Range Avg Max
Great Lakes & Plains	22,631	22,631	23,858	23,858	25,086	25,086	2	.	.
West & Southwest	22,858	24,077	28,245	26,689	33,912	35,246	6	.	.
ALL REGIONS	22,631	23,468	27,148	25,876	30,312	35,246	8	.	.

State Data

	Min	Q1	Mean	Median	Q3	Max	N	Range Avg Min	Range Avg Max
HI	33,912	33,912	33,912	33,912	33,912	33,912	1	.	.
IA	25,086	25,086	25,086	25,086	25,086	25,086	1	.	.
IL	22,631	22,631	22,631	22,631	22,631	22,631	1	.	.
TX	22,858	24,077	27,112	26,667	26,711	35,246	5	.	.

Degree Required Data

	Min	Q1	Mean	Median	Q3	Max	N	Range Avg Min	Range Avg Max
High School	22,858	23,468	26,890	25,394	30,312	33,912	4	.	.
Associate's	22,631	22,631	27,654	25,086	35,246	35,246	3	.	.
Bachelor's	.	.	.	.	.	.	.	.	.
Master's	.	.	.	.	.	.	.	.	.
Doctoral	.	.	.	.	.	.	.	.	.

SERIALS PROCESSING ASSISTANT - CONTINUED
Four-Year College
Regional Data

	Min	Q1	Mean	Median	Q3	Max	N	Range Avg Min	Range Avg Max
North Atlantic	25,376	30,651	35,189	32,531	40,609	48,549	8	33,509	56,971
Great Lakes & Plains	19,552	21,715	28,672	29,120	32,344	44,000	7	26,863	39,094
Southeast	17,653	23,171	25,682	26,352	28,614	31,954	10	.	.
West & Southwest	23,615	28,464	32,896	34,573	36,694	40,092	8	.	.
ALL REGIONS	17,653	25,376	30,370	30,498	34,368	48,549	33	29,078	45,053

State Data

	Min	Q1	Mean	Median	Q3	Max	N	Range Avg Min	Range Avg Max
AL	17,653	17,653	17,653	17,653	17,653	17,653	1	.	.
CO	30,144	34,368	35,598	36,497	36,890	40,092	5	.	.
GA	20,030	20,030	24,045	24,045	28,059	28,059	2	.	.
IL	29,120	29,120	29,120	29,120	29,120	29,120	1	.	.
KY	23,171	23,171	24,296	24,296	25,420	25,420	2	.	.
MA	31,200	31,200	31,200	31,200	31,200	31,200	1	.	.
MD	41,407	41,407	41,407	41,407	41,407	41,407	1	.	.
ME	30,805	30,805	30,805	30,805	30,805	30,805	1	.	.
MN	30,576	30,576	37,288	37,288	44,000	44,000	2	27,248	38,480
NY	25,376	25,376	29,619	29,619	33,863	33,863	2	.	.
OH	19,552	19,552	21,556	21,715	23,400	23,400	3	.	.
OR	34,777	34,777	34,777	34,777	34,777	34,777	1	.	.
PA	30,498	30,498	39,619	39,811	48,549	48,549	3	33,509	56,971
SC	27,284	27,284	27,284	27,284	27,284	27,284	1	.	.
SD	32,344	32,344	32,344	32,344	32,344	32,344	1	26,478	39,707
TN	31,429	31,429	31,429	31,429	31,429	31,429	1	.	.
UT	23,615	23,615	25,200	25,200	26,784	26,784	2	.	.
VA	23,200	23,200	23,200	23,200	23,200	23,200	1	.	.
WV	28,614	28,614	30,284	30,284	31,954	31,954	2	.	.

Degree Required Data

	Min	Q1	Mean	Median	Q3	Max	N	Range Avg Min	Range Avg Max
High School	17,653	21,715	29,396	30,576	34,777	41,407	15	26,863	39,094
Associate's	23,400	23,400	23,400	23,400	23,400	23,400	1	.	.
Bachelor's	23,200	27,422	32,167	30,651	35,883	48,549	16	33,509	56,971
Master's	.	.	.	.	.	.		.	.
Doctoral	.	.	.	.	.	.		.	.

SERIALS PROCESSING ASSISTANT - CONTINUED
University
(Includes ARL Data)
Regional Data

	Min	Q1	Mean	Median	Q3	Max	N	Range Avg Min	Range Avg Max
North Atlantic	19,094	27,429	34,629	35,429	39,271	47,332	13	23,067	32,240
Great Lakes & Plains	17,572	24,674	31,553	29,180	37,668	68,571	41	26,052	37,435
Southeast	17,318	22,639	27,237	27,039	32,365	37,719	51	20,363	35,589
West & Southwest	14,560	21,129	29,302	29,340	36,066	47,436	46	.	.
ALL REGIONS	14,560	23,688	29,675	28,113	35,310	68,571	151	24,387	35,687

State Data

	Min	Q1	Mean	Median	Q3	Max	N	Range Avg Min	Range Avg Max
AL	21,320	21,320	25,363	26,585	28,185	28,185	3	.	.
AR	17,318	17,449	20,431	19,584	20,225	32,365	9	.	.
AZ	31,388	33,075	35,901	35,037	37,711	43,156	6	.	.
CA	27,768	27,768	31,685	33,268	34,020	34,020	3	.	.
CO	30,912	36,036	38,321	37,884	40,032	47,436	9	.	.
CT	45,831	45,831	46,582	46,582	47,332	47,332	2	.	.
DC	27,429	27,429	27,429	27,429	27,429	27,429	2	.	.
FL	20,050	20,050	23,135	22,316	27,040	27,040	3	.	.
GA	17,818	17,818	20,229	20,229	22,639	22,639	2	.	.
IA	28,919	30,214	37,121	38,419	41,948	44,516	11	.	.
IL	20,800	27,098	31,770	34,960	35,360	37,440	6	34,216	50,190
IN	21,260	23,471	25,434	26,270	27,397	27,934	4	.	.
KY	28,142	28,142	28,142	28,142	28,142	28,142	1	.	.
LA	24,000	24,000	28,606	26,711	35,106	35,106	3	.	.
MA	36,754	36,754	38,432	39,271	39,271	39,271	3	27,040	41,600
MI	29,580	29,580	34,509	34,509	39,437	39,437	2	.	.
MN	26,707	26,707	35,235	35,235	43,763	43,763	2	.	.
NC	23,304	26,329	29,578	28,113	32,572	37,719	15	.	.
ND	17,572	18,882	21,633	22,144	24,385	24,674	4	.	.
NE	22,752	22,826	24,100	23,752	25,374	26,143	4	.	.
NM	19,943	19,943	19,943	19,943	19,943	19,943	1	.	.
NY	19,094	26,690	32,449	34,857	38,209	40,989	4	19,094	22,880
OH	27,165	28,877	38,309	29,180	37,751	68,571	5	17,888	24,679
OR	31,296	31,296	36,924	36,924	42,552	42,552	2	.	.
PA	22,591	22,591	28,533	28,533	34,475	34,475	2	.	.
SC	31,979	31,979	33,964	34,957	34,957	34,957	3	.	.
SD	24,211	24,211	24,211	24,211	24,211	24,211	1	.	.
TN	24,420	24,960	28,015	25,608	33,120	35,460	7	20,363	35,589
TX	18,024	21,121	24,441	22,858	25,769	36,841	14	.	.
UT	14,560	17,170	24,019	22,635	28,831	40,321	8	.	.
VA	26,774	30,413	32,726	34,600	34,694	37,149	5	.	.
WI	23,688	23,688	27,411	27,411	31,134	31,134	2	.	.
WY	18,840	18,840	21,480	19,944	25,656	25,656	3	.	.

Degree Required Data

	Min	Q1	Mean	Median	Q3	Max	N	Range Avg Min	Range Avg Max
High School	14,560	21,819	28,148	26,774	32,190	68,571	85	18,713	28,316
Associate's	17,572	24,674	29,671	27,429	36,066	39,271	19	.	.
Bachelor's	21,260	27,040	31,302	33,120	34,694	43,156	21	31,824	47,327
Master's	24,000	24,000	29,553	29,553	35,106	35,106	2	.	.
Doctoral	.	.	.	.	.	.		.	.

SERIALS PROCESSING ASSISTANT - CONTINUED
ALL ACADEMIC LIBRARIES
Regional Data

	Min	Q1	Mean	Median	Q3	Max	N	Range Avg Min	Range Avg Max
North Atlantic	19,094	30,498	34,842	34,475	39,811	48,549	21	26,548	40,484
Great Lakes & Plains	17,572	24,211	30,842	29,020	37,440	68,571	50	26,322	37,988
Southeast	17,318	23,171	26,982	27,039	31,954	37,719	61	20,363	35,589
West & Southwest	14,560	22,869	29,676	30,528	36,051	47,436	60	.	.
ALL REGIONS	14,560	23,844	29,689	28,163	34,957	68,571	192	25,794	38,497

State Data

	Min	Q1	Mean	Median	Q3	Max	N	Range Avg Min	Range Avg Max
AL	17,653	19,487	23,436	23,953	27,385	28,185	4	.	.
AR	17,318	17,449	20,431	19,584	20,225	32,365	9	.	.
AZ	31,388	33,075	35,901	35,037	37,711	43,156	6	.	.
CA	27,768	27,768	31,685	33,268	34,020	34,020	3	.	.
CO	30,144	34,368	37,349	36,694	40,032	47,436	14	.	.
CT	45,831	45,831	46,582	46,582	47,332	47,332	2	.	.
DC	27,429	27,429	27,429	27,429	27,429	27,429	2	.	.
FL	20,050	20,050	23,135	22,316	27,040	27,040	3	.	.
GA	17,818	18,924	22,137	21,335	25,349	28,059	4	.	.
HI	33,912	33,912	33,912	33,912	33,912	33,912	1	.	.
IA	25,086	30,214	36,118	38,044	41,948	44,516	12	.	.
IL	20,800	24,864	30,296	31,866	35,335	37,440	8	34,216	50,190
IN	21,260	23,471	25,434	26,270	27,397	27,934	4	.	.
KY	23,171	23,171	25,578	25,420	28,142	28,142	3	.	.
LA	24,000	24,000	28,606	26,711	35,106	35,106	3	.	.
MA	31,200	33,977	36,624	38,013	39,271	39,271	4	27,040	41,600
MD	41,407	41,407	41,407	41,407	41,407	41,407	1	.	.
ME	30,805	30,805	30,805	30,805	30,805	30,805	1	.	.
MI	29,580	29,580	34,509	34,509	39,437	39,437	2	.	.
MN	26,707	28,642	36,262	37,170	43,882	44,000	4	27,248	38,480
NC	23,304	26,329	29,578	28,113	32,572	37,719	15	.	.
ND	17,572	18,882	21,633	22,144	24,385	24,674	4	.	.
NE	22,752	22,826	24,100	23,752	25,374	26,143	4	.	.
NM	19,943	19,943	19,943	19,943	19,943	19,943	1	.	.
NY	19,094	25,376	31,506	34,074	35,429	40,989	6	19,094	22,880
OH	19,552	22,558	32,026	28,021	33,466	68,571	8	17,888	24,679
OR	31,296	31,296	36,208	34,777	42,552	42,552	3	.	.
PA	22,591	30,498	35,185	34,475	39,811	48,549	5	33,509	56,971
SC	27,284	29,631	32,294	33,468	34,957	34,957	4	.	.
SD	24,211	24,211	28,278	28,278	32,344	32,344	2	26,478	39,707
TN	24,420	24,996	28,442	26,558	32,274	35,460	8	20,363	35,589
TX	18,024	21,129	25,144	24,077	26,711	36,841	19	.	.
UT	14,560	19,780	24,255	23,980	26,784	40,321	10	.	.
VA	23,200	26,774	31,138	32,507	34,694	37,149	6	.	.
WI	23,688	23,688	27,411	27,411	31,134	31,134	2	.	.
WV	28,614	28,614	30,284	30,284	31,954	31,954	2	.	.
WY	18,840	18,840	21,480	19,944	25,656	25,656	3	.	.

Degree Required Data

	Min	Q1	Mean	Median	Q3	Max	N	Range Avg Min	Range Avg Max
High School	14,560	22,068	28,280	27,053	34,099	68,571	104	21,973	32,627
Associate's	17,572	24,096	29,135	27,429	35,246	39,271	23	.	.
Bachelor's	21,260	27,040	31,676	31,200	34,694	48,549	37	32,245	49,738
Master's	24,000	24,000	29,553	29,553	35,106	35,106	2	.	.
Doctoral									

COLLECTION DEVELOPMENT/MANAGEMENT

Analyzes community and library data to determine areas of the collection which need updating. Selects materials to update the collection. Performs related work as required.

Four-Year College
Regional Data

	Min	Q1	Mean	Median	Q3	Max	N	Range Avg Min	Range Avg Max
Southeast	27,198	27,198	27,198	27,198	27,198	27,198	1	.	.
West & Southwest	47,316	47,316	47,316	47,316	47,316	47,316	1	.	.
ALL REGIONS	27,198	27,198	37,257	37,257	47,316	47,316	2	.	.

State Data

	Min	Q1	Mean	Median	Q3	Max	N	Range Avg Min	Range Avg Max
CO	47,316	47,316	47,316	47,316	47,316	47,316	1	.	.
SC	27,198	27,198	27,198	27,198	27,198	27,198	1	.	.

Degree Required Data

	Min	Q1	Mean	Median	Q3	Max	N	Range Avg Min	Range Avg Max
High School	27,198	27,198	37,257	37,257	47,316	47,316	2	.	.
Associate's									
Bachelor's									
Master's									
Doctoral									

COLLECTION DEVELOPMENT/MANAGEMENT - CONTINUED
University
(Includes ARL Data)
Regional Data

	Min	Q1	Mean	Median	Q3	Max	N	Range Avg Min	Range Avg Max
North Atlantic	28,571	28,571	28,571	28,571	28,571	28,571	2	.	.
Great Lakes & Plains	44,550	44,550	45,170	45,170	45,790	45,790	2	.	.
Southeast	21,238	24,856	29,462	29,064	29,472	42,678	5	31,450	54,964
West & Southwest	20,800	23,028	38,666	31,606	36,446	88,512	6	.	.
ALL REGIONS	20,800	24,856	35,119	29,064	42,678	88,512	15	31,450	54,964

State Data

	Min	Q1	Mean	Median	Q3	Max	N	Range Avg Min	Range Avg Max
CA	88,512	88,512	88,512	88,512	88,512	88,512	1	.	.
DC	28,571	28,571	28,571	28,571	28,571	28,571	2	.	.
FL	21,238	21,238	21,238	21,238	21,238	21,238	1	.	.
IA	45,790	45,790	45,790	45,790	45,790	45,790	1	.	.
IN	44,550	44,550	44,550	44,550	44,550	44,550	1	.	.
NC	42,678	42,678	42,678	42,678	42,678	42,678	1	.	.
TN	24,856	24,856	27,797	29,064	29,472	29,472	3	31,450	54,964
TX	36,384	36,384	36,415	36,415	36,446	36,446	2	.	.
UT	20,800	20,800	23,814	23,814	26,828	26,828	2	.	.
WY	23,028	23,028	23,028	23,028	23,028	23,028	1	.	.

Degree Required Data

	Min	Q1	Mean	Median	Q3	Max	N	Range Avg Min	Range Avg Max
High School	20,800	21,238	30,759	29,064	36,446	44,550	7	.	.
Associate's	.	.	.	.	.	.		.	.
Bachelor's	24,856	28,571	30,830	28,571	29,472	42,678	5	31,450	54,964
Master's	88,512	88,512	88,512	88,512	88,512	88,512	1	.	.
Doctoral	.	.	.	.	.	.		.	.

COLLECTION DEVELOPMENT/MANAGEMENT - CONTINUED
ALL ACADEMIC LIBRARIES
Regional Data

	Min	Q1	Mean	Median	Q3	Max	N	Range Avg Min	Range Avg Max
North Atlantic	28,571	28,571	28,571	28,571	28,571	28,571	2	.	.
Great Lakes & Plains	44,550	44,550	45,170	45,170	45,790	45,790	2	.	.
Southeast	21,238	24,856	29,084	28,131	29,472	42,678	6	31,450	54,964
West & Southwest	20,800	23,028	39,902	36,384	47,316	88,512	7	.	.
ALL REGIONS	20,800	26,828	35,371	29,064	42,678	88,512	17	31,450	54,964

State Data

	Min	Q1	Mean	Median	Q3	Max	N	Range Avg Min	Range Avg Max
CA	88,512	88,512	88,512	88,512	88,512	88,512	1	.	.
CO	47,316	47,316	47,316	47,316	47,316	47,316	1	.	.
DC	28,571	28,571	28,571	28,571	28,571	28,571	2	.	.
FL	21,238	21,238	21,238	21,238	21,238	21,238	1	.	.
IA	45,790	45,790	45,790	45,790	45,790	45,790	1	.	.
IN	44,550	44,550	44,550	44,550	44,550	44,550	1	.	.
NC	42,678	42,678	42,678	42,678	42,678	42,678	1	.	.
SC	27,198	27,198	27,198	27,198	27,198	27,198	1	.	.
TN	24,856	24,856	27,797	29,064	29,472	29,472	3	31,450	54,964
TX	36,384	36,384	36,415	36,415	36,446	36,446	2	.	.
UT	20,800	20,800	23,814	23,814	26,828	26,828	2	.	.
WY	23,028	23,028	23,028	23,028	23,028	23,028	1	.	.

Degree Required Data

	Min	Q1	Mean	Median	Q3	Max	N	Range Avg Min	Range Avg Max
High School	20,800	26,828	32,203	29,064	36,446	47,316	9	.	.
Associate's	.	.	.	.	.	.		.	.
Bachelor's	24,856	28,571	30,830	28,571	29,472	42,678	5	31,450	54,964
Master's	88,512	88,512	88,512	88,512	88,512	88,512	1	.	.
Doctoral	.	.	.	.	.	.		.	.

INTER-LIBRARY LOAN ASSISTANT

Coordinates materials loaned through the inter-library loan system for patrons, other libraries and institutions. Searches databases and the Internet for inter-library loan requests utilizing ISBN, ISSN and citation numbers. Determines best sources for materials.

Two-Year College
Regional Data

	Min	Q1	Mean	Median	Q3	Max	N	Range Avg Min	Range Avg Max
North Atlantic	22,416	22,416	22,416	22,416	22,416	22,416	1	.	.
Great Lakes & Plains	15,787	18,714	25,516	23,540	24,960	44,579	5	.	.
Southeast	26,499	26,499	26,499	26,499	26,499	26,499	1	22,173	45,531
West & Southwest	23,071	23,071	27,349	27,349	31,626	31,626	2	.	.
ALL REGIONS	15,787	22,416	25,688	23,540	26,499	44,579	9	22,173	45,531

State Data

	Min	Q1	Mean	Median	Q3	Max	N	Range Avg Min	Range Avg Max
IA	18,714	18,714	21,127	21,127	23,540	23,540	2	.	.
KS	15,787	15,787	15,787	15,787	15,787	15,787	1	.	.
MD	22,416	22,416	22,416	22,416	22,416	22,416	1	.	.
MN	24,960	24,960	34,770	34,770	44,579	44,579	2	.	.
TX	23,071	23,071	27,349	27,349	31,626	31,626	2	.	.
VA	26,499	26,499	26,499	26,499	26,499	26,499	1	22,173	45,531

Degree Required Data

	Min	Q1	Mean	Median	Q3	Max	N	Range Avg Min	Range Avg Max
High School	15,787	15,787	17,251	17,251	18,714	18,714	2	.	.
Associate's	22,416	23,071	28,622	25,020	31,626	44,579	6	22,173	45,531
Bachelor's	.	.	.	.	.	.		.	.
Master's	24,960	24,960	24,960	24,960	24,960	24,960	1	.	.
Doctoral	.	.	.	.	.	.		.	.

INTER-LIBRARY LOAN ASSISTANT - CONTINUED
Four-Year College
Regional Data

	Min	Q1	Mean	Median	Q3	Max	N	Range Avg Min	Range Avg Max
North Atlantic	19,000	25,085	28,358	26,532	29,600	45,938	10	.	.
Great Lakes & Plains	10,712	22,730	26,452	28,048	31,990	35,131	14	22,554	32,198
Southeast	18,359	26,475	29,002	29,374	33,201	37,228	6	.	.
West & Southwest	16,640	21,063	32,820	37,812	38,340	46,498	7	.	.
ALL REGIONS	10,712	23,296	28,586	28,163	33,201	46,498	37	22,554	32,198

State Data

	Min	Q1	Mean	Median	Q3	Max	N	Range Avg Min	Range Avg Max
AL	18,359	18,359	18,359	18,359	18,359	18,359	1	.	.
CO	37,812	38,076	40,248	38,340	42,419	46,498	4	.	.
GA	33,201	33,201	33,201	33,201	33,201	33,201	1	.	.
IA	28,288	28,288	28,288	28,288	28,288	28,288	1	.	.
IL	18,720	18,720	23,493	19,760	32,000	32,000	3	.	.
KY	31,550	31,550	31,550	31,550	31,550	31,550	1	.	.
MD	33,485	33,485	33,485	33,485	33,485	33,485	1	.	.
ME	25,085	25,517	26,024	26,235	26,532	26,543	4	.	.
MN	29,848	29,848	33,155	34,486	35,131	35,131	3	30,472	44,928
MO	22,730	22,730	25,269	25,269	27,807	27,807	2	.	.
MT	16,640	16,640	16,640	16,640	16,640	16,640	1	.	.
ND	10,712	10,712	17,176	17,176	23,640	23,640	2	10,712	11,960
NY	23,296	23,296	26,448	26,448	29,600	29,600	2	.	.
OH	31,949	31,949	31,949	31,949	31,949	31,949	1	.	.
OR	31,050	31,050	31,050	31,050	31,050	31,050	1	.	.
PA	19,000	19,000	31,034	28,163	45,938	45,938	3	.	.
SC	27,198	27,198	27,198	27,198	27,198	27,198	1	.	.
SD	23,271	23,271	27,631	27,631	31,990	31,990	2	26,478	39,707
UT	21,063	21,063	21,063	21,063	21,063	21,063	1	.	.
VA	26,475	26,475	26,475	26,475	26,475	26,475	1	.	.
WV	37,228	37,228	37,228	37,228	37,228	37,228	1	.	.

Degree Required Data

	Min	Q1	Mean	Median	Q3	Max	N	Range Avg Min	Range Avg Max
High School	10,712	22,335	27,810	28,399	33,986	38,340	12	22,554	32,198
Associate's	19,760	22,730	29,902	23,296	37,228	46,498	5	.	.
Bachelor's	16,640	23,640	28,384	28,163	31,949	45,938	19	.	.
Master's	.	.	.	.	.	.	.	.	.
Doctoral	.	.	.	.	.	.	.	.	.

INTER-LIBRARY LOAN ASSISTANT - CONTINUED
University
(Includes ARL Data)
Regional Data

	Min	Q1	Mean	Median	Q3	Max	N	Range Avg Min	Range Avg Max
North Atlantic	16,420	27,768	34,424	33,690	39,270	56,521	31	22,880	22,880
Great Lakes & Plains	18,100	23,358	30,700	28,594	35,851	80,000	61	22,585	33,729
Southeast	12,792	21,581	25,557	25,948	28,706	39,850	64	18,886	33,030
West & Southwest	18,720	23,088	28,252	26,350	31,296	47,436	54	.	.
ALL REGIONS	12,792	23,088	29,053	27,775	32,730	80,000	210	21,697	32,198

State Data

	Min	Q1	Mean	Median	Q3	Max	N	Range Avg Min	Range Avg Max
AL	19,220	21,613	26,960	26,198	30,494	39,850	8	.	.
AR	15,535	17,769	21,229	19,368	23,745	37,170	12	.	.
AZ	24,388	25,789	30,712	28,913	35,117	37,083	9	.	.
CA	30,660	30,936	34,669	32,565	38,403	42,888	4	.	.
CO	23,972	31,728	37,116	38,220	39,180	47,436	9	.	.
CT	43,307	43,307	49,914	49,914	56,521	56,521	2	.	.
DC	16,420	16,420	21,924	21,924	27,429	27,429	2	.	.
FL	18,925	21,317	25,079	26,776	28,195	29,131	8	.	.
GA	12,792	15,591	20,090	20,334	24,589	26,900	4	.	.
IA	28,898	31,571	39,102	41,948	45,790	45,790	10	.	.
IL	18,100	27,098	30,735	31,821	33,946	41,101	17	24,950	38,480
IN	19,240	21,996	24,708	23,452	28,562	29,795	12	.	.
KY	34,186	34,186	34,186	34,186	34,186	34,186	1	.	.
LA	24,000	24,000	29,232	26,484	37,211	37,211	3	.	.
MA	28,954	35,404	39,428	39,270	41,835	49,971	12	.	.
MD	27,768	28,353	30,393	30,685	32,433	32,433	4	.	.
MI	26,664	26,664	28,756	28,410	31,195	31,195	3	.	.
MN	27,250	27,560	31,441	27,872	35,521	39,004	5	.	.
MO	19,130	19,130	19,130	19,130	19,130	19,130	1	.	.
NC	23,073	26,266	28,020	28,291	29,652	32,361	12	.	.
ND	18,255	18,255	21,033	21,991	22,854	22,854	3	.	.
NE	20,401	20,401	23,991	25,513	26,058	26,058	3	.	.
NM	19,943	19,943	23,783	23,783	27,623	27,623	2	.	.
NY	22,880	26,099	31,272	30,857	35,429	48,000	9	22,880	22,880
OH	27,311	35,851	44,422	36,456	42,491	80,000	5	21,008	30,562
OR	21,276	21,276	26,224	26,100	31,296	31,296	3	.	.
PA	19,152	19,152	23,649	23,649	28,145	28,145	2	.	.
SC	26,289	26,289	27,529	28,059	28,238	28,238	3	.	.
SD	22,111	22,111	22,111	22,111	22,111	22,111	1	.	.
TN	20,571	21,704	24,695	24,957	26,515	30,636	8	18,886	33,030
TX	18,768	20,042	23,609	23,904	26,236	30,380	12	.	.
UT	18,720	20,625	22,996	20,925	23,462	31,250	5	.	.
VA	22,880	25,132	29,196	28,766	31,060	38,142	5	.	.
WA	30,564	30,564	30,564	30,564	30,564	30,564	2	.	.
WI	20,790	20,790	20,790	20,790	20,790	20,790	1	.	.
WY	19,884	22,560	23,853	23,586	24,834	28,980	8	.	.

Degree Required Data

	Min	Q1	Mean	Median	Q3	Max	N	Range Avg Min	Range Avg Max
High School	12,792	22,111	28,500	27,648	31,821	80,000	126	18,855	30,217
Associate's	18,255	25,789	30,107	28,594	35,419	49,971	19	24,950	38,480
Bachelor's	16,420	24,762	29,360	27,892	34,051	43,307	36	.	.
Master's	33,690	33,690	33,690	33,690	33,690	33,690	1	.	.
Doctoral	.	.	.	.	.	.	.	.	.

INTER-LIBRARY LOAN ASSISTANT - CONTINUED
ALL ACADEMIC LIBRARIES
Regional Data

	Min	Q1	Mean	Median	Q3	Max	N	Range Avg Min	Range Avg Max
North Atlantic	16,420	26,520	32,693	31,401	39,270	56,521	42	22,880	22,880
Great Lakes & Plains	10,712	23,182	29,633	28,411	34,216	80,000	80	22,573	33,155
Southeast	12,792	22,277	25,862	26,289	28,850	39,850	71	19,982	37,197
West & Southwest	16,640	23,071	28,731	27,183	33,917	47,436	63	.	.
ALL REGIONS	10,712	23,081	28,867	27,724	32,581	80,000	256	21,951	33,309

State Data

	Min	Q1	Mean	Median	Q3	Max	N	Range Avg Min	Range Avg Max
AL	18,359	20,885	26,004	23,005	29,995	39,850	9	.	.
AR	15,535	17,769	21,229	19,368	23,745	37,170	12	.	.
AZ	24,388	25,789	30,712	28,913	35,117	37,083	9	.	.
CA	30,660	30,936	34,669	32,565	38,403	42,888	4	.	.
CO	23,972	37,812	38,079	38,340	39,180	47,436	13	.	.
CT	43,307	43,307	49,914	49,914	56,521	56,521	2	.	.
DC	16,420	16,420	21,924	21,924	27,429	27,429	2	.	.
FL	18,925	21,317	25,079	26,776	28,195	29,131	8	.	.
GA	12,792	18,390	22,712	22,277	26,900	33,201	5	.	.
IA	18,714	28,898	35,505	36,018	41,948	45,790	13	.	.
IL	18,100	24,419	29,648	31,510	33,613	41,101	20	24,950	38,480
IN	19,240	21,996	24,708	23,452	28,562	29,795	12	.	.
KS	15,787	15,787	15,787	15,787	15,787	15,787	1	.	.
KY	31,550	31,550	32,868	32,868	34,186	34,186	2	.	.
LA	24,000	24,000	29,232	26,484	37,211	37,211	3	.	.
MA	28,954	35,404	39,428	39,270	41,835	49,971	12	.	.
MD	22,416	27,768	29,579	30,685	32,433	33,485	6	.	.
ME	25,085	25,517	26,024	26,235	26,532	26,543	4	.	.
MI	26,664	26,664	28,756	28,410	31,195	31,195	3	.	.
MN	24,960	27,560	32,621	32,167	35,521	44,579	10	30,472	44,928
MO	19,130	19,130	23,222	22,730	27,807	27,807	3	.	.
MT	16,640	16,640	16,640	16,640	16,640	16,640	1	.	.
NC	23,073	26,266	28,020	28,291	29,652	32,361	12	.	.
ND	10,712	18,255	19,490	21,991	22,854	23,640	5	10,712	11,960
NE	20,401	20,401	23,991	25,513	26,058	26,058	3	.	.
NM	19,943	19,943	23,783	23,783	27,623	27,623	2	.	.
NY	22,880	23,296	30,395	29,600	35,429	48,000	11	22,880	22,880
OH	27,311	31,949	42,343	36,154	42,491	80,000	6	21,008	30,562
OR	21,276	23,688	27,431	28,575	31,173	31,296	4	.	.
PA	19,000	19,152	28,080	28,145	28,163	45,938	5	.	.
SC	26,289	26,743	27,446	27,628	28,148	28,238	4	.	.
SD	22,111	22,111	25,791	23,271	31,990	31,990	3	26,478	39,707
TN	20,571	21,704	24,695	24,957	26,515	30,636	8	18,886	33,030
TX	18,768	20,104	24,143	24,016	26,600	31,626	14	.	.
UT	18,720	20,625	22,674	20,994	23,462	31,250	6	.	.
VA	22,880	25,132	28,422	26,499	31,060	38,142	7	22,173	45,531
WA	30,564	30,564	30,564	30,564	30,564	30,564	2	.	.
WI	20,790	20,790	20,790	20,790	20,790	20,790	1	.	.
WV	37,228	37,228	37,228	37,228	37,228	37,228	1	.	.
WY	19,884	22,560	23,853	23,586	24,834	28,980	8	.	.

Degree Required Data

	Min	Q1	Mean	Median	Q3	Max	N	Range Avg Min	Range Avg Max
High School	10,712	21,444	28,280	27,463	31,980	80,000	140	20,440	31,066
Associate's	18,255	23,296	29,776	27,500	35,419	49,971	30	24,024	40,830
Bachelor's	16,420	24,356	29,023	28,160	32,000	45,938	55	.	.
Master's	24,960	24,960	29,325	29,325	33,690	33,690	2	.	.
Doctoral	.	.	.	.	.	.	.	.	.

DRIVER

Drives a library vehicle to pick-up and deliver library material between libraries, systems and branches. Determines sequence of loading for delivery purposes. Performs basic maintenance on vehicle. Informs supervisor when additional vehicle maintenance is necessary.

Four-Year College
Regional Data

	Min	Q1	Mean	Median	Q3	Max	N	Range Avg Min	Range Avg Max
North Atlantic	25,501	25,501	25,501	25,501	25,501	25,501	1	22,298	37,898
ALL REGIONS	25,501	25,501	25,501	25,501	25,501	25,501	1	22,298	37,898

State Data

	Min	Q1	Mean	Median	Q3	Max	N	Range Avg Min	Range Avg Max
PA	25,501	25,501	25,501	25,501	25,501	25,501	1	22,298	37,898

Degree Required Data

	Min	Q1	Mean	Median	Q3	Max	N	Range Avg Min	Range Avg Max
High School	25,501	25,501	25,501	25,501	25,501	25,501	1	22,298	37,898
Associate's	.	.	.	.	.	.		.	.
Bachelor's	.	.	.	.	.	.		.	.
Master's	.	.	.	.	.	.		.	.
Doctoral	.	.	.	.	.	.		.	.

DRIVER - CONTINUED
University
(Includes ARL Data)
Regional Data

	Min	Q1	Mean	Median	Q3	Max	N	Range Avg Min	Range Avg Max
North Atlantic	27,429	27,429	28,416	28,416	29,403	29,403	4		.
Great Lakes & Plains	25,102	28,954	29,459	30,276	30,846	32,115	5		.
Southeast	15,535	20,162	23,706	23,226	25,184	32,772	10		.
ALL REGIONS	15,535	23,005	26,211	27,429	29,403	32,772	19		.

State Data

	Min	Q1	Mean	Median	Q3	Max	N	Range Avg Min	Range Avg Max
AL	23,005	23,005	23,005	23,005	23,005	23,005	1		.
AR	15,535	15,535	15,535	15,535	15,535	15,535	1		.
DC	27,429	27,429	27,429	27,429	27,429	27,429	2		.
IA	30,276	30,276	30,276	30,276	30,276	30,276	1		.
IN	28,954	28,954	30,638	30,846	32,115	32,115	3		.
MD	29,403	29,403	29,403	29,403	29,403	29,403	2		.
NC	20,162	23,447	24,543	25,050	25,184	28,870	5		.
NE	25,102	25,102	25,102	25,102	25,102	25,102	1		.
SC	20,141	20,141	20,141	20,141	20,141	20,141	1		.
TN	22,896	22,896	27,834	27,834	32,772	32,772	2		.

Degree Required Data

	Min	Q1	Mean	Median	Q3	Max	N	Range Avg Min	Range Avg Max
High School	15,535	22,951	26,129	27,027	29,840	32,772	16	.	.
Associate's	27,429	27,429	27,429	27,429	27,429	27,429	2	.	.
Bachelor's	.	.	.	.	.	.		.	.
Master's	.	.	.	.	.	.		.	.
Doctoral	.	.	.	.	.	.		.	.

DRIVER - CONTINUED
ALL ACADEMIC LIBRARIES
Regional Data

	Min	Q1	Mean	Median	Q3	Max	N	Range Avg Min	Range Avg Max
North Atlantic	25,501	27,429	27,833	27,429	29,403	29,403	5	22,298	37,898
Great Lakes & Plains	25,102	28,954	29,459	30,276	30,846	32,115	5	.	.
Southeast	15,535	20,162	23,706	23,226	25,184	32,772	10	.	.
ALL REGIONS	15,535	23,226	26,176	26,465	29,403	32,772	20	22,298	37,898

State Data

	Min	Q1	Mean	Median	Q3	Max	N	Range Avg Min	Range Avg Max
AL	23,005	23,005	23,005	23,005	23,005	23,005	1	.	.
AR	15,535	15,535	15,535	15,535	15,535	15,535	1	.	.
DC	27,429	27,429	27,429	27,429	27,429	27,429	2	.	.
IA	30,276	30,276	30,276	30,276	30,276	30,276	1	.	.
IN	28,954	28,954	30,638	30,846	32,115	32,115	3	.	.
MD	29,403	29,403	29,403	29,403	29,403	29,403	2	.	.
NC	20,162	23,447	24,543	25,050	25,184	28,870	5	.	.
NE	25,102	25,102	25,102	25,102	25,102	25,102	1	.	.
PA	25,501	25,501	25,501	25,501	25,501	25,501	1	22,298	37,898
SC	20,141	20,141	20,141	20,141	20,141	20,141	1	.	.
TN	22,896	22,896	27,834	27,834	32,772	32,772	2	.	.

Degree Required Data

	Min	Q1	Mean	Median	Q3	Max	N	Range Avg Min	Range Avg Max
High School	15,535	23,005	26,092	25,501	29,403	32,772	17	22,298	37,898
Associate's	27,429	27,429	27,429	27,429	27,429	27,429	2	.	.
Bachelor's	.	.	.	.	.	.		.	.
Master's	.	.	.	.	.	.		.	.
Doctoral	.	.	.	.	.	.		.	.

INFORMATION TECHNOLOGY (IT) MANAGER

Manages day-to-day IT operations including systems analysis, programming, and computer and auxiliary operations. Directs the development and maintenance of systems. Determines and recommends department budgets and analyzes controllable expenditures. May plan and coordinate the evaluation and effectiveness of existing data processing applications and the feasibility and potential value of new applications. May assist staff and patrons with troubleshooting equipment or software problems.

Two-Year College
Regional Data

	Min	Q1	Mean	Median	Q3	Max	N	Range Avg Min	Range Avg Max
Great Lakes & Plains	21,120	21,120	28,060	28,060	35,000	35,000	2	.	.
Southeast	29,706	29,706	30,477	30,477	31,248	31,248	2	.	.
West & Southwest	15,040	15,040	15,040	15,040	15,040	15,040	1	.	.
ALL REGIONS	15,040	21,120	26,423	29,706	31,248	35,000	5	.	.

State Data

	Min	Q1	Mean	Median	Q3	Max	N	Range Avg Min	Range Avg Max
AR	31,248	31,248	31,248	31,248	31,248	31,248	1	.	.
FL	29,706	29,706	29,706	29,706	29,706	29,706	1	.	.
MN	21,120	21,120	28,060	28,060	35,000	35,000	2	.	.
TX	15,040	15,040	15,040	15,040	15,040	15,040	1	.	.

Degree Required Data

	Min	Q1	Mean	Median	Q3	Max	N	Range Avg Min	Range Avg Max
High School	.	.	.	.	.	.	.	.	.
Associate's	29,706	29,706	29,706	29,706	29,706	29,706	1	.	.
Bachelor's	21,120	21,120	29,123	31,248	35,000	35,000	3	.	.
Master's	.	.	.	.	.	.	.	.	.
Doctoral	.	.	.	.	.	.	.	.	.

INFORMATION TECHNOLOGY (IT) MANAGER - CONTINUED
Four-Year College
Regional Data

	Min	Q1	Mean	Median	Q3	Max	N	Range Avg Min	Range Avg Max
North Atlantic	42,571	42,571	42,571	42,571	42,571	42,571	1	.	.
West & Southwest	42,945	42,945	42,945	42,945	42,945	42,945	1	.	.
ALL REGIONS	42,571	42,571	42,758	42,758	42,945	42,945	2	.	.

State Data

	Min	Q1	Mean	Median	Q3	Max	N	Range Avg Min	Range Avg Max
ME	42,571	42,571	42,571	42,571	42,571	42,571	1	.	.
UT	42,945	42,945	42,945	42,945	42,945	42,945	1	.	.

Degree Required Data

	Min	Q1	Mean	Median	Q3	Max	N	Range Avg Min	Range Avg Max
High School	.	.	.	.	.	.		.	.
Associate's	.	.	.	.	.	.		.	.
Bachelor's	42,571	42,571	42,571	42,571	42,571	42,571	1	.	.
Master's	42,945	42,945	42,945	42,945	42,945	42,945	1	.	.
Doctoral	.	.	.	.	.	.		.	.

INFORMATION TECHNOLOGY (IT) MANAGER - CONTINUED
University
(Includes ARL Data)
Regional Data

	Min	Q1	Mean	Median	Q3	Max	N	Range Avg Min	Range Avg Max
North Atlantic	58,399	60,478	71,517	73,301	80,765	83,723	10	.	.
Great Lakes & Plains	42,995	45,858	52,750	49,589	53,498	74,972	6	.	.
Southeast	33,227	36,000	53,133	37,449	75,838	89,521	13	.	.
West & Southwest	22,598	36,257	45,546	46,197	52,599	76,536	17	.	.
ALL REGIONS	22,598	37,449	54,276	52,363	69,154	89,521	46	.	.

State Data

	Min	Q1	Mean	Median	Q3	Max	N	Range Avg Min	Range Avg Max
AL	85,990	85,990	85,990	85,990	85,990	85,990	1	.	.
AR	56,300	56,300	56,300	56,300	56,300	56,300	1	.	.
AZ	31,412	37,226	43,789	43,478	51,346	53,448	12	.	.
CO	76,536	76,536	76,536	76,536	76,536	76,536	1	.	.
CT	60,238	60,238	60,238	60,238	60,238	60,238	1	.	.
DC	69,154	69,154	69,154	69,154	69,154	69,154	1	.	.
FL	57,152	57,152	57,152	57,152	57,152	57,152	1	.	.
GA	36,258	36,258	36,258	36,258	36,258	36,258	1	.	.
IA	74,972	74,972	74,972	74,972	74,972	74,972	1	.	.
IL	42,995	42,995	48,247	48,247	53,498	53,498	2	.	.
KS	45,858	45,858	45,858	45,858	45,858	45,858	1	.	.
LA	33,435	34,718	35,721	36,000	36,725	37,449	4	.	.
MA	58,399	58,399	58,399	58,399	58,399	58,399	1	.	.
MD	60,478	60,478	74,989	80,765	83,723	83,723	6	.	.
MI	49,780	49,780	49,780	49,780	49,780	49,780	1	.	.
NC	75,838	75,838	81,286	78,499	89,521	89,521	3	.	.
NE	49,398	49,398	49,398	49,398	49,398	49,398	1	.	.
NM	22,598	22,598	22,598	22,598	22,598	22,598	1	.	.
PA	77,447	77,447	77,447	77,447	77,447	77,447	1	.	.
SC	33,227	33,227	34,142	34,142	35,058	35,058	2	.	.
TX	31,957	31,957	43,855	43,855	55,753	55,753	2	.	.
UT	61,981	61,981	61,981	61,981	61,981	61,981	1	.	.

Degree Required Data

	Min	Q1	Mean	Median	Q3	Max	N	Range Avg Min	Range Avg Max
High School	22,598	22,598	36,189	36,189	49,780	49,780	2	.	.
Associate's	55,753	55,753	55,753	55,753	55,753	55,753	1	.	.
Bachelor's	31,412	37,449	54,698	52,599	69,154	89,521	41	.	.
Master's	.	.	.	.	.	.	.	.	.
Doctoral	.	.	.	.	.	.	.	.	.

INFORMATION TECHNOLOGY (IT) MANAGER - CONTINUED
ALL ACADEMIC LIBRARIES
Regional Data

	Min	Q1	Mean	Median	Q3	Max	N	Range Avg Min	Range Avg Max
North Atlantic	42,571	60,238	68,886	69,154	80,765	83,723	11	.	.
Great Lakes & Plains	21,120	38,998	46,578	47,628	51,639	74,972	8	.	.
Southeast	29,706	33,435	50,112	36,258	75,838	89,521	15	.	.
West & Southwest	15,040	35,365	43,804	42,945	52,599	76,536	19	.	.
ALL REGIONS	15,040	36,000	51,214	49,780	60,478	89,521	53	.	.

State Data

	Min	Q1	Mean	Median	Q3	Max	N	Range Avg Min	Range Avg Max
AL	85,990	85,990	85,990	85,990	85,990	85,990	1	.	.
AR	31,248	31,248	43,774	43,774	56,300	56,300	2	.	.
AZ	31,412	37,226	43,789	43,478	51,346	53,448	12	.	.
CO	76,536	76,536	76,536	76,536	76,536	76,536	1	.	.
CT	60,238	60,238	60,238	60,238	60,238	60,238	1	.	.
DC	69,154	69,154	69,154	69,154	69,154	69,154	1	.	.
FL	29,706	29,706	43,429	43,429	57,152	57,152	2	.	.
GA	36,258	36,258	36,258	36,258	36,258	36,258	1	.	.
IA	74,972	74,972	74,972	74,972	74,972	74,972	1	.	.
IL	42,995	42,995	48,247	48,247	53,498	53,498	2	.	.
KS	45,858	45,858	45,858	45,858	45,858	45,858	1	.	.
LA	33,435	34,718	35,721	36,000	36,725	37,449	4	.	.
MA	58,399	58,399	58,399	58,399	58,399	58,399	1	.	.
MD	60,478	60,478	74,989	80,765	83,723	83,723	6	.	.
ME	42,571	42,571	42,571	42,571	42,571	42,571	1	.	.
MI	49,780	49,780	49,780	49,780	49,780	49,780	1	.	.
MN	21,120	21,120	28,060	28,060	35,000	35,000	2	.	.
NC	75,838	75,838	81,286	78,499	89,521	89,521	3	.	.
NE	49,398	49,398	49,398	49,398	49,398	49,398	1	.	.
NM	22,598	22,598	22,598	22,598	22,598	22,598	1	.	.
PA	77,447	77,447	77,447	77,447	77,447	77,447	1	.	.
SC	33,227	33,227	34,142	34,142	35,058	35,058	2	.	.
TX	15,040	15,040	34,250	31,957	55,753	55,753	3	.	.
UT	42,945	42,945	52,463	52,463	61,981	61,981	2	.	.

Degree Required Data

	Min	Q1	Mean	Median	Q3	Max	N	Range Avg Min	Range Avg Max
High School	22,598	22,598	36,189	36,189	49,780	49,780	2	.	.
Associate's	29,706	29,706	42,730	42,730	55,753	55,753	2	.	.
Bachelor's	21,120	36,257	52,724	50,565	61,981	89,521	45	.	.
Master's	42,945	42,945	42,945	42,945	42,945	42,945	1	.	.
Doctoral	.	.	.	.	.	.		.	.

SYSTEMS ADMINISTRATOR

Manages day-to-day IT operations including systems analysis, programming, and computer and auxiliary operations. Directs the development and maintenance of systems. Determines and recommends department budgets and analyzes controllable expenditures. May plan and coordinate the evaluation and effectiveness of existing data processing applications and the feasibility and potential value of new applications. May assist staff and patrons with troubleshooting equipment or software problems.

Two-Year College
Regional Data

	Min	Q1	Mean	Median	Q3	Max	N	Range Avg Min	Range Avg Max
Southeast	35,922	35,922	35,922	35,922	35,922	35,922	1	29,120	43,680
West & Southwest	44,102	44,102	44,102	44,102	44,102	44,102	1	.	.
ALL REGIONS	35,922	35,922	40,012	40,012	44,102	44,102	2	29,120	43,680

State Data

	Min	Q1	Mean	Median	Q3	Max	N	Range Avg Min	Range Avg Max
LA	35,922	35,922	35,922	35,922	35,922	35,922	1	29,120	43,680
TX	44,102	44,102	44,102	44,102	44,102	44,102	1	.	.

Degree Required Data

	Min	Q1	Mean	Median	Q3	Max	N	Range Avg Min	Range Avg Max
High School	.	.	.	.	.	.		.	.
Associate's	35,922	35,922	40,012	40,012	44,102	44,102	2	29,120	43,680
Bachelor's	.	.	.	.	.	.		.	.
Master's	.	.	.	.	.	.		.	.
Doctoral	.	.	.	.	.	.		.	.

SYSTEMS ADMINISTRATOR - CONTINUED
Four-Year College
Regional Data

	Min	Q1	Mean	Median	Q3	Max	N	Range Avg Min	Range Avg Max
North Atlantic	32,941	32,941	49,123	49,123	65,304	65,304	2	.	.
Southeast	33,280	33,280	33,280	33,280	33,280	33,280	1	.	.
West & Southwest	41,337	50,133	53,190	51,516	54,072	68,892	5	.	.
ALL REGIONS	32,941	37,309	49,684	50,825	59,688	68,892	8	.	.

State Data

	Min	Q1	Mean	Median	Q3	Max	N	Range Avg Min	Range Avg Max
CA	50,133	50,133	50,133	50,133	50,133	50,133	1	.	.
CO	51,516	51,516	58,160	54,072	68,892	68,892	3	.	.
MD	65,304	65,304	65,304	65,304	65,304	65,304	1	.	.
PA	32,941	32,941	32,941	32,941	32,941	32,941	1	.	.
SC	33,280	33,280	33,280	33,280	33,280	33,280	1	.	.
UT	41,337	41,337	41,337	41,337	41,337	41,337	1	.	.

Degree Required Data

	Min	Q1	Mean	Median	Q3	Max	N	Range Avg Min	Range Avg Max
High School	51,516	51,516	58,160	54,072	68,892	68,892	3	.	.
Associate's								.	.
Bachelor's	32,941	32,941	38,785	33,280	50,133	50,133	3	.	.
Master's	41,337	41,337	53,321	53,321	65,304	65,304	2	.	.
Doctoral								.	.

SYSTEMS ADMINISTRATOR - CONTINUED
University
(Includes ARL Data)
Regional Data

	Min	Q1	Mean	Median	Q3	Max	N	Range Avg Min	Range Avg Max
North Atlantic	24,901	47,481	61,045	55,515	72,191	100,798	27	.	.
Great Lakes & Plains	26,645	35,254	44,511	43,870	53,392	66,930	29	26,978	34,258
Southeast	22,320	39,518	45,330	44,844	53,651	76,243	36	.	.
West & Southwest	23,348	38,052	45,907	46,002	54,089	63,651	20	.	.
ALL REGIONS	22,320	39,781	49,009	47,427	57,505	100,798	112	26,978	34,258

State Data

	Min	Q1	Mean	Median	Q3	Max	N	Range Avg Min	Range Avg Max
AL	46,460	48,730	53,925	54,645	59,120	59,950	4	.	.
AR	33,706	33,706	33,706	33,706	33,706	33,706	1	.	.
AZ	53,901	53,901	58,776	58,776	63,651	63,651	2	.	.
CA	58,008	58,008	58,008	58,008	58,008	58,008	1	.	.
CO	43,080	43,878	47,838	46,998	51,798	54,276	4	.	.
DC	24,901	24,901	34,169	34,169	43,437	43,437	2	.	.
FL	22,320	23,851	34,074	26,718	44,296	60,539	4	.	.
GA	27,050	27,050	28,122	27,793	29,194	29,851	4	.	.
IA	41,980	43,870	48,950	48,430	53,392	57,596	6	.	.
IL	29,120	44,032	47,603	49,139	57,510	58,214	5	26,978	34,258
IN	28,080	38,840	48,269	49,500	60,000	66,930	9	.	.
KY	46,213	46,213	46,213	46,213	46,213	46,213	1	.	.
LA	54,450	54,450	54,450	54,450	54,450	54,450	1	.	.
MA	45,542	47,372	51,805	54,748	55,515	55,848	5	.	.
MD	47,481	51,143	68,443	67,480	81,712	100,798	18	.	.
MI	31,757	31,757	33,506	33,506	35,254	35,254	2	.	.
MN	34,707	34,707	40,725	39,928	47,540	47,540	3	.	.
NC	43,853	44,687	53,626	45,587	61,280	76,243	9	.	.
ND	31,200	31,200	31,200	31,200	31,200	31,200	1	.	.
NE	26,645	26,645	32,327	32,327	38,009	38,009	2	.	.
NY	35,171	35,171	44,443	44,443	53,714	53,714	2	.	.
OH	39,635	39,635	39,635	39,635	39,635	39,635	1	.	.
OR	36,156	36,156	36,882	36,882	37,608	37,608	2	.	.
SC	40,480	40,480	45,905	44,612	52,623	52,623	3	.	.
TN	38,556	41,424	43,324	43,656	46,164	46,488	6	.	.
TX	23,348	31,170	35,827	33,870	42,200	48,545	5	.	.
UT	47,328	47,328	52,520	52,520	57,711	57,711	2	.	.
VA	44,577	44,577	50,910	52,852	55,300	55,300	3	.	.
WA	53,520	53,520	56,304	56,304	59,088	59,088	2	.	.
WY	38,496	38,496	40,338	40,338	42,180	42,180	2	.	.

Degree Required Data

	Min	Q1	Mean	Median	Q3	Max	N	Range Avg Min	Range Avg Max
High School	22,320	28,053	40,230	43,048	49,139	59,088	14	.	.
Associate's	29,120	31,170	37,185	38,840	42,200	44,612	7	26,978	34,258
Bachelor's	23,348	43,853	51,912	49,319	59,053	100,798	82	.	.
Master's	55,300	55,300	55,300	55,300	55,300	55,300	1	.	.
Doctoral	.	.	.	.	.	.		.	.

SYSTEMS ADMINISTRATOR - CONTINUED
ALL ACADEMIC LIBRARIES
Regional Data

	Min	Q1	Mean	Median	Q3	Max	N	Range Avg Min	Range Avg Max
North Atlantic	24,901	47,481	60,223	55,515	72,191	100,798	29	.	.
Great Lakes & Plains	26,645	35,254	44,511	43,870	53,392	66,930	29	26,978	34,258
Southeast	22,320	35,922	44,765	44,650	52,852	76,243	38	29,120	43,680
West & Southwest	23,348	41,337	47,238	47,937	54,072	68,892	26	.	.
ALL REGIONS	22,320	39,635	48,906	47,427	57,500	100,798	122	28,049	38,969

State Data

	Min	Q1	Mean	Median	Q3	Max	N	Range Avg Min	Range Avg Max
AL	46,460	48,730	53,925	54,645	59,120	59,950	4	.	.
AR	33,706	33,706	33,706	33,706	33,706	33,706	1	.	.
AZ	53,901	53,901	58,776	58,776	63,651	63,651	2	.	.
CA	50,133	50,133	54,071	54,071	58,008	58,008	2	.	.
CO	43,080	44,676	52,262	51,516	54,276	68,892	7	.	.
DC	24,901	24,901	34,169	34,169	43,437	43,437	2	.	.
FL	22,320	23,851	34,074	26,718	44,296	60,539	4	.	.
GA	27,050	27,050	28,122	27,793	29,194	29,851	4	.	.
IA	41,980	43,870	48,950	48,430	53,392	57,596	6	.	.
IL	29,120	44,032	47,603	49,139	57,510	58,214	5	26,978	34,258
IN	28,080	38,840	48,269	49,500	60,000	66,930	9	.	.
KY	46,213	46,213	46,213	46,213	46,213	46,213	1	.	.
LA	35,922	35,922	45,186	45,186	54,450	54,450	2	29,120	43,680
MA	45,542	47,372	51,805	54,748	55,515	55,848	5	.	.
MD	47,481	51,143	68,278	67,480	81,712	100,798	19	.	.
MI	31,757	31,757	33,506	33,506	35,254	35,254	2	.	.
MN	34,707	34,707	40,725	39,928	47,540	47,540	3	.	.
NC	43,853	44,687	53,626	45,587	61,280	76,243	9	.	.
ND	31,200	31,200	31,200	31,200	31,200	31,200	1	.	.
NE	26,645	26,645	32,327	32,327	38,009	38,009	2	.	.
NY	35,171	35,171	44,443	44,443	53,714	53,714	2	.	.
OH	39,635	39,635	39,635	39,635	39,635	39,635	1	.	.
OR	36,156	36,156	36,882	36,882	37,608	37,608	2	.	.
PA	32,941	32,941	32,941	32,941	32,941	32,941	1	.	.
SC	33,280	36,880	42,749	42,546	48,618	52,623	4	.	.
TN	38,556	41,424	43,324	43,656	46,164	46,488	6	.	.
TX	23,348	31,170	37,206	38,035	44,102	48,545	6	.	.
UT	41,337	41,337	48,792	47,328	57,711	57,711	3	.	.
VA	44,577	44,577	50,910	52,852	55,300	55,300	3	.	.
WA	53,520	53,520	56,304	56,304	59,088	59,088	2	.	.
WY	38,496	38,496	40,338	40,338	42,180	42,180	2	.	.

WEB CONTENT ADMINISTRATOR

Develops, provides, and authorizes website content to increase traffic, support and promote services, and gain content visibility. Manages and performs website editorial activities including gathering and researching information that enhances the value of the site. May oversee data control technicians and writers dedicated to website.

Four-Year College
Regional Data

	Min	Q1	Mean	Median	Q3	Max	N	Range Avg Min	Range Avg Max
Great Lakes & Plains	28,000	28,000	28,352	28,352	28,704	28,704	2	.	.
ALL REGIONS	28,000	28,000	28,352	28,352	28,704	28,704	2	.	.

State Data

	Min	Q1	Mean	Median	Q3	Max	N	Range Avg Min	Range Avg Max
ND	28,000	28,000	28,000	28,000	28,000	28,000	1	.	.
OH	28,704	28,704	28,704	28,704	28,704	28,704	1	.	.

Degree Required Data

	Min	Q1	Mean	Median	Q3	Max	N	Range Avg Min	Range Avg Max
High School	.	.	.	.	.	.		.	.
Associate's	28,704	28,704	28,704	28,704	28,704	28,704	1	.	.
Bachelor's	28,000	28,000	28,000	28,000	28,000	28,000	1	.	.
Master's	.	.	.	.	.	.		.	.
Doctoral	.	.	.	.	.	.		.	.

WEB CONTENT ADMINISTRATOR - CONTINUED
University
(Includes ARL Data)
Regional Data

	Min	Q1	Mean	Median	Q3	Max	N	Range Avg Min	Range Avg Max
North Atlantic	34,417	34,417	51,684	60,318	60,318	60,318	3	.	.
Great Lakes & Plains	30,857	32,572	37,225	37,950	41,878	42,143	4	.	.
Southeast	17,981	28,888	32,892	36,521	40,533	40,535	5	.	.
West & Southwest	27,708	27,708	27,708	27,708	27,708	27,708	1	.	.
ALL REGIONS	17,981	30,857	38,163	36,521	41,613	60,318	13	.	.

State Data

	Min	Q1	Mean	Median	Q3	Max	N	Range Avg Min	Range Avg Max
DC	34,417	34,417	34,417	34,417	34,417	34,417	1		.
GA	17,981	17,981	17,981	17,981	17,981	17,981	1		.
IA	41,613	41,613	41,878	41,878	42,143	42,143	2		.
MD	60,318	60,318	60,318	60,318	60,318	60,318	2		.
MO	34,287	34,287	34,287	34,287	34,287	34,287	1		.
NC	28,888	32,705	36,619	38,527	40,534	40,535	4		.
NE	30,857	30,857	30,857	30,857	30,857	30,857	1		.
TX	27,708	27,708	27,708	27,708	27,708	27,708	1		.

Degree Required Data

	Min	Q1	Mean	Median	Q3	Max	N	Range Avg Min	Range Avg Max
High School	28,888	28,888	28,888	28,888	28,888	28,888	1		.
Associate's	27,708	27,708	34,921	36,521	40,535	40,535	3		.
Bachelor's	17,981	34,417	42,475	41,613	60,318	60,318	7		.
Master's	34,287	34,287	34,287	34,287	34,287	34,287	1		.
Doctoral	.	.	.	.	.	.			.

WEB CONTENT ADMINISTRATOR - CONTINUED
ALL ACADEMIC LIBRARIES
Regional Data

	Min	Q1	Mean	Median	Q3	Max	N	Range Avg Min	Range Avg Max
North Atlantic	34,417	34,417	51,684	60,318	60,318	60,318	3		.
Great Lakes & Plains	28,000	28,704	34,267	32,572	41,613	42,143	6		.
Southeast	17,981	28,888	32,892	36,521	40,533	40,535	5		.
West & Southwest	27,708	27,708	27,708	27,708	27,708	27,708	1		.
ALL REGIONS	17,981	28,704	36,855	34,417	41,613	60,318	15		.

State Data

	Min	Q1	Mean	Median	Q3	Max	N	Range Avg Min	Range Avg Max
DC	34,417	34,417	34,417	34,417	34,417	34,417	1		.
GA	17,981	17,981	17,981	17,981	17,981	17,981	1		.
IA	41,613	41,613	41,878	41,878	42,143	42,143	2		.
MD	60,318	60,318	60,318	60,318	60,318	60,318	2		.
MO	34,287	34,287	34,287	34,287	34,287	34,287	1		.
NC	28,888	32,705	36,619	38,527	40,534	40,535	4		.
ND	28,000	28,000	28,000	28,000	28,000	28,000	1		.
NE	30,857	30,857	30,857	30,857	30,857	30,857	1		.
OH	28,704	28,704	28,704	28,704	28,704	28,704	1		.
TX	27,708	27,708	27,708	27,708	27,708	27,708	1		.

Degree Required Data

	Min	Q1	Mean	Median	Q3	Max	N	Range Avg Min	Range Avg Max
High School	28,888	28,888	28,888	28,888	28,888	28,888	1	.	.
Associate's	27,708	28,206	33,367	32,613	38,528	40,535	4	.	.
Bachelor's	17,981	31,209	40,665	41,073	51,230	60,318	8	.	.
Master's	34,287	34,287	34,287	34,287	34,287	34,287	1	.	.
Doctoral									.

WEBMASTER

Responsible for the library's Internet and or Intranet technical functions. Maps the flow of the site, creates general graphics, provides specifications to the web authors, developers, and outside vendors for the development of databases, interactive applets, and custom graphics. Supervises development efforts including content, design and production, site maintenance and updating. Acts as a liaison between the site and users.

Four-Year College
Regional Data

	Min	Q1	Mean	Median	Q3	Max	N	Range Avg Min	Range Avg Max
North Atlantic	46,530	46,530	46,530	46,530	46,530	46,530	1	.	.
ALL REGIONS	46,530	46,530	46,530	46,530	46,530	46,530	1	.	.

State Data

	Min	Q1	Mean	Median	Q3	Max	N	Range Avg Min	Range Avg Max
PA	46,530	46,530	46,530	46,530	46,530	46,530	1	.	.

Degree Required Data

	Min	Q1	Mean	Median	Q3	Max	N	Range Avg Min	Range Avg Max
High School	.	.	.	.	.	.		.	.
Associate's	.	.	.	.	.	.			.
Bachelor's	46,530	46,530	46,530	46,530	46,530	46,530	1	.	.
Master's	.	.	.	.	.	.			.
Doctoral	.	.	.	.	.	.		.	.

WEBMASTER - CONTINUED
University
(Includes ARL Data)
Regional Data

	Min	Q1	Mean	Median	Q3	Max	N	Range Avg Min	Range Avg Max
North Atlantic	42,380	50,865	61,864	59,350	72,864	86,378	4	.	.
Great Lakes & Plains	30,857	30,857	39,967	43,255	45,790	45,790	3	.	.
Southeast	21,074	28,538	39,648	41,420	47,000	55,943	7	.	.
West & Southwest	38,928	39,511	45,534	46,034	48,864	53,832	6	.	.
ALL REGIONS	21,074	39,220	45,905	45,895	51,348	86,378	20	.	.

State Data

	Min	Q1	Mean	Median	Q3	Max	N	Range Avg Min	Range Avg Max
AL	41,420	41,420	41,420	41,420	41,420	41,420	1	.	.
AR	28,538	28,538	28,538	28,538	28,538	28,538	1	.	.
CA	48,864	48,864	48,864	48,864	48,864	48,864	1	.	.
CO	46,068	46,068	49,950	49,950	53,832	53,832	2	.	.
CT	86,378	86,378	86,378	86,378	86,378	86,378	1	.	.
FL	36,638	36,638	36,638	36,638	36,638	36,638	1	.	.
IA	45,790	45,790	45,790	45,790	45,790	45,790	1	.	.
LA	21,074	21,074	21,074	21,074	21,074	21,074	1	.	.
MA	42,380	42,380	42,380	42,380	42,380	42,380	1	.	.
MD	59,350	59,350	59,350	59,350	59,350	59,350	2	.	.
MN	43,255	43,255	43,255	43,255	43,255	43,255	1	.	.
NC	46,920	46,920	46,960	46,960	47,000	47,000	2	.	.
NE	30,857	30,857	30,857	30,857	30,857	30,857	1	.	.
SC	55,943	55,943	55,943	55,943	55,943	55,943	1	.	.
TX	46,000	46,000	46,000	46,000	46,000	46,000	1	.	.
UT	39,511	39,511	39,511	39,511	39,511	39,511	1	.	.
WY	38,928	38,928	38,928	38,928	38,928	38,928	1	.	.

Degree Required Data

	Min	Q1	Mean	Median	Q3	Max	N	Range Avg Min	Range Avg Max
High School	36,638	36,638	41,283	41,420	45,790	45,790	3	.	.
Associate's	46,000	46,000	46,000	46,000	46,000	46,000	1	.	.
Bachelor's	21,074	39,511	44,744	46,920	55,943	59,350	11	.	.
Master's	86,378	86,378	86,378	86,378	86,378	86,378	1	.	.
Doctoral	.	.	.	.	.	.		.	.

WEBMASTER - CONTINUED
ALL ACADEMIC LIBRARIES
Regional Data

	Min	Q1	Mean	Median	Q3	Max	N	Range Avg Min	Range Avg Max
North Atlantic	42,380	46,530	58,798	59,350	59,350	86,378	5	.	.
Great Lakes & Plains	30,857	30,857	39,967	43,255	45,790	45,790	3	.	.
Southeast	21,074	28,538	39,648	41,420	47,000	55,943	7	.	.
West & Southwest	38,928	39,511	45,534	46,034	48,864	53,832	6	.	.
ALL REGIONS	21,074	39,511	45,935	46,000	48,864	86,378	21	.	.

State Data

	Min	Q1	Mean	Median	Q3	Max	N	Range Avg Min	Range Avg Max
AL	41,420	41,420	41,420	41,420	41,420	41,420	1	.	.
AR	28,538	28,538	28,538	28,538	28,538	28,538	1	.	.
CA	48,864	48,864	48,864	48,864	48,864	48,864	1	.	.
CO	46,068	46,068	49,950	49,950	53,832	53,832	2	.	.
CT	86,378	86,378	86,378	86,378	86,378	86,378	1	.	.
FL	36,638	36,638	36,638	36,638	36,638	36,638	1	.	.
IA	45,790	45,790	45,790	45,790	45,790	45,790	1	.	.
LA	21,074	21,074	21,074	21,074	21,074	21,074	1	.	.
MA	42,380	42,380	42,380	42,380	42,380	42,380	1	.	.
MD	59,350	59,350	59,350	59,350	59,350	59,350	2	.	.
MN	43,255	43,255	43,255	43,255	43,255	43,255	1	.	.
NC	46,920	46,920	46,960	46,960	47,000	47,000	2	.	.
NE	30,857	30,857	30,857	30,857	30,857	30,857	1	.	.
PA	46,530	46,530	46,530	46,530	46,530	46,530	1	.	.
SC	55,943	55,943	55,943	55,943	55,943	55,943	1	.	.
TX	46,000	46,000	46,000	46,000	46,000	46,000	1	.	.
UT	39,511	39,511	39,511	39,511	39,511	39,511	1	.	.
WY	38,928	38,928	38,928	38,928	38,928	38,928	1	.	.

Degree Required Data

	Min	Q1	Mean	Median	Q3	Max	N	Range Avg Min	Range Avg Max
High School	36,638	36,638	41,283	41,420	45,790	45,790	3	.	.
Associate's	46,000	46,000	46,000	46,000	46,000	46,000	1	.	.
Bachelor's	21,074	40,946	44,893	46,725	52,404	59,350	12	.	.
Master's	86,378	86,378	86,378	86,378	86,378	86,378	1	.	.
Doctoral	.	.	.	.	.	.		.	.

COMPUTER LAB ASSISTANT

Monitors the operation of adult and/or youth computer labs. Assists patrons with questions and problem resolution. Enforces computer lab rules. May assist with installation, operation and configuring of personal computer hardware and software. Investigates reoccurring problems and recommends course of action to supervisor. May perform back-up operations and print reports.

Two-Year College
Regional Data

	Min	Q1	Mean	Median	Q3	Max	N	Range Avg Min	Range Avg Max
North Atlantic	52,000	52,000	52,000	52,000	52,000	52,000	1	.	.
Great Lakes & Plains	47,981	47,981	47,981	47,981	47,981	47,981	1	.	.
Southeast	18,554	18,554	21,398	18,554	27,087	27,087	3	18,554	38,085
West & Southwest	10,800	10,800	15,834	10,800	20,868	30,936	4	.	.
ALL REGIONS	10,800	10,800	25,279	18,554	30,936	52,000	9	18,554	38,085

State Data

	Min	Q1	Mean	Median	Q3	Max	N	Range Avg Min	Range Avg Max
FL	27,087	27,087	27,087	27,087	27,087	27,087	1	.	.
MA	52,000	52,000	52,000	52,000	52,000	52,000	1	.	.
MI	47,981	47,981	47,981	47,981	47,981	47,981	1	.	.
TX	10,800	10,800	15,834	10,800	20,868	30,936	4	.	.
VA	18,554	18,554	18,554	18,554	18,554	18,554	2	18,554	38,085

Degree Required Data

	Min	Q1	Mean	Median	Q3	Max	N	Range Avg Min	Range Avg Max
High School	18,554	18,554	18,554	18,554	18,554	18,554	2	18,554	38,085
Associate's	27,087	27,087	29,012	29,012	30,936	30,936	2	.	.
Bachelor's	47,981	47,981	49,991	49,991	52,000	52,000	2	.	.
Master's	.	.	.	.	.	.		.	.
Doctoral	.	.	.	.	.	.		.	.

COMPUTER LAB ASSISTANT - CONTINUED
Four-Year College
Regional Data

	Min	Q1	Mean	Median	Q3	Max	N	Range Avg Min	Range Avg Max
North Atlantic	21,882	21,882	21,882	21,882	21,882	21,882	1	.	.
Great Lakes & Plains	30,056	30,056	30,056	30,056	30,056	30,056	1	.	.
Southeast	24,770	25,133	26,007	26,470	26,503	27,159	5	.	.
ALL REGIONS	21,882	24,770	25,996	26,470	27,159	30,056	7	.	.

State Data

	Min	Q1	Mean	Median	Q3	Max	N	Range Avg Min	Range Avg Max
OH	30,056	30,056	30,056	30,056	30,056	30,056	1	.	.
PA	21,882	21,882	21,882	21,882	21,882	21,882	1	.	.
SC	24,770	24,770	25,469	25,133	26,503	26,503	3	.	.
TN	26,470	26,470	26,470	26,470	26,470	26,470	1	.	.
WV	27,159	27,159	27,159	27,159	27,159	27,159	1	.	.

Degree Required Data

	Min	Q1	Mean	Median	Q3	Max	N	Range Avg Min	Range Avg Max
High School	27,159	27,159	27,159	27,159	27,159	27,159	1	.	.
Associate's	24,770	24,770	26,653	25,133	30,056	30,056	3	.	.
Bachelor's	21,882	21,882	24,176	24,176	26,470	26,470	2	.	.
Master's	.	.	.	.	.	.		.	.
Doctoral	.	.	.	.	.	.		.	.

COMPUTER LAB ASSISTANT - CONTINUED
University
(Includes ARL Data)
Regional Data

	Min	Q1	Mean	Median	Q3	Max	N	Range Avg Min	Range Avg Max
North Atlantic	38,792	38,792	40,060	40,694	40,694	40,694	3	.	.
Great Lakes & Plains	33,280	33,727	37,724	35,058	41,722	47,501	4	26,978	34,258
Southeast	17,222	27,540	33,233	31,704	38,952	54,150	33	25,092	43,867
West & Southwest	14,560	17,535	22,341	18,097	20,811	48,700	36	.	.
ALL REGIONS	14,560	18,097	28,580	28,493	35,828	54,150	76	25,563	41,465

State Data

	Min	Q1	Mean	Median	Q3	Max	N	Range Avg Min	Range Avg Max
AL	24,731	24,731	29,916	29,916	35,100	35,100	2	.	.
AR	17,222	20,758	24,997	25,142	30,652	31,210	5	.	.
FL	32,011	32,011	33,496	33,496	34,980	34,980	2	.	.
GA	20,889	20,889	20,889	20,889	20,889	20,889	1	.	.
IL	33,280	33,280	38,908	35,942	47,501	47,501	3	26,978	34,258
IN	34,174	34,174	34,174	34,174	34,174	34,174	1	.	.
MA	38,792	38,792	38,792	38,792	38,792	38,792	1	.	.
MD	40,694	40,694	40,694	40,694	40,694	40,694	2	.	.
NC	25,886	30,934	38,575	40,205	45,137	54,150	13	.	.
SC	30,139	30,139	30,139	30,139	30,139	30,139	1	.	.
TN	24,440	27,779	32,558	32,960	37,668	39,208	8	25,092	43,867
UT	14,560	17,368	22,152	18,097	20,280	48,700	35	.	.
VA	31,930	31,930	31,930	31,930	31,930	31,930	1	.	.
WY	28,968	28,968	28,968	28,968	28,968	28,968	1	.	.

Degree Required Data

	Min	Q1	Mean	Median	Q3	Max	N	Range Avg Min	Range Avg Max
High School	14,560	17,722	22,054	18,284	24,440	40,694	41	.	.
Associate's	27,166	30,934	37,862	33,280	45,137	54,150	11	26,978	34,258
Bachelor's	17,222	30,652	35,756	34,840	40,205	52,120	23	25,092	43,867
Master's	.	.	.	.	.	.	.	.	.
Doctoral	.	.	.	.	.	.	.	.	.

COMPUTER LAB ASSISTANT - CONTINUED
ALL ACADEMIC LIBRARIES
Regional Data

	Min	Q1	Mean	Median	Q3	Max	N	Range Avg Min	Range Avg Max
North Atlantic	21,882	38,792	38,812	40,694	40,694	52,000	5	.	.
Great Lakes & Plains	30,056	33,280	38,156	35,058	47,501	47,981	6	26,978	34,258
Southeast	17,222	25,886	31,486	30,652	35,100	54,150	41	22,476	41,554
West & Southwest	10,800	16,775	21,690	18,097	20,811	48,700	40	.	.
ALL REGIONS	10,800	18,159	28,060	27,123	35,040	54,150	92	23,227	40,338

State Data

	Min	Q1	Mean	Median	Q3	Max	N	Range Avg Min	Range Avg Max
AL	24,731	24,731	29,916	29,916	35,100	35,100	2	.	.
AR	17,222	20,758	24,997	25,142	30,652	31,210	5	.	.
FL	27,087	27,087	31,359	32,011	34,980	34,980	3	.	.
GA	20,889	20,889	20,889	20,889	20,889	20,889	1	.	.
IL	33,280	33,280	38,908	35,942	47,501	47,501	3	26,978	34,258
IN	34,174	34,174	34,174	34,174	34,174	34,174	1	.	.
MA	38,792	38,792	45,396	45,396	52,000	52,000	2	.	.
MD	40,694	40,694	40,694	40,694	40,694	40,694	2	.	.
MI	47,981	47,981	47,981	47,981	47,981	47,981	1	.	.
NC	25,886	30,934	38,575	40,205	45,137	54,150	13	.	.
OH	30,056	30,056	30,056	30,056	30,056	30,056	1	.	.
PA	21,882	21,882	21,882	21,882	21,882	21,882	1	.	.
SC	24,770	24,951	26,636	25,818	28,321	30,139	4	.	.
TN	24,440	27,540	31,881	31,704	36,384	39,208	9	25,092	43,867
TX	10,800	10,800	15,834	10,800	20,868	30,936	4	.	.
UT	14,560	17,368	22,152	18,097	20,280	48,700	35	.	.
VA	18,554	18,554	23,012	18,554	31,930	31,930	3	18,554	38,085
WV	27,159	27,159	27,159	27,159	27,159	27,159	1	.	.
WY	28,968	28,968	28,968	28,968	28,968	28,968	1	.	.

Degree Required Data

	Min	Q1	Mean	Median	Q3	Max	N	Range Avg Min	Range Avg Max
High School	14,560	17,763	22,011	18,554	24,586	40,694	44	18,554	38,085
Associate's	24,770	28,571	34,654	31,031	43,228	54,150	16	26,978	34,258
Bachelor's	17,222	30,139	35,953	34,840	44,132	52,120	27	25,092	43,867
Master's	.	.	.	.	.	.	.	.	.
Doctoral	.	.	.	.	.	.	.	.	.

ADMINISTRATIVE ASSISTANT (SECRETARY)

Performs secretarial duties for a department and its staff. Takes and transcribes dictation, and prepares correspondence. Operates word processing equipment as required. Composes correspondence from written materials provided. Maintains personal files and department records. Arranges and schedules meetings and appointments. Takes, screens, and places telephone calls, and acts as Receptionist as needed. Compiles standard reports with data that is provided.

Two-Year College
Regional Data

	Min	Q1	Mean	Median	Q3	Max	N	Range Avg Min	Range Avg Max
North Atlantic	41,709	41,709	41,709	41,709	41,709	41,709	1	.	.
Great Lakes & Plains	20,980	25,849	28,938	26,079	27,201	44,579	5	.	.
Southeast	20,360	20,360	24,362	24,362	28,363	28,363	2	.	.
West & Southwest	15,040	18,019	24,712	21,247	31,406	41,316	4	.	.
ALL REGIONS	15,040	20,989	27,831	25,964	34,840	44,579	12	.	.

State Data

	Min	Q1	Mean	Median	Q3	Max	N	Range Avg Min	Range Avg Max
CA	41,316	41,316	41,316	41,316	41,316	41,316	1	.	.
FL	28,363	28,363	28,363	28,363	28,363	28,363	1	.	.
GA	20,360	20,360	20,360	20,360	20,360	20,360	1	.	.
IA	26,079	26,079	26,079	26,079	26,079	26,079	1	.	.
IL	25,849	25,849	26,525	26,525	27,201	27,201	2	.	.
MD	41,709	41,709	41,709	41,709	41,709	41,709	1	.	.
MI	20,980	20,980	20,980	20,980	20,980	20,980	1	.	.
MN	44,579	44,579	44,579	44,579	44,579	44,579	1	.	.
TX	15,040	15,040	19,178	20,998	21,495	21,495	3	.	.

Degree Required Data

	Min	Q1	Mean	Median	Q3	Max	N	Range Avg Min	Range Avg Max
High School	20,998	21,495	27,894	25,964	28,363	44,579	6	.	.
Associate's	20,360	23,781	32,647	34,259	41,513	41,709	4	.	.
Bachelor's	.	.	.	.	.	.		.	.
Master's	.	.	.	.	.	.		.	.
Doctoral	.	.	.	.	.	.		.	.

ADMINISTRATIVE ASSISTANT (SECRETARY) - CONTINUED
Four-Year College
Regional Data

	Min	Q1	Mean	Median	Q3	Max	N	Range Avg Min	Range Avg Max
North Atlantic	18,843	23,421	26,965	26,603	28,640	37,315	5	.	.
Great Lakes & Plains	22,443	24,960	29,035	30,841	33,093	35,039	7	27,248	38,480
Southeast	17,659	19,584	28,454	28,642	34,751	37,333	7	.	.
West & Southwest	14,520	26,136	32,820	31,068	45,408	45,408	7	.	.
ALL REGIONS	14,520	24,960	29,499	28,641	34,751	45,408	26	27,248	38,480

State Data

	Min	Q1	Mean	Median	Q3	Max	N	Range Avg Min	Range Avg Max
AL	19,584	19,584	19,584	19,584	19,584	19,584	1	.	.
CO	14,520	27,792	36,600	43,236	45,408	45,408	4	.	.
GA	28,496	28,496	28,569	28,569	28,642	28,642	2	.	.
IL	24,960	24,960	24,960	24,960	24,960	24,960	1	.	.
KY	17,659	17,659	17,659	17,659	17,659	17,659	1	.	.
MN	25,251	25,251	31,128	33,093	35,039	35,039	3	27,248	38,480
MO	30,841	30,841	30,841	30,841	30,841	30,841	1	.	.
NY	23,421	23,421	30,368	30,368	37,315	37,315	2	.	.
OH	22,443	22,443	27,030	27,030	31,616	31,616	2	.	.
OR	26,136	26,136	26,136	26,136	26,136	26,136	2	.	.
PA	18,843	18,843	22,723	22,723	26,603	26,603	2	.	.
SC	34,751	34,751	34,751	34,751	34,751	34,751	1	.	.
TX	31,068	31,068	31,068	31,068	31,068	31,068	1	.	.
VT	28,640	28,640	28,640	28,640	28,640	28,640	1	.	.
WV	32,710	32,710	35,022	35,022	37,333	37,333	2	.	.

Degree Required Data

	Min	Q1	Mean	Median	Q3	Max	N	Range Avg Min	Range Avg Max
High School	14,520	23,421	28,727	28,640	31,616	45,408	17	27,248	38,480
Associate's	24,960	28,835	32,439	33,731	36,042	37,333	4	.	.
Bachelor's	17,659	26,603	29,772	28,496	35,039	41,064	5	.	.
Master's	.	.	.	.	.	.	.	.	.
Doctoral	.	.	.	.	.	.	.	.	.

ADMINISTRATIVE ASSISTANT (SECRETARY) - CONTINUED
University
(Includes ARL Data)
Regional Data

	Min	Q1	Mean	Median	Q3	Max	N	Range Avg Min	Range Avg Max
North Atlantic	20,184	29,912	33,235	32,000	35,158	47,647	30	27,040	41,600
Great Lakes & Plains	18,099	26,361	33,493	32,186	38,869	56,417	32	.	.
Southeast	16,286	25,886	29,814	30,342	32,935	55,764	39	.	.
West & Southwest	20,446	26,947	30,801	29,517	31,920	46,040	34	.	.
ALL REGIONS	16,286	26,947	31,695	30,564	35,158	56,417	135	27,040	41,600

State Data

	Min	Q1	Mean	Median	Q3	Max	N	Range Avg Min	Range Avg Max
AL	25,064	25,064	25,709	25,709	26,353	26,353	2	.	.
AR	16,286	17,257	18,262	18,519	18,596	20,652	5	.	.
AZ	27,040	27,192	30,532	29,587	30,042	46,040	10	.	.
CA	20,446	20,446	26,235	28,368	29,892	29,892	3	.	.
CO	38,976	42,900	42,937	43,572	43,722	45,516	5	.	.
CT	45,760	45,760	45,760	45,760	45,760	45,760	1	.	.
DC	27,429	27,429	29,714	29,714	32,000	32,000	2	.	.
FL	28,017	28,017	34,304	34,304	40,591	40,591	2	.	.
GA	24,245	24,245	27,254	27,254	30,263	30,263	2	.	.
IA	28,919	30,756	37,756	37,574	44,819	46,827	8	.	.
IL	24,960	34,278	38,739	36,634	43,514	56,417	6	.	.
IN	18,099	22,568	30,147	29,224	36,878	44,888	6	.	.
KY	26,042	26,042	26,042	26,042	26,042	26,042	1	.	.
LA	35,429	35,429	35,429	35,429	35,429	35,429	1	.	.
MA	20,184	27,040	37,355	41,112	47,036	47,647	6	27,040	41,600
MD	27,479	29,912	31,399	31,426	33,420	35,158	14	.	.
MI	26,202	26,202	26,202	26,202	26,202	26,202	1	.	.
MN	26,520	27,695	33,541	34,060	39,388	39,526	4	.	.
MO	25,610	25,610	25,610	25,610	25,610	25,610	1	.	.
MT	22,134	22,134	22,134	22,134	22,134	22,134	1	.	.
NC	24,850	27,335	31,030	31,583	32,935	37,140	15	.	.
NE	27,280	27,280	27,337	27,337	27,394	27,394	2	.	.
NM	25,071	25,071	25,071	25,071	25,071	25,071	1	.	.
NY	29,453	29,453	32,675	34,286	34,286	34,286	3	.	.
OH	23,400	23,400	29,457	29,457	35,513	35,513	2	.	.
PA	24,991	28,310	32,532	34,192	36,754	36,754	4	.	.
SC	22,395	30,441	35,186	32,287	35,044	55,764	5	.	.
SD	25,714	25,714	25,714	25,714	25,714	25,714	1	.	.
TN	25,958	25,958	30,729	31,572	34,656	34,656	3	.	.
TX	24,000	26,250	28,650	27,928	31,908	33,280	12	.	.
UT	26,947	26,947	26,947	26,947	26,947	26,947	1	.	.
VA	30,264	30,264	33,959	30,342	41,270	41,270	3	.	.
WA	30,564	30,564	30,564	30,564	30,564	30,564	1	.	.
WI	31,134	31,134	31,134	31,134	31,134	31,134	1	.	.

Degree Required Data

	Min	Q1	Mean	Median	Q3	Max	N	Range Avg Min	Range Avg Max
High School	16,286	26,500	30,943	30,770	34,286	47,036	93	.	.
Associate's	18,099	26,994	28,704	27,718	30,042	47,647	16	.	.
Bachelor's	20,446	28,017	35,882	32,000	41,505	56,417	19	27,040	41,600
Master's	.	.	.	.	.	.	.	.	.
Doctoral	.	.	.	.	.	.	.	.	.

ADMINISTRATIVE ASSISTANT (SECRETARY) - CONTINUED
ALL ACADEMIC LIBRARIES
Regional Data

	Min	Q1	Mean	Median	Q3	Max	N	Range Avg Min	Range Avg Max
North Atlantic	18,843	28,060	32,600	31,815	35,956	47,647	36	27,040	41,600
Great Lakes & Plains	18,099	25,781	32,266	30,988	37,649	56,417	44	27,248	38,480
Southeast	16,286	25,475	29,389	30,264	32,935	55,764	48	.	.
West & Southwest	14,520	26,136	30,574	29,500	32,952	46,040	45	.	.
ALL REGIONS	14,520	26,136	31,097	30,263	35,039	56,417	173	27,144	40,040

State Data

	Min	Q1	Mean	Median	Q3	Max	N	Range Avg Min	Range Avg Max
AL	19,584	19,584	23,667	25,064	26,353	26,353	3	.	.
AR	16,286	17,257	18,262	18,519	18,596	20,652	5	.	.
AZ	27,040	27,192	30,532	29,587	30,042	46,040	10	.	.
CA	20,446	24,407	30,006	29,130	35,604	41,316	4	.	.
CO	14,520	41,064	40,121	43,572	45,408	45,516	9	.	.
CT	45,760	45,760	45,760	45,760	45,760	45,760	1	.	.
DC	27,429	27,429	29,714	29,714	32,000	32,000	2	.	.
FL	28,017	28,017	32,324	28,363	40,591	40,591	3	.	.
GA	20,360	24,245	26,401	28,496	28,642	30,263	5	.	.
IA	26,079	30,192	36,458	36,728	43,848	46,827	9	.	.
IL	24,960	25,849	34,494	34,278	38,490	56,417	9	.	.
IN	18,099	22,568	30,147	29,224	36,878	44,888	6	.	.
KY	17,659	17,659	21,850	21,850	26,042	26,042	2	.	.
LA	35,429	35,429	35,429	35,429	35,429	35,429	1	.	.
MA	20,184	27,040	37,355	41,112	47,036	47,647	6	27,040	41,600
MD	27,479	29,912	32,086	31,426	33,420	41,709	15	.	.
MI	20,980	20,980	23,591	23,591	26,202	26,202	2	.	.
MN	25,251	27,695	34,016	34,066	39,388	44,579	8	27,248	38,480
MO	25,610	25,610	28,226	28,226	30,841	30,841	2	.	.
MT	22,134	22,134	22,134	22,134	22,134	22,134	1	.	.
NC	24,850	27,335	31,030	31,583	32,935	37,140	15	.	.
NE	27,280	27,280	27,337	27,337	27,394	27,394	2	.	.
NM	25,071	25,071	25,071	25,071	25,071	25,071	1	.	.
NY	23,421	29,453	31,752	34,286	34,286	37,315	5	.	.
OH	22,443	22,922	28,243	27,508	33,565	35,513	4	.	.
OR	26,136	26,136	26,136	26,136	26,136	26,136	2	.	.
PA	18,843	24,991	29,262	29,116	36,754	36,754	6	.	.
SC	22,395	30,441	35,114	33,519	35,044	55,764	6	.	.
SD	25,714	25,714	25,714	25,714	25,714	25,714	1	.	.
TN	25,958	25,958	30,729	31,572	34,656	34,656	3	.	.
TX	15,040	24,649	27,025	27,225	31,482	33,280	16	.	.
UT	26,947	26,947	26,947	26,947	26,947	26,947	1	.	.
VA	30,264	30,264	33,959	30,342	41,270	41,270	3	.	.
VT	28,640	28,640	28,640	28,640	28,640	28,640	1	.	.
WA	30,564	30,564	30,564	30,564	30,564	30,564	1	.	.
WI	31,134	31,134	31,134	31,134	31,134	31,134	1	.	.
WV	32,710	32,710	35,022	35,022	37,333	37,333	2	.	.

Degree Required Data

	Min	Q1	Mean	Median	Q3	Max	N	Range Avg Min	Range Avg Max
High School	14,520	26,021	30,461	30,303	34,025	47,036	116	27,248	38,480
Associate's	18,099	26,994	29,983	28,771	33,731	47,647	24	.	.
Bachelor's	17,659	27,529	34,609	31,960	41,167	56,417	24	27,040	41,600
Master's	.	.	.	.	.	.	.	.	.
Doctoral	.	.	.	.	.	.	.	.	.

RECEPTIONIST

Operates multiple line telephone console or PBX switchboard and greets visitors. Receives incoming calls, secures identity of callers, and connects to proper parties. Takes and relays messages. Places outgoing calls. Announces and directs calls to proper party. Registers individuals and issues visitor badges. Maintains required records. Performs a wide variety of clerical duties as time permits, such as word processing, record posting and maintenance.

University
(Includes ARL Data)
Regional Data

	Min	Q1	Mean	Median	Q3	Max	N	Range Avg Min	Range Avg Max
North Atlantic	27,429	31,264	33,478	31,264	37,551	39,881	5	.	.
Great Lakes & Plains	27,912	27,912	31,047	31,200	34,029	34,029	3	22,922	42,702
Southeast	20,781	22,000	24,700	25,153	26,714	28,850	5	.	.
West & Southwest	16,762	16,762	18,960	19,939	20,180	20,180	3	.	.
ALL REGIONS	16,762	21,391	27,557	27,670	31,264	39,881	16	22,922	42,702

State Data

	Min	Q1	Mean	Median	Q3	Max	N	Range Avg Min	Range Avg Max
DC	27,429	27,429	27,429	27,429	27,429	27,429	1	.	.
FL	20,781	20,781	24,216	25,153	26,714	26,714	3	.	.
IL	31,200	31,200	32,614	32,614	34,029	34,029	2	22,922	42,702
MA	37,551	37,551	38,716	38,716	39,881	39,881	2	.	.
MD	31,264	31,264	31,264	31,264	31,264	31,264	2	.	.
NC	28,850	28,850	28,850	28,850	28,850	28,850	1	.	.
NE	27,912	27,912	27,912	27,912	27,912	27,912	1	.	.
TX	20,180	20,180	20,180	20,180	20,180	20,180	1	.	.
UT	19,939	19,939	19,939	19,939	19,939	19,939	1	.	.
VA	22,000	22,000	22,000	22,000	22,000	22,000	1	.	.
WY	16,762	16,762	16,762	16,762	16,762	16,762	1	.	.

Degree Required Data

	Min	Q1	Mean	Median	Q3	Max	N	Range Avg Min	Range Avg Max
High School	19,939	22,000	28,340	27,782	31,264	39,881	10	.	.
Associate's	27,429	27,429	29,314	29,314	31,200	31,200	2	22,922	42,702
Bachelor's	20,180	20,180	20,180	20,180	20,180	20,180	1	.	.
Master's	.	.	.	.	.	.	.	.	.
Doctoral	.	.	.	.	.	.	.	.	.

RECEPTIONIST - CONTINUED
ALL ACADEMIC LIBRARIES
Regional Data

	Min	Q1	Mean	Median	Q3	Max	N	Range Avg Min	Range Avg Max
North Atlantic	27,429	31,264	33,478	31,264	37,551	39,881	5		
Great Lakes & Plains	27,912	27,912	31,047	31,200	34,029	34,029	3	22,922	42,702
Southeast	20,781	22,000	24,700	25,153	26,714	28,850	5		
West & Southwest	16,762	16,762	18,960	19,939	20,180	20,180	3		
ALL REGIONS	16,762	21,391	27,557	27,670	31,264	39,881	16	22,922	42,702

State Data

	Min	Q1	Mean	Median	Q3	Max	N	Range Avg Min	Range Avg Max
DC	27,429	27,429	27,429	27,429	27,429	27,429	1		
FL	20,781	20,781	24,216	25,153	26,714	26,714	3		
IL	31,200	31,200	32,614	32,614	34,029	34,029	2	22,922	42,702
MA	37,551	37,551	38,716	38,716	39,881	39,881	2		
MD	31,264	31,264	31,264	31,264	31,264	31,264	2		
NC	28,850	28,850	28,850	28,850	28,850	28,850	1		
NE	27,912	27,912	27,912	27,912	27,912	27,912	1		
TX	20,180	20,180	20,180	20,180	20,180	20,180	1		
UT	19,939	19,939	19,939	19,939	19,939	19,939	1		
VA	22,000	22,000	22,000	22,000	22,000	22,000	1		
WY	16,762	16,762	16,762	16,762	16,762	16,762	1		

Degree Required Data

	Min	Q1	Mean	Median	Q3	Max	N	Range Avg Min	Range Avg Max
High School	19,939	22,000	28,340	27,782	31,264	39,881	10		
Associate's	27,429	27,429	29,314	29,314	31,200	31,200	2	22,922	42,702
Bachelor's	20,180	20,180	20,180	20,180	20,180	20,180	1		
Master's	.	.	.	.	.	.	.		
Doctoral	.	.	.	.	.	.	.		

OFFICE MANAGER

Assumes direct responsibility for dictation, filing, mail, communications, and printing departments. Implements and follows through on general office policies. Confers with other departments regarding the purchasing of office equipment, systems, and procedures affecting more than one department, and the hiring and transferring of employees and office salary structure. Prepares payroll tax returns and performs payroll accounting for organization as required. Maintains retention schedule for library records.

Two-Year College
Regional Data

	Min	Q1	Mean	Median	Q3	Max	N	Range Avg Min	Range Avg Max
Southeast	38,460	38,460	38,460	38,460	38,460	38,460	1		
West & Southwest	39,672	39,672	39,672	39,672	39,672	39,672	1		
ALL REGIONS	38,460	38,460	39,066	39,066	39,672	39,672	2		

State Data

	Min	Q1	Mean	Median	Q3	Max	N	Range Avg Min	Range Avg Max
AL	38,460	38,460	38,460	38,460	38,460	38,460	1	.	.
HI	39,672	39,672	39,672	39,672	39,672	39,672	1	.	.

Degree Required Data

	Min	Q1	Mean	Median	Q3	Max	N	Range Avg Min	Range Avg Max
High School	39,672	39,672	39,672	39,672	39,672	39,672	1	.	.
Associate's	.	.	.	.	.	.		.	.
Bachelor's	38,460	38,460	38,460	38,460	38,460	38,460	1	.	.
Master's	.	.	.	.	.	.		.	.
Doctoral	.	.	.	.	.	.		.	.

OFFICE MANAGER - CONTINUED
Four-Year College
Regional Data

	Min	Q1	Mean	Median	Q3	Max	N	Range Avg Min	Range Avg Max
North Atlantic	26,499	31,790	35,582	38,154	39,374	39,520	4	28,413	48,298
Great Lakes & Plains	23,192	23,192	24,596	24,596	26,000	26,000	2	.	.
West & Southwest	34,800	34,800	34,800	34,800	34,800	34,800	1	.	.
ALL REGIONS	23,192	26,000	32,331	34,800	39,229	39,520	7	28,413	48,298

State Data

	Min	Q1	Mean	Median	Q3	Max	N	Range Avg Min	Range Avg Max
CO	34,800	34,800	34,800	34,800	34,800	34,800	1	.	.
MA	39,520	39,520	39,520	39,520	39,520	39,520	1	.	.
ME	26,499	26,499	31,790	31,790	37,080	37,080	2	.	.
OH	23,192	23,192	24,596	24,596	26,000	26,000	2	.	.
PA	39,229	39,229	39,229	39,229	39,229	39,229	1	28,413	48,298

Degree Required Data

	Min	Q1	Mean	Median	Q3	Max	N	Range Avg Min	Range Avg Max
High School	23,192	23,192	30,136	30,136	37,080	37,080	2	.	.
Associate's	26,000	26,000	30,400	30,400	34,800	34,800	2	.	.
Bachelor's	26,499	26,499	35,083	39,229	39,520	39,520	3	28,413	48,298
Master's	.	.	.	.	.	.		.	.
Doctoral	.	.	.	.	.	.		.	.

OFFICE MANAGER - CONTINUED
University
(Includes ARL Data)
Regional Data

	Min	Q1	Mean	Median	Q3	Max	N	Range Avg Min	Range Avg Max
North Atlantic	28,000	39,881	45,236	42,936	53,000	67,429	13	.	.
Great Lakes & Plains	27,523	33,154	38,914	40,065	46,205	47,910	12	.	.
Southeast	22,426	26,761	30,636	29,537	35,682	39,568	12	.	.
West & Southwest	30,303	39,013	45,767	40,049	48,504	109,485	17	.	.
ALL REGIONS	22,426	32,517	40,754	39,321	46,490	109,485	54	.	.

State Data

	Min	Q1	Mean	Median	Q3	Max	N	Range Avg Min	Range Avg Max
AZ	30,303	30,965	37,194	33,828	43,424	50,818	4	.	.
CA	40,049	40,049	40,049	40,049	40,049	40,049	1	.	.
CO	47,700	47,700	47,700	47,700	47,700	47,700	1	.	.
CT	55,538	55,538	55,538	55,538	55,538	55,538	1	.	.
DC	37,240	37,240	37,240	37,240	37,240	37,240	1	.	.
FL	29,245	29,245	29,245	29,245	29,245	29,245	1	.	.
GA	28,000	28,000	28,000	28,000	28,000	28,000	1	.	.
IL	42,667	44,293	45,983	46,678	47,674	47,910	4	.	.
IN	27,523	30,657	33,979	33,797	37,302	40,800	4	.	.
KY	38,189	38,189	38,189	38,189	38,189	38,189	1	.	.
LA	36,677	36,677	36,677	36,677	36,677	36,677	1	.	.
MA	36,111	36,111	41,997	39,881	50,000	50,000	3	.	.
MD	41,000	41,000	45,646	42,936	53,000	53,000	6	.	.
MI	39,331	39,331	42,910	42,910	46,490	46,490	2	.	.
NC	22,426	23,542	26,816	27,243	30,091	30,354	4	.	.
ND	28,784	28,784	28,784	28,784	28,784	28,784	1	.	.
NE	32,517	32,517	32,517	32,517	32,517	32,517	1	.	.
NY	28,000	28,000	47,714	47,714	67,429	67,429	2	.	.
OR	45,000	45,000	45,000	45,000	45,000	45,000	1	.	.
SC	28,484	28,484	28,484	28,484	28,484	28,484	1	.	.
TN	25,522	25,522	25,522	25,522	25,522	25,522	1	.	.
TX	39,013	39,013	41,729	39,210	40,867	53,062	6	.	.
UT	35,000	35,000	35,000	35,000	35,000	35,000	1	.	.
VA	34,686	34,686	37,127	37,127	39,568	39,568	2	.	.
WA	48,504	48,504	70,379	53,148	109,485	109,485	3	.	.

Degree Required Data

	Min	Q1	Mean	Median	Q3	Max	N	Range Avg Min	Range Avg Max
High School	22,426	29,828	38,557	39,107	46,490	55,538	21	.	.
Associate's	27,523	29,152	39,334	35,515	45,193	67,429	8	.	.
Bachelor's	28,000	36,111	40,322	40,049	42,936	53,148	21	.	.
Master's	109,485	109,485	109,485	109,485	109,485	109,485	1	.	.
Doctoral									

OFFICE MANAGER - CONTINUED
ALL ACADEMIC LIBRARIES
Regional Data

	Min	Q1	Mean	Median	Q3	Max	N	Range Avg Min	Range Avg Max
North Atlantic	26,499	37,240	42,965	41,000	50,000	67,429	17	28,413	48,298
Great Lakes & Plains	23,192	28,784	36,869	36,567	45,920	47,910	14	.	.
Southeast	22,426	28,000	31,238	29,828	36,677	39,568	13	.	.
West & Southwest	30,303	36,029	44,869	39,672	48,504	109,485	19	.	.
ALL REGIONS	22,426	31,626	39,765	39,107	45,000	109,485	63	28,413	48,298

State Data

	Min	Q1	Mean	Median	Q3	Max	N	Range Avg Min	Range Avg Max
AL	38,460	38,460	38,460	38,460	38,460	38,460	1	.	.
AZ	30,303	30,965	37,194	33,828	43,424	50,818	4	.	.
CA	40,049	40,049	40,049	40,049	40,049	40,049	1	.	.
CO	34,800	34,800	41,250	41,250	47,700	47,700	2	.	.
CT	55,538	55,538	55,538	55,538	55,538	55,538	1	.	.
DC	37,240	37,240	37,240	37,240	37,240	37,240	1	.	.
FL	29,245	29,245	29,245	29,245	29,245	29,245	1	.	.
GA	28,000	28,000	28,000	28,000	28,000	28,000	1	.	.
HI	39,672	39,672	39,672	39,672	39,672	39,672	1	.	.
IL	42,667	44,293	45,983	46,678	47,674	47,910	4	.	.
IN	27,523	30,657	33,979	33,797	37,302	40,800	4	.	.
KY	38,189	38,189	38,189	38,189	38,189	38,189	1	.	.
LA	36,677	36,677	36,677	36,677	36,677	36,677	1	.	.
MA	36,111	37,816	41,378	39,700	44,940	50,000	4	.	.
MD	41,000	41,000	45,646	42,936	53,000	53,000	6	.	.
ME	26,499	26,499	31,790	31,790	37,080	37,080	2	.	.
MI	39,331	39,331	42,910	42,910	46,490	46,490	2	.	.
NC	22,426	23,542	26,816	27,243	30,091	30,354	4	.	.
ND	28,784	28,784	28,784	28,784	28,784	28,784	1	.	.
NE	32,517	32,517	32,517	32,517	32,517	32,517	1	.	.
NY	28,000	28,000	47,714	47,714	67,429	67,429	2	.	.
OH	23,192	23,192	24,596	24,596	26,000	26,000	2	.	.
OR	45,000	45,000	45,000	45,000	45,000	45,000	1	.	.
PA	39,229	39,229	39,229	39,229	39,229	39,229	1	28,413	48,298
SC	28,484	28,484	28,484	28,484	28,484	28,484	1	.	.
TN	25,522	25,522	25,522	25,522	25,522	25,522	1	.	.
TX	39,013	39,013	41,729	39,210	40,867	53,062	6	.	.
UT	35,000	35,000	35,000	35,000	35,000	35,000	1	.	.
VA	34,686	34,686	37,127	37,127	39,568	39,568	2	.	.
WA	48,504	48,504	70,379	53,148	109,485	109,485	3	.	.

Degree Required Data

	Min	Q1	Mean	Median	Q3	Max	N	Range Avg Min	Range Avg Max
High School	22,426	29,537	37,902	39,060	46,205	55,538	24	.	.
Associate's	26,000	28,000	37,547	34,900	39,568	67,429	10	.	.
Bachelor's	26,499	36,111	39,619	39,312	42,936	53,148	25	28,413	48,298
Master's	109,485	109,485	109,485	109,485	109,485	109,485	1	.	.
Doctoral	.	.	.	.	.	.		.	.

PUBLIC RELATIONS OFFICER

Promotes and administers public relations policies and programs such as special events, news articles, and audio and visual communication media. Maintains relations with newspaper, radio and TV media, community groups and agencies, school districts and Board of Trustees.

University
(Includes ARL Data)
Regional Data

	Min	Q1	Mean	Median	Q3	Max	N	Range Avg Min	Range Avg Max
North Atlantic	40,713	40,713	57,555	65,976	65,976	65,976	3	.	.
Great Lakes & Plains	38,603	38,603	39,301	39,301	40,000	40,000	2	.	.
Southeast	30,657	32,313	34,351	34,012	36,390	38,724	4	.	.
West & Southwest	27,288	27,288	34,301	35,616	40,000	40,000	3	.	.
ALL REGIONS	27,288	34,012	40,965	38,663	40,356	65,976	12	.	.

State Data

	Min	Q1	Mean	Median	Q3	Max	N	Range Avg Min	Range Avg Max
IA	38,603	38,603	38,603	38,603	38,603	38,603	1	.	.
IN	40,000	40,000	40,000	40,000	40,000	40,000	1	.	.
MA	40,713	40,713	40,713	40,713	40,713	40,713	1	.	.
MD	65,976	65,976	65,976	65,976	65,976	65,976	2	.	.
NC	30,657	30,657	30,657	30,657	30,657	30,657	1	.	.
SC	33,968	33,968	34,012	34,012	34,057	34,057	2	.	.
TN	38,724	38,724	38,724	38,724	38,724	38,724	1	.	.
UT	40,000	40,000	40,000	40,000	40,000	40,000	1	.	.
WY	27,288	27,288	31,452	31,452	35,616	35,616	2	.	.

Degree Required Data

	Min	Q1	Mean	Median	Q3	Max	N	Range Avg Min	Range Avg Max
High School	30,657	30,657	35,685	35,685	40,713	40,713	2	.	.
Associate's	.	.	.	.	.	.		.	.
Bachelor's	33,968	36,330	44,663	39,362	52,988	65,976	8	.	.
Master's	.	.	.	.	.	.		.	.
Doctoral	.	.	.	.	.	.		.	.

PUBLIC RELATIONS OFFICER - CONTINUED
ALL ACADEMIC LIBRARIES
Regional Data

	Min	Q1	Mean	Median	Q3	Max	N	Range Avg Min	Range Avg Max
North Atlantic	40,713	40,713	57,555	65,976	65,976	65,976	3	.	.
Great Lakes & Plains	38,603	38,603	39,301	39,301	40,000	40,000	2	.	.
Southeast	30,657	32,313	34,351	34,012	36,390	38,724	4	.	.
West & Southwest	27,288	27,288	34,301	35,616	40,000	40,000	3	.	.
ALL REGIONS	27,288	34,012	40,965	38,663	40,356	65,976	12	.	.

State Data

	Min	Q1	Mean	Median	Q3	Max	N	Range Avg Min	Range Avg Max
IA	38,603	38,603	38,603	38,603	38,603	38,603	1	.	.
IN	40,000	40,000	40,000	40,000	40,000	40,000	1	.	.
MA	40,713	40,713	40,713	40,713	40,713	40,713	1	.	.
MD	65,976	65,976	65,976	65,976	65,976	65,976	2	.	.
NC	30,657	30,657	30,657	30,657	30,657	30,657	1	.	.
SC	33,968	33,968	34,012	34,012	34,057	34,057	2	.	.
TN	38,724	38,724	38,724	38,724	38,724	38,724	1	.	.
UT	40,000	40,000	40,000	40,000	40,000	40,000	1	.	.
WY	27,288	27,288	31,452	31,452	35,616	35,616	2	.	.

Degree Required Data

	Min	Q1	Mean	Median	Q3	Max	N	Range Avg Min	Range Avg Max
High School	30,657	30,657	35,685	35,685	40,713	40,713	2	.	.
Associate's	.	.	.	.	.	.		.	.
Bachelor's	33,968	36,330	44,663	39,362	52,988	65,976	8	.	.
Master's	.	.	.	.	.	.		.	.
Doctoral	.	.	.	.	.	.		.	.

GRAPHIC ARTIST

Designs unique, original materials based on aesthetic trends. Plans layout and creates materials such as brochures, manuals, advertisements, reports, newsletters and forms using a variety of desktop publishing software. Researches and recommends the purchase of related software and hardware. Organizes and implements desktop publishing and operating methods and procedures.

Two-Year College
Regional Data

	Min	Q1	Mean	Median	Q3	Max	N	Range Avg Min	Range Avg Max
Great Lakes & Plains	33,580	33,580	33,580	33,580	33,580	33,580	1	.	.
West & Southwest	25,678	25,678	33,244	32,676	41,378	41,378	3	.	.
ALL REGIONS	25,678	29,177	33,328	33,128	37,479	41,378	4	.	.

State Data

	Min	Q1	Mean	Median	Q3	Max	N	Range Avg Min	Range Avg Max
MI	33,580	33,580	33,580	33,580	33,580	33,580	1	.	.
TX	25,678	25,678	33,244	32,676	41,378	41,378	3	.	.

Degree Required Data

	Min	Q1	Mean	Median	Q3	Max	N	Range Avg Min	Range Avg Max
High School	.	.	.	.	.	.	.	.	.
Associate's	25,678	25,678	33,244	32,676	41,378	41,378	3	.	.
Bachelor's	.	.	.	.	.	.	.	.	.
Master's	.	.	.	.	.	.	.	.	.
Doctoral	.	.	.	.	.	.	.	.	.

GRAPHIC ARTIST - CONTINUED
Four-Year College
Regional Data

	Min	Q1	Mean	Median	Q3	Max	N	Range Avg Min	Range Avg Max
North Atlantic	51,738	51,738	51,738	51,738	51,738	51,738	1	.	.
Great Lakes & Plains	26,603	26,603	26,603	26,603	26,603	26,603	1	.	.
ALL REGIONS	26,603	26,603	39,171	39,171	51,738	51,738	2	.	.

State Data

	Min	Q1	Mean	Median	Q3	Max	N	Range Avg Min	Range Avg Max
MD	51,738	51,738	51,738	51,738	51,738	51,738	1	.	.
OH	26,603	26,603	26,603	26,603	26,603	26,603	1	.	.

Degree Required Data

	Min	Q1	Mean	Median	Q3	Max	N	Range Avg Min	Range Avg Max
High School	.	.	.	.	.	.	.	.	.
Associate's	26,603	26,603	26,603	26,603	26,603	26,603	1	.	.
Bachelor's	51,738	51,738	51,738	51,738	51,738	51,738	1	.	.
Master's	.	.	.	.	.	.	.	.	.
Doctoral	.	.	.	.	.	.	.	.	.

GRAPHIC ARTIST - CONTINUED
University
(Includes ARL Data)
Regional Data

	Min	Q1	Mean	Median	Q3	Max	N	Range Avg Min	Range Avg Max
North Atlantic	22,802	35,348	45,007	51,280	54,666	54,666	4	.	.
Great Lakes & Plains	28,283	28,283	40,184	33,280	58,988	58,988	3	34,216	50,190
Southeast	24,440	24,440	31,064	33,628	35,124	35,124	3	21,944	38,334
West & Southwest	37,395	37,395	38,698	38,698	40,000	40,000	2	.	.
ALL REGIONS	22,802	30,782	39,264	36,260	51,280	58,988	12	28,080	44,262

State Data

	Min	Q1	Mean	Median	Q3	Max	N	Range Avg Min	Range Avg Max
AR	33,628	33,628	33,628	33,628	33,628	33,628	1	.	.
AZ	37,395	37,395	37,395	37,395	37,395	37,395	1	.	.
DC	22,802	22,802	22,802	22,802	22,802	22,802	1	.	.
IL	33,280	33,280	33,280	33,280	33,280	33,280	1	34,216	50,190
IN	58,988	58,988	58,988	58,988	58,988	58,988	1	.	.
MD	54,666	54,666	54,666	54,666	54,666	54,666	2	.	.
NE	28,283	28,283	28,283	28,283	28,283	28,283	1	.	.
NM	40,000	40,000	40,000	40,000	40,000	40,000	1	.	.
PA	47,894	47,894	47,894	47,894	47,894	47,894	1	.	.
TN	24,440	24,440	29,782	29,782	35,124	35,124	2	21,944	38,334

Degree Required Data

	Min	Q1	Mean	Median	Q3	Max	N	Range Avg Min	Range Avg Max
High School	58,988	58,988	58,988	58,988	58,988	58,988	1	.	.
Associate's	47,894	47,894	47,894	47,894	47,894	47,894	1	.	.
Bachelor's	22,802	33,280	37,334	35,124	40,000	54,666	9	28,080	44,262
Master's	.	.	.	.	.	.	.	.	.
Doctoral	.	.	.	.	.	.	.	.	.

GRAPHIC ARTIST - CONTINUED
ALL ACADEMIC LIBRARIES
Regional Data

	Min	Q1	Mean	Median	Q3	Max	N	Range Avg Min	Range Avg Max
North Atlantic	22,802	47,894	46,353	51,738	54,666	54,666	5	.	.
Great Lakes & Plains	26,603	28,283	36,147	33,280	33,580	58,988	5	34,216	50,190
Southeast	24,440	24,440	31,064	33,628	35,124	35,124	3	21,944	38,334
West & Southwest	25,678	32,676	35,425	37,395	40,000	41,378	5	.	.
ALL REGIONS	22,802	28,283	37,934	34,376	47,894	58,988	18	28,080	44,262

State Data

	Min	Q1	Mean	Median	Q3	Max	N	Range Avg Min	Range Avg Max
AR	33,628	33,628	33,628	33,628	33,628	33,628	1	.	.
AZ	37,395	37,395	37,395	37,395	37,395	37,395	1	.	.
DC	22,802	22,802	22,802	22,802	22,802	22,802	1	.	.
IL	33,280	33,280	33,280	33,280	33,280	33,280	1	34,216	50,190
IN	58,988	58,988	58,988	58,988	58,988	58,988	1	.	.
MD	51,738	51,738	53,690	54,666	54,666	54,666	3	.	.
MI	33,580	33,580	33,580	33,580	33,580	33,580	1	.	.
NE	28,283	28,283	28,283	28,283	28,283	28,283	1	.	.
NM	40,000	40,000	40,000	40,000	40,000	40,000	1	.	.
OH	26,603	26,603	26,603	26,603	26,603	26,603	1	.	.
PA	47,894	47,894	47,894	47,894	47,894	47,894	1	.	.
TN	24,440	24,440	29,782	29,782	35,124	35,124	2	21,944	38,334
TX	25,678	25,678	33,244	32,676	41,378	41,378	3	.	.

Degree Required Data

	Min	Q1	Mean	Median	Q3	Max	N	Range Avg Min	Range Avg Max
High School	58,988	58,988	58,988	58,988	58,988	58,988	1	.	.
Associate's	25,678	26,603	34,846	32,676	41,378	47,894	5	.	.
Bachelor's	22,802	33,280	38,774	36,260	51,738	54,666	10	28,080	44,262
Master's	.	.	.	.	.	.	.	.	.
Doctoral	.	.	.	.	.	.	.	.	.

VOLUNTEER COORDINATOR

Coordinates all volunteers and volunteer programs. Assesses volunteer needs. Recruits, screens and places volunteers. Works with staff ensure proper orientation given and evaluation of performance. May develop and coordinate volunteer recognition programs.

University
(Includes ARL Data)
Regional Data

	Min	Q1	Mean	Median	Q3	Max	N	Range Avg Min	Range Avg Max
Southeast	51,065	51,065	51,065	51,065	51,065	51,065	1	.	.
ALL REGIONS	51,065	51,065	51,065	51,065	51,065	51,065	1	.	.

State Data

	Min	Q1	Mean	Median	Q3	Max	N	Range Avg Min	Range Avg Max
NC	51,065	51,065	51,065	51,065	51,065	51,065	1	.	.

Degree Required Data

	Min	Q1	Mean	Median	Q3	Max	N	Range Avg Min	Range Avg Max
High School	51,065	51,065	51,065	51,065	51,065	51,065	1	.	.
Associate's	.	.	.	.	.	.	.	.	.
Bachelor's	.	.	.	.	.	.	.	.	.
Master's	.	.	.	.	.	.	.	.	.
Doctoral	.	.	.	.	.	.	.	.	.

VOLUNTEER COORDINATOR - CONTINUED
ALL ACADEMIC LIBRARIES
Regional Data

	Min	Q1	Mean	Median	Q3	Max	N	Range Avg Min	Range Avg Max
Southeast	51,065	51,065	51,065	51,065	51,065	51,065	1	.	.
ALL REGIONS	51,065	51,065	51,065	51,065	51,065	51,065	1	.	.

State Data

	Min	Q1	Mean	Median	Q3	Max	N	Range Avg Min	Range Avg Max
NC	51,065	51,065	51,065	51,065	51,065	51,065	1	.	.

Degree Required Data

	Min	Q1	Mean	Median	Q3	Max	N	Range Avg Min	Range Avg Max
High School	51,065	51,065	51,065	51,065	51,065	51,065	1	.	.
Associate's	.	.	.	.	.	.	.	.	.
Bachelor's	.	.	.	.	.	.	.	.	.
Master's	.	.	.	.	.	.	.	.	.
Doctoral	.	.	.	.	.	.	.	.	.

SENIOR ACCOUNTANT

Oversees clerical activities in connection with payables, debits, or credits. Prepares work sheets, analyzes to verify accuracy, prepares monthly journal entries, statements, monthly balance sheet, monthly statements, profit and loss, subsidiary, and other analyses and statements, following prescribed procedures.

Four-Year College
Regional Data

	Min	Q1	Mean	Median	Q3	Max	N	Range Avg Min	Range Avg Max
West & Southwest	44,940	44,940	44,940	44,940	44,940	44,940	1	.	.
ALL REGIONS	44,940	44,940	44,940	44,940	44,940	44,940	1	.	.

State Data

	Min	Q1	Mean	Median	Q3	Max	N	Range Avg Min	Range Avg Max
CO	44,940	44,940	44,940	44,940	44,940	44,940	1	.	.

Degree Required Data

	Min	Q1	Mean	Median	Q3	Max	N	Range Avg Min	Range Avg Max
High School	44,940	44,940	44,940	44,940	44,940	44,940	1	.	.
Associate's	.	.	.	.	.	.	.	.	.
Bachelor's	.	.	.	.	.	.	.	.	.
Master's	.	.	.	.	.	.	.	.	.
Doctoral	.	.	.	.	.	.	.	.	.

SENIOR ACCOUNTANT - CONTINUED
University
(Includes ARL Data)
Regional Data

	Min	Q1	Mean	Median	Q3	Max	N	Range Avg Min	Range Avg Max
North Atlantic	19,966	47,036	48,608	57,623	57,623	60,791	5	.	.
Great Lakes & Plains	22,910	31,000	43,074	45,222	56,100	58,000	7	.	.
Southeast	28,980	41,800	45,009	46,178	48,943	62,670	9	.	.
West & Southwest	24,012	32,416	37,483	39,821	43,368	46,000	10	.	.
ALL REGIONS	19,966	36,166	42,725	43,548	48,943	62,670	31	.	.

State Data

	Min	Q1	Mean	Median	Q3	Max	N	Range Avg Min	Range Avg Max
AL	50,170	50,170	50,170	50,170	50,170	50,170	1	.	.
AR	41,800	41,800	41,800	41,800	41,800	41,800	1	.	.
AZ	26,806	32,034	35,927	38,279	39,821	40,345	4	.	.
CO	43,368	43,368	43,752	43,752	44,136	44,136	2	.	.
DC	19,966	19,966	19,966	19,966	19,966	19,966	1	.	.
FL	46,630	46,630	46,630	46,630	46,630	46,630	1	.	.
IA	46,351	46,351	52,176	52,176	58,000	58,000	2	.	.
IL	41,933	41,933	43,578	43,578	45,222	45,222	2	.	.
IN	56,100	56,100	56,100	56,100	56,100	56,100	1	.	.
MA	47,036	47,036	53,914	53,914	60,791	60,791	2	.	.
MD	57,623	57,623	57,623	57,623	57,623	57,623	2	.	.
NC	43,548	43,548	46,223	46,178	48,943	48,943	3	.	.
NE	31,000	31,000	31,000	31,000	31,000	31,000	1	.	.
OH	22,910	22,910	22,910	22,910	22,910	22,910	1	.	.
SC	36,166	36,166	49,418	49,418	62,670	62,670	2	.	.
TN	28,980	28,980	28,980	28,980	28,980	28,980	1	.	.
UT	24,012	24,012	34,143	32,416	46,000	46,000	3	.	.
WY	41,184	41,184	41,184	41,184	41,184	41,184	1	.	.

Degree Required Data

	Min	Q1	Mean	Median	Q3	Max	N	Range Avg Min	Range Avg Max
High School	24,012	24,012	35,524	35,524	47,036	47,036	2	.	.
Associate's	22,910	26,806	33,324	37,262	39,296	40,345	5	.	.
Bachelor's	19,966	41,800	45,497	46,178	56,100	60,791	19	.	.
Master's	62,670	62,670	62,670	62,670	62,670	62,670	1	.	.
Doctoral	.	.	.	.	.	.		.	.

SENIOR ACCOUNTANT - CONTINUED
ALL ACADEMIC LIBRARIES
Regional Data

	Min	Q1	Mean	Median	Q3	Max	N	Range Avg Min	Range Avg Max
North Atlantic	19,966	47,036	48,608	57,623	57,623	60,791	5	.	.
Great Lakes & Plains	22,910	31,000	43,074	45,222	56,100	58,000	7	.	.
Southeast	28,980	41,800	45,009	46,178	48,943	62,670	9	.	.
West & Southwest	24,012	32,416	38,160	40,345	44,136	46,000	11	.	.
ALL REGIONS	19,966	36,714	42,794	43,842	47,989	62,670	32	.	.

State Data

	Min	Q1	Mean	Median	Q3	Max	N	Range Avg Min	Range Avg Max
AL	50,170	50,170	50,170	50,170	50,170	50,170	1	.	.
AR	41,800	41,800	41,800	41,800	41,800	41,800	1	.	.
AZ	26,806	32,034	35,927	38,279	39,821	40,345	4	.	.
CO	43,368	43,368	44,148	44,136	44,940	44,940	3	.	.
DC	19,966	19,966	19,966	19,966	19,966	19,966	1	.	.
FL	46,630	46,630	46,630	46,630	46,630	46,630	1	.	.
IA	46,351	46,351	52,176	52,176	58,000	58,000	2	.	.
IL	41,933	41,933	43,578	43,578	45,222	45,222	2	.	.
IN	56,100	56,100	56,100	56,100	56,100	56,100	1	.	.
MA	47,036	47,036	53,914	53,914	60,791	60,791	2	.	.
MD	57,623	57,623	57,623	57,623	57,623	57,623	2	.	.
NC	43,548	43,548	46,223	46,178	48,943	48,943	3	.	.
NE	31,000	31,000	31,000	31,000	31,000	31,000	1	.	.
OH	22,910	22,910	22,910	22,910	22,910	22,910	1	.	.
SC	36,166	36,166	49,418	49,418	62,670	62,670	2	.	.
TN	28,980	28,980	28,980	28,980	28,980	28,980	1	.	.
UT	24,012	24,012	34,143	32,416	46,000	46,000	3	.	.
WY	41,184	41,184	41,184	41,184	41,184	41,184	1	.	.

Degree Required Data

	Min	Q1	Mean	Median	Q3	Max	N	Range Avg Min	Range Avg Max
High School	24,012	24,012	38,663	44,940	47,036	47,036	3	.	.
Associate's	22,910	26,806	33,324	37,262	39,296	40,345	5	.	.
Bachelor's	19,966	41,800	45,497	46,178	56,100	60,791	19	.	.
Master's	62,670	62,670	62,670	62,670	62,670	62,670	1	.	.
Doctoral	.	.	.	.	.	.		.	.

ACCOUNTANT

Computes and prepares reports and analyses as requested by organization personnel. Calculates and checks work sheets prior to closing general ledger. Posts, balances, and reconciles general ledger accounts. Prepares profit and loss statement and balance sheets, and compute required financial statements and statistical reports as directed. Computes, checks, and files tax returns.

Four-Year College
Regional Data

	Min	Q1	Mean	Median	Q3	Max	N	Range Avg Min	Range Avg Max
North Atlantic	47,685	47,685	47,685	47,685	47,685	47,685	1	.	.
Great Lakes & Plains	28,413	28,413	28,413	28,413	28,413	28,413	1	.	.
Southeast	41,743	41,743	41,743	41,743	41,743	41,743	1	.	.
West & Southwest	40,926	40,926	40,926	40,926	40,926	40,926	1	.	.
ALL REGIONS	28,413	34,670	39,692	41,334	44,714	47,685	4		.

State Data

	Min	Q1	Mean	Median	Q3	Max	N	Range Avg Min	Range Avg Max
OH	28,413	28,413	28,413	28,413	28,413	28,413	1	.	.
PA	47,685	47,685	47,685	47,685	47,685	47,685	1	.	.
UT	40,926	40,926	40,926	40,926	40,926	40,926	1	.	.
WV	41,743	41,743	41,743	41,743	41,743	41,743	1	.	.

Degree Required Data

	Min	Q1	Mean	Median	Q3	Max	N	Range Avg Min	Range Avg Max
High School	.	.	.	.	.	.		.	.
Associate's	.	.	.	.	.	.		.	.
Bachelor's	28,413	28,413	39,280	41,743	47,685	47,685	3	.	.
Master's	40,926	40,926	40,926	40,926	40,926	40,926	1	.	.
Doctoral	.	.	.	.	.	.		.	.

ACCOUNTANT - CONTINUED
University
(Includes ARL Data)
Regional Data

	Min	Q1	Mean	Median	Q3	Max	N	Range Avg Min	Range Avg Max
North Atlantic	41,278	41,278	41,278	41,278	41,278	41,278	1	.	.
Great Lakes & Plains	22,956	33,290	39,656	43,645	45,867	48,532	6	.	.
Southeast	29,198	31,715	34,494	34,014	38,297	38,666	7	.	.
West & Southwest	25,159	32,722	34,895	35,162	36,170	51,288	12	.	.
ALL REGIONS	22,956	33,058	36,131	35,780	38,666	51,288	26	.	.

State Data

	Min	Q1	Mean	Median	Q3	Max	N	Range Avg Min	Range Avg Max
AZ	25,159	33,107	32,756	34,705	34,705	36,106	5	.	.
CO	51,288	51,288	51,288	51,288	51,288	51,288	1	.	.
FL	29,198	29,198	31,642	31,715	34,014	34,014	3	.	.
IA	42,721	42,721	45,274	44,568	48,532	48,532	3	.	.
IL	45,867	45,867	45,867	45,867	45,867	45,867	1	.	.
LA	33,058	33,058	33,058	33,058	33,058	33,058	1	.	.
NC	38,297	38,297	38,481	38,481	38,666	38,666	2	.	.
ND	22,956	22,956	22,956	22,956	22,956	22,956	1	.	.
PA	41,278	41,278	41,278	41,278	41,278	41,278	1	.	.
SC	36,508	36,508	36,508	36,508	36,508	36,508	1	.	.
SD	33,290	33,290	33,290	33,290	33,290	33,290	1	.	.
TX	36,620	36,620	36,620	36,620	36,620	36,620	1	.	.
UT	32,336	32,336	34,730	35,619	36,234	36,234	3	.	.
WY	26,916	26,916	31,428	31,428	35,940	35,940	2	.	.

Degree Required Data

	Min	Q1	Mean	Median	Q3	Max	N	Range Avg Min	Range Avg Max
High School	29,198	31,715	35,106	34,014	38,297	42,721	7	.	.
Associate's	22,956	25,159	31,123	33,906	34,705	36,106	6	.	.
Bachelor's	32,336	35,619	39,278	37,643	44,568	48,532	10	.	.
Master's	.	.	.	.	.	.		.	.
Doctoral	.	.	.	.	.	.		.	.

ACCOUNTANT - CONTINUED
ALL ACADEMIC LIBRARIES
Regional Data

	Min	Q1	Mean	Median	Q3	Max	N	Range Avg Min	Range Avg Max
North Atlantic	41,278	41,278	44,481	44,481	47,685	47,685	2	.	.
Great Lakes & Plains	22,956	28,413	38,050	42,721	45,867	48,532	7	.	.
Southeast	29,198	32,387	35,400	35,261	38,481	41,743	8	.	.
West & Southwest	25,159	33,107	35,359	35,619	36,234	51,288	13	.	.
ALL REGIONS	22,956	33,058	36,606	36,023	41,278	51,288	30	.	.

State Data

	Min	Q1	Mean	Median	Q3	Max	N	Range Avg Min	Range Avg Max
AZ	25,159	33,107	32,756	34,705	34,705	36,106	5	.	.
CO	51,288	51,288	51,288	51,288	51,288	51,288	1	.	.
FL	29,198	29,198	31,642	31,715	34,014	34,014	3	.	.
IA	42,721	42,721	45,274	44,568	48,532	48,532	3	.	.
IL	45,867	45,867	45,867	45,867	45,867	45,867	1	.	.
LA	33,058	33,058	33,058	33,058	33,058	33,058	1	.	.
NC	38,297	38,297	38,481	38,481	38,666	38,666	2	.	.
ND	22,956	22,956	22,956	22,956	22,956	22,956	1	.	.
OH	28,413	28,413	28,413	28,413	28,413	28,413	1	.	.
PA	41,278	41,278	44,481	44,481	47,685	47,685	2	.	.
SC	36,508	36,508	36,508	36,508	36,508	36,508	1	.	.
SD	33,290	33,290	33,290	33,290	33,290	33,290	1	.	.
TX	36,620	36,620	36,620	36,620	36,620	36,620	1	.	.
UT	32,336	33,978	36,279	35,927	38,580	40,926	4	.	.
WV	41,743	41,743	41,743	41,743	41,743	41,743	1	.	.
WY	26,916	26,916	31,428	31,428	35,940	35,940	2	.	.

Degree Required Data

	Min	Q1	Mean	Median	Q3	Max	N	Range Avg Min	Range Avg Max
High School	29,198	31,715	35,106	34,014	38,297	42,721	7	.	.
Associate's	22,956	25,159	31,123	33,906	34,705	36,106	6	.	.
Bachelor's	28,413	35,619	39,278	38,666	44,568	48,532	13	.	.
Master's	40,926	40,926	40,926	40,926	40,926	40,926	1	.	.
Doctoral	.	.	.	.	.	.		.	.

BOOKKEEPER

Performs diversified duties in maintaining accounting records. Verifies credits and deductions. Checks allocation of charges on bills payable. Maintains and balances petty cash account. Pays minor expenses, prepares daily cash balance figures, and weekly transaction report. Checks employee expense accounts. Prepares monthly receipts and disbursement summaries, takes trial balances, locates discrepancies, and reconciles bank statements. Compiles special reports. Analyzes facts to determine action to be taken, within the limits of standard practice.

Two-Year College
Regional Data

	Min	Q1	Mean	Median	Q3	Max	N	Range Avg Min	Range Avg Max
Great Lakes & Plains	44,056	44,056	44,056	44,056	44,056	44,056	1	.	.
ALL REGIONS	44,056	44,056	44,056	44,056	44,056	44,056	1	.	.

State Data

	Min	Q1	Mean	Median	Q3	Max	N	Range Avg Min	Range Avg Max
MI	44,056	44,056	44,056	44,056	44,056	44,056	1	.	.

Degree Required Data

	Min	Q1	Mean	Median	Q3	Max	N	Range Avg Min	Range Avg Max
High School	.	.	.					.	.
Associate's	.	.	.					.	.
Bachelor's	.	.	.					.	.
Master's	.	.	.					.	.
Doctoral	.	.	.					.	.

BOOKKEEPER - CONTINUED
Four-Year College
Regional Data

	Min	Q1	Mean	Median	Q3	Max	N	Range Avg Min	Range Avg Max
Southeast	25,872	25,872	25,872	25,872	25,872	25,872	1	.	.
West & Southwest	27,816	27,816	27,816	27,816	27,816	27,816	1	.	.
ALL REGIONS	25,872	25,872	26,844	26,844	27,816	27,816	2	.	.

State Data

	Min	Q1	Mean	Median	Q3	Max	N	Range Avg Min	Range Avg Max
CO	27,816	27,816	27,816	27,816	27,816	27,816	1	.	.
VA	25,872	25,872	25,872	25,872	25,872	25,872	1	.	.

Degree Required Data

	Min	Q1	Mean	Median	Q3	Max	N	Range Avg Min	Range Avg Max
High School	27,816	27,816	27,816	27,816	27,816	27,816	1	.	.
Associate's	.	.	.	.	.	.		.	.
Bachelor's	25,872	25,872	25,872	25,872	25,872	25,872	1	.	.
Master's	.	.	.	.	.	.		.	.
Doctoral	.	.	.	.	.	.		.	.

BOOKKEEPER - CONTINUED
University
(Includes ARL Data)
Regional Data

	Min	Q1	Mean	Median	Q3	Max	N	Range Avg Min	Range Avg Max
North Atlantic	32,171	36,830	40,201	41,746	43,572	45,143	4	.	.
Great Lakes & Plains	28,600	34,650	37,707	38,086	41,948	46,020	7	27,955	45,843
Southeast	19,683	21,790	27,856	26,193	31,645	44,503	12	18,886	33,030
West & Southwest	24,744	24,744	37,196	42,708	44,136	44,136	3	.	.
ALL REGIONS	19,683	25,902	33,485	33,669	41,948	46,020	26	23,421	39,437

State Data

	Min	Q1	Mean	Median	Q3	Max	N	Range Avg Min	Range Avg Max
AL	30,600	30,600	30,600	30,600	30,600	30,600	1	.	.
AR	19,683	19,683	22,793	22,793	25,902	25,902	2	.	.
CO	42,708	42,708	43,422	43,422	44,136	44,136	2	.	.
DC	45,143	45,143	45,143	45,143	45,143	45,143	1	.	.
FL	21,756	21,756	21,790	21,790	21,823	21,823	2	.	.
GA	30,512	30,512	30,512	30,512	30,512	30,512	1	.	.
IA	36,227	37,157	38,670	38,253	40,184	41,948	4	.	.
IL	34,650	34,650	34,650	34,650	34,650	34,650	1	.	.
MA	32,171	32,171	36,830	36,830	41,489	41,489	2	.	.
MI	28,600	28,600	28,600	28,600	28,600	28,600	1	.	.
NC	32,689	32,689	32,689	32,689	32,689	32,689	1	.	.
OH	46,020	46,020	46,020	46,020	46,020	46,020	1	27,955	45,843
PA	42,002	42,002	42,002	42,002	42,002	42,002	1	.	.
TN	21,674	21,674	23,513	22,380	26,484	26,484	3	18,886	33,030
VA	36,261	36,261	40,382	40,382	44,503	44,503	2	.	.
WY	24,744	24,744	24,744	24,744	24,744	24,744	1	.	.

Degree Required Data

	Min	Q1	Mean	Median	Q3	Max	N	Range Avg Min	Range Avg Max
High School	19,683	22,102	30,376	29,600	36,368	46,020	16	23,421	39,437
Associate's	30,512	30,512	33,387	33,387	36,261	36,261	2	.	.
Bachelor's	44,503	44,503	44,823	44,823	45,143	45,143	2	.	.
Master's	.	.	.	.	.	.		.	.
Doctoral	.	.	.	.	.	.		.	.

BOOKKEEPER - CONTINUED
ALL ACADEMIC LIBRARIES
Regional Data

	Min	Q1	Mean	Median	Q3	Max	N	Range Avg Min	Range Avg Max
North Atlantic	32,171	36,830	40,201	41,746	43,572	45,143	4	.	.
Great Lakes & Plains	28,600	35,438	38,501	38,253	43,002	46,020	8	27,955	45,843
Southeast	19,683	21,823	27,703	25,902	30,600	44,503	13	18,886	33,030
West & Southwest	24,744	26,280	34,851	35,262	43,422	44,136	4	.	.
ALL REGIONS	19,683	25,902	33,391	32,689	41,948	46,020	29	23,421	39,437

State Data

	Min	Q1	Mean	Median	Q3	Max	N	Range Avg Min	Range Avg Max
AL	30,600	30,600	30,600	30,600	30,600	30,600	1	.	.
AR	19,683	19,683	22,793	22,793	25,902	25,902	2	.	.
CO	27,816	27,816	38,220	42,708	44,136	44,136	3	.	.
DC	45,143	45,143	45,143	45,143	45,143	45,143	1	.	.
FL	21,756	21,756	21,790	21,790	21,823	21,823	2	.	.
GA	30,512	30,512	30,512	30,512	30,512	30,512	1	.	.
IA	36,227	37,157	38,670	38,253	40,184	41,948	4	.	.
IL	34,650	34,650	34,650	34,650	34,650	34,650	1	.	.
MA	32,171	32,171	36,830	36,830	41,489	41,489	2	.	.
MI	28,600	28,600	36,328	36,328	44,056	44,056	2	.	.
NC	32,689	32,689	32,689	32,689	32,689	32,689	1	.	.
OH	46,020	46,020	46,020	46,020	46,020	46,020	1	27,955	45,843
PA	42,002	42,002	42,002	42,002	42,002	42,002	1	.	.
TN	21,674	21,674	23,513	22,380	26,484	26,484	3	18,886	33,030
VA	25,872	25,872	35,545	36,261	44,503	44,503	3	.	.
WY	24,744	24,744	24,744	24,744	24,744	24,744	1	.	.

Degree Required Data

	Min	Q1	Mean	Median	Q3	Max	N	Range Avg Min	Range Avg Max
High School	19,683	22,380	30,225	28,600	34,650	46,020	17	23,421	39,437
Associate's	30,512	30,512	33,387	33,387	36,261	36,261	2	.	.
Bachelor's	25,872	25,872	38,506	44,503	45,143	45,143	3	.	.
Master's	.	.	.	.	.	.	.	.	.
Doctoral	.	.	.	.	.	.	.	.	.

PAYROLL ADMINISTRATOR

Makes a variety of computations on employee overtime, shift premium, and various payroll deductions, following standard procedures, to prepare payroll. Summarizes and reconciles payroll sheets. Investigates and resolves payroll problems, responding to employee requests. Maintains and updates data base records. Generates federal and state tax documents. Prepares special payroll analysis reports.

University
(Includes ARL Data)
Regional Data

	Min	Q1	Mean	Median	Q3	Max	N	Range Avg Min	Range Avg Max
North Atlantic	48,385	48,385	48,385	48,385	48,385	48,385	2	.	.
Great Lakes & Plains	47,857	47,857	58,595	58,595	69,333	69,333	2	.	.
Southeast	26,000	26,000	27,939	27,217	30,600	30,600	3	.	.
West & Southwest	31,633	31,633	31,633	31,633	31,633	31,633	1	.	.
ALL REGIONS	26,000	28,909	41,176	39,745	48,385	69,333	8	.	.

State Data

	Min	Q1	Mean	Median	Q3	Max	N	Range Avg Min	Range Avg Max
AL	30,600	30,600	30,600	30,600	30,600	30,600	1	.	.
FL	27,217	27,217	27,217	27,217	27,217	27,217	1	.	.
IA	47,857	47,857	47,857	47,857	47,857	47,857	1	.	.
IL	69,333	69,333	69,333	69,333	69,333	69,333	1	.	.
MD	48,385	48,385	48,385	48,385	48,385	48,385	2	.	.
NC	26,000	26,000	26,000	26,000	26,000	26,000	1	.	.
UT	31,633	31,633	31,633	31,633	31,633	31,633	1	.	.

Degree Required Data

	Min	Q1	Mean	Median	Q3	Max	N	Range Avg Min	Range Avg Max
High School	26,000	27,217	35,370	31,117	48,385	48,385	6	.	.
Associate's	.	.	.	.	.	.		.	.
Bachelor's	69,333	69,333	69,333	69,333	69,333	69,333	1	.	.
Master's	.	.	.	.	.	.		.	.
Doctoral	.	.	.	.	.	.		.	.

PAYROLL ADMINISTRATOR - CONTINUED
ALL ACADEMIC LIBRARIES
Regional Data

	Min	Q1	Mean	Median	Q3	Max	N	Range Avg Min	Range Avg Max
North Atlantic	48,385	48,385	48,385	48,385	48,385	48,385	2	.	.
Great Lakes & Plains	47,857	47,857	58,595	58,595	69,333	69,333	2	.	.
Southeast	26,000	26,000	27,939	27,217	30,600	30,600	3	.	.
West & Southwest	31,633	31,633	31,633	31,633	31,633	31,633	1	.	.
ALL REGIONS	26,000	28,909	41,176	39,745	48,385	69,333	8	.	.

State Data

	Min	Q1	Mean	Median	Q3	Max	N	Range Avg Min	Range Avg Max
AL	30,600	30,600	30,600	30,600	30,600	30,600	1	.	.
FL	27,217	27,217	27,217	27,217	27,217	27,217	1	.	.
IA	47,857	47,857	47,857	47,857	47,857	47,857	1	.	.
IL	69,333	69,333	69,333	69,333	69,333	69,333	1	.	.
MD	48,385	48,385	48,385	48,385	48,385	48,385	2	.	.
NC	26,000	26,000	26,000	26,000	26,000	26,000	1	.	.
UT	31,633	31,633	31,633	31,633	31,633	31,633	1	.	.

Degree Required Data

	Min	Q1	Mean	Median	Q3	Max	N	Range Avg Min	Range Avg Max
High School	26,000	27,217	35,370	31,117	48,385	48,385	6	.	.
Associate's	.	.	.	.	.	.	.	.	.
Bachelor's	69,333	69,333	69,333	69,333	69,333	69,333	1	.	.
Master's	.	.	.	.	.	.	.	.	.
Doctoral	.	.	.	.	.	.	.	.	.

HUMAN RESOURCES MANAGER

General responsibility for all personnel activities, such as employment, training, wage and salary administration, safety and working conditions, employee counseling, and personnel records. Investigates, advises, and prepares policies affecting personnel, and consults and advises on interpretation and administration. Conducts union contract negotiations as required. Advises management on interpretation of policy.

**Four-Year College
Regional Data**

	Min	Q1	Mean	Median	Q3	Max	N	Range Avg Min	Range Avg Max
West & Southwest	44,964	44,964	44,964	44,964	44,964	44,964	1	.	.
ALL REGIONS	44,964	44,964	44,964	44,964	44,964	44,964	1	.	.

State Data

	Min	Q1	Mean	Median	Q3	Max	N	Range Avg Min	Range Avg Max
CO	44,964	44,964	44,964	44,964	44,964	44,964	1	.	.

Degree Required Data

	Min	Q1	Mean	Median	Q3	Max	N	Range Avg Min	Range Avg Max
High School	44,964	44,964	44,964	44,964	44,964	44,964	1	.	.
Associate's	.	.	.	.	.	.	.	.	.
Bachelor's	.	.	.	.	.	.	.	.	.
Master's	.	.	.	.	.	.	.	.	.
Doctoral	.	.	.	.	.	.	.	.	.

HUMAN RESOURCES MANAGER - CONTINUED
University
(Includes ARL Data)
Regional Data

	Min	Q1	Mean	Median	Q3	Max	N	Range Avg Min	Range Avg Max
North Atlantic	57,564	57,564	57,662	57,711	57,711	57,711	3	.	.
Great Lakes & Plains	53,699	53,699	55,725	54,570	58,906	58,906	3	.	.
Southeast	34,800	36,067	40,777	37,271	44,423	54,830	6	.	.
West & Southwest	33,036	33,643	44,139	40,883	52,758	65,510	8	.	.
ALL REGIONS	33,036	36,352	46,897	45,323	57,637	65,510	20	.	.

State Data

	Min	Q1	Mean	Median	Q3	Max	N	Range Avg Min	Range Avg Max
AL	54,830	54,830	54,830	54,830	54,830	54,830	1	.	.
AZ	45,130	45,130	55,320	55,320	65,510	65,510	2	.	.
CA	33,036	33,036	33,036	33,036	33,036	33,036	2	.	.
CO	45,516	45,516	45,516	45,516	45,516	45,516	1	.	.
IA	53,699	53,699	53,699	53,699	53,699	53,699	1	.	.
IL	58,906	58,906	58,906	58,906	58,906	58,906	1	.	.
IN	54,570	54,570	54,570	54,570	54,570	54,570	1	.	.
LA	34,800	34,800	34,800	34,800	34,800	34,800	1	.	.
MA	57,564	57,564	57,564	57,564	57,564	57,564	1	.	.
MD	57,711	57,711	57,711	57,711	57,711	57,711	2	.	.
NC	36,766	36,766	36,766	36,766	36,766	36,766	1	.	.
SC	36,067	36,067	40,245	40,245	44,423	44,423	2	.	.
TN	37,776	37,776	37,776	37,776	37,776	37,776	1	.	.
TX	34,250	34,250	34,250	34,250	34,250	34,250	1	.	.
UT	60,000	60,000	60,000	60,000	60,000	60,000	1	.	.
WY	36,636	36,636	36,636	36,636	36,636	36,636	1	.	.

Degree Required Data

	Min	Q1	Mean	Median	Q3	Max	N	Range Avg Min	Range Avg Max
High School	34,250	34,250	36,264	36,766	37,776	37,776	3	.	.
Associate's	33,036	33,036	33,036	33,036	33,036	33,036	2	.	.
Bachelor's	34,800	45,130	52,379	54,830	57,711	65,510	13	.	.
Master's	.	.	.	.	.	.		.	.
Doctoral	.	.	.	.	.	.		.	.

HUMAN RESOURCES MANAGER - CONTINUED
ALL ACADEMIC LIBRARIES
Regional Data

	Min	Q1	Mean	Median	Q3	Max	N	Range Avg Min	Range Avg Max
North Atlantic	57,564	57,564	57,662	57,711	57,711	57,711	3	.	.
Great Lakes & Plains	53,699	53,699	55,725	54,570	58,906	58,906	3	.	.
Southeast	34,800	36,067	40,777	37,271	44,423	54,830	6	.	.
West & Southwest	33,036	34,250	44,231	44,964	45,516	65,510	9	.	.
ALL REGIONS	33,036	36,636	46,805	45,130	57,564	65,510	21	.	.

State Data

	Min	Q1	Mean	Median	Q3	Max	N	Range Avg Min	Range Avg Max
AL	54,830	54,830	54,830	54,830	54,830	54,830	1	.	.
AZ	45,130	45,130	55,320	55,320	65,510	65,510	2	.	.
CA	33,036	33,036	33,036	33,036	33,036	33,036	2	.	.
CO	44,964	44,964	45,240	45,240	45,516	45,516	2	.	.
IA	53,699	53,699	53,699	53,699	53,699	53,699	1	.	.
IL	58,906	58,906	58,906	58,906	58,906	58,906	1	.	.
IN	54,570	54,570	54,570	54,570	54,570	54,570	1	.	.
LA	34,800	34,800	34,800	34,800	34,800	34,800	1	.	.
MA	57,564	57,564	57,564	57,564	57,564	57,564	1	.	.
MD	57,711	57,711	57,711	57,711	57,711	57,711	2	.	.
NC	36,766	36,766	36,766	36,766	36,766	36,766	1	.	.
SC	36,067	36,067	40,245	40,245	44,423	44,423	2	.	.
TN	37,776	37,776	37,776	37,776	37,776	37,776	1	.	.
TX	34,250	34,250	34,250	34,250	34,250	34,250	1	.	.
UT	60,000	60,000	60,000	60,000	60,000	60,000	1	.	.
WY	36,636	36,636	36,636	36,636	36,636	36,636	1	.	.

Degree Required Data

	Min	Q1	Mean	Median	Q3	Max	N	Range Avg Min	Range Avg Max
High School	34,250	35,508	38,439	37,271	41,370	44,964	4	.	.
Associate's	33,036	33,036	33,036	33,036	33,036	33,036	2	.	.
Bachelor's	34,800	45,130	52,379	54,830	57,711	65,510	13	.	.
Master's	.	.	.	.	.	.		.	.
Doctoral	.	.	.	.	.	.		.	.

HUMAN RESOURCES ASSISTANT

Organizes and maintains records, and files government reports as scheduled. Maintains employment statistical data and prepares related reports. Assists in employment activities involving interviewing, verifying qualifications, and checking references. Assists in administering employee benefit programs. Responds to employee inquiries on matters related to library programs and activities.

Four-Year College
Regional Data

	Min	Q1	Mean	Median	Q3	Max	N	Range Avg Min	Range Avg Max
West & Southwest	39,384	39,384	39,384	39,384	39,384	39,384	1	.	.
ALL REGIONS	39,384	39,384	39,384	39,384	39,384	39,384	1	.	.

State Data

	Min	Q1	Mean	Median	Q3	Max	N	Range Avg Min	Range Avg Max
CO	39,384	39,384	39,384	39,384	39,384	39,384	1	.	.

Degree Required Data

	Min	Q1	Mean	Median	Q3	Max	N	Range Avg Min	Range Avg Max
High School	39,384	39,384	39,384	39,384	39,384	39,384	1	.	.
Associate's	.	.	.	.	.	.		.	.
Bachelor's	.	.	.	.	.	.		.	.
Master's	.	.	.	.	.	.		.	.
Doctoral	.	.	.	.	.	.		.	.

HUMAN RESOURCES ASSISTANT - CONTINUED
University
(Includes ARL Data)
Regional Data

	Min	Q1	Mean	Median	Q3	Max	N	Range Avg Min	Range Avg Max
North Atlantic	39,707	39,707	43,079	42,494	47,036	47,036	3	.	.
Great Lakes & Plains	37,461	37,461	42,094	40,000	48,820	48,820	3	.	.
Southeast	19,575	25,121	26,633	27,317	28,307	32,000	8	18,886	33,030
West & Southwest	38,027	38,027	38,366	38,120	38,952	38,952	3	.	.
ALL REGIONS	19,575	28,050	34,334	37,461	39,707	48,820	17	18,886	33,030

State Data

	Min	Q1	Mean	Median	Q3	Max	N	Range Avg Min	Range Avg Max
AR	19,575	19,575	23,079	23,079	26,583	26,583	2	.	.
CO	38,027	38,027	38,489	38,489	38,952	38,952	2	.	.
DC	39,707	39,707	41,101	41,101	42,494	42,494	2	.	.
IA	40,000	40,000	44,410	44,410	48,820	48,820	2	.	.
IL	37,461	37,461	37,461	37,461	37,461	37,461	1	.	.
MA	47,036	47,036	47,036	47,036	47,036	47,036	1	.	.
NC	28,050	28,050	29,420	28,209	32,000	32,000	3	.	.
SC	28,404	28,404	28,404	28,404	28,404	28,404	1	.	.
TN	23,878	23,878	25,121	25,121	26,364	26,364	2	18,886	33,030
UT	38,120	38,120	38,120	38,120	38,120	38,120	1	.	.

Degree Required Data

	Min	Q1	Mean	Median	Q3	Max	N	Range Avg Min	Range Avg Max
High School	19,575	26,364	31,980	28,307	37,461	48,820	10	18,886	33,030
Associate's	.	.	.	.	.	.		.	.
Bachelor's	26,583	38,120	37,381	39,707	40,000	42,494	5	.	.
Master's	.	.	.	.	.	.		.	.
Doctoral	.	.	.	.	.	.		.	.

HUMAN RESOURCES ASSISTANT - CONTINUED
ALL ACADEMIC LIBRARIES
Regional Data

	Min	Q1	Mean	Median	Q3	Max	N	Range Avg Min	Range Avg Max
North Atlantic	39,707	39,707	43,079	42,494	47,036	47,036	3	.	.
Great Lakes & Plains	37,461	37,461	42,094	40,000	48,820	48,820	3	.	.
Southeast	19,575	25,121	26,633	27,317	28,307	32,000	8	18,886	33,030
West & Southwest	38,027	38,073	38,621	38,536	39,168	39,384	4	.	.
ALL REGIONS	19,575	28,050	34,615	37,744	39,707	48,820	18	18,886	33,030

State Data

	Min	Q1	Mean	Median	Q3	Max	N	Range Avg Min	Range Avg Max
AR	19,575	19,575	23,079	23,079	26,583	26,583	2	.	.
CO	38,027	38,027	38,788	38,952	39,384	39,384	3	.	.
DC	39,707	39,707	41,101	41,101	42,494	42,494	2	.	.
IA	40,000	40,000	44,410	44,410	48,820	48,820	2	.	.
IL	37,461	37,461	37,461	37,461	37,461	37,461	1	.	.
MA	47,036	47,036	47,036	47,036	47,036	47,036	1	.	.
NC	28,050	28,050	29,420	28,209	32,000	32,000	3	.	.
SC	28,404	28,404	28,404	28,404	28,404	28,404	1	.	.
TN	23,878	23,878	25,121	25,121	26,364	26,364	2	18,886	33,030
UT	38,120	38,120	38,120	38,120	38,120	38,120	1	.	.

Degree Required Data

	Min	Q1	Mean	Median	Q3	Max	N	Range Avg Min	Range Avg Max
High School	19,575	26,364	32,653	28,404	39,384	48,820	11	18,886	33,030
Associate's	.	.	.	.	.	.		.	.
Bachelor's	26,583	38,120	37,381	39,707	40,000	42,494	5	.	.
Master's	.	.	.	.	.	.		.	.
Doctoral	.	.	.	.	.	.		.	.

FACILITY ENGINEERING MANAGER (MAINTENANCE)

Responsible for grounds, buildings, and building equipment. Supervises the installation, maintenance, and repair of: electrical, gas, air, and water installations; fire sprinklers; the operation of building equipment and facilities; janitorial services; and the maintenance of grounds. Works with outside contractors and architects on building construction as necessary. Plans, lays out, and assigns work, involving diagnosing and remedying difficult problems. Reports defective equipment and recommends the replacement of obsolete or damaged equipment when estimates of repair costs are excessive. Expedites building repairs in construction to avoid production delays. Performs normal supervisory functions in a department with seldom more than 10 persons.

University
(Includes ARL Data)
Regional Data

	Min	Q1	Mean	Median	Q3	Max	N	Range Avg Min	Range Avg Max
North Atlantic	48,982	48,982	56,106	56,106	63,231	63,231	4	.	.
Great Lakes & Plains	24,960	33,280	40,211	42,525	47,141	50,832	4	23,109	42,578
Southeast	23,985	29,744	34,782	34,212	37,727	48,814	6	25,459	44,512
West & Southwest	47,904	47,904	49,660	49,125	51,952	51,952	3	.	.
ALL REGIONS	23,985	34,850	43,702	47,904	49,125	63,231	17	23,892	43,222

State Data

	Min	Q1	Mean	Median	Q3	Max	N	Range Avg Min	Range Avg Max
AL	23,985	23,985	23,985	23,985	23,985	23,985	1	.	.
AR	33,573	33,573	33,573	33,573	33,573	33,573	1	.	.
AZ	51,952	51,952	51,952	51,952	51,952	51,952	1	.	.
CO	47,904	47,904	47,904	47,904	47,904	47,904	1	.	.
IA	50,832	50,832	50,832	50,832	50,832	50,832	1	.	.
IL	24,960	24,960	33,280	33,280	41,600	41,600	2	23,109	42,578
IN	43,450	43,450	43,450	43,450	43,450	43,450	1	.	.
MD	48,982	48,982	56,106	56,106	63,231	63,231	4	.	.
NC	34,850	34,850	40,464	37,727	48,814	48,814	3	.	.
TN	29,744	29,744	29,744	29,744	29,744	29,744	1	25,459	44,512
UT	49,125	49,125	49,125	49,125	49,125	49,125	1	.	.

Degree Required Data

	Min	Q1	Mean	Median	Q3	Max	N	Range Avg Min	Range Avg Max
High School	23,985	29,744	39,450	41,600	48,814	50,832	7	24,378	43,482
Associate's	24,960	24,960	29,905	29,905	34,850	34,850	2	22,922	42,702
Bachelor's	33,573	48,982	51,297	49,125	63,231	63,231	7	.	.
Master's	.	.	.	.	.	.	.	.	.
Doctoral	.	.	.	.	.	.	.	.	.

FACILITY ENGINEERING MANAGER (MAINTENANCE) - CONTINUED
ALL ACADEMIC LIBRARIES
Regional Data

	Min	Q1	Mean	Median	Q3	Max	N	Range Avg Min	Range Avg Max
North Atlantic	48,982	48,982	56,106	56,106	63,231	63,231	4	.	.
Great Lakes & Plains	24,960	33,280	40,211	42,525	47,141	50,832	4	23,109	42,578
Southeast	23,985	29,744	34,782	34,212	37,727	48,814	6	25,459	44,512
West & Southwest	47,904	47,904	49,660	49,125	51,952	51,952	3	.	.
ALL REGIONS	23,985	34,850	43,702	47,904	49,125	63,231	17	23,892	43,222

State Data

	Min	Q1	Mean	Median	Q3	Max	N	Range Avg Min	Range Avg Max
AL	23,985	23,985	23,985	23,985	23,985	23,985	1	.	.
AR	33,573	33,573	33,573	33,573	33,573	33,573	1	.	.
AZ	51,952	51,952	51,952	51,952	51,952	51,952	1	.	.
CO	47,904	47,904	47,904	47,904	47,904	47,904	1	.	.
IA	50,832	50,832	50,832	50,832	50,832	50,832	1	.	.
IL	24,960	24,960	33,280	33,280	41,600	41,600	2	23,109	42,578
IN	43,450	43,450	43,450	43,450	43,450	43,450	1	.	.
MD	48,982	48,982	56,106	56,106	63,231	63,231	4	.	.
NC	34,850	34,850	40,464	37,727	48,814	48,814	3	.	.
TN	29,744	29,744	29,744	29,744	29,744	29,744	1	25,459	44,512
UT	49,125	49,125	49,125	49,125	49,125	49,125	1	.	.

Degree Required Data

	Min	Q1	Mean	Median	Q3	Max	N	Range Avg Min	Range Avg Max
High School	23,985	29,744	39,450	41,600	48,814	50,832	7	24,378	43,482
Associate's	24,960	24,960	29,905	29,905	34,850	34,850	2	22,922	42,702
Bachelor's	33,573	48,982	51,297	49,125	63,231	63,231	7	.	.
Master's	.	.	.	.	.	.		.	.
Doctoral	.	.	.	.	.	.		.	.

BUILDING MAINTENANCE

Performs routine and preventive maintenance as directed. Performs various repairs requiring general knowledge of carpentry, plumbing, HVAC, and electrical and mechanical repair. Operates lawn mowing and snow blowing equipment. Arranges meeting rooms for special events.

University
(Includes ARL Data)
Regional Data

	Min	Q1	Mean	Median	Q3	Max	N	Range Avg Min	Range Avg Max
North Atlantic	37,240	37,240	37,240	37,240	37,240	37,240	1	.	.
Great Lakes & Plains	15,344	15,344	22,482	22,482	29,619	29,619	2	.	.
Southeast	23,873	23,873	26,437	25,104	30,334	30,334	3	.	.
West & Southwest	22,091	22,484	24,955	22,905	27,082	32,260	6	.	.
ALL REGIONS	15,344	22,601	25,937	24,489	29,977	37,240	12	.	.

State Data

	Min	Q1	Mean	Median	Q3	Max	N	Range Avg Min	Range Avg Max
AZ	22,091	22,091	24,587	24,587	27,082	27,082	2	.	.
DC	37,240	37,240	37,240	37,240	37,240	37,240	1	.	.
IN	29,619	29,619	29,619	29,619	29,619	29,619	1	.	.
NC	23,873	23,873	27,104	27,104	30,334	30,334	2	.	.
OH	15,344	15,344	15,344	15,344	15,344	15,344	1	.	.
TN	25,104	25,104	25,104	25,104	25,104	25,104	1	.	.
TX	22,484	22,484	22,484	22,484	22,484	22,484	1	.	.
UT	22,717	22,717	26,023	23,093	32,260	32,260	3	.	.

Degree Required Data

	Min	Q1	Mean	Median	Q3	Max	N	Range Avg Min	Range Avg Max
High School	15,344	22,484	24,909	23,873	29,619	32,260	11	.	.
Associate's	.	.	.	.	.	.		.	.
Bachelor's	37,240	37,240	37,240	37,240	37,240	37,240	1	.	.
Master's	.	.	.	.	.	.		.	.
Doctoral	.	.	.	.	.	.		.	.

BUILDING MAINTENANCE - CONTINUED
ALL ACADEMIC LIBRARIES
Regional Data

	Min	Q1	Mean	Median	Q3	Max	N	Range Avg Min	Range Avg Max
North Atlantic	37,240	37,240	37,240	37,240	37,240	37,240	1	.	.
Great Lakes & Plains	15,344	15,344	22,482	22,482	29,619	29,619	2	.	.
Southeast	23,873	23,873	26,437	25,104	30,334	30,334	3	.	.
West & Southwest	22,091	22,484	24,955	22,905	27,082	32,260	6	.	.
ALL REGIONS	15,344	22,601	25,937	24,489	29,977	37,240	12	.	.

State Data

	Min	Q1	Mean	Median	Q3	Max	N	Range Avg Min	Range Avg Max
AZ	22,091	22,091	24,587	24,587	27,082	27,082	2	.	
DC	37,240	37,240	37,240	37,240	37,240	37,240	1	.	
IN	29,619	29,619	29,619	29,619	29,619	29,619	1	.	
NC	23,873	23,873	27,104	27,104	30,334	30,334	2	.	
OH	15,344	15,344	15,344	15,344	15,344	15,344	1	.	
TN	25,104	25,104	25,104	25,104	25,104	25,104	1	.	
TX	22,484	22,484	22,484	22,484	22,484	22,484	1	.	
UT	22,717	22,717	26,023	23,093	32,260	32,260	3	.	

Degree Required Data

	Min	Q1	Mean	Median	Q3	Max	N	Range Avg Min	Range Avg Max
High School	15,344	22,484	24,909	23,873	29,619	32,260	11	.	
Associate's								.	
Bachelor's	37,240	37,240	37,240	37,240	37,240	37,240	1	.	
Master's								.	
Doctoral								.	

SECURITY (DISCIPLINE MONITOR)

Makes regular watch rounds of premises outside of scheduled working hours, where frequency of trips and stations is prescribed. Checks buildings, equipment and materials for leaks, fires, unauthorized individuals and other conditions. Ensures that all entrances and windows are secured, and that elevator and fire doors are closed. Makes written report of all irregularities or unusual circumstances.

University
(Includes ARL Data)
Regional Data

	Min	Q1	Mean	Median	Q3	Max	N	Range Avg Min	Range Avg Max
North Atlantic	31,838	31,838	36,082	34,809	38,827	44,373	6	.	
Southeast	20,359	20,359	22,254	23,071	23,333	23,333	3	.	
West & Southwest	18,720	19,187	23,757	19,760	25,746	40,740	12	.	
ALL REGIONS	18,720	19,760	27,064	23,071	33,668	44,373	21	.	

State Data

	Min	Q1	Mean	Median	Q3	Max	N	Range Avg Min	Range Avg Max
CO	30,900	30,900	35,820	35,820	40,740	40,740	2	.	
GA	23,333	23,333	23,333	23,333	23,333	23,333	1	.	
MA	31,838	31,838	36,109	33,668	38,827	44,373	5	.	
PA	35,949	35,949	35,949	35,949	35,949	35,949	1	.	
SC	20,359	20,359	21,715	21,715	23,071	23,071	2	.	
UT	18,720	18,720	21,345	19,760	19,760	38,000	10	.	

Degree Required Data

	Min	Q1	Mean	Median	Q3	Max	N	Range Avg Min	Range Avg Max
High School	18,720	19,760	25,731	20,359	31,838	44,373	17	.	.
Associate's	35,949	35,949	35,949	35,949	35,949	35,949	1	.	.
Bachelor's	23,333	23,333	23,333	23,333	23,333	23,333	1	.	.
Master's	.	.	.	.	.	.	.	.	.
Doctoral	.	.	.	.	.	.	.	.	.

SECURITY (DISCIPLINE MONITOR) - CONTINUED
ALL ACADEMIC LIBRARIES
Regional Data

	Min	Q1	Mean	Median	Q3	Max	N	Range Avg Min	Range Avg Max
North Atlantic	31,838	31,838	36,082	34,809	38,827	44,373	6	.	.
Southeast	20,359	20,359	22,254	23,071	23,333	23,333	3	.	.
West & Southwest	18,720	19,187	23,757	19,760	25,746	40,740	12	.	.
ALL REGIONS	18,720	19,760	27,064	23,071	33,668	44,373	21	.	.

State Data

	Min	Q1	Mean	Median	Q3	Max	N	Range Avg Min	Range Avg Max
CO	30,900	30,900	35,820	35,820	40,740	40,740	2	.	.
GA	23,333	23,333	23,333	23,333	23,333	23,333	1	.	.
MA	31,838	31,838	36,109	33,668	38,827	44,373	5	.	.
PA	35,949	35,949	35,949	35,949	35,949	35,949	1	.	.
SC	20,359	20,359	21,715	21,715	23,071	23,071	2	.	.
UT	18,720	18,720	21,345	19,760	19,760	38,000	10	.	.

Degree Required Data

	Min	Q1	Mean	Median	Q3	Max	N	Range Avg Min	Range Avg Max
High School	18,720	19,760	25,731	20,359	31,838	44,373	17	.	.
Associate's	35,949	35,949	35,949	35,949	35,949	35,949	1	.	.
Bachelor's	23,333	23,333	23,333	23,333	23,333	23,333	1	.	.
Master's	.	.	.	.	.	.	.	.	.
Doctoral	.	.	.	.	.	.	.	.	.

DEVELOPMENT MANAGER

Manages and may participate in all aspects of library's annual fund development program. Identifies potential donors and maintains donor database. Responsible for maintaining budgets of delegated programs and may supervise staff.

University
(Includes ARL Data)
Regional Data

	Min	Q1	Mean	Median	Q3	Max	N	Range Avg Min	Range Avg Max
North Atlantic	21,275	41,489	50,627	55,000	65,500	65,500	6	.	.
Great Lakes & Plains	32,000	32,000	49,508	49,508	67,015	67,015	2	.	.
Southeast	50,503	54,647	63,915	61,330	71,556	85,754	8	.	.
West & Southwest	41,184	41,184	51,060	51,060	60,935	60,935	2	.	.
ALL REGIONS	21,275	50,503	56,457	57,080	65,500	85,754	18	.	.

State Data

	Min	Q1	Mean	Median	Q3	Max	N	Range Avg Min	Range Avg Max
AL	59,160	59,160	59,160	59,160	59,160	59,160	1	.	.
AR	68,000	68,000	68,000	68,000	68,000	68,000	1	.	.
AZ	60,935	60,935	60,935	60,935	60,935	60,935	1	.	.
FL	63,500	63,500	63,500	63,500	63,500	63,500	1	.	.
IN	67,015	67,015	67,015	67,015	67,015	67,015	1	.	.
MA	41,489	41,489	41,489	41,489	41,489	41,489	1	.	.
MD	55,000	55,000	60,250	60,250	65,500	65,500	4	.	.
MI	32,000	32,000	32,000	32,000	32,000	32,000	1	.	.
NC	50,503	50,503	60,205	55,000	75,111	75,111	3	.	.
PA	21,275	21,275	21,275	21,275	21,275	21,275	1	.	.
SC	54,294	54,294	70,024	70,024	85,754	85,754	2	.	.
WY	41,184	41,184	41,184	41,184	41,184	41,184	1	.	.

Degree Required Data

	Min	Q1	Mean	Median	Q3	Max	N	Range Avg Min	Range Avg Max
High School	32,000	32,000	36,745	36,745	41,489	41,489	2	.	.
Associate's	.	.	.	.	.	.		.	.
Bachelor's	21,275	55,000	58,066	59,160	65,500	75,111	13	.	.
Master's	60,935	60,935	73,344	73,344	85,754	85,754	2	.	.
Doctoral	.	.	.	.	.	.		.	.

DEVELOPMENT MANAGER - CONTINUED
ALL ACADEMIC LIBRARIES
Regional Data

	Min	Q1	Mean	Median	Q3	Max	N	Range Avg Min	Range Avg Max
North Atlantic	21,275	41,489	50,627	55,000	65,500	65,500	6	.	.
Great Lakes & Plains	32,000	32,000	49,508	49,508	67,015	67,015	2	.	.
Southeast	50,503	54,647	63,915	61,330	71,556	85,754	8	.	.
West & Southwest	41,184	41,184	51,060	51,060	60,935	60,935	2	.	.
ALL REGIONS	21,275	50,503	56,457	57,080	65,500	85,754	18	.	.

State Data

	Min	Q1	Mean	Median	Q3	Max	N	Range Avg Min	Range Avg Max
AL	59,160	59,160	59,160	59,160	59,160	59,160	1	.	.
AR	68,000	68,000	68,000	68,000	68,000	68,000	1	.	.
AZ	60,935	60,935	60,935	60,935	60,935	60,935	1	.	.
FL	63,500	63,500	63,500	63,500	63,500	63,500	1	.	.
IN	67,015	67,015	67,015	67,015	67,015	67,015	1	.	.
MA	41,489	41,489	41,489	41,489	41,489	41,489	1	.	.
MD	55,000	55,000	60,250	60,250	65,500	65,500	4	.	.
MI	32,000	32,000	32,000	32,000	32,000	32,000	1	.	.
NC	50,503	50,503	60,205	55,000	75,111	75,111	3	.	.
PA	21,275	21,275	21,275	21,275	21,275	21,275	1	.	.
SC	54,294	54,294	70,024	70,024	85,754	85,754	2	.	.
WY	41,184	41,184	41,184	41,184	41,184	41,184	1	.	.

Degree Required Data

	Min	Q1	Mean	Median	Q3	Max	N	Range Avg Min	Range Avg Max
High School	32,000	32,000	36,745	36,745	41,489	41,489	2	.	.
Associate's	.	.	.	.	.	.	.	.	.
Bachelor's	21,275	55,000	58,066	59,160	65,500	75,111	13	.	.
Master's	60,935	60,935	73,344	73,344	85,754	85,754	2	.	.
Doctoral	.	.	.	.	.	.	.	.	.

GRANT PROPOSAL WRITER

Researches and investigates grant opportunities. Prepares grant proposals in accordance with funder's giving policies, guidelines, and criteria.

University
(Includes ARL Data)
Regional Data

	Min	Q1	Mean	Median	Q3	Max	N	Range Avg Min	Range Avg Max
Great Lakes & Plains	48,402	48,402	48,402	48,402	48,402	48,402	1	.	.
Southeast	34,359	34,359	34,359	34,359	34,359	34,359	1	.	.
West & Southwest	54,672	54,672	57,846	57,846	61,020	61,020	2	.	.
ALL REGIONS	34,359	41,381	49,613	51,537	57,846	61,020	4	.	.

Discussion

Summary of Results

Those interested in a particular type of library or type of library work, or a particular region will have their own way of drawing conclusions from the results of this survey. Because this is the first *Non-MLS Salary Survey*, we are reporting all of the data. As mentioned in the Results section, the low response rate (24.5 percent) negatively impacted the significance of the state data, and in some cases the regional data. The responses from 836 libraries yielded 26,937 individual salaries ranging from $10,707 (federal minimum wage was $5.15/hour) to $141,924 across sixty-two (62) positions. A more meaningful way to summarize is to look at mean salaries paid to particular types of positions in classes of libraries in particular states and regions of the United States, mindful of the number of responses in each case.

The authors thank every single respondent for completing this survey. This was a daunting task for many. We also appreciate respondents' support of the value of collecting these data for an important segment of librarianship. We also appreciate the advice received to improve the survey in years to come.

Library Class	Minimum Salary	Maximum Salary
Very Small Public	$10,712	$68,640
Small Public	$10,712	$120,000
Medium Public	$10,707	$141,924
Large Public	$10,711	$101,920
Very Large Public	$12,480	$130,686
Two-year College	$10,800	$66,286
Four-year College	$10,712	$68,892
University	$12,792	$109,485
ARL	$13,374	$89,521

Mean Salaries by Type of Position

The means of sixty-two (62) positions are shown in the order the positions appear in the survey in Table 1. Data presented in the public libraries tables for the categories

are distinguished by population served as follows:

Very Small	serving less than 10,000
Small	serving 10,000–24,999
Medium	serving 25,000–99,999
Large	serving 100,000–499,999
Very large	serving 500,000 or more

Data presented in the academic library tables for the categories are distinguished by Two-Year Colleges, Four-Year Colleges and Universities (including ARL). Blanks or dashes appear when no data were reported by a particular library type or size.

Salaries by Type of Library

For all sixty-two (62) position categories, the highest academic library salary reported was $109,485 for an Office Manager at a University in the West & Southwest region. The highest public library salary reported was $141,924 for a Human Resources Manager in a Medium Public library in the North Atlantic region.

Complicating Factors

There are unforeseen complications with any new survey, and this one was no exception. Complications occurred in the sampling methodology, in not limiting responses to full time positions, and in the overall complexity of positions within the classes of responding libraries. However, this survey also shares many of the complicating factors associated with conducting a salary survey of this size. The most significant factors were:

- Inaugural survey
- Full-time and part-time salary normalization
- Degree required
- Salaries above $40,000
- Salaries below $20,000
- Position descriptions
- No position responses
- State level data collection
- Non-responses

Inaugural Survey

This is the first time that the ALA-APA has asked for this data from the nation's public and academic libraries. The *Non-MLS Salary Survey* includes sixty-two (62) positions, which made completing the salary data for each incumbent a significant task for the staff member(s) responsible, particularly if the data were compiled manually.

Respondents indicated that it would be helpful to have received more advanced notification of the survey. Also, the original letters were not addressed to the attention of the "Library Director," which meant they did not always reach the appropriate staff, particularly on academic campuses.

Finally, the survey completion time was short—less than six weeks—beginning in early February with an extended deadline of March 17th. The timeframe was recommended by The Management Association of Illinois to ensure completion of both surveys on schedule.

Full-Time and Part-Time Salary Normalization

The questionnaire asked about salaries for full-time and part-time incumbents, exempt and non-exempt, paid by the library.[1] Smaller libraries depend on part-time staff at all levels, and it is not unusual for staff in support positions to be part-time. If no hours were designated, 40 hours was assumed. All part-time salaries were converted to full-time salaries, based on a 40-hour workweek, for the purposes of analysis. All full-time salaries were also converted, based on hourly wage calculations, to a 40-hour work week.

Degree Required

Almost all of the sixty-two (62) positions listed a high school diploma, associate's or bachelor's degree as the minimum educational requirement. Fewer than 1 percent reported a master's or doctoral degree requirement for any particular position. Bachelor's degrees were the minimum for the following positions: Associate Librarians, Information Technology Managers,

Systems Administrators, Web Content Administrators, Webmasters, Public Relations Officers, Graphic Artists, Volunteer Coordinators, Senior Accountants, Accountants, Human Resources Managers, Development Managers and Grant Proposal Writers.

For public libraries, hiring may be determined by Knowledge, Skills and Abilities (KSAs) and may combine education and experience. Both public and academic job descriptions may ask for the MLS or equivalent. Respondents were instructed to use their judgment about whether an MLS is typically hired or occupied the position. For jobs that specifically required the Library Technical Assistant Associate's Degree, the Associate's Degree category was adequate.

Salaries Above $40,000

In public libraries (Table 1), there were fifty-seven (57) occurrences of *average* salaries above $40,000. The highest average salary was $84,569 (12 reported salaries) for the Development Manager position in Very Large public libraries. The Senior Accountant position in all five public library classes had mean salaries from $40,539 (Small; 2 reported salaries) to $65,029 (Very Large; 22 reported salaries). The Human Resources Managers position in four public library classes had mean salaries of $45,760 (Small; 1 reported salary) to $80,039 (Very Large; 26 reported salaries). Of the 70 salaries reported for Senior Accountants that included educational requirements, 50 list a bachelor's degree as the minimum. Of the 70 salaries reported for Human Resources Managers that included educational requirements, 46 list a bachelor's degree as the minimum educational requirement.

In academic libraries (Table 2), there were thirty-two (32) occurrences of *average* salaries above $40,000. The highest average salary was $64,217 (6 reported salaries) for the Development Manager position in ARL member libraries. The Systems Administrator position in all four academic library classes had mean salaries from $40,012 (Two-Year; 2 reported salaries) to $49,685 (ARL; 39 reported salaries). The Information Technology (IT) Manager, Webmaster, Senior Accoun-

---

1. DEFINITION OF EXEMPT VERSUS NON-EXEMPT EMPLOYEES—The terms "exempt" and "non-exempt" refer to an employee's status under the Fair Labor Standards Act (FLSA) and whether or not the position must be paid time and one half for all hours worked over 40 in a workweek (non-exempt) or if they are "exempt" from the overtime requirements. In order for a position to be "exempt," it must meet one of four main categories - executive supervises 2 or more FTEs), professional (i.e., MLS degreed librarian), administrative (making decisions of importance which requires independent judgment and discretion on matters of importance to the business of the organization), or outside sales. The Management Association of Illinois.

tant and Human Resources Managers position in three academic library classes had mean salaries of above $40,000. For IT Managers, the averages were $42,758 (Four-Year; 2 reported salaries) to $55,848 (University; 25 reported salaries). For Webmasters, the averages were $45,367 (ARL; 9 reported salaries) to $46,530 (Four-Year; 1 reported salary). For Senior Accountants, the averages were $42,506 (University; 10 reported salaries) to $44,940 (Four-Year; 1 reported salary). For Human Resources Managers, the averages were $44,964 (Four-Year; 1 reported salary) to $47,446 (ARL; 11 reported salaries). Of the 28 salaries reported for Senior Accountants that included educational requirements, 19 list a bachelor's degree as the minimum. Of the 19 salaries reported for Human Resources Managers that included educational requirements, 13 list a bachelor's degree as the minimum educational requirement.

Salaries Below $20,000

The lowest average public library salaries (Table 2) were found in the Very Small through Medium sized public libraries. Keep in mind that many of these mean salaries are based on one case, such as the Associate Librarian—Government Documents as the lowest mean for public library positions at $12,480 and which was reported in Great Lakes & Plains Region. In all, there were fifteen means for all regions that were below $20,000. Three of the lowest salary averages were reported, from $14,727 to $16,065, were for the Shelver/Page position. Of the 1,675 salaries reported for Shelvers/Pages that included educational requirements, 1,671 (all but four) listed a high school diploma as the minimum. In fact, some incumbents were still in high school. In contrast, 1,300 of 2,471 of all the Associate Librarian positions, reported required a bachelor's degree (47 percent).

The lowest average academic library salaries (Table 2) were found across the classes of libraries. The lowest, $13,027, was reported for Shelvers/Pages in Two-Year Colleges. This mean is based on seven reported salaries. In all, there were nine means for all regions that were below $20,000. Examples of other lower paid positions, based on averages for the four regions, were Clerk—Adult Services (Four-Year; $15,585; 58 reported salaries); Clerk—Government Documents (ARL; $16,997; 9 reported salaries); and Processing Assistant (Two-Year; $16,658; 3 reported salaries). Of the 105 salaries reported for Processing Assistants that included educational requirements, 84 listed a high school diploma as the minimum (80 percent).

Position Descriptions

For every salary survey, there were exceptions to the positions we chose to include. This survey was particularly challenging because libraries, regardless of type, use a variety of titles to capture the nature of the work that does not require a Master's Degree in Library and Information Studies (MLS). In addition to the 37 titles included in the supplementary question of the 2004 *Survey of Librarian Salaries*, there were 2,571 other unique titles submitted by respondents (See Figure 1). Many of these titles were incorporated into the 62 positions included in the survey. Included were functional areas; excluded were most steps and classifications, such as Senior Library Clerk or Library Assistant II, because they are usually meaningful primarily in the context of particular library systems.

The positions were chosen to reflect titles prevalent in public and academic settings. It was hoped that the respondents would accept that there would be some positions that were not present in one or the other and ignore those positions. It was not efficient to attempt to separate the titles, which proved a wise decision since there were so few titles for which no academic or no public library had an incumbent (see No Position Responses below). The instructions asked respondents "to provide us with data for each of the positions in your organization that match at least 70 percent to our job descriptions." It was also hoped that respondents would consider the essence of the position description, rather than whether it matched exactly how they defined their own positions.

In this era of team-based staffing, flat management, innovative staff scheduling and declining budgets, appointing staff to just one position was troublesome for many. Respondents had difficulty ascribing even a majority of time to one position. In libraries where one person performs several tasks, the respondent chose the predominant activity rather than the component tasks of the position.

And still, there were positions not included in title or description in this survey. These may be added in future surveys. The data for Associate Librarians encompassed salaries for many highly responsible positions, including Directors and non-MLS Librarians, for which there was no other appropriate category. A few respondents expressed that there should have been more extensive positioning for circulation staff, technology support and managers in all functional areas.

There were low numbers of responses for some positions, particularly by small public and academic

Table 1. Mean Salaries by Position and Library Type—Public

Title	Very Small Public	Small Public	Medium Public	Large Public	Very Large Public
Associate Librarian—Adult Services	$24,228	$29,711	$28,105	$30,973	$37,038
Associate Librarian—Archives and Special Collection	$22,288	$28,258	$34,760	$31,663	$30,511
Associate Librarian—Children's Services/Young Adult	$27,382	$29,980	$33,735	$32,030	$38,763
Associate Librarian—Government Documents	$12,480	$22,603	-	$24,593	$37,205
Associate Librarian—Instructional Services/Literacy	-	-	$57,809	$44,037	$38,408
Associate Librarian—Reference/Information Services	$25,906	$31,126	$30,456	$33,461	$36,303
Associate Librarian—Outreach/Bookmobile	$29,848	$22,101	$33,502	$32,949	$38,233
Associate Librarian—Media Services	$26,926	$35,624	$66,023	$34,403	$41,131
Associate Librarian—Technical Assistance	$29,409	$27,783	$32,786	$33,091	$29,492
Library Tech Assistant—Adult Services	$24,385	$24,839	$29,054	$27,666	$32,546
Library Tech Assistant—Archives & Special Collections	$21,893	$24,440	$38,050	$29,037	$41,090
Library Tech Assistant—Children's & YA Srvcs	$22,510	$27,141	$29,420	$29,165	$31,322
Library Tech Assistant—Government Documents	-	$37,706	$28,101	$30,872	$38,954
Library Tech Assistant—Instructional Services/Literacy	-	-	$39,007	$34,075	$40,349
Library Tech Assistant—Reference/Information Services	$26,897	$28,503	$28,544	$30,146	$31,637
Library Tech Assistant—Outreach/Bookmobile	$26,920	$21,410	$28,154	$28,897	$35,180
Library Tech Assistant—Media Services	-	$32,854	$32,170	$29,312	$39,667
Library Tech Assistant—Acquisitions	$27,822	$32,811	$34,119	$32,517	$42,909
Library Tech Assistant—Cataloging	$23,428	$27,921	$30,407	$30,965	$41,392
Clerk—Adult Services	$20,231	$23,245	$20,893	$25,881	$32,419
Clerk—Archives and Special Collections	$18,390	$25,902	$16,267	$24,715	$31,508
Clerk—Children's Services/Young Adult Services	$19,917	$23,210	$21,958	$25,127	$26,922
Clerk—Government Documents	-	-	$23,370	$32,005	$28,784
Clerk—Instructional Services/Literacy	-	-	$33,381	$29,262	$43,989
Clerk—Reference/Information Services	$25,484	$23,606	$22,063	$24,695	$27,056
Clerk—Outreach/Bookmobile	$24,274	$13,520	$26,701	$24,466	$32,843
Clerk—Media Services	$37,835	$26,978	$22,185	$28,681	$30,383
Clerk—Acquisitions	$26,516	$25,116	$34,817	$29,513	$31,291
Clerk—Circulation	$20,295	$23,505	$23,792	$25,672	$29,166
Clerk—Accounting (Payables)	$24,518	$33,076	$32,795	$30,068	$33,827
Shelver/Page	$14,727	$15,820	$16,065	$16,394	$19,596
Bookmobile Driver	$20,832	$13,520	$25,818	$27,288	$33,581
Copy Cataloger	$31,096	$30,613	$31,175	$31,477	$37,912
Book Repairer	$19,448	$21,163	$23,397	$24,576	$28,358
Processing Assistant	$22,248	$20,374	$23,572	$26,584	$33,009
Serials Processing Assistant	$16,806	$24,532	$29,628	$28,600	$31,046
Collection Development/Management	-	$32,032	$25,175	$37,730	$55,718
Inter-Library Loan Assistant	$23,398	$26,811	$26,715	$28,084	$33,758
Driver	-	-	$24,370	$25,181	$29,986
Information Technology (IT) Manager	$31,440	$32,952	$47,074	$56,719	$74,379
Systems Administrator	$34,601	$33,942	$42,763	$44,822	$60,375
Web Content Administrator	$20,800	$41,600	$44,793	$46,891	$51,256
Webmaster	$37,440	$33,300	$37,080	$45,888	$53,396

Table 1. Mean Salaries by Position and Library Type—Public, continued

Title	Very Small Public	Small Public	Medium Public	Large Public	Very Large Public
Computer Lab Assistant	-	$18,925	$21,597	$24,358	$51,953
Administrative Assistant (Secretary)	$26,468	$29,670	$36,837	$35,046	$39,879
Receptionist	-	$20,280	$27,446	$28,258	$32,063
Office Manager	$21,035	$36,958	$40,099	$40,183	$53,154
Public Relations Officer	$32,773	$38,597	$42,215	$45,297	$59,481
Graphic Artist	-	$39,977	$36,447	$36,775	$42,821
Volunteer Coordinator	$16,120	$31,627	$37,981	$35,395	$48,903
Senior Accountant	$41,843	$40,539	$47,785	$56,192	$65,029
Accountant	$20,263	$41,701	$44,606	$41,916	$45,493
Bookkeeper	$26,884	$33,606	$35,169	$33,699	$36,901
Payroll Administrator	-	$29,280	$40,374	$36,011	$42,363
Human Resources Manager	$37,440	$45,760	$57,845	$53,832	$80,039
Human Resources Assistant	-	-	$36,344	$32,832	$41,465
Facility Engineering Manager (Maintenance)	$48,402	$36,771	$44,997	$45,992	$58,041
Building Maintenance	$21,574	$27,756	$33,712	$31,639	$41,854
Janitorial Cleaner	$23,646	$24,259	$25,641	$25,091	$31,452
Security (Discipline Monitor)	-	$26,230	$27,795	$25,394	$31,624
Development Manager	$32,000	$31,200	$55,139	$58,566	$84,569
Grant Proposal Writer	-	-	-	$45,970	$60,243

Table 2. Mean Salaries by Position and Library Type—Academic

Title	Two-Year	Four-Year	University	ARL
Associate Librarian—Adult Services	$30,415	$25,146	$28,302	$37,882
Associate Librarian—Archives and Special Collection	-	$37,732	$41,031	$39,931
Associate Librarian—Children's Services/Young Adult	-	-	$29,786	-
Associate Librarian—Government Documents	$33,333	$30,183	$31,092	$43,458
Associate Librarian—Instructional Services/Literacy	$25,213	$24,000	$40,412	$32,258
Associate Librarian—Reference/Information Services	$31,902	$32,108	$33,207	$38,025
Associate Librarian—Outreach/Bookmobile	-	-	$39,010	-
Associate Librarian—Media Services	$24,261	$32,358	$38,541	$35,441
Associate Librarian—Technical Assistance	$29,616	$28,225	$33,111	$39,025
Library Tech Assistant—Adult Services	$27,680	$22,530	$27,970	$38,142
Library Tech Assistant—Archives & Special Collections	$18,806	$27,760	$30,435	$33,210
Library Tech Assistant—Children's & YA Srvcs	-	$27,159	$29,431	-
Library Tech Assistant—Government Documents	$36,341	$40,326	$28,310	$32,305
Library Tech Assistant—Instructional Services/Literacy	$26,932	$47,316	$32,337	$30,873
Library Tech Assistant—Reference/Information Services	$24,070	$34,453	$30,136	$29,782
Library Tech Assistant—Outreach/Bookmobile	-	-	$25,560	-
Library Tech Assistant—Media Services	$21,093	$32,401	$30,045	$32,751
Library Tech Assistant—Acquisitions	$29,178	$30,750	$29,070	$30,705
Library Tech Assistant—Cataloging	$29,093	$30,693	$28,923	$34,259
Clerk—Adult Services	$20,584	$15,585	$26,122	-
Clerk—Archives and Special Collections	-	$27,243	$28,333	$25,521

Table 2. Mean Salaries by Position and Library Type—Academic, continued

Title	Two-Year	Four-Year	University	ARL
Clerk—Children's Services/Young Adult Services	-	-	$29,873	-
Clerk—Government Documents	-	$27,318	$22,977	$16,997
Clerk—Instructional Services/Literacy	-	-	$26,125	-
Clerk—Reference/Information Services	$23,301	$23,506	$24,595	$17,699
Clerk—Outreach/Bookmobile	-	-	$16,690	-
Clerk—Media Services	$31,121	$26,532	$27,158	$27,003
Clerk—Acquisitions	$22,158	$29,671	$31,109	$25,555
Clerk—Circulation	$20,357	$26,220	$26,060	$25,740
Clerk—Accounting (Payables)	$30,210	$33,582	$28,983	$29,850
Shelver/Page	$13,027	$22,332	$15,925	$23,422
Bookmobile Driver	-	-	-	$21,753
Copy Cataloger	$24,119	$32,256	$31,159	$33,485
Book Repairer	$18,720	$34,311	$27,660	$24,908
Processing Assistant	$16,658	$26,738	$25,598	$28,788
Serials Processing Assistant	$27,148	$30,370	$28,491	$32,139
Collection Development/Management	-	$37,257	$38,179	$31,623
Inter-Library Loan Assistant	$25,688	$28,586	$28,050	$31,102
Driver	-	$25,501	$25,093	$26,864
Information Technology (IT) Manager	$26,423	$42,758	$55,848	$52,404
Systems Administrator	$40,012	$49,684	$48,648	$49,685
Web Content Administrator	-	$28,352	$38,151	$38,204
Webmaster	-	$46,530	$46,345	$45,367
Computer Lab Assistant	$25,279	$25,996	$30,702	$27,822
Administrative Assistant (Secretary)	$27,831	$29,499	$30,321	$33,888
Receptionist	-	-	$25,275	$31,360
Office Manager	$39,066	$32,331	$41,884	$37,527
Public Relations Officer	-	-	$45,782	$37,523
Graphic Artist	$33,328	$39,171	$40,991	$36,846
Volunteer Coordinator	-	-	-	$51,065
Senior Accountant	-	$44,940	$42,506	$42,829
Accountant	-	$39,692	$33,727	$38,534
Bookkeeper	$44,056	$26,844	$32,300	$34,868
Payroll Administrator	-	-	$38,647	$43,706
Human Resources Manager	-	$44,964	$46,226	$47,446
Human Resources Assistant	-	$39,384	$31,353	$35,576
Facility Engineering Manager (Maintenance)	-	-	$42,599	$44,944
Building Maintenance	-	-	$26,351	$25,730
Janitorial Cleaner	-	-	-	-
Security (Discipline Monitor)	-	-	$26,547	$27,150
Development Manager	-	-	$52,576	$64,217
Grant Proposal Writer	-	-	-	$49,613

libraries. Many of them were unsurprising. There were no Associate Librarian—Children's Services/Young Adult in most colleges, nor were there Associate Librarians—Literacy in most colleges, ARL member libraries or smaller public libraries. There were few non-MLS Literacy staff in academic libraries. Either these positions do not exist or they require an MLS. There were few majority-dedicated bookmobile drivers, which may be an issue of employees sharing this with other duties. Surprisingly, there were three bookmobile drivers in ARL member libraries. Library Technical Assistant (LTA) positions are most prevalent in public libraries. There was one Children's LTA in Four-Year Colleges and eight in Universities. Only one Very Small public library had an Archives LTA; two Small public libraries and two Two-Year Colleges had that position. There were no copy catalogers reported by smaller libraries in two regions. Book repairers are mainly in Very Large public libraries and ARL member libraries.

No Position Responses

All positions had at least one library response. The following is a list of positions for which no library in that category responded.

PUBLIC, small through medium—These libraries typically have one or a few staff performing a variety of duties. The positions below are either unavailable in smaller libraries or they are occupied by MLS-degreed staff.

Very Small public libraries
- Associate Librarian—Instructional Services/Literacy
- Clerk—Government Documents
- Clerk—Instructional Services/Literacy
- Collection Development/Management
- Computer Lab Assistant
- Driver
- Grant Proposal Writer
- Graphic Artist
- Human Resources Assistant
- Library Tech Assistant—Government Documents
- Library Tech Assistant—Instructional Services/Literacy
- Library Tech Assistant—Media Services
- Payroll Administrator
- Receptionist
- Security

Small public libraries
- Associate Librarian—Instructional Services/Literacy
- Clerk—Government Documents
- Clerk—Instructional Services/Literacy
- Driver
- Grant Proposal Writer
- Human Resources Assistant
- Library Tech Assistant—Instructional Services/Literacy

Medium public libraries
- Associate Librarian—Government Documents
- Grant Proposal Writer

ACADEMIC—On campuses, there are generally other departments that perform and fund many of the positions below. Additionally, there are some positions and functions that are outside the service mission of academic libraries (e.g., Adult Services and Children's Services/Young Adult Services). In Two-Year Colleges, Webmasters, Accountants and Human Resources staff may be in different departments, paid by different sources, or occupied by MLS staff.

Two-Year College
- Accountant
- Associate Librarian—Archives and Special Collection
- Associate Librarian—Children's Services/Young Adult
- Associate Librarian—Outreach/Bookmobile
- Bookmobile Driver
- Building Maintenance
- Clerk—Archives and Special Collections
- Clerk—Children's Services/Young Adult Services
- Clerk—Government Documents
- Clerk—Instructional Services/Literacy
- Clerk—Outreach/Bookmobile
- Collection Development/Management
- Development Manager
- Driver
- Facility Engineering Manager (Maintenance)
- Grant Proposal Writer
- Human Resources Assistant
- Human Resources Manager
- Janitorial Cleaner
- Payroll Administrator
- Public Relations Officer
- Receptionist

- Security (Discipline Monitor)
- Senior Accountant
- Volunteer Coordinator
- Web Content Administrator
- Webmaster

Four-Year Colleges
- Associate Librarian—Children's Services/Young Adult
- Associate Librarian—Outreach/Bookmobile
- Bookmobile Driver
- Building Maintenance
- Clerk—Children's Services/Young Adult Services
- Clerk—Instructional Services/Literacy
- Clerk—Outreach/Bookmobile
- Development Manager
- Facility Engineering Manager (Maintenance)
- Grant Proposal Writer
- Janitorial Cleaner
- Library Tech Assistant—Outreach/Bookmobile
- Payroll Administrator
- Public Relations Officer
- Receptionist
- Security (Discipline Monitor)
- Volunteer Coordinator

Universities
- Bookmobile Driver
- Grant Proposal Writer
- Janitorial Cleaner
- Volunteer Coordinator
- ARL Member Libraries
- Associate Librarian—Children's Services/Young Adult Services
- Associate Librarian—Outreach/Bookmobile
- Clerk—Adult Services
- Clerk—Children's Services/Young Adult Services
- Clerk—Instructional Services/Literacy
- Clerk—Outreach/Bookmobile
- Janitorial Cleaner
- Library Tech Assistant—Children's Services/Young Adult Services
- Library Tech Assistant—Outreach/Bookmobile

State-Level Data Collection

The sample frame, 1,983 public and 1,435 academic libraries, was determined to collect statistically significant responses to support state-level analysis. Although the overall response rates were too low to support state-level analysis, all of the state-level responses are included.

Figure 1. "Other" Support Staff Titles Reported by 10 or More Libraries

Job Title	Libraries Reporting Use of Job Title	Job Title	Libraries Reporting Use of Job Title	Job Title	Libraries Reporting Use of Job Title
Custodian	41	Library Technical Assistant	17	Acquisitions Supervisor	11
Secretary	35	Circulation Clerk	16	Head of Circulation	11
Cataloging Assistant	30	Office Manager	16	Interlibrary Loan Assistant	11
Administrative Secretary	28	Executive Secretary	15	Librarian II	11
Library Specialist	27	Facilities Manager	15	Library Assistant I	11
Senior Library Assistant	25	Graphic Artist	15	Library Assistant III	11
Senior Library Clerk	25	Graphic Designer	15	Maintenance Supervisor	11
Reference Assistant	23	Reference Librarian	15	Receptionist	11
Bookkeeper	22	Cataloger	14	Senior Clerk	11
Library Clerk	22	Circulation Coordinator	14	Supervising Library Assistant	11
Account Clerk	20	Courier	13	Volunteer Coordinator	11
Accountant	19	Page	13	Children's Librarian	10
Acquisitions Assistant	19	Librarian I	12	Computer Operator	10
Library Assistant II	17	Acquisitions Coordinator	11	Principal Library Clerk	10

Davis, Denise M. 2005. Library Support Staff Job Titles. American Library Association, Office for Research and Statistics. http://www.ala.org/ala/ors/reports/libsupjobtitles.htm.

Readers are encouraged to be conscious of the number of responses when using the data. We anticipate higher response levels in the future.

Non-Responses

In total, 75.5 percent of institutions did not respond to the survey. A small number of academic and public libraries asked to be removed from the sample, and reasons given included being a private institution, lack of time and staff shortages. ☐

Appendix A. Survey Questionnaire

2006 NON-MLS PERSONNEL SALARY SURVEY

PLEASE PRINT

userID: *(listed on cover letter)*: _____

Name of Library _____

Questionnaire completed by _____

Phone (include area code) _____ Ext. _____

E-Mail Address _____

COMPLETED SURVEY DUE MARCH 3, 2006

Demographic Data

1. What is the number of <u>full time</u> **non-MLS** employees employed by your organization? (required)
   _____ Non-Exempt
   _____ Exempt

2. What is the number of <u>part time</u> **non-MLS** employees employed by your organization? (required)
   _____ Non-Exempt
   _____ Exempt

3. Projected 12-month salary increase for <u>Non-Exempt</u> employees _____ %

4. Projected 12-month salary increase for <u>Exempt</u> employees _____ %

5. How many non-MLS staff have faculty status (academic libraries only)? _____

6. How many hours per week must an employee work to be considered full time? (required)

   _____ hrs/wk

7. Is there a maximum number of hours per week part-time employees are allowed to work?
   ❏ No maximum
   ❏ Yes, maximum of _____ hours per week

b. Professionals:
- ☐ Yes, all employees
- ☐ Yes, some employees
- ☐ No

9.   If yes, which union/local? _____

10. How many of your staff report being a member of the following U.S. Census Bureau categories of race/ethnicity (assumption)?
- a. White, non-Hispanic _____
- b. Black/African-American _____
- c. Hispanic/Latino _____
- d. Asian/Pacific Islander _____
- e. American Indian _____

INSTRUCTIONS

The 2006 Non-MLS Personnel Salary Survey is being co-sponsored by the **American Library Association – Allied Professional Association** and the **American Library Association**.

PARTICIPATION OPTIONS (all found at http://www.hrsource.org/ala.asp):

1. **Participate online.** See the cover letter for your userID/password. This is our preferred method of receiving your information.
2. **Participate via spreadsheet.** Download our MS Excel spreadsheet and e-mail it back to Jean Hannon: jhannon@hrsource.org.
3. **Participate on paper.** Use the enclosed sheets to record your information using the job descriptions to match your jobs. Then fax or mail back the library demographic information sheet and data form(s) when you are done to:

> The Management Association of Illinois
> Attn: Compensation Department
> 1400 Opus Place, Suite 500
> Downers Grove, IL 60515
> 630-963-2800 FAX

MATCHING JOBS

This survey requests annual salaries paid to all full-time and part-time positions which **do not require** a master's degree accredited or recognized by the American Library Association (but which may require another advanced degree).

Read the position descriptions carefully and compare them to jobs in your organization. If the responsibilities of a job in the survey align with your position by 70% or better, report data for the matched position. If jobs do not coincide with those in the survey by at least 70%, do not report data for that job.

For staff working in multiple departments, attribute their salary to the department that pays the majority of the salary or to the department where the person spends the majority of his/her time. We recognize that your library may be organized differently or may place a particular functional area in another departmental category. Please report positions in the functional area that most closely matches the position title and tasks.

REPORTING PAY

Use the following **2006 Non-MLS Personnel Salary Survey Pay Data Sheet** to provide us with data for each of the positions in your organization that match at least 70% to our job descriptions. Each row in the spreadsheet should represent one incumbent at your organization as we do not want averages, we want actual pay data. Report salaries paid by the library budget which are filled as of February 1, 2006. **If a position is currently vacant, do not report anything for that position.**

JOB CODE
Please provide the job code from the survey job descriptions for each incumbent for which you are reporting data.

JOB TITLE
Please provide the job title from the survey job descriptions for each incumbent for which you are reporting data.

ACTUAL BASE SALARY
Salaries are defined as actual **straight time** pay. Do not provide averages. Do not include benefits, overtime premiums, shift differentials, bonuses, or any other incentives or variable pay components.

REGULAR HOURS PER WEEK
Please list the amount of hours each incumbent works on a regular basis. If no hours are designated, 40 is assumed.

RATE REPORTED BY (PAY BASIS)
Report salaries only according to the basis on which you pay them, i.e., 1 or H = Hourly, 2 or W = Weekly, 3 or M = Monthly, or 4 or A = Annually. Do not convert other bases or time periods.

RANGE MINIMUM
Report the beginning salary (range minimum) for each position.

RANGE MAXIMUM
Report the salary cap, if any (range maximum) for each position.

DEGREE REQUIRED
Please use the following to report what degree is required for the position (not what degree current incumbents have earned): 1 or HS = High School, 2 or AA = Associates degree, 3 or BA = Bachelors degree, 4 or MA = Masters degree and 5 or PhD = Doctoral degree.

QUESTIONS?
If you have any questions or problems completing this questionnaire, please contact Jean Hannon at (800) 448-4584 ext. 238 or jhannon@hrsource.org.

FOR YOUR RECORDS:
KEEP A COPY OF REPORTED DATA

JOB DESCRIPTIONS

PUBLIC SERVICES

Associate Librarian (non-MLS degreed)

Provides assistance to patrons including topical research and material location. Assists patrons with the use of library resources and equipment. Screens the collection for outdated or unused materials following established guidelines. May perform managerial and administrative duties.

Use the following Job Codes based on the Department assigned to:

1. **Adult Services** – *provides access to materials, services and programs intended to meet the needs of the adult users of a public library.*
2. **Archives and Special Collections** – *manages and maintains collection; identifies and appraises records, authenticates, describes and documents, facilitates access and use, preserves and conserves, and exhibits collection.*
3. **Children's Services/Young Adult Services** – *provides services intended for children and youth through twelfth grade; develops collection, provides homework and reader's advisory services, and develops age appropriate programs.*
4. **Government Documents** – *provides access to publications of the U.S. federal government such as transcripts of hearings and text of bills, resolutions, statutes, reports, charters, treaties, periodicals and statistics.*
5. **Instructional Services/Literacy** – *advances learning, teaching and research with respect to information literacy in higher education; assists patrons to develop the ability to read and write.*
6. **Reference/Information Services** – *assists patrons with questions; instructs in the selection and use of appropriate tools and techniques for finding information; conducts searches for materials; contributes to reference collection development.*
7. **Outreach/Bookmobile** – *provides services and programs to homebound, disabled, institutionalized or other underserved patrons.*
8. **Media Services** – *develops and manages non-print library materials such as files, video recordings, audio recordings, CD-ROMs, computer software, etc.*
9. **Technical Assistance** - *acquires, organizes (bibliographic control), physically processes and maintains library collections.*

Library Technical Assistant

Provides basic assistance to patrons referring patrons to Librarian for professional assistance. Locates materials and information for patrons. May complete routine copy cataloging. Assists with special programming.

Use the following Job Codes based on the Department assigned to:

10. **Adult Services** – *provides access to materials, services and programs intended to meet the needs of the adult users of a public library.*
11. **Archives and Special Collections** – *manages and maintains collection; identifies and appraises records, authenticates, describes and documents, facilitates access and use, preserves and conserves, and exhibits collection.*
12. **Children's Services/Young Adult Services** – *provides services intended for children and youths through twelfth grade; develops collection, provides homework and reader's advisory services, and develops age appropriate programs.*
13. **Government Documents** – *provides access to publications of the U.S. federal government such as transcripts of hearings and text of bills, resolutions, statutes, reports, charters, treaties, periodicals and statistics.*
14. **Instructional Services/Literacy** – *advances learning, teaching and research with respect to information literacy in higher education; assists patrons to develop the ability to read and write.*
15. **Reference/Information Services** – *assists patrons with questions; instructs in the selection and use of appropriate tools and techniques for finding information; conducts searches for materials; contributes to reference collection development.*
16. **Outreach/Bookmobile** – *provides services and programs to homebound, disabled, institutionalized or other underserved patrons.*

Library Technical Assistant, continued

17. **Media Services** – *develops and manages non-print library materials such as files, video recordings, audio recordings, CD-ROMs, computer software, etc.*
18. **Acquisitions** –*selects, orders, and receives new materials and maintains accurate records of such transactions.*
19. **Cataloging** - *prepares bibliographic records to represent the items acquired by the library, including bibliographic description, subject analysis, and classification.*

Clerk

Performs routine duties required the use of a variety of forms, reports or procedures. Provides basic patron assistance: sets up computer stations, locates materials, provides information. Maintains departmental or area records. Performs miscellaneous clerical duties such as filing, typing, sorting or photocopying.

Use the following Job Codes based on the Department assigned to:

20. **Adult Services** – *provides access to materials, services and programs intended to meet the needs of the adult users of a public library.*
21. **Archives and Special Collections** – *manages and maintains collection; identifies and appraises records, authenticates, describes and documents, facilitates access and use, preserves and conserves, and exhibits collection.*
22. **Children's Services/Young Adult Services** – *provides services intended for children and youths through twelfth grade; develops collection, provides homework and reader's advisory services, and develops age appropriate programs.*
23. **Government Documents** – *provides access to publications of the U.S. federal government such as transcripts of hearings and text of bills, resolutions, statutes, reports, charters, treaties, periodicals and statistics.*
24. **Instructional Services/Literacy** – *advances learning, teaching and research with respect to information literacy in higher education; assists patrons to develop the ability to read and write.*
25. **Reference/Information Services** – *assists patrons with questions; instructs in the selection and use of appropriate tools and techniques for finding information; conducts searches for materials; contributes to reference collection development.*
26. **Outreach/Bookmobile** – *provides services and programs to homebound, disabled, institutionalized or other underserved patrons.*
27. **Media Services** – *develops and manages non-print library materials such as files, video recordings, audio recordings, CD-ROMs, computer software, etc.*
28. **Acquisitions Clerk** – *orders and receives new materials; works with collections staff to determine most appropriate sources; checks shipments to ensure correct quantity, material and quality.*
29. **Circulation Clerk** – *checks in and out materials; inspects materials for damage, verifies due date and calculates fine; assists patrons with basic informational questions; sorts materials and prepares for reshelving; issues and updates identification cards according to established procedures.*
30. **Accounting Clerk (Payables)** – *processes vendor invoices, matches with purchase order, verifies payment authorization, computes discount, assigns budgetary account, draws checks and prepares for mailing; maintains vendor records and files; performs miscellaneous bookkeeping duties as required.*

31. Shelver/Page

Moves and unloads carts. Shelves materials in appropriate locations. Shelf-reads assigned areas and straightens collection as needed. Removes out-of-place materials for reshelving.

32. Bookmobile Driver

Loads and unloads materials. Drives to and from specified locations. Assists patrons with material selection. Checks in and out materials.

TECHNICAL SERVICES

33. Copy Cataloger
Performs copy cataloging for print and non-print materials using OCLC, AACRII, MARC, DDC and local consortium standards. Edits previously cataloged materials. Serves a resource for other library personnel concerning cataloging rules and practices.

34. Book Repairer
Checks the condition of the materials and determines the most suitable method of repairing. Recreates packaging, labels and barcodes.

35. Processing Assistant
Prepares materials for placement throughout the library. Prepares spines, labels and barcodes. May send materials to outside bindery for processing. May perform simple repairs as needed. Transfers processed materials to appropriate department.

36. Serials Processing Assistant
Orders, receives and prepares library subscriptions. Updates online systems to reflect holdings, locations and identity. Monitors subscription status, processes invoices and renewals, and resolves issues with vendors as needed.

37. Collection Development/Management
Analyzes community and library data to determine areas of the collection which need updating. Selects materials to update the collection. Performs related work as required.

38. Inter-Library Loan Assistant
Coordinates materials loaned through the inter-library loan system for patrons, other libraries and institutions. Searches databases and the Internet for inter-library loan requests utilizing ISBN, ISSN and citation numbers. Determines best sources for materials.

39. Driver
Drives a library vehicle to pick-up and deliver library material between libraries, systems and branches. Determines sequence of loading for delivery purposes. Performs basic maintenance on vehicle. Informs supervisor when additional vehicle maintenance is necessary.

TECHNOLOGY SUPPORT

40. Information Technology (IT) Manager
Manages day-to-day IT operations including systems analysis, programming, and computer and auxiliary operations. Directs the development and maintenance of systems. Determines and recommends department budgets and analyzes controllable expenditures. May plan and coordinate the evaluation and effectiveness of existing data processing applications and the feasibility and potential value of new applications. May assist staff and patrons with troubleshooting equipment or software problems.

41. Systems Administrator
Provides system management and operation support to the activities and resources required to provide quality computer operations processing and applications system resource management and availability. Sets up and implements standards for computer operations, uses software support tools to process scheduling, reports, report generation, database administration, system data backups, performance tuning and security. Troubleshoots and resolves problems associated with local and wide area network environments. Has responsibilities for dealing with hardware and software vendors and technical support issues. Troubleshoots PC software, coordinates with help desk and sets connections to broadband/baseband networks.

42. Web Content Administrator
Develops, provides, and authorizes website content to increase traffic, support and promote services, and gain content visibility. Manages and performs website editorial activities including gathering and researching information that enhances the value of the site. May oversee data control technicians and writers dedicated to website.

43. Webmaster
Responsible for the library's Internet and or Intranet technical functions. Maps the flow of the site, creates general graphics, provides specifications to the web authors, developers, and outside vendors for the development of databases, interactive applets, and custom graphics. Supervises development efforts including content, design and production, site maintenance and updating. Acts as a liaison between the site and users.

44. Computer Lab Assistant
Monitors the operation of adult and/or youth computer labs. Assists patrons with questions and problem resolution. Enforces computer lab rules. May assist with installation, operation and configuring of personal computer hardware and software. Investigates reoccurring problems and recommends course of action to supervisor. May perform back-up operations and print reports.

GENERAL ADMINISTRATION

45. Administrative Assistant (Secretary)
Performs secretarial duties for a department and its staff. Takes and transcribes dictation, and prepares correspondence. Operates word processing equipment as required. Composes correspondence from written materials provided. Maintains personal files and department records. Arranges and schedules meetings and appointments. Takes, screens, and places telephone calls, and acts as Receptionist as needed. Compiles standard reports with data that is provided.

46. Receptionist
Operates multiple line telephone console or PBX switchboard and greets visitors. Receives incoming calls, secures identity of callers, and connects to proper parties. Takes and relays messages. Places outgoing calls. Announces and directs calls to proper party. Registers individuals and issues visitor badges. Maintains required records. Performs a wide variety of clerical duties as time permits, such as word processing, record posting and maintenance.

47. Office Manager
Assumes direct responsibility for dictation, filing, mail, communications, and printing departments. Implements and follows through on general office policies. Confers with other departments regarding the purchasing of office equipment, systems, and procedures affecting more than one department, and the hiring and transferring of employees and office salary structure. Prepares payroll tax returns and performs payroll accounting for organization as required. Maintains retention schedule for library records.

48. Public Relations Officer
Promotes and administers public relations policies and programs such as special events, news articles, and audio and visual communication media. Maintains relations with newspaper, radio and TV media, community groups and agencies, school districts and Board of Trustees.

49. Graphic Artist
Designs unique, original materials based on aesthetic trends. Plans layout and creates materials such as brochures, manuals, advertisements, reports, newsletters and forms using a variety of desktop publishing software. Researches and recommends the purchase of related software and hardware. Organizes and implements desktop publishing and operating methods and procedures.

50. Volunteer Coordinator
Coordinates all volunteers and volunteer programs. Assesses volunteer needs. Recruits, screens and places volunteers. Works with staff ensure proper orientation given and evaluation of performance. May develop and coordinate volunteer recognition programs.

51. Senior Accountant

Oversees clerical activities in connection with payables, debits, or credits. Prepares work sheets, analyzes to verify accuracy, prepares monthly journal entries, statements, monthly balance sheet, monthly statements, profit and loss, subsidiary, and other analyses and statements, following prescribed procedures.

52. Accountant

Computes and prepares reports and analyses as requested by organization personnel. Calculates and checks work sheets prior to closing general ledger. Posts, balances, and reconciles general ledger accounts. Prepares profit and loss statement and balance sheets, and compute required financial statements and statistical reports as directed. Computes, checks, and files tax returns.

53. Bookkeeper

Performs diversified duties in maintaining accounting records. Verifies credits and deductions. Checks allocation of charges on bills payable. Maintains and balances petty cash account. Pays minor expenses, prepares daily cash balance figures, and weekly transaction report. Checks employee expense accounts. Prepares monthly receipts and disbursement summaries, takes trial balances, locates discrepancies, and reconciles bank statements. Compiles special reports. Analyzes facts to determine action to be taken, within the limits of standard practice.

54. Payroll Administrator

Makes a variety of computations on employee overtime, shift premium, and various payroll deductions, following standard procedures, to prepare payroll. Summarizes and reconciles payroll sheets. Investigates and resolves payroll problems, responding to employee requests. Maintains and updates data base records. Generates federal and state tax documents. Prepares special payroll analysis reports.

55. Human Resources Manager

General responsibility for all personnel activities, such as employment, training, wage and salary administration, safety and working conditions, employee counseling, and personnel records. Investigates, advises, and prepares policies affecting personnel, and consults and advises on interpretation and administration. Conducts union contract negotiations as required. Advises management on interpretation of policy.

56. Human Resources Assistant

Organizes and maintains records, and files government reports as scheduled. Maintains employment statistical data and prepares related reports. Assists in employment activities involving interviewing, verifying qualifications, and checking references. Assists in administering employee benefit programs. Responds to employee inquiries on matters related to library programs and activities.

57. Facility Engineering Manager (Maintenance)

Responsible for grounds, buildings, and building equipment. Supervises the installation, maintenance, and repair of: electrical, gas, air, and water installations; fire sprinklers; the operation of building equipment and facilities; janitorial services; and the maintenance of grounds. Works with outside contractors and architects on building construction as necessary. Plans, lays out, and assigns work, involving diagnosing and remedying difficult problems. Reports defective equipment and recommends the replacement of obsolete or damaged equipment when estimates of repair costs are excessive. Expedites building repairs in construction to avoid production delays. Performs normal supervisory functions in a department with seldom more than 10 persons.

58. Building Maintenance

Performs routine and preventive maintenance as directed. Performs various repairs requiring general knowledge of carpentry, plumbing, HVAC, and electrical and mechanical repair. Operates lawn mowing and snow blowing equipment. Arranges meeting rooms for special events.

59. Janitorial Cleaner

Cleans assigned areas using power equipment as needed. Cleans drinking fountains, offices partition windows, washrooms, toilets and lavatories. Replenishes supplies.

60. Security (Discipline Monitor)

Makes regular watch rounds of premises outside of scheduled working hours, where frequency of trips and stations is prescribed. Checks buildings, equipment and materials for leaks, fires, unauthorized individuals and other conditions. Ensures that all entrances and windows are secured, and that elevator and fire doors are closed. Makes written report of all irregularities or unusual circumstances.

61. Development Manager

Manages and may participate in all aspects of library's annual fund development program. Identifies potential donors and maintains donor database. Responsible for maintaining budgets of delegated programs and may supervise staff.

62. Grant Proposal Writer

Researches and investigates grant opportunities. Prepares grant proposals in accordance with funder's giving policies, guidelines, and criteria.

Appendix B. Methodology

Formation of Library Groups

As in previous years, the survey samples were selected from two library universes—public and academic. The public library universe included all public libraries and was stratified into 5 classes using the 2003 public library file: Very Small, serving populations less than 10,000; Small, serving 10,000–24,999; Medium, serving 25,000–99,999; Large, serving 100,000–499,999; and, Very Large, serving 500,000 or more.

The academic library universe was stratified into four categories: Two-year College, Four-Year College, and University (including Association for Research Libraries members' data) using the 2004 post-survey file provided by the U.S. Census Bureau for the purposes of this study. This file includes codes for the categories created by the Carnegie Foundation for the Advancement of Teaching in 1994. Our "Two-Year College" corresponds to the Carnegie category "Associate of Arts." Our "Four-Year College" category corresponds to the Carnegie Categories "Baccalaureate I and II." Our "University" includes the Carnegie categories "Master's I and II, Doctoral I and II, and Research I and II."

Within each of these eight classes, libraries were further stratified by state and into four geographic areas used frequently by National Center for Education Statistics (NCES): North Atlantic, Great Lakes & Plains, Southeast, West & Southwest. A list of states included in each region is provided in Table B1. As in previous surveys, the eight library classes and four geographic areas were combined to form thirty-two groups from which samples were selected. Tables B2-B10 show the size of each group, the size of the sample, and the size of the return.

Sample Selection and Return

The sample frame for each type/size/geographic strata was determined by using a proportional sampling procedure that took into account the size of the population in each group and the expected return rate for the survey. The public library sample was selected using a file from the NCES containing 2003 data on all public libraries reported by state library agencies as part of the Federal State Cooperative System for Public Library Data (FSCS). The file includes data on all ALA-accredited and non-ALA-accredited MLS and other staff. Before selecting the sample, The Management Association of Illinois dropped from the sampling frame libraries with two or fewer such personnel and libraries that had refused to respond to previous salary surveys. One thousand nine hundred and eighty-three (1,983) public libraries were surveyed.

The procedure for selecting the academic library sample was similar to the procedure followed in previous years for the *Survey of Librarian Salaries*. The Association created a sampling frame using the NCES universe file for academic libraries. This file includes data on the number of staff who are "librarians and other professionals." Before selecting the sample, The Association dropped from the sampling frame libraries with two or fewer of such personnel and libraries that had refused to respond to previous salary surveys. Also removed were institutions that had closed (3), and two (2) that could not be confirmed from either the 2000 or 2003 NCES data file. Then The Association screened out several sets of institutions—those categorized as "specialized" by the Carnegie Corporation for the Advancement of Teaching. Those institutions offer degrees ranging from the bachelor's to the doctorate, at least 50 percent of which are in a single specialized field, e.g., "theological seminaries, Bible colleges, and other institutions offering degrees in religion," and "Schools of art, music, and design." Specialized institutions often declined to respond in the early years of the *Survey of Librarian Salaries*. Also excluded were four sets of institutions whose individual members had been unable to respond in the past. In New York, the seventeen institutions that are part of the City University of New York were removed because librarians there have full academic status and salary is not related to position description. Public Two-Year schools in California were removed for the same reason, as were the fourteen members of the state university system in Pennsylvania. Also in Pennsylvania, we removed all but the main campus of Pennsylvania State University because librarians at other campuses declined to respond in the past and referred us to the main campus. One thousand four hundred thirty-five (1,435) academic libraries were surveyed.

A total of 3,418 surveys were sent and a total of 836 responses were analyzed for this report.

Procedure

The cover letter was mailed in early February 2006 to academic and public libraries with directions for participating online, participating using MS Excel spreadsheets, or downloading and printing a paper survey. A separate letter was sent to ARL members. Large libraries were mailed a copy of the questionnaire, but also were given the option of participating online, using MS Excel spreadsheets, or returning their paper survey to The Association. Data from paper surveys received at The Association were entered online by Association staff. A reminder postcard was sent to all non-respondents in March. The web survey closed on March 17 and all responses were cleaned, then analyzed using SPSS for Windows.

Participating members of the Association of Research Libraries (ARL), which included 123 of the largest university libraries in the U.S., also were able to choose

among the following participation methods: using the same form they use for ARL surveys, participating online, emailing a MS Excel spreadsheet, or completing it on paper.

Table B-1. States in Four Regions of the U.S.

North Atlantic	Great Lakes & Plains	Southeast	West & Southwest
Connecticut	Illinois	Alabama	Alaska
Delaware	Indiana	Arkansas	Arizona
District of	Iowa	Florida	California
Columbia	Kansas	Georgia	Colorado
Maine	Michigan	Kentucky	Hawaii
Maryland	Minnesota	Louisiana	Idaho
Massachusetts	Missouri	Mississippi	Montana
New Hampshire	Nebraska	North Carolina	Nevada
New Jersey	North Dakota	South Carolina	New Mexico
New York	Ohio	Tennessee	Oklahoma
Pennsylvania	South Dakota	Virginia	Oregon
Rhode Island	Wisconsin	West Virginia	Texas
Vermont			Utah
			Washington
			Wyoming

Source: *Statistics of Public Libraries, 1977–1978* (NCES, 1982).

Table B-2. Very Large Public Libraries: Size of Universe, Return

	Universe	Return	
	#	#	% of Universe
North Atlantic	12	3	25.00
Great Lakes & Plains	11	8	72.27
Southeast	18	9	50.00
West & Southwest	35	17	48.57
TOTAL	76	37	48.68

Table B-3. Large Public Libraries: Size of Universe, Return

	Universe	Return	
	#	#	% of Universe
North Atlantic	47	19	40.42
Great Lakes & Plains	66	25	37.87
Southeast	110	28	25.45
West & Southwest	114	39	34.21
TOTAL	337	111	32.94

Table B-4. Medium-Sized Public Libraries: Size of Universe, Return

	Universe	return	
	#	#	% of Universe
North Atlantic	173	42	24.27
Great Lakes & Plains	127	41	32.28
Southeast	109	31	28.44
West & Southwest	96	31	32.29
TOTAL	505	145	28.71

Table B-5. Small Public Libraries:
Size of Universe, Return

	Universe	Return	
	#	#	% of Universe
North Atlantic	187	41	21.92
Great Lakes & Plains	172	50	29.06
Southeast	70	13	18.57
West & Southwest	94	17	18.08
TOTAL	523	121	23.13

Table B-6. Very Small Public Libraries:
Size of Universe, Return

	Universe	Return	
	#	#	% of Universe
North Atlantic	172	42	24.41
Great Lakes & Plains	236	76	32.20
Southeast	38	10	26.31
West & Southwest	96	25	26.04
TOTAL	542	153	28.22

Table B-7. Two-Year College Libraries:
Size of Universe, Return

	Universe	Return	
	#	#	% of Universe
North Atlantic	111	7	6.30
Great Lakes & Plains	123	21	17.07
Southeast	123	20	16.26
West & Southwest	148	11	7.43
TOTAL	505	59	11.68

Table B-8. Four-Year College Libraries:
Size of Universe, Return

	Universe	Return	
	#	#	% of Universe
North Atlantic	98	17	17.34
Great Lakes & Plains	113	25	22.12
Southeast	117	26	22.22
West & Southwest	60	15	25.00
TOTAL	388	83	21.39

Table B-9. University and ARL Libraries:
Size of Universe, Return

	Universe	return	
	#	#	% of Universe
North Atlantic	159	26	16.4
Great Lakes & Plains	141	38	27.0
Southeast	123	38	30.9
West & Southwest	119	25	21.0
TOTAL	542	127	23.4

Table B-10. All Libraries Surveyed:
Size of Universe, Return

	Universe	Return	
	#	#	% of Universe
North Atlantic	959	197	20.54
Great Lakes & Plains	989	284	28.71
Southeast	708	175	24.71
West & Southwest	762	180	23.62
TOTAL	3418	836	24.45

Appendix C. Cover Letters

February 6, 2006

«library»
«address1»
«city», «state» «zip»

| **For Online Participation:** |
| UserID: «userid» |
| Password: «password» (case sensitive) |

Dear Colleague:

As you know, ALA has collected and published salary information on librarians with ALA-accredited masters degrees since 1982. In 2006, we are conducting the first annual non-Masters in Library Science (non-MLS) Salary Survey! The American Library Association-Allied Professional Association (ALA-APA) and American Library Association (ALA) are conducting this survey in response to the need to have accurate and current information about how the spectrum of library staff is compensated. Many libraries have no data for analysis of non-MLS salaries, and prior to this survey the only detailed national tool was the bi-annual support staff survey by *Library Mosaics: The Magazine for Support Staff*, which is no longer in publication.

Your library has been selected to participate in both the non-MLS and MLS salary surveys for 2006. Both are coordinated by the ALA-APA as part of its mission of "improving the salaries and status of library workers." ALA-APA continues to work in consultation with the ALA Office for Research and Statistics on both of these studies. This year the data is being collected with the assistance of The Management Association of Illinois. The non-MLS survey will be administered first, then the MLS survey. The survey period for both is January-May 2006.

Because your library is one of a scientifically selected sample for this new survey series, your response is essential to the success of the survey. Your library has a unique identifier for the survey. We understand that it will take some time to complete the survey so you may choose among several methods, including using a web-based form, emailing a MS Excel spreadsheet or completing it on paper. The instructions are on the enclosed page.

We want a successful survey and will work with you to ensure your library's response. If you have any questions, problems, or technical difficulties, please contact The Management Association of Illinois' Survey Department at 800-448-4584.

Please complete the non-MLS questionnaire by March 3, 2006 You will be notified about the MLS questionnaire, sent separately, in March. As a thank you for your participation, all participants are entitled to a 25% discount on the price of the report. (Mention this discount when you place the order. The non-MLS report will be published in May 2006 and the MLS in September. Both will be available for purchase through the ALA Store.)

Thank you very much for your cooperation as we launch this new survey, and your continued support of the long-standing MLS Salary Survey.

Sincerely yours,

Keith Michael Fiels
Executive Director
American Library Association and American Library Association-Allied Professional Association

*P.S. In order to ensure the validity of the survey results, reminders will be sent to
non-respondents. However, we would rather spend the postage money on other services.
Please help our budget by responding promptly to the online survey.*

February 6, 2006

For Online Participation:
UserID:
Password:

Dear Library Director/Dean:

As you know, ALA has collected and published salary information on librarians with ALA-accredited masters degrees since 1982. In 2006, we are conducting the first annual non-Masters in Library Science (non-MLS) Salary Survey! The American Library Association-Allied Professional Association (ALA-APA) and American Library Association (ALA) are conducting this survey in response to the need for accurate and current information about how the spectrum of library staff are compensated. Many libraries have no data for analysis of non-MLS salaries, and prior to this survey the only detailed national tool was the bi-annual support staff survey by *Library Mosaics: The Magazine for Support Staff*, which is no longer in publication.

The Librarian Salary Survey includes ARL libraries to ensure that the summary data we report represents the full range of academic, as well as public, libraries. We ask Association for Research Libraries (ARL) members who are in our sample for permission to use the data already submitted to ARL for the positions described on our librarian questionnaire. ***This year, we are asking that you also provide, for this non-MLS salary survey, salaries for the staff not included in the ARL survey (librarians and professionals).*** We understand that it will take some time to complete the survey so you may choose among several methods, including using the same form you use for ARL, a web-based form, emailing a MS Excel spreadsheet, or completing it on paper. The instructions are on the enclosed page.

We want a successful survey and will work with you to ensure your library's response. If you have any questions, problems, or technical difficulties, please contact The Management Association of Illinois' Survey Department at 800-448-4584.

Improving the salary data collected about the profession is important to ALA-APA and ALA. We look forward to your continued participation and your feedback. Thank you very much for your cooperation with the 2006 survey. If you have questions, please call me at 1-800-545-2433, ext. 2424 or send e-mail to jgrady@ala.org.

Sincerely yours,

Jenifer Grady

Jenifer Grady
Director, ALA-APA

Appendix C. Directory of State Libraries Reporting Salary Data

compiled by the American Library Association,
Office for Research and Statistics

Directory of State Libraries Reporting Salary Data - 2005

State	Does your state library collect salary data for professional and/or paraprofessional library staff (e.g., public, academic, school. or special)?	If yes, with what frequency? yearly __ other (please specify)	If your state library collects salary data, what is the most current year of salary data you have?	Salary Survey URL
Alabama	No			
Alaska	Yes	Yearly	Stopped in 2003	
Arizona	Yes	Yearly	2003-2004	
Arkansas	Yes	Bi-annually	2004	
California	Yes	Yearly	2003-2004	
Colorado	Yes	Yearly	2005	
Connecticut	Yes	Yearly	2005	
Delaware	NOT REPORTED			
District of Columbia	NOT REPORTED			
Florida	Sort-of	Yearly	2005	
Georgia	Yes	Yearly	2004	
Hawaii	NOT REPORTED			
Idaho	No			
Illinois	Yes	Yearly	2004	
Indiana	Yes	Yearly	2004	
Iowa	Yes	Yearly	2004	
Kansas	Yes	Yearly	2004	
Kentucky	Yes	First-Time	2006	
Louisiana	No			
Maine	No			
Maryland	Yes	Yearly	2005	
Massachusetts	Yes	Yearly	2004	
Michigan	Yes	Yearly	2003	
Minnesota	Yes	Yearly	2004	
Mississippi	No			
Missouri	NOT REPORTED			
Montana	Yes		2005	
Nebraska	Yes	Yearly	2004	
Nevada	No			
New Hampshire	Yes	Yearly	2003	http://www.nh.gov/nhsl/ldss/NHstats2003.xls
New Jersey	Yes	Yearly	2004	
New Mexico	No			
New York	Yes	Yearly	2004	
North Carolina	Yes	Yearly	2003-2004	
North Dakota	NOT REPORTED			
Ohio	Yes	Yearly	2004	
Oklahoma	Yes	Yearly	2005	
Oregon	Yes	Yearly	2004-2005	http://oregon.gov/OSL/LD/statsploregon.shtm
Pennsylvania	Yes	Yearly	2005	
Rhode Island	Yes	Yearly	2005	
South Carolina	Yes	Yearly	2004	
South Dakota	No			
Tennessee	Yes	Yearly	2004	
Texas	No			
Utah	NOT REPORTED			
Vermont	No			
Virgin Islands	No			
Virginia	Yes	Yearly	2004	
Washington	Yes	Yearly	2004	
West Virginia	Yes	Bi-annually	2006	
Wisconsin	No			
Wyoming	Yes	Yearly	2004	